Frommer's

Edition

Singapore & Malaysia

by Jennifer Eveland

IDG Books Worldwide, Inc.
An International Data Group Company
Foster City, CA • Chicago, IL • Indianapolis, IN • New York, NY

ABOUT THE AUTHOR

As a child expatriate, **Jennifer Eveland** fell in love with Singapore and Southeast Asia. After writing the first edition of this Singapore and Malaysia guide in 1997–98 she spent most of 1999 living in Thailand updating *Frommer's Thailand,* 4th Edition, and contributing chapters on all three countries to *Frommer's Southeast Asia.* She currently lives in Singapore, and, surprisingly, has yet to be caned.

IDG BOOKS WORLDWIDE, INC.

An International Data Group Company
919 E. Hillsdale Blvd.
Suite 400
Foster City, CA 94404

Find us online at **www.frommers.com**

ISBN 0-02-863516-7
ISSN 1093-6971

Editor: Matt Hannafin
Production Editor: Donna Wright
Photo Editor: Richard Fox
Design by Michele Laseau
Staff Cartographers: John Decamillis, Roberta Stockwell, Elizabeth Puhl
Page Creation by Kendra Span and Linda Quigley

SPECIAL SALES

Contents

List of Maps

ACKNOWLEDGMENTS

I'd like to extend my appreciation to Kok Yul Chin at the Singapore Tourism Board for all her help, and to Linda "Mom" Eveland, who crept intrepid through the streets with me chatting up shop owners, street-side vendors, and every other fascinating soul we found. To all the wonderful people who provided me with great information along the way, and helped make my travels (and this book) so colorful, a big *Terimah Kasih* and *Xie Xie* to you all! And, last but not least, a very special thanks to my Onanies for their friendship, fun, and support: SuLi Chen and Avinash Garde ("The Strange Couple Upstairs"), Vijay "Banana Leaf" Ahuja, and Antonio "Alpha Dog" Muci. We got a lot of funny.

And to Matt Hannafin. You know I can never thank you enough.

AN INVITATION TO THE READER

In researching this book, we discovered many wonderful places—hotels, restaurants, shops, and more. We're sure you'll find others. Please tell us about them, so we can share the information with your fellow travelers in upcoming editions. If you were disappointed with a recommendation, we'd love to know that, too. Please write to:

Frommer's Singapore & Malaysia, 2nd Edition
Frommer's Travel Guides
1633 Broadway
New York, NY 10019

AN ADDITIONAL NOTE

Please be advised that travel information is subject to change at any time—and this is especially true of prices. We therefore suggest that you write or call ahead for confirmation when making your travel plans. The author, editors, and publisher cannot be held responsible for the experiences of readers while traveling. Your safety is important to us, however, so we encourage you to stay alert and be aware of your surroundings. Keep a close eye on cameras, purses, and wallets, all favorite targets of thieves and pickpockets.

WHAT THE SYMBOLS MEAN

✪ Frommer's Favorites

Our favorite places and experiences—outstanding for quality, value, or both.

The following abbreviations are used for credit cards:

AE	American Express	EURO	Eurocard
CB	Carte Blanche	JCB	Japan Credit Bank
DC	Diners Club	MC	MasterCard
DISC	Discover	V	Visa
ER	EnRoute		

FIND FROMMER'S ONLINE

www.frommers.com offers up-to-the-minute listings on almost 200 cities around the globe—including the latest bargains and candid, personal articles updated daily by Arthur Frommer himself. No other Web site offers such comprehensive and timely coverage of the world of travel.

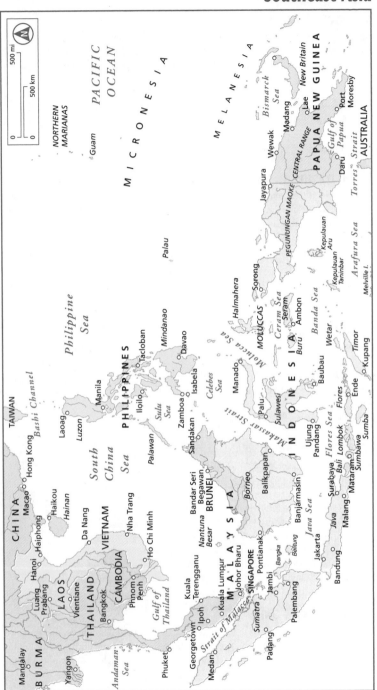

Southeast Asia

The Best of Singapore & Malaysia

I could spend a lifetime exploring Singapore. I'm in awe of the cultural mysteries and exotic beauty of the city's old mosques and temples. As I pass the facades of buildings that mark history, I get nostalgic for old tales of colonial romance. Towering overhead, present-day Singapore glistens with the wealth of modern miracles. And when I smell incense and spice and jasmine swirling in wet topical breezes, I can close my eyes and know exactly where I am.

Each time I stay here, new curiosities present themselves to me. Singapore thrives on a history that has absorbed a multitude of foreign elements over almost 2 centuries, melding them into a unique modern national identity. Beginning with the landing of Sir Stamford Raffles in 1819, add to the mix the original Malay inhabitants, immigrating waves of Chinese traders and workers, Indian businessmen and laborers, Arab merchants, British colonials, European adventure-seekers, and an assortment of Southeast Asian settlers—this tiny island rose from the ingenuity of those who worked and lived together here. Today, all recognize each group's importance to the heritage of the land, each adding unique contributions to a culture and identity we know as Singaporean.

I'll confess, many travelers complain to me about how westernized Singapore is. For many, a vacation in Asia should be filled with culture shock, unfamiliar traditions, and curious adventures. Today's travel philosophy seems to be that the more underdeveloped and obscure a country is, the more "authentic" the experience will be. But poor Singapore—all those lovely opium-stained coolies and toothless rickshaw pullers are now driving BMWs and exchanging cellular phone numbers. How could anyone possibly find this place so fascinating?

With all its shopping malls, fast-food outlets, imported fashion, and steel skyscrapers, Singapore could look like any other contemporary city you've ever visited—but to peel through the layers is to understand that life here is far more complex. While the outer layers are startlingly Western, just underneath lies a curious area where East blends with West in language, cuisine, attitude, and style. At the core, you'll find a sensibility rooted in the cultural heritage of values, religion, superstition, and memory. In Singapore, nothing is ever as it appears to be.

For me this is where the fascination begins. I detect so many things familiar in this city, only to discover how these imported ideas have been altered to fit the local identity. Like the Singaporean shophouse—a jumble of colonial architectural mandates, European tastes, Chinese superstitions, and Malay finery. Or Singlish, the unofficial local tongue, which combines English language with Chinese grammar, common Malay phrases, and Hokkien slang to form a patois unique to this part of the world. This transformation of cultures has been going on for almost 2 centuries. So, in a sense, Singapore is no different today than it was 100 years ago. And in this I find my "authentic" travel experience.

When the urban jungle gets me crazy, I escape to **Malaysia.** Even Kuala Lumpur, the capital city, seems relaxed in comparison to Singapore. In fact, many Singaporeans look to their northern neighbor for the perfect vacation, taking advantage of its pristine and exciting national forests and marine parks, relaxing on picture-perfect beaches in either sophisticated resorts or quaint bungalows, taking in culture in its small towns, shopping for inexpensive handicrafts, or eating some of the finest food in Southeast Asia. Malaysia offers something for everyone—history, culture, adventure, romance, mystery, nature, and relaxation—without the glaring buzz of an overdeveloped tourism industry. It almost makes me overjoyed that few tourists venture here.

My favorite part of Malaysia, however, is the warmth of its people. I have yet to travel in this country without collecting remarkable tales of hospitality, openness, and generosity. I've found the Malaysian people to be genuine in their approach to foreign visitors, another fine by-product of the underdeveloped tourism industry. For those who want to find a nice little corner of paradise, Malaysia could be your answer.

I've crept down alleys, wandered the streets of cities and towns, combed beaches, and trekked jungles to seek out the most exciting things that Singapore and Malaysia have to offer. In this volume I've presented the sights and attractions of these countries with insight into historical, cultural, and modern significance to bring you a complete appreciation of all you are about to experience. I've peeked in every shop door, chatting up the local characters inside. I've eaten local food until I can't move. I've stayed out all night. I've done it all and written about it here. I can only hope you will love Singapore and Malaysia as much as I do.

1 Frommer's Favorite Singapore Experiences

- **Sipping a Singapore Sling at the Long Bar:** Ahhhh, the Long Bar. Home of the Singapore Sling. I like to come in the afternoons, before the tourist rush. Sheltered by long timber shutters that close out the tropical sun, the air cooled by lazy punkahs (small fans that wave gently back and forth above), you can sit back in old rattan chairs and have your saronged waitress serve you sticky alcoholic creations while you toss back a few dainty crab cakes. Life can be so decadent. Okay, so the punkahs are electric, and, come to think of it, the place is air-conditioned (not to mention that it costs a small fortune), but it's fun to imagine the days when Somerset Maugham, Rudyard Kipling, or Charlie Chaplin would be sitting at the bar sipping Slings and spinning exotic tales of their world travels. Drink up, my friend; it's a lovely high. See chapter 8.

- **Witnessing Bloody Traditions:** Every so often, a magical Saturday night comes around when you can witness the Kuda Kepang, which is not your average traditional dance. It features young men on wooden horses who move like warriors, whirling and spinning and slapping the horses to shake intimidating sounds out of them. Accompanied by rhythmic and repetitive traditional Malay music, the warriors dance in unison, staging battles with each other until by the end of a long series of dances, the horsemen are in a trance. A pot of burning frankincense is produced, from which they all inhale. After that, all hell breaks loose. The dancers are whipped, fed glass—which they chew and swallow hungrily—walk on glass shards, and shred entire coconuts with their teeth. While the whipping appears somewhat staged, I assure you the rest is real. It's a traditional dance that's taken very seriously both by the dancers and by the huge and mostly Malay crowds that gather for it. What's more, the next day the dancers don't recall what they did—and they're never injured. Unfortunately, the dance is not performed on a regular basis. The group works mostly for private ceremonies and gatherings, and appears at **Malay Village** (☎ 65/748-4700) on the off Saturday night when they don't have a gig. Call ahead to find out if they'll be performing. See chapters 5 and 8.

If you're not able to catch a performance, but still want a little ceremonial gore, check out the calendar of events in chapter 2. During the Thaipusam Festival, men pierce their bodies with skewers, and during the Thimithi Festival they walk on burning coals. To celebrate the Birthday of the Monkey God, Chinese priests will slice themselves with sharp implements and write chants and prayers with their own blood.

- **Checking Out the Orchard Road Scene:** You can't find better people watching than on Orchard Road every Saturday afternoon, when it seems like every Singaporean crawls out of the woodwork to join the parade of shoppers, strollers, hipsters, posers, lovers, geeks, and gabbers. Everybody is here, milling around every mall, clustered around every sidewalk bench, checking everybody out. At the corner of Scotts Road and Orchard, just under the Marriott, there's an al fresco cafe where you'll find local celebrities hanging out to see and be seen. International celebrities and models have been spotted here on occasion, too. In the mix, you're bound to see most every tourist on the island, coming around to see what all the excitement is about.

  On Saturdays, school lets out early, so the malls are filled with mobs of bored teenagers, kicking around, trying to look cool, and watching the music videos in the front window of the HMV music store in The Heeren. Moms and dads also have half-days at the office, so the strip takes on the feel of an obstacle course, as all the parents race around wielding strollers, trying to run errands while they have the chance. Meanwhile, outside in the shady areas, you can see crowds of *amahs* (housekeepers) and workers relaxing and catching up on the latest news on their free afternoon.

  For some, the scene is a madhouse to be avoided; for others, it's a chance to watch life on a typical Saturday afternoon in downtown Singapore. And it is typical, 'cause however huge and delightful the scene is for tourists, it's just part of everyday reality for residents of the Garden City. See chapter 7.

2 Frommer's Favorite Malaysia Experiences

- **Opening Your Mind to Good Medicine:** The first time I went to Tioman Island I was appalled by the rows of A-frame shacks that passed themselves off as bungalows. "I wouldn't let my dog sleep in one of these! Who's your architect—Lassie? Call the concierge, there's been a terrible mistake! Good Lord, where's the *minibar?!*"

  Needless to say, my first day in the doghouse was nutty. The rustic little cabin felt like it would fall apart at the first breeze. Really, I've stayed in more attractive places at summer camp. The concrete latrine in the rear was as back-to-basics as you could get, save going outside behind a tree. But I somehow survived my first night, cold shower and all.

The next day, after strolling around the kampung village, lazing about at the beach, chatting with friendly locals and fellow travelers, eating great barbecued fish and drinking some cold beer, I had to admit, the place had its charm. And I also had to admit my doghouse was starting to look rather cozy. No annoying telephones, no loud TVs, no distractions. Just peace.

By my third day, I began to redecorate. Drape a little sarong over the window here, place another mosquito candle on the table there, sweep out the sand; it was my little home. I couldn't remember the last time I'd felt so laid-back and satisfied. The hectic world I'd left behind began to look more and more insane with each passing day. And as the years of stress melted away, I couldn't imagine why anyone would ever want more from life than this. Civilization is so overrated. See chapter 11.

- **Experiencing Kampung Hospitality:** Pakcik (uncle) was just slightly older than his ancient Mercedes, but his price was right, so I hired him for the day to drive me around Kota Bharu. Sometime after lunch, during a stop at the kite-maker's house, I spotted a beautiful gasing, a wood and steel Malay top. It would be the perfect gift for my brother! I just had to have one.

  Well, the kite-maker didn't want to give his up, but Pakcik had a few ideas. After coming up empty at the local shops, he took on my quest with personal conviction. Off we drove through the outskirts of town, the sights becoming more and more rural. He turned down a dirt road, past grazing water buffaloes lazing near rice paddies. Soon the fields turned to jungle, and a small kampung village appeared in the trees. I watched out the window as we passed traditional wooden stilt houses where grannies fanned themselves on the porch watching the children chase chickens in the yard. Beside each house, colorful batik sarongs waved in the breeze.

  The path wound to the house of Pakcik's nephew. I was welcomed inside with curiosity, perhaps the first foreigner to visit. They offered me a straw mat, which I used to join the others resting comfortably on the floor. Within minutes, an audience of neighbors gathered around, plucking fruits from the trees in the yard for me. I listened as Pakcik told them of my search for a gasing, and was surprised to see every person scatter. That afternoon I was offered every gasing in the village.

  My afternoon in Pakcik's kampung is one of my most cherished memories, and a most meaningful experience. You see, as Southeast Asia becomes increasingly affluent and globalized, this way of life becomes steadily endangered. It's a lifestyle that for many urban Malaysians captures the spirit of the good life—simple days when joy was free. And everyone will be proud to show you; all you need is an open heart and a big smile. Malaysian hospitality never ceases to amaze me.

3 The Best Small Towns & Villages

- **Kuala Terengganu** (Malaysia): The capital of Malaysian handicrafts has yet to be plotted on any standard tourist itinerary. Explore the city's cottage industries and experience a more orthodox side of Malaysian Islam in this quiet cultural gem. See chapter 11.
- **Any Kampung** (Tioman Island, Malaysia): Even though Tioman was developed for the tourism industry, you'll never think this place is overdeveloped. The

casual and rustic nature of the island's tiny beach villages holds firm, and those who seek escape rarely leave disappointed. See chapter 11.

- **Malacca** (Malaysia): As perhaps the oldest trading port in Malaysia, this town hosted a wide array of international traders: Arabs, Portuguese, Dutch, English, Indian, and Chinese, all of whom left their stamp. See chapter 10.
- **Cameron Highlands** (Malaysia): When the tropical heat gets you down, head for the hills. The colonials favored this cooling retreat for growing tea and roses and for building lovely Tudor country homes. See chapter 10.

4 The Best Beaches

- **Tanjung Rhu** (Langkawi, Malaysia): Perhaps one of the most stunning beaches in Malaysia, this wide gorgeous stretch of white sand hugs a crystal clear, deep blue cove. Even Alex Garland would be impressed. See chapter 10.
- **Kumpung Juara** (Tioman Island, Malaysia): This beach is what they mean when they say *isolated.* Be prepared to live like Robinson Crusoe—in tiny huts, many with no electricity at all. But, oh, the beach! Most visitors don't get to this part of the island, so many times you can have it all to yourself. See chapter 11.
- **Central Beach** (Sentosa Island, Singapore): This is just about the best beach you'll find in Singapore, which isn't really known for its beaches. It's lively, with water sports and beach activities plus food and drink. However, if you really need pristine seclusion, you'll have to head for Malaysia. See chapter 5.
- **Cherating** (Malaysia): If you're a leatherback turtle, you'll think the best beach in the world is just north of Cherating. Every spring and summer, these giant sea creatures come ashore to lay their eggs, so if you're in town from May to June you might catch a look at the hatchlings. Meanwhile, during the turtles' off-season, international windsurfing and water-board enthusiasts gather annually for competitions at this world famous spot. See chapter 11.

5 The Most Exciting Outdoor Adventures

- **Trekking in Taman Negara** (Malaysia): With suitable options for all budgets, levels of comfort, and desired adventure, peninsular Malaysia's largest national park opens the wonders of primary rain forest and the creatures who dwell in it to everyone. From the canopy walk high atop the forest to night watches for nocturnal life, this adventure is as stunning as it is informative. See chapter 11.
- **Scuba diving at Sipadan** (Malaysia): One of the top-10 dive sites in the world, the reefs off the eastern coast of Sabah draw adventure divers from all parts of the globe. If scuba is your game, this is your dream come true. Better yet, highly qualified operators can arrange everything for you from Kota Kinabalu. See chapter 12.
- **Sungai Buloh Nature Reserve** (Singapore): Every year during the winter months, flocks of migrating birds from as far north as Siberia vacation in the warm waters of this unique mangrove swamp park. Easily traversed via wooden walkway, the park will never disappoint for some stunning wildlife shots. See chapter 5.

6 The Most Fascinating Temples, Churches & Mosques

- **Thian Hock Keng** (Singapore): One of Singapore's oldest Chinese temples, it is a fascinating testimony to Chinese Buddhism as it combines with traditional Confucian beliefs and natural Taoist principles. Equally fascinating is the modern world that carries on just outside the old temple's doors. See chapter 5.
- **Jalan Tokong, Malacca** (Malaysia): This street, in the historical heart of the city, supports a Malay mosque, a Chinese temple, and a Hindu temple existing peacefully side by side—the perfect example of how the many foreign religions that came to Southeast Asia shaped its communities and learned to coexist in harmony. See chapter 10.
- **Armenian Church** (Singapore): While not the biggest Christian house of worship in the city, it is perhaps one of the most charming in its architectural simplicity, tropical practicality, and spiritual tranquility. See chapter 5.
- **Hajjah Fatimah Mosque** (Singapore): I love this mosque for its eclectic mix of religious symbols and architectural influences. To me, it represents not just the Singaporean ability to absorb so many different ideas, but also a Muslim appreciation and openness toward many cultures. See chapter 5.

7 The Most Interesting Museums

- **Images of Singapore** (Sentosa Island, Singapore): No one has done a better job than this museum in chronicling the horrors of the World War II Pacific Theater and Japanese occupation in Southeast Asia. Video and audio displays take you on a journey through Singapore's experience. The grand finale, the Surrender Chambers, features life-sized wax-figure dioramas of the fateful events. See chapter 5.
- **Penang Museum and Art Gallery** (Penang, Malaysia): A slick display of Penang's colonial history and multicultural heritage, this place is chock-full of fascinating tidbits about the people, places, and events of this curious island. Plus, it doesn't hurt that the air-conditioning works very well! See chapter 10.
- **Asian Civilisations Museum** (Singapore): One of the newer displays on the block, this extremely well-presented museum documents the evolutionary and cultural history of the region's major ethnic groups. A very informative afternoon. See chapter 5.
- **State Museums of Malacca** (Malaysia): This small city has more museums than any other city in the country, with some unusual displays such as kites and Malaysian literature. See chapter 10.

8 The Best Luxury Resorts & Hotels

- **Raffles Hotel** (Singapore): For old-world opulence, Raffles is second to none. It's pure fantasy of the days when tigers still lurked around the perimeters. See chapter 3.
- **The Four Seasons** (Singapore): Elegance and warmth combine to make this place a good bet. Consider a regular room here before you book a suite elsewhere. See chapter 3.
- **The Regent** (Kuala Lumpur, Malaysia): For my money, the Regent offers the smartest decor and the best service and selection of facilities in the whole city. See chapter 10.

- **The Aryani Resort** (Kuala Terengganu, Malaysia): An exotic retreat, Aryani combines local Terengganu flavors with all the pampering you'd want from a get-away resort. See chapter 11.
- **Shangri-La's Rasa Sayang Resort** (Penang, Malaysia): The oldest resort on the beach has claimed the best stretch of sand and snuggled the most imaginative modern, yet traditionally designed resort into the gardens just beyond. See chapter 10.
- **The Datai** (Langkawi, Malaysia): The Datai is as stunning as any of the best resorts Phuket and Bali have to offer, without the Phuket or Bali price tag. See chapter 10.

9 The Best Hotel Bargains

- **RELC International Hotel** (Singapore): For a safe and simple place to call home in Singapore, RELC can't be beat. One wonders how they keep costs so low when their location is so good. See chapter 3.
- **Traders Hotel** (Singapore): Value-for-money is the name of the game, with all sorts of promotional packages, self-service launderettes, vending machines, and a checkout lounge just a few of the offerings that make this the most convenient hotel in the city. See chapter 3.
- **Swiss-Inn** (Kuala Lumpur, Malaysia): Location, location, location! Right in the center of Kuala Lumpur's bustling Chinatown, the Swiss-Inn is the perennial favorite for travelers here. A comfortable choice, plus it's so close to everything. See chapter 10.
- **Heeren House** (Malacca, Malaysia): Bargain or no bargain, this boutique hotel in the heart of the old city is *the* place to stay in Malacca if you want to really get a feel of the local atmosphere. See chapter 10.
- **Telang Usan Hotel** (Kuching, Malaysia): An informal place, Telang Usan is homey and quaint, and within walking distance of many major attractions in Kuching. See chapter 12.

10 The Best Local Dining Experiences

- **Hawker Centers** (Singapore & Malaysia): Think of them as shopping malls for food—*great* food! For local cuisine, who needs a menu with pictures when you can walk around and select anything you want as it's prepared before your eyes. See chapters 4, 10, 11, and 12.
- **Gurney Drive** (Penang, Malaysia): Penang is the king of Asian cuisine, from Chinese to Malay to Indian and everything else in between. This large hawker center by the sea is a great introduction to Penang. See chapter 10.
- **Imperial Herbal** (Singapore): In the Chinese tradition of yin and yang, dishes are prepared under the supervision of the house doctor, a traditional healer who will be glad to "prescribe" the perfect cure for whatever ails you. See chapter 4.
- **Chile Crab at UDMC Seafood Centre** (Singapore): A true Singaporean favorite, chile crabs will cause every local to rise up in argument over where you can find the best in town. Head out to UDMC to try the juicy crabs cooked in a sweet chile sauce. Prepare to get messy! See chapter 4.

11 The Best Markets

- **Arab Street** (Singapore): Even though Singapore is a shopper's paradise, it could still use more places like Arab Street. Small shops selling everything from textiles to handicrafts line the street. Bargaining is welcome. See chapter 7.
- **Central Market** (Kuala Lumpur, Malaysia): One-stop shopping for all the rich arts and handicrafts Malaysia produces, and it's air-conditioned! See chapter 10.
- **Central Market** (Kuala Terengganu, Malaysia): This huge bustling market turned me into a shopping freak! All of the handicrafts Terengannu is famous for come concentrated in one exciting experience: batik, songket cloth, brass ware, basket weaving—the list goes on. See chapter 11.
- **Petaling Street, Kuala Lumpur** (Malaysia): This night market gets very, very crowded and crazy with all who come for watches, handbags, computer software, video CDs (which aren't exactly DVDs but can be played on a DVD player), and all manner of blatant disregard for international copyright laws. See chapter 10.

12 The Best Shopping Bargains

- **Silver Filigree Jewelry** (Malaysia): This fine silver is worked into detailed filigree jewelry designs to make brooches, necklaces, bracelets, and other fine jewelry.
- **Pewter** (Malaysia): Malaysia is the home of Selangor Pewter, one of the largest manufacturers of pewter in the world, and their many showrooms have all sorts of items to choose from. See the Kuala Lumpur shopping section in chapter 10 for KL locations. For locations in Penang, Malacca, and Johor call the Selangor hotline at ☎ 03/422-1000.
- **Knockoffs & Pirate Goods** (Singapore & Malaysia): Check out how real those watches look! And so cheap! You can find them at any night market. Ever dream of owning a Gucci? Have I got a deal for you! Can I tell you about pirate video CDs and computer software without getting my book banned? Uh, okay, whatever you do, *don't buy these items!*
- **Batik** (Singapore & Malaysia): While most of the batiks you find in Singapore come from Indonesia, most in Malaysia are made at factories that you can often tour. The Indonesian prints usually show traditional motif and colors, while Malaysian designs can be far more modern. Look for batik silk as well. See chapters 7, 10, and 11.
- **Handicrafts in Kuala Terengganu** (Malaysia): You can fill your entire gift list in a matter of minutes with a trip to the central market, home to so many Malaysian handicrafts. Likewise, nearby Kota Bharu's cottage industries produce great textiles, silver, and basket weaving, plus fun items like kites and musical instruments. See chapter 11.

13 The Best Nightlife

- **Singapore, the whole city.** Nightlife is becoming increasingly sophisticated in Singapore, where locals have more money for recreation and fun. Take the time to choose the place that suits your personality. Jazz club? Techno disco? Cocktail lounge? Wine bar? Good old pub? They have it all. See chapter 8.
- **Bangsar** (near Kuala Lumpur, Malaysia): Folks in Kuala Lumpur know to go to Bangsar for nighttime excitement. A couple of blocks of concentrated restaurants, cafes, discos, pubs, and wine bars will tickle any fancy. Good people-watching, too. See chapter 10.

Planning a Trip to Singapore

2

The seasoned traveler usually has as many stories of travel nightmares as he does of glorious experiences—your luggage gets sent to Timbuktu, your hotel reservations get mixed up, and your taxi driver takes you to Lord-knows-where. The good news about traveling to Singapore? This place *works!* A seamless communications infrastructure means that you can plan your own trip, without a middleman travel agent, and still have everything go as smoothly as if you were on an organized coach tour. Reliable phone lines, fax technology, and Internet presence makes advance planning a breeze. Of course it helps that so many Singaporeans speak fluent English. Additionally, the Singapore Tourism Board (STB) is a wealthy and well-oiled machine that has anticipated the needs of travelers.

The STB is perhaps one of the most visible government agencies in Singapore, and it's impossible for any tourist to get out of the country without encountering at least one of its many publications or postings or coming face-to-face with one of its innumerable representatives. If you have access to one of its offices before your trip, it's a great source of information. (STB's international offices are listed under "Visitor Information," below.)

In this chapter, I'll run through the nuts and bolts of travel to Singapore, letting you in on everything from how much your money will buy, to the best time of year to travel and what to wear, to what sea creatures to watch out for if you go swimming.

1 Singapore's Regions in Brief

On a world map, Singapore is nothing more than a speck nestled in the heart of Southeast Asia, at the tip of the Malaysian Peninsula. In the north, it's linked to Malaysia by a causeway over the Strait of Johor, which is its only physical connection to any other body of land. To the south, the Straits of Singapore separate the island from Indonesia, which you can sometimes see from the tops of high buildings and even from some beaches. Farther north, above Malaysia, are Thailand, Burma, Cambodia, and Vietnam; to the east, East Malaysia, Borneo, and Brunei; to the northeast, the Philippine Islands; and stretching from west to south are the islands of Indonesia.

The country is made up of one main island, Singapore, and around 60 smaller ones, some of which—like Sentosa, Pulau Ubin, Kusu, and

St. John's Island—are popular retreats. The main island is shaped like a flat, horizontal diamond, measuring in at just over 42 kilometers (25 miles) from east to west and almost 23 kilometers (14 miles) north to south. With a total land area of only 584.8 square kilometers (351 sq. miles), Singapore is almost shockingly tiny.

Singapore's geographical position, sitting approximately 137 kilometers (82 miles) north of the equator, means that its climate offers uniform temperatures, plentiful rainfall, and high, high humidity.

Don't come expecting a dramatic landscape. Mostly, the profile Singapore presents to the world is undramatic. Small, rolling hills are about the norm, and much of the island is little more than 15 meters (50 ft.) above sea level, with its highest peak, Bukit Timah, rising only 163 meters above sea level. There are a few ridges to the west and southwest. Mount Faber, rising behind the World Trade Centre, is actually a ridge. The coast is almost entirely flat, with maybe a couple of sea cliffs here or there. Actually, the shoreline has changed considerably since the early years of settlement due to major land reclamation projects and swamp drainage. Much of this work was done in colonial times, but here's a figure to play with: From 1964 to 1997, Singapore's Housing Development Board reclaimed more than 2,680 hectares (or 6,620 sq. acres) of land. If you play with those numbers (2,680 ÷ 33 years) you get about 81 hectares per year. That's a lot of land. Think about it this way: Even if you leave Singapore thinking you've seen it all, there will always be something new to see when you come back.

As a city-state, Singapore is basically a city that *is* the country. That doesn't necessarily mean that the entire country is urban, but that the whole of the country and the city is "Singapore," without provincial divisions.

Singapore does, however, have an urban center and smaller suburban neighborhoods: The urban area centers around the Singapore River at the southern point of the island, and within it are neighborhood divisions: the **Historic District** (also referred to as the city center or cultural district), **Chinatown, Tanjong Pagar** (which is oftentimes lumped together with Chinatown due to its close proximity), the **Orchard Road area, Little India,** and **Kampong Glam** (also referred to as the Arab District).

Just beyond the urban area lie suburban neighborhoods. Some older suburbs, like **Katong** and **Geylang,** date from the turn of the 20th century. Others are new, and are therefore referred to as "HDB New Towns." (HDB stands for "Housing Development Board," the government agency responsible for public housing.) HDB New Towns such as **Ang Mo Kio** or **Toa Payoh** are clusters of public housing units, each with their own network of supporting businesses: provision shops, restaurants, health-care facilities, and sometimes shopping malls.

FINDING AN ADDRESS

Unless you're familiar with a particular street, it is unfortunately difficult to distinguish what neighborhood a place is located in using only the written address. Most addresses are simply a number and a street name. Postal codes won't give you much of a clue either.

One exception is addresses in the New Towns, in which you'll see the name of the neighborhood in the body of the address. These neighborhoods are blocks of buildings, each with a corresponding block number that will appear in the address—for example, "Lorong Toa Payoh, Blk #14." It may help to know that in Malay *lorong* is lane, *jalan* is street, and *bukit* is hill. These designations appear quite frequently in Singapore.

One clue for locating shops in shopping malls and offices or apartments in large buildings: Numbers for these addresses are written as, for example, #03-15. Where you

Singapore

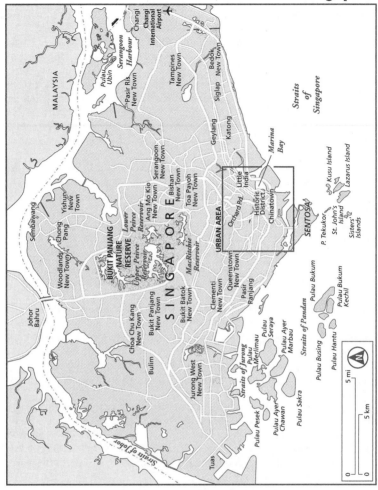

see this, the first set of digits represents the level (in this case the third floor) of the place, and the second set represents the location on the floor numerically. Where you see, say, #03-15/16/17, the place occupies three storefront or office units. Generally, you won't get lost in malls or offices. Almost all places have directories on the ground floor.

Here's something I've found to be handy in helping me find my way around: Almost all cabbies have a copy of a book called **The Singapore Street Directory,** which includes very detailed road maps for the whole island. You can look places up with just the name of the road, and know where you need to go. This is particularly helpful when you find one of the few cabbies with poor English, a new guy, or one who has never heard of the place you need to go. If you can find it for him on the map, he can take you there.

THE CITY

The urban center of Singapore spans quite far from edge to edge, so walking from one end to the other—say, from Tanjong Pagar to Kampong Glam—might be a bit much.

However, once you become handy with local maps, you'll be constantly surprised at how close the individual districts are to one another.

The main focal point of the city is the **Singapore River,** which on a map is located at the southern point of the island, flowing west to east into the Marina. It's here that Sir Stamford Raffles, a British administrator, landed and built his settlement for the East India Trading Company. As trade prospered, the banks of the river were expanded to handle commerce, behind which neighborhoods and administrative offices took root. In 1822, Raffles developed a Town Plan, which allocated neighborhoods to each of the races who'd come in droves to find work and begin new lives. The lines drawn then still remain today, shaping the major ethnic enclaves within the city limits.

On the south bank of the river, *go-downs* (warehouses) were built along the waterside, behind which offices and residences sprang up for the Chinese community of merchants and coolie laborers who worked the river and sea trade. Raffles named this section **Chinatown,** a name that stands today.

Neighboring Chinatown to the southwest is **Tanjong Pagar,** a small district where wealthy Chinese and Eurasians built plantations and manors. With the development of the steamship, Keppel Harbour, a deep natural harbor just off the shore of Tanjong Pagar, was built up to receive the larger vessels. Tanjong Pagar quickly developed into a commercial and residential area filled with workers who flocked there to support the industry.

In these early days, both Chinatown and Tanjong Pagar were amazing sites of city activity. Row houses lined the streets, with shops on the bottom floors and homes on the second and third floors. Chinese coolie laborers commonly lived 16 to a room, and the area flourished with gambling casinos, clubs, and opium dens where they would spend their spare time and money. Indians also thronged to the area to work on the docks, a small reminder that although races had their own areas, they were never exclusive communities.

As recently as the 1970s, a walk down the streets in this area was an adventure: The shops housed Chinese craftsmen and artists; on the streets, hawkers peddled food and other merchandise. Calligrapher scribes set up shop on sidewalks to write letters for a fee. Housewives would bustle, running their daily errands; children would dash out of every corner; and bamboo poles hung laundry from upper stories. Today, however, both of these districts are sleepy by comparison. Modern HDB apartment buildings have siphoned residents off to the suburbs, and though the Urban Redevelopment Authority has renovated many of the old shophouses in an attempt to preserve history, they're now tenanted by law offices and architectural, public relations, and advertising firms. About the only time you'll see this place hustle anymore is during weekday lunchtime, when all the professionals dash out for a bite.

The **north bank** was originally reserved for colonial administrative buildings, and is today commonly referred to as the **Historic District.** The center point was The Padang, the field on which the Europeans would play sports and hold outdoor ceremonies. Around the field, the Parliament Building, Supreme Court, City Hall, and other municipal buildings sprang up in grand style, and behind these buildings, Government Hill—the present-day **Fort Canning Park**—was the home of the governors. The Esplanade along the waterfront was a center for European social activities and music gatherings, when colonists would don their finest Western styles and walk the park under parasols or cruise in horse-drawn carriages. These days, the Historic District is still the center of most of the government's operations, and close by high-rise hotels and shopping malls have been built. The area on the bank of the river is celebrated as Raffles's landing site.

Factoid

It's estimated that up to 50,000 expatriates live in Singapore. Japanese make up the greatest percentage of these, followed by Americans, British, Germans, Swiss, Canadians, French, and Dutch. The high concentration of Western residents is evident in the density of expatriate schools in the Holland Village area.

To the northwest of the Historic District, in the areas along **Orchard Road and Tanglin,** a residential area was created for Europeans and Eurasians. Homes and plantations were eventually replaced by apartment buildings and shops, and in the early 1970s, luxury hotels ushered tourism into the area in full force. In the 1980s, huge shopping malls sprang up along the sides of Orchard Road, turning the landscape into the shopping hub it continues to be. The Tanglin area is home to most of the foreign embassies in Singapore.

The original landscape of **Little India** made it a natural location for an Indian settlement, as the Indians were the original cattle hands and traders in Singapore; the area's natural grasses and springs provided their cattle with food and water, while bamboo groves supplied necessary lumber for their pens. Later, with the establishment of a jail nearby, Indian convict laborers, and the Indian workers who supplied services to them, came to the area for work and ended up staying. Today, while fewer Indians actually reside in this district, Little India is still the heartbeat of Indian culture in Singapore; shops here sell the clothing, cultural, and religious items, and imported goods from "back home" that keep the Indian community linked to their cultural heritage. Although the Indian community in Singapore is a minority in its numbers, you wouldn't think so on Sundays, when all the workers have their day off and come to the streets here to socialize and relax.

Like Little India, the area around **Bugis Street** is adjacent to the Historic District. This neighborhood was originally allocated for the Bugis settlers who came from the island of Celebes, part of Indonesia. The Bugis were welcomed in Singapore, and because they originated from a society based on seafaring and trading, they became master shipbuilders. Today, regrettably, nothing remains of Bugis culture outside of the national museums. In fact, for most locals, Bugis Street is better remembered as a 1970s den of iniquity where transvestites, transsexuals, and other sex performers would stage seedy Bangkok-style shows and beauty contests. The government "cleaned up" Bugis Street in the 1980s, so that all that remains is a huge shopping mall and a sanitized night market.

Kampong Glam, the neighborhood beyond Bugis Street, was given to Sultan Hussein and his family as part of his agreement to turn control of Singapore over to Raffles. Here he built his *istana* (palace) and the Sultan Mosque, and the area subsequently filled with Malay and Arab Muslims who imparted a distinct Islamic flavor to the neighborhood. The presence of the Sultan Mosque assures that the area remains a focal point of Singapore Muslim society, but the istana has fallen into disrepair and serves as a sad reminder of the economic condition into which Singapore's Malay community has fallen. **Arab Street** is perhaps the most popular area attraction for tourists and locals, who come to find deals on textiles and regional crafts.

Two areas of the city center are relatively new, having been built atop huge parcels of reclaimed land. Where the eastern edges of Chinatown and Tanjong Pagar once touched the water's edge, land reclamation created the present-day downtown business district, which is named after its central thoroughfare, **Shenton Way.** This Wall Street–like district is home to the magnificent skyscrapers that grace Singapore's

Urban Singapore Neighborhoods

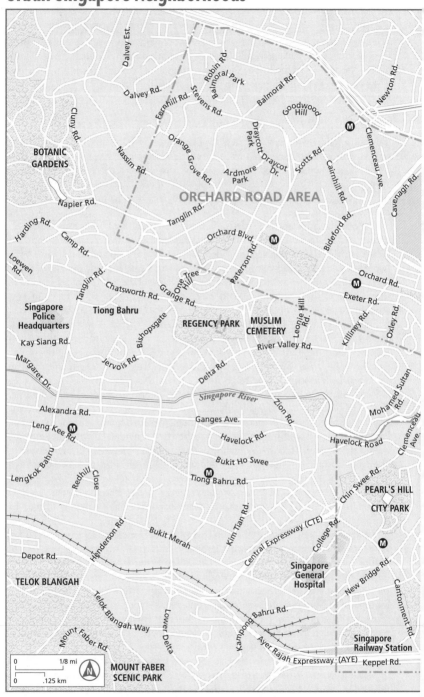

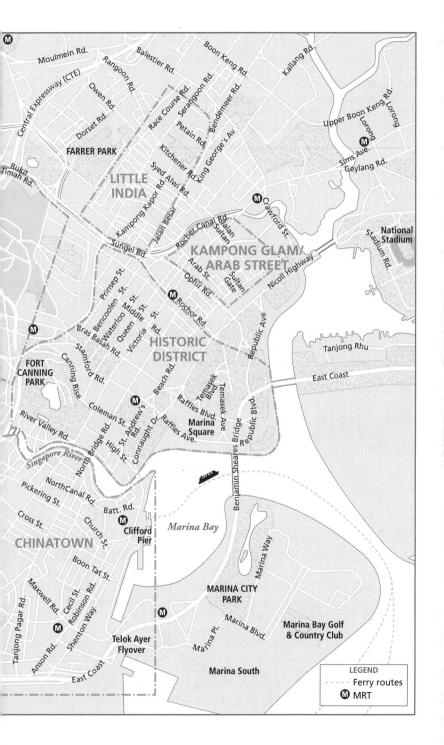

15

skyline and to the banks and businesses that have made the place an international financial capital. During weekday business hours (9am to 5pm), Shenton Way is packed with scurrying businesspeople. After hours and on weekends, it's nothing more than a quiet forest of concrete, metal, and glass.

The other reclaimed area is **Marina Bay,** on the other side of the river, just east of the Historic District. **Suntec City,** Southeast Asia's largest convention and exhibition center, is located here, and has become the linchpin of a thriving hotel, shopping mall, and amusement zone.

SUBURBAN SINGAPORE

With rapid urbanization in the 20th century, plantations and farms turned into sub-urban residential areas, many with their own ethnic roots.

To the east of the city is **Katong,** a famous residential district inhabited primarily by Peranakan (Straits Chinese) and Eurasian families. Its streets were, and still are, lined with Peranakan-style terrace houses, a residential variation of the shophouse found in commercial districts. The Peranakans and Eurasians were tolerant groups, a result of interracial marriages and multicultural family life, who created a close-knit community with a laid-back feeling that's carried over to the present day. Main streets are still lined with Peranakan restaurants and there are many Catholic churches and schools that served the Eurasians.

As public transportation opened up the eastern sections of the island, neighbor-hoods extended farther out. **Geylang,** the neighborhood just beyond Katong, was and still is primarily a Malay district. Joo Chiat and Geylang roads are lined with antiques shops and restaurants where halal foods—corresponding to Islamic dietary laws—are served. Today, a lot of the shophouses have been renovated, but it's still a good area to find housewares, fabrics, and modern furniture shops. **Joo Chiat Complex** (601 Joo Chiat Rd., at the corner of Geylang Road and across the street from Malay Village) has shops with Muslim religious artifacts, fabrics, and Indo-Malay pop and traditional recordings. At night, parts of Geylang are notorious for an illegal but tolerated prostitution industry.

Also to the east is **Changi Village,** at the far eastern tip of the island. It was built as the residential area of a British military post, but the Brits are gone now and Changi is pretty quiet. In recent years, however, restaurants and nightspots have opened here, making for a nice time outside of the urban center's hustle and bustle. From the pub-lic beach here you can see Singapore's northern islands, and parts of Malaysia and Indonesia. The one really notable aspect of the place is that it's where you pick up **fer-ries** to Pulau Ubin and Malaysia.

From the main urban center, if you head west, you'll find an old neighborhood, **Tiong Bahru.** Its original inhabitants were Chinese from the Chinatown and Tanjong Pagar districts, and the neighborhood remains largely Chinese today. In the 1960s, the Housing Development Board replaced small homes and makeshift housing with high-rise public apartment housing. The younger generations have moved on to bigger housing in the new estates, leaving the place mostly populated by the elderly.

Located west of Tiong Bahru, **Holland Village** is another famous neighborhood that's become a tourist attraction in its own right. Its nucleus of shops carries mer-chandise catering to Westerners, many of whom reside in the vicinity. Despite the Western customers, these aren't necessarily Western goods, but rather the kind of rattan furnishing, baskets, pottery, and other regional goods that you find adding color to otherwise Western-style homes.

THE "NEW TOWNS"

In the 1960s, to deal with the growing Singapore population, the HDB created a scheme to build residential areas along an imaginary circle around the Central Water Catchment Reserve in the center of the island. These New Towns would consist of blocks of high-rise public apartments around which shops, markets, and restaurants could settle to support the residents. Kampungs, villages, farms, and orchards were leveled, swamps were drained, and local streams were turned into concrete channels to make way for New Towns such as Bedok, Tampines, Pasir Ris, Toa Payoh, Bishan, Ang Mo Kio, Yishun, Woodlands, and Clementi, which sprang up in all parts of the island. One trip on a subway and all these names become familiar, as the Mass Rapid Transit System (MRT) was brought into the scheme to provide affordable transportation to all the towns.

Since 1960, more than 766,570 government apartments have been built. That's a lot of Singaporeans living in public housing. But however appealing the scheme sounded at first, residents in New Towns have their complaints. The apartments have become extremely expensive, and long waiting lists are filled with couples who wish to buy their first homes and families who need to upgrade to larger digs. Beyond questions of expense, though, there's the fact that the New Towns are singularly *depressing*, with block after block of similarly characterless high-rises looming overhead and compartmentalized living creating an urban anonymity between the many inhabitants. Certain towns are said to have their own identities, stemming from larger populations of one ethnic group or another or from a particular majority age group, but even this modest differentiation is under attack by various government initiatives aimed at interspersing the races and encouraging a "Singaporean" national homogeneity.

The Singapore Tourism Board has developed a **half-day tour** of these New Towns, plus other suburban districts. For more information about this tour, see chapter 6, "Strolling & Touring Around Singapore."

2 Visitor Information

The long arm of the Singapore Tourism Board (STB) reaches many overseas audiences through its branch offices, which will gladly provide brochures and booklets to help you plan your trip, and through their Web site, at **www.newasia-singapore.com**. The STB also has Web sites with special tips directed specifically for American and Canadian travelers. If you're traveling from the States, look up **www.singapore-usa.com**; from Canada, try **www.singapore-ca.com**.

IN THE UNITED STATES
- **New York:** 590 Fifth Ave., 12th Floor, New York, NY 10036 (☎ **212/ 302-4861;** fax 212/302-4801)
- **Chicago:** Two Prudential Plaza, 180 North Stetson Ave., Suite 2615, Chicago, IL 60601 (☎ **312/938-1888;** fax 312/938-0086)
- **Los Angeles:** 8484 Wilshire Blvd., Suite 510, Beverly Hills, CA 90211 (☎ **323/ 852-1901;** fax 323/852-0129)

IN CANADA
- **Toronto:** The Standard Life Centre, 121 King St. West, Suite 1000, Toronto, Ontario, Canada M5H 3T9 (☎ **416/363-8898;** fax 416/363-5752)

IN THE UNITED KINGDOM
- **London:** 1st Floor, Carrington House, 126–130 Regent St., London W1R 5FE, United Kingdom (☎ **207/4370033;** fax 207/7342191)

Kampung Life

When modern, hectic, business-like society gets them down, many modern Singaporeans look back with longing to the days when life was simple, and when they do, the kampung villages always come to mind.

Kampung (sometimes *kampong*) is Malay for "village," and once upon a time, many of Singapore's rural laborers and fishermen—mostly Malays but also Chinese and Indians—lived in these villages, small clusters of houses that were built from wood and *attap* (thatch) and raised on stilts, irrespective of whether they rested on swampland or dry earth. Built along the shores of the island and close to jungles, the buildings were nestled in backdrops of idyllic greenery, surrounded by banana and coconut groves and marshes. Homes had land for chicken coops and kitchen gardens, and backyards in which children could play; villages had central wells, provision shops, and sometimes a mosque. Despite their poverty, the kampung villages represented community.

The 1950s and 1960s were the heydays of kampung life. Later, the houses were "improved" with corrugated metal, concrete, and wallboard, all of which rusted and rotted over time, making the kampungs look more like slums than the homely villages they once were. Inside, modernization brought government-mandated running water and plumbing, and even electrical appliances like TVs, refrigerators, and telephones, but all in all, life was hardly opulent.

Today, this entire way of life is just a memory. Every last kampung on the main island has been razed, the inhabitants relocated by the government to public housing estates. Many former kampung inhabitants have had a difficult time adjusting to life in concrete high-rises, with no front porch or back yard, and neighbors who are too busy to remember their names. Perhaps that's why Singaporeans have recently been so ardently debating the development of Pulau Ubin, a small island to the north of the main island. The government has plans to make the small island into an HDB New Town, complete with an MRT (Mass Rapid Transit System) line linking it to the rest of the country—and severing it from its meaningful past. Despite the truth—that kampung life reflected poverty and struggle—the memory of them remains a link to older days that, however irrelevant to the modern world and however romanticized, still warms the hearts of many Singaporeans.

IN AUSTRALIA & NEW ZEALAND
- **Sydney:** Level 11, AWA Building, 47 York St., Sydney NSW 2000, Australia (☎ **2/9290-2888**; fax 2/9290-2555)

IN SINGAPORE
- **Tourism Court:** 1 Orchard Spring Lane, across the street from Traders Hotel (☎ **65/736-6622;** fax 65/736-9423. Their toll-free Touristline in Singapore is ☎ **1800/736-2000**)

3 Entry Requirements

To enter Singapore, you must have a valid passport. Visitors from the United States, Canada, Australia, New Zealand, and the United Kingdom are not required to obtain a visa prior to their arrival. A **Social Visit Pass** (with combined social and business status) good for up to 30 days will be awarded upon entry for travelers arriving by plane, or for 14 days if your trip is by ship or overland from Malaysia. Good news for U.S. passport holders: In fall 1999 the United States allowed Singaporeans to travel socially in the United States without a visa, so Singapore has reciprocated by allowing Americans a 3-month social/business-class Social Visit Pass upon entry. Be advised,this and all other types of passes are at the discretion of the Immigration officer, who may not award you the full amount of time. Singapore is trying to cut down on foreigners living here without proper documentation—many make illegal "Visa Runs" to Malaysia to allow them to stay longer in Singapore. However, if this is your first trip to Singapore, you should have no problems.

OBTAINING A VISA

If you do plan a stay longer than that granted by the Social Visit Pass, direct your visa inquiries to Singapore representative offices in your home country.

IN THE UNITED STATES

- **Washington, D.C.:** The Embassy of the Republic of Singapore, 3501 International Place NW, Washington, DC 20008 (☎ **202/537-3100;** fax 202/ 537-0876)
- **New York:** The Permanent Mission of Singapore to the United Nations, 231 E. 51st St., New York, NY 10022 (☎ **212/826-0840;** fax 212/826-2964)

IN CANADA

- **Vancouver:** Singapore High Consulate-General, Suite 1305, 999 W. Hastings St., Vancouver, British Columbia, V6C 2W2 Canada (☎ **604/669-5115;** fax 604/669-5153)

IN THE UNITED KINGDOM

- **London:** Singapore High Commission, 9 Wilton Crescent, London, SW 1X 8SA, United Kingdom (☎ **71/235-8315;** fax 71/245-6583)

IN AUSTRALIA

- **Canberra:** Singapore High Commission, 17 Forster Crescent, Yarralumla ACT 2600, Canberra, Australia (☎ **6/273-3944;** fax 6/273-3260)

IN NEW ZEALAND

- **Wellington:** Singapore High Commissioner, 17 Kabul St., Khandallah, P.O. Box 13-140, Wellington, New Zealand (☎ **4/479-2076;** fax 4/479-2315)

IN SINGAPORE

The Singapore Immigration & Registration (SIR) Department operates a 24-hour automated inquiry system for questions about visa requirements at ☎ **65/391-6100,** but if you need to speak to a representative, call between the hours of 8am and 5pm Monday through Friday, or 8am and 1pm on Saturday. The Singapore Immigration & Registration office is located at 10 Kallang Rd., SIR Building (above the Lavender MRT station). Business hours are Monday through Friday 8am to 5pm and Saturdays 8am to 1pm. For immigration information on the net, visit the Ministry of Home Affairs Web site at **www.mha.gov.sg**.

   If you need to extend your visa, apply at the SIR directly. You'll be required to process standard forms, and you'll need a letter of sponsorship from a Singapore citizen. Visa extensions are awarded completely at the discretion of the officer handling your request.

If you overstay your visa, report immediately to the SIR. Even the most conscientious travelers can overstay their visas. At immigration, you'll be asked to hand over your passport, departure record, your airline ticket to prove your return flight, and you'll be asked to write a letter to explain why you did not depart on time. They'll ask you to return the next day to retrieve your documents. In certain cases they may even require that you undergo an interview with an immigration official. If this happens, I strongly recommend that you act very humble, grovel, and beg forgiveness. The minimum fine for overstaying is S$50 (US$29.95), but the officer can charge you more. Again, it's at his discretion. If you are unfortunate enough to have overstayed for over a month or two, you may be arrested and punished, which means jail time or caning. How about that for a holiday story to take back to your friends?

If you need to replace travel documents while in Singapore, or have other problems, the foreign mission contacts are as follows: **United States,** 27 Napier Rd. (☎ **65/476-9100;** open Monday to Friday 8:30am to 5:15pm); **Canada,** 80 Anson Rd., #14/15-00 IBM Towers (☎ **65/325-3200;** open Monday to Friday 8:30am to 12:30pm and 1:30 to 4:30pm); **United Kingdom,** Tanglin Road (☎ **65/473-9333;** open Monday to Friday 8:30am to 5pm); **Australia,** 25 Napier Rd. (☎ **65/836-4100;** open Monday to Friday 8:30am to 12:30pm and 1:30 to 4:30pm); **New Zealand,** 391A Orchard Rd., Ngee Ann City Tower A #15-06 (☎ **65/235-9966;** open Monday to Friday 8:30am to 5pm).

CUSTOMS REGULATIONS

There's no restriction on the amount of currency you can bring into Singapore. For those over 18 years of age who have arrived from countries other than Malaysia and have spent more than 48 hours outside Singapore, allowable duty-free concessions are 1 liter of spirits; 1 liter of wine; and 1 liter of either port, sherry, or beer, all of which must be intended for personal consumption only. There are no duty-free concessions on cigarettes or other tobacco items. If you exceed the duty-free limitations, you can bring your excess items in upon payment of goods and services tax (GST) and Customs duty.

Upon departure, you'll be required to pay a **departure tax** of S$15 (US$9). Nowadays, this tax is usually added onto your airfare. Ask your airline if this is the case. If not, coupons for the amount can be purchased at most hotels, travel agencies, and airline offices.

PROHIBITED ITEMS   The following items are not allowed through Customs unless you have authorization or an import permit: animals; birds and their by-products; plants; endangered species or items made from these species; arms and explosives; bulletproof clothing; toy guns of any type; weapons, including decorative swords and knives; cigarette lighters in the shape of pistols; toy coins; pornographic prerecorded videotapes and cassettes, books, or magazines; controlled substances; poisons; and materials that may be considered treasonable (plutonium, military maps—that kind of thing). For all pharmaceutical drugs, especially sleeping pills, depressants, or stimulants, you must provide a prescription from your physician authorizing personal use for your well-being. All inquiries can be directed to the **Customs Office** at Changi International Airport (☎ **65/542-7058**) or to the automated Customs hot line at ☎ **65/355-2000** (Monday to Friday 8am to 5pm, Sat 8am to noon). A detailed rundown can be found on the net at the Ministry of Home Affairs home page **www.mha.gov.sg.**

Whatever You Do, Don't Drop Your Chewing Gum

According to the Customs office here, as a visitor it's perfectly legal for you to bring a packet or two of chewing gum into Singapore for your own personal consumption, and you can chew it on the streets or anywhere else you like. It is, however, illegal to sell or buy chewing gum within Singapore itself. Why? This is the story I heard.

After Singapore built the MRT subway system, truly a remarkable feat of engineering and efficiency, the government brought visiting international dignitaries to the system to show off their pride and joy. When the train pulled into the station, the doors jammed, and complete and irremediable embarrassment ensued. When the authorities demanded an investigation into the problem, it was found that someone had jammed chewing gum into the door mechanism. As a result, the government banned chewing gum, asserting that Singaporeans were unable to responsibly dispose of the stuff.

By the way, the Customs officer warned me (with a chuckle) that if a visitor arrived with more than just a few small packs, he might be suspected of chewing gum trafficking, in which case the offending material would simply be confiscated for the duration of the offender's stay, and returned upon departure.

If you do try to bring in any of the above articles, they will be confiscated and you will need to defend yourself to the relevant authorities. Pornographic materials will be confiscated, and upon occasion, videotapes will be returned with questionable scenes erased. And—my favorite part—you will be charged a small sum for the "service."

Another tip: You may be carrying items that are perfectly legal elsewhere, but aren't legal here. Keep in mind to report the following items to Customs officers upon entry: any sort of video cassette, decorative weapons (say, if you've bought a lovely antique keris dagger in Malaysia), or pornographic materials. If they find these items on you and you've failed to declare them, you could be punished with a fine. You may be ordered by Customs to unpack your bags to reveal the contents inside. As a leisure traveler, you should rarely have any problems along these lines, but it's always better to be aware. By the way, on a nice note, if you have been asked to empty your cases, the officers are required to help you repack if they're not too busy.

SINGAPORE'S DRUG POLICY   With all of the publicity surrounding the issue, Singapore's strict drug policy shouldn't need recapitulation, but here it is: Importing, selling, or using illegal narcotics is absolutely forbidden. Punishments are severe, up to and including the death penalty (automatic for morphine quantities exceeding 30 grams, heroin exceeding 15 grams, cocaine 30 grams, marijuana 500 grams, hashish 200 grams, opium 1.2 kilograms, and methamphetamines 250 grams). If you're carrying smaller sums (anything above: morphine 3 grams, heroin 2 grams, cocaine 3 grams, marijuana 15 grams, hashish 10 grams, opium 100 grams, and methamphetamines 25 grams) you'll still be considered to have intent to traffic, and may face the death penalty if you can't prove otherwise. If you're crazy enough to try to bring these things into the country and you are caught, no measure of appeal to your home consulate will grant you any special attention.

It should be noted that even with these drug laws, narcotics abuse still continues in Singapore. Despite aggressive government campaigns to stop drug abuse, casual marijuana consumption continues in underground circles. I also hear many rumors about growing opiate addiction problems, and in recent years there's been trouble among Singaporean youth involving the most recent fashionable drugs, Ecstasy and metham- phetamines. Do yourself a favor: If you're in an area where you suspect illegal drug consumption is taking place, get the hell away from there as fast as you can. Con- sumption charges include 5 to 30 years imprisonment and caning. Things have become so strict that Singaporeans are even accountable for drug abuses committed overseas—a Singaporean who fails a urine analysis after an overseas trip faces the same penalties as if the offense were committed in the country. If narcotics are an impor- tant part of your vacation enjoyment, reconsider Singapore. Frommer's has a wonder- ful travel guide available for Amsterdam, which I'd recommend you take a peek at.

THE TOURIST REFUND SCHEME

Singapore has a great incentive for travelers to drop big bucks: the Tourist Refund Scheme. If you purchase goods at a value of S$300 (US$179.65) or more at a shop that displays the Tax Free Shopping sign, Customs will reimburse the 3% GST (goods and services tax) you paid for the purchase. You are allowed to pool receipts from dif- ferent retailers for purchases of S$100 (US$59.90) or more. Here's how it works: When you purchase the item(s), apply with the retailer for a Tax Free Shopping Check. When you're leaving Singapore, present your Shopping Checks and the items purchased at the Tax Refund Counters located in the Departure Hall at Changi Air- port's terminals 1 or 2. Within 12 weeks, you'll receive a check for the GST refund— or, if you used a credit card for the purchase, your bill can be credited (a surcharge may be levied). For more information, contact the **Singapore Tourism Board** at ☎ 800/736-2000.

4 Money

The local currency unit is the **Singapore dollar.** It's commonly referred to as the "Sing dollar," and retail prices are often marked as S$ (a designation I've used throughout this book). Notes are issued in denominations of S$1, S$2, S$5, S$10, S$50, S$100, S$500, and S$1,000. Notes vary in size and color from denomination to denomina- tion. Coins are issued in denominations of S1¢, S5¢, S10¢, S20¢, S50¢, and the fat, gold-colored S$1. Singapore has an interchangeability agreement with Brunei, so the Brunei dollar is accepted as equal to the Singapore dollar.

Singapore's currency weathered the Southeast Asian economic crisis in 1997 rather successfully, so if you were hoping for a more favorable exchange rate, you're looking in the wrong place; the Sing dollar has decreased in value only slightly from precrisis rates. At the time of this writing, exchange rates on the Singapore dollar were as fol- lows: US$1 = S$1.67, Can$1 = S$1.14, £1 = S$2.70, A$1 = S$1.07, NZ$1 = S85¢. These are the exchange rates used throughout this book, but before you begin bud- geting your trip, I suggest you obtain the latest conversions so you don't suffer any shocks at the last minute. A neat and easy customizable currency conversion program can be found on the Internet through CNN's Web site at **www.cnn.com/TRAVEL/ ESSENTIALS,** and there's a great interactive table at **www.xe.net/ict.**

CURRENCY EXCHANGE   While hotels and banks will perform currency exchanges, you'll get a better rate at any one of the many money changers that can be found in all the shopping malls and major shopping districts (look for the certificate of government authorization). Many shops are also authorized to change money, and will display signs to that effect. Money changers usually give you the official going rate for the day, and sometimes the difference in rate between hotels and money changers

Singapore Dollar Conversion Chart

S$	U.S.$	Can$	A$	NZ$	U.K.£
.10	$0.06	$0.09	$0.09	$0.12	£0.04
.20	$0.12	$0.18	$0.19	$0.24	£0.07
.50	$0.30	$0.44	$0.47	$0.59	£0.19
1.00	$0.60	$0.90	$0.95	$1.20	£0.35
2.00	$1.20	$1.75	$1.85	$2.35	£0.75
5.00	$3.00	$4.40	$4.65	$5.90	£1.85
10.00	$6.00	$8.75	$9.35	$11.75	£3.70
20.00	$12.00	$17.55	$18.70	$23.55	£7.401
50.00	$29.95	$43.85	$46.75	$58.80	£18.50
100.00	$59.90	$87.70	$93.45	$117.65	£37.05
500.00	$299.40	$438.60	$467.30	$588.25	£185.20
1000.00	$598.80	$877.20	$934.60	$1,176.45	£370.35

can be as much as US8¢ to the dollar. Lastly, while some hotels and shops may accept your foreign currency as payment, they will always calculate the exchange rate in their favor.

AUTOMATED TELLER MACHINES   Singapore has thousands of conveniently located 24-hour automated teller machines (ATMs). Whether you're in your hotel, a shopping mall, or a suburban neighborhood, I'd be surprised if you're more than 1 or 2 blocks from an ATM—ask your concierge or any passerby and they can direct you. With debit cards on the MasterCard/Cirrus or Visa/PLUS systems, you can withdraw Singapore currency from any of these machines, and your bank will deduct the amount from your account at that day's official exchange rate. This is a very good way to access cash for the most favorable currency rate, but make sure you check with your bank before you leave home, to find out what your daily withdrawal limits are. It's also a good idea to keep track of ATM charges—while Singapore banks do not charge for the service, your home financial institution can levy a fee of up to US$1.50 per transaction for this convenience.

TRAVELER'S CHECKS   The two most easily recognizable traveler's checks in Singapore are issued from American Express and Thomas Cook. They can be cashed at banks and hotels, but money changers will cash them at the day's official exchange rate (as opposed to charging a fee or giving their own rate). Upon occasion they may try to charge a fee, but if you indicate you'll take your business elsewhere they may change their minds. To cash a traveler's check you will need to show your passport. Occasionally, an international driver's license or your driver's license from home will suffice.

CREDIT CARDS   American Express (AE) is accepted widely, as are Diners Club (DC), MasterCard (MC), Japan Credit Bank (JCB), and Visa (V), though you'll find that some budget hotels, smaller shops, and restaurants will accept no credit cards at all. Purchases made with credit cards will appear on your bill at the exchange rate on the day your charge is posted, *not* what the rate was on the day the purchase was made. It's also worth noting that if your signature is slightly different on the slip than it is on

What Things Cost in Singapore

Taxi from the airport to city center	S$22 (US$13.15)
MRT from Orchard to Chinese Garden stations	S$1.30 (US$0.80)
Local telephone call	S10¢ (3 min.) (US$0.06)
Double room at an expensive hotel	S$350 (US$209.60)
Double room at a moderate hotel	S$250 (US$149.70)
Double room at an inexpensive hotel	S$120 (US$71.85)
Dinner for one at an expensive restaurant	S$60 (US$35.95)
Dinner for one at a moderate restaurant	S$25 (US$14.95)
Dinner for one at an inexpensive restaurant	S$5 (US$3)
Glass of beer	S$9.00 (US$5.40)
Coca-Cola	S$1.10 (US$0.65)
Cup of coffee at common coffee shop	S70¢ (US$0.42)
Cup of coffee at Starbucks, Coffee Club, and so on	S$3 (US$1.80)
Roll of 36-exposure color film	S$4.50 (US$2.70)
Admission to the National History Museum	S$3 (US$1.80)
Movie ticket	S$9 (US$5.40)

your card, shop owners will make you redo the slip. They're real sticklers for signature details, so don't leave out a middle initial or forget to cross a T.

American Express is a recommended asset for all who venture overseas. Their Charge Card Guarantee Service allows you to cash personal checks up to US$1,000 every 21 calendar days while you travel. (Note that if the checks are not honored by your financial institution, American Express will charge it to your bill and will freeze your account until the entire amount is recovered.) For more information, check the American Express Web site at **www.americanexpress.com**.

In Singapore, the American Express office the 24-hour membership services hot line is ☎ **1800/732-2244.** The 24-hour traveler's check refund hot line is ☎ 1800/ 738-3383.

MasterCard has toll-free access to report lost or stolen cards. In Singapore dial ☎ **1800/110-0113** to reach MasterCard's Global Service Emergency Assistance for International Travelers.

For **Visa's** Emergency Assistance number call their local toll-free hot line at ☎ **1800/580-7500.**

For both MasterCard and Visa, there are other services available, but it depends on the type of card you hold and the institution that issued it. Contact your issuing institution before your trip to find out what travel benefits you're eligible to receive.

WIRING FUNDS Although some other travel books report the contrary, Western Union does not operate in Singapore. However, there are alternatives. **Thomas Cook Overseas Ltd.** can wire funds to and from other international Thomas Cook locations or can wire money from any Thomas Cook to your bank account. The telegraphic transfer service costs S$20 (US$12) per transaction, regardless of the amount transferred. Also through the Thomas Cook office, you can send and receive MoneyGram transfers. Fees are based on a graded scale, with transfers of US$1,000 carrying a charge of US$50. (*Note:* Only U.S. currency can be handled through the MoneyGram service.) It takes only 10 to 15 minutes to send or receive money with either wire transfer option. Thomas Cook will also draft traveler's checks in foreign currencies for a charge of 1% of the total amount. The Singapore Thomas Cook office is located at 50 Raffles Place on the ground floor of the Singapore Landtower Building (walk along Change Alley to find the office). Or you can call them at ☎ **65/ 538-8133.** They are open Monday to Friday 9am to 5:30pm, Saturday 9am to 1pm; but for transactions, they request you show up well before closing time.

5 When to Go

CLIMATE

At approximately 137 kilometers (82 miles) north of the equator, with exposure to the sea on three sides, it's a sure bet that Singapore will be hot and humid year-round. Temperatures remain uniform, with a daily average of 80.6°F (26.7°C), afternoon temperatures reaching as high as 87.44°F (30.8°C), and an average sunrise temperature as low as 75.03°F (23.9°C). Relative humidity often exceeds 90% at night and in the early morning. Even on a "dry" afternoon, don't expect it to drop much below 60%. (The daily average is 84.4% relative humidity.) Rain falls year-round, much of it coming down in sudden downpours that end abruptly and are followed immediately by the sun. Don't expect it to cool off any after a shower, though. On the contrary, downpours leave the air thick and heavy as water quickly evaporates from pavement and hot surfaces. The annual rainfall is 94.08 inches (2,352mm).

Weather patterns in Singapore are dominated by two periods: the **Northeast Monsoon** and the **Southwest Monsoon.** While these seasons are called monsoons, they are not necessarily of the "bend-the-palms-and-blow-your-beach-shack-down" variety. The distinctions are observed merely to keep track of wind directions, which at one time were important for sea merchants but nowadays only mark what small seasonal changes Singapore has.

The Northeast Monsoon occurs between December and March, when temperatures are slightly cooler, relatively speaking, than other times of the year. Even in December, though, one of the "cooler" months, you can still break a sweat past midnight. The heaviest rainfall occurs between November and January, with daily showers that sometimes last for long periods of time; at other times, it comes down in short heavy gusts and goes quickly away. Wind speeds are rarely anything more than light. The Southwest Monsoon falls between June and September. Temperatures are higher and, interestingly, it's during this time of year that Singapore gets the *least* rain (with the very least reported in July).

In between monsoons, thunderstorms are frequent. Also interesting, the number of daylight hours and number of nighttime hours remains almost constant year-round. February is the sunniest month, while December is generally more overcast.

CLOTHING CONSIDERATIONS   Common sense will tell you that the ideal clothes to pack are lightweight, loose fitting, and of natural fibers. To ward off the tropical heat, many public places are air-conditioned to Arctic-freeze temperatures, so it's a good idea to bring a light sweater or jacket so you'll have something warm if you're stuck in the theater, in a restaurant, or on a tour bus for hours—it's also helpful if you plan on going in and out of air-conditioning frequently throughout the day. These types of sudden temperature changes have been known to ruin many vacations with summer colds.

Another good consideration is to bring shoes that fit you very loosely. If you come from colder climates, your feet will swell from the heat, as well as from being on them all day while you're taking in the sights. Don't even trust your favorite pair. If they're a snug fit, they'll turn into your worst enemies before long, and nothing feels worse than having to pinch your feet into tight and uncomfortable shoes when you want to have fun.

For sightseeing, shorts and T-shirts are probably the most comfortable attire, but keep in mind if you plan to visit a mosque that neither men nor women are permitted to wear shorts, and women are not permitted to wear miniskirts or sleeveless, backless, or low-cut tops. As for footwear, if you can find slip-on shoes that are comfortable for walking, they'd be the most convenient, as all mosques, temples, and private residences will require you to remove your shoes at the door.

Most restaurants and nightclubs will request attire that is "dress casual," meaning a shirt and slacks for men and a dress or skirt/slacks and top for women. Because of the heat, many places are forgiving when it comes to dress codes—you can't be expected to be a fashion plate all the time; however, when formal attire is required, you should take it seriously. Men will be expected to appear in a jacket and tie and women in dress slacks or a formal dress. This will only be the case at very expensive restaurants or high-toned events. As far as clothing style is concerned, Singaporeans can be quite fashion conscious. If you look like you've just popped out of a safari in the jungles of Borneo, you'll be an odd sight on Singapore's urban streets.

Calendar of Public Holidays & Events

There are 11 official public holidays: New Year's Day, Chinese New Year or Lunar New Year (2 days), Hari Raya Puasa, Good Friday, Hari Raya Haji, Labour Day, Vesak Day, National Day, Deepavali, and Christmas Day. On these days, expect government offices, banks, and some shops to be closed.

Holidays and festivals are well publicized by the **Singapore Tourism Board** (STB), which loves to introduce the world to the joys of all Singapore's cultures. A call or visit to an STB office either before your trip or once you arrive will let you know the what, where, and when of all that's happening during your stay. See the listing of STB offices in the United States, Canada, the United Kingdom, and Australia under "Visitor Information," earlier in this chapter. Its Web site at **www.newasia-singapore.com** also has information about upcoming holidays and festivals.

January/February

- **New Year's Day.** The first day of the calendar year is celebrated in Singapore by all races and religions. New Year's Eve in Singapore is always cause for parties and celebrations similar to those in the West. Look for special events and parties at restaurants and nightclubs, but don't expect to find a lot of taxis around when you need one! January 1.

- ✪ **Lunar New Year or Chinese New Year.** If you want to catch the biggest event in the Chinese calendar and pretty much the biggest in Singapore, come during the Chinese New Year celebrations, which include parades and festivals. Two days, late January/early February. For details, see the box, "Ringing in the New Year, Chinese-Style," below.

- ✪ **Thaipusam Festival.** If you're lucky enough to be in Singapore during this event, you're in for a bizarre cultural treat. This annual festival is celebrated by Hindus to give thanks to Lord Subramaniam, the child god who represents virtue, youth,

Ringing in the New Year, Chinese-Style

Chinese New Year, a 15-day celebration of the new year according to the lunar calendar, is the most important festival of the Chinese culture and a huge occasion in Singapore. It was originally called *Chun Jie* or Spring Festival, to celebrate the passing of winter and spring's promise of a fertile and prosperous growing season. In modern times, it is still seen as a chance to put the past behind and start afresh, with new hopes for prosperity, health, and luck. During the celebration, homes and businesses display large red banners with the characters *Gong Xi Fa Cai,* which mean "Wishing you great prosperity." Stores generally mark up prices dramatically just before the New Year to cash in on the opportunity. Outside of homes, the Chinese hang the character Fu, which means "luck." The fu is usually hung upside down because in Chinese the words for "luck upside down" sound similar to the words for "luck arrives." Red, symbolizing luck and prosperity, is predominant in banners and is the color of the *hong bao,* packets of money given to children and single young adults by parents and married friends. Money is given in even dollar amounts (as even numbers are considered auspicious) and should be opened in private. Oranges and tangerines are given as gifts (also in even numbers), symbolizing gold and luck, both in their colors and in Chinese puns. Also important—in most places, but unfortunately not Singapore, where they're banned—are noisy firecrackers, which are believed to ward off evil spirits and also serve (through their noise) as a sign of life.

New Year's Day, the first day of celebration, generally falls somewhere between January 21 and February 19. In preparation for New Year's Day, the Chinese pay off old debts (since debt is believed to lead to bad luck in the coming year if not taken care of) and clean their homes from tip to toe, sweeping the floors in a symbolic clearing away of old misfortunes. All cleaning is done before New Year's Eve because New Year's Day is auspicious, and to sweep on this day would be to sweep away good luck. (So hide your broom.) New Year's Eve is the night of the reunion feast, where family members gather and invite the spirits of deceased ancestors to gather for a meal, the centerpiece of which is a large fish to symbolize unity.

New Year's is a time for rejoicing with family and friends, praying to ancestors, and, in Singapore, going to the Chingay parade, a brilliant procession of dragon dances, stilt walkers, and floats, that heads down Orchard Road. While the first and second days are spent visiting friends and family, the third is considered unlucky for visiting, and most people return to work.

The final day of the celebration, the 15th day, is the Lantern Festival, which coincides with the first full moon of the new year. Paper lanterns are hung in doorways, which to Westerners is a romantic backdrop for this day, which the Chinese consider auspicious for lovers.

beauty, and valor. During Thaipusam, male Hindus who have made prayers to Subramaniam for special wishes must carry *kavadis* in gratitude. These huge steel racks are decorated with flowers and fruits and are held onto the men's bodies by skewers and hooks that pierce the skin. Carrying the *kavadis,* the devotees parade from Sri Perumal Temple in Little India to Chettiar's Temple on Tank Road, where family members remove the heavy structures. For an additional spectacle, they will pierce their tongues and cheeks with skewers and hang fruits from hooks in their flesh. The devotees have all undergone strict diet and prayer before the festival, and it is reported that, afterward, no scars remain. Late January/early February.

Hari Raya Puasa. Hari Raya Puasa marks the end of Ramadan, the Muslim month of fasting during daylight hours. During Ramadan, food stalls line up around the Sultan Mosque in Kampong Glam, ready to sell Malay and Indian food at sundown. It's a 3-day celebration (though only the first day is a public holiday) of thanksgiving dinners, and non-Muslims are often invited to these feasts, as the holiday symbolizes an openness of heart and mind and a renewed sense of community. During the course of the three evenings, Geylang—the neighborhood centered around Geylang Road—is decorated with lights and banners and the whole area is open for a giant *pasar malam,* or night market. Late January/early February.

March/April

- **Good Friday.** Churches and cathedrals hold special services on this Christian holiday to remember the crucifixion of Christ. St. Joseph's on Victoria Street holds an annual candlelight procession. Late March/early April.

- **Qing Ming (All Souls' Day).** Qing Ming, or All Souls' Day, was originally a celebration of spring. On this day, Chinese families have picnics at ancestral graves, cleaning the graves and pulling weeds, lighting red candles, burning joss sticks and "Hell Money" (paper money whose smoke rises to the afterworld to be used by the ancestors), and bringing rice, wine, and flowers for the deceased in a show of ancestral piety. Early April.

- **The Singapore International Film Festival.** This event showcases critically acclaimed works, including international films and Singaporean short productions. The year 1999 marked the 12th year this event has taken place—it's become a renowned showcase for Asian films, which constitute 40% of those featured. The festival includes competitions, workshops, and tributes to filmmakers. Information can be obtained from its Web site at http://filmfest.asia-online.com.sg. You can order tickets through TicketCharge over the phone by calling ☎ 65/296-2929, via e-mail at booking@ticketcharge.net, or at many locations throughout the city. See "The Performing Arts" section in chapter 8 for exact locations. April.

- **Hari Raya Haji.** One of the five pillars of Islam involves making a pilgrimage to Mecca at least once in a lifetime, and Hari Raya Haji is celebrated the day after pilgrims make this annual voyage to fulfill their spiritual promise. Muslims who have made the journey adopt the title of Haji (for men) and Hajjah (for women). After morning prayers, sheep and goats are sacrificed and their meat is distributed to poor families. Late April/early May.

May

- **Vesak Day.** Buddhist shrines and temples are adorned with banners, lights, and flowers and worshippers gather to pray and chant in observance of the birth, enlightenment, and death of the Buddha, which all occurred on this day. Good places to watch the festivities, unless you're afraid of crowds, are the Temple of a Thousand Lights in Little India or Thian Hock Keng Temple in Chinatown. On this day, Buddhists will refrain from eating meat, donate food to the poor, and set animals (especially birds) free to show kindness and generosity. It falls on the full moon of the fifth month of the lunar calendar—which means somewhere around mid-May.

June

✪ **Festival of Asian Performing Arts.** During this monthlong festival, first-class local, regional, and international music and dance performances are staged in a number of venues. The cultural performances, some modern and some traditional, are always excellent and are highly recommended. Contact the Singapore Tourism Board (STB) for a full program with details of each event. June.

July

- **The Singapore Food Festival.** Local chefs compete for honors in this monthlong exhibition of international culinary delights. It's a good time to be eating in Singapore, as restaurants feature the brand-new creations they have entered in the events. Contact the STB for details. July.
- **The Great Singapore Sale.** This is a monthlong promotion to increase retail sales, and most shops will advertise huge savings for the entire month. It's well publicized with red banners all over Orchard Road. July.
- **Singapore World Invitational Dragon Boat Races.** The annual dragon boat races are held to remember the fate of Qu Yuan, a patriot and poet during the Warring States period in Chinese history (475–221 B.C.), who threw himself into a river to end his suffering at watching his state fall into ruin under the hands of corrupt leadership. The people searched for him in boats shaped like dragons, beating gongs and throwing rice dumplings into the water to distract the River Dragon. Today, the dragon boat races are an international event, with rowing teams from 20 countries coming together to compete. Drums are still beaten, and rice dumplings are still a traditional favorite. Contact the STB for information. Late June / early July.
- **Maulidin Nabi.** Muslims celebrate the birth of the Prophet Mohammed on this day. Sultan Mosque is the center of the action for Muslims who come to chant in praise. July 17.

August

✪ **National Day.** On August 9, 1965, Singapore separated from the Federation of Malaysia, becoming an independent republic. Singaporeans celebrate this as a sort of independence day, with a grand parade with spectacular floats and marching bands. They also stage a fireworks display in the evening. August 9.

- **Festival of the Hungry Ghosts.** The Chinese believe that once a year the gates of purgatory are opened and all the souls inside are let loose to wander among the living. These are the poor souls who either died violent deaths or whose families failed to pay them respects after they died—fates that cause them to menace people as much as they can. To appease the spirits and prevent evil from falling upon themselves, the Chinese burn joss, Hell money, and paper replicas of luxury items, the latter two meant to appear in the afterworld for greedy ghosts to use. The main celebration is on the 15th day of the 7th month of the lunar calendar, and is celebrated with huge feasts to settle hungry ghosts. At markets, altars are placed under tents. Chinese operas are performed throughout the month to entertain the spirits and make them more docile. For information on these performances, call the **Chinese Theatre Circle,** 5 Smith St. (☎ **65/ 323-4862**). They perform excerpts from classic operas every Wednesday and Friday evenings year-round at Clarke Quay (see chapter 8 for more details), but may stage special full-length operas for the occasion. You can also try the STB, which will tell you if there are any visiting operas performing around the city.

September

- **The Mooncake and Lantern Festivals.** Traditionally called the midautumn festival, it was celebrated to give thanks for a plentiful harvest. The origins date from the Sung Dynasty (A.D. 970–1279) when Chinese officials would exchange round mirrors as gifts to represent the moon and symbolize good health and success. Today, the holiday is celebrated by eating moon cakes, which are sort of like little round hockey pucks filled with lotus seeds or red bean paste and a salted duck egg yolk. Children light colorful plastic or paper lanterns shaped like fish, birds, butterflies, and, more recently, cartoon characters. There's an annual lantern display and competition out at the Chinese Garden, with acrobatic performances, lion dances, and night bazaars. Late September/early October.

October/November

- **Navarathiri Festival.** During this 9-day festival, Hindus make offerings to the wives of Shiva, Vishnu, and Brahma. The center point in the evenings is Chettiar's Temple (at 15 Tank Rd.), where dances and musical performances are staged. Performances begin around 7:30pm. Contact the STB for information. Late October/early November.

- **Deepavali.** Hindus and Sikhs celebrate Deepavali as the first day of their calendar. The new year is ushered in with new clothing, social feasts, and gatherings. It's a beautiful holiday, with Hindu temples aglow from the tiny earthen candles placed in cutouts up the sides of the buildings. Hindus believe that the souls of the deceased come to earth during this time, and the candles help to light their way back to heaven. During the celebration, **Serangoon Road** in Little India is a crazy display of colored lights and decorative arches. Children love this holiday, as it is customary to hand out sweets, especially to the little ones, and many businesspeople choose this time to close their books from the year's accounts and start afresh. Late October/early November.

- ✪ **Thimithi Festival.** Thimithi begins at the Sri Perumal Temple in Little India and makes its way in parade fashion to the Sri Mariamman Temple in Chinatown. Outside the temple, a bed of hot coals is prepared and a priest will lead the way, walking first over the coals, to be followed one at a time by devotees. Crowds gather to watch the spectacle, which begins around 5pm. Make sure you're early so you can find a good spot. Contact the STB for information. Late October/early November.

- **Birthday of the Monkey God.** In the Chinese temples ceremonies are performed by mediums who pierce their faces and tongues and write prayers with the blood. In the temple courtyards you can see Chinese operas and puppet shows. The **Tan Si Chong Su Temple** on Magazine Road, upriver from Boat Quay, is a good bet for seeing the ceremonies. Contact the STB for information. Late September/early October.

- **Festival of the Nine-Emperor God.** During this celebration, held over the first 9 days of the 9th month of the lunar calendar (to the Chinese, the double nines are particularly auspicious), temples are packed with worshippers, hawkers sell religious items outside, and Chinese operas are performed for the Nine-Emperor God, a composite of nine former emperors who control the prosperity and health of worshippers. At the height of the festival, priests write prayers with their own blood. On the 9th day, the festival closes as the Nine-Emperor God's spirit, contained in an urn, is sent to sea on a small decorated boat. Contact the STB for information. Late October.

- **Pilgrimage to Kusu Island.** During this monthlong period, plan your trips to Kusu Island wisely, as the place becomes a mob scene. Throughout the month (the lunar month, that is), Chinese travel to this small island to visit the temple there and pray for another year of health and wealth. See chapter 8 for more information on Kusu. October/November.

December
- **Christmas Light-Up.** Orchard Road is brilliant in bright and colorful streams of Christmas lights and garlands. All of the hotels and shopping malls participate, dressed in the usual Christmas regalia of nativity scenes and Santa Clauses. November 15 through January 2.
- **Christmas Day.** On this day, Christian Singaporeans celebrate the birth of Christ. December 25.

6 Health & Insurance

BEATING THE HEAT & HUMIDITY
As Singapore's climate guarantees heat and humidity year-round, you should remember to take precautions. Make sure you give yourself plenty of time to relax and regroup on arrival to adjust your body to the new climate (and to the new time, if there is a time difference for you). Also, *drink plenty of water.* This may seem obvious, but remember that tea, coffee, colas, and alcohol dehydrate the body and should never be substituted for water if you're thirsty. Singapore's tap water is absolutely potable, so you don't have to worry about any wee beasties floating around in your glass.

Avoid overexposure to the sun. The tropical sun will burn you like thin toast in no time at all. You may also feel more lethargic than usual. This is typical in the heat, so take things easy and you'll be fine. Be careful of the air-conditioning, though. It's nice and cooling, but if you're prone to catching a chill, or find yourself moving in and out of air-conditioned buildings a lot, you can wind up with a horrible summer cold.

DIETARY PRECAUTIONS
Generally speaking, you'll have no more problems with the food in Singapore than you will in your hometown, barring any digestive problems you may experience simply because you're not used to the ingredients. All the same sanitary rules apply, too—for instance, as at home, you should thoroughly wash the fruits or vegetables you buy, to rinse away any bacteria.

Chinese restaurants in Singapore still use monosodium glutamate (MSG), the flavor enhancer that was blamed for everything from fluid retention to migraine headaches, and has been squeezed out of most Chinese restaurant cuisine in the West. The MSG connection has just started to catch on here, but not in full force. Many restaurants can now prepare dishes without MSG upon request, but smaller places will probably think you're insane for asking.

DISEASES
Singapore doesn't require that you have any **vaccinations** to enter the country, but strongly recommends immunization against diphtheria, tetanus, hepatitis A and B, and typhoid. If you're particularly worried, follow their advice; if you're the intrepid type, ignore it.

While there's no risk of contracting malaria (the country's been declared malaria-free for decades by the World Health Organization), there is a similar deadly virus, **dengue fever** (also just called dengue), that's carried by mosquitoes and has no immunization. Dengue fever is a problem in the tropics around the world; however, Singapore has an aggressive campaign to prevent the responsible mosquitoes from breeding, spraying dark corners with insecticide and enforcing laws so people mop up pools of stagnant water. Symptoms of dengue fever include sudden fever and tiny red spotty rashes on the body. If you suspect you've contracted dengue, seek medical attention immediately (see the listing of hospitals under "Fast Facts" later in this chapter). If left untreated, this disease can cause internal hemorrhaging and even death. Your best protection is to wear insect repellent, especially if you're heading out to the zoo, bird park, or any of the gardens or nature preserves.

OCEAN SAFETY

The worst thing that can happen to you in the ocean is injury caused by sea creatures. Sea urchins crawl along the ocean bed, and stonefish, stingrays, and cone shells will sting if provoked. Even if you're staying by the shore, at certain times of the year jellyfish get washed in pretty close. The best protection is to wear hard rubber tennis shoes or fins at all times while in the water—and don't taunt any strange fish.

If you're unfortunate enough to get a sea urchin splinter, you can neutralize the poison by soaking the wound in hot water for 30 minutes to an hour. The spines can't be removed like splinters, but if they're small, your body can dissolve them. If they're large, seek medical attention.

Stings from creatures like stonefish, stingrays, and cone shells can be very painful and can even lead to respiratory paralysis. If you are stung, remain calm and, if possible, try to keep the wound well below the level of your heart. You can put hot water on the wound and use a tourniquet (not on a joint), but be sure to seek medical attention for all such injuries.

For jellyfish stings, first douse the wound with a disinfectant and put on meat tenderizer. (Which I'm sure you'll just happen to have in your beach kit!) Don't rub the area; instead, sprinkle talcum powder on it—which causes the stings to stick together—and scrape them off.

DANGEROUS ANIMALS & PLANTS

Singapore has a whole slew of **snakes,** and they're not only in the deepest, darkest parts of the island—sometimes, they're forced from their homes by construction and left to look for trouble in more populated areas. The venomous kinds are cobras, kraits, coral snakes, pit vipers, and sea snakes. If you encounter a sea snake, don't splash around, as this will just encourage an attack.

If you're bitten by a snake, keep yourself calm, try to position the wounded area below the level of your heart, and wrap a tourniquet loosely above the wound (but not on a joint). Don't take any aspirin or other medications unless it's an over-the-counter pain reliever that doesn't contain aspirin. There are only two facilities in Singapore with snake antivenin, **Singapore General Hospital,** Outram Road (☎ 65/ 321-4103), and **National University Hospital,** 5 Lower Kent Ridge Rd. (☎ 65/ 772-5000).

Dangerous insects are scorpions, spiders, centipedes, bees, and wasps. If stung, wash the area with disinfectant and apply ice to reduce the pain and prevent the venom from being absorbed further. If you have an allergic reaction, seek medical help.

There are a lot of **plants** in Singapore that have poisonous parts. Some of the more common ones are common bamboo, arcea palm, frangipani, mango tree, papaya, and tapioca. Only parts of these plants are poisonous. If you're unsure, just don't nibble on anything strange.

INSURANCE

There are three kinds of travel insurance: trip cancellation, medical, and lost luggage coverage. **Trip cancellation insurance** is a good idea if you have paid a large portion of your vacation expenses up front (it generally costs approximately 6% to 8% of the total value of your vacation). The other two types of insurance, however, don't make sense for most travelers. Rule number one: Check your existing policies before you buy any additional coverage.

Your existing health insurance should cover you if you get sick while on vacation (though if you belong to an HMO, you should check to see whether you are fully covered when away from home). If you need hospital treatment, most health insurance plans and HMOs will cover out-of-country hospital visits and procedures, at least to some extent. However, most make you pay the bills up front at the time of care, and you'll get a refund after you've returned and filed all the paperwork. Members of **Blue Cross/Blue Shield** can now use their cards at select hospitals in most major cities worldwide (☎ **800/810-BLUE** or www.bluecares.com/blue/bluecard/wwn for a list of hospitals). For independent travel health-insurance providers, see below. Your homeowner's insurance should cover stolen luggage. The airlines are responsible for $1,250 on domestic flights if they lose your luggage; if you plan to carry anything more valuable than that, keep it in your carry-on bag.

The differences between travel assistance and insurance are often blurred, but in general the former offers on-the-spot assistance and 24-hour hot lines (mostly oriented toward medical problems), while the latter reimburses you for travel problems (medical, travel, or otherwise) after you have filed the paperwork. The coverage you should consider will depend on how much protection is already contained in your existing health insurance or other policies. Some credit- and charge-card companies may insure you against travel accidents if you buy plane, train, or bus tickets with their cards. Before purchasing additional insurance, read your policies and agreements over carefully. Call your insurers or credit/charge-card companies if you have any questions.

Some credit cards (American Express and certain gold and platinum Visa and MasterCards, for example) offer automatic flight insurance against death or dismemberment in case of an airplane crash.

Among the reputable issuers of travel insurance are: **Access America,** 6600 W. Broad St., Richmond, VA 23230 (☎ 800/284-8300); **Tele-Trip Company,** Mutual of Omaha Plaza, Omaha, NE 68175 (☎ 800/228-9792); **Travel Guard International,** 1145 Clark St., Stevens Point, WI 54481 (☎ 800/826-1300); **Travel Insured International, Inc.,** P.O. Box 280568, East Hartford, CT 06128 (☎ 800/243-3174); **Columbus Travel Insurance,** 279 High St., Croydon CR0 1QH (☎ 0171/375-0011 in London; www2.columbusdirect.com/columbusdirect); **International SOS Assistance,** P.O. Box 11568, Philadelphia PA 11916 (☎ 800/523-8930 or 215/244-1500), strictly an assistance company; and **Travelex Insurance Services,** P.O. Box 9408, Garden City, NY 11530-9408 (☎ 800/228-9792).

Companies specializing in accident and medical care include: **MEDEX International,** P.O. Box 5375, Timonium, MD 21094-5375 (☎ 888/MEDEX-00 or 410/453-6300; fax 410/453-6301; www.medexassist.com); **Travel Assistance International** (Worldwide Assistance Services, Inc.), 1133 15th St. NW, Suite 400, Washington, DC 20005 (☎ 800/821-2828 or 202/828-5894; fax 202/828-5896); and **The Divers Alert Network** (DAN) (☎ 800/446-2671 or 919/684-2948), which insures scuba divers.

7 Tips for Travelers with Special Needs

TRAVELERS WITH DISABILITIES

If you haven't checked it out already, there's a Web site called Global Access (www.geocities.com/Paris/1502), with tips on trip planning, links to resources, and shared experiences from disabled travelers. (Despite the Web address, it discusses travel other than to Paris.) There's also a handy free guide called *Access Singapore,* put together by the Singapore Council of Social Services, with charts to rate accessibility features of hotels, airports, places of interest, shops, and public buildings. To get one, contact the **Singapore Tourism Board (STB)** at ☎ **1800/736-2000.** (See "Visitor Information" earlier in this chapter for international STB offices.)

Most hotels have accessible rooms, and some cab companies offer special van services. I've found most of the newer buildings are constructed with access ramps for wheelchairs, but older buildings are very problematic, especially the shophouses, with narrow sidewalks and many uneven steps.

SENIORS

Around the world, most countries won't consider you eligible for senior citizen's discount until you reach maybe 60 or 65 years of age. However, in Singapore it's common to see 55 as the starting age for benefits. My poor mother (who's not yet old enough to qualify back home) had a shock when she was asked her age at the National Museum. She saved a few dollars, but was a bit sore about it! Most attractions and museums have discounted admission for senior citizens. Hotels, airlines, and tour operators will also quote you discounted packages if you request senior rates.

The STB will also help plan your trip, and can offer its own advice for senior travelers. Regarding this service, here's my advice: If you work out your itinerary with the help of STB, make sure you're firm about time constraints. Many of the tours and daily itineraries are rushed, with little time for a rest here and there. A common complaint is exhaustion by the end of just 1 day. In the heat, this is not only uncomfortable, but dangerous as well.

GAY & LESBIAN TRAVELERS

In a highly publicized December 11, 1998, interview on CNN, Senior Minister Lee Kuan Yew was asked by an anonymous caller about the future of gays in Singapore. The senior minister responded, "Well, it's not a matter which I can decide or any government can decide. It's a question of what a society considers acceptable. And as you know, Singaporeans are by and large a very conservative, orthodox society . . . I would say, completely different from . . . the United Sates and I don't think an aggressive gay rights movement would help. But what we are doing as a government is to leave people to live their own lives as long as they don't impinge on other people. I mean, we don't harass anybody." Naturally, the conservative government doesn't support such alternative lifestyles; however, gay and lesbian culture is alive and well in Singapore. What you'll find is that older gays and lesbians are more conservative and therefore less open to discussion, while the younger generations have very few qualms about describing the local scene and their personal experiences as gay men or lesbians in Singapore.

There are tons of Web sites on the Internet for gays and lesbians in Singapore. Start at **www2.best.com/~utopia/tipssing.htm,** an extremely comprehensive "insider" collection of current events, meeting places, travel tips, topical Web discussions, and links to resources. Chapter 8 lists some gay and lesbian clubs and karaoke lounges that are all nice places with friendly folks.

FAMILIES

Because of their focus on business travelers, hotels in Singapore are not especially geared toward children. You can get extra beds in hotel rooms (this can cost anywhere from S$15 to S$50 (US$9 to US$29.95), and most hotels will arrange a baby-sitter for you on request, though most ask for at least 24 hours notice. While almost all hotels have pools to keep the kiddies cool and happy, only two, the **YMCA International House** and **Metro YMCA,** have lifeguards on duty, and only one, **Shangri-La's Rasa Sentosa Resort,** has activity programs specifically for children. See chapter 3 for more information on these hotels.

Children have their own special rates of admission for just about every attraction and museum. The cutoff age for children is usually 12 years of age, but if your kids are older, be sure to ask if the attraction has a student rate for teens. If the kids get edgy during all the "boring" historical and cultural aspects of your trip, plan a morning visit to the **Singapore Zoological Gardens** or out to Sentosa Island's **Fantasy Island water park.** These are the two places where I can almost guarantee they (and you) will have a great time.

In Singapore, childhood innocence is revered, so you will rarely find crimes being committed against them. You can rest assured that if your child is missing, he or she is probably just around the corner looking for you—maybe even with the help of a concerned Singaporean.

Given the strictures of Muslim culture, women who are **breast-feeding** should strictly limit the activity to private places. In the West it may be acceptable, but here it'll just freak people out.

BUSINESSPEOPLE

Businesspeople, Singapore is your town. Every hotel has special accommodations for business travelers, which can include nicer rooms; higher floors; free extras such as newspapers, shoe shines, and suit pressings; and club lounges where you can have a free breakfast and evening cocktails while you watch CNN or work on one of the hotel's PCs.

Most multinational corporations have accounts with major hotel chains, so your firm may tell you where to stay. If you make your arrangements on your own, though, remember that every hotel has a corporate rate, which is sometimes up to 40% off the going room rate.

Refer to "Singapore's People, Etiquette & Customs" later in this chapter before your first meeting, so you know how to greet people and trade business cards in the appropriate style.

8 Getting There

BY PLANE

If you're hunting for the best airfare, there are a few things you can do. First, plan your trip for the low-volume season, which runs from September 1 to November 30. Between January 1 and May 31, you'll pay the highest fares. Plan your travel on weekdays only, and, if you can, plan to stay for at least a full week. Book your reservations in advance—waiting until the last minute can mean you'll pay sky-high rates. Also, if you have access to the Internet, there are a number of great sites that'll search out super fares for you. See the "Flying for Less: Tips for Getting the Best Airfares," box for more hints.

FROM THE UNITED STATES

Singapore Airlines (☎ 800/742-3333 in the U.S.; 65/223-6030 in Singapore; www.singaporeair.com) has a daily flight from New York, two daily flights from Los Angeles, two daily flights from San Francisco (only one on Sunday), and a flight four times weekly from Newark, New Jersey. Flights originating from the East Coast travel over Europe, stopping in either Frankfurt or Amsterdam. Flights from the West Coast stopover in either Tokyo or Hong Kong.

United Airlines (☎ 800/241-6522; 65/873-3533 in Singapore; www.ual.com) has daily flights connecting pretty much every major city in the United States with Singapore via the Pacific route. Expect a stopover in Tokyo en route.

Northwest Airlines (☎ 800/447-4747; 65/336-3371 in Singapore; www.nwa.com) links all major U.S. airports with daily direct flights to Singapore from the following ports of exit: New York, Detroit, Minneapolis, Los Angeles, Seattle, and San Francisco, with direct flights from Las Vegas on Mondays and Thursdays only. All flights have one short stopover in Tokyo.

FROM CANADA

Singapore Airlines (☎ 604/681-7488; 65/223-6030 in Singapore; www.singaporeair.com) has flights from Vancouver three times a week, with a stopover in Seoul.

FROM THE UNITED KINGDOM

Singapore Airlines (☎ 181/747-0007 in London; 161-832-3346 in Manchester; 65/223-6030 in Singapore; www.singaporeair.com) has three daily flights departing from London's Heathrow Airport with a daily connection from Manchester. Depending on the day of departure, these flights stopover in either Amsterdam, Zurich, or Bombay.

British Airways (☎ 0345/222111 local call from anywhere within the U.K.; 65/839-7788 in Singapore; www.british-airways.com) has daily nonstop flights from London.

Quantas Airways Ltd. (☎ 0345/747767; 65/839-7788 in Singapore; www.quantas.com) has daily nonstop flights on weekdays and flights twice daily on weekends from London.

FROM AUSTRALIA

Singapore Airlines (☎ 65/223-6030 in Singapore; www.singaporeair.com) has twice-daily flights from Melbourne (☎ 3/9254-0300) and Sydney (☎ 2/9350-0100); three dailies from Perth (☎ 8/9265-0500); a daily from Brisbane (☎ 7/3259-0717); flights from Adelaide (☎ 8/8203-0800) four times a week; and from Cairns (☎ 70/317-538) three times a week.

Quantas Airways Ltd. (☎ 2/131313 toll free; 65/839-7788 in Singapore; www.quantas.com) links all major airports in Australia with daily direct flights to Singapore from Sydney and Melbourne.

British Airways (☎ 8/9425-7711 in Perth; 7/3223-3133 in Brisbane; 65/839-7788 in Singapore; www.british-airways.com) has daily flights from Perth and Brisbane. British Airways and Quantas work in partnership to provide routing from Australia, so be sure to consult Quantas for connecting flights form your city.

FROM NEW ZEALAND

Singapore Airlines (☎ 3032129 in Auckland; 3668003 in Christchurch; www.singaporeair.com) has daily flights from Auckland and Christchurch.

Air New Zealand (☎ 0800/737000; www.airnewzealand.co.nz) has daily flights from Christchurch and a daily flight from Auckland in partnership with Singapore Airlines (so you can still use or accumulate frequent-flyer miles for this trip).

GETTING INTO TOWN FROM THE AIRPORT

Most visitors to Singapore will land at **Changi International Airport,** which is located toward the far eastern corner of the island. Compared to so many other international airports, Changi is a dream come true, providing clean and very efficient space and facilities. Expect to find in-transit accommodations, restaurants, duty-free shops, money changers, ATMs, car-rental desks, accommodation assistance, and tourist information all marked with clear signs. When you arrive, keep your eyes peeled for the many Singapore Tourism Board brochures that are so handily displayed throughout the terminal.

The city is easily accessible by public transportation. A **taxi** trip to the city center will cost around S$22 to S$25 (US$13.15 to $14.95) and takes around 20 minutes. You'll traverse the wide Airport Boulevard to the Pan-Island Expressway (PIE) or the East Coast Parkway (ECP), past public housing estates and other residential neighborhoods in the eastern part of the island, over causeways, and into the city center.

CityCab offers an **airport shuttle,** a six-seater maxicab that traverses between the airport and the major hotel areas. It covers most hotels, and is very flexible about drop-offs and pickups within the central areas, including MRT (subway) stations. Bookings are made at the airport shuttle counter in the arrival terminal or by calling ☎ 65/553-3880. Pay S$7 (US$4.20) for adults and S$5 (US$3) for children directly to the driver.

A couple of **buses** run from the airport into the city as well. SBS bus no. 16 will take you on a route to Orchard Road and Raffles City (in the Historic District). SBS bus no. 36 runs a direct route to and from the airport and Orchard Road. Both bus stops are located in the basement of the arrival terminal. A trip to town will be about S$1.30 (US$.78).

For **arrival and departure information,** you can call Changi International Airport toll-free at ☎ 1800/542-4422.

BY TRAIN

The Keretapi Tanah Melayu Berhad railroad company runs express and local trains from **Malaysia to Singapore** four times daily. In Kuala Lumpur, contact KTM at ☎ 03/274-7434, or see their Web site at www.ktmb.com.my. The fare from KL is RM60 (US$15.80), RM26 (US$6.85), and RM14.80 (US$3.90) for first-, second-, and third-class travel, respectively. Further details on KTM service are listed in chapter 9. All trains let you off at the Singapore Railway Station (☎ 65/222-5165) on Keppel Road in Tanjong Pagar, not far from the city center. Money-changing services are available in the station. A taxi into town is not expensive from here.

The *Eastern & Oriental Express,* sister to the *Venice Simplon-Orient-Express,* runs once a week between Singapore and Bangkok in exquisite luxury, with occasional departures between Bangkok and Chiang Mai. For international reservations from the U.S. and Canada call ☎ 800/524-2420, from Australia ☎ 3/9699-9766, from New Zealand ☎ 9/379-3708, and from the U.K. ☎ 171/805-5100. From Singapore and Malaysia contact E&O in Singapore at (☎ 65/392-3500).

BY BUS

Buses to Singapore from almost all cities in Malaysia will let you off at either the Ban Sen Terminal at the corner of Queen Street and Arab Street in Kampong Glam or at

Flying for Less: Tips for Getting the Best Airfares

Passengers within the same airplane cabin rarely pay the same fare for their seats. Business travelers who need to purchase tickets at the last minute, change their itinerary at a moment's notice, or get home before the weekend pay the premium rate, known as the full fare. Passengers who can book their ticket long in advance, who don't mind staying over Saturday night, or who are willing to travel on a Tuesday, Wednesday, or Thursday after 7pm, will pay a fraction of the full fare. Here are a few other easy ways to save.

1. Periodically airlines lower prices on their most popular routes. Check your newspaper for advertised discounts or call the airlines directly and ask if any **pro-motional rates** or special fares are available. If your schedule is flexible, ask if you can secure a cheaper fare by staying an extra day or by flying midweek. (Many airlines won't volunteer this information.) If you already hold a ticket when a sale breaks, it may even pay to exchange your ticket, which usually incurs a $50 to $75 charge.

    Note, however, that the lowest-priced fares are often nonrefundable, require advance purchase of 1 to 3 weeks and a certain length of stay, and carry penalties for changing dates of travel.

2. **Consolidators,** also known as bucket shops, are a good place to find low fares. Consolidators buy seats in bulk from the airlines and then sell them back to the public at prices below even the airlines' discounted rates. Their small boxed ads usually run in the Sunday travel section at the bottom of the page. Before you pay, however, ask for a confirmation number from the consolidator and then call the airline itself to confirm your seat. Be prepared to book your ticket with a different consolidator if the airline can't confirm your reservation. Also be aware that bucket shop tickets are usually non-refundable or rigged with stiff cancellation penalties, often as high as 50% to 75% of the ticket price.

    Council Travel (☎ **800/226-8624;** www.counciltravel.com) and **STA Travel** (☎ **800/781-4040;** www.sta.travel.com) cater especially to young travelers, but their bargain-basement prices are available to people of all ages. **Travel Bargains** (☎ **800/AIR-FARE;** www.1800airfare.com) was formerly owned by TWA but now offers the deepest discounts on many other airlines, with a 4-day advance purchase. Other reliable consolidators include **1-800-FLY-CHEAP** (www.1800flycheap.com); **TFI Tours International** (☎ **800/ 745-8000** or 212/736-1140), which serves as a clearinghouse for unused seats; or "rebators" such as **Travel Avenue** (☎ **800/333-3335** or 312/ 876-1116) and the **Smart Traveller** (☎ **800/448-3338** in the U.S., or 305/448-3338), which rebate part of their commissions to you.

3. **Search the Internet** for cheap fares—though it's still best to compare your findings with the research of a dedicated travel agent, if you're lucky enough

the crossroads of Lavender Street and Kallang Bahru. From Kuala Lumpur buses leave from the **Kuala Lumpur Railway Station** (Plusliner/NICE, ☎04227-2760), costs around RM55/US$14.45. Buses from Johor Bharu depart from **Larkin Bus Terminal** (Singapore-Johor Ekspress, ☎ 07/223-2276), RM2.40/US$0.63.

to have one, especially when you're booking more than just a flight. A few of the better-respected virtual travel agents are **Travelocity** (www.travelocity.com) and **Microsoft Expedia** (www.expedia.com). Just enter the dates you want to fly and the cities you want to visit, and the computer roots out the lowest fares. Expedia's site will e-mail you the best airfare deal once a week if you so choose. Travelocity uses the SABRE computer reservations system that most travel agents use, and has a "Last Minute Deals" database that advertises really cheap fares for those who can get away at a moment's notice.

4. Great last-minute deals are also available through a free e-mail service, provided directly by the airlines, called **E-savers.** Each week, the airline sends you a list of discounted flights, usually leaving the upcoming Friday or Saturday, and returning the following Monday or Tuesday. You can sign up for all the major airlines at once by logging on to **Smarter Living** (www.smarterliving.com), or go to each individual airline's Web site.

5. **Book a seat on a charter flight.** Discounted fares have pared the number available, but they can still be found. Most charter operators advertise and sell their seats through travel agents, thus making these local professionals your best source of information for available flights. Before deciding to take a charter flight, however, check the restrictions on the ticket: You may be asked to purchase a tour package, to pay in advance, to be amenable if the day of departure is changed, to pay a service charge, to fly on an airline you're not familiar with (this usually is not the case), and to pay harsh penalties if you cancel. Also, you'll have to be understanding if the charter doesn't fill up and is canceled up to 10 days before departure. Summer charters fill up more quickly than others and are almost sure to fly, but if you decide on a charter flight, seriously consider cancellation and baggage insurance.

6. **Look into courier flights.** Companies that hire couriers use your luggage allowance for their business baggage; in return, you get a deeply discounted ticket. Flights are often offered at the last minute, and you may have to arrange a pretrip interview to make sure you're right for the job. **Now Voyager,** open Monday to Friday from 10am to 5:30pm and Saturday from noon to 4:30pm (☎ **212/431-1616**), flies from New York. Now Voyager also offers noncourier discounted fares, so call the company even if you don't want to fly as a courier.

7. **Join a travel club** such as **Moment's Notice** (☎ **718/234-6295**) or **Sears Discount Travel Club** (☎ **800/433-9383,** or 800/255-1487 to join), which supply unsold tickets at discounted prices. You pay an annual membership fee to get the club's hot line number. Of course, you're limited to what's available, so you have to be flexible.

BY FERRY

From the **Johor Ferry Terminal** (☎ 07/251-7404) in Tanjung Belungkor on the East coast of Malaysia you can catch a FerryLink ferry four times daily and be in Singapore in 45 minutes. One-way fare for adults is MR15 (US$3.95). The ferry lets you off at Changi Ferry Terminal (no phone) on the east coast of Singapore. Taxis do not ply this route, so call a CityCab at ☎ 65/552-2222 to come fetch you. *Also note:* Changi Ferry Terminal does not have money-changing services. FerryLink's Singapore contact numbers are ☎ 65/545-3600; fax 65/545-5040.

From **Tioman Island** you can catch an Auto Batam Ferries and Tours ferry to Singapore at the Berjaya Jetty every day at 2:30pm, Please note this service does not operate from mid-October to early March due to the monsoon season. The ferries let you off at Singapore's Tanah Merah Ferry Terminal, in the eastern part of the island. The terminal has money-changing facilities and a taxi queue outside. Auto Batam's contact in Singapore is ☎ **65/271-4866.**

Tanah Merah Ferry Terminal is also home to companies that serve nearby Batam, a popular day trip, and Bintan, an Indonesian island resort area.

PACKAGE TOURS & ESCORTED TOURS

Before you start your search for the lowest airfare, you may want to consider booking your flight as part of a travel package such as an escorted tour or a package tour. Packaged travel may not be the option for you if you like to navigate on a whim. If you like to plan your coordinates in advance, however, many package options will enable you to do just that, and will save you money in the process.

ESCORTED TOURS

Some people love escorted tours. They let you relax and take you to the maximum number of sights in the minimum amount of time with the least amount of hassle. If you do choose an escorted tour, you should ask a few simple questions before you buy:

1. **What is the cancellation policy?** Do they require a deposit? Can they cancel the trip if they don't get enough people? Do you get a refund if they cancel? If you cancel? How late can you cancel if you are unable to go? When do you pay in full?

2. **How busy is the schedule?** How much sightseeing do they plan each day? Do they allow ample time for relaxing by the pool, shopping, or wandering?

3. **What is the size of the group?** The smaller the group, the more flexible the itinerary, and the less time you'll spend waiting for people to get on and off the bus. Tour operators may be evasive about this because they may not know the exact size of the group until everybody has made their reservations; but they should be able to give you a rough estimate. Some tours have a minimum group size and may cancel the tour if they don't book enough people.

4. **What is included in the price?** Don't assume anything. You may have to pay for transportation to and from the airport. A box lunch may be included in an excursion, but drinks might cost extra. Beer might be included, but wine might not. Can you opt out of certain activities? Are all your meals planned in advance? Can you choose your entree at dinner, or does everybody get the same chicken cutlet?

Note: If you choose an escorted tour, think strongly about purchasing travel insurance from an independent agency, especially if the tour operator asks you to pay up front. (See discussion of travel insurance later in this chapter.) One final caveat: Since escorted tour prices are based on double occupancy, the single traveler is usually penalized.

PACKAGE TOURS

Package tours are not the same thing as escorted tours. They are simply a way to buy airfare and accommodations at the same time. In many cases, a package that includes airfare, hotel, and transportation to and from the airport will cost you less than just the flight alone would have, had you booked it yourself. That's because packages are sold in bulk to tour operators, who then resell them to the public at a cost that drastically undercuts standard rates.

Packages vary widely, however. Some offer a better class of hotels than others. Some offer the same hotels for lower prices. Some offer flights on scheduled airlines, while others book charters. In some packages, your choice of accommodations and travel days may be limited. Some packages let you choose between escorted vacations and independent vacations; others will allow you to add on just a few excursions or escorted day trips (also at lower prices than you could locate on your own) without booking an entirely escorted tour. Each destination usually has one or two packagers that are usually cheaper than the rest because they buy in even greater bulk. If you spend the time to shop around, you will save in the long run.

FINDING A PACKAGE DEAL

The best place to start your search is the travel section of your local Sunday newspaper. Also check the ads in the back of national travel magazines like *Travel & Leisure, National Geographic Traveler,* and *Condé Nast Traveller.* **Liberty Travel,** one of the biggest packagers in the northeast United States, usually boasts a full-page ad in Sunday papers. You won't get much in the way of service, but you will get a good deal. Check your local directory for one of its many local branches nationwide, or visit the Liberty Web site at www.libertytravel.com. **American Express Vacations** (☎ 800/241-1700; www.leisureweb.com) is another option. Check out its **Last Minute Travel Bargains** site, offered in conjunction with **Continental Airlines** (www.americanexpress.com/travel/lastminutetravel/default.asp), with deeply discounted vacations packages and reduced airline fares that differ from the E-savers bargains that Continental e-mails weekly to subscribers.

Another good resource is the airlines themselves, which often package their flights together with accommodations. Fly-by-night packagers are uncommon, but they do exist; when you buy your package through the airline, however, you can be pretty sure that the company will still be in business when your departure date arrives. Singapore Airlines, in partnership with many travel-related businesses here, has a special New Singapore Stopover Package. If you book passage with Singapore Airlines, for an additional US$30 you can take advantage of free admission to many attractions, free transportation on the Hop-On Trolley, and special discounts on hotel rooms, dining, shopping, and more. For details, contact Singapore Airlines at the phone numbers listed under "By Plane," above, or check their Web site at www.singaporeair.com.

The biggest hotel chains and resorts also offer package deals. If you already know where you want to stay, call the resort itself and ask if they offer land/air packages.

Among the most experienced and knowledgeable tour operators specializing in Southeast Asia are **Absolute Asia,** 180 Varick St., 16th Fl., New York, NY 10014 (☎ 800/736-8187; www.absoluteasia.com.), and **East Quest,** One Union Square West, Suite 606, New York, NY 10013 (☎ 800/638-3449; www.eastquest1@aol.com). Both companies offer a diverse blend of cultural and adventure travel programs and will customize tours and design itineraries to suit each individual's particular interest. People traveling with Absolute Asia have three options: follow the itinerary as is, combine it with another itinerary, or design their own trip.

Explore Worldwide, c/o the Adventure Center, 1311 63rd St., Suite 200, Emeryville, CA 94608 (☎ 800/227-8747; 800/661-7265 Trek Holidays, in Canada; 1-800/221-931 Adventure World, in Australia), offers adventure and cultural group tours to Southeast Asia, including several to Malaysia and one that covers Singapore and Malaysia.

9 Getting Around

The many inexpensive mass transit options make getting around Singapore pretty easy. Of course, **taxis** always simplify the ground transportation dilemma. They're also very affordable, and, by and large, drivers are helpful and honest if not downright personable. The **Mass Rapid Transit (MRT)** subway service has four lines that run over two main routes (roughly east-west and north-south) and are very easy to figure out. **Buses** present more of a challenge because there are so many routes snaking all over the island, but they're a great way to see the country while getting where you want to go. In the bus section, below, I've thrown in some tips that will hopefully demystify the bus experience for you.

Of course, if you're just strolling around the urban limits, many of the sights within the various neighborhoods are within walking distance, and indeed, some of the neighborhoods are only short walks from each other—getting from Chinatown to the Historic District only requires crossing over the Singapore River, and from Little India to Kampong Glam is not far at all. However, I advise against trying to get from, say, Chinatown (in the west) to Kampong Glam (in the east). The distance can be somewhat prohibitive, especially in the heat.

BY PUBLIC TRANSPORTATION

Stored-fare **TransitLink fare cards** can be used on both the subway and the buses, and can be purchased at TransitLink offices in the MRT stations. These save you the bother of trying to dig up exact change for bus meters; plus, if you transfer from a bus to the MRT, or between buses, you'll save S25¢. The card does carry a S$2 (US$1.20) deposit—for a S$12 (US$7.20) initial investment, you'll get S$10 (US$6) worth of travel credit. At the end of your stay, you can cash in your card for the remaining value, and still get one extra trip for about S10¢.

BY MASS RAPID TRANSIT (MRT)

The MRT is Singapore's subway system. It's cool, clean, safe, and reliable, providing service from the far west reaches of the island to the far east parts on the east-west line and running in a loop around the north part of the island on the north-south line. The lines are color coded to make it easy to find the train you're looking for (see the MRT map in this chapter for specifics). The two lines intersect at the Raffles Place Interchange in Chinatown/Shenton Way, at City Hall in the Historic District, and in the western part of the island at the Jurong East Interchange. (By the way, don't let the "East" fool you—Jurong East is actually in the western part of the island.) MRT operating hours vary between lines and stops, with the earliest train beginning service daily at 5:15am and the last train ending at 12:47am.

Fares range from S60¢ to S$1.50 (US$0.36 to US$0.90), depending on which stations you travel between. System charts are prominently displayed in all MRT stations to help you find your appropriate fare, which you pay with a TransitLink fare card. Single-fare cards can be purchased at vending machines at MRT stations. See above for information on stored-fare cards. (*One caution:* A fare card cannot be used by two people for the same trip; each must have his own.)

TransitLink also has a Special Edition Tourist Souvenir Ticket, which is good for MRT use only. For S$7 (US$4.20) you can buy a fare card with S$6 (US$3.60) stored value, which you can take home as a souvenir after your trip. It saves you a dollar off the standard deposit, but no refunds can be mad on leftover value.

For more information, call TransitLink TeleInfo at ☎ **1800/779-9366** (daily 24 hours).

MRT Transit System

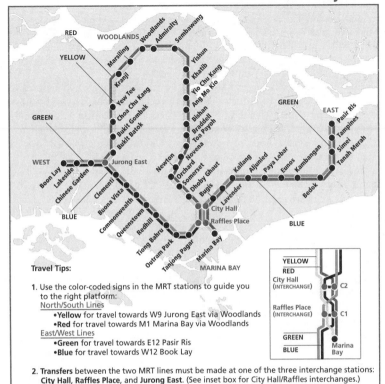

Travel Tips:

1. Use the color-coded signs in the MRT stations to guide you to the right platform:
   North/South Lines
   - **Yellow** for travel towards W9 Jurong East via Woodlands
   - **Red** for travel towards M1 Marina Bay via Woodlands
   East/West Lines
   - **Green** for travel towards E12 Pasir Ris
   - **Blue** for travel towards W12 Book Lay

2. **Transfers** between the two MRT lines must be made at one of the three interchange stations: **City Hall**, **Raffles Place**, and **Jurong East**. (See inset box for City Hall/Raffles interchanges.)

By Bus

Singapore's bus system comprises an extensive web of routes that reach virtually everywhere on the island. It can be intimidating for newcomers, but once you get your feet wet, you'll feel right at home. There are two main bus services, **SBS (Singapore Bus Service)** and **TIBS (Trans-Island Bus Service).** Most buses are clean, but not all are air-conditioned.

Start off first by purchasing the latest edition of the **TransitLink Guide** for about S$1.40 (US$0.84) at the TransitLink office in any MRT station, at a bus interchange, or at selected bookstores around the city. This tiny book is a very handy guide that details each route and stop, indicating connections with MRT stations and fares for each trip. Next to the guide, the best thing to do is simply ask people for help. At any crowded bus stop there will always be somebody who speaks English and is willing to help out a lost stranger. You can also ask the bus driver where you need to go, and he'll tell you the fare, how to get there, and even when to get off.

All buses have a couple of fare machines close to the driver. Feed the machine your TransitLink card then push the button with the corresponding fare (it's pretty much an honor system to make sure you pay the correct rate). You'll get a receipt back with your fare stamped on it. Sometimes the authorities come around and check to see that people are paying the correct fare, and if you've made a mistake, this is a good time to play up the ignorant tourist routine—otherwise you could be charged the highest fare as punishment. The best thing to do? Ask the driver to tell you the correct fare for where you want to go. It'll be anywhere between S$.55 and S$1.50 (US$0.33 and US$0.90). If you're paying cash, be sure to have exact change; place the coins in the box by the driver and announce your fare to him. He'll issue a ticket, which will pop out of a slot on one of the TransitLink machines.

The **Tourist Day Ticket** is a great deal for travelers. The 1-day pass costs S$10 (US$6), and is good for 12 rides on either SBS or TIBS buses or the MRT. Using one of these will save you having to worry about calculating the correct fare or coming up with exact change. You can pick one up at any TransitLink office and at hotels, money changers, provisioner shops, or travel agents. Unfortunately, there's no handy sign identifying which shops sell them, so you'll have to ask around.

For more information, contact either of the two operating bus lines during standard business hours: **Singapore Bus Service** (SBS) (☎ 1800/287-2727) or the **Trans-Island Bus Service** (TIBS) (☎ 1800/482-5433).

BY TROLLEY

You have a couple of trolley options; both services are offered for the convenience of travelers, making stops at most major tourist destinations. The **Singapore Trolley** shuttles down Orchard Road, through the Historic District and over the Singapore River, and down to Marina Square. For S$14.90 (US$8.90) adults and S$9.90 (US$5.95) children, you can enjoy unlimited rides during your stay (this price also includes a free riverboat tour). Buy your tickets either from your hotel's front desk or directly from the driver. Call Singapore Explorer at ☎ **65/339-6833.**

Singapore Airlines hosts the SIA Hop-on bus. Plying between Bugis Junction, Suntec City, the Historic District, the Singapore River, Chinatown, and the Singapore Botanic Gardens, the Hop-on comes every 30 minutes between the hours of 8:30am and 7pm. Unlimited rides for one day cost S$5 (US$3) adults and S$3 (US$1.80) children. Buy your tickets from your hotel's front desk, from a Singapore Airlines office, or from the bus drivers. If you've traveled to Singapore via Singapore Airlines, you're entitled to free passage aboard the Hop-on. Just show your ticket to the driver. For more information call Singapore Airlines at ☎ 65/223-6030.

BY TAXI

Taxis are a very convenient and affordable way to get around Singapore, and there's every chance you'll get a good conversation with the driver into the bargain (see "Frommer's Favorite Singapore Experiences" in chapter 1). Despite this, I advise against relying completely on taxicabs, since Singapore's excellent public transportation system will take you practically anywhere you need to go for a fraction of the price. Even in the middle of nowhere there's always a bus route to take you to familiar territory—just remember to keep your TransitLink Guide (see above) handy, so you'll know where the bus you're about to hop is headed.

In town, all of the shopping malls, hotels, and major buildings have taxi queues, which you're expected to use. During lunch hours and the evening rush, the queues can be very long; though by and large taxis are convenient, don't count on finding one fast during the evening rush hours between 5pm and 7pm. Especially if it's raining, you'll be waiting for an hour, easy. Everybody wants a cab at this time, and for some strange reason this is the time the cabbies choose to change shifts. Brilliant. During this time, I recommend you call to book a taxi pickup. You pay a little extra, but believe me, some days it can really be worth it.

Most destinations in the main parts of the island can be reached fairly inexpensively, while trips to the outlying attractions can cost between S$10 and S$15

(US$6 and US$9) one-way. If you're at an attraction or restaurant outside of the central part of the city where it is more difficult to hail a cab on the street, you can ask the cashier or service counter attendant to call a taxi for you. The extra charge for pickup is between S$2.80 and S$3.20 (US$1.70 and US$1.90) depending on the cab company (Comfort is the cheapest). Call these main cab companies for bookings: **CityCab** (cash payment ☎ 65/552-2222; credit-card payment ☎ 65/553-8888), **Comfort** (☎ 65/ 552-1111), and **TIBS** (☎ 65/481-1211).

All taxis charge the metered fare, which is S$2.40 (US$1.45) for the first kilometer and S10¢ for each additional 225 to 240 meters or 30 seconds of waiting. Extra fares are levied on top of the metered fare depending on where you're going and when you go. At times, figuring your fare seems more like a riddle. Here's a summary:

Trips during peak hours: Between the hours of 7:30 and 9:30am Monday to Friday, 4:30 to 7pm Monday to Friday, and 11:30am to 2pm on Saturdays, trips will carry an additional S$1 (US$0.60) peak-period surcharge. But if you're traveling outside the Central Business District (CBD), you won't need to pay this surcharge during the morning rush. (To accurately outline the boundaries of the CBD, I'd need to fill a couple of encyclopedic volumes, so for this purpose, let's just say it's basically Orchard Road, the Historic District, Chinatown, and Shenton Way—basically.)

Additional charges rack up each time you travel through an Electronic Road Pricing (ERP) scheme underpass. On the Central Expressway (CTE), Pan-Island Expressway (PIE), and selected thoroughfares in the CBD, charges from S30¢ to S$1.70 (US$0.18 to US$1) are calculated by an electronic box on the driver's dashboard. The driver will add this amount to your fare.

And for special torture, here's some **more charges:** From midnight to 6am, add 50% to your fare. From 6pm on the eve of a public holiday to midnight the following day, you pay an additional S$1. From Changi or Seletar Airports add S$3 (US$1.80). And for credit-card payments add 10%.

BY CAR

Singapore's public transportation systems are so extensive, efficient, and inexpensive that you shouldn't need a car to enjoy your stay. In fact, I don't advise it. While most hotels and restaurants and many attractions do have parking facilities, parking in lots can be expensive, and on-street parking is by prepurchased, color-coded parking tickets that are confusing for even Singaporeans to use. In addition, if you're not accustomed to driving on the left side of the road, you'll need to take the time to pick up a new skill.

There is also the business of the Electronic Road Pricing (ERP) scheme, which I talked about in the taxi section, above. Private cars are all equipped with an ERP box on the dashboard. The driver buys a stored-value ERP card to feed to the machine, and with each trip through an ERP underpass, the correct amount is automatically deducted from the card. Car-rental agencies will all provide ERP boxes for your car, and can also give you an ERP stored-value card. The amount you use will be added to your bill. Or you can purchase your own stored-value card (S$22/US$13.15) from any local bank. Tickets for public parking can be purchased at any gas station.

RENTING A CAR

There are two main impediments to renting a car in Singapore, but if you're really determined, you can overcome them.

The first problem involves **licensing:** You'll be required to produce an International Driver's License, which you should obtain in your home country before your trip. You can get one in Singapore, but first you must get a Singapore Driver's License, which you then convert to an international one—kinda impractical if you're on vacation or just in town quickly for business. It's a mess of red tape, but if you want to try, you can start by calling the Driving License Section of the **Traffic Police Department** at ☎ **65/221-0000.**

The second problem involves **cost:** Because of heavy government taxes aimed at reducing traffic congestion and air pollution, everything to do with cars in Singapore is outlandishly expensive—the going price for a simple Toyota Corolla, for instance, can be as high as S$125,000 (US$74,850). This attempt to reduce automobile traffic is also extended to you, the traveler, through rental charges up to S$1,000 (US$599) plus taxes for 1 week's rental of the smallest car on the lot.

One of the few good reasons to rent a car is if you plan to **drive into Malaysia.** Back in the 1970s, driving in Malaysia was risky because of highway bandits. These days, though, it's relatively safe traveling, and thanks to the new toll road—the North-South Highway from Singapore all the way up to the Thai border—it's pretty convenient (see chapter 10 for more on this subject, and on renting a car in Malaysia rather than Singapore, which can save you some cash). Two good places to seek out a rental car are:

- **Avis:** Changi Airport Terminal 2 (☎ **65/542-8855**), Boulevard Hotel (☎ **65/737-1668**). You must be at least 23 years old to rent, and the minimum rental period is 24 hours. Rates in Singapore run from S$175 (US$104.80) for a Mitsubishi Lancer to S$315 (US$188.60) for a Mitsubishi Gallant daily and S$1,050 (US$628.75) to S$1,890 (US$1,131.75) weekly, respectively. For travel to Malaysia, the daily rates are S$200 (US$119.75) for the Lancer to S$355 (US$212.55) for the Gallant or S$1,225 (US$733.55) to S$2,170 (US$1,299.40) weekly, respectively. One-way rentals are available, with varying drop-off fees for Malacca, Kuala Lumpur, Kuantan, Terengganu, Kota Bahru, Alor Setar, Ipoh, and Penang. All major credit cards are accepted.

- **Hertz:** Changi Airport Terminal 2, Arrival Meeting Hall South (☎ **65/542-5300**), or 125 Tanglin Rd., Tudor Court Shopping Gallery (☎ **1800/734-4646**). You must be at least 21 years of age to rent and the minimum rental period is 24 hours. Daily rates for rental within Singapore run from S$199 (US$119.15) for a Mitsubishi Lancer to S$559 (US$334.75) for a BMW or Mercedes Benz, and S$1,194 (US$714.95) to S$3,354 (US$2,008.40) per week, respectively. Hertz does not rent luxury cars for driving to Malaysia. For Malaysia driving, Hertz will charge an extra S$25 (US$14.95) per day. For one-way trips to Malaysia there are varying drop-off charges for Johor Bahru, Kuala Lumpur, Kuantan, and Penang. Hertz accepts all major credit cards.

In addition, both rental agencies offer **hourly rentals** of chauffeur-driven vehicles. Through Avis you can book a chauffeur-driven Mercedes Benz for S$60 (US$35.95) per hour, with a 3-hour minimum. Hertz also has luxury car and driver bookings at S$68 (US$40.70) per hour with a 5-hour minimum, but also rents smaller cars (like the Lancer) for S$48 (US$28.75) per hour (minimum 5 hrs.) Due to the high expense, it's not really practical to hire a car and driver for sightseeing purposes.

10 Suggested Itineraries

Probably because most people see Singapore as a jumping-off point for other Southeast Asian destinations, the average visitor spends only 3.5 days here. A jumping-off point it certainly is, but I assure you, you'll have no problem filling your days if you stay for a week or more.

Following are suggested itineraries for a trip lasting the standard 3.5 days, but if you're staying for at least a week, take a look at the really great itinerary I've included for you. It's made up of theme days that will walk you through the major cultures and influences in Singapore, from the colonial period all the way up to Singapore today. The itinerary is very relaxed, and includes sights, attractions, shopping, and recommended dining experiences that, at the end, will have given you a well-rounded view of what this small but wonderful country is all about.

If You Have 3.5 Days

Day 1   Take a walking tour of the **Historic District** (chapter 6), and visit the **National Museum** and the **Asian Civilisations Museum** (chapter 5). If you have time, try to catch the **Singapore Art Museum** (also chapter 5). Spend your evening at one of the many bars and restaurants on **Boat Quay** and **Clarke Quay** (see chapters 4 and 8).

Day 2   Take the Little India walking tour followed by the Arab Street/Kampong Glam tour (both in chapter 6). Feel free to take your time and shop along the way. Try the murtabak at Zam Zam's (also in chapter 6). Check in with STB to find out what cultural programs are currently running, or see chapter 8 for more details

Day 3   Take the Chinatown walking tour (chapter 5) in the morning and spend the afternoon at Orchard Road, shopping and people-watching (chapter 7). Have a seafood dinner out at Long Beach Seafood Restaurant (chapter 4).

Day 4   Only a half-day to work with here, so spend the morning at the Singapore Botanic Gardens (chapter 5).

If You Have a Week

Day 1: Chinese Day   This will be an easy day, since it's your first day in Singapore and I don't want to exhaust you. Begin with a **walking tour of Chinatown,** past the temples and little shops selling Chinese herbs and bric-a-brac (see chapter 6). Break up your day with a nice lunch at **Chen Fu Ji Fried Rice** on Erskine Road (chapter 4). In the afternoon, head for **The Tea Village** on Erskine Road for a traditional Chinese tea ceremony (chapter 4) and a little rest. At 6:30pm head for Clarke Quay, where you can watch players dressed in Cantonese opera garb for the 7:45 performance of Chinese opera classics (chapter 8). The recommended Chinese dinner experience is at **Imperial Herbal** at the Metropole Hotel (chapter 4). For night owls, check out the **The Next Page** on Mohamed Sultan Lane (chapter 8). Let the giant portrait of a smiling Mao Zedong fill your dreams at the end of Chinese Day.

Day 2: Malay Day   Start off with the **walking tour of Kampong Glam,** filled with Malay and Muslim heritage, and **Arab Street,** for great shopping (both in chapter 6). A good lunch suggestion is to have murtabak, a Muslim specialty, at **Zam Zam's** on North Bridge Road, just behind Sultan's Mosque. In the afternoon, take the MRT out to Paya Lebar (in Geylang) for a little shopping at **Malay Village** (chapter 5) and, if you're around for the weekend, the traditional dance performances there (chapter 8). If you're hearty, take a walk down Joo Chiat Road to East Coast Road. Hang a left and across the street and down a ways you'll find the **Katong Antique House,** filled with Peranakan antiques that will bring Straits Chinese heritage to life (chapter 7). When you're starving from all this sightseeing, finish off your day at Clarke Quay's **Satay Club,** where you can try Malaysia's number one contribution to Singaporean food: those sweet delicious bits of barbecued meats dipped in a spicy peanut sauce. Yum!

Day 3: Indian Day   Naturally, Indian Day starts with the morning **walking tour of Little India** (chapter 6). Have lunch at either **Muthu's Curry** on Race Course

Road (chapter 4) or at my favorite, **Komala Vilas** on Buffalo Road (chapter 4). Don't forget to check out the stacks and cases of Indian silk and gold jewelry at **Mustapha's** (chapter 7). In the afternoon, head over to **Chettiar's Temple** on Tank Road (chapter 5). Have dinner accompanied by live Indian music at the **Tandoor** in the Parkview Holiday Inn (chapter 4).

Day 4: Colonial Day   Take the **Historic District walking tour** (chapter 6), and while you're at the **Raffles Hotel,** stop in for lunch at the **Tiffin Room,** just like the colonists used to do (chapter 4). There's some great shopping at the **Raffles Hotel Arcade** and in **Raffles City Shopping Centre** for modern Western fashions (chapter 7). After you've spent your savings, spend the rest of the afternoon with a cool **Singapore Sling at the Long Bar** in Raffles Hotel (chapter 8). If you want the true decadent dining experience, go back to your hotel, scrub up, and head to the **Raffles Grill** (chapter 4). See what's playing at the **Singapore Symphony Orchestra,** or check to see if there's a touring production of a West End show (chapter 8)—or maybe take a **trishaw ride** around the Colonial District.

Day 5: Nature Day   Have a glorious breakfast at the Songbird Terrace at the **Jurong BirdPark** (chapter 5). Later, head over to the **Singapore Botanic Gardens** (chapter 5), and take a lovely walk through the place after catching a quick lunch at the **hawker center** by the front gate on Cluny Road. (Make sure you try the Roti John—it's the best in Singapore!) After a delightful stroll through the gardens and the **National Orchid Garden,** head up to the **Singapore Zoological Gardens** (chapter 5) for a fantastic afternoon with the animals.

If you like your nature just a tad wilder, visit **Sungei Buloh Nature Park** in the morning (chapter 5) to watch the birds, and then head to **Bukit Timah Nature Reserve** (chapter 5) for a stroll through primary rain forest.

You can have a nice local dinner at the Singapore Zoological Gardens' **Night Safari,** and stick around for a wonderful adventure into the lives of some nocturnal creatures, or catch a cab to either **Long Beach Seafood** or **UDMC** (chapter 4) to taste some of the local sea creature varieties. For true animal nightlife, go to Velvet Underground at **Zouk** (chapter 8)—the nocturnal creatures there will put the animals at the Night Safari to shame. Or, walk down **Boat Quay** (chapter 8), select your favorite bar, and take your drink by the side of the river.

Day 6: Singapore Heritage Day   Soak up the culture at the **National Museum** (chapter 5) then head over to the **Asian Civilisations Museum** (chapter 5) for a glimpse of Singapore in the context of its Asian neighbors. For the shoppers among you, nothing is more perfect than a day at **Tanglin Shopping Centre** or out at Dempsey Road browsing through all the antiques shops, which display Chinese, Peranakan, Malay, and Indonesian treasures (chapter 7). Have dinner at **Newton hawker center** (chapter 4), where you can try out all the local specialties. Then head down to **Peranakan Place** in the evening for a stroll down Emerald Hill Road to take a peek at some of the exquisite private residences in the old renovated shophouses. **No. 5 Emerald Hill** is a great little bar in an old shophouse, or try **Que Pasa,** a great little wine bar in the shophouse just next door. Call some of the local theater groups or dance troupes to see if you can catch a cultural performance (chapter 8).

Day 7: Modern Singapore Day   Take a morning **bumboat ride** up and down the Singapore River and out into the harbor (chapter 6) to fill yourself up with the beautiful panorama of the cityscape. Then cruise the shopping malls of the **Orchard Road** tourist shopping mecca (chapter 7). When you can't take any more, have a quiet time at the **Singapore Art Museum,** taking in all the local, regional, and international artwork in splendid display (chapter 5). From there, it's a short walk to **Doc Cheng's,** modern Singapore's tongue-in-cheek answer to Chinese heritage (chapter 4). Tonight is the night to check out a modern Singapore **theater performance** or see if any local films are running to wrap up all of your experiences and learn how modern-day Singaporeans enfold their culture and history into the contemporary context (chapter 8). If you're a nightclubber, go to **Neo Pharaohs** on Cairnhill Road, a nice example of how cosmopolitan Singapore can be. Now, run down to **Johnny Two Thumbs Tattoo** at 14 Scotts Rd. #04-15 (☎ 65/737-4861) for a souvenir that will last a lifetime. (*Just kidding*—and don't blame me if you do it.) Stay out all night, then run to catch your plane!

11 Singapore's People, Etiquette & Customs
THE PEOPLE

Many tourists come to Singapore for the shopping or the culture or the sights, but I go for the people, who are some of the most fascinating, open, and friendly folk I've ever met. Most often, when you travel in foreign lands, the people you meet are other international travelers. In Singapore, however, the friends you make will be Singaporeans—I almost guarantee it. And if you're ever lost or need help, there will always be someone with a friendly face who'll volunteer to assist.

The median age of the population is around 32, which means the younger generations, who tend to be on the cosmopolitan and worldly side, rule local trends. I hate to generalize, but the younger set tends to be yuppie in every sense of the word. Most are professionally oriented, and while they work hard, they play hard also, from going out to nightclubs to traveling around the region and the world.

There's an ever-present image consciousness, fueled by heavy consumerism. Fashion, cars, and social scenes are in. Money is in. Success is in. Young Singaporeans strive for what they call the five Cs—career, condo, car, cash, and credit cards—and it sometimes seems they'll stop at nothing to achieve them.

Which leads me to the local term *kiasu,* used to describe a person who is afraid to miss out on anything—so afraid, in fact, that he's willing to make a fool of himself trying to grab everything he can. "Mr. Kiasu" is a popular cartoon character who epitomizes the kiasu stereotype. The proverbial village idiot, he piles his plate high at buffets to get every last penny's worth of food, wrestles through crowds at sales to get the bargains, and will go to every extent to outdo his neighbors and peers. Unfortunately, he represents a real phenomenon among the young people, who are aggressively competitive and struggle to keep up with anything new. Stop by a bookstore and pick up one of the Mr. Kiasu cartoon books for a hilarious look at his misadventures and a bit of tongue-in-cheek insight into local culture.

As with any modern society, while the younger generations are busy finding their niche in the world, it is the older generations that keep traditional cultures alive. Singapore's population, now at three million people, is a mix of Chinese (77%), Malays (14.2%), Indians (7.2%), and others, including Eurasians (1.2%). Though the country is overwhelmingly Chinese, the government has embraced all local heritage, recognizing religious holidays and festivals and promoting racial harmony in its policies, all as part of its plan to foster a single national identity, molded from the disparate cultural backgrounds of the Singaporean populace. They've even commissioned the National Association of Registered Tour Guides to take schoolchildren to cultural districts and places of historical significance to teach respect for their heritage, and to let them peer through the multicultural prism of what it is to be "Singaporean."

Unfortunately, this government social planning may have contributed to one of the common problems that's plaguing Singapore's younger generations today: a lack of identity. No longer immersed in the traditions of their own ethnic groups; growing up with so many cultural influences, both from inside Singapore and from outside its borders; and with traditional values being rapidly replaced by commercialism and a whole new set of opportunities, it's not surprising to hear so many young people ask, "Who am I?"

THE CHINESE

When Raffles opened Singapore's port for free trade, junk-loads of Chinese immigrated to find their fortunes. Most were poor workers from China's southern regions, who brought with them different cultures and dialects from their respective places of origin. Of the mix, the **Hokkiens** (from Fujian province) are the largest percentage of Chinese in Singapore at 42%, followed by the **Teochews** (from Guangdong province), **Cantonese** (also from Guangdong), **Hakkas** (from central China), and finally the **Hiananese** (from Hainan island), at 6%.

Most of the Chinese are Buddhist, a philosophy based on the teachings of ancient Indian philosopher and teacher Gautama Buddha (the Enlightened One) and focused on the Three Jewels that serve as a spiritual guide: They are the Buddha, the Dharma (his teachings), and the Sangha (monastic order). The Chinese in Singapore combine Buddhism with Taoism and Confucianism, which accounts for Buddhist temples that are structurally aligned according to the Taoist practice of *feng shui* (see below), with altars to the Taoist deity Kuan Yin and ancestral tablets that contest to the Confucian values of filial piety.

Feng shui, also called "geomancy," derives from the Taoist belief that people must always live in harmony with their surroundings. More than a simple "Don't litter" kind of message, it's a philosophy that applies to every kind of human environment, from homes to businesses, and says that if you place a home and its furnishing a particular way you can either enhance your luck, health, and wealth or invite doom. The belief is that *chi,* or positive energy, flows through people, buildings, and landscapes; if your home is not properly aligned, this chi can either get trapped and turn into bad stagnant energy, or be chased out of your house altogether. So true to these theories are the Chinese that businesses will pay exorbitant amounts to have their feng shui masters come in to consult on their interior decor and even on major construction plans, and will follow their advice to the last detail.

Characteristically, the Chinese are very superstitious, with numbers playing a critical role in everyday decisions, preferring auspicious numbers for automobile license plates, and choosing dates that contain lucky numbers for business openings. Here's another superstition: Don't leave your chopsticks sticking up in your rice bowl. It invites hungry ghosts.

THE MALAYS

When Raffles arrived, Malays had already inhabited the island, fishing the waters and trading with other local seafaring people. Many more were to immigrate in the decades to follow.

Although Singapore's Malay population is very low today, the unofficial national language, Singlish, contains a heavy dose of Malay influence, some of the best-loved local dishes are Malay, and even the national anthem is sung in Malay. The shame is that, while Malays are recognized as the original inhabitants, they constantly feel the sting of the Chinese domination of Singaporean culture and policy, and represent an unbalanced percentage of the economically disadvantaged classes, with the lowest levels of education and the highest number of criminal offenders. The government prides itself on policies to promote racial harmony, but it is widely accepted that Malays occupy jobs on the low scale of the economy. Even in the military, while there are many Malays in the enlisted troops, there are almost none in the officers' ranks. Some people have explained the economic discrimination as a language barrier: Malays are less likely to learn English, and even less likely to learn Chinese, which is a major strike against them in the job market.

Islam has been by far the most common religion among Malays since it was introduced to the Malaysian Peninsula around the year 1303. The religion's strict moral code, based on the Qur'an (or Koran), God's revelation to the Prophet Mohammed, is upheld by the faithful in Singapore, with many Malay women covering their heads and Muslim dietary laws influencing all Malay dishes. The younger generations are not as orthodox, and are seen less and less in the mosques, much to the dismay of their elders.

THE PERANAKANS

Until recently, you didn't hear much about the Peranakans (also called Straits Chinese), who were a subculture of the colonial era that grew out of intermarriage between the Chinese and Malays. However, recent trends to embrace Singapore's heritage have rekindled interest in this small yet influential group, who are unique to Singapore and Malaysia.

In the early days of Singapore, immigration of Chinese women was forbidden, so many Chinese men found wives in the native Malay population. The resultant ethnic group, the Peranakans, formed their own culture from a mixing of Chinese and Malay traditions. This mixed heritage allowed them to become strong economic and political players, oftentimes serving as middlemen between Chinese, Europeans, and other locals. Peranakan shophouses combined traditional Chinese and Malay elements, with European influence thrown in. Their pottery used Chinese styles and decorations, but in more flamboyant colors, reflecting Malaysian tastes, and their locally well-known cuisine combined Chinese preparation with locally found ingredients. The clothing worn by Peranakan ladies (or *Nonyas;* Peranakan men were called *Babas*) is also locally famous—the delicately embroidered *kebaya* is worn over a sarong, and the elegant beaded slippers are the most dainty things you've ever seen.

Peranakan literally means "Straits-born," so, technically speaking, all people born in Malaysia can argue they are Peranakan, and in a lot of literature you may see the term used broadly. Today, though, with many Singaporeans able to trace their heritage to this ethnic group, a heritage society has developed to support their interests and keep their culture alive.

THE INDIANS

Many Indians were aboard Raffles's ship when it landed on the banks of the Singapore River, so this group has always been counted as Singapore's first immigrants. In the following decades many more Indians would follow them to find work and wealth, many finding positions in the government as clerks, teachers, and traders.

In 1825, hundreds of Indians who had been in prison in Bencoolen (Sumatra) were transferred to Singapore, where they worked as convict laborers. These Indian convicts built many of the government buildings and cathedrals—for instance St. Andrew's

Cathedral, Sri Mariamman Temple, and the Istana—and worked on the heavy-duty municipal projects. Eventually, they served their sentences and assimilated into society, many remaining in Singapore.

Most Indian immigrants were from the southern regions of India, and from such ethnic groups as the Tamils, Malayalis, Punjabis, and Gujratis. So, despite Little India's reputation as an Indian enclave, the Indian population in fact split into groups based on racial divisions and settled in pockets all over the city. The Indians were also divided between religious affiliation. While most were Hindu—which revolves around the Holy Trinity of Shiva, Vishnu, and Brahma, but includes many, many other male and female deities, all of which are considered parts of the same God—Indian religious groups also included Muslims, Christians, Sikhs, and Buddhists.

The Indians tend to be an informal and warm people, adding their own brand of casual ease to Singapore, but any Singaporean will tell you that one of the most precious contributions the Indians made is their cuisine. Indian restaurants are well patronized by all ethnic groups because the southern Indian vegetarian cooking is the only food that can be enjoyed by any Singaporean, no matter what cultural or religious dietary laws he may have.

Recently, Indians have become somewhat discontented with life in Singapore, feeling overwhelmed by a Chinese government they feel promotes Chinese culture. Indians are some of the most open critics of government practices.

ETIQUETTE TIPS

Here's a delicate one, but there's no way to get around it: Only use your right hand in social interaction. Why? Because in Indian and Muslim society, the left hand is used only for bathroom chores. Not only should you eat with your right hand and give and receive all gifts with your right hand, but you should make sure all gestures, especially pointing (and, even *more* especially, pointing in temples and mosques), are made with your right hand. By the way, you should also be sure to point with your knuckle rather than your finger, to be more polite.

The other important etiquette tip is to remember to **remove your shoes** before entering places of worship (except for churches and synagogues) and all private residences. The private residence part is very important. I have yet to meet a local family that does not leave its shoes at the door.

A **traditional Indian greeting** is a slight bow with your palms pressed together in front of your chest. In these modern times, though, a handshake will usually do. When greeting an older man or especially a woman, wait for a gesture, then follow suit.

The **traditional Malay greeting,** called the *salaam,* is still practiced in Malaysia, but is rarely seen in Singapore. In this practice, both parties extend their hands to lightly touch each others', then touch their hearts with their fingertips. This is only done between members of the same sex. While Malay men will offer the more common handshake, always remember that Muslim women are not allowed to touch men to whom they are not related by blood or marriage. A simple smile and nod is fine.

Ladies, if seated on the floor, should never sit with their legs crossed in front of them—instead, always tuck your legs to the side. Both men and women should also be careful not to show the bottoms of their feet. If you cross your legs while on the floor or in a chair, don't point your soles toward other people—it's very rude. Also be careful not to use your foot to point or gesture, as this is also insulting.

Muslims who have traveled to Mecca take the prefix Haji, for males, and Hajjah for females, before their names. Feel free to use these titles if you know the person you're talking with has made the pilgrimage; it's a real mark of pride for them.

As for **Chinese etiquette and customs,** that can be rough. So many elements of Chinese culture make no sense to Westerners that I couldn't possibly cover the whole range. The younger generations are not as strict as the older folks about these points of cultural etiquette, but if you find yourself in a situation, even common sense can't make you a good judge of proper etiquette. You could give a beautiful brush painting to a Chinese as a gift, and the tiniest bird in the background could be a bad omen laying a curse on all of their future generations. Seriously.

If you are invited to a Chinese occasion or need to buy a gift for someone, the best thing you can possibly do is consult a Chinese person for advice. This is where hotel staff come in handy. What color should I wear? What is the proper attire? Will this gift be nice? You'll thank them later.

I can give you some basic rules of thumb that will help:

- **Don't wear all white or all black if you're invited to a festive occasion;** these colors are for mourning. The same is pretty much true for all-blue and all-green outfits. Reds, pinks, oranges, and yellows are great for such gatherings.
- **Gifts should never be knives, clocks, or handkerchiefs,** and don't send *anybody* white flowers. (The sharp blades of knives symbolize the severing of a friendship; in Cantonese, the word for clock sounds the same as the word for funeral; handkerchiefs bring to mind tears and sadness; and white is the color of funeral mourning.)
- **When giving money,** an even amount in a red envelope is presented on auspicious occasions, and an odd number in a white envelope is presented at funerals. There's no correct amount, but if there's a meal involved, the amount should at least cover the cost. By the way, the Chinese do not open gifts in public.
- The main rules regarding **table manners** revolve around the use of chopsticks. Don't stick them upright in any dish, don't gesture with them, and don't suck on them. Dropped chopsticks are also considered bad luck.

As for **greetings,** Chinese men and women are all pretty well accustomed to the standard handshake.

If you're conducting business in Singapore, you'll most likely be **exchanging business cards.** All Chinese Singaporeans present and receive business cards using both hands, as if giving or accepting a gift. If a card is given to you, read it and make a comment about it. "Nice card" or "You're the *director* of the department!" will do. Hang on to it a bit before putting it away—to stow it immediately is a sign of disrespect.

USEFUL MALAY PHRASES

Bahasa Malaysia, the Malay language, is spoken commonly in Singapore. In addition to Malays, many Indians and Chinese talk the talk, which is a common language in markets and shops. Knowing a few phrases can sometimes get you better deals, as the shop owner may think you're an expatriate rather than a tourist. Written Malay uses the same alphabet as English, so it's easy to read. Sounding out the syllables phonetically is fairly simple. One note on pronunciation: Where a *k* appears at the end of a word, "swallow" the sound, or just don't pronounce the k in a hard fashion.

Greetings

Good morning	Selamat pagi (sell-*ah*-mat *pah*-gee)
Good night	Selamat malam (sell-*ah*-mat *mah*-lahm)
How are you?	Apa khabar? (*ah*-pah *kah*-bar)
I'm fine	Khabar baik (*kah*-bar *bah*-ee)

Common Phrases

Thank you	Terimah kasih (ter-*ee*-mah *kah*-see)
You're welcome	Sama-sama (*sah*-mah *sah*-mah)
What does this mean?	Apa makna ini? (*ah*-pah *mahk*-nah *ee*-nee)
What time is it?	Pukul berapa? (*poo*-kool ber-*ah*-pah)
Is this seat taken?	Ada orang duduk di sini? (*ah*-dah *ohr*-ahng *doo*-doo dee *see*-nee)

Handy Phrases

Where is . . .	Di mana (dee *mah*-nah) . . .
the toilet?	tandas? (*tan*-dahs)
a coin phone?	pondok telefon? (*pohn*-doh *teh*-leh-fohn)
a taxi stand?	perhentian teksi? (pehr-*hen*-tyohn *tek*-see)

Taxi Talk

How far is it?	Berapa juah? (behr-*ah*-pah *joo*-ah)
Stop here please	Tolong berhenti di sini (*toh*-long behr-*hen*-tee dee *see*-nee)

Shopping Talk

I'm just looking around	Saya hanya melihat-lihat saja (*sah*-yah *hahn*-yah meh-*lee*-haht *lee*-haht *sah*-jah)
What is the price?	Berapa harganya? (behr-*ah*-pah hahr-*gahn*-yah)
This is too expensive	Ini terlalu mahal (*ee*-nee tehr-*lah*-loo mah-*hahl*)
Is that your lowest price?	Adakah ini harga yang paling rendah? (*ah*-dah-kah *ee*-nee *hahr*-gah yahng *pah*-ling *ren*-dah)
Do you accept credit cards?	Adakah kamu menerima kad kredit? (*ah*-dah-kah *kah*-moo mehn-eh-*ree*-mah kahd *krehd*-eet)

In Case You Need a Doctor

I need a doctor	Saya hendak berjumpa doktor (*sah*-yah *hen*-dah behr-*joom*-pah *dohk*-tohr)
I am allergic to antibiotics	Saya alergik kepada antibiotik (*sah*-yah ah-*ler*-jihk keh-*pah*-dah ahn-tee-bee-*oh*-tee)
I am seeing double	Penglihatan saya berlapis (*pehng*-lee-hah-tahn *sah*-yah behr-*lah*-pees)

Fast Facts: Singapore

American Express The American Express office is located at #01-04/05 Winslan House, Killiney Road (a short walk from Orchard Rd.). The direct line for travel services is ☎ **65/235-5788.** The 24-hour membership services hot line is ☎ **1800/732-2244.** The 24-hour traveler's check refund hot line is ☎ **1800/738-3383.** See the "Money" section earlier in this chapter for more details on member privileges.

Baby-Sitters Most hotels will arrange for a reliable baby-sitter with at least 24 hours advance notice.

Business Hours **Shopping centers** are open Monday through Saturday from 10am to 8pm, and stay open until 10pm on some public holidays. **Banks** are open from 9:30am to 3pm Monday through Friday, and from 9am to 11am on Saturdays. **Restaurants** open at lunchtime from around 11am to 2:30pm, and for dinner they reopen at around 6pm and take the last order sometime around 10pm. **Nightclubs** stay open until midnight on weekdays and until 2am on Fridays and Saturdays. **Government offices** are open from 9am to 5pm Monday through Friday and from 9am to 3pm on Saturdays. **Post offices** conduct business from 8:30am to 5pm on weekdays and from 8:30am to 1pm on Saturdays.

Cameras & Film   There are many camera equipment shops in the malls on **Orchard Road,** and some will take repairs. Avoid the shops in Far East Plaza and Lucky Plaza, as these are not as reputable. Film is readily available everywhere at prices comparable to the West. Many of the major shopping centers have fast and inexpensive film-developing services, and developing quality is generally excellent.

Climate   See "When to Go" earlier in this chapter.

Credit Cards   To report lost or stolen credit cards, the number to call for **American Express** is ☎ **1800/732-2244.** For **MasterCard,** the toll-free Emergency Assistance hot line is ☎ **1800/110-0113**. For **Visa,** call toll-free ☎ **1800/110-0344.** If your **Diners Club** card is lost or stolen, call locally ☎ **65/292-7055.**

Crime   Because of harsh laws, strict enforcement, and traditional cultural beliefs, there is not a lot of crime in Singapore. Murder and rape are almost nonexistent. A few pickpockets do creep around tourist-populated areas, though, so take care. All hotels have either a safe-deposit box in the rooms or a safe behind the front desk. The only other thieves you need to be aware of are shop owners who may overcharge you for purchases, all in the sport of savvy salesmanship. To defend yourself, see chapter 7 for tips on how to bargain effectively, and have a ball negotiating your way to some great prices.

Also, you probably don't want to become a criminal yourself. Violations that bring on large fines include littering, jaywalking, smoking in prohibited areas, and failing to obey taxi queues (meaning that if there's a taxi queue nearby, it's against the law to hail a cab out of the queue).

The number to call for a **police emergency** is ☎ **999.**

Currency   See "Money" earlier in this chapter.

Customs   See "Customs Regulations" earlier in this chapter.

Dentists   Dental care in Singapore is excellent, and most procedures will cost less than they would at home. Some hospitals offer emergency dental care at affordable rates, should you need dental care during your trip.

Doctors   Most hotels have in-house doctors on call 24 hours a day. A visit to a private physician can cost anywhere from S$25 to S$100 (US$15 to $60). In the event of a medical emergency call ☎ **995** for an ambulance.

Driving Rules   See "Getting Around" earlier in this chapter.

Drug Laws   If you are caught in possession of morphine quantities exceeding 30 grams, heroin exceeding 15 grams, cocaine 30 grams, marijuana 500 grams, hashish 200 grams, or opium 1.2 grams, the Singapore government will consider you to be a drug trafficker and you will receive the death penalty—no questions asked. See the "Customs Regulations" section earlier in this chapter for more details.

Electricity   Standard electrical current is 220 volts AC (50 cycles). Consult your concierge to see if your hotel has converters and plug adapters in-house for you to use. If you are using sensitive equipment, do not trust the cheap voltage transformers. Nowadays, a lot of electrical equipment—including portable radios and laptop computers—comes with built-in converters, so you can follow the manufacturer's directions for changing them over. FYI, videocassettes taped on different voltage currents are recorded on machines with different record and playback cycles. Prerecorded videotapes are not interchangeable between currents unless you have special equipment that can play either kind.

Embassies & Consulates   See "Visitor Information & Entry Requirements" earlier in this chapter.

Emergencies   For police dial ☎ **999.** For medical or fire emergencies call ☎ **995.**

Etiquette   See "Singapore's People, Etiquette & Customs" earlier in this chapter.

Hairdressers/Barbers   Most major hotels have unisex salons, and you can find them in many shopping malls as well. For the gentleman who wants a really special shave 'n' a haircut, you can always try the back alley behind the Allsagoff School off Sultan Road in Kampong Glam. They don't make places like these anymore.

Hitchhiking   Definitely not recommended in Singapore. Heaven knows what punishment you'll invite.

Holidays   See the "Calendar of Public Holidays & Events" earlier in this chapter.

Hospitals   If you need to seek emergency medical attention, go to either of the following centrally located private hospitals: **Mount Elizabeth Hospital Ltd.,** 3 Mount Elizabeth Rd., near Orchard Road (☎ **65/737-2666**), or **Singapore General Hospital,** Outram Road, in Chinatown (☎ **65/222-3322**). Medical care in Singapore is of superior quality. In fact, throngs of ASEAN (Association of Southeast Asian Nations) neighbors make annual trips to Singapore for their physical examinations and other medical treatments. You can be assured of excellent care, should you need it.

Internet   Internet cafes are becoming common throughout the city, with usage costs between S$4 and S$5 (US$2.40–$3) per hour (keep in mind, if you use the Internet in your hotel's business center, you'll pay a much higher price). Almost every shopping mall has one, especially along Orchard Road, and there are cyber-cafes in both terminals at Changi Airport. In town, along Orchard Road, try **Cyber Arena Internet Point II,** Cuppage Terrace, 39 Orchard Rd. (☎ **65/ 738-1540**), or **E-Net Cyberspace,** 1 Scotts Rd., Shaw Centre #05-10 (☎ **65/ 835-2338**). In the Historic District, there are a few in Stamford House, just across from City Hall MRT Station. Check out **Chills Café,** #01-01 Stamford House, 39 Stamford Rd. (☎ **65/883-1016**).

Language   The official languages are Malay, Chinese (Mandarin), Tamil, and English. Malay is the national language while English is the language for government operations, law, and major financial transactions. Most Singaporeans are at least bilingual, with many speaking one or more dialects of Chinese, English, and some Malay.

Laundry   Almost all Singaporeans have washing machines in their homes, so the concept of self-service laundry is not terribly common here. There are some laundries listed in the Singapore Yellow Pages directory, but most of them are out in the Housing Board developments, so it may be a trek. A few hotels offer self-service launderettes, and most of them have a laundry service, but you'll pay inflated prices for clean clothes. (I've noted which hotels provide these facilities/services in chapter 3.)

Liquor Laws   The legal age for alcohol purchase and consumption is 18 years. Some of the smaller clubs rarely check identification, but the larger ones will, and sometimes require patrons to be 21 years old to enter, just to weed out younger crowds. Public drunk-and-disorderly behavior is against the law, and may snag you for up to S$1,000 in fines for the first offense, or even imprisonment—which is unlikely, but still a great way to ruin a vacation. There are strict drinking and driving laws, and roadblocks are set up on weekends to catch party people on their way home to the housing developments.

Mail   Most hotels have mail services at the front counter. **Singapore Post** has centrally located offices at #04-15 Ngee Ann City/Takashimaya Shopping Centre (☎ 65/738-6899); Tang's department store at 320 Orchard Rd. #03-00 (☎ 65/738-5899); Chinatown Point, 133 New Bridge Rd. #02-42/43/44 (☎ 65/538-7899); Change Alley, 16 Collyer Quay #02-02 Hitachi Tower (☎ 65/538-6899); and at 231 Bain St. #01-03 Bras Basah Complex (☎ 65/ 339-8899). Plus there are five branches at Changi International Airport. For all general inquiries, dial ☎ 65/1605 for the Singapore Post hot line.

The going rate for international airmail letters to North America and Europe is S$1 (US$0.06) for 20 grams plus S35¢ (US$0.21) for each additional 10 grams. For international airmail service to Australia and New Zealand, the rate is S70¢ (US$0.42) for 20 grams plus S30¢ (US$0.18) for each additional 10 grams. Postcards and aerograms to all destinations are S50¢ (US$0.30).

Your hotel will accept mail sent for you at its address. American Express has a special mail delivery and holding deal for card members.

Maps   The *Singapore Street Directory,* a book detailing every section of the island, is carried by most taxi drivers, and can be very helpful if you're trying to get someplace and he either doesn't know where it is or can't understand you. The street listing in the front will direct you to the corresponding map. A good cabbie can take it from there. Other good maps of the major city areas can be found in free STB publications, while there are also a few commercially produced maps sold in all major bookstores here.

Newspapers & Magazines   Local English newspapers available are the *International Herald Tribune, The Business Times, The Straits Times,* and *USA Today International.* Following an article criticizing the Singapore government, the *Asian Wall Street Journal* was banned from wide distribution in Singapore. Most of the major hotels are allowed to carry it, though, so ask around and you can find one. *The New Paper* is an "alternative publication" that may be a useful source for finding out what's happening around town. Major hotels, bookstores, and magazine shops sell a wide variety of international magazines.

Pets   Singapore has strict quarantine regulations, and I'll be shocked if you can find a hotel that will take pets. Keep poochie at home.

Pharmacies/Chemists   Guardian Pharmacies fills prescriptions with name brand drugs (from a licensed physician within Singapore), and carries a large selection of toiletry items. Convenient locations include #B1-05 Centrepoint Shopping Centre (☎ 65/737-4835), Changi International Airport Terminal 2 (☎ 65/545-4233), #02-139 Marina Square (☎ 65/333-9565), and #B1-04 Raffles Place MRT Station (☎ 65/535-2762).

Police   Given the strict law enforcement reputation in Singapore, you can bet the officers here don't have the greatest senses of humor. If you find yourself being questioned about anything, big or small, be dead serious and most respectful. For emergencies, call ☎ **999.** If you need to call the police headquarters, dial ☎ **65/235-9111.**

If you are arrested, you have the right to legal council, but only when the police decide you can exercise that right. You get no call unless they give you permission. Bottom line: Don't get arrested.

Radio/TV   There are five channels in Singapore, four of which are mostly English-language programming. These days, more shows are being produced locally, but there's still a heavy rotation of the latest hits from the United States, the United Kingdom, and Australia. The larger hotels all have HBO and some have CNN, as well as other satellite programming.

There are five FM radio stations, which broadcast in all of the national languages.

Rest Rooms/Toilets   Rest rooms are easy to find in Singapore and most of the time they are clean. Note that the authorities levy fines for not flushing, though I've never seen anyone actually come in and check. The more modern facilities will have toilet bowls, but you won't get out of Singapore alive without encountering a "squatty potty"—a small porcelain bowl in the floor over which you are expected to hover. Be prepared. If you head out to beach areas or to surrounding islands, bring spare tissue. Every once in a blue moon, I've encountered some old lady who stands outside the door and charges you a dime to use the toilet, but it's rare.

Safety   Singapore is a pretty safe place by any standards. There's very little violent crime, even late at night. If you stay out, there's very little worry about making it home safe. If your children are missing, they probably aren't kidnapped, but are being consoled by a friendly passerby while you search for them. This may sound naive, but the Chinese are culturally a very family-oriented people, and most would never dream of harming a child.

In recent years, some pickpocketing has been reported. Hotel safe-deposit boxes are the best way to secure valuables, and traveler's checks solve theft problems in a jiff.

Smoking   It's against the law to smoke in public buses, elevators, theaters, cinemas, air-conditioned restaurants, shopping centers, government offices, and taxi queues.

Taxes   Many hotels and restaurants will advertise rates followed by "+++." The first + is the goods and services tax (GST), which is levied at 3% of the purchase. The second + is 1% cess (a 1% tax levied by the STB on all tourism-related activities). The third is a 10% gratuity. See the "Customs Regulations" section earlier in this chapter for information on the GST Tourist Refund Scheme, which lets you recover the GST for purchases of goods over S$300 (US$179.65) in value.

Taxis   See "Getting Around" earlier in this chapter.

Telephone Dialing Info at a Glance

- **To place a call from your home country to Singapore:** Dial the international access code (011 in the U.S., 0011 in Australia, or 00 in the U.K., Ireland, and New Zealand), plus the country code (**65**), plus the seven-digit phone number (for example, 011-65/000-0000). Note that many hotels have toll-free numbers for calling from all these countries; where this is the case, I've listed them in the individual hotel reviews.
- **To call Malaysia from Singapore:** Via an operator, dial 109. To call direct, dial the access code for the trunk line that links the two countries (007) plus Malaysia's country code (60) plus the city code and the number (for example, 005-60/000-0000).
- **To place a direct international call from Singapore:** Dial the international access code (001), the country code (U.S. and Canada 1, Australia 61, Republic of Ireland 353, New Zealand 64, U.K. 44), the area or city code, and the number.
- **To reach the international operator:** Dial 104.
- **To place a call within Singapore:** Dial the seven-digit number. The "65" prefix need not be used. Toll-free numbers in Singapore use the standard "1-800" prefix.
- Other useful numbers are for the **time** (☎ **1711**), and for the **weather** (☎ **65/542-7788**). For **telephone directory assistance,** dial **100**.

Telegrams & Wiring Money   See "Money" earlier in this chapter for information on wiring money. To send a telegram, consult your hotel. Many of them offer this service for a fee.

Telephones & Faxes   Almost all hotels will send faxes locally and internationally for you and add the charge to your bill.

   Public phones are abundant and can be operated by coins or by phone cards, which can be purchased in increments of S$2, S$5, and S$10 (US$1.20, US$3, and US$6) values at post offices, provisioners shops, and some money changers. The charge for a local call is S10¢ (US $.06) for 3 minutes. A tone will interrupt your call when your time is up to remind you to add another coin. Calls to numbers beginning with 1800 are toll free within Singapore.

   International Direct Dialing (IDD) is the long-distance service used by most hotels, businesses, and private residences in Singapore, with direct dialing to 218 countries. Depending on where you are calling, there is rarely a delay or echo on the line, and reception is incredibly clear.

   Before you leave your home country, contact your long-distance provider to see if they offer a **long-distance calling card,** which will allow you to access their international operators and have your calls charged to your home phone bill at their rates. Singapore has some of the lowest international call rates in the world, but unfortunately, hotels charge a whopping surcharge for these calls.

Time   Singapore Standard Time is 8 hours ahead of Greenwich mean time (GMT). International time differences will change during daylight saving or summer time. Basic time differences are: New York –13, Los Angeles –16,

Montreal −13, Vancouver −16, London −8, Brisbane +3, Darwin +1, Melbourne +2, Sydney +3, and Auckland +4. For the current time within Singapore, call ☎ **1711.**

Tipping   Tipping is discouraged at hotels, bars, and in taxis. Basically, the deal here is not to tip. A gratuity is automatically added into guest checks, and there's no need to slip anyone an extra buck for carrying bags or such. It's not expected.

Tourist Offices   See "Visitor Information & Entry Requirements" earlier in this chapter.

Water   Tap water in Singapore passes World Health Organization standards and is potable.

Yellow Pages   The Singapore Yellow Pages is the place to start for any need that may come up. They are standard in most hotel rooms. They're rarely found at public phones, but shopkeepers may let you take a peek at theirs if you ask nicely.

Singapore Accommodations

At last count, the number of official (gazetted) hotels in Singapore was more than 100, and the number of hotel rooms was somewhere more than 30,000. Now here's another fact to chew over: On any given night, an average 75% of these rooms are occupied, mostly by business travelers. International business is the Singaporean hotel industry's bread and butter, so competition between hotels is fierce, causing them to invest in the most high-priced renovations of the most deluxe-super-royal-regal executive facilities, all in an attempt to lure business folks and—eventually, it is hoped—land lucrative corporate accounts.

Of course, this all means that budget accommodations are not a high priority on the island. Between the business community's demand for luxury on the one hand and the inflated Singaporean real estate market on the other, room prices tend to be high. What this means for leisure travelers is that you may end up paying for a business center you'll never use or a 24-hour stress-reliever masseuse you'll never call—and all this without the benefit of a corporate discount rate.

Don't fret, though: I'm here to tell you that there's a range of accommodations out there—you just have to know where to find 'em. In this chapter, I'll help you pick the right accommodations for you, based on your vacation goals and your travel budget, so you can make the most of your stay.

CHOOSING YOUR NEIGHBORHOOD

In considering where you'll stay, think about what you'll be doing in Singapore—that way, you can choose a hotel that's close to the particular action that suits you. (On the other hand, since Singapore is a small place and public transportation is excellent, nothing's really ever too far away.)

Orchard Road has the largest cluster of hotels in the city, and is right in the heart of Singaporean shopping mania—the malls and wide sidewalks where locals and tourists stroll to see and be seen. The **Historic District** has hotels that are near museums and sights, while those in **Marina Bay** center more around the business professionals who come to Singapore for Suntec City, the giant convention and exhibition center located there. **Chinatown** and **Tanjong Pagar** have some lovely boutique hotels in quaint back streets, and **Shenton Way** has a couple of high-rise places for the convenience of people doing

Urban Singapore Accommodations

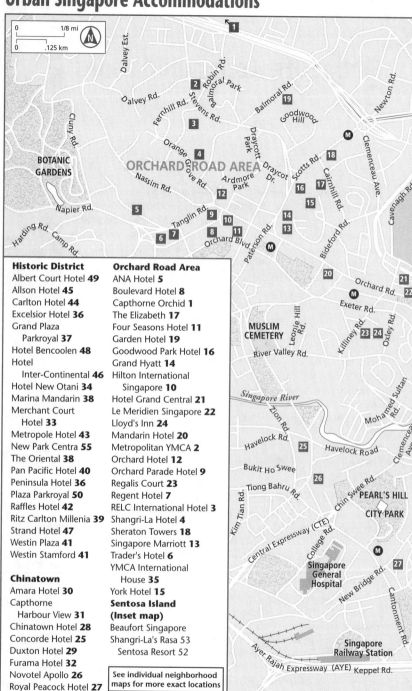

Historic District
Albert Court Hotel **49**
Allson Hotel **45**
Carlton Hotel **44**
Excelsior Hotel **36**
Grand Plaza
  Parkroyal **37**
Hotel Bencoolen **48**
Hotel
  Inter-Continental **46**
Hotel New Otani **34**
Marina Mandarin **38**
Merchant Court
  Hotel **33**
Metropole Hotel **43**
New Park Centra **55**
The Oriental **38**
Pan Pacific Hotel **40**
Peninsula Hotel **36**
Plaza Parkroyal **50**
Raffles Hotel **42**
Ritz Carlton Millenia **39**
Strand Hotel **47**
Westin Plaza **41**
Westin Stamford **41**

Chinatown
Amara Hotel **30**
Capthorne
  Harbour View **31**
Chinatown Hotel **28**
Concorde Hotel **25**
Duxton Hotel **29**
Furama Hotel **32**
Novotel Apollo **26**
Royal Peacock Hotel **27**

Orchard Road Area
ANA Hotel **5**
Boulevard Hotel **8**
Capthorne Orchid **1**
The Elizabeth **17**
Four Seasons Hotel **11**
Garden Hotel **19**
Goodwood Park Hotel **16**
Grand Hyatt **14**
Hilton International
  Singapore **10**
Hotel Grand Central **21**
Le Meridien Singapore **22**
Lloyd's Inn **24**
Mandarin Hotel **20**
Metropolitan YMCA **2**
Orchard Hotel **12**
Orchard Parade Hotel **9**
Regalis Court **23**
Regent Hotel **7**
RELC International Hotel **3**
Shangri-La Hotel **4**
Sheraton Towers **18**
Singapore Marriott **13**
Trader's Hotel **6**
YMCA International
  House **35**
York Hotel **15**

**Sentosa Island
(Inset map)**
Beaufort Singapore
Shangri-La's Rasa **53**
  Sentosa Resort **52**

See individual neighborhood
maps for more exact locations

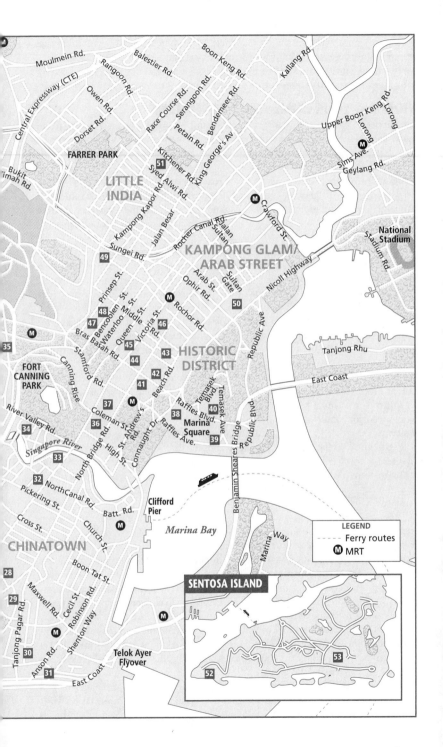

business in the downtown business district. Many hotels have free morning and evening shuttle buses to Orchard Road, Suntec City, and Shenton Way. I've also listed two hotels on **Sentosa,** an island to the south that's a popular day or weekend trip for many Singaporeans. (It's connected to Singapore by a causeway.)

CHOOSING YOUR HOME AWAY FROM HOME

What appeals to you? A big, flashy, internationalist palace or a smaller, homier place? Hyatt, Sheraton, Hilton, and Hotel Intercontinental are just a few of the international chain hotels you will find in Singapore. Many hotels, such as the Mandarin, the Shangri-La, and the Hilton, were built in the seventies, during Singapore's economic boom; and while they've seen many major renovations over the years, they're not as flashy as the newer properties. One benefit, however, is these older hotels sometimes have larger rooms and more landscaped ground space. For the most part, the modern hotels are nondescript towers—though the Westin has the distinction of being the tallest hotel in the world.

The newest trend is the **boutique hotel.** Conceived as part of the Urban Restoration Authority's renewal plans, rows of old shophouses and buildings in ethnic areas like Chinatown and Tanjong Pagar have been restored and transformed into small, lovely hotels. Places like Albert Court Hotel, the Duxton, and the Royal Peacock are beautiful examples of local flavor turned into elegant accommodations. While these places can put you closer to the heart of Singapore, they do have their drawbacks—for one, both the hotels and their rooms are small and, due to building codes and a lack of space, they're unable to provide facilities like swimming pools, Jacuzzis, or fitness centers.

While **budget hotels** have very limited facilities and interior stylings that never made it much past 1979, you can always expect a clean room. What's more, service can sometimes be more personal in smaller hotels, where front desk staff has fewer faces to recognize and is accustomed to helping guests with the sorts of things a business center or concierge would handle in a larger hotel. Par for the course, many of the guests in these places are backpackers, and mostly Western backpackers at that. However, you will see some ASEAN (Association of Southeast Asian Nations) people staying in these places. *One note:* The budget accommodations listed here are places decent enough for any standards. While cheaper digs are available, the rooms can be dreary and depressing, musty and old, or downright sleazy.

Unless you choose one of the extreme budget hotels, there are some standard features you can expect to find everywhere. While no hotels offer a courtesy car or limousine, many have **courtesy shuttles** to popular parts of town. Security key cards are catching on, as are in-room safes (yes, even in safe and secure Singapore). You'll also see in-house movies and sometimes CNN on your TV, as well as a nifty interactive service that lets you check on your hotel bill, order room service, and get general information on Singapore with the touch of a button. Voice mail is gaining popularity, and fax services can always be provided upon request. You'll find most places have adequate fitness center facilities, almost all of which offer a range of massage treatments. Pools tend to be on the small side, and Jacuzzis are often placed in men's and women's locker rooms, making it impossible for couples to use them together. While tour desks are in some lobbies, car-rental desks are rare.

The Singapore Tourism Board (STB) recently launched a new campaign to pull hotel concierges into its loop with updated and accurate **visitor information** via a computer link to STB information resources. I've indicated in the text which hotels offer this service.

Making Hotel Reservations Online

The Web site **www.asia-hotels.com** offers an Internet-based hotel reservation system for up to 6,500 hotels in Asia, including Singapore and Malaysia. The site offers competitive room rates through their Internet booking service, and lists detailed information on each hotel and resort. There's no charge for their service—hotels pick up the tab.

Many of the finest **restaurants** in Singapore are located in hotels, whether they are operated by the hotel directly or just inhabiting rented space. Some hotels can have up to five or six restaurants, each serving a different cuisine. Generally, you can expect these restaurants to be more expensive than places not located in hotels. In each hotel review, the distinguished restaurants have been noted; these restaurants are also fully reviewed in chapter 4.

RATES

Let's talk money. Rates for double rooms range from as low as S$80 (US$47.90) at the Strand on Bencoolen (a famous backpacker's strip) to as high as S$650 (US$389.20) a night at the exclusive Raffles Hotel. Average rooms are usually in the S$200 to S$300 (US$119.75 to US$179.65) range, but keep in mind that **although all prices listed in this book are the going rates, they rarely represent what you'll actually pay.** In fact, you should *never* have to pay the advertised rate in a Singapore hotel, as many offer promotional rates. When you call for your reservation, always ask what special deals they are running and how you can get the lowest price for your room. Many times hotels that have just completed renovations offer discounts, and most have special weekend or long-term stay programs. Also be sure to inquire about free add-ons. Complimentary breakfast and other services can have added value that make a difference in the end.

For the purposes of this guide, I've divided hotels into the categories **very expensive,** S$400 (US$239.50) and up; **expensive,** S$300 to S$400 (US$179.65 to US$239.50); **moderate,** S$200 to S$300 (US$119.75 to US$179.65); and **inexpensive,** under S$200 (US$119.75).

TAXES & SERVICE CHARGES

All rates listed are in Singapore dollars, with U.S. dollar equivalents provided as well (remember to check the exchange rate when you're planning, though, since it may fluctuate). Most rates do not include the so-called "+++" taxes and charges: the 10% service charge, 3% goods and services tax (GST), and 1% cess (a 1% tax levied by the STB on all tourism-related activities). Keep these in mind when figuring your budget. Some budget hotels will quote discount rates inclusive of all taxes.

THE BUSY SEASON

The busy season is from January to around June. In the late summer months, business travel dies down and hotels try to make up for drooping occupancy rates by going after the leisure market. In fall, even tourism drops off somewhat, making the season ripe for budget-minded visitors. These may be the best times to get a deal. Probably the worst time to negotiate will be between Christmas and the Chinese New Year, when folks travel on vacation and to see their families.

MAKING RESERVATIONS ON THE GROUND

If you are not able to make a reservation before your trip, there is a **reservation service** available at Changi International Airport. The Singapore Hotel Association operates desks in both Terminals 1 and 2, with reservation services based upon room availability for many hotels. Discounts for these arrangements are sometimes as high as 30%. The desks are open daily from 7:30am to 11:30pm.

1 Best Bets

- **Best Feng Shui:** No doubt about it, for a little extra good vibes, stay at the **Grand Hyatt Singapore.** This hotel suffered from low occupancy rates until it consulted a Chinese monk to put the structure in harmony with its surrounding elements, seen and unseen. The day after the recommended adjustments were completed (at quite some cost), the hotel reopened and immediately ran at full capacity for 3 days straight.
- **Best Romantic Hideaway:** The **Beaufort,** on Singapore's Sentosa island is a favorite spot for honeymooners. Request dinner anywhere (even in the woods or by the sea) and they will make your dreams come true.
- **Best Hotels for the Suit & Tie Set:** While all of the international hotels have good executive club facilities, the **Grand Hyatt Singapore** has the most exciting rooms. Very powerful. Go get 'em.
- **Best Hotel for History Nuts:** **Raffles Hotel** and the **Goodwood Park Hotel** are both historical landmarks.
- **Best Local-Flavor Accommodations:** The **Albert Court Hotel** and the **Hotel Inter-Continental's** Shophouse Rooms have captured a truly lovely local feel and combined it with the comfort of a modern facility. You can experience Singaporean culture without leaving your room.
- **Best View:** From the upper floors of the **Westin Stamford Hotel** you can see all the way across the water to Indonesia. The **Marina Mandarin** has gorgeous views of the marina on one side of the hotel, while the **Ritz-Carlton** has spectacular views on both sides. **Shangri-La's Rasa Sentosa Resort** on Sentosa has to be given a special award for the breathtaking view of the beach and surrounding seas. At night, the lights from docked ships twinkle on the horizon. It's simply gorgeous.
- **Best View from a Tub:** You have to see it to believe it, but every huge bathtub in the **Ritz-Carlton** sits just beneath an octagonal picture window with views of the harbor and marina. You can sightsee while you have a soak!
- **Best Pool:** The **Beaufort Sentosa, Singapore** has a large outdoor pool tiled in midnight blue specked with mica. During the day it glistens almost black; at night it shimmers emerald green. The pool at **Shangri-La's Rasa Sentosa Resort** is a mass of curvy spaces with lots of fun pool equipment to play around with. The kiddie pool has rock slides that will make you wish you were 9 again.
- **Most High-Profile Address:** If you live to impress, **Raffles Hotel** is where you will stay. It was the first choice of Michael Jackson and every other famous figure to pass through Singapore since God knows when.
- **Best Hotels for Shopaholics:** Anywhere on Orchard Road.
- **Best Hotel for Tourists Who Don't Want to Miss Anything:** **Traders Hotel** is located right across the street from the headquarters of the Singapore Tourism Board (STB).

- **Best Hotels for Penny-Pinchers:** I challenge you to find better value for your money than at **RELC International Hotel.**
- **Best Hotel for Backpackers:** The **Strand** is the freshest in its class. And while hostels are not common in Singapore, the **YMCA International** is a clean and safe alternative.
- **Best Hotel for Tree Huggers:** The **Shangri-La** and the **Beaufort Sentosa, Singapore** boast extensive gardens and live up to expectations.
- **Best Spa:** The **Grand Plaza Hotel,** the **Plaza,** and the **Four Seasons.** See the feature "The Best of Singapore's Spas" later in this chapter to find out why.
- **Best Butt Kissing:** The **Four Seasons** will pamper you like a VIP, with style and grace.

2 The Historic District

VERY EXPENSIVE

✪ **Raffles Hotel.** 1 Beach Rd., Singapore 189673. ☎ **800/525-4800** in the U.S. and Canada, 008/251-958 in Australia, 0800/441098 in New Zealand, 0800/964470 in the U.K., or 65/337-1886. Fax 65/339-7650. www.raffles.com. E-mail: raffles@pacific.net.sg. 104 suites. A/C MINIBAR TV TEL. S\$650–S\$6,000 (US\$389.20–US\$3,592.80) suite. AE, DC, JCB, MC, V. Near City Hall MRT.

Raffles Hotel has been legendary since its establishment in 1887. Named after Singapore's first British colonial administrator, Sir Stamford Raffles, it was founded by the Armenian Sarkies brothers. Originally, it was a bungalow, but by the 1920s and 1930s it had expanded to become a mecca for celebrities like Charlie Chaplin and Douglas Fairbanks, for writers like Somerset Maugham and Noël Coward, and for various and sundry kings, sultans, and politicians. Always at the center of Singapore's colonial high life, it's hosted balls, tea dances, and jazz functions, and during World War II was the last rallying point for the British in the face of Japanese occupation and the first place for refugee prisoners of war released from concentration camps. In 1987, the Raffles Hotel was declared a landmark and restored to its early-20th-century splendor, with grand arches, 14-foot molded ceilings with spinning fans, tiled teak and marble floors, Oriental carpets, and period furnishings. Outside, the facade of the main building was similarly restored, complete with the elegant cast-iron portico and the verandas that encircle the upper stories.

Because it is a national landmark, thousands of people pass through the open lobby each day, so in addition there's a private inner lobby marked off for "residents" only. Nothing feels better than walking along the dark teak floors of the verandahs, past little rattan-furnished relaxation areas overlooking the green tropical courtyards. Each suite entrance is like a private apartment door: Enter past the living and dining area dressed in Oriental carpets and reproduction furniture, then pass through louvered doors into the bedroom with its four-poster bed and beautiful armoire, ceiling fan twirling high above. Now imagine you're a colonial traveler, fresh in town from a long ocean voyage. Raffles is the only hotel in Singapore where you can still fully play out this fantasy, and it can be a lot of fun.

Dining/Diversions: Accommodations aside, the hotel's restaurants and nightlife also draw the crowds, who come to eat at the Tiffin Room, Raffles Grill, and Doc Cheng's (all reviewed in chapter 4) and to lounge in the Bar and Billiards Room and Long Bar.

Amenities: Services include in-room VCR with video rental, in-room data port and fax machine, personal butler service, 24-hour room service, and voice mail. The outdoor pool is small, but it's open 24 hours a day (quite unique) and it's very private.

Other facilities like a business center; fitness center with Jacuzzi, sauna, steam room, and massage; and beauty salon are fairly standard; but the Raffles Hotel arcade also houses a theater playhouse, Raffles Culinary Academy, the Raffles Hotel Museum, and 65 exclusive boutiques.

✪ **The Ritz-Carlton, Millenia Singapore.** 7 Raffles Ave., Singapore 039799. ☎ **800/ 241-3333** in the U.S. and Canada, or 65/337-8888. Fax 65/338-0001. www.ritzcarlton.com. E-mail: reservation@ritz-carlton.com.sg. 608 units. A/C MINIBAR TV TEL. S$430–S$475 (US$257.50–US$284.45) double; S$550–S$5,000 (US$329.35–US$2,994) suite. AE, DC, JCB, MC, V. 10-min. walk to City Hall MRT.

Touted as the ultimate in Singapore luxury hotels, The Ritz-Carlton, Millenia is just that, but you have to love ultramodern design. The space-age lobby is like a science museum: The sculptures and artworks displayed throughout this place are very daring and innovative. Luckily for residents, the guest rooms display a great deal of warmth and coziness in comparison. All rooms have spectacular views of either Kallang Bay or the more majestic Marina Bay. Even the bathrooms have views, as the huge tubs are placed under octagonal picture windows so you can gaze as you bathe. Oh, the decadence! Guest rooms here are about 25% larger than most five-star rooms elsewhere, providing ample space for lovely seating areas, big two-poster beds, and full walk-in closets.

Dining: Aside from the elegant Greenhouse (the hotel's coffee shop), there's the Summer Pavilion, set in an atmospheric lotus garden and serving Cantonese delicacies, while the popular Snappers specializes in excellent regional seafood favorites.

Amenities: Services here—in-house movies, 24-hour room service, and voice mail—seem standard compared to other hotels in this price category, which tend to offer some nice luxury perks. On the other hand, a spa and fitness center with massage, sauna, steam, hot and cold plunge pools, and an outdoor tennis court will keep you active and destressed. The hotel pool is a gorgeous 25-meter Greco-Roman monster done in streaks of shimmering blue tile, with a Jacuzzi tucked beneath a cascading waterfall. Follow the covered pathway from the lobby right into the heart of the Marina area's huge shopping malls.

EXPENSIVE

Carlton Hotel Singapore. 76 Bras Basah Rd., Singapore 189558. ☎ **65/338-8333.** Fax 65/339-6866. www.carlton.com.sg. E-mail: roomreservations@carlton.com.sg. 477 units. A/C MINIBAR TV TEL. S$320 (US$191.60) double; S$600 (US$359.30) suite. AE, DC, JCB, MC, V. 5-min. walk to City Hall MRT.

The most appealing features of the Carlton are its location in the heart of the Historic District and the view from its front rooms—of the harbor, river, and financial district, plus an aerial view of the entire CHIJMES block, just across the street. Make sure you specify rooms with the views, as the back view (or "city view") is not nearly as spectacular. The lobby is a dimly lit space distinguished by garden plantings and lots of marble and oak, creating an atmosphere that's much more inviting than the austere and cold grandeur of a lot of its competitors. (*Note:* The coin fountain in the lobby collects money for the Kidney Dialysis Foundation—toss a couple of coins in.) The rooms have large sunny windows and a nice, casual ambience, but aren't much by way of counter and closet space. The small bathrooms have very good showers.

Dining: Carlton has fewer in-house restaurant choices than other hotels in this category. For Western food in a casual atmosphere, try Café Victoria; for Cantonese and dim sum, there's Wah Lock.

Amenities: In addition to standard hotel services, the Carlton offers in-house movies, 24-hour room service, and concierge with computer link to STB. Facilities

Historic District Accommodations

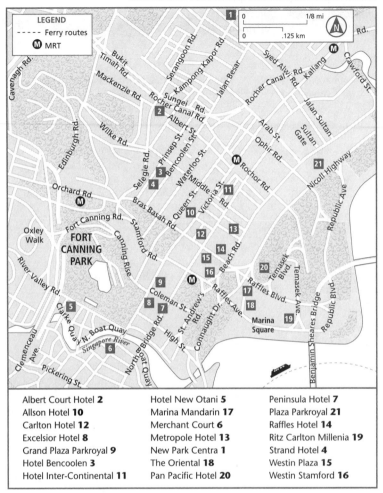

Albert Court Hotel **2**	Hotel New Otani **5**	Peninsula Hotel **7**
Allson Hotel **10**	Marina Mandarin **17**	Plaza Parkroyal **21**
Carlton Hotel **12**	Merchant Court **6**	Raffles Hotel **14**
Excelsior Hotel **8**	Metropole Hotel **13**	Ritz Carlton Millenia **19**
Grand Plaza Parkroyal **9**	New Park Centra **1**	Strand Hotel **4**
Hotel Bencoolen **3**	The Oriental **18**	Westin Plaza **15**
Hotel Inter-Continental **11**	Pan Pacific Hotel **20**	Westin Stamford **16**

include Jacuzzi, sauna, a tour desk, and a beauty salon. Unfortunately, for a hotel in this price range, the fitness center facilities, pool area, and business center are not as modern, well equipped, or attractive as the competition.

Grand Plaza Parkroyal. 10 Coleman St., Singapore 179809. ☎ **800/44-UTELL** in the U.S. and Canada, or 65/336-3456. Fax 65/339-9311. E-mail: gph01@pacific.net.sg. 338 units. A/C MINIBAR TV TEL. S$300–S$320 (US$179.65–US$191.60) double; S$500–S$1,200 (US$299.40–US$718.55) suite. AE, DC, JCB, MC, V. 5-min. walk to City Hall MRT.

The Grand Plaza was built on top of (and incorporating) 2 blocks of prewar shophouses, and you can see hints of shophouse detail throughout the lobby, which is otherwise like any other hotel's. The old alleyway that ran between the shophouse blocks has been transformed into a courtyard where dinner is served alfresco. The hotel is located at the corner of Coleman and Hill streets, just across from the Armenian Church, the Asian Civilisations Museum, the Singapore Arts Museum, and Fort Canning Park—and if that's not convenient enough, a shuttle will take you to Orchard Road. Guest rooms are of average size, have considerable closet space, and sport sharp

---

ⓘ Family-Friendly Hotels

Unfortunately, Singapore's hotels are geared so heavily to the business traveler that very few have good facilities for families. For every rule there's an exception, of course, and in Singapore that exception is the truly phenomenal **Shangri-La's Rasa Sentosa Resort** (see page 94). For the younger kids, there's a day-care center with activities, lunches, and nap time. A video arcade and table tennis games keep older kids occupied, and the kiddie pool has rock-formation slides that are a childhood dream come true. For teens, the Rasa Sentosa offers nature walks, rock climbing, beach volleyball, and windsurfing, and has in-line skates for rent. Basically, they offer all you could ever want to make your kids' vacation as good as yours, and even have a little quiet time to yourself.

The inexpensive **YMCA International House** (see page 93) is a good deal for traveling families. The rooms are big enough for extra beds, the pool has a full-time lifeguard on duty, and the McDonald's in the lobby means the kids won't go hungry if they turn up their noses at the local fare.

The **Novotel Apollo Singapore** (see page 79) is out of the way, but the rooms are big and each one has a sofa bed. Games by the pool keep the kids busy when you're too pooped to care, and a self-service launderette helps cut laundry costs.

Italian contemporary furniture in natural tones, with homey touches like snugly comforters on all the beds.

Dining/Diversions: St. Gregory's brasserie sets up a buffet of Western selections three times daily, but for something more formal, resident Chinese restaurant Hua Yuen comes highly recommended. Rolf's Knie bar and deli is a different twist on a lobby bar, with cocktails plus light snacks.

Amenities: All rooms feature in-house movie programming and voice mail, plus 24-hour room service and concierge with computer link to STB. From the outdoor pool you can see the steeple of the Armenian Church across the street—the same view you get from the modern fitness center. There's also a beauty salon and a small shopping arcade. The hotel's Saint Gregory Marine Spa is Singapore's largest and most exclusive. There are 20 private treatment rooms where you can enjoy hydrotherapy baths, jet showers, Jacuzzis, steam baths, facial and body treatments, and massage therapies.

✪ **Hotel Inter-Continental Singapore.** 80 Middle Rd., Singapore 188966 (near Bugis Junction). ☎ **800/327-0200** in the U.S. and Canada, 008/221-335 in Australia (Sydney 02/9232-1199), 800/442-215 in New Zealand, 0345/581-444 in the U.K. (London 181/847-2277), or 65/338-7600. Fax 65/338-7366. www.interconti.com. E-mail: singapore@ interconti.com. 406 units. A/C MINIBAR TV TEL. S$410 (US$245.51) double; S$580–S$3,800 (US$347.30–US$2,275.45) suite. AE, DC, JCB, MC, V. Bugis MRT.

The government let Inter-Continental build a hotel in this spot with one ironclad stipulation: The hotel chain had to retain the original shophouses on the block and incorporate them into the hotel design. No preservation, no hotel. Reinforcing the foundation, Hotel Inter-Continental built up from there, giving touches of old architectural style to the lobby, lounge, and other public areas on the bottom floors while imbuing it with the feel of a modern hotel. Features like beamed ceilings and wooden staircases are warmly accentuated with Chinese and European antique reproductions, Oriental carpets, and local artworks. The second and third floors have "Shophouse Rooms" styled with such Peranakan trappings as carved hardwood furnishings and floral linens, and with homey touches like potted plants and carpets over wooden floors. These rooms are very unique, presenting a surprising element of local flair that you don't often find in large chain hotels. Guest rooms on higher levels are large, with formal European styling and large luxurious bathrooms.

Dining/Diversions: The Inter-Continental's restaurants spill out into neighboring Parco Bugis Junction shopping mall, making the choices here extensive: The Olive Tree for Mediterranean food, Pimai Thai for very good Thai cuisine, Essence for spa cuisine, Man Fu Yuan for superb Chinese cuisine, a poolside cafe and a delicatessen, plus Sketches, a pasta bar (which I've reviewed in chapter 4). Add on the huge Victoria Bar and lobby lounge, and you never have to leave the building.

Amenities: Although the pool area has a terrible view, the space is beautifully landscaped, with a wooden deck and comfortable lounge chairs. Other facilities include a 24-hour fitness center with sauna, outdoor Jacuzzi, business center, self-service launderette and tennis court. The hotel also provides in-house movies, in-room data port with fax machine, butler service, 24-hour room service, voice mail, and concierge with computer link to STB.

✪ **Marina Mandarin Singapore.** 6 Raffles Blvd., Marina Square, Singapore 039594. ☎ **65/338-3388.** Fax 65/339-4977. www.marina-mandarin.com.sg. E-mail: mmsrevn@pacific.net.sg. 575 units. S$340–S$420 (US$203.60–US$251.50) double; S$460 (US$275.45) executive club; S$600–S$3,000 (US$359.30–US$1,796.40) suite. AE, DC, JCB, MC, V. 10-min. walk to City Hall MRT.

There are a few hotels in the Marina Bay area built around the atrium concept, and of them, this one is the loveliest. The atrium lobby opens up to ceiling skylights 21 stories above, guest corridor balconies fringed with vines line the sides, and in the center hangs a glistening metal mobile sculpture in red and gold. One of the most surprising details is the melodic chirping of caged songbirds, which fills the open space every morning. In the evening, live classical music from the lobby bar drifts upward.

The guest rooms are equally impressive: large and cool, with two desk spaces and balconies standard for each room. Try to get the Marina view for that famous Shenton Way skyline towering above the bay. All bathrooms have double sinks, a separate shower and tub, and a bidet.

Dining: At Marina Mandarin you can choose from Italian at their Restorante Bologna, Cantonese at Peach Blossom, or Continental cuisine at their coffee shop.

Amenities: A 24-hour business center, in-room data ports with fax machine, butler service, 24-hour room service, and voice mail make this place convenient for business. You can work out the kinks at their large outdoor pool; in the fitness center, with aerobics and massage, Jacuzzi, sauna, and steam room; or on the squash court or two outdoor tennis courts. In-house movies, beauty salon, and a number of boutiques round out the package.

The Oriental, Singapore. 5 Raffles Ave., Marina Square, Singapore 039797. ☎ **800/526-6566** in the U.S. and Canada, or 65/338-0066. Fax 65/339-9537. 523 units. A/C MINI-BAR TV TEL. S$370 (US$221.55) double; S$460 (US$275.45) suite. AE, DC, JCB, MC, V. 10-min. walk to City Hall MRT. INTERNATIONAL.

Another atrium-concept hotel, the Oriental has just recently knocked down some of the walls in its atrium lobby to expand it outward. The new space is occupied by Café des Artistes, a big bright lobby restaurant dedicated to the local arts scene. The theme plays out in two- and three-dimensional creations throughout, plus scheduled performance events at the neighboring Gallery. Guest rooms at The Oriental are large and modern, and for an additional S$30 you can have the harbor view, which on the higher floors is worth the money.

Dining: The feather in The Oriental's cap, Café des Artistes celebrates local fine arts, while the relaxed Pronto by the Poolside serves light Italian meals al fresco. Cherry Garden has won numerous awards for its fine Hunan fare.

Amenities: In-house movies, in-room data port with fax machine, 24-hour room service, voice mail, and a concierge computer linked to STB provide a good range of services for both business and leisure travelers. Tennis is available through courts shared with the Marina Mandarin, and other facilities include a Jacuzzi, sauna, a steam room, a beauty salon, and a number of boutiques. The hotel pool has a nice, relaxed garden atmosphere. Next to the pool, the brand-new fitness center includes an outdoor weight center with a view of the city.

The Pan Pacific Hotel Singapore. 7 Raffles Blvd., Marina Square, Singapore 039595 (near Suntec City). ☎ **800/327-8585** in the U.S. and Canada, 800/525-900 in Australia, 800/447-555 in New Zealand, 800/96-94-96 in the U.K., or 65/336-8111. Fax 65/339-1861. www.panpac.com. E-mail: reservations@panpacifichotel.com.sg. 800 units. A/C MINIBAR TV TEL. S$320–S$340 (US$191.60–US$203.60) double; S$450–S$480 (US$269.45–US$287.45) suite. AE, DC, JCB, MC, V. 10-min. walk to City Hall MRT.

Because of its location and design, the Pan Pacific Hotel competes heavily with the Marina Mandarin and the Oriental, all grabbing up their share of business travelers and Suntec City Convention Center guests. In doing so, Pan Pacific has included a new service that is quite noteworthy: high-speed fiber-optic Internet access in each room (for your own laptop), and optional mobile phones upon check-in for forwarding calls from the hotel's main number. Leisure travelers probably won't find tremendous use for these services; however, Pan Pacific is still a fine choice for comfortable and convenient accommodations. The atrium lobby has been newly renovated from its previous dark and looming presence to a brighter, more airy feel. Guest rooms are good-size and comfy, with luxurious marble bathrooms.

Dining: Walk through a lovely rock garden to Keyaki Japanese restaurant, with an atmosphere as fine as its food, or try Korean barbecue and steamboat buffet at Summer House. Tuscany, the hotel's addition to Singaporean Italian options, isn't as exciting as the other choices.

Amenities: The hotel facilities are great: The large pool sports an underwater sound system; the fitness center is huge and state-of-the-art, with aerobics classes, massage, and a very large indoor Jacuzzi; and there are boutiques, two outdoor tennis courts, a beauty salon, and business center. In-house movies, in-room data ports with fax and Internet access, butler service, 24-hour room service, voice mail, and a tour desk add convenience.

MODERATE

Allison Hotel Singapore. 101 Victoria St., Singapore 188018. ☎ **65/336-0811.** Fax 65/339-7019. www.allsonhotels.com. E-mail: allson.sales@pacific.net.sg. 450 units. A/C MINIBAR TV TEL. S$250 (US$149.70) double; S$450 (US$269.45) suite. AE, DC, JCB, MC, V. 5-min. walk from Bugis Junction MRT.

The Allison Hotel has a great location right on Victoria Street: You walk one way and you're having fun at Bugis Junction; walk the other, you're in the heart of the city center. Sporting a large, open lobby and spacious public areas, the Allison reserved most of the nicest details for the guest floors. You enter into the guest rooms through beautiful carved rosewood doors, and even the less expensive rooms have Ming-style beds, tables, cabinets, and armchairs, plus colorful floral fabrics that are a welcome change from the usual any-city/anywhere room decor you generally see. The bathrooms are not as elaborate as some, and are small, but a welcome overhaul of the plumbing has corrected a persnickety lack of hot water that plagued the hotel for years. Hotel facilities include a small outdoor pool; a fitness center with massage, Jacuzzi, sauna, and steam; a beauty salon; and a number of boutiques. The warm and inviting Liu Hsiang Lou Szechuan restaurant is located off the main lobby on the second floor (see chapter 4 for a review).

Excelsior Hotel. 5 Coleman St., Singapore 179805. ☎ **65/338-7733.** Fax 65/339-3847. 271 units. A/C MINIBAR TV TEL. S$240–S$270 (US$143.70–US$161.70) double; S$440–S$1,400 (US$263.45–US$838.30) suite. AE, DC, JCB, MC, V. 5-min. walk to City Hall MRT.

The Excelsior is not the most stylish place, but it—and its sister hotel the Peninsula—always runs at high occupancy rates due to low room rates and good arrangements with travel agents and tour group organizers. The majority of guests are tour groups and independent leisure travelers, many from Australia. Rooms, both deluxe and superior, are exactly the same aside from altitude: The former are on higher floors and have a few more amenities (such as slightly nicer toiletries). Headboards on the beds are a very bizarre peacock design, and sofa seating areas are tucked into small window bays. Check out the very unusual and oh-so-tacky two-story bird sculpture in the fifth-floor stairwell. Gracious.

There's no business center, but secretarial services are available. Hotel facilities include a small outdoor pool and use of the fitness center at the Peninsula Hotel, next door. One plus: The hotel is very accommodating about flight departure schedules and will let you stay and even use the shower while waiting for an evening flight.

Hotel New Otani Singapore. 177A River Valley Rd., Singapore 179031. ☎ **800/ 421-8795** in the U.S. and Canada, 800/273-2294 in California, or 65/338-3333. Fax 65/339-2854. www.newotani.co.jp. E-mail: newotani@singnet.com.sg. 408 units. A/C MINI-BAR TV TEL. S$300–S$320 (US$179.65–US$191.60) double; S$600–S$700 (US$359.30–US$419.15) suite. AE, DC, JCB, MC, V. Far from MRT stations.

The Hotel New Otani sits along the Singapore River just next to Clarke Quay (a popular spot for nightlife, dining, and shopping) and a stroll away from the Historic District. At night, you have access to nearby Boat Quay bars and restaurants to one side and to the unique clubs of Mohamed Sultan Road on the other. The hotel was renovated in 1993, and recent additions (to all rooms) include multimedia PCs with Microsoft Office and tourist information. Internet access and computer games are also available for an extra charge. All rooms have small balconies with good views of the river, the financial district, Fort Canning Park, and Chinatown, and the standard rooms have large luxurious bathrooms like those you typically see in more deluxe accommodations. Facilities include a large outdoor pool and a fitness center with aerobics, a Jacuzzi, sauna, facials, and massage (you can even get a massage poolside). The hotel runs daily shuttle service to Orchard Road, Shenton Way, and Marina Square.

Peninsula Hotel. 3 Coleman St., Singapore 179804. ☎ **800/223-0888** in the U.S. and Canada, 0800/252840 in the U.K., or 65/337-2200. Fax 65/336-3020. 307 units. A/C MINIBAR TV TEL. S$240–S$260 (US$143.70–US$155.70) double; S$360–S$440 (US$215.55–US$263.45) suite. AE, DC, JCB, MC, V. 5-min. walk to City Hall MRT.

Not extraordinary, but not a bad place at all, the Peninsula caters mostly to tourist markets, and busloads of people can sometimes be found milling about the lobby. Security is tight, with card-key access to guest floors. Rooms are large, but furnishings are not overly inviting. Some rooms have a harbor view that's worth asking for. Be warned if you are tall: Bathroom shower nozzles are positioned very low. Hotel facilities include a small outdoor pool and a small fitness center. The Peninsula is the sister hotel to the Excelsior (see above), so it shares facilities in neighboring buildings filling 1 whole city block in a central location.

Plaza Parkroyal. 7500A Beach Rd., Singapore 199591. ☎ **65/298-0011.** Fax 65/296-3600. 350 units. A/C MINIBAR TV TEL. S$270 (US$161.70) double; S$550 (US$329.35) suite. AE, DC, JCB, MC, V. 10-min. walk to Bugis MRT.

Situated just across from the Arab Street and Kampong Glam areas, you're a little off the beaten track at the Plaza Hotel—you'll need to take buses or taxis just about everywhere—but the trade-off is that if you stick around you can take advantage of the gorgeous and luxurious recreation and relaxation facilities, which include a half-size Olympic pool with a diving board (a rarity in Singapore), a dreamy sundeck decorated in a lazy-days Balinese-style tropical motif, and a Bali-themed poolside cafe, cooled by ceiling fans. Two gyms to the side have plenty of space and new equipment, but the most exquisite facility of all is the spa. Designed with the help of Susan-Jane Beers, expert on Indonesian herbs, the spa has body scrubs, healing massages, and beauty treatments that incorporate wet and dry applications of Indonesian herbs, some of which are grown fresh on the hotel's rooftop. Guest rooms are fine and exactly what you'd want for the price. Other hotel facilities include outdoor and indoor Jacuzzis, sauna, and steam room.

✪ **The Westin Stamford & Westin Plaza.** 2 Stamford Rd., Singapore 178882. ☎ **800/WESTIN-1** in the U.S. and Canada, or 65/338-8585. Fax 65/338-2862. www.westinsingapore.com. E-mail: westin1@singnet.com.sg. 2,046 units. A/C MINIBAR TV TEL. Westin Stamford: S$340–S$360 (US$203.60–US$215.55) double; S$380 (US$227.55) executive club; S$450–S$1,700 (US$269.45–US$1,017.95) suite. Westin Plaza: S$360–S$380 (US$215.55–US$227.55) double; S$400 (US$239.50) executive club. AE, DC, JCB, MC, V. City Centre MRT.

The combined Westin Stamford and Westin Plaza hotels, an impressive complex comprising 2,046 combined guest rooms, the Raffles City Convention Centre, plus 12 food and beverage outlets, sits directly atop the Raffles City Shopping Complex and City Hall MRT station just in the center of town. Both hotels opened in 1986, with special acclaim for The Westin Stamford as the Guinness Book of World Records' tallest hotel in the world. Its 70 floors measure in at 226.13 meters (735 ft.) and offer some pretty spectacular views. Funny thing: The rooms in The Westin Stamford are less expensive than those in The Westin Plaza. Go for the views, and save money!

Guest rooms are slightly larger than average and feature balconies; the rooms' light pastel decor gives a feeling of freshness. If you plan to conduct business in Singapore, The Westin offers guest offices for S$390 (US$234). Ask about their weekend promotional rates.

Facilities include a large outdoor pool; 24-hour fitness center with aerobics, Jacuzzi, sauna, and steam room; six outdoor tennis courts; two squash courts; and table tennis. The excellent Compass Rose restaurant, perched right at the top of the hotel, sports stunning views in addition to some mighty scrumptious meals. (See chapter 4 for a full review.)

INEXPENSIVE
✪ **Albert Court Hotel.** 180 Albert St., Singapore 189971. ☎ **65/339-3939.** Fax 65/339-3252. www.fareast.com.sg/hotels. E-mail: sales.mktg@albertcourt.com.sg. 136 units. A/C MINIBAR TV TEL. S$120 (US$71.85) double. AE, DC, JCB, MC, V. 5-min. walk to Bugis MRT.

The Albert Court was first conceived as part of the Urban Renewal Authority's master plan to revitalize this block, which involved the restoration of two rows of prewar shophouses. The eight-story boutique hotel that emerged has all the Western comforts but has retained the charm of its shophouse roots. Decorators placed local Peranakan touches everywhere from the carved teak panels in traditional floral design to the antique china cups used for tea service in the rooms. (Guaranteed: The sight of these cups brings misty-eyed nostalgia to the hearts of Singaporeans.) Guest room details like the teak molding, floral batik bedspreads, bathroom tiles in bright Peranakan colors, and old-time brass electrical switches give this place true local charm and distinction. Room service is available from 7am to 11pm.

Hotel Bencoolen. 47 Bencoolen St., Singapore 189626. ☎ **65/336-0822.** Fax 65/336-2250. 89 units. A/C TV TEL. S$98 (US$58.70) double. MC, V. 10-min. walk to City Hall MRT.

Bencoolen is the signature backpacker hotel on the block, and it is definitely budget minded through and through: To get into the place you have to enter through the ground-level parking lot; the rooms are on the small side, and filled with old and oddly matched furnishings; and the double beds are two twins pushed together. Even the walls are strange combinations of painted concrete, tiles, and padded paneling. The showers here are a nightmare, with handheld shower nozzles and no clips on the walls on which to hang them. Executive rooms are slightly nicer—the same size, but with bigger closets, a small desk area, and a TV set, hair dryer, and fridge in each. For only US$5 more a night, I'd say go for it. The hotel has a rooftop restaurant, and parking is available.

Metropole Hotel. 41 Seah St., Singapore 188396. ☎ **65/336-3611.** Fax 65/339-3610. 54 units. A/C TV TEL. S$142–S$161 (US$85.05–US$96.40) standard to studio deluxe. Rates include breakfast. AE, DC, JCB, MC, V. 5-min. walk to City Hall MRT.

Located at the corner of Beach Road and Seah Street, the Metropole Hotel is right next to the Raffles Hotel, which means you'll either enjoy the proximity or feel like a passenger in steerage staring up at first class. The lobby is nothing to speak of, and the rooms are sparsely furnished and on the musty side, with desks, a stock-it-yourself fridge, radios, small windows, small closets, and no views. Baby-sitting and fax services are available. Sure, the rates include breakfast, but you could do better at the Strand (see below) for less money. A coffeehouse and the Imperial Herbal restaurant (reviewed in chapter 4 and a good place for the cure to what ails you) are on the premises.

New Park Centra. 181 Kitchener Rd., Singapore 208533. ☎ **65/291-5533.** Fax 65/297-2827. 531 units. A/C MINIBAR TV TEL. S$140 (US$83.85) double; S$200 (US$119.75) suite. AE, DC, JCB, MC, V. 15-min. walk to Lavender MRT.

Located on the edge of the Historic District (technically in Little India), this hotel is close to some of the best mosques and temples in Singapore, but far from just about everything else (including the MRT station, which is a confusing 15-minute walk, cutting through apartment blocks). Nevertheless, the staff is courteous and the guest rooms have been recently renovated with new, tasteful furnishings. The high-ceilinged guest rooms are very comfortable, have excellent storage space for luggage and clothing, and offer unique views across the rooftops of the busy shophouse neighborhood surrounding the hotel. Though the tiled bathrooms are spotless, they could use refurbishing, as the tiles appear shabby in comparison to the marble stylings of newer hotel bathrooms. The fitness center is practical, with few luxuries, but at least they have piped-in music for workout motivation. The pool is equally utilitarian, and there are plastic chairs on the sparse sundeck. There's a self-service launderette and a shopping arcade on the premises.

✪ **Strand Hotel.** 25 Bencoolen St., Singapore 189619. ☎ **65/338-1866.** Fax 65/338-1330. 130 units. A/C TV TEL. S$65 (US$38.90) double; S$80 (US$47.90) triple; S$100 (US$59.90) 4-person sharing. AE, DC, MC, V. 10-min. walk to City Hall MRT.

The Strand is by far the best of the backpacker places in Singapore. The lobby is far nicer than you'd expect, and your S$65 a night gets you a clean and neat room. Although there are some hints that you really are staying in a budget hotel—older decor and uncoordinated furniture sets, for instance—the place provides some little niceties, like hotel stationery. The no-frills bathrooms are clean and adequate. There are no coffee- and tea-making facilities, but there is 24-hour room service and a cafe on the premises. Free parking is available.

3 Chinatown

EXPENSIVE

✪ **Duxton Hotel.** 83 Duxton Rd., Singapore 089540. ☎ **800/552-6844** in the U.S. and Canada, 800/251-664 in Australia, 800/446-110 in New Zealand, or 65/227-7678. Fax 65/227-1232. http://duxtonhotels.com.sg. E-mail: duxton@singnet.com.sg. 50 units. A/C MINIBAR TV TEL. S$180 (US$107.80) double; S$240 (US$143.70) suite. Rates include full English breakfast. AE, DC, JCB, MC, V. 5-min. walk to Tanjong Pagar MRT.

The Duxton was one of the first accommodations in Singapore to experiment with the boutique hotel concept, transforming its shophouse structure into a small hotel and doing it with an elegance that's earned great international acclaim. From the outside, the place has old-world charm equal to any lamplit European cobblestone street, but step inside and there are very few details to remind you that you are in a quaint old shophouse—or in the historic Chinese district, for that matter. It's a sophisticated and romantic little place, done entirely in turn-of-the-century styling that includes reproduction Chippendale furniture, hand-painted wall papers, and pen-and-ink Audubon-style drawings. Each room is different (to fit the structure of the building), but even with the limited spaces they have to work with, they've succeeded in creating rooms that feel airy and open. Garden suites feature a lovely little courtyard.

Dining: Duxton houses the finest French restaurant in town, L'Aigle d'Or, which is terrifically authentic, receiving the highest reviews year after year from local and international dining critics (see review in chapter 4).

Amenities: Regulations do not allow for pools and space does not allow for fitness centers (they will arrange access to a nearby fitness center for you), but you do get complimentary chocolates, fruit basket, mineral water, and shoe-shine services, and a free shuttle to Shenton Way and Orchard Road. Secretarial services are also available.

Merchant Court Hotel. 20 Merchant Rd., Singapore 058281. ☎ **800/637-7200** in the U.S. and Canada, 800/655-147 in Australia, 800/442-519 in New Zealand, 800/252-840 in the U.K., or 65/337-2288. Fax 65/334-0606. www.raffles.com/ril. 476 units. A/C MINIBAR TV TEL. S$305–S$335 (US$182.65–US$200.60) double; S$810–S$1,500 (US$485.05–US$898.20) suite. AE, DC, JCB, MC, V. 10- min. walk to Raffles Place MRT.

Merchant Court's convenient location and facilities make it very popular with leisure travelers. Situated on the Singapore River, the hotel has easy access not only to Chinatown and the Historic District, but also to Clarke Quay and Boat Quay, with their multitude of dining and nightlife options. While this new hotel's guest rooms aren't the biggest in the city, I never felt claustrophobic due to the large windows, fresh decor, and cooling atmosphere. Try to get a room with a view of the river or landscaped pool area.

Dining: The hotel has only one cafe/coffee shop facility—smart planning, as most guests prefer to hop out to one of the great restaurants along the river close by.

Amenities: Convenience is provided by a self-service launderette, drink and snack vending machines on each floor, and unstocked minibar fridge, so you can buy your own provisions. The hotel touts itself as a city hotel with a resort feel, with landscaped

Chinatown Accommodations

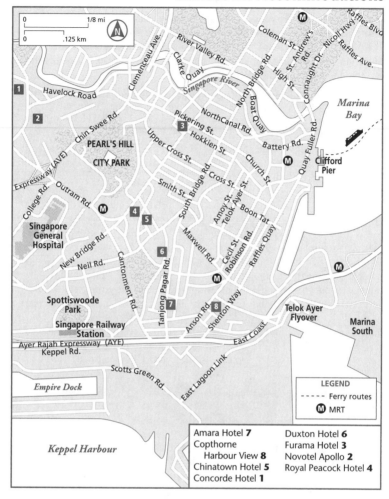

LEGEND
- - - - - Ferry routes
Ⓜ MRT

Amara Hotel **7**	Duxton Hotel **6**
Copthorne	Furama Hotel **3**
Harbour View **8**	Novotel Apollo **2**
Chinatown Hotel **5**	Royal Peacock Hotel **4**
Concorde Hotel **1**	

pool area (with a view of the river). Other facilities include in-house movies, a health spa, and a fitness center with sauna, steam, massage, and Jacuzzi.

MODERATE

Amara Singapore. 165 Tanjong Pagar Rd., Singapore 088539. ☎ **65/224-4488.** Fax 65/224-3910. E-mail: reserv@amara.com.sg. 338 units. A/C MINIBAR TV TEL. S$250 (US$150) double; S$270–S$330 (US$161.70–US$197.60) executive club; S$350–S$650 (US$209.60–US$389.20) suite. AE, DC, JCB, MC, V. 5-min. walk to Tanjong Pagar MRT.

Amara, located in the Shenton Way financial district, attracts primarily business travelers, so if your vacation includes a little business too, this hotel puts you closer to the action. If you're simply in town for a vacation, though, Amara probably isn't your best choice. The top eight floors of this hotel are reserved for the corporate set—not only do they have better views, but modern decor and services attractive to business visitors as well. Rooms on the Leisure Floors have an unappealing combination of green and white painted furniture, and have very little to offer in terms of views. The hotel does have other convenience facilities like a self-service launderette and ice machines and shoe polishers on each floor, plus the usual: a large outdoor pool, a fitness center, Jacuzzi, sauna, two outdoor tennis courts, a jogging track, and a shopping arcade. At press time the hotel had plans for a major renovation, but couldn't specify dates, so call ahead to find out more information.

Concorde Hotel Singapore. 317 Outram Rd., Singapore 169075. ☎ **65/733-0188.** Fax 65/733-0989. www.concorde.net. E-mail: singapore@concorde.net. 515 units. A/C MINIBAR TV TEL. S$230–S$320 (US$137.70–US$191.60) double; S$400–S$1,500 (US$239.50–US$898.20) suite. AE, DC, JCB, MC, V. 15-min. walk to Outram MRT.

This place originally opened as the Glass Hotel, a name Concorde has found difficult to shake, since its curving facades are covered to the seams with smoky windows. That famous facade recently underwent a face-lift, along with the hotel's large circular atrium and many guest rooms. The newly refurbished rooms are airy and spacious, with new furniture in simple contemporary style. The bathrooms, while not as opulent as some, are still as comfortable as home. Hotel facilities include a fitness center, one outdoor tennis court, a beauty salon, and a number of shops. There are three pools: one small private pool for the Presidential Suite; the sixth-floor guest pool (also spruced up with recent renovations); and the rooftop pool, for executive club floor guests. None of the pools are particularly luxurious, and there are no Jacuzzis or sauna, but the view from the rooftop pool has been used by many filmmakers over the years. Although the Concorde only has two restaurants to choose from, Xin Cuisine Chinese Restaurant is one of the city's top restaurants for healthy Chinese fare—very popular with lunchtime business folks who come for dian xin (dim sum). The Concorde's location is not exactly central, but if the government builds another bridge across the Singapore River—as it may—access to Orchard Road, Clarke Quay, and the Historic District will be much easier.

Copthorne Harbour View Singapore. 81 Anson Rd., Singapore 079908. ☎ **65/224-1133.** Fax 65/222-0749. www.harbourview.com.sg. 416 units. A/C TV TEL. S$300 (US$179.65) double; S$600 (US$359.30) suite. AE, DC, JCB, MC, V. 5-min. walk to Tanjong Pagar MRT.

Because of its proximity to Shenton Way, Harbour View has a very high proportion of business guests, which explains the lobby TV monitors that display Changi International Airport arrival and departure schedules and international weather forecasts. But poor Harbour View has changed management firms a few times in the past 3 years, which explains why the facility was in a bit of a shambles when I wrote the first edition of this book. Luckily, Copthorne has come along since then, ushering in a new scheme for total refurbishment including all guest rooms, restaurants, function rooms, lobby, and public areas. Renovations are scheduled for completion in fall 2000, so booking here should promise some sparkling new facilities.

Furama Hotel Singapore. 60 Eu Tong Sen St., Singapore 059804. ☎ **65/533-3888.** Fax 65/534-1489. E-mail: fhsg@furama-hotels.com. 355 units. A/C MINIBAR TV TEL. S$220 (US$131.75) double; S$350 (US$209.60) suite. AE, DC, JCB, MC, V. 10-min. walk to Outram MRT.

Located smack-dab between the heart of Chinatown and the Boat Quay and Clarke Quay areas, the Furama is a good moderately priced choice if you want to be near shopping and nightlife. The first high-rise hotel built in Chinatown, it has a funky, arching multilevel rooftop that always attracts attention. Guest rooms are good-size and as cozy as home, and the bathrooms are large, leaving you plenty of space to spread out. One small drawback is the lack of any foyer or entranceway between the corridors and the rooms themselves—the doors just open right in. Hotel facilities include a small outdoor pool, a small fitness center with Jacuzzi, and a shopping arcade.

Novotel Apollo Singapore. 405 Havelock Rd., Singapore 169633. ☎ **65/733-2081.** Fax 65/733-1588. E-mail: aposin@mbox2.singnet.com.sg. 368 units. A/C MINIBAR TV TEL. S$240–S$280 (US$143.70–US$167.65) double; S$400 (US$239.50) suite. AE, DC, JCB, MC, V. 15-min. walk to Outram MRT.

Novotel has just recently taken over the management of this property, an older hotel that has just undergone construction of a new wing. Called the Tropical Wing, it caters primarily to corporate travelers, featuring a fully modern facility with large rooms and all new furnishings. The construction project also included enlargement of the lobby with a comfortable lobby lounge, a new outdoor pool and Jacuzzi, outdoor tennis courts, and a huge ballroom. The old wing, called the Tower Block, has slightly less expensive rooms, and at the time of writing was just beginning a major refurbishment scheduled for completion in December 2000. Make sure you request the Tropical Wing during this time to avoid construction noise and wallpaper glue fumes. If you're staying here, you may find yourself dependent on taxi transportation, as the MRT is a bit far, but the location is still within short taxi hops around the city.

INEXPENSIVE

✪ **Chinatown Hotel.** 12–16 Teck Lim Rd., Singapore 088388. ☎ **65/225-5166.** Fax 65/225-3912. www.chinatownhotel.com. E-mail: enquiries@chinatownhotel.com. 42 units. A/C TV TEL. S$80–S$90 (US$47.90–US$53.90) double. AE, DC, MC, V. 5-min. walk to Outram MRT.

Chinatown Hotel definitely has its pros and cons, but for clean rooms, friendly service, and a good rate, it's one of my favorites. *Be prepared:* Because this is a boutique hotel with limited space, the rooms, though modern and well maintained, are tiny, and the bathrooms *are* the shower—just a showerhead coming out of the wall as you stand in front of the sink. Some rooms have no windows, so specify when you make reservations if you're fond of natural light. Guest room TVs have one movie channel, and some rooms have been recently supplied with coffee- and tea-making facilities, hair dryers (unique for this price category), and unstocked refrigerators. Or you can enjoy free coffee, tea, and toast in the lobby. Larger hotels will charge higher rates so you can enjoy the luxury of a pool, fitness center, and multiple food and beverage outlets; but if you're in town to get out and see Singapore, it's nice to know you won't pay for things you'll never use. Besides, the folks at the front counter will always remember your name and are very professional without being impersonal.

The Royal Peacock. 55 Keong Saik Rd., Singapore 089158. ☎ **65/223-3522.** Fax 65/221-1770. 79 units. A/C MINIBAR TV TEL. S$150 (US$89.80) double with no window, S$185 (US$110.80) double with window; S$240 (US$143.70) junior suite. AE, DC, MC, V. 5-min. walk to Outram MRT.

In the center of Chinatown's historic red-light district is one of Singapore' smallest boutique hotels, the Royal Peacock. Occupying 10 restored prewar shophouses, the place is tiny but colorful inside and out. As with other hotels of this type, the existing shophouse structure and strict restoration regulations make very small rooms de rigueur, but you've got to wonder about the hotel's decision to decorate them in the darkest colors they could find: Each room has one wall painted deep red, and purple carpet is used throughout. It's visually exciting, sure, but it makes you (or me, at least) feel claustrophobic. Adding to the problem is the fact that the less expensive rooms have no windows, and, where there are windows, the rooms just small squares. Yikes.

All told, though, and even taking these criticisms into account, the rooms have flair. All have pretty wooden sleigh beds, and the bathrooms—which, due to restoration regulations, don't have tubs—are separated from the rooms with louvered shutters and are done in terra-cotta tiles. Rumor has it they're rethinking the entire design scheme. Room service is available for lunch and dinner till 10:30pm, and secretarial services are available as well.

4 Orchard Road Area

VERY EXPENSIVE

✪ Four Seasons Hotel Singapore. 190 Orchard Blvd., Singapore 248646. ☎ **800/ 332-3442** in the U.S., 800/268-6282 in Canada, or 65/734-1110. Fax 65/733-0682. www.fourseasons.com. E-mail: fssrez@magix.com.sg. 254 units. A/C MINIBAR TV TEL. S$475–S$500 (US$284.45–US$299.40) double; S$530 (US$317.35) executive club; S$620–S$4,500 (US$371.25–US$2,694.60) suite. AE, DC, JCB, MC, V. 5-min. walk to Orchard MRT.

A lot of upmarket hotels will try to convince you that staying with them is like visiting a wealthy friend. Four Seasons actually delivers. The guest rooms are very spacious and inviting, and even the standard rooms have creature comforts you'd expect from a suite, such as complimentary fruit, terry bathrobes and slippers, CD and video disc players, and an extensive complimentary video disc and CD library that the concierge is just waiting to deliver selections from to your room. Each room has two-line speaker-phones with voice mail and an additional data port. The Italian marble bathrooms have double vanities, deep tubs, bidets, and surround speakers from the TV and stereo. Did I mention remote-control drapes? Everything here is comfort and elegance done to perfection (in fact, the beds here are *so* comfortable that they've sold almost 100 in the gift shop—no kidding!). In the waiting area off the lobby you can sink into soft sofas and appreciate the antiques and artwork selected from the owner's private collection. Consider a standard room here before a suite in a less expensive hotel. You won't regret it.

Dining/Diversions: Jiang-Nan Chun, with its art nouveau decor and gourmet Cantonese cuisine, consistently presents a fabulous dining experience. Seasons' American cuisine can also cook up delicious dishes that are low in fat, cholesterol, sodium, and evil calories, while traditional English tea is served at the cozy Terrace Lounge.

Amenities: I don't even know where to begin! The fitness center has a state-of-the-art gymnasium with TV monitors, videos, tape players and CD and video disk players, a virtual reality bike, aerobics, sauna, steam rooms, massage, facials, body wraps and aromatherapy treatments, and a staff of fitness professionals. Want more? How about a flotation tank and a Mind Gear Syncro-Energiser (a brain relaxer that uses pulsing lights), a billiards room, and an OptiGolf Indoor Pro-Golf System. Two indoor, air-conditioned tennis courts and two outdoor courts are staffed with a resident professional tennis coach to provide instruction or play a game. There are two pools: a 20-meter lap pool and a rooftop sundeck pool, both with adjacent Jacuzzis.

✪ Goodwood Park Hotel. 22 Scotts Rd., Singapore 228221. ☎ **800/772-3890** in the U.S., 800/665-5919 in Canada, 800/89-95-20 in the U.K., or 65/737-7411. Fax 65/732-8558. 235 units. A/C MINIBAR TV TEL. S$425–S$465 (US$254.50–US$278.45) double; S$615–S$650 (US$368.25–US$389.20) poolside suite; S$888–S$3,000 (US$531.75–US$1,796.40) suite. AE, DC, JCB, MC, V. 5-min. walk to Orchard MRT.

The Goodwood Park Hotel, a national landmark built in 1900, resembles a castle along the Rhine—having served originally as the Teutonia Club, a social club for the

Orchard Road Area Accommodations

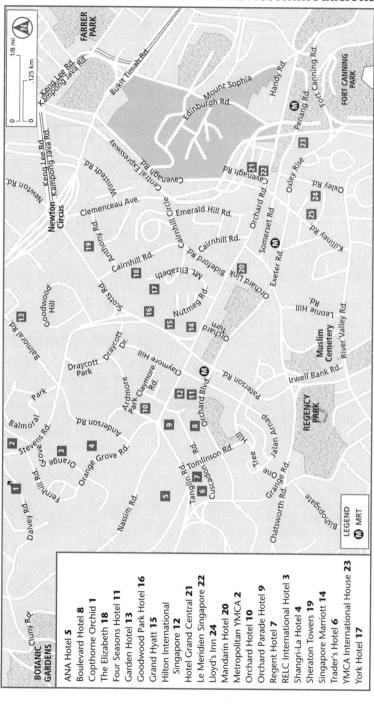

BOTANIC GARDENS

FARRER PARK

FORT CANNING PARK

MUSLIM CEMETERY

REGENCY PARK

LEGEND
M MRT

ANA Hotel 5
Boulevard Hotel 8
Copthorne Orchid 1
The Elizabeth 18
Four Seasons Hotel 11
Garden Hotel 13
Goodwood Park Hotel 16
Grand Hyatt 15
Hilton International Singapore 12
Hotel Grand Central 21
Le Meridien Singapore 22
Lloyd's Inn 24
Mandarin Hotel 20
Metropolitan YMCA 2
Orchard Hotel 10
Orchard Parade Hotel 9
Regent Hotel 7
RELC International Hotel 3
Shangri-La Hotel 4
Sheraton Towers 19
Singapore Marriott 14
Trader's Hotel 6
YMCA International House 23
York Hotel 17

81

German community. During World War II, high-ranking Japanese military used it as a residence, and three years later it served as a British war crimes court before being converted into a hotel. Since then the hotel has expanded from 60 rooms to 235, and has hosted a long list of international celebrities and dignitaries.

For the money, there are more luxurious facilities, but while most hotels have bigger and better business and fitness centers (Goodwood has *the* smallest fitness center), only the Raffles Hotel can rival Goodwood Park's historic significance. The poolside suites off the Mayfair Pool are fabulous in slate tiles and polished wood, offering direct access to the small Mayfair Pool with its lush Balinese-style landscaping. There are also suites off the main pool, which is much larger but offers little privacy from the lobby and surrounding restaurants. The original building has large and airy guest rooms, but beware of the showers, which have handheld showerheads that clip to the wall, making it difficult to aim and impossible to keep the water from splashing out all over the bathroom floor. The extremely attentive staff always serves with a smile.

Dining: Goodwood hosts some fine dining, including excellent Italian cuisine at Bice Ristorante Italiano, mouthwatering Chinese food at Chang Jiang, the finest Continental fare at Gordon Grill, and a full range of top-quality Japanese cuisine at Shima (all reviewed in the next chapter).

Amenities: Facilities and services include in-house movies, in-room data port with fax machine, butler service, and voice mail. Of the two outdoor pools, the Mayfair pool is by far more exotic. There's a beauty salon, gift shop, and tour desk.

✪ **Grand Hyatt Singapore.** 10–12 Scotts Rd., Singapore 228211. ☎ **800/228-9000** in the U.S., or 65/738-1234. Fax 65/732-1696. www.hyatt.com. 693 units. S$340–S$450 (US$203.60–US$269.45) double; S$490–S$3,800 (US$293.40–US$2,275.45) suite. AE, DC, JCB, MC, V. Near Orchard MRT.

Rumor has it that, despite its fantastic location, this hotel was doing pretty poorly until they had a feng shui master come in and evaluate it for redecorating. According to the Chinese monk, because the lobby entrance was a wall of flat glass doors that ran parallel to the long reception desk in front, all the hotel's money was flowing from the desk right out the doors and into the street. To correct the problem, the doors are now set at right angles to each other, a fountain was built in the rear, and the reception was moved around a corner to the right of the lobby. Since then, the hotel has enjoyed some of the highest occupancy rates in town. Feng shui or not, the new decor is modern, sleek, and sophisticated, an elegant combination of polished black marble and deep wood. Quiet corridors with great artwork lead to bright guest rooms distinguished by small glass-enclosed alcoves looking over the hotel gardens. Bathrooms are large, with lots of marble counter space.

Dining/Diversions: Mezza9, one of the latest darlings of the trendy dining scene, deserves its reputation for excellent food (Western, Japanese, and Chinese mix) and ambience. It's definitely for those who wish to be seen. Pete's Place is more down-to-earth, and the Italian selections are good. Grand Hyatt's contribution to the nightclub scene brings us Brix, reviewed in chapter 8, with live bands and dancing.

Amenities: Two lush tropical gardens decorate the hotel and pool area, with rock formations, flowers, and a total of 16 waterfalls. There's also a children's slide pool, two floodlit tennis courts, and an air-conditioned badminton court. The fitness center has modern equipment, TV monitors, landscaped Jacuzzi, sauna and steam room areas, aerobics classes, and massage and beauty treatments. There also is a beauty salon, business center, and shopping arcade. Rooms feature in-house movies, data ports, voice mail, and butler service, while a tour desk and a concierge with computer link to STB will help you with everything.

The Best of Singapore's Spas

After a long day on your feet sightseeing in the hot sun, I'll bet I know what you want: a massage, a soak in a hydrotherapy tub, or a nice herbal or floral wrap. (This all before a relaxing and romantic dinner, of course.) Most of the major hotels have massage rooms in their fitness centers, but a few offer luxurious facilities that go above and beyond the call of relaxation and hedonistic beauty pleasures. Here's the best:

At the Grand Plaza Hotel's **Saint Gregory Marine Spa,** 10 Coleman St. #01-23 (☎ **65/432-5588**), even nonguests can make advance appointments to enjoy services in quiet and peaceful surroundings. The spa treatments center around water. Pools are snuggled in amidst lush green plants, with soothing sounds of waves lilting through the air. The focal treatments are the hydrotherapy baths, but you can also get jet showers, steam baths, facials and body treatments, and hand, foot, and body massage. The 20-room center has separate facilities for men and women, but couples can enjoy VIP suites for treatments for two.

The gorgeous, Bali-style spa at the Plaza Hotel's **Plaza Fitness Club,** 7500 Beach Rd., Level Three (☎ **65/298-0011**), has exotic details right down to the floors, which are bejeweled with tiny seashells. Treatments have been developed by Susan-Jane Beers, a local authority on Indonesian herbal health and beauty treatments. Enjoy aromatherapy, wet or dry herbal and floral wraps, body and facial massage, and foot reflexology.

If exercise and relaxation are high on your list of vacation priorities, consider staying at the **Four Seasons Hotel Singapore,** 190 Orchard Rd. (☎ **65/ 734-1110**). Its fitness center is perhaps the best at any hotel on the island, covering two floors and with state-of-the-art exercise facilities as well as personal trainers and nutrition guides. Massages use both Asian and European techniques, and facials, body wraps, and aromatherapy treatments are also available. If you're into this sort of thing, there's even a flotation tank—à la Michael Jackson—and something called a Mind Gear Syncro-Energiser, which relaxes the brain with pulsing light.

Many shopping arcades have outlets advertising **foot reflexology,** a technique whose popularity is just booming these days. Foot reflexology uses pressure techniques to massage the feet in spots that correspond to various parts of your body, relaxing the whole body while only touching the feet. A lot of these places aren't worth the money or time, as the certificate requirements for practitioners aren't exactly demanding. I do recommend one place, though: **Vincien Foot Reflexology** in the Tanglin Shopping Centre at 19 Tanglin Rd. #03-44 (☎ **65/ 739-9639**). Call ahead for an appointment and request Bernard, a retired businessman whose lifetime hobbies have included chi gong (Chinese energy transfer), Reiki (Japanese energy transfer), foot reflexology, and Swedish massage, to name only a few. He comes into the shop by appointment only, and because his heart and soul are in his work, he is worth every penny you pay him. Forty-minute foot reflexology treatments start at an affordable S$30 (US$17.95). A full hour is only S$40 (US$23.95). Full body treatments are S$80 (US$47.90) for 1 hour.

EXPENSIVE

ANA Hotel Singapore. 16 Nassim Hill, Singapore 258467. ☎ **800/ANA-HOTELS** in the U.S. and Canada, or 65/732-1222. Fax 65/235-1516. www.anahotel.com.sg. E-mail: enquiries@ anahotel.com.sg. 456 units. A/C MINIBAR TV TEL. S$300–S$330 (US$179.65–US$197.60) double; S$360 (US$215.55) cabana double or executive club; S$400–S$2,000 (US$239.50– US$1,197.60) suite. AE, DC, JCB, MC, V. 10-min. walk to Orchard MRT.

ANA is located in the embassy area and a 10-minute walk from the Botanic Gardens, which is the perfect place for a morning jog or an evening stroll. From the outside, the modern building is plain, while on the inside, everything is turn-of-the-century, European-style decor—no hints of Asia at all. The rooms are a good size and sport the latest interactive system for hotel service, shopping, and video-on-demand directly through your TV. The bathrooms have clip-on showerheads, which can be inconvenient. Cabana rooms with poolside patios are available. On an interesting note, ANA is, I believe, the only hotel in the city to target women travelers. Special security measures, phone call and visitor screening, plus pretty guest room amenities reach out to this increasing market. In their brochure they guarantee "for dining, our restaurant staff are most discreet and will seat the lone lady traveler where she will not feel any discomfort eating alone"! As a lone lady traveler, I love seeing things like this. Thanks, but I'll just sit at the bar.

Dining/Diversions: You don't have to be a lone lady traveler to enjoy Japanese food at Unkai. It suits a Japanese hotel chain to have excellent Japanese cuisine. After, you can have a drink or dance at Ridley's.

Amenities: Standard offerings: in-house movies, in-room data port, 24-hour room service, and a tour desk. Facilities include a business center, an outdoor pool, plus the Legends Health and Fitness Centre, which, in addition to a gym, has massage, sauna, and steam facilities.

Hilton International Singapore. 581 Orchard Rd., Singapore 238883. ☎ **800/ 445-8667** in the U.S., or 65/737-2233. Fax 65/732-2917. E-mail: hiltels@pacific.net.sg. 423 units. S$270–S$300 (US$161.70–US$179.65) double; S$310 (US$185.65) club; S$850 (US$509) suite. AE, DC, MC, V. Near Orchard MRT.

There may be newer hotels along Orchard Road, but if you count the luxury cars that drive up to the valet at the Hilton, you'll know this is still a good address to have while staying in Singapore. Probably the most famous feature of the Hilton is its shopping arcade, where you can find your Donna Karan, Louis Vuitton, Gucci—all the greats. Ask the concierge for a pager, and they'll page you for important calls while you window-shop or try some of the 45 fragrant vodkas at the lobby bar. Security is guaranteed through key-activated elevators to the guest floors. With all this, the guest rooms should be pretty sumptuous, no? Well, no. The rooms are simpler than you'd expect, with nothing flashy or overdone. There are floor-to-ceiling windows in each, and while views in the front of the hotel are of Orchard Road and the Thai Embassy property, views in the back are not so hot.

Dining/Diversions: I love the Harbour Grill, with its great service and fabulous menu (I've reviewed it in the next chapter), but for something a bit more casual, Checkers has a daily international buffet. The highlight here? Caspia Bar's above-mentioned vodka list.

Amenities: Hotel facilities include a 24-hour business center, in-house movies, in-room data port with fax machine, voice mail, a tour desk, a small outdoor pool, and a modern fitness center with sauna and steam.

Le Meridien Singapore. 100 Orchard Rd., Singapore 238840. ☎ **800/543-4300** in the U.S. and Canada, 800/622240 in Australia, 0800/454040 in New Zealand, 0800/404040 in the U.K., or 65/733-8855. Fax 65/732-7886. www.lemeridien-hotels.com. E-mail: meriorch@asianconnect.com. 407 units. A/C MINIBAR TV TEL. S$300–S$330 (US$179.65–US$197.60) double; S$360 (US$215.55) executive club; S$1,400–S$1,800 (US$838.30–US$1,077.85) suite. AE, DC, MC, V. Dhoby Ghaut/Somerset MRT.

Atrium lobbies are big in Singapore, and I think Le Meridien's is the original, and one of the brightest. Long, straight corridors look out into the huge, open, skylighted space and down to the colorful lobby lounge decorated with plants and fresh flowers. Just at the southern tip of Orchard Road, Le Meridien offers good access to shopping activities, plus the attractions of the nearby Historic District.

Standard rooms are light and fresh with simple European decor and subtle Chinese accents. Voice mail and extra data ports for laptop usage make for convenience, and some rooms have balconies. Bathrooms are state-of-the-art. The Jade and Opal suites are the best spaces, but the executive club facilities are not as attractive as other hotels in this category.

Dining/Diversions: There's not much to speak of here in terms of hotel dining—a coffee house and a lobby bar, but the tiny Nogawa Japanese restaurant rents space just off the lobby to serve sushi and sashimi at affordable prices.

Amenities: Le Meridien offers VCRs in all rooms, 24-hour room service, a tour desk, and concierge with computer link to STB, plus a small outdoor pool and a large fitness center with aerobics and sauna.

Mandarin Singapore. 333 Orchard Rd., Singapore 238867. ☎ **800/380-9957** in the U.S. and Canada, or 65/737-4411. Fax 65/235-6688. www.meritus-hotels.com. E-mail: rmresvn@singnet.com.sg. 1,235 units. A/C MINIBAR TV TEL S$400 (US$239.50) double; S$450 (US$269.45) club; S$580–S$2,800 (US$347.30–US$1,676.65) suite. AE, DC, JCB, MC, V. Near Orchard MRT.

Smack in the center of Orchard Road is the Mandarin Hotel, a two-tower complex with Singapore's most famous revolving restaurant topping it off like a little hat. The 39-story Main Tower opened in 1973, and with the opening of the South Wing 10 years later the number of rooms expanded to 1,200. Massive renovations of both wings and most of the facilities were completed in 1995. True to its name, the hotel is decorated in Chinese style, from the huge lobby mural of the "87 Taoist Immortals" to the black-and-red Ming-design carpet murals and black lacquer-style guest room entrances. The South Wing is predominantly for leisure travelers, who have access to the tower from the side of the hotel off Orchard Road. The guest rooms here are slightly smaller and furnished with Chinese-style dark wood modular units. The guest rooms in the Main Tower are brighter and larger. All bathrooms have bidets and scales.

Dining: The revolving restaurant, the Top of the M, serves Continental cuisine while you gaze on a 360° view of the city. The restaurant 333 (Triple Three) spreads an amazing Western buffet daily. The Chatterbox is a good place to try local favorites, including their award-winning Hainanese Chicken Rice, while Pine Court delights with its mix of Chinese cuisines. (I've reviewed the last two in chapter 4.)

Amenities: In-house movies, 24-hour room service, voice mail, a tour desk, and concierge with computer link to STB round out services offered. Hotel facilities include an outdoor tennis court, squash court, a midsize outdoor pool, business center, a busy shopping arcade, and a large fitness center with aerobics, Jacuzzi, sauna, and steam.

Orchard Hotel Singapore. 442 Orchard Rd., Singapore 238879. ☎ **800/465-6486** in the U.S. and Canada, 800/655147 in Australia (Sydney 02/92237422), 0800/442519 in New Zealand, 0800/252854 in the U.K., or 65/734-7766. Fax 65/733-5482. E-mail: orcharde@singnet.com.sg. 680 units. A/C MINIBAR TV TEL. S$320–S$360 (US$191.60–US$215.55) double; S$430 (US$257.50) club; S$650–S$1,800 (US$389.20–US$1,077.85) suite. AE, DC, JCB, MC, V. 5-min. walk to Orchard MRT.

Just this past year, the Orchard completed a major renovation of its guest rooms, lobby, and facilities, and the new touches add a lot of comfort and style. While their Harvest Rooms (at the high end of the price range) are done in tasteful and attractive florals, the less expensive doubles sport the kind of unassuming pastels you'd expect to see in just about any hotel room. The rooms are just slightly smaller than most, and have an interactive TV system for guest room services.

Dining: The Orchard Café performs coffee shop duties, while your only fine dining choice, Hua Ting, gets high marks for Cantonese cuisine that's first rate at an affordable price.

Amenities: Facilities include a midsize outdoor pool, a fitness center with sauna, a shopping mall, and business center. Rooms have in-house movies, plus there's 24-hour room service, a tour desk, and a concierge with computer link to STB.

The Regent Singapore. 1 Cuscaden Rd., Singapore 249715. ☎ **800/545-4000** in the U.S. and Canada, 1800/022-800 in Australia, 0800/440-800 in New Zealand, 0800/28-22-45 in the U.K., or 65/733-8888. Fax 65/732-8838. www.regenthotels.com. E-mail: seha. hussein@fourseasons.com. 441 units. A/C MINIBAR TV TEL. S$350–S$370 (US$209.60–US$221.55) double; S$550–S$1,300 (US$329.35–US$778.45) suite. 10-min. walk to Orchard MRT.

The Regent is tucked between Cuscaden and Tanglin roads, right across the street from the Singapore Tourism Board office—quite convenient. And check out the lobby in this place! It's a huge, three-level atrium affair with windows on three sides, a skylight, fountains, plenty of small private meeting nooks, and Jetsons-style raised walkways. The generous-size rooms have high ceilings and are decorated with Southeast Asian–style fabrics, but the bathrooms are smaller than at most other comparable hotels. You have to request coffee- and tea-making facilities in your room; otherwise the service is free in the tea lounge, which also serves a high tea the old-fashioned way—on silver tray service, not buffet.

Dining: The highlight here, Summer Palace, is one of the city's finest venues for fabulous Cantonese dishes, but be prepared to pay for it. Maxim's de Paris's classical French cuisine can't compete with some of the other French restaurants in the city, but the poolside buffet can be nice.

Amenities: Expect in-house movies, in-room data ports with fax machine, 24-hour room service, voice mail, and a tour desk, and a concierge with computer link to STB. Hotel facilities include a business center with private office space rental and secretarial support; a small outdoor pool; and a midsize, modern fitness center with Jacuzzi, steam, massage, and beauty treatments.

✪ **Shangri-La Hotel.** Orange Grove Rd., Singapore 258350. ☎ **800/942-5050** in the U.S. and Canada, 800/222448 in Australia, 0800/442179 in New Zealand, or 65/737-3644. Fax 65/733-3257. www.shangri-la.com. 760 units. A/C MINIBAR TV TEL. S$405 (US$242.50) Tower double; S$490 (US$293.40) Garden double; S$440 (US$263.45) horizon club; S$550 (US$329.35) Valley double; S$1,000–S$3,200 (US$598.80–US$1,916.15) suite. AE, DC, JCB, MC, V. 10-min. walk to Orchard MRT.

It may not be as centrally located as other hotels in the area, but the Shangri-La is a lovely place, with strolling gardens, a putting course, and an outdoor pool paradise that are great diversions from the hustle and bustle all around. Maybe that's why visiting VIPs like George Bush, Benazir Bhutto, and Nelson Mandela have all stayed here.

The hotel has three wings: The Tower Wing is the oldest, housing the lobby and most of the guest rooms, which were recently renovated. The Garden Wing's bougainvillea-laden balconies, half of which overlook the tropical atrium with its cascading waterfall and exotic plants, drip with tropical magic—these rooms feel the most like resort rooms. The exclusive Valley Wing has a private entrance and very spacious rooms, linked to the main tower by a sky bridge that looks out over the hotel's 6 hectares (15 acres) of landscaped lawns, fruit trees, and flowers.

Dining/Diversions: Shang Palace and Nadaman provide Chinese and Japanese dining, while Shangri-La is opening a new restaurant in late 2000 to add to your choices. High tea on the Rose Veranda is lovely.

Amenities: Rooms in all wings have interactive TV with in-house movies, and fax machines are available on request. Services and facilities include 24-hour room service, a tour desk, a concierge with computer link to STB, a business center, beauty salon, and gift shop, two pools (one large outdoor and one small heated indoor), four tennis courts, two squash courts, and a fitness center with hot and cold Jacuzzis, steam, sauna, and massage.

Sheraton Towers Singapore. 39 Scotts Rd., Singapore 228230. ☎ **800/325-3535** in the U.S. and Canada, 800/073535 in Australia, 0800/443535 in New Zealand, 0800/353535 in the U.K., or 65/737-6888. Fax 65/737-1072. www.sheraton.com. 410 units. S$370–S$430 (US$221.55–US$257.50) double; S$510 (US$305.40) cabana room; S$700–S$2,800 (US$419.15–US$1,676.65) suite. AE, DC, JCB, MC, V. 5-min. walk to Newton MRT.

One of the first things you see when you walk into the lobby of the Sheraton Towers is the service awards the place has won; check in, and you'll begin to see why they won 'em. With the Deluxe (standard) room they'll give you a suit pressing on arrival, daily newspaper delivery, shoe-shine service, and complimentary movies. Upgrade to a Tower room and you get a personal butler, complimentary nightly cocktails and morning breakfast, free laundry, free local calls, your own pants press, and free use of the personal trainer in the fitness center. The Cabana rooms, off the pool area, have all the services of the Tower Wing in a very private resort room. Get a suite here only if you are very fond of the color peach.

Dining: For sophisticated dining and melt-in-your-mouth Chinese fare, Li Bai (reviewed in chapter 4) remains one of the city's most respected fine dining establishments. The newer Domvs gives you the option of dining on northern Italian cuisine, while the coffee shop off the lobby serves the daily local and Western breakfast, lunch, tea, and dinner selections.

Amenities: Hotel facilities include a business center, newly renovated pool with a fine view of the surrounding trees, and a small fitness center with a sauna but, curiously, no windows. A short list of services includes in-house movies and in-room data ports.

Singapore Marriott Hotel. 320 Orchard Rd., Singapore 238865. ☎ **800/228-9290** in the U.S. and Canada, 1800/251-259 in Australia (Sydney 02/299-1614), 0800/22-12-22 in the U.K., or 65/735-5800. Fax 65/735-9800. www.marriott.com. E-mail: mhrs.sindt.dors@ marriott.com. 373 units. A/C MINIBAR TV TEL. S$380 (US$227.55) double; S$420 (US$251.50) executive club; S$650–S$1,880 (US$389.20–US$1,125.75) suite. AE, DC, JCB, MC, V. Orchard MRT.

You can't get a better location than at the corner of Orchard and Scotts roads. Marriott's green-roofed pagoda tower is a well-recognized landmark on Orchard Road, but guest rooms inside tend to be smaller than average to fit in the octagonal structure. Luckily the current refurbishing scheme plans to add lively colors to brighten the spaces (these should be mostly completed by the time this book hits the stores). The palatial lobby compensates for the cramped pagoda: You enter through sheets of water flowing over black marble, feng shui style, into a seating area nestled between nine towering preserved palm trees. The sidewalk cafe off the lobby is a favorite place for international and Singaporean celebrities who like to be seen.

Marriott, which took over management of this property in 1995, caters to the business traveler, so the rooms on the club floors get most of the hotel's attention. The club lounge, for instance, has a great view and there's not a tacky detail in the comfortable seating and dining areas.

Dining: The Crossroads Café, on the corner of Orchard and Scotts roads, gets packed daily because of its great location—a good opportunity for people-watching—while just inside, the Marriott cafe serves daily breakfast and lunch buffets. Another cafe, next to the landscaped pool, provides light meals and snacks throughout the day. For fine dining, try the Wan Hao Chinese Restaurant.

Amenities: Data ports, three phones, and voice mail are standard in all the hotel's rooms, as are in-house movies and an iron and ironing board. Marriott's business center runs round-the-clock, while other facilities include a half-size outdoor basketball court and a very deep, midsize outdoor pool with a nice view and great inexpensive snack bar. The fitness center (also open 24-hours!) has aerobics, Jacuzzi, sauna, and steam room. Tang's, Singapore's largest indigenous department store, is located just adjacent to the hotel.

MODERATE

Boulevard Hotel. 200 Orchard Blvd., Singapore 248647. ☎ **800/635-0980** in the U.S., 0800/899515 in the U.K., or 65/737-2911. Fax 65/737-8449. 521 units. A/C MINIBAR TV TEL. S$150 (US$89.80) double; S$325 (US$194.60) suite. AE, DC, JCB, MC, V. 15-min. walk to Orchard MRT.

Orchard Boulevard runs parallel to Orchard Road, the main hub of it all, and yet Orchard Boulevard has trees and chirping birds, which makes the Boulevard Hotel close to the action, but more relaxing. Unlike most hotels in Singapore, this place caters less to business guests and more to the leisure set, as evidenced by the lobby, which is still bustling at 10am with excited travelers from all over the world (at this point in the morning, most other hotels have shipped their guests off to work).

This is yet another hotel built around an atrium concept, only Boulevard's atrium is not as open and airy as most. A giant metallic monument to prosperity towers up the shaft of the atrium. It's rather plain by day, but dramatic when it's lit at night. Guest rooms in the Cuscaden Wing—the oldest part of the hotel, built in 1976—are good size, decorated in darker hues, and are less expensive than the guest rooms in the newer Orchard Wing, built in 1984. Hotel facilities include a fitness center with sauna, two midsize outdoor pools, and shops. Boulevard's pastry shop, next to the coffee shop, is famous for its chicken pies, a tasty and inexpensive treat.

Copthorne Orchid Singapore. 214 Dunearn Rd., Singapore 299526. ☎ **800/637-7200** in the U.S. and Canada, 800/442-519 in Australia, or 65/250-3322. Fax 65/250-9292. www.singapore-hotel.com.sg. E-mail: roomres@orchidsing.com.sg. 440 units. A/C MINIBAR TV TEL. S$220–S$240 (US$131.75–US$143.710) double; S$300 (US$179.65) family; S$300–S$480 (US$179.65–US$287.45) suite. AE, DC, MC, V. Far from MRT stations.

The Copthorne hotel management chain has recently taken over the Orchid, which was formerly under Novotel management (so it may still be referred to as Novotel around town). Lobby renovations in 1997 redesigned the space in a very open and contemporary style, with straight lines and light wood paneling à la IKEA. Of course, the renovations were not without the addition of a lucky koi pond, full of golden fish to bring you luck and fortune, and nestled in an adorable, brightly painted courtyard that can be viewed from the lobby bar. The pond runs from the courtyard under the floor of the bar to a pool and fountain inside. The newness of this part of the hotel adds contrast to the older sections—as you walk down the covered but otherwise open-air corridors, you can see signs of age. Nevertheless, guest rooms here are big and fairly pleasant, with tall stucco walls and high ceilings. The rooms in the Plymouth Wing to the back of the complex have a sofa bed in addition to the regular beds, and offer plenty of desk and counter space.

The hotel has installed interactive GuestServe TV, a service that allows you to check on your bill and access information about hotel facilities and Singapore tourism information. There's also a self-service launderette, shopping, a free shuttle to Orchard Road for the convenience of guests, and a health center with massage, sauna, and steam room. The hotel's worst feature is probably its pool, which has pretty landscaping but is on the ground level, separated from a noisy main street by only a vine-covered fence. There's a game area with a billiards table to the side.

The Elizabeth Singapore. 24 Mount Elizabeth, Singapore 228518. ☎ **65/738-1188.** Fax 65/732-3866. E-mail: elizabethrsvn@pacific.net.sg. 256 units. A/C MINIBAR TV TEL. S$300–S$340 (US$179.65–US$203.60) double; S$650–S$950 (US$389.20–US$568.85) suite. AE, DC, JCB, MC, V. 10-min. walk to Orchard MRT.

This small, quaint hotel has cozy rooms and the most friendly and accommodating staff around. Done in dark, cool European styling throughout, from the lobby to the guest rooms, this modern hotel's most dramatic feature is the lobby area's fantastic cascading waterfalls, which drop over a vertical tropical rock-and-plant garden nestled behind three-story-high glass panels. Both the business center and fitness center are small, but the pool is in a pretty, columned courtyard—and they pipe in underwater music. Other facilities include a gift shop, and, for those of you in the mood for cuddly, a specialty teddy bear shop.

Orchard Parade Hotel. 1 Tanglin Rd., Singapore 247905. ☎ **65/737-1133.** Fax 65/733-0242. www.farest.com.sg/hotels. 387 units. A/C MINIBAR TV TEL. S$280–S$360 (US$167.65–US$215.55) double; S$380–S$460 (US$227.55–US$275.45) family studio; S$400 (US$239.50) junior suite; S$480–S$1,200 (US$287.45–US$718.55) suite. AE, DC, JCB, MC, V. Orchard MRT.

In a mad dash to compete, every hotel in Singapore is either planning a renovation, currently renovating, or just finishing one up. Orchard Parade is no exception. Its new renovation took 2 years and S$40 million to redo the swimming pool, guest rooms, lobby, driveway, front entrance, and food and beverage outlets. The result is a fine hotel decorated in a Mediterranean theme integrating marble mosaics, plaster walls, beamed ceilings, and wrought-iron railings. The large pool on the sixth-floor roof features colorful tiles and draping arbors, a motif carried over through the new fitness center. If it's important to you, you need to specify a room with a view here. Just outside, a long terrace along Orchard Road hosts many restaurant choices, the most popular of which, Modestos, serves good pasta and pizzas at an affordable price.

✪ Traders Hotel Singapore. 1A Cuscaden Rd., Singapore 249716. ☎ **800/942-5050** in the U.S. and Canada, 800/222448 in Australia, 0800/442179 in New Zealand, or 65/738-2222. Fax 65/831-4314. www.shangri-la.com. 543 units. A/C TV TEL. S$275–S$320 (US$164.65–US$191.60) double; S$355 (US$212.55) club; S$490–S$1,000 (US$293.40–US$598.80) studio apt. and suite. AE, DC, JCB, MC, V. 10-min. walk to Orchard MRT.

A fantastic bargain for leisure travelers in Singapore, Traders advertises itself as a "value-for-money" hotel. A spin-off of Shangri-La (see above), this hotel anticipates the special needs of travelers and tries on all levels to accommodate them. Rooms have an empty fridge that can be stocked from the supermarket next door (show your room card key at nearby Tanglin Mall for discounts from many of the shops); there are spanking clean self-service launderette facilities with ironing boards on six floors; and

Feng Shui & Singaporean Society

Have you ever noticed how some homes seem to give off terrific vibes the moment you enter the front door while others leave you feeling disturbed and wanting to get out fast? The Chinese believe *feng shui* (pronounced "fung *shway*" and meaning "wind and water") has a lot to do with these positive and negative feelings.

The earliest record of feng shui dates from the Han Dynasty (202 B.C. to A.D. 220) and the practice is still widely followed and highly regarded in Asia today. In essence, the idea of feng shui revolves around the way physical surroundings relate to the invisible flow of *chi* (positive energy), which must move smoothly throughout the home or business in order for life to play itself out beneficially. Walls, doors, windows, or furnishings can throw off this flow through their color, balance, placement, or proportion—even by their points on the compass. Your bed, for example, placed on the wrong wall or facing the wrong way, could encourage chi to rush into a room and out again, taking wealth and health with it. If your bed is situated directly under an exposed beam, you might as well make a standing appointment with the chiropractor, 'cause that's some *baaad* feng shui.

In Singapore, company presidents regularly call upon feng shui masters to rearrange their office furniture, and the master is usually the first person called in on new construction jobs, to assess the building plans for their adherence to good feng shui practices. It's not uncommon to hear stories about buildings being partially torn down late in the construction process, simply because a master hadn't examined the plans earlier and, when finally consulted, had deemed that the structure did not promote good feng shui. The extra cost is considered a valid investment—after all, what's a few dollars saved now if bad feng shui will later cause the business to fail? For the average homeowner who doesn't want to consult a feng shui master (or can't afford to), a plethora of books are available to advise on creating successful living spaces.

For every life situation there's a feng shui solution. And don't worry what people will think when they see those four purple candles in the corner of your living room or the pair of wooden flutes dangling from an exposed beam. Let 'em laugh—you'll be grinning all the way to the bank.

there are vending machines and ice machines. They even provide a hospitality lounge for guests to use after checkout, with seating areas, work spaces with data ports, card phones, safe-deposit boxes, vending machines, and a shower.

Guest rooms are smaller than average, but feature child-size sofa beds and large drawers for storage. The large, landscaped pool area has a great poolside al fresco cafe, Ah Hoi's Kitchen, serving up tasty Chinese dishes at reasonable prices. Hotel facilities include a data port in each room and a fitness center with outdoor Jacuzzi, sauna, steam, and massage and facial services. Services include voice mail, free shuttle service to Orchard Road, Shangri-La Hotel, Shangri-La Rasa Sentosa Resort, Suntec City, and Shenton Way business district. Be sure to ask about promotion rates when you book your room. If you're planning to stay longer than 2 weeks, they have a long-stay program that offers discount meals, laundry and business center services, and half-price launderette tokens.

York Hotel Singapore. 21 Mount Elizabeth, Singapore 228516. ☎ **800/223-5652** in the U.S. and Canada, 800/553-549 in Australia, 800/447-555 in New Zealand, 800/89-88-52 in the U.K., or 65/737-0511. Fax 65/732-1217. www.yorkhotel.com.sg. E-mail: enquiry@yorkhotel.com.sg. 406 units. A/C MINIBAR TV TEL. S$265–S$285 (US$158.70–US$170.65) double; S$260 (US$155.70) cabana; S$400 (US$239.50) split-level cabana; S$430–S$910 (US$257.50–US$544.90) suite. AE, DC, JCB, MC, V. 10-min. walk to Orchard MRT.

This small tourist-class hotel can boast some of the most consistently professional and courteous staff I've encountered. A short walk from Orchard, York is convenient though far enough removed to provide a relaxing atmosphere. A recent renovation has redressed previously flavorless rooms in a sharp contemporary style in light woods, natural tones, and simple lines. Combined with an already spacious room, the result is an airy, cooling effect. Bathrooms throughout are downright huge. Cabana rooms look out to a pool and sundeck decorated with giant palms. Despite surrounding buildings, it doesn't feel claustrophobic, as do some of the more centrally situated hotels. There's a Jacuzzi, but the business center is tiny and there's no fitness center. Guests in single-occupancy rooms are often upgraded to doubles.

INEXPENSIVE

Garden Hotel Singapore. 14 Balmoral Rd., Singapore 259800. ☎ **65/235-3344.** Fax 65/235-9730. E-mail: garden@pacific.net.sg. 216 units. A/C TV TEL. S$190 (US$113.75) double; S$210 (US$125.75) cabana; S$200 (US$119.75) family; S$300 (US$179.65) suite. AE, DC, JCB, MC, V. 15-min. walk to Newton MRT.

This five-story hotel is a discreet building in a quiet prime residential neighborhood north of the Orchard Road area—and that's its main downfall: It's pretty far out from where all the action is. (The hotel compensates with a free shuttle to Orchard Road and to the Marina area.) Other than location, this is a fine place to stay. It serves a mostly Western market of leisure travelers and families, discouraging tour groups to avoid noisy throngs loitering around the lobby area and crashing the food and beverage outlets at feeding times. The good news is that 95% of the guest rooms have balconies. The bad news is, some of them are *indoors,* with a view of the atrium coffee shop, so make sure you get one with an outside view. The rooms here are average-size and bright, and guest rooms in the west wing have been recently refurbished. Garden Hotel has two pools, a rooftop pool that gets good sun and a small ground-level landscaped pool in a courtyard surrounded by large cabana rooms. Inexpensive babysitting services are available, and hotel facilities include gift shops and a midsize fitness center with sauna.

Hotel Grand Central, Singapore. 22 Cavenagh Rd./Orchard Rd., Singapore 229617. ☎ **800/331006** in Australia, or 65/733-3922. Fax 65/733-6022. 390 units. A/C MINIBAR TV TEL. S$210–S$230 (US$125.75–US$137.70) double; S$300 (US$179.65) suite. AE, DC, MC, V. Somerset MRT.

Most of the hotels in this price category are at least a 10-minute walk outside the main drag, but Hotel Grand Central is right on it, with an exclusive Orchard Road address. The hotel always runs at high occupancy, its lobby a hustle and bustle of mostly ASEAN (Association of Southeast Asian Nations) vacation travelers who, truth to tell, seem to have worn dull the front counter staff's service edge. The building was originally eight floors, but recent renovations added an extra floor to the top, which houses executive club rooms. The corridors are on the dreary side, and the guest rooms and bathrooms are a little run-down. Windows are positioned high, so there's not much in the way of views—although rooms in the center of the building offer views of rooms on the opposite side, if that's your idea of fun. Facilities include a small fitness center with Jacuzzi and sauna, a beauty salon, and a shopping arcade, and the hotel offers a full range of services (excluding concierge). To the side of the rooftop pool is a special corner reserved for dead hotel houseplants—a tip-off that maybe this isn't the most luxurious place on Orchard Road.

Lloyd's Inn. 2 Lloyd Rd., Singapore 239091. ☎ **65/737-7309.** Fax 65/737-7847. 34 units. A/C TV TEL. S$65 (US$38.90) double. MC, V. 10-min. walk to Somerset MRT.

Lloyd's is a budget motel in every sense. It's a two-story building on a relatively quiet, low-traffic street. The corridors are open-air and the rooms are small, with a definite budget feeling, though all have air-conditioning and phones. Each room has its own bathroom, though they tend to be mildewy. The published rates include the "+++" taxes (see "Taxes & Service Charges," above); there's no discount offered for long-term stays; you must pay for your room when you check in; and if you use a credit card, it'll cost you an extra 2%. As for the parking, this place is squeezed into its lot like a snail in its shell, so there's room for about two cars—and that's it. No pool, no fitness center, no nothing—you got your room; that's what you got.

Metropolitan YMCA Singapore. 60 Stevens Rd., Singapore 257854. ☎ **65/737-7755.** Fax 65/235-5528. E-mail: lodge@mymca.org.sg. 91 units. A/C TV TEL. S$65–S$95 (US$38.90–US$56.90) double; S$80–S$110 (US$47.90–US$65.85) family; S$125 (US$74.85) suite. AE, DC, JCB, MC, V. 15-min. walk to Newton MRT.

This place is a little out of the way and the rooms are looking a little on the older side, but they're clean and efficient. One oddity here: The least expensive rooms have no windows; for sunlight, you'll have to pay a little extra. There are nine family rooms outfitted with either three twin beds or a double and a twin. The family rooms are the same size as the other rooms, but the bathrooms are bigger and there's a lot more closet space. In early 1998, a new multipurpose fitness center opened here, installed all new equipment, and hired a trainer. The pool is a nice size, as is the kiddie pool, and there's a lifeguard on duty from 9am to 9pm daily. No dorm rooms are available, but concierge, dry cleaning, laundry, and secretarial services are. Plus, there's a self-service launderette, a coffee shop, a tour desk, and a shuttle service to Orchard Road.

Regalis Court. 64 Lloyd Rd., Singapore 239113. ☎ **65/734-7117.** Fax 65/736-1651. 43 units. A/C TV TEL. S$145–S$165 (US$86.85–US$98.80) double. Rates include continental breakfast. AE, DC, JCB, MC, V. 10-min. walk from Somerset MRT.

For a bit of local charm at an affordable price, Regalis Court is a favorite. Centrally located just a 10-minute walk from Orchard Road, this old charming bungalow has been restored beautifully and outfitted with Peranakan-inspired touches. Everything here will make you feel as if you're staying in a quaint guest house rather than a hotel, from the open-air lobby (under the porte cochere) and corridors to the guest rooms, which have comforting touches like teakwood furnishings, textile wall hangings, Oriental throws over wooden floors, and bamboo chick blinds to keep out the sun. Although guest rooms are slightly smaller than conventional rooms, they are still quite comfortable. Facilities are few. Laundry services, a steam room, and car hire are also offered.

✪ **RELC International Hotel.** 30 Orange Grove Rd., Singapore 258352. ☎ **65/737-9044.** Fax 65/733-9976. www.hotel-web.com. E-mail: relcih@singnet.com.sg. 128 units. A/C TV TEL. S$110 (US$65.85) double; S$165 (US$98.80) suite. Rates include American breakfast for 2. DC, JCB, MC, V. 10-min. walk to Orchard MRT.

For real value, my money is on RELC. Sure the location is terrific (only a 10-minute walk to Orchard Road), but the added value is in the quality of the facility. I found the service and convenience here superior to some hotels in the higher priced categories. RELC has four types of rooms—superior twin, executive twin, Hollywood queen, and alcove suite—but no matter what the size, none of the rooms ever feel cluttered, close, or cramped. All rooms have balconies, TVs with two movie channels, and a fridge with free juice boxes and snacks. Bathrooms are large, with full-length tubs and hair dryers standard. If you're interested in the higher-priced rooms, I'd choose the

Hollywood queen over the alcove suite—its decor is better and it can sleep a family very comfortably. The "superior" rooms don't have coffee- and tea-making facilities. A self-service launderette is available.

✪ **YMCA International House.** 1 Orchard Rd., Singapore 238824. ☎ **65/336-6000.** Fax 65/337-3140. 109 units. A/C TV TEL. S$89.25 (US$53.45) double; S$106 (US$63.45) family room; S$114.70 (US$68.70) superior room; S$28.35 (US$16.95) dormitory. Non-YMCA members must pay S$5 (US$3) temporary membership fee at check-in. AE, DC, JCB, MC, V. Near Dhoby Ghaut MRT.

Of the two YMCAs in Singapore, this one has the better location. At the lower end of Orchard Road, it's only a short walk to the Dhoby Ghaut MRT station, making it very convenient for getting around via mass transit. The guest rooms have just been renovated and have private bathrooms that are better than I've seen at some much pricier hotels. All rooms have air-conditioning, a telephone (with free local calls), color television, and a stock-it-yourself refrigerator. The dormitories are small, dark, and quiet, with two bunk beds per room. Across the hall are men's and women's locker rooms for showering. Most of the public areas have no air-conditioning, including the old fitness facility, billiards center, and squash courts—so be warned: They can become unbearably hot. The rooftop pool is nothing to write home about, but there is a full-time lifeguard on duty. There's a coffee shop and a McDonald's in the lobby. The hotel staff is amazingly friendly.

5 Sentosa Island

There are only two hotel properties on Sentosa Island, the Shangri-La Rasa Sentosa, located right on the water and designed for families and fun, and the Beaufort, located close to the water and even closer to golfing, and designed for secluded, romantic getaways.

✪ **The Beaufort.** 2 Bukit Manis Rd., Sentosa, Singapore 099891. ☎ **800/457-4000** in the U.S. and Canada, 1800/801-855 in Australia, 0800/55-65-55 in the U.K., or 65/275-0331. Fax 65/275-0228. www.beaufort.com.sg. E-mail: rsvn@beaufort.com.sg. 214 units. A/C MINIBAR TV TEL. S$380 (US$227.55) double; S$450 (US$269.45) suite; S$1,500 (US$898.20) villa. AE, DC, JCB, MC, V. See "Sentosa Island" in chapter 5 for public transportation.

Designed with romance in mind, the Beaufort's small resort-style buildings, fashioned after the famous resorts of Phuket, Thailand, are connected with covered walkways encircling lily ponds and courtyard gardens. Here, the designers have done a great job combining clean modern lines with tropical touches to produce a sophisticated getaway with relaxing charm. Lazy terraces and cozy alcoves tucked all over the grounds invite guests to unwind in privacy—perfect for intimate candlelight dinners that can be requested anywhere you like.

The standard guest rooms in the five-story hotel building are small but stunning, featuring camphor burl wood doors and accents, Thai silk screens in dreamy blues and greens, and deep tubs and separate showers in the bathrooms, surrounded by thick celadon green tiling and sleek black granite details. Ask for views of the golf course, which are prettier than the views of the hotel courtyards and buildings. Butlers wait round the clock to serve you—a standard feature for all rooms, but if you want the ultimate, the Beaufort's Garden Villas deliver privacy and luxury in little houses with individual pools.

In a tree just behind the open-air lobby, look for Tommy the monkey, which sometimes hangs out with one or two of its wives or kids. You have to love any resort that has a resident monkey family.

Dining: A terrace cafe provides Asian and Western meals three times daily, while Siggi's on the Cliff hosts a sumptuous seafood barbecue nightly.

Amenities: Hotel facilities include VCR and video rentals for suites, and in-house movies for standard category rooms. The pool (one of my favorites in Singapore) seduces with midnight-blue tiles, which look black and sexy by day and like shimmering emeralds by night. The tree-lined sundeck looks out to ships in the harbor. A large health club, located in a separate restored colonial building, features a gym, Jacuzzi, and sauna. Three floodlit tennis courts (with coach), two squash courts, a 20-meter lap pool, and an archery range are available for guest use, as are mountainbike rentals for tooling around the island. Ask about the special packages for honeymoon and golf excursions.

○ **Shangri-La's Rasa Sentosa Resort.** 101 Siloso Rd., Sentosa, Singapore 098970. ☎ **800/942-5050** in the U.S. and Canada, 1800/222-448 in Australia, 0800/442-179 in New Zealand, or 65/275-0100. Fax 65/275-0355. www.shangri-la.com. E-mail: Reservations@ rasa-sentosa.com.sg. 459 units. A/C MINIBAR TV TEL. Weekdays S$280 (US$167.65) hill-view double, S$320 (US$191.60) cabana double or pool double, S$350 (US$209.60) deluxe seafacing double; from S$550 (US$329.35) terrace rooms and suites. Weekends S$340 (US$203.60) hill-view double, S$370 (US$221.55) cabana double or pool double, S$400 (US$239.50) deluxe sea-facing double. AE, DC, JCB, MC, V. See "Sentosa Island" in chapter 5 for public transportation.

Set on an immaculate white sandy beach fringed with coconut palms, Shangri-La's Rasa Sentosa Resort is Singapore's only true beachfront hotel. It's frequented by Singaporeans looking to get away from it all, but as a visitor to Singapore you may find it isolated from the city's attractions. Still, you can always take advantage of the resort's complimentary shuttle service for trips to the action, only to return to the serenity of the resort at the end of a busy day.

Great outdoor activities make the Rasa Sentosa particularly attractive. The resort's extensive recreational facilities, including a sea-sports center, offer windsurfing, sailing, and paddle skiing. Other facilities include a large outdoor free-form swimming pool, a jogging track, aqua bike rentals, an outdoor Jacuzzi, and a fully equipped spa with gym, sauna, body and facial treatments, hydromassage, and massage therapies. The hotel also organizes nature walks, cycling tours, rock-wall climbing, and beach volleyball. For children, there is a separate pool with water slides (no lifeguard, though), a playground, a nursery, and a video arcade. There are five outlets providing an array of dining choices such as sizzling barbecue on the terrace, cafe-style Asian and international favorites, and sumptuous seafood served under the stars.

As for the rooms, the decision between whether to take the hill-view room or the slightly more expensive sea-facing room is a no-brainer: The view of the sea is exceptional, and if you don't go for it, you'll be missing out on glorious mornings, throwing back the curtains, and taking in the view from the balcony.

Singapore Dining 4

Take three million people, put 'em on a tiny island for their whole lives, and what have you got? Three million people looking for new things to entertain them. Sure, the sights and attractions can keep visitors occupied for weeks, but how many times can you go to Sentosa before it becomes the same old same old? The locals have seen and done it all.

So what do Singaporeans do for boredom relief? They eat. Dining out in Singapore is the central focus of family quality time, the best excuse for getting together with friends, and the proper way to close that business deal. That's why you find such a huge selection of local, regional, and international cuisine here, served in settings that range from bustling hawker centers to grand and glamorous palaces of gastronomy. But to simply say "If You Like Food You'll Love Singapore!" doesn't do justice to the modern concept of eating in this place. The various ethnic restaurants, with their traditional decor and serving styles, hold their own special sense of theater for foreigners; but Singaporeans don't stop there, dreaming up new concepts in cuisine and ambience to add fresh dimensions to the fine art of dining. For a twist, new variations on traditions pop up, like the French-service Chinese cuisine at Chang Jiang or the East-meets-West New Asia cuisine dished up at Doc Cheng's. Theme restaurants turn regular meals into attractions. Take, for example, Imperial Herbal's intriguing predinner medical examination or House of Mao's Cultural Revolution menu.

Recent figures say Singapore has over 2,000 eating establishments, so you'll never be at a loss for a place to go. In this chapter, I'll begin by providing an overview of the main types of traditional cuisine to help you decide, and also list those signature dishes that each style has contributed to the "local cuisine," dishes that have crossed cultures to become time-honored favorites—the Singaporean equivalent to bangers and mash or burgers and fries. These suggestions are especially helpful when navigating the endless choices at hawker centers.

The restaurants I've chosen for review in this chapter offer a cross-cut of cuisine and price range, and were selected for superb quality or authenticity of dishes. Some were selected for the sheer experience, whether it's a stunning view or just plain old fun. Beyond this list, you're sure to discover favorites of your own without having to look too far.

A good place to start is right in your hotel. Many of Singapore's best restaurants are in its hotels, whether they're run by the hotel itself or operated by outfits just renting the space. Hotels generally offer a wide variety of cuisine, and coffee shops almost always have Western selections. Shopping malls have everything from food courts with local fast food to mid-priced and upmarket establishments. Western fast-food outlets are always easy to find—McDonald's burgers, Dunkin' Donuts, or Starbucks coffee—but if you want something a little more local, you'll find coffee shops (called *kopitiam*) and small home-cookin' mom-and-pop joints down every back street. Then there are hawker centers, where, under one roof, the meal choices go on and on.

1 One Little Island, Lots & Lots of Choices

CHINESE CUISINE

The large Chinese population in Singapore makes this obviously the most common type of food you'll find, and by right, any good description of Singaporean food should begin with the most prevalent Chinese regional styles. Many Chinese restaurants in the West are lumped into one category—Chinese—with only mild acknowledgment of Szechuan and dim sum. But China's a big place, and its size is reflected in its many different tastes, ingredients, and preparation styles.

CANTONESE CUISINE   Cantonese-style food is what you usually find in the West: Your stir-fries, wontons, and sweet-and-sour sauces all come from this southern region. Cantonese cooks emphasize freshness of ingredients, which explains why some Cantonese homemakers will shop up to three times a day for the freshest picks. Typical preparation involves quick stir-frying in light oil, or steaming for tender meats and crisp, flavorful vegetables. These are topped off with light sauces that are sometimes sweet. Cantonese-style food also includes roasted meats like suckling pig and the red-roasted pork that's ever present in Western Chinese dishes. Compared to northern styles of Chinese cuisine, Cantonese food can be bland, especially when sauces and broths are overthickened and slimy. Singaporean palates demand the standard dish of chile condiment at the table, which sometimes helps the flavor. One hearty Cantonese dish that has made it to local cuisine fame is **clay pot rice,** which is rice cooked with chicken, Chinese sausage, and mushrooms, prepared in—you guessed it—a clay pot.

The Cantonese are also responsible for **dim sum** (or *tim sum,* as you'll sometimes see it written around Singapore). Meaning "little hearts," dim sum is a variety of deep-fried or steamed buns, spring rolls, dumplings, meatballs, spare ribs, and a host of other tasty treats. It's a favorite in Singapore, especially for lunch. At a dim sum buffet wheel carts of dishes are moved from table to table and you simply point to what looks nice. Food is served in small portions, sometimes still in the steamer. Take only one item on your plate at a time, and stack the empty plates as you finish each one. Traditionally, you'd be charged by the plate, but sometimes you can find great all-you-can-eat buffets for a good price.

BEIJING CUISINE   Beijing-style food, its rich garlic and bean-paste flavoring betraying just a touch of chili, comes to us from the north of China and is the food of the emperors. Another difference is that you'll find mutton on a northern Chinese menu, but certainly not on any southern menu. The most famous Beijing-style dish is **Beijing duck** (also known as Peking duck). The crispy skin is pulled away and cut into pieces, which you then wrap in thin pancakes with spring onion and a touch of sweet plum sauce. The meat is served later in a dish that's equally scrumptious.

SHANGHAI CUISINE   Shanghai-style cuisine is similar to Beijing-style but tends to be more oily. Because of its proximity to the sea, Shanghai recipes also include more fish. The exotic **drunken prawns** and the popular **drunken chicken** are both from this regional style, as is the mysterious **bird's nest soup,** made from swift's nests.

SZECHUAN CUISINE   Szechuan-style cuisine, second only to Cantonese in the West, also relies on the rich flavors of garlic, sesame oil, and bean paste, but is heavier on the chiles than Shanghai cuisine—*much* heavier on the chiles. Sugar is also sometimes added to create tangy sauces. Some dishes can really pack a punch, but there are many Szechuan dishes that are not spicy. Popular are **chicken with dried chiles** and **hot-and-sour soup.** Another regional variation, **Hunan-style food,** is also renowned for its fiery spice, and can be distinguished from Szechuan-style by its darker sauces.

TEOCHEW CUISINE   Teochew-style cuisine uses fish as its main ingredient, and is also known for its light soups. Many dishes are steamed, and in fact **steamboat,** which is a popular poolside menu item in hotels, gets its origins from this style. For steamboat, boiling broth is brought to the table, and you dunk pieces of fish, meat, and vegetables into it, à la fondue. Other Teochew contributions to local cuisine are the **Teochew fish ball,** a springy ball made from pounded fish with salt and water served in a noodle soup, and the traditional Singaporean breakfast dish **congee** (or moi), which is rice porridge served with fried fish, salted vegetables, and sometimes boiled egg. Also, if you see **braised goose** on the menu, you're definitely in a Teochew restaurant.

HOKKIEN CUISINE   Although the Hokkiens are the most prevalent dialect group in Singapore, their style of cuisine rarely makes it to restaurant tables, basically because it's simple and homely. Two dishes that have made it as local cuisine favorites are the **oyster omelette,** flavored with garlic and soy, and **Hokkien mee,** which is thick wheat noodles with seafood, meat, and vegetables in a heavy sauce.

HAKKA CUISINE   If Hokkien food is simple and homely, Hakka food is the homeliest of the homely. Flavored with glutinous rice wine, many dishes feature tofu and minced seafood and meats. Hakkas are also known for not wasting an animal body part—not exactly a hallmark of haute cuisine. Good dishes to try are **salt-baked chicken** and **minced seafood** wrapped in a fried tofu cake.

NOTES ON THE CHINESE PALATE

A very touchy topic for many Westerners: Chinese cuisine employs many a strange ingredient that sometimes makes the unaccustomed stomach queasy. A saying from way back in my family goes, "The Chinese will eat anything that doesn't eat them first," and it's almost true. Turtle, sea urchin, and sea cucumber are all popular Singaporean dishes, though their meats are unpleasantly mushy to those accustomed to more Western tastes. Many Singaporeans devour these creatures for their taste and some for their health-giving and restorative powers. In fact, some Chinese restaurants are creating dishes using unusual ingredients, which they claim balance the body's energy (its yin and yang) to promote health, beauty, and longevity. Indeed, frog's glands are pretty tasty in scrambled eggs, and the next day your skin will glow like never before!

On the more appealing side are other Chinese-inspired local favorites like carrot cake (white radishes that are steamed and pounded until soft, then fried in egg, garlic, and chile), Hokkien bak ku teh (boiled pork ribs in a seasoned soup), Teochew kway teow (stir-fried rice noodles with egg, prawns, and fish), and the number one favorite for foreigners, Hainanese chicken rice (boiled sliced chicken breast served over rice cooked in chicken stock).

New Asia cuisine has been hitting the market hard as globalization takes control of Singaporean palates. Also called "fusion food," this cuisine combines Eastern and Western ingredients and cooking styles for a whole new eating experience. Some of it works, some of it doesn't, but true gourmet connoisseurs consider it all a culinary atrocity.

MALAY CUISINE

Malay cuisine combines Indonesian and Thai flavors, blending ginger, turmeric, chiles, lemongrass, and dried shrimp paste to make unique curries. Heavy on coconut milk and peanuts, Malay food can at times be on the sweet side. The most popular Malay curries are **rendang,** a dry, dark, and heavy coconut-based curry served over meat; **sambal,** a red and spicy chile sauce; and **sambal belacan,** a condiment of fresh chiles, dried shrimp paste, and lime juice.

The ultimate Malay dish in Singapore is **satay,** sweet barbecued meat kabobs dipped in chile peanut sauce. Another popular dish is **roti john,** minced mutton and onion in French bread that's dipped in egg and fried. **Nasi lemak**—coconut rice surrounded by an assortment of fried anchovies, peanuts, prawns, egg, and sambal—is primarily a breakfast dish, but can be eaten anytime.

PERANAKAN CUISINE

Peranakan cuisine came out of the Straits-born Chinese community and combines such mainland Chinese ingredients as noodles and oyster sauces with local Malay flavors of coconut milk and peanuts. **Laksa lemak** is a great example of the combination, mixing Chinese rice flour noodles into a soup of Malay-style spicy coconut cream with chunks of seafood and tofu. And **otak otak** is all the rage. It's toasted mashed fish with coconut milk and chile, wrapped in a banana leaf and grilled over flames.

INDIAN CUISINE

SOUTHERN INDIAN CUISINE   Southern Indian food is a superhot blend of spices in a coconut milk base. Rice is the staple, along with thin breads such as prata and dosai, which are good for curling into shovels to scoop up drippy curries. Vegetarian dishes are abundant, a result of Hindu-mandated vegetarianism, and use lots of chickpeas and lentils in curry and chili gravies. **Vindaloo,** meat or poultry in a tangy and spicy sauce, is also well known.

Banana leaf restaurants, surely the most interesting way to experience southern Indian food in Singapore, serve up meals on banana leaves cut like place mats. It's very informal. Spoons and forks are provided, but if you want to act local and use your hands, remember to use your right hand only (see "Singapore's People, Etiquette & Customs" in chapter 2), and don't forget to wash up before and after at the tap.

One tip for eating very spicy foods is to mix a larger proportion of rice to gravy. Don't drink in between bites, but eat through the burn. Your brow may sweat but your mouth will build a tolerance as you eat, and the flavors will come through more fully.

NORTHERN INDIAN CUISINE   Northern Indian food combines yogurts and creams with a milder, more delicate blend of herbs and chiles than is found in its southern neighbor. It's served most often with breads like fluffy nans and flat chapatis. Marinated meats like chicken or fish, cooked in the tandoor clay oven, are always the highlight of a northern Indian meal.

Northern Indian restaurants are more upmarket and expensive than the southern ones, but while they offer more of the comforts associated with dining out, the southern banana leaf experience is more of an adventure.

Some Singaporean variations on Indian cuisine are **mee goreng,** fried noodles with chile and curry gravy, and **fish head curry,** a giant fish head simmered in a broth of coconut curry, chiles, and fragrant seasonings.

Muslim influences on Indian food have produced the **murtabak,** a fried prata filled with minced meat, onion, and egg. Between the Muslims' dietary laws (halal) forbidding pork and the Hindus' regard for the sacred cow, Indian food is the one cuisine that can be eaten by every kind of Singaporean.

SEAFOOD

One cannot describe Singaporean food without mentioning the abundance of fresh seafood. But most important is the uniquely Singaporean **chile crab,** chopped and smothered in a thick tangy chile sauce. Restaurants hold competitions to judge who has the best, and everyone has his favorite—one local sent me all the way out to Pong-gol, on the north coast, to find his pick of "The Best Chile Crab." **Pepper crabs** and **black pepper crayfish** are also a thrill. Instead of chile sauce, these shellfish are served in a thick black-pepper-and-soy sauce.

FRUITS

A walk through a wet market at any time of year will show you just what wonders the tropics can produce. Varieties of banana, fresh coconut, papaya, mango, and pineapple are just a few of the fresh and juicy fruits available year-round; in addition, Southeast Asia has an amazing selection of exotic and almost unimaginable fruits. From the light and juicy **star fruit** to the red and hairy **rambutan,** they are all worthy of a try, either whole or juiced.

Dare it if you will, the fruit to sample—the veritable king of fruits—is the **durian,** a large, green, spiky fruit that, when cut open, smells worse than old tennis shoes. The "best" ones are in season every June, when Singaporeans go wild over them. In case you're curious, the fruit has a creamy texture and tastes lightly sweet and deeply musky.

One interesting note on fruits: The Chinese believe that foods contain either yin or yang qualities with corresponding "heaty" and "cooling" effects. Fried foods and hot soups are heaty and therefore should be kept to a minimum in the tropics, and the same is true for some fruits. Whereas watermelon, star fruit, and oranges are cooling, mangoes, litchi, and especially durians are heaty. Taking too many heaty foods is believed to result in a sore throat, for which the best remedy is Chinese tea.

2 Tips on Dining

Of course, in any foreign land, the exotic cuisine isn't the only thing that keeps you guessing. Lucky for you, the following tips will make dining no problem.

HOURS   Most restaurants are open for lunch as early as 11am, but close around 2:30 or 3pm to give them a chance to set up for dinner, which begins around 6pm. Where closing times are listed, that is the time when the last order is taken.

TIPPING   Don't tip. Restaurants always add a gratuity to the bill, and to give extra cash can be embarrassing for the wait staff.

RESERVATIONS   Some restaurants, especially the more fashionable or upscale ones, may require that reservations be made up to a couple days in advance. Reservations are always recommended for Saturday and Sunday lunch and dinner, as eating is a favorite national pastime and a lot of families take meals out for weekend quality time.

ATTIRE   Because Singapore is so hot, "dress casual" (meaning a shirt and slacks for men and a dress or skirt/slacks and top for women) is always a safe bet in moderate to

Urban Singapore Dining

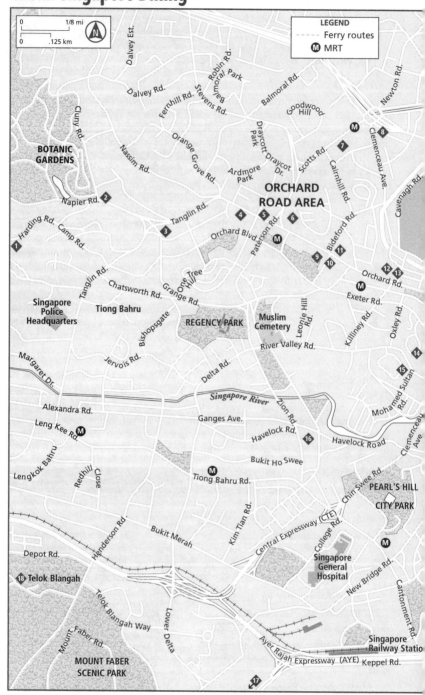

LEGEND
- - - - Ferry routes
Ⓜ MRT

BOTANIC GARDENS

ORCHARD ROAD AREA

Singapore Police Headquarters

Tiong Bahru

REGENCY PARK

Muslim Cemetery

PEARL'S HILL CITY PARK

Singapore General Hospital

MOUNT FABER SCENIC PARK

Telok Blangah

Singapore Railway Station

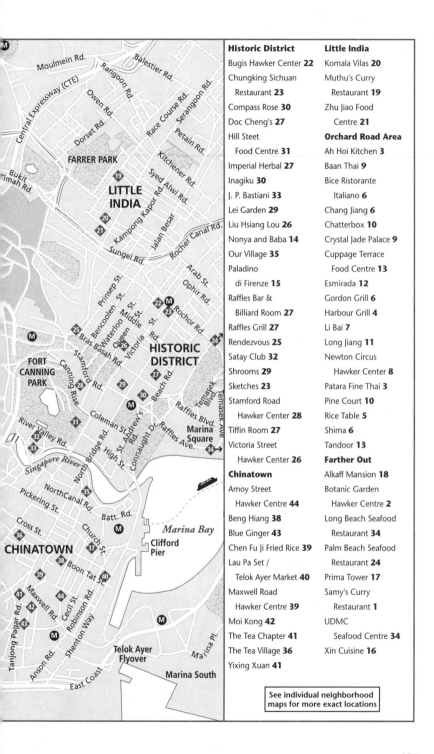

Historic District
Bugis Hawker Center **22**
Chungking Sichuan
  Restaurant **23**
Compass Rose **30**
Doc Cheng's **27**
Hill Steet
  Food Centre **31**
Imperial Herbal **27**
Inagiku **30**
J. P. Bastiani **33**
Lei Garden **29**
Liu Hsiang Lou **26**
Nonya and Baba **14**
Our Village **35**
Paladino
  di Firenze **15**
Raffles Bar &
  Billiard Room **27**
Raffles Grill **27**
Rendezvous **25**
Satay Club **32**
Shrooms **29**
Sketches **23**
Stamford Road
  Hawker Center **28**
Tiffin Room **27**
Victoria Street
  Hawker Center **26**
Chinatown
Amoy Street
  Hawker Centre **44**
Beng Hiang **38**
Blue Ginger **43**
Chen Fu Ji Fried Rice **39**
Lau Pa Set /
  Telok Ayer Market **40**
Maxwell Road
  Hawker Centre **39**
Moi Kong **42**
The Tea Chapter **41**
The Tea Village **36**
Yixing Xuan **41**

Little India
Komala Vilas **20**
Muthu's Curry
  Restaurant **19**
Zhu Jiao Food
  Centre **21**
Orchard Road Area
Ah Hoi Kitchen **3**
Baan Thai **9**
Bice Ristorante
  Italiano **6**
Chang Jiang **6**
Chatterbox **10**
Crystal Jade Palace **9**
Cuppage Terrace
  Food Centre **13**
Esmirada **12**
Gordon Grill **6**
Harbour Grill **4**
Li Bai **7**
Long Jiang **11**
Newton Circus
  Hawker Center **8**
Patara Fine Thai **3**
Pine Court **10**
Rice Table **5**
Shima **6**
Tandoor **13**
Farther Out
Alkaff Mansion **18**
Botanic Garden
  Hawker Centre **2**
Long Beach Seafood
  Restaurant **34**
Palm Beach Seafood
  Restaurant **24**
Prima Tower **17**
Samy's Curry
  Restaurant **1**
UDMC
  Seafood Centre **34**
Xin Cuisine **16**

See individual neighborhood
maps for more exact locations

101

expensive restaurants. For the very expensive restaurants, formal is required. For the cheap places, come as you are, as long as you're decent.

ORDERING WINE WITH DINNER   Singaporeans have become more wine savvy in recent years, and have begun importing estate-bottled wines from California, Australia, New Zealand, France, and Germany. However, these bottles are heavily taxed. A bottle of wine with dinner starts at around S$50 and a single glass runs between S$10 and S$25 (US$6 and US$15), depending on the wine and the restaurant. Chinese restaurants usually don't charge corkage fees for bringing your own.

ORGANIZATION OF RESTAURANT LISTINGS   I've organized the restaurants in this chapter in a few different ways. First, I've grouped them in a simple list by style of cuisine, so if you decide you want a nice Peranakan dinner, for instance, you can scope out your choices all together before referring to the individual restaurant reviews. Second, I've arranged the reviews into four basic neighborhoods: the Historic District, Chinatown, Little India, and the Orchard Road area. Within these divisions, I've arranged them by price. Keep in mind that the divisions by neighborhood are almost as arbitrary as they were when Stamford Raffles created them in 1822. Everything in the city is relatively close and easily accessible, so don't think you should plan your meals by the neighborhood your hotel sits in when a short taxi ride will take you where you really want to go.

I've selected the restaurants listed here because they have some of the best food and most memorable atmospheres, but there are hundreds of other restaurants serving any kind of food in a variety of price ranges. Many magazines on dining in Singapore are available at newsstands and can help you find other favorite restaurants. A good place to start is with *Wine & Dine*, available just about anywhere. (And if you find any restaurants that are really super, drop a line or an e-mail to let me know about 'em—the addresses are on page ix.)

LUNCH COSTS   Lunch at a hawker center can be as cheap as S$3.50 (US$2.10), truly a bargain. Many places have set-price buffet lunches, but these can be as high as S$45 (US$26.95). Indian restaurants are great deals for inexpensive buffet lunches, which can be found as reasonably as S$10 (US$6) per person for all you can eat.

DINNER COSTS   In this chapter, prices for Western restaurants list the range for standard entrees and prices for Asian restaurants list the range for small dishes intended for two. As a guideline, here are the relative costs for dinner in each category of restaurant, without wine, beer, cocktails, or coffee, and ordered either à la carte or from a set-price menu:

- **Very Expensive:** At a very expensive restaurant, you can expect to pay as much as S$145 (US$86.85) per person. The more expensive cuisines are Continental and Japanese, but a full-course Cantonese dinner, especially if you throw in shark's fin, can be up to S$125 to S$150 (US$74.85 to US$89.80) per person.
- **Expensive:** At an expensive restaurant, expect dinner to run between S$50 and S$80 (US$29.95 and US$47.90) per person.
- **Moderate:** At a moderate restaurant, dinner for one can be as low as S$25 (US$14.95) and as high as S$50 (US$29.95).
- **Inexpensive:** Some inexpensive dinners can be under S$5 (US$3) at hawker stalls, and up to around S$15 (US$9) for one if you eat at local restaurants. Fortunately, Singapore is not only a haven for cultural gastric diversity, but it's also possible to eat exotic foods here to your heart's content, all while maintaining a shoestring budget.

Best Bets for Breakfast

The local Singaporean breakfast, available all over the island, rarely appeals to Westerners. **Congee,** a soupy rice porridge, comes with salted egg, dried anchovies, and other assorted foreign objects that make my stomach cringe at 7 in the morning (before my coffee kicks in). Still, you can pick up some in any hawker center for about S$2 (US$1.20), or pay a lot more in hotel coffee shops (read: They're overpriced).

When you're looking for a good breakfast nosh, you have to be careful in general of your hotel's coffee shop. Most hotels offer a standard buffet breakfast, and many are incredibly impressive, with an enormous selection of fruits, cereals, baked goods, eggs, meats, and dairy items. But most cost between S$15 and S$25 (US$9 and US$15), quite an expense for a meal that's usually "eat and run." There are many other alternatives, however. I recommend asking your concierge for the nearest cafe/coffee shop. Starbucks, The Coffee Bean & Tea Leaf, Spinelli, Seattle Coffee Company, Java Coast, and Dunkin' Donuts all have outlets in all corners of the city. A cup of coffee and scone will come to just over S$5 (US$3). (*Also note:* Many hotels provide an electric kettle with instant coffee and tea bags standard in every room.)

If the breakfast buffet does appeal to you, try the **Marriott Café** in the Singapore Marriott Hotel, where you can eat all you like for S$15 (US$9); it's one of the less expensive but better quality breakfast buffets around. Raffles Hotel's **Ah Teng's Bakery** (daily 7am to 11pm) has a nice set-price breakfast for only S$6 (US$3.60), and is great if you're staying in the historic district area. For something special, every Sunday and on Public Holidays, the **Garden Seafood Restaurant** at Goodwood Park Hotel serves a massive and excellent selection of Hong Kong–style dim sum for only S$12.80 (US$7.65) per person (8 to 10:30am).

3 Best Bets

- **Best View:** Perched atop the Westin Stamford, the **Compass Rose** (page 106) offers views of Singapore, Malaysia, and Indonesia that are as glorious as the food.
- **Most Romantic:** Take a lesson from the Italians. **Paladino di Firenze** (page 108) is intimate and charming and the food is very sensual.
- **The Most Delectable Chinese Food You've Ever Eaten: Li Bai** (page 116) has an ever-changing menu of traditional recipes and new creations that will melt in your mouth.
- **Tastiest Scorpion:** At **Imperial Herbal** (page 109) it's the macho dish to order, and after the house physician gives you a checkup, he'll have the kitchen add specific herbs to your dish that will cure your ailments.
- **Best Aquarium Display:** No respectable Chinese restaurant is without the obligatory live seafood display in full view of the clientele. My favorite is the Wall-o'-Aquariums at **Long Beach Seafood Restaurant** (page 120).
- **Best Wait Staff:** The folks at **Esmirada** (page 116) are under strict house orders to have as much fun as the patrons. Breaking bread hasn't been this joyous in a long time.
- **Best Wine List:** The wine steward at **Raffles Grill** (page 106) will suggest the perfect wine for each course.

- **Best Chile-and-Pepper Crabs:** Every Singaporean has an opinion about where the best chile-and-pepper crabs are. At **UDMC** (page 121) there are eight restaurants to choose from, each one excellent and inexpensive. You're bound to find a good one here.
- **Best Performance by a Leading Man with a Ginsu Knife:** Gather round the grill at **Shima** (page 117) for some good traditional Japanese showmanship.
- **Best Vegetarian Feast:** Lucky for vegetarians, Hindus don't eat meat, and since there are lots of Hindus in Singapore, there's also lots of vegetarian restaurants. **Komala Vilas** (page 113) has the best Indian vegetarian dishes, and you can confirm this with any local. Order the dosai.
- **Hottest Indian Food You'll Ever Eat:** The sweat will drip from your brow, your nose will run, and your eyes will tear when you eat at **Samy's Curry Restaurant** (page 121). You have my promise.
- **Best Local Tradition:** Everybody loves satay, and in Singapore they've devoted a whole club—the **Satay Club** (page 123)—to the little Malay shish kebabs. It's touristy, but still, it's a tradition.
- **Best Place to Experiment with Local Cuisine:** Of course the hawker centers are the best place, but if you prefer a more modern atmosphere, try **Chatterbox** (page 119). The staff is very helpful, and the selection is very complete. It may not be exactly authentic, but it's pretty close.
- **Best Caesar Salad:** At the **Harbour Grill** (page 116), it's better than making your own. The ingredients are brought out on a cart, and you direct the chef for your own blend of dressing.

4 Restaurants by Cuisine

CHINESE
Chinese Mixed Cuisines
Chungking Szechuan Restaurant (Parco Bugis Junction, Historic District, *M*)
Pine Court (Mandarin Hotel, Orchard Road, *M*)

Beijing
Prima Tower Revolving (Keppel Road, Shenton Way Business District, see section 9, *M*)

Cantonese
Crystal Jade Palace (Takashimaya Shopping Centre, Orchard Road, *M*)
Lei Garden (CHIJMES, Historic District, *E*)
Li Bai (Sheraton Towers, near Newton MRT, Orchard Road, *E*)
Xin Cuisine (also serves Herbal cuisine; Concorde Hotel, Outram Road, see section 9, *M*)

Hakka
Moi Kong (Murray Street, Chinatown, *I*)

Herbal
Imperial Herbal (Metropole Hotel, near Raffles Hotel, Historic District, *M*)
Xin Cuisine (also Cantonese; Concorde Hotel, Outram Road, see section 9, *M*)

Hokkien
Beng Hiang (Amoy Street, Chinatown, *I*)

New Asia
Doc Cheng's (Raffles Hotel Arcade, Historic District, *M*)

Shanghainese
Chang Jiang (Goodwood Park Hotel, off Orchard Road, *E*)

Key to Abbreviations: *VE* = Very Expensive   *E* = Expensive   *M* = Moderate   *I* = Inexpensive

Szechuan/Hunan

House of Mao (China Square Food Centre, Chinatown, *M*)

Liu Hsiang Lou (Allson Hotel, Historic District, near Bugis Junction, *M*)

Long Jiang (Crown Prince Hotel, Orchard Road, *M*)

CONTINENTAL

Compass Rose (The Westin Stamford, Historic District, *E*)

Gordon Grill (Goodwood Park Hotel, off Orchard Road, *E*)

Harbour Grill (Hilton International Singapore, Orchard Road, *E*)

FRENCH

L'Aigle d'Or (Duxton Hotel, Chinatown, *VE*)

Raffles Grill (Raffles Hotel, Historic District, *VE*)

FUSION

Doc Cheng's (Raffles Hotel, Historic District, *M*)

Shrooms (CHIJMES, Historic District, *M*)

INDIAN (NORTHERN)

Our Village (Boat Quay, Historic District, *I*)

Tandoor (Holiday Inn Parkview, off Orchard Road, *M*)

INDIAN (SOUTHERN)

Komala Vilas (Serangoon Road, Little India, *I*)

Muthu's Curry Restaurant (Race Course Road, Little India, *I*)

Samy's Curry Restaurant (Dempsey Road, western Singapore, see section 9, *M*)

Tiffin Room (Raffles Hotel, Historic District, *E*)

ITALIAN

Bice Ristorante Italiano (Goodwood Park Hotel, off Orchard Road, *E*)

Paladino di Firenze (Mohamed Sultan Road, Historic District, *E*)

Sketches (Parco Bugis Junction, Historic District, *I*)

JAPANESE

Inagiku (The Westin Plaza, Historic District, *VE*)

Shima (Goodwood Park Hotel, off Orchard Road, *E*)

MALAY/INDONESIAN

Alkaff Mansion (Telok Blangah Hill Park, near Mount Faber, see section 9, *E*)

Rendezvous (Rendezvous Hotel, Historic District, *I*)

Satay Club (Clarke Quay Festival Village, Hawker Center, Historic District, *I*)

The Rice Table (Orchard Road, *I*)

MEDITERRANEAN

Esmirada (Orchard Road at Peranakan Place, *E*)

J.P. Bastiani (Clarke Quay, Historic District, *E*)

PERANAKAN

Blue Ginger (Tanjong Pagar Road, Tanjong Pagar/Chinatown, *I*)

Nonya and Baba (River Valley Road, Historic District, *I*)

SEAFOOD

Long Beach Seafood Restaurant (East Coast Parkway, see section 9, *M*)

Palm Beach Seafood Restaurant (Stadium Walk, Kallang Park, see section 9, *M*)

UDMC Seafood Centre (East Coast Parkway, *I*)

SINGAPOREAN

Ah Hoi's Kitchen (Trader's Hotel, off Orchard Road, *M*)

Chatterbox (Mandarin Hotel, Orchard Road, *I*)

Chen Fu Ji Fried Rice (Chinatown, *I*)

THAI

Baan Thai (Ngee Ann City, Orchard Road, *M*)

Patara Fine Thai (Tanglin Mall, off Orchard Road, *M*)

5 The Historic District

VERY EXPENSIVE

Inagiku. The Westin Plaza Level 3, 2 Stamford Rd. ☎ **65/431-6156.** Reservations recommended. Set lunch S$30–S$50 (US$17.95–US$29.95); set dinner S$60–S$180 (US$35.95–US$107.80). AE, DC, JCB, MC, V. Daily noon–2:30pm and 6:30–10:30pm. JAPANESE.

At Inagiku, you'll have excellent Japanese food that gets top marks for ingredients, preparation, and presentation. In delicately lighted and subtle decor, you can enjoy house favorites like sashimi, tempura, and teppanyaki—with separate dining areas for tempura and a sushi bar. The tokusen sashimi morikimi is masterful in its presentation: An assortment of raw fish—including salmon, prawns, and clams—is laid out in an ice-filled shell inside of which nestles the skeleton of a whole fish. It's odd and delightful at the same time. I recommend the tempura moriawase, a combination of seafood and vegetables that's very lightly deep fried. Also highly recommended are the teppanyaki prawns. In addition to sake, there is also have a good selection of wines.

✪ **Raffles Grill.** Raffles Hotel, 1 Beach Rd. ☎ **65/331-1611.** Reservations recommended. Entrees S$42–S$52 (US$25.15–US$31.15); set dinner S$120 and S$130 (US$71.85 and US$77.85) per person. AE, DC, MC, V. Mon–Fri noon–2:30pm and 7–10pm; Sat–Sun 7–10pm. FRENCH.

Dining in the grande dame of Singapore achieves a level of sophistication unmatched by any other five-star restaurant. The architectural charm and historic significance of the old hotel will transform dinner into a cultural event, but don't just come here for the ambience; the food is outstanding as well. Three set dinners allow you to select from the à la carte menu dishes like roasted veal tenderloin or roasted rack of suckling pig, the latter a highly recommended choice for its juicy meat under crispy mouth-watering skin. The 400-label wine list (going back to 1890 vintages) could be a history lesson, and if you'd like you can request the cellar master to select a wine to match each course. The fabulously attentive service from the wait staff will make you feel like you own the place. Formal dress is required.

EXPENSIVE

✪ **Compass Rose.** The Westin Stamford, 2 Stamford Rd., Level 70. ☎ **65/338-8585.** Reservations recommended. Buffet lunch Mon–Sat S$36 (US$21.55), Sun and public holidays S$41.90 (US$25.10); dinner entrees S$40.50–S$45 (US$24.25–US$26.95). AE, DC, JCB, MC, V. Daily noon–2:30pm and 6:30–10:30pm. CONTINENTAL.

What a view! From the top of the Westin Stamford, the tallest hotel in the world, you can see out past the marina to Malaysia and Indonesia—and the restaurant's three-tier design means every table has a view. It's decorated with contemporary-styled Roman arches, pediments, and columns; and when the sun sets, the whole place turns the many colors of the sky. Lunch is an extensive display of seafood served in a host of international recipes, with chefs searing scallops to order. Don't even talk about the dessert buffet—it's so tantalizing you'll think the altitude has gotten to your head. Dinner is à la carte, with dishes inspired by lighter tastes and low-fat recipes. Try the peppered lobster tail and sea scallops with hot garlic sauce. The Dutch veal tenderloin and grilled goose liver is served with a pumpkin rosette, carrot, and tarragon cream sauce. For dessert, order the sample plate.

J.P. Bastiani. 3A River Valley Rd., Clarke Quay Merchant's Court #01-12. ☎ **65/433-0156.** Reservations recommended for lunch, necessary for dinner. Entrees S$29–S$42 (US$17.35–US$25.15). AE, DC, MC, V. Mon–Fri 11:30am–2:30pm and 6:30–10:30pm; Sat–Sun 6:30–11pm. MEDITERRANEAN.

Historic District Dining

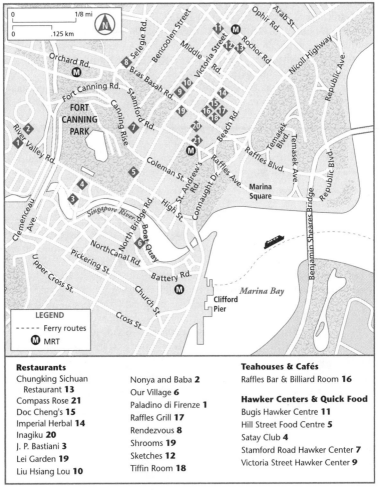

Restaurants

Chungking Sichuan
  Restaurant **13**
Compass Rose **21**
Doc Cheng's **15**
Imperial Herbal **14**
Inagiku **20**
J. P. Bastiani **3**
Lei Garden **19**
Liu Hsiang Lou **10**

Nonya and Baba **2**
Our Village **6**
Paladino di Firenze **1**
Raffles Grill **17**
Rendezvous **8**
Shrooms **19**
Sketches **12**
Tiffin Room **18**

Teahouses & Cafés

Raffles Bar & Billiard Room **16**

Hawker Centers & Quick Food

Bugis Hawker Centre **11**
Hill Street Food Centre **5**
Satay Club **4**
Stamford Road Hawker Center **7**
Victoria Street Hawker Center **9**

The real-life J. P. Bastiani owned a pineapple cannery at Clarke Quay; today, he lends his name to this cozy Mediterranean place, with its walled courtyard patio in the back for cocktails, a wine cellar with a huge international collection on the first floor, and a gorgeous dining room upstairs that's just dripping with romance. Their seafood dishes are the best, with a choice of a delicious coriander-crusted salmon with ginger and onion confit, or the pan-roasted sea bass, which is stuffed with leeks and potato. You can also try one of their excellent meat entrees such as rack of lamb or filet mignon. The dishes are rich and servings are quite large, so make a mental note in advance to save room for their fantastic tiramisu.

✪ **Lei Garden.** 30 Victoria St., CHIJMES #01-24. ☎ **65/339-3822.** Reservations required. Small dishes S$18–S$58 (US$10.80–US$34.75). AE, DC, JCB, MC, V. Daily 11:30am–2:30pm and 6–10:30pm. CANTONESE.

Lei Garden, with three locations in Singapore, six in Hong Kong and Kowloon, and two in Guangzhou, lives up to a great reputation for the highest quality Cantonese cuisine in one of the most elegant settings. Actually, of the three local branches, this one is special for the unique ambience of CHIJMES just outside its towering picture windows. Highly recommended dishes are the "Buddha jumps over the wall," a very popular Chinese soup made from abalone, fish maw (stomach), shark's fin, and Chinese ham. It's generally served only on special occasions. To make the beggar's chicken, they take a whole stuffed chicken and wrap and bake it in a lotus leaf covered in yam, which makes the chicken moist with a delicate flavor you'll never forget. For either of these dishes, you must place your order at least 24 hours in advance when you make your dinner reservation. Also try the barbecued Peking duck, which is exquisite. A small selection of French and Chinese wines is available.

✪ **Paladino di Firenze.** 7 Mohamed Sultan Rd. (off River Valley Rd.). ☎ **65/738-0917.** Reservations required for dinner. Entrees S$38–S$48 (US$22.75–US$28.75). AE, DC, JCB, MC, V. Daily noon–2:30pm and 7–10:30pm. NORTHERN ITALIAN.

This has to be one of the most romantic and cozy restaurants in Singapore. There's not a lot of space in its old restored shophouse setting, but they don't overcrowd the tables, separating little areas with plantings and crazy little metal trees. Whitewashed exposed-brick walls and oriental carpets on the floor create a homey feeling, while copper- and gold-colored tablecloths add shimmer in the candlelight. The northern Italian cuisine here is excellent. The Crespelle alla Paladino are Tuscan-inspired home-made crepes filled with beef, fresh mushrooms, and Parmesan; but the osso bucco, braised veal shanks, is the most highly recommended dish here. There is a large selection of wines to choose from. Make your reservations early because this place is small and very popular. After dinner, stroll the trendy clubs along Mohamed Sultan Road.

Tiffin Room. Raffles Hotel, 1 Beach Rd. ☎ **65/337-1886.** Reservations recommended. All meals served buffet style. Breakfast S$30 (US$17.95); lunch S$35 (US$20.95); high tea S$26.50 (US$15.85); dinner S$45 (US$26.95). AE, DC, JCB, MC, V. Daily 7:30–10am, noon–2pm, 3:30pm–5pm (high tea), and 7–10pm. SOUTHERN INDIAN/TIFFIN CURRY.

Tiffin curry came from India and is named after the three-tiered containers that Indian workers would use to carry their lunch. The tiffin box idea was stolen by the British colonists, who changed around the recipes a bit so they weren't as spicy. The cuisine that evolved is pretty much what you'll find served at Raffles's Tiffin Room, where a buffet spread lets you select from a variety of curries, chutneys, rice, and Indian breads. The restaurant is just inside the lobby entrance of Raffles Hotel and carries the trademark Raffles elegance throughout its decor.

MODERATE

Chungking Szechuan Restaurant. 200 Victoria St., #02-53/54 Parco Bugis Junction. ☎ **65/337-9915.** Reservations recommended. Small dishes S$8–S$48 (US$4.80–US$28.75). AE, DC, JCB, MC, V. Mon–Fri 11:15am–2:30pm and 6:15–10:30pm. SZECHUAN/CANTONESE.

In a large, well-lit space, Chunking doesn't have a hint of Chinese kitsch typical to other restaurants of this category, but rather chooses a more contemporary understated decor. Located on the second floor of Parco Bugis Junction shopping mall, its large windows open up the room and provide views of the streets below, which are flanked with shophouses. The menu features dishes that blend two styles: Cantonese and spicy Szechuan. The Szechuan smoked duck is a favorite, either a half or full bird, smoked with Chinese tea leaves and herbs in a sweet black sauce. For a lighter dish, try the steamed fillet of codfish deep fried in a soybean crust topped with a light soy sauce.

Deep-fried live prawns with special peppercorn Szechuan sauce leave a tingle in the mouth, but never fear, the staff is very flexible about spice. Chungking also serves the standard dim sum lunch. The owner is a wine connoisseur, and has stocked some lovely wines, but they'll never charge corkage if you bring your own.

✪ Doc Cheng's. Raffles Hotel Arcade #02-20, Level 2. ☎ **65/331-1761.** Reservations recommended. Entrees S$21.50–S$31.50 (US$12.85–US$18.85). AE, DC, MC, V. Mon–Fri noon–2pm and 7–10pm; Sat–Sun 7–10pm. FUSION.

Doc Cheng's calls itself "The Restaurant for Restorative Foods," but you won't find any ancient Chinese secrets here. Doc Cheng, the hero of the joint, was part man and part mythological colonial figure. Educated in Western medicine in England, he was a sought-after physician who became a local celebrity and notorious drunk. His concept of restorative foods is therefore rather skewed, but the restaurant banks on the decadence of the attraction and serves up "transethnic" dishes smothered in tongue-in-cheek humor. Guest chefs make the menu ever changing—the latest and greatest, an unbelievably scrumptious tamarind charcoal beef short ribs dish on portobello mushrooms. Equally well prepared (though lighter) is the charcoal-fried shutome swordfish on risotto. The house wine is a Riesling (sweet wines are more popular with Singaporeans) from Raffles's own vineyard. Three separate dining areas allow you to dine under the verandah, on the patio, or in cozy booths inside.

✪ Imperial Herbal. Metropole Hotel, 3rd Floor, 41 Seah St. (near Raffles Hotel). ☎ **65/ 337-0491.** Reservations recommended for lunch, necessary for dinner. Small dishes S$14–S$24 (US$8.40–US$14.35). AE, DC, JCB, MC, V. Daily 11:30am–2:30pm and 6:30–10:30pm. HERBAL.

People come again and again for the healing powers of the food served here, enriched with herbs and other secret ingredients prescribed by a resident Chinese herbalist. Upon entering, go to the right, where you'll find the herb counter. The herbalist, who is also trained in Western medicine, will ask for the symptoms of what ails you and take your pulse. While you sit and order, he'll prepare a packet of ingredients and ship them off to the kitchen, where they'll be added to the food in preparation. Surprisingly, dishes turn out tasty, without the anticipated medicinal aftertaste. If all this isn't wild enough for you, order the scorpion.

The herbalist is in-house every day but Sunday. It's always good to call ahead, though, as he's the main attraction. When you leave, present him with a small *ang pau*—a gift of cash in a red envelope—maybe S$5 or S$7 (US$3 or US$4.20). Red envelopes are available in any card or gift shop.

Liu Hsiang Lou. Allson Hotel, 101 Victoria St. ☎ **65/336-0811.** Reservations recommended but not necessary. Small dishes S$12–S$44 (US$7.20–US$26.35). AE, DC, JCB, MC, V. Daily 11:30am–2:30pm and 6:30–10:30pm. SZECHUAN.

As you enter there's a veritable zoo of tanks filled with lobsters, long-neck clams, and frogs—you can buddy up to your dinner while you wait for your table. In addition to seafood, Liu Hsiang Lou also specializes in amazingly tender venison, which can be prepared sautéed with black pepper, dried red chile, garlic, or chives. Camphor- and tea-smoked duck is a fragrant and delicious Szechuan specialty, and it is prepared marinated in authentic style and bring it out in thin slices for you to wrap in pancakes with plum sauce. Soon hock is fish steamed with a tasty mix of tofu, mushrooms, vegetables, and chile. The most popular dishes are the sautéed diced chicken with dried red chile and the sour and spicy soup with shredded meat and fish maw (stomach). In addition, they have lunch hour dim sum. Carved rosewood chairs and landscape paintings make for a warm atmosphere.

Shrooms. CHIJMES, 30 Victoria St. ☎ **65/336-2268.** Reservations recommended. Entrees S$31–S$36.50 (US$18.55–US$21.85). AE, DC, JCB, MC, V. Daily 11:30am–2:30pm and 6:30–10:30pm. FUSION.

In one of the most exquisite locations in the city—atop the CHIJMES complex—Shrooms occupies a glorious hall in elegant sparse-contempo style; however, the atmosphere is wonderfully casual. With a mixture of Indian, Chinese, and Western selections, there'll be something for everyone on this menu; but I highly recommend the tandoori selections (both breads and meats), which are just are perfect. Shrooms also operates a cafe downstairs, with lighter choices (the tandoori sandwich is weird and amazing at the same time). After dinner, the place turns into a nightclub, so stick around.

INEXPENSIVE

Bukhara. 3C River Valley Rd., #01-44 Clarke Quay. ☎ **65/338-1411.** Reservations recommended. Buffet lunch S$13.60 (US$8.15), buffet dinner S$19.90 (US$11.90). AE, DC, JCB, MC, V. Daily noon–2:30pm and 6:30–10:30pm. NORTHERN INDIAN.

I like to recommend Bukhara for the buffet, which is a great way to savor many treats without going over the top with the expense. Tandoori lamb kabobs, fish, prawns, chicken, and more will make meat lovers' eyes pop—the food just keeps coming. Plu, tandoori veggies like cauliflower and stuffed potatoes and peppers are quite good. The decor is a little bit India-kitsch, with carved stonelike accents and beat-up wooden chairs. The buffet includes breads and dal. You can also order from an à la carte menu of standard northern Indian fare. If you're in Clarke Quay, this is the best choice in this price range.

✪ **Nonya and Baba.** 262 River Valley Rd. (close to the Imperial Hotel). ☎ **65/734-1386.** Reservations recommended. Small dishes S$6–S$8 (US$3.60–US$4.80). AE, DC, JCB, MC, V. Daily 11am–2:30pm and 6–9:45pm. PERANAKAN.

Like a little Peranakan coffee shop, Nonya and Baba serves a menu of traditional standards from time-honored recipes. It's frequented by locals, many of whom come to eat Straits-Chinese comfort food like Mom used to make. The menu has about 16 dishes, with photos and very detailed descriptions of the preparations and ingredients of each, and the staff is willing and able to help you decide. Sambal udang, a dry sambal over prawns and tomatoes, seems to be a favorite for Westerners. The same goes for the satay ayam (chicken satay). Otak otak, a fish cake with chile and shrimp paste wrapped in banana leaf and grilled, makes a great snack. However, a most special dish is the Ayam Buah Keluak, whose preparation time includes 3 days to soak-crack the hard Indonesian nuts to get to the black paste inside, which is then mixed with shrimp and pork, restuffed, then fried. The ambience here is very local, with coffee shop–style marble-top tables and chairs à la Peranakan. The walls are decorated with framed kebayas (formal Nonya embroidered blouses), some batiks, and photos of the house specialties.

✪ **Our Village.** 46 Boat Quay (take elevator to 5th floor). ☎ **65/538-3058.** Reservations recommended on weekends. Entrees S$9–S$20 (US$5.40–US$12). AE, MC, V. Mon–Fri 11:30am–1:30pm and 6–10:30pm; Sat–Sun 6–10:30pm. NORTHERN INDIAN.

With its antique white walls stuccoed in delicate and exotic patterns and glistening with tiny silver mirrors, you'll feel like you're in an Indian fairyland here. Even the ceiling twinkles with silver stars, and hanging lanterns provide a subtle glow for the heavenly atmosphere—it's a perfect setting for a delicate dinner. Everything here is handmade from hand-selected imported ingredients, some of them coming from secret sources. In fact, the staff is so protective of its recipes, you'd almost think their secret ingredient was opium—and you'll be floating so high after tasting the food that it might as well be. There are vegetarian selections as well as meats (no beef or pork) prepared in luscious gravies or in the tandoor oven. The dishes are light and healthy, with all natural ingredients and not too much salt.

Rendezvous. #02-02 Hotel Rendezvous, 9 Bras Basah Rd. ☎ **65/339-7508.** Reservations not necessary. Meat dishes sold per piece S$3–S$5 (US$1.80–US$3). AE, DC, MC, V. Daily 11am–9pm. Closed on public holidays. INDO-MALAY.

I was sad when, after a few months away from Singapore, I couldn't find Rendezvous at its previous location in Raffles City Shopping Center, only to learn it had shifted to a nicer space at the new (coincidentally named?) Rendezvous Hotel. Line up to select from a large number of Malay dishes, cafeteria style, like sambal squid in a spicy sauce of chile and shrimp paste, and beef rendang, in a dark spicy curry gravy. The wait staff will bring your order to your table. The coffee shop setting is as far from glamorous as the last Rendezvous, but on the wall black-and-white photos trace the restaurant's history back to its opening in the early '50s. It's a great place to experiment with a new cuisine.

Sketches. 200 Victoria St., #01-85/86/87 Parco Bugis Junction. ☎ **65/339-8386.** S$10.50 (US$6.30) hungry; S$14.50 (US$8.70) starving. AE, DC, JCB, MC, V. Daily 11am–10pm. ITALIAN.

Pasta is always an easy and agreeable choice, and sometimes when you're traveling, familiar tastes can be welcome from time to time. Not only is this place fast, inexpensive, and good, it's also pretty unique. The concept is "Design-a-Pasta," where they give you a menu on which is a series of boxes you check off: one set for pasta type; one set for sauce type; another for add-ins like meats, mushrooms, and garlic; and boxes for chile, Parmesan, and pine nuts. The kitchen is in the center of the restaurant, with bar seating all around. This is the best place to be if you want to watch those cooks hustle through menu card after menu card—it's a great show. You can also sit at one of the tables in the restaurant or out on the patio inside the shopping mall, but then you'd miss the fun of eating here.

6 Chinatown

VERY EXPENSIVE

✪ **L'Aigle d'Or.** 83 Duxton Rd., Duxton Hotel. ☎ **65/227-7678.** Reservations recommended. Entrees S$75–S$96 (US$44.90–US$57.50); set lunch S$36 (US$21.60). AE, DC, MC, V. Daily noon–2pm and 7–10pm. FRENCH.

L'Aigle d'Or's reputation in Singapore is second to none, and after you dine here, you'll understand why. The French menu is perfection, the setting is classic, and the staff is extremely attentive and charming. Like many of the other European restaurants in Singapore, their menu changes regularly with the seasons, so you may find different dishes than on your last visit. This time around the menu featured a gorgeous veal rib, panfried and tender. For something different, try the panfried foie gras and rhubarb ravioli, a current house specialty and unbelievably tasty in a tangy raspberry sauce. As you would expect, the wine list is top of the line, the cheese selection is excellent, and the desserts are unmentionable. If you're looking for someplace truly special, you can't do better.

MODERATE

✪ **House of Mao.** 51 Telok Ayer St., #03-02 China Square Food Centre. ☎ **65/533-0660.** Reservations recommended. Entrees S$8–S$34. (US$4.80–$20.35). AE, DC, JCB, MC, V. Daily 11:30am–2:30pm and 6:30–10pm. HUNAN.

Only in Singapore will you find a Cultural Revolution theme restaurant. Start with the Gang of Four cocktail before ordering your Long March chicken—you think I'm kidding. Actually, for a campy place, the food is great: Hunan style, which means plenty of chile. The viceroy chicken was supposed to be real spicy, but I found it quite nice and tangy. Venison is also featured on the menu, as well as a nice assortment of vegetable and (very flavorful) tofu dishes. *Vegetarians beware:* All these dishes are prepared with some sort of shredded meats. I laughed out loud at the hilarious menu, the Red Guard staff uniforms, and the memorabilia. Maybe Mao really will live to be a thousand years old after all.

INEXPENSIVE

Beng Hiang. 112-116 Amoy St. ☎ **65/221-6695.** Reservations recommended on weekends. Small dishes S$8–S$20 (US$4.80–US$12). AE, MC, V. Daily 11:30am–2:30pm and 6–9:30pm. HOKKIEN.

This modest little place is perhaps the best way to find Hokkien food. Situated in a shophouse on Amoy Street in the heart of Hokkien Chinatown, you can have a taste of a cuisine rarely found in restaurants. The spiced sausage and fried prawn balls are served dry to be dipped in sweet black soy sauce. Fish maw thick soup is similar to a shark's fin soup, and has egg, mushrooms, crabmeat, carrots, and shredded bamboo. Hokkien-style noodles with pork and prawn is the most popular dish. Calligraphy and Chinese landscape paintings make the low-key decor pretty.

Blue Ginger. 97 Tanjong Pagar Rd. ☎ **65/222-3928.** Reservations required for lunch, recommended for dinner. Entrees S$6.50–S$22.80 (US$3.90–US$13.65). AE, MC, V. Daily 11:30am–2:30pm and 6–10pm. PERANAKAN.

The standard belief is that Malay and Peranakan cooking is reserved for home-cooked meals, and therefore restaurants are not as plentiful—and where they do exist, are very informal. Not so at Blue Ginger, where traditional and modern mix beautifully in a style so fitting for Singapore. Snuggled in a shophouse, the decor combines clean and neat lines of contemporary styling with paintings by local artists and touches of Peranakan flair like carved wooden screens. The cuisine is Peranakan from traditional recipes, making for some very authentic food—definitely something you can't get back home. A good appetizer is the ngo heong: fried rolls of pork and prawn that are deliciously flavored with spices but not at all hot. A wonderful entree is the ayam panggang "Blue Ginger," really tender grilled boneless thigh and drumstick with a mild coconut-milk sauce. One of the most popular dishes is the ayam buah keluak, a traditional chicken dish made with a hard black Indonesian nut with sweet meat inside. The favorite dessert here is durian chendol, red beans and pandan jelly in coconut milk with durian puree. Served with shaved ice on top, it smells strong.

Chen Fu Ji Fried Rice. 7 Erskine Rd. ☎ **65/323-0260.** Reservations not accepted. S$10–S$20 (US$6–US$12). No credit cards. Daily noon–2:30pm and 6–9:45pm. SINGAPOREAN CUISINE/FRIED RICE.

With bright green walls glaring under fluorescent lighting, the fast-food ambience is nothing to write home about, but once you try the fried rice here, you'll never be able to eat it anywhere else again, ever. These people take loving care of each fluffy grain, frying the egg evenly throughout. The other ingredients are added abundantly, and there's no hint of oil. On the top is a crown of shredded crabmeat. If you've never been an aficionado, you'll be one now. Other dishes are served here to accompany the fried rice, and their soups are also very good.

Moi Kong. 22 Murray St. (between Maxwell House and Fairfield Methodist Church). ☎ **65/221-7758.** Reservations recommended on weekends. Small dishes S$4–S$30 (US$2.40–US$17.95). AE, MC, V. Daily 11:30am–2:30pm and 5:30–10pm. HAKKA.

Chinatown Dining

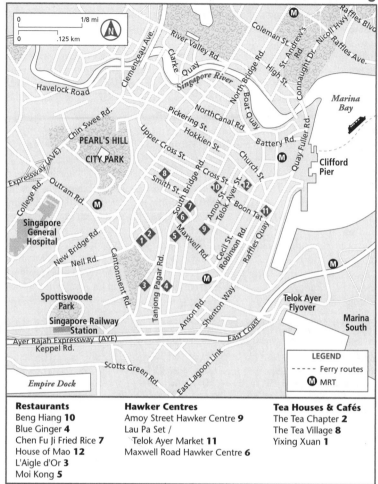

Restaurants
Beng Hiang **10**
Blue Ginger **4**
Chen Fu Ji Fried Rice **7**
House of Mao **12**
L'Aigle d'Or **3**
Moi Kong **5**

Hawker Centres
Amoy Street Hawker Centre **9**
Lau Pa Set /
  Telok Ayer Market **11**
Maxwell Road Hawker Centre **6**

Tea Houses & Cafés
The Tea Chapter **2**
The Tea Village **8**
Yixing Xuan **1**

Located down a back alley called Murray Food Court, Moi Kong is a restaurant that looks more like somebody's kitchen, from the plastic tablecloths and dishes to tea served in simple glasses. The staff is very helpful about offering suggestions from the Hakka menu, dishes that are heavier on tofu and flavored more with homemade Chinese wine. Try house specialties like red wine prawn or salted chicken baked and served plain. The deep-fried bean curd stuffed with minced pork and fish is a traditional standard and can be served either dry or braised with black bean sauce. If you don't believe the food here is top rate, just ask Jackie Chan, whose happy photos are on the wall by the cash register!

7 Little India

✪ **Komala Vilas.** 76/78 Serangoon Rd.). ☎ **65/293-6980.** Reservations not accepted. Dosai S$2 (US$1.20); lunch for 2 S$8 (US$4.80). No credit cards. Daily 11:30am–3pm and 6:30–10:30pm. SOUTHERN INDIAN.

Komala Vilas is famous with Singaporeans of every race. Don't expect the height of ambience—it's pure fast food—but to sit here during a packed and noisy lunch hour is to see all walks of life come through the doors. Vegetarian dishes southern-Indian style, so there's nothing fancy about the food; it's just plain good. Order the dosai, a huge, thin pancake used to scoop up luscious and hearty gravies and curries. Even for carnivores, it's very satisfying. What's more, it's cheap: two samosas, dosai, and an assortment of stew-style gravies (dal) for two are only S$8 (US$4.80) with tea. For a quick fast-food meal, this place is second to none.

Muthu's Curry Restaurant. 76/78 Race Course Rd. ☎ **65/293-2389** or 65/293-7029. Reservations not accepted. Entrees S$3.50–S$6.50 (US$2.10–US$3.90); fish head curry from S$16 (US$9.55). AE, DC, JCB, MC, V. Daily 10am–10pm. SOUTHERN INDIAN.

We're not talking the height of dining elegance here. It's more like somebody's kitchen where the chairs don't match, but you know there's got to be a reason why this place is packed at mealtimes with a crowd of folks from construction workers to business-people. The list of specialties is long and includes crab masala, chicken biryani, and mutton curry, and fish cutlet and fried chicken sold by the piece. Of course you can get the local favorite, fish head curry (this is a great place to try it). The fish head floats in a huge portion of curry soup, its eye staring and teeth grinning. The cheek meat is the best part of the fish, but to be real polite, let your friend eat the eye. Go toward the end of mealtime, so you don't get lost in the rush and can find staff with more time to help you out.

8 Orchard Road Area

EXPENSIVE

Bice Ristorante Italiano. Goodwood Park Hotel, 22 Scotts Rd. ☎ **65/735-3711.** Entrees S$24–S$45 (US$14.35–US$26.95). AE, DC, MC, V. Daily noon–3:30pm and 6–10:30pm. Closed Christmas, New Year's, and Chinese New Year. ITALIAN.

Beatrice—or "Mama Bice" as she's known in Italy—opened her first restaurant in Milano 2 years ago, and has since opened two others, one in New York and one in Singapore. There's plenty of space, carved out into dining areas by plantings and unique displays of wooden shipping crates. Their chef hails from Milan and serves Mama Bice's family recipes of flavors inspired by her northern Italian ancestry. The lamb is tender and fresh and the pasta a perfect al dente. Because of the space, the wait for a table is short, but the bar as you walk in is a nice place to have a glass of wine before your meal. Bice has the largest selection of Italian wines in the city.

Chang Jiang. Goodwood Park Hotel, 22 Scotts Rd. ☎ **65/730-1752.** Reservations recommended. Small dishes S$15–S$58 (US$9–US$34.75). AE, DC, JCB, MC, V. Daily noon–2:30pm and 7–10:30pm. SHANGHAINESE.

The small and elegant Chang Jiang is a unique blend of Chinese food and European style. A fine setting, which mixes refined Continental ambience with Chinese accents, has a view of the courtyard and pool of the historic Goodwood Park Hotel through its large draped picture windows. The food is Chinese, but the service is French Gueri-don style, in which dishes are presented to diners and taken to a side table to be por-tioned into individual servings. Some dishes are prepared while you watch, especially coffee, which is a veritable chemistry showcase. A couple of the more sumptuous dishes are the tangy and crunchy crisp eel wuxi and the sweet batter-dipped prawns with sesame seed and salad sauce. If you order the Beijing Duck, after the traditional pancake dish they serve the shredded meat in a delicious sauce with green bean noodles.

Orchard Road Area Dining

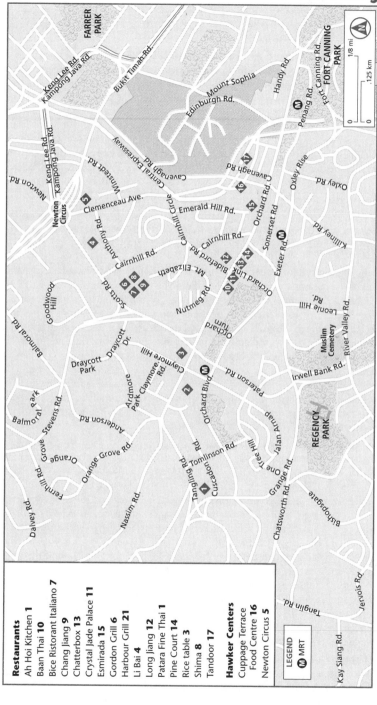

Restaurants
Ah Hoi Kitchen **1**
Baan Thai **10**
Bice Ristorant Italiano **7**
Chang Jiang **9**
Chatterbox **13**
Crystal Jade Palace **11**
Esmirada **15**
Gordon Grill **6**
Harbour Grill **21**
Li Bai **4**
Long Jiang **12**
Patara Fine Thai **1**
Pine Court **14**
Rice table **3**
Shima **8**
Tandoor **17**

Hawker Centers
Cuppage Terrace
Food Centre **16**
Newton Circus **5**

LEGEND
Ⓜ MRT

✪ **Esmirada.** 180 Orchard Rd., #01-01 Peranakan Place ☎ **65/735-3476.** Reservations recommended for dinner. Entrees S$24–S$42 (US$14.35–US$25.15). AE, DC, MC, V. Daily noon–midnight. MEDITERRANEAN.

Ask any expatriate about restaurants and you'll hear about Esmirada. This place revels in the joys of good food and drink, bringing laughter and fun to the traditional act of breaking bread with friends and family. Evening meals can get loud and lively, so don't be surprised if the whole place gets up and dances on the tables. (And don't be surprised if your waiter joins in!) The menu is easy: There's one dish each from Italy, Spain, Greece, France, Yugoslavia, Portugal, and Morocco, and they never change. Huge portions are served family style, from big bowls of salad to shish kebab skewers hanging from a rack, all placed in the center of the table so everyone can dig in. Don't even bother with paella anywhere else—this is the best. The place is small, so make your reservations early. Stucco walls, wrought-iron details, and terra-cotta floors are mixed with wooden Indonesian tables and chairs with kilim cushions in an East-meets-West style that works very nicely.

Gordon Grill. Goodwood Park Hotel, 22 Scotts Rd. ☎ **65/730-1744.** Reservations recommended. Entrees S$32–S$50 and up (US$19.15–US$29.95). AE, DC, JCB, MC, V. Daily noon–2.30pm, and 7–11:30. ENGLISH/SCOTTISH.

Bringing meat and potatoes to the high life, Gordon Grill wheels out a carving cart full of the most tender prime rib and sirloin you could imagine, cut to your desired thickness. The menu of traditional English and Scottish fare includes house specialties like the panfried goose liver with apple and port wine sauce appetizer and the house recipe for (perfect) lobster bisque. Featured entrees are the mixed seafood grill of lobster, garoupa (grouper), scallops, and prawns in a lemon butter sauce and roast duck breast glazed with honey and black pepper. The traditional English sherry trifle is the dessert to order here, but if you want a little taste of everything, the dessert variation lets you have small portions of each dessert, with fresh fruit. The dining room, which is small and warmly set with dark tartan carpeting and portraits of stately Scotsmen, feels more comfortable than claustrophobic, and light piano music drifts in from the lounge next door. Dress formal.

✪ **Harbour Grill.** Hilton International Singapore, 581 Orchard Rd. ☎ **65/730-3393.** Reservations recommended. Entrees S$34–S$36 (US$20.35–US$21.55). Two courses S$55 (US$32.95), 3 courses S$75 (US$44.90), or 4 courses S$90 (US$53.90) per person. AE, DC, MC, V. Daily noon–2:30pm and 7–10:30pm. CONTINENTAL.

Grilled seafood and U.S. prime rib are perfectly prepared and served with attentive style in this award-winning restaurant. The Continental cuisine is lighter than most, with recipes that focus on the natural freshness of their ingredients rather than on creams and fat. Caesar salad is made at your table so you can request your preferred blend of ingredients, and the oyster bar serves fresh oysters from around the world. For the main course, the prime rib is the best and most requested entree, but the rack of lamb is another option worth considering—it melts in your mouth. Guest chefs from international culinary capitals are flown in for monthly specials. The place is small and cozy, with exposed brick and a finishing kitchen in the dining room. Windows have been replaced with murals of the Singapore harbor in the 1850s, but in the evenings it is still airy and fresh feeling.

✪ **Li Bai.** Sheraton Towers, 39 Scotts Rd. ☎ **65/839-5623.** Reservations required. Entrees S$18–S$48 and up (US$10.80–US$28.75). AE, DC, MC, V. Daily noon–2:30pm and 6:30–10:30pm. CANTONESE.

Chinese restaurants are typically unimaginative in the decor department—slapping up a landscape brush painting or two here and there is sometimes about as far as they go. Not at Li Bai, though, which is very sleekly decorated in contemporary black and red lacquer, with huge vases of soft pussy willows dotted about. Creative chefs and guest chefs turn out a constantly evolving menu, refining specialties, and jade and silver chopsticks and white bone china add opulent touches to their flawless meals. Make sure you ask for their most recent creations—they're guaranteed to please. Or, try the farm chicken smoked with jasmine tea, a succulent dish. The crab fried rice is fabulous, with generous chunks of fresh meat, and the beef in mushroom and garlic brown sauce is some of the tenderest meat you'll ever feast upon. The wine list is international, with many vintages to choose from.

✪ **Shima.** Goodwood Park Hotel, 22 Scotts Rd. ☎ **65/734-6281.** Reservations recommended. Set dinner S$39–S$100 and up per person (US$23.35–US$59.90). AE, DC, JCB, MC, V. Daily noon–2:30pm and 6:30–10:30pm. JAPANESE.

Downstairs is the tiny sushi and sashimi bar in clean and simple sushi-bar style. Upstairs is the main restaurant, a sprawling space divided up into specialty groupings of tables depending on your desired meal, from the teppanyaki grill to the yakinuku barbecue at the table. Its dark and cozy clubhouse feel brightens with area lighting for each table, creating interesting visuals as you walk in. The menu is complete, from a Japanese steamboat buffet to the best kobe beef in Singapore. For the most sumptuous feast with theater, go for the grill, prepared table-side with all the chopping, slicing, dicing, and cleaver-juggling you could want. Special sets are featured, and the lunch menu is discounted quite a bit. Specify what you intend to eat when you make your reservations.

MODERATE

✪ **Ah Hoi's Kitchen.** Traders Hotel, 1A Cuscaden Rd., 4th level. ☎ **65/831-4373.** Reservations recommended. Entrees S$8–S$26.50 (US$4.80–$15.85). AE, DC, JCB, MC, V. Daily 11:30am–2:30pm and 6:30–10:30pm. SINGAPOREAN.

I like Ah Hoi's for its casual charm and its selection of authentic local cuisine. The menu is extensive, specializing in local favorites like fried black pepper kuay teow (noodles), sambal kang kong (vegetable), and fabulous grilled seafood. The al fresco poolside pavilion location gives it a real "vacation in the tropics" sort of relaxed feel— think of a hawker center without the dingy florescent bulbs, greasy tables, and sludgy floor. Also good here is the chile crab—if you can't make it out to the seafood places on the east coast of the island, it's the best alternative for tasting this local treat. Make sure you order the fresh lime juice. It's very cooling.

Baan Thai. 381 Orchard Rd., #04-23 Ngee Ann City. ☎ **65/735-5562.** Reservations recommended. Entrees S$9–S$35 (US$5.40–US$20.95). AE, DC, JCB, MC, V. Daily 11am–2:30pm and 6:30–10:30pm. THAI.

Spotless and well lit, Baan Thai is fitted out with an exotic decor, from the giant Thai Buddha that greets you in the reception area to dining nooks sectioned off with carved wooden screens. Every detail is beautifully integrated, from hanging oil lamps to antique artworks and curio items down to the celadon green plates. A fiery dish to try is the pla khao lard plik, charcoal-grilled garoupa (grouper) topped with chile. The phad Thai is fried rice noodles with prawn and chicken in a tamarind, chile, and peanut sauce. Thai green curry gravy combines lemongrass, lemon leaf, garlic, and green chile in a base of coconut and is served over your choice of chicken, pork, or beef. It's nice and spicy, but the cook will adjust the spice to taste upon request. Or you can go for the green curry, a traditional Thai favorite, and very good here.

Crystal Jade Palace. 391 Orchard Rd., #04-19 Ngee Ann City. ☎ **65/735-2388.** Reservations required. Small dishes S$12–S$38 (US$7.20–US$22.75); set lunch for 2 from S$50 (US$29.95). AE, DC, JCB, MC, V. Daily 11:30am–2:30pm and 6:30–10:30pm. CANTONESE.

Although Crystal Jade Palace is an upmarket choice, it's a fantastic way to try Chinese food as it was intended. From the aquariums of soon-to-be-seafood-delights at the entrance you can survey the rows of big round tables (and some small ones, too) packed with happy diners, feasting away. The food here is authentic Cantonese, prepared by Hong Kong master chefs. Dim sum, fresh seafood, and barbecue dishes accompany exotic shark's fin and baby abalone. Scallop dishes are very popular and can be prepared either sautéed with cashews, chile, and soy; panfried with chiles, white pepper, and salt; or sautéed with green vegetables. The tender panfried cod in light honey sauce proves worthy of its reputation as a time-honored favorite. For a unique soup, try the double-boiled winter melon with mixed meats, mushrooms, crab, and dried scallops served in the halved melon shell. You can order Chinese or French wines to accompany your meal.

Long Jiang. Crown Prince Hotel, 270 Orchard Rd. ☎ **65/734-9056.** Reservations required Sat–Sun, and public holidays. Buffet lunch S$28 (US$16.75), buffet dinner S$32 (US$19.15). AE, DC, JCB, MC, V. Daily buffet lunch 11:45am–2:30pm, buffet dinner 7–10:30pm. SZECHUAN.

Long Jiang is the best way for beginners to experiment with Chinese Szechuan cuisine. Lunch and dinner are served all-you-can-eat buffet style, but rather than trek up to a lukewarm spread with plate in hand, you can eyeball a menu complete with photos of each dish. The portions are small, and you can order as many as you like, which means you can try different tastes without committing to only one or two dishes you're not sure about. They also have an à la carte menu with specialties like crispy chicken with hot sesame sauce, fried string beans with minced meat, and sautéed prawn with dried chile (which is only moderately spicy). The atmosphere is rather plain, with some Chinese touches.

Patara Fine Thai. #03-14 Tanglin Mall, 163 Tanglin Rd. ☎ **65/737-0818.** Reservations recommended for lunch, required for dinner. Entrees S$17–S$30 (US$10.20–US$17.95). AE, DC, MC, V. Daily noon–2:30pm and 6–10:30pm. THAI.

Patara may say fine dining in its name, but the food here is home cooking: not too haute, not too traditional. Seafood and vegetables are big here. Deep-fried garoupa (grouper) is served in a sweet sauce with chile that can be added sparingly upon request. Curries are popular, too. The roast duck curry in red curry paste with tomatoes, rambutans, and pineapple is juicy and hot. For something really different, Patara's own invention, the Thai taco isn't exactly traditional, but is good, filled with chicken, shrimp, and sprouts. Their green curry, one of my favorites, is perhaps the best in town. Their Thai-style iced tea (which isn't on the menu, so you'll have to ask for it) is fragrant and flowery. A small selection of wines is also available.

Pine Court. Mandarin Singapore, 333 Orchard Rd. (take the express elevator to the 35th floor). ☎ **65/831-6262.** Reservations recommended. Small dishes S$16–S$46 (US$9.60–US$27.55). AE, DC, JCB, MC, V. Daily noon–3pm and 6:30–11pm. CHINESE MIX.

The decor at Pine Court is stunning. Carved rosewood screens on the walls are like geometric lace, and little clusters of delicate wood and white paper lanterns cast a warm glow from the high ceilings. During dinner, and while music plays, the giant silk screen landscape painting against the far wall is transformed through visual effects to represent each season. Pine Court was once a Beijing-style restaurant, and even though they now serve many different kinds of Chinese cuisine, the Peking duck remains a favorite and will never leave the menu. The sautéed mixed seafood served in a yam basket is comprised of stir-fried scallops, prawns, and garoupa (grouper) with vegetables in a lightly fried basket that's very tasty—it's a great presentation. Another great dish is the specialty crispy roast chicken (whole or half), with the skin left on and seasoned with soy sauce.

Tandoor. Holiday Inn Parkview, 11 Cavenagh Rd. ☎ **65/730-0153.** Reservations recommended. Entrees S$11–S$40 (US$6.60–$23.95). AE, DC, MC, V. Daily noon–2:30pm and 7–10:30pm. NORTHERN INDIAN.

Live music takes center stage in this small restaurant, adorned with carpets, artwork, and wood floors and furnishings. Entrees prepared in their tandoor oven come out flavorful and not as salty as most tandoori dishes. The tandoori lobster is rich, but the chef's specialty is crab lababdar: crabmeat, onions, and tomato sautéed in a coconut gravy. Fresh cottage cheese is made in-house for fresh and light saag panir, a favorite here. Chefs keep a close eye on the spices to ensure the spice enhances the flavor rather than drowning it out—more times than not, customers ask them to add *more* spices. A final course of creamy masala tea perks you up and aids digestion. If you're curious, the tandoor oven is behind a glass wall in the back, so you can watch them prepare your food.

INEXPENSIVE

❂ **Chatterbox.** Mandarin Hotel, 333 Orchard Rd. ☎ **65/737-4411.** Reservations recommended for lunch and dinner. Entrees S$15–S$39 (US$9–US$23.35). AE, DC, JCB, MC, V. Daily 24 hours. SINGAPOREAN/WESTERN.

If you'd like to try the local favorites but don't want to deal with street food, then Chatterbox is the place for you. Their Hainanese chicken rice is highly acclaimed, and other dishes—like nasi lemak, laksa, and carrot cake—are as close to the street as you can get. For a quick and tasty snack, order tahu goreng, deep-fried tofu in peanut chile sauce. This is also a good place to experiment with some of those really weird local drinks. Chin chow is the dark brown grass jelly drink; cendol is green jelly, red beans, palm sugar, and coconut milk; and bandung is the pink rose syrup milk with jelly. For dessert, order the ever-favorite sago pudding, made from the hearts of the sago palm. This informal and lively coffee shop dishes out room service for the Mandarin Hotel and is open 24 hours a day.

❂ **The Rice Table.** International Building, 360 Orchard Rd., #02-09, ☎ **65/835-3783.** Reservations not necessary. Lunch buffet S$12.80 (US$7.65), dinner buffet S$18.50 (US$11.10). AE, DC, MC, V. Tues–Sun noon–2:30pm and 6–9:30pm. INDONESIAN.

Indonesian Dutch rijsttafel, a service of many small Indonesian dishes (up to almost 20) with rice, is imitated buffet style at the Rice Table, so if the rijsttafel at Alkaff Mansion (see section 9) tickles your fancy but you don't want to drop the kind of money they charge, you can try something similar here. Stuff yourself on favorite Indo-Malay wonders like beef rendang, chicken satay, otak otak, and sotong assam (squid) for a very reasonable price. Their recipes are nice and tasty. Expect to pay extra for your drinks and desserts.

9 Restaurants a Little Farther Out

Many travelers will choose to eat in town for convenience, and while there's plenty of great dining in the more central areas, there are some other really fantastic dining finds if you're willing to hop in a cab for 10 or 15 minutes. These places are worth the trip—for a chance to dine along the water at UDMC or amid lush terrace gardens at Alkaff

Mansion, or to just go for superior seafood at Long Beach Seafood Restaurant. And don't worry about finding your way back: Most places always have cabs milling about. If not, restaurant staff will always help you call a taxi.

EXPENSIVE

✪ **Alkaff Mansion.** 10 Telok Blangah Green (off Henderson Rd.), Telok Blangah Hill Park. ☎ **65/278-6979.** Reservations recommended. Set rijstaffel menu S\$60 (US\$35.95) per person; buffet S\$35 (US\$20.95) per person. AE, DC, JCB, MC, V. Daily 7pm–midnight. INDONESIAN.

Alkaff Mansion was built by the wealthy Arab Alkaff family not as a home, but as a place to throw elaborate parties; and true to its mission, Alkaff Mansion is tops for elegant ambience. The mansion allows for indoor and outdoor patio dining at small tables glistening with starched white linens and small candles. The forest outside is a stunning backdrop. The dinner cuisine here is rijsttafel—home-style Indonesian fare that was influenced by Dutch tastes and is served in set menus that rotate weekly. A typical set dinner might include gado gado (a cold salad with sweet peanut sauce) and a soup. To announce the main course, a gong is sounded and ladies dressed in traditional kebaya sarongs carry out the dishes on platters. Main courses include the siakap masak asam turnis (fish in a tangy sauce); the udang kara kuning, which is a great choice for lobster; and the crayfish in chile sauce. In rijstaffel tradition, the dinner is served with rice, which is accompanied by an array of condiments like varieties of sambal and achar. Downstairs, Alkaff serves a huge buffet with nightly changing themes. I strongly recommend this place for a truly unique and memorable dining experience.

MODERATE

✪ **Long Beach Seafood Restaurant.** 1018 East Coast Pkwy. ☎ **65/445-8833.** Reservations recommended. Seafood is sold by weight according to seasonal prices. Most dishes S\$9–S\$16 (US\$5.40–US\$9.60). AE, DC, JCB, MC, V. Daily 5pm–1:15am. SEAFOOD.

They really pack 'em in at this place. Tables are crammed together in what resembles a big indoor pavilion, complete with festive lights and the sounds of mighty feasting. This is one of the best places for fresh seafood of all kinds: fish like garoupa (grouper), sea bass, marble goby, and kingfish, and other creatures of the sea from prawns to crayfish. The chile crab here is good, but the house specialty is really the pepper crab, chopped and deliciously smothered in a thick concoction of black pepper and soy. Huge chunks of crayfish are also tasty in the black pepper sauce, and can be served in variations like barbecue, sambal, steamed with garlic, or in a bean sauce. Don't forget to order buns so you can sop up the sauce. You can also get vegetable, chicken, beef, or venison dishes to complement, or choose from their menu selection of local favorites.

Palm Beach Seafood Restaurant. 5 Stadium Walk, #03-04 Leisure Park. ☎ **65/ 344-3088.** Reservations strongly recommended for weekends. Seafood is sold by the gram according to seasonal prices. Most small dishes between S\$12–S\$28 (US\$7.20–US\$16.75). AE, MC, V. Daily noon–2:30pm and 6–11:30pm. SEAFOOD.

When eating scrumptious local seafood you usually find yourself in some casual open-air setting or extremely underdressed dining hall, so don't let the upscale setting at Palm Beach fool you: The food is as great as any dingy seaside joint, and very reasonably priced. Australian lobster graces the finest dish here—cooked in a clay pot with coconut milk and chile sauce. Their chile crab is also great, but to me it seems a bit "local" for such a swank place. Besides, it's very messy. A gift shop outside lets you bring home jars of hot pot sauce, achar (sweet sauce), chile sauce, and sambal.

Prima Tower. 201 Keppel Rd. ☎ **65/272-8822.** Reservations required. Small dishes S$14–S$50 (US$8.40–US$29.95) and up. AE, DC, MC, V. Daily 11am–2:30pm and 6:30–10:30pm. Closed Chinese New Year. BEIJING.

One of the main attractions here is the fact that the restaurant revolves, giving you an ever-changing view of the city from your table. The other main attraction is the food, which is Beijing-style Chinese. Naturally, the best dish is the Peking duck, which has been a house specialty since this restaurant opened 20 years ago. All of the noodles for the noodle dishes are prepared in-house using traditional recipes and techniques, so the word of the day is *fresh*. Try them with minced pork and chopped cucumber in a sweet sauce. The restaurant manager comes to each table to present the daily specials. It's a good time to chat him up for the best dishes and ask questions about the menu.

Xin Cuisine. Concorde Hotel, 317 Outram Rd., Level 4. ☎ **65/732-3337.** Reservations recommended. Small dishes S$10–S$30 (US$6–US$17.95). AE, DC, JCB, MC, V. Daily noon–2.30pm and 6:30–10:30pm. HERBAL/CANTONESE.

A recent trend is to bring back the Chinese tradition of preparing foods that have special qualities for beauty, health, and vitality, balancing the body's yin and yang and restoring energy. Xin (new) cuisine transforms these concepts into light and flavorful creations, listed in a menu that's literally a book. The chef is famous for East-meets-West creations, but be assured, the cuisine is mostly Chinese. The concentrated seafood soup with chicken and spinach is a light and delicious broth that's neither too thick nor thin and has chunks of meat and shredded spinach. Stewed Mongolian rack of lamb is obviously not Cantonese, but is as tender as butter and served in a sweet brown sauce with buns to soak up the gravy. The steamed eggplant with toasted sesame seed is fantastic, with warm tender slices served in soy sauce. For the more adventurous, they serve up a mean hasma scrambled egg whites. Hasma is frog glands, which are believed to improve the complexion. The dish is a little alarming to some, but served with a hint of ginger and scooped onto walnut melba toast, it's actually quite nice.

INEXPENSIVE

✪ UDMC Seafood Centre. Block 1202 East Coast Pkwy. Seafood dishes are charged by weight, with dishes from around S$12 (US$7.20). AE, DC, MC, V. Daily 5pm–midnight. SEAFOOD.

Eight seafood restaurants are lined side by side in 2 blocks, their fronts open to the view of the sea outside. UDMC is a fantastic way to eat seafood Singapore style, in the open air, in restaurants that are more like grand stalls than anything else. Eat the famous local chile crab and pepper crab here, along with all sorts of squid, fish, and scallop dishes. Noodle dishes are also available, as are vegetable dishes and other meats. But the seafood is the thing to come for. Of the eight restaurants, there's no saying which is the best, as everyone seems to have their own opinions about this one or that one (personally, I like Jumbo at the far eastern end of the row). Some restaurants accept Japan Credit Bank. Have a nice stroll along the walkway and gaze out to the water while you decide which one to go for.

✪ Samy's Curry Restaurant. Block 25 Dempsey Rd. ☎ **65/472-2080.** Reservations not accepted. Sold by the scoop or piece, S80¢–S$3 (US$0.50–US$1.80). V. Daily 11am–3pm and 6–10pm. No alcohol served. SOUTHERN INDIAN.

There are many places in Singapore to get good southern Indian banana leaf (see description under "One Little Island, Lots & Lots of Choices," above), but none quite so unique as Samy's out at Dempsey Road. Part of the Singapore Civil Service

Clubhouse, at lunchtime nonmembers must pay S50¢ (US$.30) to get in the door. Not that there's much of a door, because Samy's is situated in a huge, high-ceilinged, open-air hall, with shutters thrown back and fans whirring above. Wash your hands at the back and have a seat, and soon someone will slap a banana leaf place mat in front of you. A blob of white rice will be placed in the center, and then buckets of vegetables, chicken, mutton, fish, prawn, and you name it will be brought out, swimming in the richest and spiciest curries to ever pass your lips. Take a peek in each bucket, shake your head yes when you see one you like, and a scoop will be dumped on your banana leaf. Eat with your right hand or with a fork and spoon. When you're done, wipe the sweat from your brow, fold the banana leaf away from you, and place your tableware on top. Samy's serves no alcohol, but the fresh lime juice is nice and cooling.

10 Hawker Centers

Hawker centers—large groupings of informal open-air food stalls—were Singapore's answer to fast and cheap food in the days before McDonald's came along, and are still the best way to sample every kind of Singaporean cuisine. They can be intimidating for newcomers, especially during the busy lunch or dinner rush, when they turn into fast-paced carnivals; so if it's your first time, try this: First, walk around to every stall to see what they have to offer. The stalls will have large signs displaying principal menu items, and you should feel free to ask questions, too, before placing your order. Special stalls have drinks only. The fresh lime goes with any dish, but to be truly local, grab a giant bottle of Tiger beer.

Next, find a table. Some stalls have their own tables for you to use; otherwise, sit anywhere you can and when you order let the hawker know where you are (tables usually have numbers to simplify). If it's crowded and you find a couple of free seats at an already occupied table, politely ask if they are taken; and if the answer is no, have a seat—it's perfectly customary. Your food will be brought to you, and you are expected to pay upon delivery. When you're finished, don't clear your own plates, and don't stack them. Some stalls may observe strict religious customs that require different plates for different foods, and getting other scraps on their plates may be offensive.

For the record, all hawkers are licensed by the government, which inspects them and enforces health standards.

The most notorious hawker center in Singapore is **Newton.** Located at Newton Circus, the intersection of Scotts Road, Newton Road, and Bukit Timah/Dunearn Road, this place is notorious, as opposed to famous, for being an overcommercialized tourist spectacle where busloads of foreigners come and gawk at the Singaporean fast-food experience. It's slightly more expensive than other hawker centers, and if you go, be very careful about ordering seafood—they may bring you more than you asked for, and overcharge you for it. All in all, if you want to check it out, it is a good initiation before moving on to the real places. **Lau Pa Set Festival Village** (Telok Ayer Market) is located in Chinatown at the corner of Raffles Way and Boon Tat Street, and sometimes gets touristy, too; but for the record, both Newton and Lau Pa Set are open 24 hours.

For a more authentic experience **in Chinatown,** try the center at the end of Amoy Street near Telok Ayer Road, or the one at the corner of Maxwell Road and South Bridge Road (though the latter is known for being frighteningly dingy).

In the Historic District there are a few. Try the one on Hill Street next to the Central Fire Station or the one on Stamford Road between the National Museum and

Armenian Street intersection. You'll also find a couple on Victoria Street on either side of Allson Hotel, and another at Bugis night market.

In Little India, Zhujiao Centre is a nice-size hawker center. **On Orchard Road,** try Cuppage Terrace, just beyond the Centrepoint Shopping Centre.

Outside of the Singapore Botanic Garden, on Cluny Road near Napier Road, is another place that's worth mentioning because you can get the best roti john in Singapore there.

One place that's been near and dear to Singaporeans for years (though now they've mostly been chased away by overcommercialization) is the ✪ **Satay Club.** It used to be down at the Esplanade, but constant building and land reclamation efforts moved it around a bunch of times, and so they eventually moved it to Clarke Quay off River Valley Road. Yes, it is very touristy now, but still worth a visit. Satay, by the way, is perhaps the most popular Malay dish of all time. The small kabobs of meat are skewered onto the stiff veins of palm leaves and barbecued over a hibachi. Order them by the stick. They come with cucumbers and onion on the side, and a bowl of peanut chile sauce to dunk it all in. Find yourself a table, get some beer, order yourself up a whole plate, and you'll be happy as a clam, whether you look like a tourist or not.

11 Cafe Society

In Singapore, traditions such as British high tea and the Chinese tea ceremony live side by side with a growing coffee culture. These popular hangouts are all over the city. Here are a few places to try.

BRITISH HIGH TEA

Two fabulous places to take high tea in style are at **Raffles Bar & Billiard Room** at Raffles Hotel, 1 Beach Rd. (☎ 65/331-1746), and **The Compass Rose Café** at the Westin Stamford, 2 Stamford Rd. (☎ 65/431-5707). Both places are lovely, if pricey. The buffet will cost anywhere between S$25 and S$45 (US$14.95 to US$26.95). High tea is served in the afternoons until 5 or 5:30pm.

CHINESE TEA

There are a few places in Chinatown where tea is still as important today as it has always been in Chinese culture. The **Tea Village,** 27-31 Erskine Rd. (☎ 65/221-7825), **The Tea Chapter,** 11A Neil Rd. (☎ 65/226-1175), and **Yixing Xuan,** 23-25 Neil Rd. (☎ 65/224-6961), offer tranquil respites from the day and cultural insight into Chinese tea appreciation.

CAFES

Western-style coffee joints have been popping up left and right all over the island, so coffee-addicted travelers can rest assured that in the morning their favorite blends are brewing close by—as long as you don't mind spending S$4 (US$2.40) for a cup of brew. Within the city, good places to try are **The Coffee Club,** with branches in Takashimaya Shopping Centre (☎ 65/735-7368) and Boat Quay (☎ 65/538-0061), **Beans & Brew** at 230 Victoria St. #B1-13, (☎ 65/337-8525), or **The Coffee Connection,** with branches at Parco Bugis Junction (☎ 65/339-7758) and Clarke Quay (☎ 65/336-1121). But you won't be at a loss for a coffee shop—they're literally everywhere.

5 Singapore Attractions

Of Singapore's many sights and attractions, I enjoy the historic and cultural sights the most. The city's many old buildings and well-presented museum displays bring history to life. Chinese and Hindu temples and Muslim mosques welcome curious observers to discover their culture as they play out their daily activities, and the country's natural parks make the great outdoors easily accessible from even the most urban neighborhood. That's the best benefit of traveling in Singapore: Most attractions are situated within the heart of the city, and those that lie outside the urban center can still be easily reached.

Singapore also has a multitude of planned attractions for visitors and locals alike. Theme parks devoted to cultural heritage, sporting fun, and even kitsch amusement pop up all over the place. While some of these can be a little too Disneyland for many peoples' tastes, some are fun, especially if you're traveling with children. In this chapter I've outlined the many attractions here, provided historic and cultural information to help you appreciate each sight in its local context, and given you the truth about those attractions I think you could really skip, so you don't waste your time and money finding out for yourself. To help you plan your activities, I've put stars next to those attractions I've enjoyed the most—either for significance, excellent planning, or just plain curiosity.

I've divided this chapter into the main sections of the urban center—the Historic District, Chinatown, Little India, Kampong Glam, and Orchard Road, where you'll find the more historic sights of the city—and those outside the city, to the west, north, and east, where you'll find large areas dedicated to nature reserves, a zoo, and other wildlife attractions, theme parks, and sprawling temple complexes, all easily accessible by public transportation or a cab ride. As a kicker, I'll take you to Sentosa (a small island to the south that's packed from shore to shore with amusements, adventure theme parks, historic exhibits, nature displays, and outdoor activities for families), and to some of the smaller outlying islands, and will fill you in on sports and recreation options.

When you're traveling to attractions outside the urban area, I recommend keeping this book handy—taxis are not always easy to find, so you may need to refer to the guide to call for a pick up or use the bus and MRT system, route numbers for which I've included with listings of most non-central attractions.

A note: Many of the sights to see in Singapore are not of the "pay your fee and see the show" variety, but rather historic buildings, monuments, and places of religious worship. The city's historic buildings, such as City Hall or Parliament House, must be appreciated from the outside, their significance lying in their unique architecture and historical context combined with the sensual effect of the surrounding city. Monuments and statues tell the stories of events and heroes important to Singapore both in the past and present. The places of worship listed in this chapter are open to the public and free of entrance charge. Expect temples to be open from sunup to sundown. Visiting hours are not specific to the hour, but, unless it's a holiday (when hours may be extended), you can expect these places to be open during daylight hours.

1 The Historic District

Fort Canning Park. Major entrances are from the Hill St. Food Centre, Percival Rd. (Drama Centre), Fort Canning Aquarium, National Library Carpark, and Canning Walk (behind Park Mall). Free admission. Dhoby Gaut or City Hall MRT.

These days, Fort Canning Park is known for great views out over Singapore, but in days past it served as the site of Raffles's home and the island's first botanical garden. Its history goes back even farther, though: Excavations over the years have unearthed ancient brick foundations and artifacts that gave a certain credence to the island natives' belief that their royal ancestors lived and were buried on the site. Fourteenth-century Javanese gold ornaments were excavated and placed on display at the Singapore History Museum. Atop the hill, a mysterious keramat, or sacred grave, marks the burial site of Iskander Shah (also known as Parameswara), the Palembang ruler who came to Singapore in the late 1300s before settling in Malacca. The debate surrounding the truth of this account doesn't hinder those who come to pay homage and worship at the site, which is well maintained within the park.

From the start Raffles chose this hill to build his home (at the site of the present-day lookout point), which later became residence for Singapore's Residents and Governors. In 1860, the house was torn down to make way for Fort Canning, which was built to quell British fears of invasion but instead quickly became the laughingstock of the island. The location was ideal for spotting invaders from the sea, but defending Singapore? Not likely. The cannons' range was such that their shells couldn't possibly have made it all the way out to an attacking ship—instead, most of the town below would have been destroyed. In 1907, the fort was demolished for a reservoir. Today, the only reminders of the old fort are some of the walls and the Fort Gate, a deep stone structure. Behind its huge wooden door you'll find a narrow staircase that leads to the roof of the structure.

Raffles also chose this as the location for the first botanical garden on the island. The garden was short-lived due to lack of funding; however, the park still has a pretty interesting selection of plants and trees, like the cannonball tree with its large round seed pods, and the cotton tree, whose pods open to reveal fluffy white "cotton" that was commonly used for stuffing pillows and mattresses. In many parts, these plants are well marked along the pathways. Also look for the ASEAN sculpture garden; five members of the Association of Southeast Asian Nations each donated a work for the park in 1982 to represent the region's unity.

Fort Canning was also the site of a **European cemetery.** To make improvements in the park, the graves were exhumed and the stones placed within the walls surrounding the outdoor performance field that slopes from the Music and Drama Society building. A large Gothic monument was erected in memory of James Napier Brooke, infant son of William Napier, Singapore's first Law Agent, and his wife, Maria Frances,

Urban Singapore Attractions

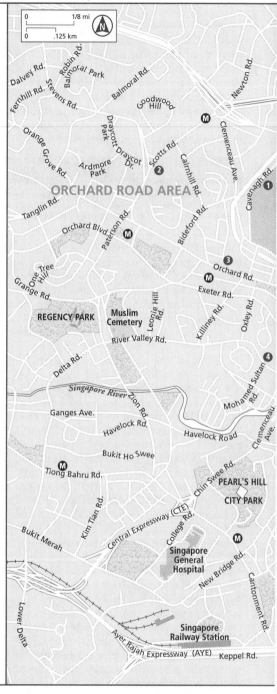

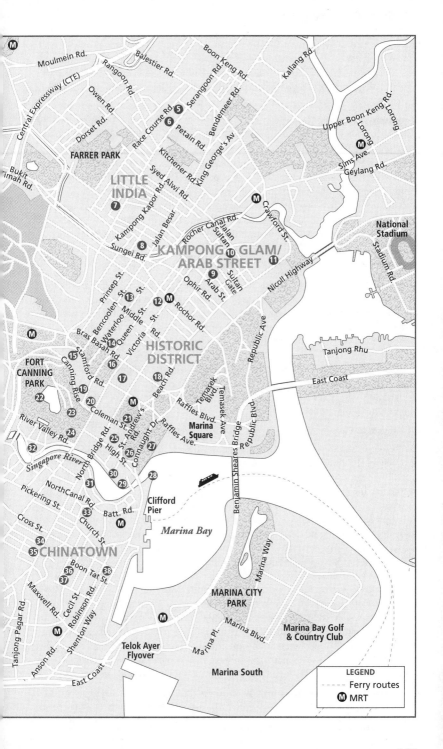

FARRER PARK

LITTLE INDIA

Moulmein Rd.
Balestier Rd.
Boon Keng Rd.
Kallang Rd.
Central Expressway (CTE)
Rangoon Rd.
Owen Rd.
Dorset Rd.
Race Course Rd.
Serangoon Rd.
Bendemeer Rd.
King George's Av.
Upper Boon Keng Rd.
Lorong
Sims Ave.
Geylang Rd.
Bukit Timah Rd.
Kitchener Rd.
Syed Alwi Rd.
Kampong Kapor Rd.
Jalan Besar
Rocher Canal Rd.
Jalan Sultan
Crawford St.
National Stadium
Sungei Rd.

KAMPONG GLAM/
ARAB STREET

Sultan Cafe
Arab St.
Ophir Rd.
Nicoll Highway
Stadium Rd.

Prinsep St.
St.
Bencoolen St.
Middle St.
Rochor Rd.
Bras Basah Rd.
Waterloo St.
Queen St.
Victoria St.

HISTORIC
DISTRICT

Republic Ave.
Tanjong Rhu
East Coast

FORT
CANNING
PARK

Stamford Rd.
Canning Rise
Coleman St.
Beach Rd.
Raffles Blvd.
Temasek Ave.
Temasek Blvd.
Republic Blvd.

River Valley Rd.
St. Andrew's Rd.
Connaught Dr.
Raffles Ave.

Marina
Square

Singapore River
North Bridge Rd.
High St.

North Canal Rd.
Pickering St.
Batt. Rd.
Church St.
Clifford
Pier
Marina Bay

Benjamin Sheares Bridge

Cross St.

CHINATOWN
Boon Tat St.

Maxwell Rd.
Cecil St.
Robinson Rd.
Shenton Way
Anson Rd.
Tanjong Pagar Rd.
East Coast

MARINA CITY
PARK
Marina Way
Marina Pl.
Marina Blvd.

Marina Bay Golf
& Country Club

Telok Ayer
Flyover
Marina South

LEGEND
Ferry routes
M MRT

127

the widow of prolific architect George Coleman. Although no records exist, Coleman probably designed the cupolas as well as two small monuments over unknown graves. The Music and Drama Society building itself was built in 1938. Close by, in the wall, are the tombstones of Coleman and of Jose D'Almeida, a wealthy Portuguese merchant.

Singapore Philatelic Museum. 23B Coleman St. ☎ **65/337-3888.** Adults S$2 (US$1.20), children and seniors S$1 (US$0.60). Tues–Sun 9am–4:30pm. Take the MRT to City Hall and walk toward Coleman St.

This building, constructed in 1895 to house the Methodist Book Room, recently underwent a S$7 million restoration and reopened as the Philatelic Museum in 1995. Exhibits include a fine collection of old stamps issued to commemorate historically important events, first-day covers, antique printing plates, postal service memorabilia, and private collections. Visitors can trace the development of a stamp from idea to the finished sheet, and you can even design your own. Free guided tours are available upon request.

Hill Street Building. Hill St. at the corner of River Valley Rd., on Fort Canning Park.

Originally built to house the British Police Force, the building was sited directly across from Chinatown for easy access to quell the frequent gang fights. Later it became home to the National Archives and it is believed that inquisitions and torture were carried out in the basement during the Japanese occupation (see appendix). Former National Archive employees have claimed to have seen ghosts of tortured souls sitting at their desks.

Unfortunately, you are not allowed to wander inside to see the ghosties yourself. You'll have to satisfy yourself by appreciating the architectural beauty of the outside of the building, which has been somewhat blurred by the recent painting of the window frames—in rainbow colors.

✪ **Armenian Church.** 60 Hill St., across from the Grand Plaza Hotel.

Of all colonial buildings, the Armenian Church (more formally called the Church of St. Gregory the Illuminator) is one of the most beautiful examples of early architectural style here. Designed by George Coleman, one of Singapore's most prolific and talented architects, it is his finest work. Although there were many alterations in the last century, the main style of the structure still dominates. The round congregation hall is powerful in its simplicity, its long louvered windows letting in cooling breezes while keeping out the imposing sunlight. Roman Doric columns support symmetrical porticos that protect the structure from rain. All in all, it's a wonderful achievement of combined European eclectic tastes and tropical necessity.

The first permanent Christian church in Singapore, it was funded primarily by the Armenian community, which was at one time quite powerful. Today, few Singaporeans can trace their heritage back to this influential group of immigrants. The church was consecrated in 1836, and the last appointed priest serving the parish retired in 1936. Although regular Armenian services are no longer held, other religious organizations make use of the church from time to time. The cemetery in the back of the church is the burial site of many prominent Armenians, including Ashgen Agnes Joachim, discoverer of the Vanda Miss Joachim, Singapore's national flower.

✪ **Asian Civilisations Museum.** 39 Armenian St. ☎ **65/332-3015.** Adults S$3 (US$1.80), children and seniors S$1.50 (US$0.90). Tues–Sun 9am–5:30pm (extended hours Wed until 9pm). Free guided tours in English Tues–Fri 11am, 2pm, and 3:30pm, with an extra tour on weekends at 2:45. City Hall MRT, and follow Stamford Rd. to Armenian St.

The old Tao Nan School, which dates from 1910, was completely renovated and reopened in 1997 to house the Asian Civilisations Museum. Beautiful and clear exhibits display fine collections of jade, calligraphy, ceramics, furniture, and artworks, all offering visitors the chance to trace the archipelago's rich Chinese heritage. Changing exhibits in the temporary galleries represent the other Asian civilizations. This museum is actually the first half of a two-phase project; the second is scheduled to open in late 2000 in the Empress Place Building, so look for it.

✪ **Singapore History Museum.** Stamford Rd., across the street from Bras Basah Park. ☎ **65/375-2510.** National Heritage Board Web site www.museum.org.sg/nhb.html. Adults S$3 (US$1.80), children and seniors S$1.50 (US$0.90). Museum admission plus 3-D movie ticket adults S$4 (US$2.40), children and seniors S$2 (US$1.20). Tues–Sun 9am–5:30pm (extended hours Wed until 9am). Free guided tours in English Tues–Fri 11am and 2pm, with an extra tour on weekends at 3:30pm. "The Singapore Story—Overcoming the Odds: A 3-D Experience" show times Tues–Sun every hour between 10:30am and 3:30pm.

Raffles Museum was opened in 1887, in a handsome example of neo-Palladian architecture designed by colonial architect Henry McCallum. It was the first of its kind in Southeast Asia, housing a superb collection of regional natural history specimens and ethnographic displays. In both 1907 and 1916, the museum outgrew its space and was enlarged. Renamed the National Museum in 1969, its collections went through a transformation, focusing on Singapore's history rather than that of the archipelago. Several years later, it became known as the Singapore History Museum. While the small museum's lack of space limits the number and size of exhibits, several are quite interesting. I always enjoy the Audubon-style pen-and-inks commissioned by first Resident William Farquhar. Take the time to read the accompanying descriptions, which point out the many flaws in the artists' knowledge of basic anatomy and botany. Also interesting are 20 dioramas portraying events from the settlement's early days to modern times. An interesting note: At one time the descriptions that accompanied the dioramas raked the Japanese over the coals for the horrors committed during their World War II occupation. In recent years, the Japanese requested they change these to a less offensive account, and the museum responded with silence. Today, while other dioramas have paragraphs of description, these few have maybe one or two lines each. Period. Finally, "Rumah Baba" shows through costumes and household and ceremonial items the unique culture of the Peranakans, or Straits-born Chinese. Additional visiting exhibits change frequently.

Kuan Yin Thong Hood Cho Temple. Waterloo St., about 1½ blocks from Bras Basah Rd. Open to the public during the day.

It's said that whatever you wish for within the walls of Kuan Yin Temple comes true, so get in line and have your wishes ready. It must work, as there's a steady stream of people on auspicious days of the Chinese calendar. The procedure is simple: Wear shoes easily slipped off before entering the temple. Light several joss sticks. Pray to the local god, pray to the sky god, then turn to the side and pray some more. Now pick up the container filled with inscriptions and shake it until one stick falls out. After that, head for the interpretation box office to get a piece of paper with verses in Mandarin and English to look up what your particular inscription means. (For a small fee, there are interpreters outside.) Now for the payback: If your wish comes true, be prepared to return to the temple and offer fruits and flowers to say thanks (oranges, pears, and apples are a thoughtful choice and jasmine petals are especially nice). Be careful what you wish for. Once you're back home and that job promotion comes through, your new manager might nix another vacation so soon. To be on the safe side, bring the goods with you when you make your wish.

✪ **Singapore Art Museum.** 71 Bras Basah Rd. ☎ **65/332-3222.** www.museum.org.sg/
nhb.html. Adults S$3 (US$1.80), children and seniors S$1.50 (US$0.90). Tues–Sun 9am–
5:30pm (extended hours Wed until 9pm). Free guided tours in English Tues–Fri 11am and
2pm, with additional weekend tour at 3:30pm. City Hall MRT, across Bras Basah Park from the
Singapore History Museum.

The Singapore Art Museum (SAM) officially opened in 1996 to house an impressive
collection of over 3,000 pieces of art and sculpture, most of it by Singaporean and
Malay artists. Limited space requires the curators to display only a small number at a
time, but these are incorporated in interesting exhibits to illustrate particular artistic
styles, social themes, or historical concepts. A large collection of Southeast Asian
pieces rotates regularly, as well as visiting international exhibits. Besides the main halls,
the museum offers up a gift shop with fine souvenir ideas, a cafe, a conservation lab-
oratory, an auditorium, and the E-mage Gallery, where multimedia presentations
include not only the museum's own acquisitions but other works from public and private collections in the region as well. Once a Catholic boys' school established in 1852,
SAM has retained some visible reminders of its former occupants: Above the front
door of the main building you can still see inscribed "St. Joseph's Institution," and a
bronze-toned, cast-iron statue of St. John Baptist de la Salle with two children stands
in its original place.

Cathedral of the Good Shepherd. 4 Queen St., at the corner of Queen St. and Bras Basah
Rd. Open to the public during the day.

This cathedral was Singapore's first permanent Catholic church. Built in the 1840s, it
brought together many elements of a fractured parish. In the early days of the colony,
the Portuguese Mission thought itself the fount of the Holy Roman Empire's presence
on the island, and so the French Bishop was reduced to holding services at the home
of a Mr. McSwiney on Bras Basah Road; a dissenting Portuguese priest held forth at a
certain Dr. d'Ameida's residence; and the Spanish priest was so reduced that we don't
even know where he held his services. These folks were none too pleased with
their makeshift houses of worship and so banded together to establish their own
cathedral—the Cathedral of the Good Shepherd. Designed in a Latin cross pattern,
much of its architecture is reminiscent of St. Martin-In-The-Fields and St. Paul's in
Covent Garden. The Archbishop's residence, in contrast, is a simple two-story bungalow with enclosed verandahs and a portico. Also on the grounds are the Resident's
Quarters and the Priests' Residence, the latter more ornate in design, with elaborate
plasterwork.

✪ **CHIJMES (Convent of the Holy Infant Jesus).** 30 Victoria St. Free admission. 1-hour
historical tour in English Mon–Fri 11am and 3pm, Sat 11am, S$5 (US$3) per person.

Entering this bustling enclave of retail shops, restaurants, and nightspots, it's difficult
to imagine this was once a convent which, at its founding in 1854, consisted of a lone,
simply constructed bungalow. After decades of buildings and add-ons, this collection
of unique yet perfectly blended structures—a school, a private residence, an orphanage, a stunning Gothic chapel, and many others—were enclosed within walls, form-
ing peaceful courtyards and open spaces encompassing an entire city block. Legend
has it the small door on the corner of Bras Basah and Victoria streets welcomed hundreds of orphan babies, girl children who were born during inauspicious years or to
poor families who just appeared on the stoop each morning. In late 1983, the convent
relocated to the suburbs, and some of the block was leveled to make way for the MRT
Headquarters. Thankfully, most of the block survived and the Singapore government, in
planning the renovation of this desirable piece of real estate, wisely kept the integrity of
the architecture. For an evening out, the atmosphere at CHIJMES is exquisitely

Historic District Attractions

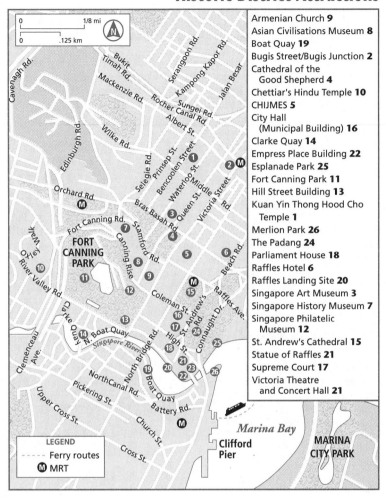

Armenian Church **9**
Asian Civilisations Museum **8**
Boat Quay **19**
Bugis Street/Bugis Junction **2**
Cathedral of the
    Good Shepherd **4**
Chettiar's Hindu Temple **10**
CHIJMES **5**
City Hall
    (Municipal Building) **16**
Clarke Quay **14**
Empress Place Building **22**
Esplanade Park **25**
Fort Canning Park **11**
Hill Street Building **13**
Kuan Yin Thong Hood Cho
    Temple **1**
Merlion Park **26**
The Padang **24**
Parliament House **18**
Raffles Hotel **6**
Raffles Landing Site **20**
Singapore Art Museum **3**
Singapore History Museum **7**
Singapore Philatelic
    Museum **12**
St. Andrew's Cathedral **15**
Statue of Raffles **21**
Supreme Court **17**
Victoria Theatre
    and Concert Hall **21**

LEGEND
----- Ferry routes
Ⓜ MRT

romantic. At the same time, you can enjoy a special decadence when you party in one of the popular bars here.

A note on the name: CHIJMES is pronounced "Chimes"; the "Chij," as noted, stands for Convent of the Holy Infant Jesus, and the "mes" was just added on so they could pronounce it "Chimes." No foolin'.

✪ Raffles Hotel. 1 Beach Rd. ☎ 65/337-1886.

Built in 1887 to accommodate the increasing upper-class trade, Raffles Hotel was originally only a couple of bungalows with 10 rooms, but, oh, the view of the sea was perfection. The owners, Armenian brothers named Sarkies, already had a couple of prosperous hotels in Southeast Asia (the Eastern & Oriental in Penang and The Strand in Rangoon) and were well versed in the business. It wasn't long before they added a pair of wings and completed the main building—and reading rooms, verandas, dining rooms, a grand lobby, the Bar and Billiards Room, a ballroom, and a string of shops. By 1899, electricity was turning the cooling fans and providing the pleasing glow of comfort.

As it made its madcap dash through the twenties, the hotel was the place to see and be seen. Vacancies were unheard of. Hungry Singaporeans and guests from other hotels, eager for a glimpse of the fabulous dining room, were turned away for lack of reservations. The crowded ballroom was jumping every night of the week. It was during this time that Raffles's guest book included famous authors like Somerset Maugham, Rudyard Kipling, Joseph Conrad and Noël Coward. These were indeed the glory years, but the lovely glimmer from the chandeliers soon faded with the stark arrival of the Great Depression. Raffles managed to limp through that dark time—and, darker still, through the Japanese occupation—and later pull back from the brink of bankruptcy to undergo modernization in the fifties. But fresher, brighter, more opulent hotels were taking root on Orchard Road, pushing the "grand old lady" to the back seat.

The hotel was in limbo for a period of time due to legal matters, and in 1961 it passed through several financial institutions to land on the doorstep of the Development Bank of Singapore (DBS). It was probably this journey that saved the Raffles from a haphazard renovation nightmare. Instead, history-minded renovators selected 1915 as a benchmark and, with a few changes here and there, faithfully restored the hotel to that era's magnificence and splendor. Today, the hotel's restaurants and nightlife draw thousands of visitors daily to its open lobby, its theater playhouse, the Raffles Hotel Museum, and 65 exclusive boutiques. Its 15 restaurants and bars—especially the Tiffin Room, Raffles Grill, and Doc Cheng's, all reviewed in chapter 4—are a wonder, as is its famous Bar and Billiards Room and Long Bar.

Bugis Street/Bugis Junction. Bugis MRT stop, across from Parco Bugis Junction shopping mall.

If you happened to visit Singapore in the seventies, and remember Bugis as a haven for transvestites and sex shows, you're in for a big surprise. Bugis Street ain't what it used to be. In place of the decadence is a giant shopping mall, Parco Bugis Junction. A little of the past still lingers at the **Boom Boom Room** (#02-04 New Bugis Village, 3 New Bridge Road; ☎ 65/339-8187), where nightly shows feature the most beautiful transvestites belting out hits by Barbra Streisand and Judy Garland. (See chapter 8 for a full write-up.) There's also a night market with a few bargains on cheap chic, curio items, accessories, and video discs.

The area around Bugis Street has a more benign history. The Bugis, fierce and respected warriors, were some of the first people to settle on Singapore in its early years. Raffles took note of their boatbuilding skills and, as part of his master town plan, included Bugis Town to attract more of them to the island.

✪ **St. Andrew's Cathedral.** Coleman St., between North Bridge Rd. and St. Andrew's Rd., across from the Padang. Open during daylight hours.

Designed by George Coleman; erected on a site selected by Sir Stamford Raffles himself; named for the patron saint of Scotland, St. Andrew; and primarily funded by Singapore's Scottish community, the first St. Andrew's was the colonials' Anglican Church. Completed toward the end of the 1830s, its tower and spire were added several years later to accord the edifice more stature. By 1852, because of massive damage sustained from lightning strikes, the cathedral was deemed unsafe and torn down. The cathedral that now stands on the site was completed in 1860. Of English Gothic Revival design, the cathedral is one of the few standing churches of this style in the region. The spire resembles the steeple of the Salisbury Cathedral—another tribute from the colonials to Mother England. Not only English residents but Christian Chinese, Indians, continental Europeans, and Malays consider this to be their center of worship.

Colonial Architecture 101

Three major players were influential in defining Singapore's early style. **George Drumgold Coleman,** an Irish architect who spent some time in Calcutta and later Java building private homes for wealthy merchants, visited Singapore (where he met Stamford Raffles), and returned to stay in 1826. By 1833, he'd been appointed superintendent of public works. A prolific builder, his designs set the fashion for Singapore's architecture of the day. Only three of his buildings remain today, but they're all exceptional: **Parliament House** (Maxwell House, which unfortunately has been renovated beyond recognition), the **Armenian Church,** and the **Caldwell House** in CHIJMES. Coleman also built many merchants' homes, offices, shops, and go-downs (shed-type warehouses), chiefly in a neo-Palladian style. Because the Singaporean climate was like that of the Mediterranean, he used many of that region's architectural elements, such as verandas and porticos for shade, courtyard gardens for cool tranquillity, large windows and doors for air circulation, and tall ceilings to capture and hold the rising warm air. Local materials figured into his constructions, mostly timber from up-country jungles, locally quarried granite, and Chinese and Malacca bricks.

During this colonial period, Singapore served as the dumping ground for India's penal system, and prisoners were continually brought here to work in the quarries and brick foundries, and in the jungles, felling timber. Coleman had the idea to use these convicts for construction, and they played an important role in helping to shape Singapore's style, as many brought with them a superb knowledge of southern Indian plasterwork and construction skills.

Major J. F. A. McNair, a colonial engineer, continued Coleman's neo-Palladian style in his works, including the **Istana** and **Sri Temasek.** Following the English residence styles of India, he designed many fine country homes for the British expatriates, incorporating elements of the Italian Renaissance, a lifelong fascination of his.

Trained in London, **Regent Alfred John Bidwell** came to the Straits Settlements around 1895. Not long after his arrival in Singapore, he joined the prestigious architecture firm Swan and Maclaren. Bidwell had a thorough knowledge of what was fashionable for the times; for example, the Queen Anne style for his **Goodwood Hotel Tower Wing** also incorporated European influences then in vogue in Britain and on the Continent. Bidwell was also responsible for designing the Main Building and the Bras Basah wings of the **Raffles Hotel,** keeping the integrity of the original edifice intact. Bidwell's renovations to the **Victoria Theatre and Concert Hall** remained true to the original design, built 50 years earlier in Victorian Revival style.

The plasterwork of St. Andrew's inside walls used a material called Madras chunam, which, though peculiar, was a common building material here in the 1880s. A combination of shell lime (without the sand) was mixed with egg whites and coarse sugar or jaggery until it took on the consistency of a stiff paste. The mixture was thinned to a workable consistency with water in which coconut husks had steeped, and was then applied to the surface, allowed to dry, and polished with rock crystal or smooth stones to a most lustrous patina. Who would've thought?

The original church bell was presented to the cathedral by Maria Revere Balestier, the daughter of famed American patriot Paul Revere. The bell now stands in the Singapore History Museum.

City Hall (Municipal Building). St. Andrew's Rd., across from the Padang. Entrance to the visitor's gallery is permitted, but all other areas are off-limits.

During the Japanese occupation, City Hall was a major headquarters, and it was here in 1945 that Admiral Lord Louis Mountbatten accepted the Japanese surrender. In 1951, the Royal Proclamation from King George VI was read here declaring that Singapore would henceforth be known as a city. Fourteen years later, Prime Minister Lee Kuan Yew announced to its citizens that Singapore would henceforth be called an independent republic.

City Hall, along with the Supreme Court, was judiciously sited to take full advantage of the prime location. Magnificent Corinthian columns march across the front of the symmetrically designed building, while inside, two courtyards lend an ambience of informality to otherwise officious surroundings. For all its magnificence and historical fame, however, its architect, F. D. Meadows, relied too heavily on European influence. The many windows afford no protection from the sun, and the entrance leaves pedestrians unsheltered from the elements. In defining the very nobility of the Singapore government, it appears the Singaporean climate wasn't taken into consideration.

Supreme Court. St. Andrew's Rd., across from the Padang. Closed to visitors, but worth seeing from the outside.

The Supreme Court stands on the site of the old Hotel de L'Europe, a rival of the Raffles Hotel until it went bankrupt in the 1930s. The court's structure, a classical style favored for official buildings the world over, was completed in 1939. With its spare adornment and architectural simplicity, the edifice has a no-nonsense, utilitarian attitude, and the sculptures across the front, executed by the Italian sculptor Cavaliere Rodolpho Nolli, echo what transpires within. *Justice* is the most breathtaking, standing 2.7 meters (9 ft.) high and weighing almost 4 tons. Kneeling on either side of her are representations of *Supplication* and *Thankfulness.* To the far left are *Deceit* and *Violence.* To the far right, a bull represents *Prosperity* and two children hold wheat, to depict *Abundance.*

Two and a half million bricks were used in building this structure, but take a moment to note the stonework: It's fake! Really a gypsum type of plaster, it was applied by Chinese plasterers who'd fled from Shanghai during the Sino-Japanese conflict, and molded to give the appearance of granite.

While taking in the exterior, look up at the dome, which is a copy of the dome of St. Paul's Cathedral in London. The dome covers the courtyard, which is surrounded by the four major portions of the Supreme Court building.

The Padang. St. Andrew's Rd. and Connaught Dr.

This large field—officially called Padang Besar but known as the Padang—has witnessed its share of historical events. Bordered on one end by the Singapore Recreation Club and on the other end by the Singapore Cricket Club, and flanked by City Hall, the area was once known as Raffles Plain. Upon Raffles' return to the island in 1822, he was angry that Resident Farquhar had allowed merchants to move into the area he had originally intended for government buildings. All building permits were rescinded and a new site for the commercial district was planned for the area across the Singapore River. The Padang became the official center point for the government quarters, around which the Esplanade and City Hall were built. On weekends the Padang hosts cricket and rugby matches, in season.

Today the Padang is mainly used for public and sporting events—pleasant activities—but in the 1940s it felt more forlorn footsteps when the invading Japanese forced the entire European community onto the field. There they waited while the occupation officers dickered over a suitable location for the "conquered." Presently, they ordered all British, Australian, and Allied troops as well as European prisoners on the 22-kilometer march to Changi.

An interesting side note: Frank Ward, designer of the Supreme Court, had big plans for the Padang and surrounding buildings. He would have demolished the Cricket Club, Parliament House, and the Victoria Hall & Theatre to erect an enormous government block if World War II hadn't arrived, ruining his chances.

Parliament House. 1 High St., at the south end of the Padang, next to the Supreme Court. Closed to the general public, but worth seeing from the outside.

Parliament House, built in 1826, is probably Singapore's oldest surviving structure, even though it has been renovated so many times it no longer looks the way it was originally constructed. It was designed as a home for John Argyle Maxwell, a Scottish merchant, but before it was completed, the government rented it to house the court and other government offices. In 1939, when the new Supreme Court was completed, the judiciary moved in; then, in 1953, following a major renovation, Maxwell's House was renamed Parliament House, and was turned over to the legislature.

The original house was designed by architect George D. Coleman, who had helped Raffles with his Town Plan of 1822. Coleman's design was in the English neo-Palladian style. Simple and well suited to the tropics, this style was popular at the time with Calcutta merchants. Major alterations have left very little behind of Coleman's design, however, replacing it with an eclectic French classical style, but some of his work survives. Today, the building has been transformed once again, into part of a larger S$80 million Parliament Complex.

The bronze elephant in front of Parliament House was a gift to Singapore in 1872 from His Majesty Somdeth Phra Paraminda Maha Chulalongkorn (Rama V), Supreme King of Siam, as a token of gratitude following his stay the previous year.

Victoria Theatre and Concert Hall. 9 Empress Place, at the southern end of the Padang. ☎ 65/339-6120.

Designed by colonial engineer John Bennett in a Victorian Revival style that was fashionable in Britain at the time, the theater portion was built in 1862 as the Town Hall. Victoria Memorial Hall was built in 1905 as a memorial to Queen Victoria, retaining the same style of the old building. The clock tower was added a year later. In 1909, with its name changed to Victoria Theatre, the hall opened with an amateur production of the *Pirates of Penzance*. Another notable performance occurred when Noël Coward passed through Singapore and stepped in at the last moment to help out a traveling English theatrical company that had lost a leading man. The building looks much the same as it did then, though of course the interiors have been modernized. It was completely renovated in 1979, conserving all the original details, and was renamed Victoria Concert Hall. It has since housed the Singapore Symphony Orchestra and various performance companies. (See chapter 8 for details.)

Statue of Raffles. Victoria Theatre and Concert Hall.

This sculpture of Sir Stamford Raffles was erected on the Padang in 1887 and moved to its present position after getting in the way of one too many cricket matches. During the Japanese occupation, the statue was placed in the Singapore History Museum (then the Raffles Museum), and was replaced here in 1945. The local joke is that Raffles's arm is outstretched to the Bank of China building, and his pockets are empty. (Translation: In terms of wealth in Singapore, it's Chinese one, Brits nil.)

Empress Place Building. 1 Empress Place, at the southern end of the Padang next to the Parliament Building.

Standing as a symbol of British colonial authority as travelers entered the Singapore River, Empress Place Building housed almost the entire government bureaucracy around the year 1905, and was a government office until the 1980s, housing the Registry of Births and Deaths and the Citizenship Registry. Every Singaporean at some point passed through its doors. In the late 1980s, the government offices moved out and the building was restored as an historical cultural exhibition venue.

The oldest portion is the part nearest Parliament House; it was designed by colonial engineer J. F. A. McNair and built by convict labor between June 1864 and December 1867. Four major additions and other renovations have been faithful to his original design. Inside, there are many surviving details, including plaster moldings, cornices, and architraves. It is currently being renovated as the second phase of the Asian Civilisations Museum.

Raffles Landing Site. North Boat Quay.

The polymarble statue at this site was unveiled in 1972. It was made from plaster casts of the original 1887 figure located in front of the Victoria Theatre and Concert Hall (see above), and stands on what is believed to be the site where Sir Stamford Raffles landed on January 29, 1819.

ALONG THE RIVER

The Singapore River had always been the heart of life in Singapore even before Raffles landed, but for many years during the 20th century life here was dead—quite literally. Rapid urban development that began in the 1950s turned the river into a giant sewer, killing all plant and animal life in it. In the mid-1980s, though, the government began a large and surprisingly successful cleanup project; and shortly thereafter, the buildings at Boat Quay and Clarke Quay were restored. Now the areas on both banks of the river offer entertainment, food, and pubs day and night.

Boat Quay. Located on the south bank of the Singapore River between Cavenagh Bridge and Elgin Bridge.

Known as "the belly of the carp" by the local Chinese because of its shape, this area was once notorious for its opium dens and coolie shops. Nowadays, thriving restaurants boast every cuisine imaginable and the rocking nightlife offers up a variety of sounds—jazz, rock, blues, Indian, and Caribe—that are lively enough to get any couch potato tapping his feet. See chapters 4 and 8 for dining and nightlife suggestions, and remember to pronounce quay *key* if you don't want people to look at you funny.

Clarke Quay. River Valley Rd. west of Coleman Bridge.

The largest of the waterfront developments, Clarke Quay was named for the second governor of Singapore, Sir Andrew Clarke. In the 1880s, a pineapple cannery, iron foundry, and numerous warehouses made this area bustle. Today, with 60 restored warehouses hosting restaurants and a shopping section known as Clarke Quay Factory Stores, the Quay still hops. **River House,** formerly the home of a *towkay* (company president), occupies the oldest building. The **Bar Gelateria Bellavista** ice cream parlor (River Valley Rd. at Coleman Bridge) was once the ice house. On Thursdays and

Fridays from 6:30 to 8:15pm, enthusiasts can catch a **Chinese opera performance** and makeup demonstration—it's a treat to watch. Get up early on Sunday, forgo the comics section and take in the **flea market,** which opens at 9am and lasts all day. You'll find lots of bargains on unusual finds.

Merlion Park. South bank, at the mouth of the Singapore River, near the Anderson Bridge. Free admission. Daily 7am–10pm.

The Merlion is Singapore's half-lion, half-fish national symbol, the lion representing Singapore's roots as the "Lion City" and the fish representing the nation's close ties to the sea. Bet you think a magical and awe-inspiring beast like this has been around in tales for hundreds of years, right? No such luck. Rather, he was the creation of some scheming mind at the Singapore Tourism Board in the early 1970s. Talk about the collision of ancient culture and the modern world. Despite the Merlion's commercial beginnings, he's been adopted as the national symbol and spouts continuously every day at the mouth of the Singapore River from 10am to noon. Aside from the beastie himself, there's nothing to do in the park, and in fact, the best Merlion viewing can actually be done from Esplanade Park (see below).

Esplanade Park. Connaught Dr., on the marina, running from the mouth of the Singapore River along the Padang to Raffles Ave. Open daily until midnight.

Esplanade Park and Queen Elizabeth Walk, two of the most famous parks in Singapore, were established in 1943 on land reclaimed from the sea. Several memorials are located here. The first is a fountain built in 1857 to honor **Tan Kim Seng,** who gave a great sum of money toward the building of a waterworks. Another monument, **the Cenotaph,** commemorates the 124 Singaporeans who died in World War I; it was dedicated by the Prince of Wales. On the reverse side, the names of those who died in World War II have been inscribed. The third prominent memorial is dedicated to **Major General Lim Bo Seng,** a member of the Singaporean underground resistance in World War II who was captured and killed by the Japanese. His memorial was unveiled in 1954 on the 10th anniversary of his death. These days, the park is a little bit of a mess due to the nearby construction of Singapore's new Theatres on the Bay, modeled after the Sydney Opera House.

Chettiar's Hindu Temple (aka the Tank Road Temple). 15 Tank Rd., close to the intersection of Clemenceau Ave. and River Valley Rd.

One of the richest and grandest of its kind in Southeast Asia, the Tank Road Temple is most famous for a **thoonganai maadam,** a statue of an elephant's backside in a seated position. It's said that there are only four others of the kind, located in four temples in India.

The original temple was completed in 1860, restored in 1962, and practically rebuilt in 1984. The many sculptures of Hindu deities and the carved Kamalam-patterned rosewood doors, arches, and columns were executed by architect-sculptors imported from Madras, India, specifically for the job. The Hindu child god, Lord Muruga, rules over the temple and is visible in one form or another wherever you look. Also notice the statues of the god Shiva and his wife, Kali, captured in their lively dance competition. The story goes that Kali was winning the competition, so Shiva lifted his leg above his head, something a woman wasn't thought capable of doing. He won and quit dancing—good thing, too, since every time Shiva did a little jig he destroyed part of the world.

Outside in the courtyard are statues of the wedding of Lord Muruga; his brother, Ganesh; another brother, Vishnu; and their father, Shiva; along with Brahma, the creator of all.

Used daily for worship, the temple is also the culmination point of Thaipusam, a celebration of thanks, and the Festival of Navarathiri (see chapter 2).

2 Chinatown/Tanjong Pagar

Wak Hai Cheng Bio Temple. 30-B Phillip St., at the corner of Phillip St. and Church St.

Like most of Singapore's Chinese temples, Wak Hai Cheng Bio had its start as a simple wood-and-thatch shrine where sailors, when they got off their ships, would go to express their gratitude for sailing safely to their destination. Before the major land reclamation projects shifted the shoreline outward, the temple was close to the water's edge, and so it was named "Temple of the Calm Sea Built by the Guangzhou People." It's a Teochew temple, located in a part of Chinatown populated mostly by the Teochews.

Inside the Taoist temple walls are two blocks, the one on the left devoted to Ma Po Cho, the Mother of Heavenly Sages, who protects travelers and ensures a safe journey. The one on the left is devoted to Siong Tek Kong, the god of business. Both are as important to the Chinese community today as they were way back when. Look for the statue of the Gambler Brother, with coins around his neck. The Chinese pray to him for wealth and luck, and in olden days would put opium on his lips. This custom is still practiced today, only now they use a black herbal paste called *koyo*, which is conveniently legal.

Inside the temple you can buy joss sticks and paper for S$2.50. Three joss sticks are for heaven, your parents, and yourself, to be burned before the altar. Three corresponding packets of elaborately decorated paper and gold leaf are to be burned outside in the gourd-shaped kilns (gourd being a symbol of health). The joss or "wishing paper," four thin sheets stamped with black and red characters, has many meanings. The red sheet is for luck (red being particularly auspicious) and the other three are to wash away your sins, for a long life, and for your wishes to be carried to heaven. Even if you are not Taoist, you're more than welcome to burn the joss.

The temple itself is quite a visual treat, with ceramic figurines and pagodas adorning the roof, and every nook and cranny of the structure adorned with tiny three-dimensional reliefs that depict scenes from Chinese operas. The spiral joss hanging in the courtyard adds an additional picturesque effect.

Nagore Durgha Shrine. 140 Telok Ayer St., at the corner of Telok Ayer St. and Boon Tat St. ☎ 65/324-0021.

Although this is a Muslim place of worship, it is not a mosque, but a shrine, built to commemorate a visit to the island by a Muslim holy man of the Chulia people (Muslim merchants and moneylenders from India's Coromandel Coast), who was traveling around Southeast Asia spreading the word of Indian Islam. The most interesting visual feature is its facade: Two arched windows flank an arched doorway, with columns in between. Above these is a "miniature palace"—a massive replica of the facade of a palace, with tiny cutout windows and a small arched doorway in the middle. The cutouts in white plaster make it look like lace. From the corners of the facade, two 14-level minarets rise, with three little domed cutouts on each level and onion domes on top. Inside, the prayer halls and two shrines are painted and decorated in shockingly tacky colors.

There is controversy surrounding the dates that the shrine was built. The government, upon naming the Nagore Durgha a national monument, claimed it was built sometime in the 1820s; however, Nagoreallauddeen, who is the 15th descendant of

Chinatown Attractions

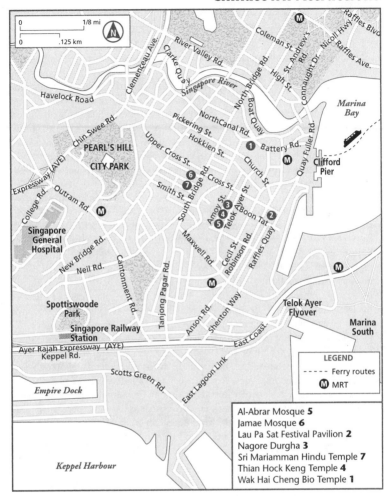

LEGEND
- - - - Ferry routes
Ⓜ MRT

Al-Abrar Mosque **5**
Jamae Mosque **6**
Lau Pa Sat Festival Pavilion **2**
Nagore Durgha **3**
Sri Mariamman Hindu Temple **7**
Thian Hock Keng Temple **4**
Wak Hai Cheng Bio Temple **1**

the holy man for whom the shrine is named, claims it was built many years before. According to Nagoreallauddeen, the shrine was first built out of wood and attap, and was later rebuilt from limestone in 1815, four years before the arrival of Sir Stamford Raffles. In 1818, rebuilding materials were imported from India to construct the present shrine. The government has no historical records to prove the previous existence of the shrine at that time. Nagoreallauddeen, who sits daily in the office just to the right in the entrance hall, is fighting to have his date made official, and has covered the government plaque to the left of the front door, which declares the shrine a national monument. He'll tell you the whole story of the building and of his lineage if you ask, but he doesn't speak English, so try to grab a translator.

✪ **Thian Hock Keng Temple.** 158 Telok Ayer St., $^1/_2$ block beyond Nagore Durgha Shrine.

Thian Hock Keng, the "Temple of Heavenly Bliss," is one of the oldest Chinese temples in Singapore. Before land reclamation, when the shoreline came right up to Telok

The Shophouses of Singapore

The shophouses that line many of Singapore's streets are perhaps the architectural feature travelers find most memorable about this city. These row houses were southern Asia's answer to urban commercial and residential buildings through the early 1800s and into the first half of the 20th century. Their design was perfect. Ground floors were occupied by shops or coffeehouses, while the upper floors were homes—an ideal situation for mom-and-pop operations. The rows of uniform buildings fit perfectly within the grid of the city streets, while inside air shafts and vents let air and sunlight circulate throughout. Out front, many of the shophouses featured ornately decorated facades, while the "five-foot-ways" (covered sidewalks) formed by the shophouses' projecting second stories shielded pedestrians from sun and rain.

Most of the shophouses were built between 1840 and 1960, and differ slightly depending on their period of construction. The earliest houses were built between 1840 and 1860. The style of architecture, imaginatively called the **Early Shophouse Style**, is easy to detect. These houses are low and squat, rising never more than two stories each. On the second floor, the one or two rectangular windows are plain, as are the facades. Sometimes the beam moldings give them a heavy appearance that's clumsy looking compared to the more delicate styles of the later shophouses. What minimal ornamentation exists sometimes reflects the ethnic background of the families who lived inside. Two good examples of this style are at 72 Arab St. and 68 Bussorah St., out in Kampong Glam, or the squat houses at the corner of Amoy and Boon Tat streets in Chinatown.

As time went by, demand for high ceilings inside the newer shophouses meant that the houses themselves grew to greater heights. Windows started to show simple arches, and were adorned with timber shutters, sometimes with glass panels. Simple vents started to appear that were part functional and part decorative. This style, called the **First Transitional Shophouse Style,** can be seen at 118 Serangoon Rd. or 23 Kerbau Rd. in Little India.

Ayer Road, the first Chinese sailors landed here and immediately built a shrine, a small wood-and-thatch structure, to pray to the goddess Ma Po Cho for allowing their voyage to be safely completed. For each subsequent boatload of Chinese sailors, the shrine was always the first stop upon landing. Ma Po Cho, the Mother of the Heavenly Sages, was the patron goddess of sailors, and every Chinese junk of the day had an altar dedicated to her.

The temple that stands today was built in 1841 over the shrine with funds from the Hokkien community, led by the efforts of two Malacca-born philanthropists, Tan Tock Seng and Tan Kim Seng. All of the building materials were imported from China, except for the gates, which came from Glasgow, Scotland, and the tiles on the facade, which are from Holland. The doorway is flanked by two lions, a male with a ball to symbolize strength and a female with a cup to symbolize fertility. On the door are door gods, mythical beasts made from the combined body parts of many animals. Note the wooden bar that sits at the foot of the temple entrance (as do similar bars in so many Chinese temples). This serves a couple of purposes: First, it keeps out wandering ghosts, who cannot cross over the barrier. Second, it forces anyone entering the temple to look down as they cross, bowing their head in humility. Just inside the door are granite tablets that record the temple's history.

The transitional shophouse led into what is called the **Late Shophouse Style.** These houses were built between 1900 and 1940, and are the most ornamental of all of the shophouse styles. Second stories had three windows, sometimes separated by ornamental columns. They were decorated in bright colors with features borrowed from many different cultures. Chinese panel frescoes, wooden Malay fringes around the eaves, colorful ceramic tile work (many tiles were imported from Holland), and floral plasterwork make these shophouses stand out from the rest. Good examples of this style are found at 121 Serangoon Rd. in Little India and at 101 Jalan Sultan in Kampong Glam.

When the **Second Transitional Shophouse Style** came along in the period of the Late Shophouse Style, designers began to pull away from the flamboyant decor of previous structures and concentrated on a more streamlined design. Elements of art deco began to creep in as ceramic tile designs combined with geometric window panels and balustrades. By the 1930s, the **Art Deco Shophouse Style** was in full swing, with classical streamlining of columns. No decorative tiles can be found on the facades, but the houses were made striking by their uniformity from house to house down an entire block. Usually this style of shophouse has a prominently displayed plaque with its date of construction. You can see this style at 148 and 150 Neil Rd. in Chinatown, and at 79 Serangoon Rd. in Little India.

One feature that was common to the houses, but is seen very rarely these days, is the **pintu pagar,** a type of front door that consisted of a pair of half doors, often intricately carved and painted, which had larger timber doors behind them. The pintu pagar design allowed the large doors to remain open during the day, letting in light and breezes yet ensuring a little privacy for the people inside. Along the same lines are the first-story windows, many of which have no glass, but just bars to keep out robbers and let air circulate.

Ahead at the main altar is Ma Po Cho, and on either side are statues of the Protector of Life and the God of War. To the side of the main hall is a Gambler Brother statue, prayed to for luck and riches. From here you can see the temple's construction of brackets and beams, fitting snugly together and carved with war heroes, saints, flowers, and animals, all in red and black lacquer and gilded in gold. Behind the main hall is an altar to Kuan Yin, the Goddess of Mercy. On either side of her are the sun and moon gods.

To the left of the courtyard are the ancestral tablets. In keeping with Confucian filial piety, each represents a soul. The tablets with red paper are for souls still alive. Also in the temple complex is a pagoda and a number of outer buildings that at one time housed a school and community associations.

Al-Abrar Mosque. 192 Telok Ayer St., near the corner of Telok Ayer St. and Amoy St., near Thian Hock Keng Temple.

This mosque was originally erected as a thatched building in 1827 and was also called Masjid Chulia and Kuchu Palli, which in Tamil means "hut mosque." The building that stands today was built in the 1850s, and even though it faces Mecca, the complex conforms with the grid of the neighborhood's city streets. In the late 1980s, the mosque underwent major renovations that enlarged the mihrab and stripped away some of the ornamental qualities of the columns in the building. The one-story prayer hall was extended upward into a two-story gallery. Little touches like the timber window panels and fanlight windows have been carried over into the new renovations.

Lau Pa Sat Festival Pavilion. 18 Raffles Quay, located in the entire block flanked by Robinson Rd., Cross St., Shenton Way, and Boon Tat St.

Though it used to be well beloved, the locals think this place has become an atrocity. Once the happy little hawker center known as Telok Ayer Market, it began life as a wet market, selling fruits, vegetables, and other foodstuffs. Now it's part hawker center, part Western fast-food outlets, and all tourist.

It all began on Market Street in 1823, in a structure that was later torn down, redesigned, and rebuilt by G. D. Coleman. Close to the water, seafood could be unloaded fresh off the pier. After the land in Telok Ayer Basin was reclaimed in 1879, the market was moved to its present home, a James MacRitchie design that kept the original octagonal shape and was constructed of 3,000 prefab cast-iron elements brought in from Europe.

In the 1970s, as the financial district began to develop, the pavilion was dominated by hawkers who fed the lunchtime business crowd. In the mid-eighties, the structure was torn down to make way for the MRT construction and then meticulously put back together, puzzle piece by puzzle piece. By 1989, the market was once again an urban landmark, but it sat vacant until Scotts Holdings successfully tendered to convert it into a festival market. At this time, numerous changes were made to the building, which was renamed Lau Pa Sat ("Old Market") in acknowledgment of the name by which the market had been known by generations of Singaporeans. By the way, Lau Pa Sat is one of the few hawker centers that's open 24 hours, in case you need a coffee or snack before retiring.

✪ **Sri Mariamman Hindu Temple.** 244 South Bridge Rd., at the corner of South Bridge Rd. and Pagoda St.

As the oldest Hindu temple in Singapore, Sri Mariamman has been the central point of Hindu tradition and culture. In its early years, the temple housed new immigrants while they established themselves and also served as social center for the community. Today, the main celebration here is the Thimithi Festival in October or November (see chapter 2). The shrine is dedicated to the goddess Sri Mariamman, who is known for curing disease (a very important goddess to have around in those days), but as is the case at all other Hindu temples, the entire pantheon of Hindu gods are present to be worshipped as well. On either side of the gopuram are statues of Shiva and Vishnu, while inside are two smaller shrines to Vinayagar and Sri Ararvan. Also note the sacred cows that lounge along the top of the temple walls.

The temple originated as a small wood-and-thatch shrine founded by Naraina Pillai, an Indian merchant who came to Singapore with Raffles' first expedition and found his fortune in trade. In the main hall of the temple is the small god that Pillai originally placed here.

✪ **Jamae Mosque.** 18 South Bridge Rd., at the corner of South Bridge Rd. and Mosque St.

Jamae Mosque was built by the Chulias, Tamil Muslims who were some of the earlier immigrants to Singapore, and who had a very influential hold over Indian Muslim life centered in the Chinatown area. It was the Chulias who built not only this mosque, but Masjid Al-Abrar and the Nagore Durgha Shrine as well. Jamae Mosque dates from 1827, but wasn't completed until the early 1830s. The mosque stands today almost exactly as it did then.

While the front gate is typical of mosques you'd see in southern India, inside most of the buildings reflect the neoclassical style of architecture introduced in administrative buildings and homes designed by George Coleman and favored by the Europeans. There are also some Malay touches in the timber work. A small shrine inside, which may be the oldest part of the mosque, was erected to memorialize a local religious leader, Muhammad Salih Valinva.

3 Little India

Abdul Gafoor Mosque. 41 Dunlop St., between Perak Rd. and Jalan Besar.

Abdul Gafoor Mosque is actually a mosque complex consisting of the original mosque, a row of shophouses facing Dunlop Street, a prayer hall, and another row of houses ornamented with crescent moons and stars, facing the mosque. The original mosque was called Masjid Al-Abrar, and is commemorated on a granite plaque above what could have been either the entrance gate or the mosque itself. It still stands, and even though it is badly dilapidated, retains some of its original beauty. One beautiful detail is the sunburst above the main entrance, its rays decorated with Arabic calligraphy.

The surrounding shophouses were built in 1887 and 1903 by Sheik Abdul Gafoor, and their income paid for the start of the new mosque on the site 7 years later. Gafoor passed away before the mosque's completion, and although he'd willed the entire complex to his son, the latter's mismanagement of the affair led the government to pass control to the Mohammeden Endowments Board, who saw the mosque to completion in 1927.

Restoration of the shophouses is underway, including transformation of the facing shophouses into a religious school.

✪ Sri Veerama Kaliamman Temple. On Serangoon Rd. at Veerasamy Rd. Daily 8am–noon and 5:30–8:30pm.

This Hindu temple is primarily for the worship of Shiva's wife Kali, who destroys ignorance, maintains world order, and blesses those who strive for knowledge of God. The box on the walkway to the front entrance is for smashing coconuts, a symbolic smashing of the ego, asking God to show "the humble way." The coconuts have two small "eyes" at one end so they can "see" the personal obstacles to humility they are being asked to smash.

Inside the temple in the main hall are three altars, the center one for Kali (depicted with 16 arms and wearing a necklace of human skulls) and two altars on either side for her two sons—Ganesh, the elephant god, and Murugan, the four-headed child god. To the right is an altar with nine statues representing the nine planets. Circle the altar and pray to your planet for help with a specific trouble.

Around the left side of the main hall, the first tier of the gopuram tells the story of how Ganesh got his elephant head. A small dais in the rear left corner of the temple compound is an altar to Sri Periyachi, a very mean looking woman with a heart of gold. She punishes women who say and do things to make others feel bad. She also punishes men—under her feet is an exploiter of ladies.

Here's a bit of trivia: Red ash, as opposed to white, is applied to the forehead after prayers are offered in a temple devoted to a female god.

Sri Perumal Temple. 397 Serangoon Rd., ¹/₂ block past Perumal Rd. Best times to visit are daily 7–11am or 5–7:30pm.

Sri Perumal Temple is devoted to the worship of Vishnu. As part of the Hindu trinity, Vishnu is the sustainer balancing out Brahma the creator and Shiva the destroyer.

An Introduction to Hindu Temples

The gopuram is the giveaway—the tiered roof piled high with brightly colored statues of gods and goddesses. Definitely a Hindu temple. So what are they all doing up there? It's because in India, what with the caste system and all, the lower classes were at one time not permitted inside the temple, so having these statues on the outside meant they could still pray without actually entering. Furthermore, while each temple is dedicated to a particular deity, all the gods are represented, in keeping with the Hindu belief that although there are many gods, they are all one god. So everyone is up there, in poses or scenes that depict stories from Hindu religious lore. Sometimes there are brightly colored flowers, birds, and animals as well—especially sacred cows. So why are some of them blue? It's because blue is the color of the sky, and to paint the gods blue meant that they, like the sky, are far-reaching and ever present.

There's no special way to pray in these temples, but by custom, most will pray first to Ganesh, the god with the elephant head, who is the remover of obstacles, especially those that can hinder one's closeness to god. Another interesting prayer ritual happens in the temple's main hall around a small dais that holds nine gods, one for each planet. Devotees who need a particular wish fulfilled will circle the dais, praying to their astrological planet god for their wish to come true.

The location of Hindu temples is neither by accident nor by Raffles's Town Plan. By tradition, they must always be built near a source of fresh water so that every morning, before prayer, all of the statues can be bathed. The water runs off a spout somewhere outside the main hall, from which devotees take the water and touch their heads.

Non-Hindus are welcome in the temples to walk around and explore. **Temple etiquette** asks that you first remove your shoes, and if you need to point to something, out of respect, please use your right hand, and don't point with your index finger.

When the world is out of whack, he rushes to its aid, reincarnating himself to show mankind that there are always new directions for development.

On the first tier to the left of the front entrance on the gopuram, statues depict Vishnu's nine reincarnations. Rama, the sixth incarnation, is with Hanuman, the monkey god, who helped him in the fierce battle to free his wife from kidnapping. Krishna, shown reclining amidst devotees, is the eighth incarnation and a hero of many Hindu legends, most notably the Bhagavad-Gita. Also up there is the half-and-half bird Garuda, Vishnu's steed. Inside the temple are altars to Vishnu, his two wives, and Garuda.

The temple was built in 1855, and was most recently renovated in 1992. During Thaipusam, the main festival celebrated here (see chapter 2), male devotees who have made vows over the year carry kavadi—huge steel racks decorated with flowers and fruits and held onto their bodies by skewers and hooks—to show their thanks and devotion, while women carry milk pots in a parade from Sri Perumal Temple to Chettiar's Temple on Tank Road.

✪ **Sakya Muni Buddha Gaya (Temple of a Thousand Lights).** On Race Course Rd., 1 block past Perumal Rd. Daily 7:30am–4:45pm.

Thai elements influence this temple, from the chedi (stupa) roofline to the huge Thai-style Buddha image inside. Often this temple is brushed off as strange and tacky, but there are all sorts of surprises inside, making the place a veritable Buddha theme park. On the right side of the altar, statues of baby boddhisattvas receive toys and sweets from worshippers. Around the base of the altar, murals depict scenes from the life of Prince Siddhartha (Buddha) as he searches for enlightenment. Follow them around to the back of the hall and you'll find a small doorway to a chamber under the altar. Another Buddha image reclines inside, this one shown at the end of his life, beneath the Yellow Seraka tree. On the left side of the main part of the hall is a replica of a footprint left by the Buddha in Ceylon. Next to that is a wheel of fortune. For 50¢ you get one spin.

4 Arab Street/Kampong Glam

✪ **Sultan Mosque.** 3 Muscat St. Daily 9am–1pm and 2–4pm. No visiting is allowed during mass congregation Fri 11:30am–2:30pm.

Though there are more than 80 mosques on the island of Singapore, Sultan Mosque is the real center of the Muslim community. The mosque that stands today is the second Sultan Mosque to be built on this site. The first was built in 1826, partially funded by the East India Company as part of their agreement to leave Kampong Glam to Sultan Hussein and his family in return for sovereign rights to Singapore. The present mosque was built in 1928 and was funded by donations from the Muslim community. The Saracenic flavor of the onion domes, topped with crescent moons and stars, is complemented by Mogul cupolas. Funny thing, though: The mosque was designed by an Irish guy named Denis Santry, who was working for the architectural firm Swan and McLaren.

Other interesting facts about the mosque: Its dome base is a ring of black bottles; the carpeting was donated by a prince of Saudi Arabia and bears his emblem; and at the back of the compound, North Bridge Road has a kink in it, showing where the mosque invaded the nicely planned urban grid pattern. Also, if you make your way through the chink where the back of the building almost touches the compound wall, peer inside the makam to see the royal graves. They open the makam doors on Friday mornings and afternoons.

Sultan Mosque, like all the others, does not permit shorts, miniskirts, low necklines, or other revealing clothing to be worn inside. However, they do realize that non-Muslim travelers like to be comfortable as they tour around, and provide cloaks free of charge. They hang just to the right as you walk up the stairs.

✪ **Istana Kampong Glam.** Located at the end of Sultan Gate, 1 block past the intersection of Sultan Gate, Bagdad St., and Pahang St. This is a private residence, therefore no entry is permitted.

The Istana Kampong Glam hardly seems a fitting palace for Singapore's former royal family, but there's a fascinating and controversial story behind its current state of sad disrepair. In 1819, Sultan Hussein signed the original treaty that permitted the British East India Trading Company to set up operations in Singapore. Then, in 1824, he signed a new treaty in which he gave up his sovereign rights to the country in return for Kampong Glam (which became his personal residence) and an annual stipend for himself and his descendants. Shortly after his death some 11 years later, his son, Sultan Ali, built the palace. The family fortunes began to dwindle over the years that followed, and a decades-long dispute arose between Ali's descendants over ownership rights to the estate. In the late 1890s, they went to court, where it was decided that

An Introduction to Mosques

To appreciate what's going on in the mosques in Singapore, here's a little background on some of the styles and symbols behind these exotic buildings. I have also included some tips that will help non-Muslims feel right at home.

The rule of thumb for Mosques is that they all face Mecca. Lucky for these buildings (and for Singaporean urban planners), most of the major mosques in Singapore have managed to fit within the grid of city streets quite nicely, with few major angles or corners jutting into the surrounding streets. One fine example of a mosque that obeys the Mecca rule but disregards zoning orders is Sultan Mosque in Kampong Glam. A peek around the back will reveal how the road is crooked to make way for the building.

The mosques in Singapore are a wonderful blend of Muslim influences from around the world. The grand Sultan Mosque has the familiar onion dome and Moorish stylings of the Arabic Muslim influence. The smaller but fascinating Hajjah Fatimah Mosque is a real blend of cultures, from Muslim to Chinese to even Christian—testimony to Islam's tolerance of other cultural symbols. On the other hand, the mosques in Chinatown, such as Jamae Mosque and the Nagore Durgha Shrine, are Saracenic in style, a style that originated in India in the late 19th century, mixing traditional styles of Indian and Muslim architecture with British conventionality.

Each mosque has typical features such as a **minaret,** a skinny tower from which the call to prayer was sounded (before recorded broadcasts), and a **mihrab,** a niche in the main hall which faces Mecca and in front of which the imam prays, his voice bouncing from inside and resonating throughout the mosque during prayers. You will also notice that there are no statues to speak of. Some mosques will have a **makam,** a burial site within the building for royalty and esteemed benefactors. This room is usually locked, but sometimes can be opened upon request. To the side of the main prayer hall there's always an **ablution area,** a place for worshippers to wash the exposed parts of their bodies before prayers, to show their respect. This is a custom for all Muslims, whether they pray in the mosque or at home. It is believed that the custom began in Islam's early days, before modern plumbing, and was intended to reduce the smell of so many people crammed into one small hall on those hot Middle Eastern days.

When visiting the mosques in Singapore, and anywhere else for that matter, there are some important rules of **etiquette** to follow. Appropriate dress is required. For both men and women, shorts are prohibited, and you must remove your shoes before you enter. For women, please do not wear short skirts or sleeveless, backless, or low-cut tops (although modern Singaporean Muslims do not require women to cover their heads before entering). Also remember: Never enter the main prayer hall. This area is reserved for Muslims only. Women should also tread lightly around this area, as it's forbidden for women to enter. No cameras or video cameras are allowed, and remember to turn off cellular phones and pagers. Friday is the Sabbath day, and you should not plan on going to the mosques between 11am and 2pm on this day.

no one had the rights as the successor to the sultanate, and the land was reverted to the state, though the family was allowed to remain in the house. Trouble is, since the place had become state owned, the family lost the authority to improve the buildings of the compound, which is why they've fallen into the dilapidated condition you see today. Any day now, Sultan Hussein's family will be given the boot and the place will be spruced up to house Kampong Glam cultural exhibits.

It's not known who designed the Istana, but many believe it was George Coleman (see the box, "Colonial Architecture 101," earlier in this chapter), who, in addition to official buildings, also contracted himself out to design personal residences. The style certainly resembles signature elements found in some of his other works.

The house to the left before the main gate of the Istana compound is called **Gedong Kuning,** or Yellow Mansion. It was the home of Tenkgu Mahmoud, the heir to Kampong Glam. When he died, it was purchased by local Javanese businessman Haji Yusof, the Belt Merchant. His descendants still live in the house.

Alsagoff Arab School. 121 Jalan Sultan, across from Sultan Plaza.

Built in 1912, the school was named for Syed Ahmad Alsagoff, a wealthy Arab merchant and philanthropist who was very influential in Singapore's early colonial days and who died in 1906. It is the oldest girls' school in Singapore, and was the island's first Muslim school.

✪ **Hajjah Fatimah Mosque.** 4001 Beach Rd., past Jalan Sultan.

Hajjah Fatimah was a wealthy businesswoman from Malacca and something of a local socialite. She married a Bugis prince from Celebes, and their only child, a daughter, married Syed Ahmed Alsagoff, son of Arab trader and philanthropist Syed Abdul Rahman Alsagoff. Hajjah Fatimah had originally built a home on this site, but after it had been robbed a couple of times and later set fire to, she decided to build a mosque here and moved to another home.

Inside the high walls of the compound are the prayer hall, an ablution area, gardens and mausoleums, and a few other buildings. You can walk around the main prayer halls to the garden cemeteries, where flat square headstones mark the graves of women and round ones mark the graves of men. Hajjah Fatimah is buried in a private room to the side of the main prayer hall, along with her daughter and son-in-law.

The minaret tower in the front was designed by an unknown European architect and could be a copy of the original spire of St. Andrew's Cathedral. The tower leans a little, a fact that's much more noticeable from the inside. On the outside of the tower is a bleeding heart—an unexpected place to find such a downright Christian symbol. It's a great example of what makes this mosque so charming—all the combined influences of Moorish, Chinese, and European architectural styles.

5 Orchard Road Area

The Istana and Sri Temasek. Orchard Rd., between Claymore Rd. and Scotts Rd.

In 1859, the construction of Fort Canning necessitated the demolition of the original governors' residence, and the autocratic and unpopular governor-general Sir Harry St. George Ord proposed this structure be built as the new residence. Though the construction of such a large and expensive edifice was unpopular, Ord had his way, and design and construction went through, with the building mainly performed by convicts under the supervision of Maj. J. F. A. McNair, the colonial engineer and superintendent of convicts.

In its picturesque landscaped setting, Government House echoed Anglo-Indian architecture, but its symmetrical and cross-shaped plan also echoed the form of the traditional Malay istana (palace). During the occupation, the house was occupied by Field Marshal Count Terauchi, commander of the Japanese Southern Army, and

Major General Kawamura, commander of the Singapore Defense Forces. With independence, the building was renamed the Istana, and today serves as the official residence of the President of the Republic of Singapore. Used mainly for state and ceremonial occasions, the grounds are open to every citizen on selected public holidays, though they're not generally open for visits. The house's domain includes several other houses of senior colonial civil servants. The colonial secretary's residence, a typical 19th-century bungalow, is also a gazetted monument and is now called Sri Temasek.

✪ **Peranakan Place.** Located at the intersection of Emerald Hill and Orchard Rd.

Emerald Hill was once nothing more than a wide treeless street along whose sides quiet families lived in typical terrace houses—residential units similar to shophouses, with a walled courtyard in the front instead of the usual "five-foot way." Toward Orchard Road, the terrace houses turned into shophouses, with their first floors occupied by small provisioners, seamstresses, and dried-goods stores. Across Orchard was Robinsons Department Store in a plain, boxy building.

As Orchard Road developed, so did Emerald Hill. A giant shopping mall called Centrepoint was built close to the junction of the two roads, and Robinsons moved into more glitzy digs. Meanwhile, the buildings were all renovated. The shophouses close to Orchard Road became restaurants and bars and the street was closed off to vehicular traffic. Now it's an alfresco cafe, landscaped with a veritable jungle of potted foliage and peopled by colorful tourists—much different from its humble beginnings.

But as you pass Emerald Hill, don't just blow it off as a tourist trap. Walk through the cafe area and out the back onto Emerald Hill. All of the terrace houses have been redone, and magnificently. The facades have been freshly painted and the tiles polished, and the dark wood details add a contrast that is truly elegant. When these places were renovated, they could be purchased for a song, but as Singaporeans began grasping at their heritage in recent years, their value shot up, and now these homes fetch huge sums.

For a peek inside some of these wonderful places (and who doesn't like to see how the rich live?), go to a bookstore and look at *Living Legacy: Singapore's Architectural Heritage Renewed,* by Robert Powell. Gorgeous photographs take you inside a few of these homes and some other terrace houses and bungalows around the island, showing off the traditional interior details of these buildings and bringing their heritage to life.

Goodwood Park Hotel Tower Wing. 22 Scotts Rd., 1 block from Orchard Rd.

In 1861, with the Orchard Road area developing from a plantation area into a residential district popular with Europeans, Singapore's prosperous Germans purchased a piece of land on Scotts Road to build a community clubhouse, to be called the Teutonia Club. The design was entrusted to Swan and McLaren and placed in the hands of R. A. J. Bidwell, who chose for the building the lively Dutch-, French-, and English-influenced Queen Anne style, which had emerged in England in the late 19th century. The L-shaped plan enclosed two large halls linked by a prominent projecting porte cochère at the corner. The halls had generous verandahs both front and back, which separated guests from service staff and ensured adequate ventilation.

The club officially opened on September 21, 1900, but toward the end of March 1915, as the reverberations of World War I spread around the world, some 300 German nationals in Penang and Singapore were classified as enemy aliens and, together with their families, shipped to be interned in Australia. Their possessions, including the clubhouse, were confiscated and liquidated at public auction. Three brothers purchased the club, renaming it Goodwood Hall after the famous Goodwood Race-course and using it as a performance venue (for 2 nights in December 1922, ballerina Anna Pavlova performed there with her troupe) before converting it to a hotel in the late 1920s. During the Japanese occupation the hotel was used by senior Japanese officers, and after the war, the Army War Crimes Office conducted trials on the premises. Plans in the seventies that called for the replacement of the Tower Wing with a 16-story modern building, complete with bubble lift, were abandoned when it was vocally criticized by the public. Instead, a new tower, which faintly resembles the original, was built in 1978. It's only a replica, but for the record it's an official national monument. The hotel's public areas are open to nonguests.

6 Attractions Outside the Urban Area

The famous image of Singapore, promulgated by the convention board and recognizable to business travelers everywhere, is of the towering cityscape along the water's edge—but there's a reason they call this place the Garden City. Not only are there picturesque gardens and parks nestled within the urban jungle, but the urban jungle is nestled within *real* jungle. While it's true that most of the wooded areas have been replaced by suburban housing, it's also true that thousands of acres of secondary rain forest have survived the migration of Singaporeans to the suburbs. Better yet, there are still some areas with primary rain forest, some of which are accessible by paths.

What Singapore does have are spectacular **gardens,** from the well-groomed Botanical Garden to nature preserves like Bukit Timah and Sungei Buloh, where tropical rain forest and mangrove swamps are close enough to the city that you can visit them on a morning or afternoon visit. Outside the city center you'll also find **historic sites and temples** like the edifying Changi Prison Museum and the Siong Lim Temple, as well as **museums** and **science centers.**

In the late 1800s, the colonial government began to section off tracts of forest into **nature reserves** to preserve the habitats of local species of plants and animals. The first of these was the Bukit Timah Nature Reserve, established in 1883. In 1990, Singapore passed a national parks act, which established the National Parks Board to oversee not only the national parks, but also the Singapore Botanical Gardens and Fort Canning Park. The mission of the board is to preserve and promote the nature reserves as a sanctuary for wildlife, a place for plant conservation, and a resource for education and outdoor recreational activities. Today, in addition to Bukit Timah, the nature reserve system includes MacRitchie, Seletar, Pierce, and Upper Pierce reservoirs. With the exception of Bukit Timah, these places are located in the central part of the island (see "Central & Northern Singapore Attractions," below).

While the Sungei Buloh Nature Park is not under the jurisdiction of the National Parks Board, it too serves to conserve wildlife for educational and recreational purposes.

WESTERN SINGAPORE ATTRACTIONS

The attractions grouped in this section are on the west side of Singapore, beginning from the Singapore Botanic Gardens at the edge of the urban area all the way out to the Singapore Discovery Centre past Jurong. Remember, if you're traveling around this area that transportation can be problematic, as the MRT system rarely goes direct to any of these places, taxis can be hard to find, and bus routes get more complex. Keep the telephone number for taxi booking handy. Sometimes ticket sales people at each attraction can help and make the call for you.

Attractions Outside the Urban Area

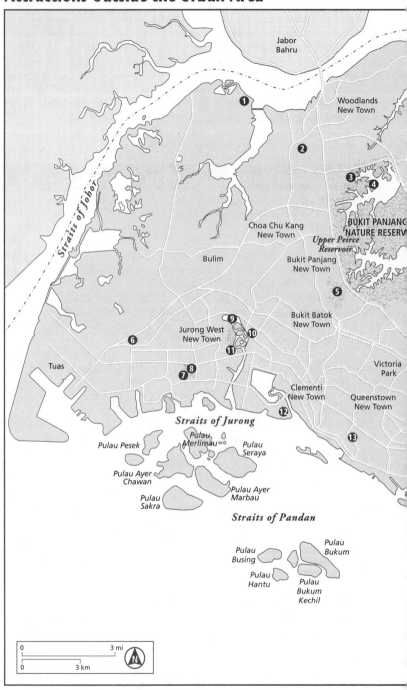

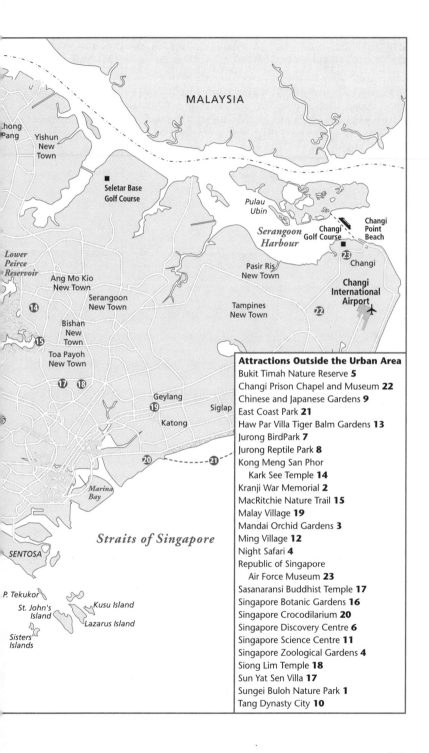

MALAYSIA

Chong
Pang

Yishun
New
Town

Seletar Base
Golf Course

Pulau
Ubin

Serangoon Harbour

Changi
Golf Course

Changi
Point
Beach

Changi

㉓

Lower
Peirce
Reservoir

Ang Mo Kio
New Town

Serangoon
New Town

Pasir Ris
New Town

Changi
International
Airport

⑭

Bishan
New
Town

Tampines
New Town

㉒

⑮

Toa Payoh
New Town

⑰ ⑱

Geylang

Siglap

⑲

Katong

⑳

㉑

Marina
Bay

SENTOSA

Straits of Singapore

P. Tekukor

St. John's
Island

Kusu Island

Lazarus Island

Sisters
Islands

Attractions Outside the Urban Area
Bukit Timah Nature Reserve **5**
Changi Prison Chapel and Museum **22**
Chinese and Japanese Gardens **9**
East Coast Park **21**
Haw Par Villa Tiger Balm Gardens **13**
Jurong BirdPark **7**
Jurong Reptile Park **8**
Kong Meng San Phor Kark See Temple **14**
Kranji War Memorial **2**
MacRitchie Nature Trail **15**
Malay Village **19**
Mandai Orchid Gardens **3**
Ming Village **12**
Night Safari **4**
Republic of Singapore Air Force Museum **23**
Sasanaransi Buddhist Temple **17**
Singapore Botanic Gardens **16**
Singapore Crocodilarium **20**
Singapore Discovery Centre **6**
Singapore Science Centre **11**
Singapore Zoological Gardens **4**
Siong Lim Temple **18**
Sun Yat Sen Villa **17**
Sungei Buloh Nature Park **1**
Tang Dynasty City **10**

Bukit Timah Nature Reserve. 177 Hindhede Dr. ☎ **1800/468-5736.** Free admission. Daily 7am–7pm. MRT to Newton, then TIBS bus no. 171 or SBS bus no. 182 to park entrance.

Bukit Timah Nature Reserve is pure primary rain forest. Believed to be as old as 1 million years, it's the only place on the island with vegetation that exists exactly as it was before the British settled here. The park is more than 81 hectares (202 acres) of soaring canopy teeming with mammals and birds and a lush undergrowth with more bugs, butterflies, and reptiles than you can shake a vine at. Here you can see more than 700 plant species, many of which are exotic ferns, plus mammals like long-tailed macaques, squirrels, and lemurs. There's a visitor center and four well-marked paths, one of which leads to Singapore's highest point. At 163 meters (535 ft.) above sea level, don't expect a nosebleed, but some of the scenic views of the island are really nice. Along another walkway is Singapore's oldest tree, estimated to be 400 years old. Also at Bukit Timah is Hindhede Quarry, which filled up with water at some point, so you can take a dip and cool off during your hike.

✪ **Jurong BirdPark.** 2 Jurong Hill. ☎ **65/265-0022.** Adults S$10.30 (US$6.15), children under 12 S$4.10 (US$2.45), seniors S$7.21 (US$4.30). Panorail adults S$2.50 (US$1.50), children under 12 S$1 (US$0.60). Mon–Fri 9am–6pm; Sat–Sun, and public holidays 8am–6pm. MRT to Boon Lay Station, transfer to SBS no. 194 or 251.

Jurong BirdPark, with a collection of 8,000 birds from more than 600 species, showcases Southeast Asian breeds plus other colorful tropical beauties, some of which are endangered. The more than 20 hectares (49$^{1}/_{2}$ acres) can be easily walked or, for a couple dollars extra, you can ride the panorail for a bird's-eye view (so to speak) of the grounds. I enjoy the Waterfall Aviary, the world's largest walk-in aviary. It's an up-close-and-personal experience with African and South American birds, plus a pretty walk over pathways and babbling brooks through landscaped tropical forest. This is where you'll also see the world's tallest man-made waterfall, but the true feat of engineering here is the panorail station, built inside the aviary. Another smaller walk-in aviary is for Southeast Asian endangered bird species; at noon every day this aviary experiences a man-made thunderstorm. The daily guided tours and regularly scheduled feeding times are enlightening. Other bird exhibits are the flamingo pools, the World of Darkness (featuring nocturnal birds), and the penguin parade, a favorite for Singaporeans, who adore all things Arctic.

Two shows feature birds of prey either acting out their natural instincts or performing falconry tricks. The **Fuji World of Hawks** is at 10am and the **King of the Skies** is at 4pm. The **All-Star Birdshow** takes place at 11am and 3pm, with trained parrots that race bikes and birds that perform all sorts of silliness, including staged birdie misbehaviors. Try to come between 9am and 11am for breakfast among hanging cages of chirping birds at the **Songbird Terrace.**

Jurong Reptile Park. 241 Jalan Ahmad Ibrahim. ☎ **65/261-8866.** Adults S$7 (US$4), children under 12 and seniors S$3.50 (US$2.10). Daily 9am–6pm. MRT to Boon Lay Station, transfer to SBS no. 194 or 251.

The newly renovated Jurong Reptile Park (fixed up just in time, as the older facility was smelling up the entire neighborhood) houses more than 50 species of reptiles from the region and around the world. Feedings are fun, as are the reptile shows (at 11:45am and 2pm daily). Snakes are happy to wrap themselves around your neck for a souvenir photo (10:30am and 5pm daily). In itself, it's no reason to trek out to Jurong, but it makes a convenient add-on to a visit to the Jurong BirdPark.

Haw Par Villa Tiger Balm Gardens. 262 Pasir Panjang Rd. ☎ **65/774-0300.** Adults S$5 (US$3), children S$2.50 (US$1.50). Daily 9am–5pm. MRT to Buona Vista and transfer to bus no. 200.

In 1935, brothers Haw Boon Haw and Haw Boon Par—creators of Tiger Balm, the camphor and menthol rub that comes in those cool little pots—took their fortune and opened Tiger Balm Gardens as a venue for teaching traditional Chinese values. They made more than 1,000 statues and life-size dioramas depicting Chinese legends and historic tales and illustrating morality and Confucian beliefs. Many of these were gruesome and bloody and some of them were really entertaining.

But Tiger Balm Gardens suffered a horrible fate. In 1985, it was converted into an amusement park and reopened as Haw Par Villa. Most of the statues and scenes were taken away and replaced with rides. Well, business did not exactly boom. In fact, the park has been losing money fast. But recently, in an attempt to regain some of the original Tiger Balm Garden edge, they replaced many of the old statues, some of which are a great backdrop for really kitschy vacation photos. Last year they also lowered the admission price from S$16 for adults to the more affordable S$5 they charge today. Catch the two theme rides: the Tales of China Boat Ride and the Wrath of the Water Gods Flume.

Tang Dynasty City. 2 Yuan Ching Rd. ☎ **65/261-1116.** Adults S$15.45 (US$9.25), children to 12 S$10.30 (US$6.15). 10am–4pm. MRT to Lakeside, then transfer to SBS no. 154 or 240.

This theme park re-creates Xian, the Chinese capital city during the Tang Dynasty (A.D. 618–907), the "Golden Age" of Chinese history for great achievements in the sciences, architecture, religion, and the arts, and for trade along the silk road. To build the reproduction city, around 80 workers who specialized in period buildings were brought in from China, as were all the green bricks and slates, roof tiles, 50,000 kilos of white jade, and almost S$5 million worth of antiques. As you make your way through the narrow streets you can check out the shops showcasing artisans who carve chops (the stone stamps carved with Chinese characters that artists use to sign paintings and calligraphy) and eggshells (real eggshells, carved with intricate and delicate lace designs), and perform the tea ceremony. In some buildings you can walk upstairs, especially at the three-story "pleasure home." The Buddhist temple that was built for the city has come into use as an actual temple for visitors to the park.

The wax museum has more than 100 historical Chinese figures including Confucius and Ghenghis Khan. And if you think wax museums are creepy, you have to see the animated figures of Sun Yat-sen and Mao Zedong shouting propaganda. There are 2,000 reproduction terra-cotta warriors in an underground tomb display, plus a Ghost Mansion, featuring Japanese-engineered illusions.

✪ **Chinese and Japanese Gardens.** 1 Chinese Garden Rd. ☎ **65/264-3455.** Adults S$4.50 (US$2.70), children S$2 (US$1.20). Daily 9am–6pm. MRT to Chinese Garden or Bus nos. 335, 180, and 154.

Situated on two islands in Jurong lake, the gardens are reached by an overpass and joined by the Bridge of Double Beauty. The **Chinese Garden** dedicates most of its area to "northern style" landscape architecture. The style of Imperial gardens, the northern style integrates brightly colored buildings with the surroundings to compensate for northern China's absence of rich plant growth and natural scenery. The Stoneboat is a replica of the stone boat at the Summer Palace in Beijing. Inside the Pure Air of the Universe building are courtyards and a pond, and there is a seven-story pagoda, the odd number of floors symbolizing continuity. Around the gardens, special attention has been paid to the placement of rock formations to resemble true nature, and also to the qualities of the rocks themselves, which can represent the forces of yin and yang, male and female, passivity or activity, and so on.

I like the Garden of Beauty, in Suzhou style, representing the southern style of land-scape architecture. Southern gardens were built predominantly by scholars, poets, and men of wealth. Sometimes called Black-and-White gardens, these smaller gardens had more fine detail, featuring subdued colors as the plants and elements of the rich natural landscape gave them plenty to work with. Inside the Suzhou garden are 2,000 pots of *penjiang* (bonsai) and displays of small rocks.

While the Chinese garden is more visually stimulating, the **Japanese garden** is intended to evoke feeling. Marble-chip paths lead the way so that as you walk you can hear your own footsteps and meditate on the sound. They also serve to slow the journey for better gazing upon the scenery. The Keisein, or "Dry Garden," uses white pebbles to create images of streams. Ten stone lanterns, a small traditional house, and a rest house are nestled between two ponds with smaller islands joined by bridges.

There are toilets situated at stops along the way, as well as benches to have a rest or to just take in the sights. Paddleboats can be rented for S$5 (US$3) per hour just outside the main entrance.

✪ **Singapore Botanic Gardens.** Main entrance at corner of Cluny Rd. and Holland Rd. ☎ **1800/471-7300** toll free in Singapore. Free admission. Daily 4am–11:30pm (closing at midnight on weekends). The National Orchid Garden adults S$2 (US$1.20), children under 12 and seniors S$1 (US$0.60). Daily 8:30am–7pm. MRT to Orchard. Take SBS no. 7, 105, 106, 123, or 174 from Orchard Blvd.

In 1822, Singapore's first botanic garden was started at Fort Canning by Sir Stamford Raffles. After it lost funding, the present Botanic Garden came into being in 1859 thanks to the efforts of a horticulture society; it was later turned over to the government for upkeep. More than just a garden, this space occupied an important place in the region's economic development when "Mad" Henry Ridley, one of the garden's directors, imported Brazilian rubber tree seedlings from Great Britain. He devised improved latex-trapping methods and led the campaign to convince reluctant coffee growers to switch plantation crops. The garden also pioneered orchid hybridization, breeding a number of internationally acclaimed varieties.

Carved out within the tropical setting lies a rose garden, sundial garden with pruned hedges, a banana plantation, a spice garden, and sculptures by international artists dotted around the area. As you wander, look for the Cannonball tree (named for its cannonball-shaped fruit), Para rubber trees, teak trees, bamboos, and a huge array of palms, including the sealing wax palm—distinguished by its bright scarlet stalks—and the rumbia palm, which bears the pearl sago. The fruit of the silk-cotton tree is a pod filled with silky stuffing that was once used for stuffing pillows. Flowers like bougainvilleas and heliconias add beautiful color.

The **National Orchid Garden** is 3 hectares (7.4 acres) of gorgeous orchids growing along landscaped walks. The English Garden features hybrids developed here and named after famous visitors to the garden—there's the Margaret Thatcher, the Benazir Bhutto, the Vaclav Havel, and more. The gift shops sell live hydroponic orchids in test tubes for unique souvenirs.

The gardens have three lakes. Symphony Lake surrounds an island band shell for "Concert in the Park" performances by the local symphony and international entertainers like Chris de Burg. Call visitor services at ☎ **65/471-7361** for performance schedules.

Singapore Science Centre. 15 Science Centre Rd., off Jurong Town Hall Rd. ☎ **65/560-3316.** www.sci-ctr.edu.sg/. Adults S$3 (US$1.80), children under 16 S$1.50 (US$0.90), seniors S$2.50 (US$1.50). Tues–Sun and public holidays 10am–6pm. Take the West Coast Attractions bus (see above) or MRT to Jurong East then SBS no. 66 or 335.

The centre features hands-on exhibits in true science-center spirit. You can play in the Atrium, Physical Sciences Gallery, Life Sciences Gallery, and the Hall of Science. Unfortunately, many of the exhibits are worn and tired from overuse and abuse. The Technology Gallery is one of the more interesting exhibits if you can wrestle the kids away from the machines, and the aromatics display, with blindfolded "guess the herb or spice" corner, is so popular they're thinking of upgrading it from temporary status. Singapore Airlines has redone the new "On Wings We Fly" Aviation Gallery. Also notable are the section on the cleaning of the Singapore River and showcased educational projects from university students. The Omni Theatre planetarium has a projection booth encased in glass so you can check out how it works.

✪ **Singapore Discovery Centre.** 510 Upper Jurong Rd. ☎ **65/792-6188.** www. asianconnect.com/sdc. Adults S$9 (US$5.40), children under 12 S$5 (US$3); simulator ride S$4 (US$2.40); Shooting Gallery S$3 (US$1.80). Tues–Fri 9am–7pm; Sat–Sun and public holidays 9am–8pm. MRT to Boon Lay; transfer to SBS no. 192 or 193.

The original plan was to build a military history museum here, but then planners began to wonder if maybe the concept wouldn't bring people running. What they came up with instead is a fascinating display of the latest military technology with hands-on exhibits that cannot be resisted—one of 19 interactive information kiosks, for instance, lets you design tanks and ships. Airborne Rangers, a virtual reality experience, lets you parachute from a plane and manipulate your landing to safety. In the motion simulator, feel your seat move in tandem with the fighter pilot on the screen. The Shooting Gallery is a computer-simulated combat firing range using real but decommissioned M16 rifles. Other attractions are an exhibit of 14 significant events in Singapore history, including the fall of Singapore, self-government, racial riots, and housing block development. And then there's Tintoy Theatre, where the robot Tintoy conducts an entertaining lecture on warfare! Tintoy fights a war, seeking the help of Sun Tzu and other ancient military tacticians. IMAX features roll at the five-story iWERKS Theatre regularly. When you get hungry, there's a fast-food court.

You can also have a 30-minute bus tour of the neighboring Singapore Air Force Training Institute free with SDC admission. Inquire about tour times at the front counter.

Ming Village. 32 Pandan Rd. ☎ **65/265-7711.** Admission and guided tour free. Daily 9am–6pm. MRT to Clementi, then SBS no. 78. Ming Village offers a free Singapore Trolley shuttle from Paragon by Sogo on Orchard Rd. and from the Raffles Hotel bus stop at 9:20am and 9:30am respectively, and also at 10:30am and 10:40am respectively.

Tour a pottery factory that employs traditional pottery-making techniques from the Ming and Qing dynasties and watch the process from mold making, hand throwing, and hand painting to glazing each piece. After the tour, shop from their large selection of beautiful antique reproduction dishes, vases, urns, and more. Certificates of authenticity are provided, which describe the history of each piece. They are happy to arrange overseas shipping for your treasures, or if you want to carry your purchase home, they'll wrap it very securely.

CENTRAL & NORTHERN SINGAPORE ATTRACTIONS
The northern part of Singapore contains most of the island's nature reserves and parks. Here's where you'll find the Singapore Zoological Gardens, in addition to some sights with historical and religious significance. Despite the presence of the **MRT** in the area, there is not any simple way to get from attraction to attraction with ease. Bus transfers to and from MRT stops is the way to go—or you could stick to taxicabs.

Kranji War Memorial. Woodlands Rd., located in the very northern part of the island. MRT to Bugis. From Rochore Rd., take SBS no. 170.

Kranji Cemetery commemorates the men and women who fought and died in World War II. Prisoners of war in a camp nearby began a burial ground here, and after the war it was enlarged to provide space for all the casualties. The Kranji War Cemetery is the site of 4,000 graves of servicemen, while the Singapore State Cemetery memorializes the names of over 20,000 who died and have no known graves. Stones are laid geometrically on a slope with a view of the Strait of Johor. The memorial itself is designed to represent the three arms of the services.

✪ **Siong Lim Temple.** 184-E Jalan Toa Payoh. Located in Toa Payoh New Town. Take MRT to Toa Payoh, then take a taxi.

This temple, in English "the Twin Groves of the Lotus Mountain Temple," has a great story behind its founding. One night in 1898, Hokkien businessman Low Kim Pong and his son had the same dream—of a golden light shining from the West. The following day, the two went to the western shore and waited until, moments before sundown, a ship appeared carrying a group of Hokkien Buddhist monks and nuns on their way to China after a pilgrimage to India. Low Kim Pong vowed to build a monastery if they would stay in Singapore. They did.

Laid out according to feng shui principles, the buildings include the Dharma Hall, a main prayer hall, and drum and bell towers. They are arranged in *cong lin* style, a rare type of monastery design with a universal layout so that no matter how vast the grounds are, any monk can find his way around. The entrance hall has granite wall panels carved with scenes from Chinese history. The main prayer hall has fantastic details in the ceiling, wood panels, and other wood carvings. In the back is a shrine to Kuan Yin, Goddess of Mercy.

Originally built amid farmland, the temple became surrounded by suburban high-rise apartments in the 1950s and 1960s, with the Toa Payoh Housing Development Board New Town project and the Pan-Island Expressway creeping close by.

✪ **Kong Meng San Phor Kark See Temple.** Bright Hill Dr. Located in the center of the island to the east of Bukit Panjang Nature Preserve. Bright Hill Dr. is off Ang Mo Kio Ave. Take MRT to Bishan, then take a taxi.

The largest and most modern religious complex on the island, this place, called Phor Kark See for short, is comprised of prayer and meditation halls, a hospice, gardens, and a vegetarian restaurant. The largest building is the Chinese-style Hall of Great Compassion. There is also the octagonal Hall of Great Virtue and a towering pagoda. For S$0.50 (US$.30) you can buy flower petals to place in a dish at the Buddha's feet. Compared to other temples on the island, Phor Kark See seems shiny—having only been built in 1981. As a result, the religious images inside carry a strange, almost artificial, cartoon air about them.

If you're curious, find the crematorium in the back of the complex. Arrive on Sundays after 1pm and wait for the funeral processions to arrive. Chairs line the side and back of the hall, and attendees do not mind if you sit quietly and observe, as long as you are respectful. The scene is not for the faint of heart, but makes for a touching moment of cultural difference and human similarity.

Sun Yat Sen Villa. 12 Tai Gin Rd., near Toa Payoh New Town. No phone. Free admission. Mon–Fri 9am–5pm; Sat–Sun and public holidays 9am–4pm. Take the MRT to Toa Payoh, then take a taxi.

Dr. Sun Yat-sen visited Singapore eight times to raise funds for his revolution in China, and made Singapore his headquarters for gaining the support of overseas

Chinese in Southeast Asia. A wealthy Chinese merchant built the villa around 1880 for his mistress, and a later owner permitted Dr. Sun Yat-sen to use it. The house reflects the classic bungalow style, which is becoming endangered in modern Singapore. Its typical bungalow features include a projecting carport with a sitting room overhead, verandas with striped blinds, second-story cast-iron railings, and first-story masonry balustrades. A covered walkway leads to the kitchen and servants' quarters in the back.

Inside, the life of Dr. Sen is traced in photos and watercolors, from his birth in southern China through his creation of a revolutionary organization. Restorations are planned to convert it into the Sun Yat Sen Nanyang Memorial Hall.

Sasanaransi Buddhist Temple. 14 Tai Gin Rd., located next to the Sun Yat Sen Villa near Toa Payoh New Town. Daily 6:30am–9pm. Chanting: Sun 9:30am, Wed 8pm, and Sat 7:30pm. Take MRT to Toa Payoh, then take a taxi.

Known simply as the Burmese Buddhist Temple, it was founded by a Burmese expatriate to serve the overseas Burmese Buddhist community. His partner, an herbal doctor also from Burma, traveled home to buy a 10-ton block of marble from which was carved the 11-foot-tall Buddha image that sits in the main hall, surrounded by an aura of brightly colored lights. The original temple was off Serangoon Road in Little India, and was moved here in 1991 at the request of the Housing Development Board. On the third story is a standing Buddha image in gold, and murals of events in the Buddha's life.

Mandai Orchid Gardens. Mandai Lake Rd., on the route to the Singapore Zoological Gardens. ☎ **65/269-1036.** Adults S$2 (US$1.20), children under 12 S50¢ (US$0.30). Daily 8:30am–5:30pm. MRT to Ang Mo Kio and SBS no. 138.

Owned and operated by Singapore Orchids Pte Ltd. to breed and cultivate hybrids for international export, the gardens double as an STB tourist attraction. Arranged in English garden style, orchid varieties are separated in beds that are surrounded by grassy lawn. Tree-growing varieties prefer the shade of the covered canopy. On display is Singapore's national flower, the Vanda Miss Joaquim, a natural hybrid in shades of light purple. Behind the gift shop is the Water Garden, where a stroll will reveal many houseplants common to the West, as you would find them in the wild.

✪ Singapore Zoological Gardens. 80 Mandai Lake Rd., at the western edge of the Bukit Panjang Nature Reserve, on the Seletar Reservoir. ☎ **65/269-3411.** www.asianconnect. com/zoo. Adults S$10.30 (US$6.15), children under 12 S$4.60 (US$2.75). Discounts for seniors. Daily 8:30am–6pm. MRT to Ang Mo Kio and take SBS no. 138.

They call themselves the Open Zoo because, rather than coop the animals in jailed enclosures, they let them roam freely in landscaped areas. Beasts of the world are kept where they are supposed to be using psychological restraints and physical barriers that are disguised behind waterfalls, vegetation, and moats. Some animals are grouped with other species to show them coexisting as they would in nature. For instance, the white rhinoceros is neighborly with the wildebeest and ostrich—not that wildebeests and ostriches make the best company, but certainly contempt is better than boredom. Guinea and pea fowl, Emperor tamarinds, and other creatures are free roaming and not shy; however, if you spot a water monitor or long-tailed macaque, know that they're not zoo residents—just locals looking for a free meal.

Major zoo features are the Primate Kingdom, Wild Africa, the Reptile Garden, the children's petting zoo, and underwater views of polar bears, sea lions, and penguins. Daily shows include primate and reptile shows at 10:30am and 2:30pm, and elephant and sea lion shows at 11:30am and 3:30pm. You can take your photograph with an orangutan, chimpanzee, or snake, and there are elephant and camel rides, too.

The literature provided includes half-day and full-day agendas to help you see the most while you're there. The best time to arrive, however, is at 9am, to have breakfast with an orangutan, which feasts on fruits, and puts on a hilarious and very memorable show. If you miss that, you can also have tea with it at 4pm. Another good time to go is just after a rain, when the animals cool off and get frisky.

✪ Night Safari. Singapore Zoological Gardens, 80 Mandai Lake Rd., at the western edge of the Bukit Panjang Nature Reserve, on the Seletar Reservoir. ☎ **65/269-3411.** www. asianconnect.com/zoo/. Adults S$15.45 (US$9.25), children under 12 S$10.30 (US$6.15). Daily 7:30pm–midnight. Ticket sales close at 11pm. Entrance Plaza, restaurant, and fast-food outlet open from 6:30pm. MRT to Ang Mo Kio and take SBS no. 138.

Singapore takes advantage of its unchanging tropical climate and static ratio of daylight to night to bring you the world's first open-concept zoo for nocturnal animals. Here, as in the zoological gardens, animals live in landscaped areas, their barriers virtually unseen by visitors. These areas are dimly lit to create a moonlit effect, and a guided tram leads you through "regions" designed to resemble the Himalayan foothills, the jungles of Africa, and, naturally, Southeast Asia. Some of the free-range prairie animals come very close to the tram. The 45-minute ride covers almost 3¹/₂ kilometers (2 miles), and has regular stops to get off and have a rest or stroll along trails for closer views of smaller creatures.

Staff, placed at regular intervals along the trails, help you find your way, though it's almost impossible to get lost along the trails; however, it is nighttime, you are in the forest, and it can be spooky. The guides are there more or less to add peace of mind (and all speak English). Flash photography is strictly prohibited, and be sure to bring plenty of insect repellent. *A weirder tip:* Check out the bathrooms. They're all open-air, Bali style.

Sungei Buloh Nature Park. 301 Neo Tiew Crescent. ☎ **65/794-1401.** Adults S$1 (US$0.60) children and seniors S50¢ (US$0.30). (Mon–Fri 7:30am–7pm; Sat–Sun and public holidays 7am–7pm. Audiovisual show Mon–Sat 9am, 11am, 1pm, 3pm and 5pm; hourly Sun and public holidays. MRT to Kranji, bus no. 925 to Kranji Reservoir Dam. Cross causeway to park entrance.

Located to the very north of the island and devoted to the wetland habitat and mangrove forests that are so common to the region, 87-hectare (218-acre) Sungei Buloh is out of the way, and not the easiest place to get to; but it's a beautiful park, with constructed paths and boardwalks taking you through tangles of mangroves, soupy marshes, grassy spots, and coconut groves. Of the flora and fauna, the most spectacular sights here are the birds, of which there are somewhere between 140 and 170 species in residence or just passing through for the winter. Of the migratory birds, some have traveled from as far as Siberia to escape the cold months from September to March. Bird observatories are set up at different spots along the paths. Also, even though you're in the middle of nowhere, Sungei Buloh has a visitor center, a cafeteria, and souvenirs.

MacRitchie Nature Trail. Central Catchment Nature Reserve. No phone. Free admission. From Orchard Rd. take bus no. 132 from the Orchard Parade Hotel. From Raffles City take bus no. 130. Get off at the bus stop near Little Sisters of the Poor. Next to Little Sisters of the Poor, follow the paved walkway, which turns into the trail.

Of all the nature reserves in Singapore, the Central Catchment Nature Reserve is the largest at 2,000 hectares (5,000 acres). Located in the center of the island, it's home to four of Singapore's reservoirs: MacRitchie, Seletar, Pierce, and Upper Pierce. The rain forest here is secondary forest, but the animals don't care; they're just as happy with the place. There's one path for walking and jogging (no bicycles allowed) that stretches 3 kilometers (1.8 miles) from its start in the southeast corner of the reserve, turning to the edge of MacRitchie Reservoir, then letting you out at the Singapore Island Country Club.

EASTERN SINGAPORE ATTRACTIONS

The East Coast leads from the edge of Singapore's urban area to the tip of the eastern part, at Changi Point. Eastern Singapore is home to the Changi International Airport, nearby Changi Prison, and the long stretch of East Coast Park along the shoreline. The **MRT** heads east in this region, but swerves northward at the end of the line. A popular **bus line** for east coast attractions not reached by MRT is the SBS no. 2, which takes you to Changi Prison, Changi Point, Malay Village, and East Coast Park (a short walk from Joo Chiat Centre).

○ **Malay Village.** 39 Geylang Serai, in the suburb of Geylang, an easy walk from the MRT station. ☎ **65/748-4700** or 65/740-8860. Free admission to village. Kampong Days and Cultural Museum adults S$5 (US$3), children S$3 (US$1.80). Mon–Fri 10am–9pm; Sat–Sun and public holidays 10am–10pm. MRT to Paya Lebar.

In 1985, Malay Village opened in Geylang as a theme village to showcase Malay culture. The Cultural Museum is a collection of artifacts from Malay culture, including household items, musical instruments, and a replica of a wedding dais and traditional beaded ceremonial bed. Kampung Days lets you walk through a kampung house (or Malay village house) as it would have looked in the 1950s and 1960s. The 25-minute **Lagenda Fantasy show** is more for kids, using multi-image projection, Surround Sound, and lights to tell tales from the Arabian Nights and the legend of Sang Nila Utama, the founder of Temasek (Singapore). The village has souvenir shops mixed with places that sell everything from antique knives to caged birds.

Two in-house groups perform **traditional Malaysian and Indonesian dances** in the late afternoons and evenings. Call during the day on Saturday to find out if they'll be performing the **Kuda Kepang** in the evening. If you're lucky enough to catch it, it's a long performance but worth the wait because at the end the dancers are put in a trance and walk on glass, eat glass, and rip coconuts to shreds with their teeth (see "Frommer's Favorite Singapore Experiences" in chapter 1 for details). Arrive early because the place gets packed with locals.

○ **Changi Prison Chapel and Museum.** 169 Sims Ave., off Upper Changi Rd., in the same general area as the airport. ☎ **65/543-0893**. Free admission. Mon–Sat 10am–5pm. Closed Sun and public holidays. Changi Prison Chapel Sun Service (all are welcome) 5:30–6:30pm. MRT to Tanah Merah station, then transfer to SBS no. 2.

Upon successful occupation of Singapore, the Japanese marched all British, Australian, and allied European prisoners to Changi by foot, where they lived in a prison camp for 3 years, suffering overcrowding, disease, and malnutrition. Prisoners were cut off from the outside world except to leave the camp for labor duties. The hospital conditions were terrible; some prisoners suffered public beatings, and many died. In an effort to keep hope alive, they built a small chapel from wood and attap. Years later, at the request of former POWs and their families and friends, the government built this replica.

The museum displays sketches by W. R. M. Haxworth and secret photos taken by George Aspinall—both men POWs who were imprisoned here. Displayed with descriptions, the pictures, along with writings and other objects from the camp, bring this period to life, depicting the day-to-day horror with a touch of high morale.

The Singapore Crocodilarium. 730 East Coast Pkwy., running along East Coast Park. ☎ **65/447-3722**. Adults S$2 (US$1.20), children under 12 S$1 (US$0.60). Daily 9am–5pm. MRT to Paya Lebar or Eunos and take a taxi.

Head to the Crocadilarium if you're interested in seeing alligators from India and four types of crocodiles—from Singapore, Africa, Louisiana, and Caiman (South Africa). Of the total 1,800 crocodiles that reside here, 500 are on display. The Singapore crocodile, one of the largest, reaches a maximum size of 5.5 meters (6 yd.) and can weigh up to 500 kilograms (1,100 lb.). They're pretty fierce because they have bigger heads, which means bigger mouths. However, midsize ones are the most dangerous to people because they have better mobility on land. Every so often the place picks up when a couple of them have a brutish fight. On a sweeter note, the Crocodilarium has approximately 400 births per year. Some young ones are on display—and they're very cute—but the Crocodilarium won't let you see the newborn babies because they're delicate and spook easily. While many of these alligators and crocodiles are intended for the booming pelt industry, some are just for show. A huge gift shop peddles crocodile products, which are made both in-house and imported from outside designers. Here you can also find ostrich hide, stingray skin, and antelope pelt goods.

The best way to get back to town is to ask the front counter to call you a cab.

Republic of Singapore Air Force Museum. Blk. 78 Cranwell Rd. off Loyang Ave. Changi Camp. Free admission. Tues–Sun 10am–4:30pm. SBS no. 2 or 9.

Established in 1988, this museum tracks the evolution of the Republic of Singapore Air Force with exhibits of historical artifacts and records and displays of aircraft, missiles, and dioramas with audiovisual effects.

East Coast Park. East Coast Pwy. No phone. Free admission. MRT to Bedok, bus no. 31, or on Sun and public holidays bus no. 401.

East Coast Park is a narrow strip of reclaimed land, only 8.5 kilometers long, tucked in between the shoreline and East Coast Parkway, and serves as a hangout for Singaporean families on the weekends. Moms and dads barbecue under the trees while the kids swim at the beach, which is nothing more than a narrow lump of grainy sand sloping into yellow-green water that has more seaweed than a sushi bar. Paths for bicycling, in-line skating, walking, or jogging run the length of the park, and are crowded on weekends and public and school holidays. On Sundays, you'll find kite flyers in the open grassy parts. The lagoon is the best place to go for bicycle and in-line skate rentals, canoeing, and windsurfing. A couple of outfits, listed in section 9, "Sports & Recreation," offer equipment rentals and instruction.

Because East Coast Park is so long, getting to the place you'd like to hang out can be a bit confusing. Many of the locators I've included sound funny (for example, Carpark C), but are recognizable landmarks for taxi drivers. Sailing, windsurfing, and other sea sports happen at the far end of the park, at the lagoon, which is closer to Changi Airport than it is to the city. Taxi drivers are all familiar with the lagoon as a landmark. Unfortunately, public transportation to the park is tough—you should bring a good map, and expect to do a little walking from any major thoroughfare.

East Coast Park is home to a few other interesting places. **UDMC Seafood Centre** (see chapter 4) is located not far from the lagoon, and **Big Splash**—Singapore's first water park with water slides, wave pools, and river rides—is not too far away, at 902 East Coast Pwy. (☎ **65/345-6762**).

7 Sentosa Island

In the 1880s, Sentosa, then known as Pulau Blakang Mati, was a hub of British military activity, with hilltop forts built to protect the harbor from sea invasion from all sides. Today, it has become a weekend getaway spot and Singapore's answer to Disneyland all rolled into one. You'll find a lot of people recommending Sentosa as a must-see on your vacation, and while many travelers do visit the island for some part of their trip, it might not be the best way to spend your time if you're only in town for a few days. Basically, for those who like to do hard-core cultural and historical-immersion vacations, Sentosa will seem too contrived and cartoonish—just check out the Images of Singapore exhibit and go home. But for those who just want a good time, it delivers.

If you tried to see everything on the island, you'd need at least 3 days, but a day is just enough to see and do the best. If you want to get out of the city, the beaches are cooling and well stocked with activities, and resorts like the Beaufort are tranquil and romantic. If you're into the museum scene, there are some very well-presented historical exhibits and nature showcases. If you want to keep the kids happy, there's a water park, theme parks, and amusement rides. For your sense of adventure, you can never go wrong with Underwater World. Free with your Sentosa admission are the Fountain Gardens and Musical Fountain, the Enchanted Garden of Tembusu, the Dragon Trail Nature Walk, and the beaches.

If you're spending the day, there are numerous restaurants and a couple of food courts. For overnights, the Shangri-La's Rasa Sentosa Resort and the Beaufort Sentosa, Singapore (see chapter 3) are popular hotel options. For general **Sentosa inquiries,** call ☎ **65/275-0388.**

GETTING THERE

Private cars are not allowed entry to the island except between the hours of 6:30pm and 3am, but there are more than a few other ways to get to Sentosa. The cable car and ferry fares are exclusive of Sentosa admission charges, which you are required to pay upon arrival; bus fares include your admission charge. **Island admission** is S$5 (US$3) for adults and S$3 (US$1.80) for children. Admission in the evenings (after 6:30pm) is S$3 (US$1.80) for adults and S$1.80 (US$1.10) for children. Tickets can be purchased at the following booths: Mount Faber Cable Car Station, World Trade Centre Ferry Departure Hall, Cable Car Towers (next to the World Trade Centre), Cable Car Plaza (on Sentosa), Sentosa Information Booth 4 (at the start of the causeway, opposite Kentucky Fried Chicken), and at Sentosa Information Booth 3 (at the end of the causeway bridge, upon entering Sentosa). Many attractions require purchase of additional tickets, which you can get at the entrance of each.

BY CABLE CAR   Cable cars depart from the top of Mount Faber and from the World Trade Centre daily from 8:30am to 9pm at a cost of S$6.90 (US$4.15) for adults and S$3.90 (US$2.35) for children. The ticket is good for round-trip, and you can decide where you choose to depart and arrive (at either Mt. Faber or World Trade Centre every 5 or 10 minutes on the Singapore side) for one price. Plan at least one trip on the cable car because the view of Singapore, Sentosa, and especially the container port is really fantastic from up there. The round-trip cable car ticket is also good for a return on the ferry, in case you've had enough view. *Be warned:* If you return to Singapore at the Mt. Faber stop, you'll have to walk down the mountain to find a cab or bus.

BY FERRY   The ferry departs from the World Trade Centre on weekdays from 9:30am to 9pm at 20-minute intervals, and on weekends and public holidays from 8:30am to 9pm at 15-minute intervals. The round-trip fare for both adults and children is S$2.30 (US$1.40), and one-way is S1.30¢ (US$0.78).

BY BUS   **Sentosa Bus Service Leisure Pte Ltd** operates bus service to and from Sentosa. Service A operates between 7:15am and 11:30pm daily from the World Trade Centre (WTC) Bus Terminal. Services C and M run from the Tiong Bahru MRT

Station between 7:20am and 11:30pm daily. Service E stops along Orchard Road at Lucky Plaza, the Mandarin Hotel, Peranakan Place, Le Meridien Hotel, Plaza Singapura, and then Bencoolen Street, POSB Headquarters, Raffles City, and Pan Pacific Hotel, and operates from 10am to 10:45pm daily. Fares run from S$6 to S$7 (US$3.60 to US$4.20) for adults and S$4 to S$5 (US$2.40 to US$3) for children, depending on which bus you catch from where. Fares are paid to the driver as you board, and the Sentosa admission fee is included in your fare. The last bus out of Sentosa is at 11:30pm.

BY TAXI   Taxis are only allowed to drop off and pick up passengers at the Beaufort Sentosa, Singapore; Shangri-La's Rasa Sentosa Resort; and NTUC Sentosa Beach Resort. The taxi fare from 6am to 6:30pm is S$3 (US$1.80) per person; however, after 6:30pm you must pay a flat fare of S$12 (US$7.20) per car. After 9pm the price drops to S$6 (US$3.60).

GETTING AROUND

Once on Sentosa, a free monorail operates from 9am to 10pm daily at 10-minute intervals to shuttle you around to the various areas. If you're staying at one of the island's major hotels, you can take advantage of their free shuttle services to get into Singapore's urban area.

SEEING THE SIGHTS

The attractions that you get free with your Sentosa admission are the **Fountain Gardens** and **Musical Fountain,** the **Enchanted Garden of Tembusu,** the **Dragon Trail Nature Walk,** and the **beaches.**

The **Fountain Gardens,** just behind the Ferry Terminal, are geometric European-style gardens with groomed pathways and shady arbors. In the center is an amphitheater of sorts, the focus of which is a fountain—actually three fountains—that creates water effects with patterns of sprays and varying heights. During regular shows throughout the day, the fountains burst to the sounds of everything from marches to Elton John. At night, they turn on the lights for color effects.

The **Flower Terrace** starts behind the Ferry Terminal through the Fountain Garden and creeps up the side of the hill beyond. The slope has a steep grade, but pathways meander to offer some relief from the climb. Still, in the heat, you won't be taking this one fast.

The **Enchanted Garden of Tembusu,** in a corner of the Fountain Garden, is a shady grove of Tembusu trees and MacArthur palms. In the evenings, the garden is lit with tiny lights for a touch of romance.

The **Dragon Trail Nature Walk** takes advantage of the island's natural forest for a 1½-kilometer (1-mile) stroll through secondary rain forest. In addition to the variety of dragon sculptures, there are also local squirrels, monkeys, lizards, and wild white cockatoos to try to spot.

Sentosa has three beaches, **Siloso Beach** on the western end and ✪ **Central Beach** and **Tanjong Beach** on the eastern end, each dressed in tall coconut palms and flowering trees. At Central Beach, deck chairs, beach umbrellas, and a variety of **watersports equipment** like pedal boats, aqua bikes, fun bugs, canoes, surfboards, and banana boats are available for hire at nominal charges. **Bicycles** are also available for hire at the bicycle kiosk at Siloso Beach. Shower and changing facilities, food kiosks, and snack bars are at rest stations. Siloso Beach is open at night for barbecue picnics, and has a really nice view of the tiny lights of ships anchored in the port. About once

Sentosa Island Attractions

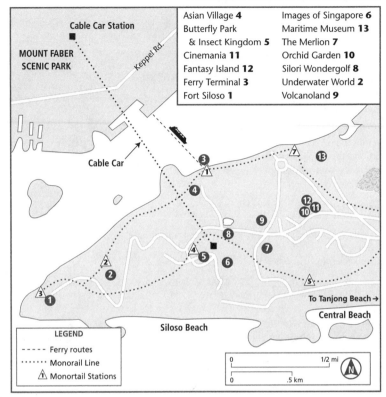

Asian Village **4**	Images of Singapore **6**
Butterfly Park	Maritime Museum **13**
& Insect Kingdom **5**	The Merlion **7**
Cinemania **11**	Orchid Garden **10**
Fantasy Island **12**	Silori Wondergolf **8**
Ferry Terminal **3**	Underwater World **2**
Fort Siloso **1**	Volcanoland **9**

LEGEND

- - - - - Ferry routes

· · · · · · Monorail Line

⚠ Monorail Stations

0 — 1/2 mi

0 — .5 km

a month, rumors spread throughout the island about a **full-moon party** on Siloso that lasts until the sun comes up. The parties are never publicized, but are anticipated by the many folks looking for an alternative to the bar scene at night. Ask around at the bars, and they'll let you know if there's something going on.

For beach activities like volleyball, check out the offerings at the Shangri-La's Rasa Sentosa Resort (see chapter 3). Hotel guests get first dibs, but many activities and equipment are available to the public at reasonable charges.

Unless noted, all of the following Sentosa attractions have admission charges separate from the Sentosa charge, and operating hours that differ from place to place.

Asian Village. ☎ 65/275-0338. Free admission. Daily 10am–9pm. Adventure Asia daily 10am–7pm. Monorail stop 1.

They set up this festival village around a tiny lake, with three zones representing the architectural moods of East, South, and Southeast Asia. Only there's no people! The original concept included bustling shops, street performers, traditional dance numbers, and regular shows in the auditorium, but not enough visitors came to the attraction, so most of the shops are empty and the dancers were laid off. You can paddleboat around the lake for S$5 (US$3) per half hour.

In the back of the village find **Adventure Asia,** with 10 rides tucked inside a shady grove. Ten bucks (US$6) gets you unlimited rides—not a bad deal.

Maritime Museum. ☎ **65/270-8855.** Free admission. Daily 10am–7pm. Closest to monorail stop 7, then walk along Gateway Ave.

Nautical paraphernalia buffs rejoice: Here's a showcase devoted to Singapore's ever-important connection to the sea. From ship models to artifacts, sea charts, and photos, the museum tells the story of 14 centuries of maritime life.

✪ **Fantasy Island.** ☎ **65/275-1088.** Adults S$16 (US$9.60), children 3–12 S$10 (US$6). Daily 10am–7pm. Monorail stop 7.

If you have a few hours and a swimsuit, this place is a great time. Try out all kinds of water slides, water tunnels, surf rides, rapids, and a simulated lazy river running around the whole park. For the little ones, there are tree houses with water toys, special slides, and a kiddie pool. Changing rooms are available, there's a food outlet, and a first-aid team is on duty.

Cinemania. ☎ **65/373-0159.** Adults S$10 (US$6), children S$6 (US$3.60). Daily 11am–8pm. Monorail stop 7.

At this 3-D audiovisual ride with motion simulator, they rotate three films at a time from a library of 25 titles like *Cosmic Pinball, Desert Duel,* and *Runaway Train.* Call ahead for titles and show times.

Sentosa Orchid Gardens. ☎ **65/278-1940.** Adults S$3.30 (US$2), children S$2 (US$1.20). Daily 9am–6:30pm. Monorail stop 1; the Orchid Garden is to the east of the Fountain Gardens.

This place is more geared toward the theme-party scene, so you're better off at the National Orchid Garden at the Singapore Botanic Gardens or at Mandai Orchids to see the best collections.

The Merlion. ☎ **65/275-0388.** Adults S$3 (US$1.80), children S$2 (US$1.20). Daily 9am–10pm. Monorail stop 1 and 4.

Imagine, if you will, 12 towering stories of that half-lion, half-fish creature, the Merlion. That's a lot of mythical beast. Admission buys you an elevator ride to the ninth floor, where you can peer out the mouth, and to the top of its head for a 360° view of Singapore, Sentosa, and even Indonesia. Be at the Fountain Gardens at 7:30, 8:30, and 9:30pm nightly for the "Rise of the Merlion" show, where they light up the thing with 16,000 fiber-optic lights and shoot red lasers out its eyes. Poor Merlion. Hope this never happens to the national symbol of *your* home country.

VolcanoLand. ☎ **65/275-1828.** Adults S$12 (US$7.20), children S$6 (US$3.60). Daily 10am–7pm. Monorail stop 1 or 4.

It's hard to say whether VolcanoLand is amusing or whether it's touristy and weird. The main attraction here is the ancient Central American "active volcano," a walk-through exhibit that takes you on a journey to the center of the Earth with a mythological explorer and his Jules Verne–style robot buddy. Inside the "volcano" there's a multimedia show about the mysteries of life and the universe and a simulated volcano eruption. Besides its being completely contrived, the special-effects creations are by far less cheesy than most. Outside the volcano in the rest of the small park are the not-very-politically-correct "Live Tribal Performances," like the Mayan Parade costume and dance ceremonies and the "Volcano Ritual Performance" to celebrate having survived the volcano's "eruption."

✪ **Images of Singapore.** ☎ **65/275-0388.** Adults S$5 (US$3), children S$3 (US$1.80). Daily 9am–9pm. Monorail stop 4.

Images of Singapore is without a doubt one of the main reasons to come to Sentosa. There are three parts to this museum/exhibit: the Pioneers of Singapore and the Surrender Chambers—which date back as far as I can remember—and Festivals of Singapore, a recent addition.

Pioneers of Singapore is an exhibit of beautifully constructed life-size dioramas that place figures like Sultan Hussein, Sir Stamford Raffles, Tan Tock Seng, and Naraina Pillai, to name just a few pioneers, in the context of Singapore's timeline and note their contributions to its development. Also interesting are the dioramas depicting scenes from the daily routines of the different cultures as they lived during colonial times. It's a great stroll that brings history to life.

The powers that be have tried to change the name of the **Surrender Chambers** to the Sentosa Wax Museum, but it still hasn't caught on because the Surrender Chambers are oh so much more than just a wax museum. The gallery leads you through authentic footage, photos, maps, and recordings of survivors to chronologically tell the story of the Pacific theater activity of World War II and how the Japanese conquered Singapore. The grand finale is a wax museum depicting, first, a scene of the British surrender and, last, another of the Japanese surrender.

Recently, Images of Singapore had added the **Festivals of Singapore,** another life-size diorama exhibit depicting a few of the major festivals and traditions of the Chinese, Malay, Indian, and Peranakan cultures in Singapore. For each group, wedding traditions are shown in complete regalia, with brief explanations of the customs. While this exhibit is not quite like being there and would be dull as a stand-alone, it's not bad tacked on to the other two. Try to catch the video presentation at the end—a tribute to Singapore's strides in "cultural integration" told in true "It's a small world after all" style.

Silori WonderGolf Sentosa. ☎ **65/275-2011.** Adults S$8–S$10 (US$4.80–US$6), children S$4–S$6 (US$2.40–US$3.60). Daily 9am–9pm. Monorail stop 4.

It's definitely miniature golf, but without the windmill. Instead, holes are made tricky using greens landscaped with rock designs and water features set on tiny terraces up the side of a steep slope. Two 18-hole courses and one 9-hole course offer differing degrees of difficulty, and during the day it gets pretty hot. To get there, either hike up the Flower Terrace or climb down the catwalk from the Cable Car Station.

Butterfly Park and Insect Kingdom Museum of Singapore. ☎ **65/275-0013.** Adults S$6 (US$3.60), children S$3 (US$1.80). Daily 9am–6:30pm. Monorail stop 4.

This walk-in enclosure provides an up-close view of some 60 live species of native butterflies, from cocoon to adult. At the Insect Kingdom, the exhibits are mostly dead, but extensive, with its collection carrying more than 2,500 bugs. Live ones to see include scorpions, tarantulas, and the very weird dead leaf mantis.

✪ **Underwater World.** ☎ **65/275-0030.** Adults S$13 (US$7.80), children S$7 (US$4.20). Daily 9am–9pm. Monorail stop 2.

Underwater World is without a doubt one of the most visited attractions on Sentosa. Everybody comes for the tunnel: 83 meters of transparent acrylic tube through which you glide on a conveyor belt, gaping at sharks, stingrays, eels, and other creatures of the sea drifting by, above and on both sides. At 11:30am, 2:30pm, and 4:30pm daily, a scuba diver hops in and feeds them by hand. In smaller tanks you can view other unusual sea life like the puffer fish and the mysteriously weedy and leafy sea dragons. Then there's the latest display of bamboo shark embryos, developing within egg cases—what's keeping you?

Kudos to their latest attractions: an **underwater walk** or **swim with the sharks.** S$96 (US$57.50) gets you 30 minutes underwater attached to a hose for fresh air while you walk through schools and play with the fish. Or the same amount buys you 90 minutes scuba diving in the shark tank. For both you must be over 18 years of age, and of course for the latter you must be able to prove scuba certification.

✪ **Fort Siloso.** ☎ **65/275-0388.** Adults S$3 (US$1.80), children S$2 (US$1.20). Daily 9am–7pm. Monorail stop 3.

Fort Siloso guarded Keppel Harbour from invasion in the 1880s. It's one of three forts built on Sentosa, and it later became a military camp in World War II. The buildings have been decorated to resemble a barracks, kitchen, laundry, and military offices as they looked back in the day. In places, you can explore the underground tunnels and ammunition holds, but they're not as extensive as you would hope they'd be.

8 The Surrounding Islands

There are 60 smaller islands ringing Singapore that are open for full- or half-day trips. The ferry rides are cool and breezy, and provide interesting up-close views of some of the larger ships docked in the harbor. The islands themselves are small and, for the most part, don't have a lot going on. The locals basically see them as little escapes from the everyday grind—peaceful respites for the family.

KUSU & ST. JOHN'S ISLANDS

Kusu Island and St. John's Island are both located to the south of Singapore proper, about a 15- to 20-minute ferry ride to Kusu from the World Trade Centre, 25 to 30 minutes to St. John's.

It's name meaning "Tortoise Island" in Chinese, there are many popular legends about how **Kusu Island** came to be. The most popular ones involve shipwrecked people, either fishermen or monks, who were rescued when a tortoise turned himself into an island. Kusu Island was originally two small islands and a reef, but in 1975, reclaimed land turned it into a (very) small getaway island. There are two places of worship: a Chinese temple and a Malay shrine. The Chinese temple becomes a zoo during "Kusu Season" in October, when thousands of Chinese devotees flock here to pray for health, prosperity, and luck. There are two swimming lagoons (the one to the north has a really beautiful view of Singapore Island), picnic facilities, toilets, and public telephones.

Historically speaking, **St. John's Island** is an unlikely place for a day trip. As far back as 1874, this place was a quarantine for Chinese immigrants sick with cholera; in the 1950s, it became a deportation holding center for Chinese Mafia thugs; and later, it was a rehab center for opium addicts. Today you'll find a mosque, holiday camps, three lagoons, bungalows, a cafeteria, a huge playing field, and basketball. It's much larger than Kusu Island, but not large enough to fill a whole day of sightseeing. Toilets and public phones are available.

Ferries leave at regular intervals and make a circular route, landing on both islands. Tickets are available from the desk at the back of the World Trade Centre. Adult tickets cost S$9 (US$5.40), and tickets for children under 12 are S$6 (US$3.60). During "Kusu Season"—the month of October—thousands of people make their way to Kusu Island to pray in the temple there, and during this month the ferry departs from Clifford Pier. To get to the World Trade Centre, take MRT to Tanjong Pagar, then bus no. 10, 97, 100, or 131. For Clifford Pier, take the MRT to Raffles and walk through Change Alley. *A small tip:* There's a Cold Storage in the World Trade Center where you can pick up water and provisions for the trip.

SISTERS ISLAND

Sisters Island, just to the west of St. John's, is not visited as regularly as the other islands because no regular ferry service has operations there. However, at **Clifford Pier** you can hire one of the water taxis—the bumboats hired by ships in the harbor for cargo and crew shuttles—to take you there. The taxi dispatchers are on the ground level, lined up with tables, folding chairs, and CB radios. Feel free to bargain, but the trip will probably cost you around S$50 (US$30). Basically, people go to Sisters Island to swim. Sisters is also a popular destination for divers, who hire boats and come for advanced scuba outings.

PULAU UBIN

My favorite island getaway has to be Ubin. Located off the northeast tip of Singapore, Pulau Ubin remains the only place in Singapore where you can find life as it used to be before urban development. Lazy kampung villages pop up along side trails perfect for a little more rugged bicycling. It's truly a great day trip for those who like to explore nature and rural scenery. Toward the end of 1999, the Singapore press carried numerous reports about government plans to develop the island for public housing, so I expect that within the next 20 years we'll see poor Ubin burdened with boxy housing estates and the hideous trappings of urban sprawl. And when they eventually extend the MRT out to the island, it's curtains for this place. See it while you can. *A side note:* Rumors have it that during the occupation the Japanese brought soldiers here to be tortured, and so some believe the place is haunted.

To get to Ubin, take bus no. 2 to Changi Village. Walk past the food court down to the water and find the ferry. There's no ticket booth, so you should just approach the captain and buy your ticket from him—it'll cost you about S$1.50. The boats leave regularly, with the last one returning from the island at 9pm.

Once you're there, bicycle-rental places along the jetty can provide you with bikes and island maps at reasonable prices. A few coffee shops cook up rudimentary meals, and you'll also find public toilets and coin phones in the more populated areas.

9 Sports & Recreation

BEACHES

Besides the beach at East Coast Park (see "Attractions Outside the Urban Area," above) and those on Sentosa Island (see above) you can try the smaller beach at Changi Village, called Changi Point. From the shore, you have a panoramic view of Malaysia, Indonesia, and several smaller islands that belong to Singapore. The beach is calm, and frequented mostly by locals who set up camps and barbecues to hang out all day. There's kayak rentals along the beach, and in Changi Village you'll find, in addition to a huge hawker center, quite a few international restaurants and pubs to hang out in and have a fresh seafood lunch when you get hungry. To get there take SBS bus no. 2 from either the Tanah Merah or Bedok MRT stations.

On Kusu and St. John's Islands there are quiet swimming lagoons, a couple of which have quite nice views of the city. Some people head out to Sisters Island for swimming, but the trip is a bit expensive for just a dip. (See "The Surrounding Islands," above.)

BICYCLE RENTAL

Bicycles are not for rent within the city limits, and traffic does not really allow for cycling on city streets, so sightseeing by bicycle is not recommended for city touring. If you plan a trip out to **Sentosa,** cycling provides a great alternative to that island's tram system, and gets you closer to the parks and nature there. For a little light cycling, most people head out to **East Coast Park,** where rentals are inexpensive, the scenery is nice on cooler days, and there are plenty of great stops for eating along the way. One favorite place where the locals go for mountain-biking sorts of adventures (and to cycle amidst the old kampung villages) is **Pulau Ubin,** off the northeast coast of Singapore.

AT EAST COAST PARK   Bicycles can be rented at East Coast Park from **Ling Choo Hong** (☎ 65/449-7305), near the hawker center at Carpark E; **SDK Recreation** (☎ 65/445-2969), near McDonald's at Carpark C; or **Wimbledon Cafeteria & Bicycle Rental** (☎ 65/444-3928), near the windsurfing rental places at the lagoon. All of these are open 7 days from about 9am to 8 or 9pm. Rentals are all in the neighborhood of S$4 (US$2.40) to S$8 (US$4.80) per hour, depending on the type and quality bike you're looking for. Identification may be requested.

ON SENTOSA ISLAND   Try **SDK Recreation** (☎ 65/272-8738), located at Siloso Beach off Siloso Road, a short walk from Underwater World (see "Sentosa Island," above). Open 7 days from around 10am to 6:30 or 7pm. Rental for a standard bicycle is S$4 (US$2.40) per hour. A mountain bike goes for S$8 (US$4.80) per hour. Identification is required.

IN PULAU UBIN   When you get off the ferry, there are a number of places to rent bikes. The shops are generally open between 8am and 6pm and will charge between S$5 (US$3) and S$8 (US$4.80) per hour, depending on which bike you choose. Most rental agents will have a map of the island for you—take it. Even though it doesn't look too impressive, it'll be a great help.

GOLF

Golf is a very popular sport in Singapore. There are quite a few clubs, and though some of them are exclusively for members only, many places are open for limited play by nonmembers. All will require you bring a par certificate.

Most hotel concierges will be glad to make arrangements for you, and this may be the best way to go. Also, it's really popular for Singaporeans go on day trips to Malaysia for the best courses. See chapters 10 and 11 for more information about golfing in Malaysia.

Changi Golf Club. 20 Netheravon Rd. ☎ **65/545-5133.**

Nonmembers can play at this private club only on weekdays. The 9-hole course is par 34, with greens fees of S$41.20 (US$24.70), or you can play it twice for S$82.40 (US$49.45). They have club and shoe rentals for around S$20 (US$12) and S$10 (US$6) respectively. A caddy for 18 holes sets you back S$25 (US$15). While on weekdays they will accept walk-ins, the club recommends advanced booking and requires it for weekend and holiday play. They may even be able to set you up with other players. The course opens at 7:30am. Last tee is 4:30pm.

Jurong Country Club. 9 Science Centre Rd. ☎ **65/560-5655.**

This private course welcomes nonmembers 7 days a week, but requests at least 48 hours advanced booking for its 18-hole, par 72 course. Greens fees cost S$95 (US$57) on weekdays and S$180 (US$108) on weekends. A caddy can be hired for S$25 (US$15) each, and shoe and club rentals are also available. First tee is between 7:15 and 8:45am. Second tee is between noon and 1:30pm. Night golf begins between 5pm and 6:30pm.

Seletar Base Golf Course. 244 Oxford St., 3 Park Lane. ☎ **65/481-4745.**

A public course, Seletar's 9-hole, par 36 course is open for everyone 7 days a week. Expect to pay greens fees of S$45 (US$27) on weekdays and S$60 (US$36) on weekends, with very low-cost golf cart and equipment rentals (all available with deposit). First tee is at 7am except for Monday through Thursday, when first tee is at 11am. Last tee is 5pm.

Sentosa Golf Club. 27 Bukit Manis Rd., Sentosa Island ☎ **65/275-0022.**

The best idea if you're traveling with your family and want to get in a game, Sentosa's many activities will keep the kids happy while you practice your swing guilt-free. This club's two 18-hole courses are each 72 par, with greens fees ranging from S$120 to S$140 (US$72 to $84) on weekdays and S$220 (US$132) on weekends and holidays. It's a bit more expensive than other courses around, but the chance to get off Singapore island for the day can be quite relaxing. Advance phone bookings are required.

IN-LINE SKATE RENTALS

East Coast Park has long stretches of paved pathways along the beach that make for some very scenic skating. Rentals are available from **Ling Choo Hong** (☎ **65/449-7305**), near the hawker center at Carpark E; and **SDK Recreation** (☎ **65/445-2969**), near McDonald's at Carpark C, for S$7 (US$4.20) per hour, including protective wear. Both are open from 9am to 8 or 9pm daily.

SCUBA DIVING

The locals are crazy about scuba diving, but are more likely to travel to Malaysia and other Southeast Asian destinations for good underwater adventures. The most common complaint is that the water surrounding Singapore is really silty—sometimes to the point where you can barely see your hand before your face. If you're still interested, the best place to try for a beginner certification course is at **SEADive Adventurers** (☎**65/251-0322**), which also organizes diving trips and offers classes up to advanced levels. **Sharkey's Dive & Travel** (☎ **65/294-0168**) also arranges diving trips.

DEEP-SEA FISHING

For something different, but very worth your time and money, Grant Pereira, Singapore's most acclaimed salty dog, takes folks out on fantastic fishing tours. With 25 years of experience fishing the waters of Southeast Asia and the rest of the world, he uses his expertise and connections to arrange weekend trips around Singapore and to neighboring Malaysia and Indonesia for great catches. Be prepared to live the life of a seaman, though. While you'll be inundated with cockroaches and saltfish on board, Mr. Pereira guarantees you'll "catch fish 'til your arms drop off." Everything is included with the price of the trip (he even has a cook on board), but you'll have to bring your own booze. And bring plenty of extra booze for Mr. Pereira—his awesome fish tales don't come cheap! (Trust me, he's the fishing buddy you've always dreamed of.) If you're up for a really unique local experience, with a little bit of advance notice he can arrange an overnight on a kelong—a Malay fishing shack in the middle of the sea, surrounded by bamboo traps. Your best bet is to contact him via e-mail well in advance of your visit at grant@tacklemall.com.sg. Or call or fax ☎ **65/583-6732.**

SPECTATOR SPORTS

Cricket season is from March to September, and at the **Singapore Cricket Club,** matches are normally played every Saturday at 11:30am and Sunday at 11am (be sure to call in advance to double-check times). The clubhouse is reserved for club members; however, all are welcome to watch from the sides. The Cricket Club is located at the Esplanade, Connaught Drive (☎ **65/338-9271**).

Horse races are held on selected Saturdays and Sundays at the **Singapore Turf Club** on Bukit Timah Road (☎ **65/879-1000**). Races are held on Wednesday evenings and on weekends. Admission to the grandstand is S$5 (US$3). Be warned these are the cheapest seats in the house. For an extra S$5, you can sit in the upper grandstands, which are air-conditioned. As a visitor, you may not wish to become a member, but the members' club is really the most comfortable place to be. Call the listed number if you're interested. Also call about limited bus services to the club. Your hotel may be close to one of their regular routes.

The **rugby** season runs from September to March. Games are held at the **Singapore Cricket Club,** the Esplanade, Connaught Drive (☎ **65/338-9271**), on Saturdays at 5:30pm (like the cricket matches, make sure you call ahead just to be sure the game is on). Visitors are welcome to watch the games, but only club members are allowed to view from the clubhouse.

TENNIS

Quite a few hotels in the city provide tennis courts for guests, many floodlit for night play (which allows you to avoid the midday heat), and even a few that can arrange lessons, so be sure to check out listings for hotel facilities in chapter 3. You'll have to travel about 15 minutes by taxi form the city center to reach the **Singapore Tennis Centre** on East Coast Parkway near the East Coast Park (☎ **65/442-5966**). Their courts are open to the public for day and evening play. Weekdays offer discount rates of S$8.50 (US$5.10) per hour, while weekday evening peak hours (between 6 and 9pm) jump to S$12.50 (US$7.50). Weekends and public holidays expect to pay S$12.50 (US$7.50) per hour also. If you need to stay closer to town, you can play at the **Tanglin Sports Centre** on Minden Road (☎ **65/473-7236**). Court costs are S$3.50 (US$2.10) per hour on weekdays, with charges upped to S$9.50 (US$5.70) on weekday nights from 6 to 10pm, on weekends, and all public holidays.

WATERSKIING

The Kallang River, located to the east of the city, has hosted quite a few international waterskiing tournaments. If this is your sport, contact the **Cowabunga Ski Centre,** the authority in Singapore. Located at Kallang Riverside Park, 10 Stadium Lane (☎ **65/344-8813**), they'll arrange lessons for adults and children and waterskiing by the hour. Beginner courses will set you back S$140 (US$84) for five half-hour lessons, while more experienced skiers can hire a boat plus equipment for S$80 (US$48) on weekdays and S$100 (US$60) on weekends. It's open on weekdays from noon to 7pm and weekends from 9am to 7pm. Call in advance for a reservation.

WINDSURFING & SAILING

You'll find both windsurf boards and sailboats for rent at the lagoon in **East Coast Park,** which is where these activities primarily take place. The largest and most reputable firm to approach has to be the **Europa Sailing Club** at 1212 East Coast Pkwy. (☎ **65/449-5118**). For S$20/hour (US$12) you can rent a small sailboat, while windsurf boards go for about the same. Expect to leave around S$30 (US$18) deposit. While Europa does offer courses, instruction is really not recommended for short-term visitors since classes usually occur over extended periods of time on a set schedule.

Strolling & Touring Around Singapore

Back in the early 19th century, Sir Stamford Raffles had a vision for a multicultural Singapore, integrating diverse immigrant communities into one economy while creating separate ethnic neighborhoods within which they'd live. The Historic District marked the center of the colonial administration, Chinatown became the heart of sea trade, Little India evolved as the home of Indian commercial activities, and Kampong Glam served as the focus of Islam and the Malay royalty. These neighborhoods were made official in his Town Plan of 1822, and amazingly enough, still stand almost 180 years later.

Modern Singapore, though, is bigger than its original neighborhoods, and what was once jungle has been cleared to create the popular suburban New Towns, which have simultaneously siphoned off many residents of the ethnic neighborhoods and, through the melting-pot effect, furthered the government's aim of molding a unified Singaporean national identity from the ethnic fragments. What are the neighborhoods like now? Many ethnic shops, restaurants, places of worship, and museums hold on, maintaining the ties between the areas and the Chinese, Indian, and Malay communities, but even this situation is under attack—curiously, by a plan designed to enshrine the neighborhoods' ethnicities.

Recognizing the importance of Singapore's individual cultures—if only for the tourist revenues they generate—the Urban Redevelopment Authority has instituted the Tourism 21 plan, whose aim it is to preserve these cultural nooks in the city by restoring buildings, adding tourist touches, and turning each area into a Thematic Zone. Sound a little like Disney, doesn't it? The plan has already begun to take hold in Chinatown, where, sadly, most of the lifestyle that made that neighborhood come alive has been forced out by the newly renovated buildings' newly high rents. What's taken their place? A lot of bland souvenir shops. At the risk of sounding alarmist, here's my prognosis: Now is perhaps the last time when a traveler to Singapore can see the remaining neighborhoods untouched by meddling government planners. You've picked a good time to come.

In this chapter, I've tailored four walking tours to the four big ethnic neighborhoods: the Historic District, Chinatown, Little India, and Arab Street/Kampong Glam. The walking tours map out the most convenient route to see all the sights in each neighborhood. While the larger sights are described in greater detail in chapter 5, in between these places lie interesting features of the city—the small details that locals take for granted and visitors take home as treasured memories. I've pointed out some of the more interesting features along the routes, and provided some information of what these small details reveal about Singapore and its people. At the end of the chapter, I've also provided write-ups on some of the more respectable tour services, if you feel you want to take a guided tour.

One final note: Though these neighborhoods were always ethnic enclaves, they were never ethnic fortresses, so no matter where you go, you'll find influences from many cultures mixed into the scene. In the Historic District, for instance, Christian churches and Hindu and Chinese temples coexist. In Chinatown, there are Indian mosques and Hindu temples. Likewise, Little India's got Chinese, Burmese, and Muslim places of worship. What I'm saying is, don't visit Little India expecting to feel you're in downtown Delhi. You're in Singapore, and in Singapore, the big mix is the essence of life.

1 Walking Tours

Walking Tour 1
The Historic District

Start: Fort Canning Park.
Finish: City Hall MRT, Stamford Road.
Time: 5 hours (excluding museum tours but including an hour for lunch).
Best Times: Anytime. In the evenings the museums and other buildings will be closed, but many of the municipal buildings are handsomely floodlit, lending an air of romance to a walk around the Padang.

When Raffles first sailed up the Singapore River he saw a small fishing and trading village along the banks and a thick overgrowth of jungle and mangrove forest creeping up a gentle hill that overlooked the harbor. Over time, the left bank of the river would be reclaimed and built up for sea trade, the right bank would be cleared for the center of government activity, and high atop the hill, he'd build his home, Government House.

The Town Plan of 1822 set aside this district, referred to in this book as the Historic District, but also called the Colonial District or the Civic Centre. The central point was **The Padang,** a large field for sports exercises and ceremonies. Around the field, government buildings were erected, each reflecting preferred British tastes of the day. European hotels popped up, as well as cultural venues, and the Esplanade by the marina became a lively focal point for the European social scene.

The oldest part of the city is **Fort Canning Park,** the hill where Raffles built his home. Its history predates Raffles; excavation sites have unearthed artifacts and small treasures from earlier trading settlements and a sacred shrine that's believed to be the final resting place of Iskander Shah, founder of Malacca. It is here that the walking tour begins. (See chapter 5 for more details on most of these sights.)

1. Begin at **Fort Canning Park.** If you follow Canning Rise to the top of the hill, you'll be at the **Battle Box,** from which you can pick up the path and follow it through the historic sites in the park. You'll finish at the entrance after the Music and Drama Academy. Walk down Canning Rise to Hill Street.

   On your right just before Hill Street is the:

2. **Philatelic Museum.** Housed in a restored 1895 building, the museum presents stamps issued to commemorate important events, first-day covers, antique printing plates, postal service memorabilia, and private collections.

At Hill Street, turn right and you'll pass the Central Fire Station on your right, followed by the Hill Street Food Centre. One block along Hill Street and on your right is the:

3. **Hill Street Building.** Since this building's erection in 1934, the local Chinese have believed it destroyed the good trading feng shui of the area. During World War II, this home of the Singapore Police Force was taken over by the occupying Japanese, who, it's rumored, practiced torture here. Tough luck seems to follow Hill Street building—recent restorations have included a new paint job, covering all the window frames in atrocious rainbow colors. In its former glory, an even coat of dingy whitewash enhanced the delicate details of the structure, especially those around the windows, which are almost lacelike.

Turn around and backtrack. On your left after you pass Canning Rise at #60 is the:

4. **Armenian Church.** Designed by famed Colonial architect George Coleman, the church was consecrated in 1836 as the first permanent Christian church in Singapore. The cemetery in the back of the church holds the graves of many Armenians. Once prominent, their heritage has lost almost all other representation in modern Singapore, the community's bloodline diluted within the other local cultures.

A bit down across the street at #47 is the:

5. **Singapore Chinese Chamber of Commerce.** The organization was founded in 1906, but this building, in an odd mix of East meets West, wasn't built until 1964. Glazed tiles and painted columns reflect Chinese palaces, while on the outer wall two dragon murals in tile are copies of a famous pair in Beijing.

Walk straight on until you reach Stamford Road. Turn left; 1 block along, at the corner of Stamford Road and Armenian Street, is the **MPH building,** named after the bookstore within. Once upon a time, MPH was the largest English bookstore in Singapore, but is now overshadowed by the larger international book outlets like Books Kinokuniya and Border's on Orchard Road.

A detour down Armenian Street will take you to the **Substation** on your right, one of the hubs of the Singapore visual and performing arts communities. Outside, posted bills advertise current exhibits and performances, while inside, a small performance space, arts gift shop, gallery, and cafe make for a nice stop. Just beyond the Substation is the:

6. **Asian Civilisations Museum.** Housed in the old Tao Nan School building, this first branch of a planned two-branch museum focuses on the Malaysian archipelago's rich Chinese heritage, presenting displays of fine jade, calligraphy, ceramics, furniture, and artworks.

Backtrack to Stamford Road and turn left. Up a way on your left is the:

7. **Singapore History Museum.** Focusing on Singaporean history, the museum's collection includes 20 dioramas that portray events from the settlement's early days to modern times.

Cross the street and cut through **Bras Basah Park** on Bencoolen Street. Bras Basah literally means "dried rice," and it was so named because this was a place to which wet rice was brought to lay out to dry. In the park today you can find rickshas lined up waiting for business. Any year now, you can expect Bras Basah Park to disappear, to make way for a new college.

At the corner of Bencoolen Street and Bras Basah Road, turn right. Turn left onto Waterloo Street, a small street that represents many different religions in one space; 2 blocks down on your left is the:

8. **Maghain Aboth Synagogue.** Built in Victorian style in 1878, it was the first synagogue in Singapore, serving a highly influential Jewish community. Before its establishment, worship was carried out in a shop on Synagogue Street, in Chinatown. Farther down Waterloo the street turns to a lively pedestrian walkway. On your left is:

9. **Sri Krishna Temple.** While there's nothing about this small temple to distinguish it from other more significant ones, it is a special point along this road, rounding out the presence of Christian, Jewish, and Chinese Buddhist places of worship with a Hindu presence. It's still a popular place of worship, with vendors outside and bustle during Hindu holidays.

Just next door to Sri Krishna you'll find:

10. **Kuan Yin Thong Hood Cho Temple.** This place is famous for granting your most fervent wishes, so read the instructions in chapter 5 and get in line.

Backtrack to Bras Basah Road; on your left will be the:

11. **Singapore Art Museum.** The museum houses a large collection of art and sculpture, most of it by Singaporean and Malay artists.

Also along Bras Basah Road, farther on your right at the corner of Bras Basah and Queen Street is the:

12. **Cathedral of the Good Shepherd.** Built in the 1840s by various congregations, it was Singapore's first permanent Catholic cathedral.

One more block along Bras Basah and you'll take a right onto Victoria Street. On your left will be:

13. **CHIJMES.** Once a large convent and orphanage, this place (whose name stands for "Convent of the Holy Infant Jesus" and is pronounced *chimes*) has turned 180° to house many popular bars, plus retail shops, restaurants, and a performance space.

From CHIJMES, take Victoria Street back past the intersection of Bras Basah and walk about 6 blocks to:

14. **Bugis Street.** Once full of sex shows and decadence, Bugis has cashed in and become a shopping center and popular night market, though you can still catch a transvestite review at the **Boom Boom Room** (see chapter 8).

Back on Bras Basah, turn right from CHIJMES or left from Bugis Street. To your right is the towering:

15. **Westin Stamford.** (See chapter 3.) The tallest hotel in the world, it sits atop Raffles City Shopping Centre. On your left is the **Raffles Hotel Arcade.** If you follow Bras Basah to the corner at Beach Road and turn left, you'll be at the entrance of the:

16. **Raffles Hotel.** (See chapters 3, 5, and 8.) Built in 1887, Raffles is a living, breathing slice of British colonial history that's still going strong. If nothing else, take a stroll through the lobby. If you have more time, check out the museum or have a Singapore Sling in the place they originated, the famous Long Bar.

☕ **TAKE A BREAK**   For a no-muss, no-fuss local lunch I'd recommend the **food court** inside Raffles City Shopping Centre. Choose from an assortment of Chinese noodles, Malay curries, Thai soups, Indian vegetarian dishes, and Singaporean favorites from any of the superclean, very inexpensive stalls. For a more upscale meal, the buffet at Raffles's **Tiffin Room** is lovely. If it's the afternoon, you could catch high tea at the **Raffles Bar and Billiards Room,** or, for a

Historic District Walking Tour

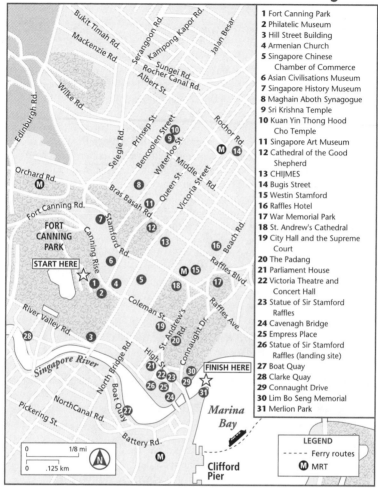

1 Fort Canning Park
2 Philatelic Museum
3 Hill Street Building
4 Armenian Church
5 Singapore Chinese Chamber of Commerce
6 Asian Civilisations Museum
7 Singapore History Museum
8 Maghain Aboth Synagogue
9 Sri Krishna Temple
10 Kuan Yin Thong Hood Cho Temple
11 Singapore Art Museum
12 Cathedral of the Good Shepherd
13 CHIJMES
14 Bugis Street
15 Westin Stamford
16 Raffles Hotel
17 War Memorial Park
18 St. Andrew's Cathedral
19 City Hall and the Supreme Court
20 The Padang
21 Parliament House
22 Victoria Theatre and Concert Hall
23 Statue of Sir Stamford Raffles
24 Cavenagh Bridge
25 Empress Place
26 Statue of Sir Stamford Raffles (landing site)
27 Boat Quay
28 Clarke Quay
29 Connaught Drive
30 Lim Bo Seng Memorial
31 Merlion Park

LEGEND
- - - - Ferry routes
Ⓜ MRT

few dollars more, take your tea at the **Compass Rose,** at the top of the Westin Stamford. The view is to die for. (See chapter 4 for details on all of these.)

From Raffles Hotel, backtrack on Beach Road and continue past the intersection at Bras Basah. On your left is:

17. War Memorial Park. This memorial was erected for the Singaporeans who lost their lives during the Japanese occupation. Because of its four columns, it is called "the chopsticks," each chopstick representing a group that died—Chinese, Malays, Indians, and Europeans and other races.

As you pass War Memorial Park, bear right onto St. Andrew's Road and look to your right to see:

18. St. Andrew's Cathedral. An earlier church designed by George Coleman stood on this site until it was struck by lightning and torn down in 1852. The present structure dates from 1860 and is of English Gothic Revival design—it's one of the few standing churches of this style in the region.

Follow St. Andrew's Road to:

19. **City Hall and the Supreme Court.** Both will be on your right. Built in a most official-looking classical style, these municipal buildings stand on some of the best real estate on the island. While there's not much for curious folks to see inside these buildings, the outside decor is worth a stop, particularly the relief carvings of Justice, Supplication, Thankfulness, Deceit, Violence, Prosperity, and Abundance along the front of the Supreme Court.

Across the street from these buildings is:

20. **The Padang.** It may only look like a playing field, but as the center around which the city was built, it has a great deal of historic significance.

After the Supreme Court, as you round the curve, bear left. Just ahead is the:

21. **Parliament House.** Once the seat of Singapore's Legislative Assembly, it's probably the oldest surviving building in the country, having been built in 1826 (though it's been substantially altered since). These days parliamentary business is conducted in the recently completed (and characterless) gray marble monstrosity that stands just behind. The bronze elephant you see out front was presented in 1872 by King Chulalongkorn, Rama V of Siam.

As you continue round the curve of St. Andrew's Road, you'll see the:

22. **Victoria Theatre and Concert Hall.** The theater portion was built in 1862 as the Town Hall, and the concert hall was built in 1905 as a memorial to Queen Victoria. Today, the Singapore Symphony Orchestra and various other companies call it home.

Cut around to the front of the theater to see the first:

23. **Statue of Sir Stamford Raffles.** Dating from 1887, the statue stood in the Padang until it got in the way of the cricket matches.

From the statue you can look across the water to see:

24. **Cavenagh Bridge.** Constructed in 1869, it linked the government center with Commercial Square across the river. It was named after Orfeur Cavenagh, who was governor of Singapore from 1859 until 1867.

From Cavenagh Bridge you can walk upriver following the pedestrian walkway along the riverbank, and pass:

25. **Empress Place.** It will be on your right. The building once housed almost the entire government bureaucracy of Singapore, and at press time it was being converted to house phase two of the Asian Civilisations Museum.

Walk a block or two along the river to the second:

26. **Statue of Sir Stamford Raffles.** This statue was made from plaster casts of the original 1887 figure located in front of the Victoria Theatre and Concert Hall (see above), and stands on what is believed to be the site where Sir Stamford Raffles landed on January 29, 1819. This is a great place to appreciate the Singapore River.

Across the river is:

27. **Boat Quay.** It's known as "the belly of the fish." It takes a little imagination to see it, but from this point (near the Raffles statue) as you look upstream and down, the shape of the river resembles a fish; the head faces downstream and the tail ends at the upstream Elgin Bridge—with Boat Quay sitting at its belly. According to Chinese feng shui, it is this belly—the luckiest part of the fish— that's made Boat Quay a commercial success throughout its history.

Also at the Raffles Landing Site, examine the trees to find a fragment of the old metal pipe banister that once marked the edge of the water. When they built up this side of the river, they cut the banister, but a small portion was embedded in the trunk of the tree, and still remains. The tree is now about 20 yards from the water's edge.

At this point you are behind the Parliament Building. If you want to continue in the strict historical vein, skip #28; if you're in the mood for a detour, however, upriver is:

28. **Clarke Quay.** A former cannery and warehouse area, Clarke Quay is now home to 60 restored warehouses that contain retail shops and restaurants. Just before it is **Elgin Bridge,** built in 1862 and named after Lord Elgin, a British High Commissioner who merely passed through Singapore in 1857 on his way to China.

Backtrack to the Raffles Landing Site, behind the Parliament Building. To the right side is Parliament Lane. Follow this back to St. Andrew's Road. Turn right and follow the curve around the Padang to:

29. **Connaught Drive.** Connaught follows along the edge of the Padang, while on its other side is a park called **Queen Elizabeth Walk,** which these days is an everlovin' mess thanks to the construction of a new concert hall. At the beginning of Queen Elizabeth Walk, **Anderson Bridge** links the Historic District to Collyer Quay. If the bridge is to your right, look slightly left to see the:

30. **Lim Bo Seng Memorial.** The statue was erected in memory of Maj. Gen. Lim Bo Seng, a member of the Singaporean underground resistance in World War II who was captured and killed by the Japanese.

On the other side of Anderson Bridge is:

31. **Merlion Park.** Here you can see Singapore's national symbol, the Merlion—half-fish, half-lion, and all-around symbol of prosperity.

Walking Tour 2
Chinatown

Start: Wak Hai Cheng Bio Temple on Phillip Street.
Finish: Chinatown Point, the Singapore Handicraft Center on New Bridge Road.
Time: 4 to 5 hours (maybe more, depending on the heat, how much time you take for lunch, and how much you like to dawdle).
Best Times: Start in the morning to give yourself enough time to see all you want without being rushed. Any day of the week should be fine.

When the first Chinese junk landed in Singapore, the sailors aboard rushed to the shore and prayed to Kuan Yin, the goddess of mercy, for bringing them safely to their destination. A small shrine was built on the shore, which became the first stop all Chinese sailors made as they landed ashore. It was nothing like today's Thian Hock Keng Temple, but hey, they had to start somewhere.

These Chinese and other merchants set up warehouses along the western bank of the Singapore River, and business offices, residences, clan associations, and coolie houses began to fill the area behind Boat Quay. In 1822, when Sir Stamford Raffles developed his Town Plan, he reserved this area for the Chinese, naming it Chinatown, a name that's stuck.

As you tour Chinatown, you may be surprised to see a Hindu Temple and even a couple of mosques. Although the area was predominantly Chinese, many Hindus and Muslims set roots here in the early days, drawn by fresh water at Spring Street (as Hindu temples must always be built on a water supply and Muslims require water for ablution before prayers) and by commerce.

For a long time, Chinatown remained basically unaltered, but that's changed recently as the Urban Redevelopment Authority (URA) has come in to renovate many of the more interesting places along the Chinatown walk. During the course of the walking tour, I'll show the contrast between the old and the new, and describe some of the effects of the URA's plan.

The tour begins on Phillip Street at:

1. **Wak Hai Cheng Bio Temple.** Built by Chinese sailors, its name means "Temple of the Calm Sea Built by the Guangzhou People." It's a Teochew temple, located in a part of Chinatown (from here to Boat Quay) that was populated mostly by the Teochews.

   From here, cross Church Street to:

2. **Telok Ayer Street.** Before major land reclamation in the 1870s, the water reached right up to Telok Ayer. As a center of commercial activity, this street was home to the earliest temples, clan associations, and entertainment houses. From the 1850s to 1870s the street was crowded with slaves, illicit activities, and awful smells, driving most of the wealthier folks to seek relocation outside the area. Notice some of the buildings to the right of the street still have flood gates to protect them from rising tides.

   As you walk down Telok Ayer Street, on your right at #76 is:

3. **Fuk Tak Chi Temple.** Dating from 1820, this is the island's oldest Chinese temple, serving as the first stop for newly arrived Chinese sailors. Built by Cantonese and Hakka, the tiny temple was smoke-filled and decrepit before a recent urban upgrading incorporated it into the Far East Complex, a very touristy attempt at reclaiming the heritage of the area. Since then, the temple has no longer been used for worship, but as a museum for a small display of historical items.

   Continue along Telok Ayer, and just at the intersection with Cross Street, on your right you'll see:

4. **Ying Fo Fui Kun.** As the headquarters of the Ying Fo Clan Association, this house was a central meeting point for Hakka immigrants from four areas in southern China. Established in 1822, the association helped newcomers find work and homes, sent money back to families, and disseminated news from China throughout the overseas Chinese community. Inside, photographs catalogue the massive 1997 restoration that took place here (there's no admission charge). I like this building for its simple but classic "scholar" style preferred by southern Chinese.

   Continue along Telok Ayer (crossing over Cross St.) and on your right as you pass Boon Tat Street you'll see:

5. **Nagore Durgha Shrine.** Built to commemorate a visit to the island by a Muslim holy man who was traveling around Southeast Asia spreading the word of Islam, there's a continuing dispute over exactly how old the place is. If you can find a translator, Nagoreallauddeen, the 15th descendant of the holy man, will tell you his side of the dispute—he's here every day.

   A little farther down on the right is:

6. **Thian Hock Keng Temple.** One of the oldest Chinese temples in Singapore, it's another one built originally by Chinese sailors and dedicated to the goddess Ma Po Cho. Note the wooden bar that runs at the foot of the entrance, keeping out wandering ghosts and, coincidentally, forcing you to bow as you enter—or at least to look down, so you don't trip.

   Still farther down Telok Ayer Street, on the right, is the:

Chinatown Walking Tour

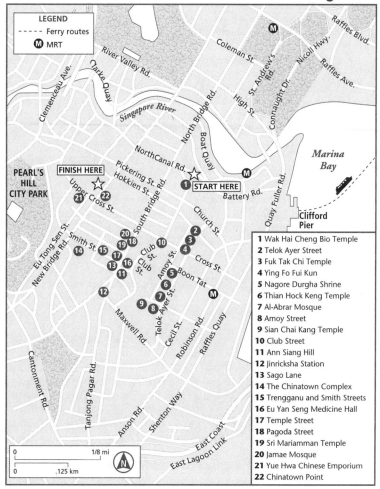

LEGEND
- - - - Ferry routes
Ⓜ MRT

PEARL'S HILL CITY PARK

FINISH HERE ☆

START HERE ☆

Marina Bay

Clifford Pier

1 Wak Hai Cheng Bio Temple
2 Telok Ayer Street
3 Fuk Tak Chi Temple
4 Ying Fo Fui Kun
5 Nagore Durgha Shrine
6 Thian Hock Keng Temple
7 Al-Abrar Mosque
8 Amoy Street
9 Sian Chai Kang Temple
10 Club Street
11 Ann Siang Hill
12 Jinricksha Station
13 Sago Lane
14 The Chinatown Complex
15 Trengganu and Smith Streets
16 Eu Yan Seng Medicine Hall
17 Temple Street
18 Pagoda Street
19 Sri Mariamman Temple
20 Jamae Mosque
21 Yue Hwa Chinese Emporium
22 Chinatown Point

7. Al-Abrar Mosque. Also known as Kuchu Palli (small mosque) and as Masjid Chulia, the original mosque on this site was a thatched hut that was probably erected not long after 1827. The present brick structure was erected in the 1850s.

Just past Al-Abrar Mosque on the right is:

8. Amoy Street. The Hokkien center of Chinatown, Amoy Street now looks peaceful during the day. About the only time you see hustle and bustle here is around lunchtime, when all the workers from Amoy's ad agencies and public relations firms head for the Amoy Street hawker center.

Beyond the hawker center, straight ahead where Amoy bends to the right, is the:

9. Sian Chai Kang Temple. A tiny shrine, this one has gained popularity recently, and is more lively these days.

Continue along Amoy Street, and when you reach the intersection of Amoy and Boon Tat streets, look at the decrepit **shophouse** on the far corner. The exposed side reveals trees that have taken root in the crumbling walls of the structure. This particular house, along with its neighbors, represents some of the oldest shop houses around. Note the squat, top-heavy structure, two square windows up top and minimal adornment. This is a great example of the shop house in its worst unrenovated state. This one looks too far gone to even be considered for renovation and might eventually be torn down. Luckily it's still here for you to see, but soon may not be.

Continue up Amoy Street to Cross Street. Turn left and walk a ways. To the left will be:

10. **Club Street.** Club Street was a famous social spot for wealthy Chinese businessmen. A fascinating collection of shophouses line the narrow street, which is now home to many law firms, media offices, and advertising agencies. It's great to come back here at night for all the cafes and bars that have become popular along this stretch. If you care for a tiny detour, head down **Mohamed Ali Lane** on your right. In one of this street's small alleys, you can find one of the city's last remaining old-style barbers, with his chair set up in the back alley. For a couple of bucks you'll get a good old-fashioned trim and ear cleaning. Back on Club Street, continuing on farther and about midway down, a small lane (also called Club Street) comes to a dead end at the **Chinese Weekly Entertainment Club,** which was built in 1892 by a local Peranakan millionaire as a gentlemen's club for the more powerful members of the Chinese community.

Turn back to the original Club Street and continue down to Ann Siang Hill; turn left.

11. **Ann Siang Hill.** The shophouses on Ann Siang Hill are gorgeous examples of decorative local architecture and all of its influences. I like the contrast between the sadly dilapidated house on the corner of Ann Siang and Club streets and the shiny examples of renovation magic around it. Some of these old buildings still have two-part pintu pagar doors—small, saloon-style swinging panels that allow both air circulation and privacy—behind which are large doors that are only used to lock up. Some of the tile work on these houses is wild. Take a look at #26 and #24 through #19.

Ann Siang Hill is also home to many **clan associations.** These family guilds were created in the early 1800s to support new Chinese immigrants to Singapore by helping them to find work. For the established Chinese clan members, the associations distributed news from the mainland, served social functions, and settled disputes. Remittance houses on the street also served to send money and messages back to folks' homes in China.

Ann Siang Hill branches off into two roads. Stay to the right and walk a block until it turns into Kadayanalur Street. Continue straight until you hit Maxwell Road, where you'll make a right and head for the intersection of Maxwell and South Bridge roads. It's a large intersection, but as you look to your left the triangular white building is the old:

12. **Jinricksha Station.** This was the depot for the thousands of rickshas that once served as regular public transportation. This spot saw many vicious fights between clans, which struggled for the most lucrative ricksha routes. The building has now been converted into restaurants.

☕ **TAKE A BREAK** For a side trek, turn toward Jinricksha Station and bear right down Neil Road. Along Neil Road are a couple of Chinese teahouses—**The Tea Chapter** (see chapter 4)—is a good spot to relax and take in a traditional Chinese tea ceremony. If you're in the mood for something more substantial than tea, stop into **Chen Fu Ji Fried Rice,** at 7 Erskine Rd. (bear right from Maxwell

Rd. at the Jinriksha Station up South Bridge Rd.). This is the best fried rice in the world. Trust me.

From the intersection at Jinricksha station, cross South Bridge Road and turn to the right. Walk along South Bridge Road until you reach Sago Lane, and turn left.

13. **Sago Lane.** This short street was named after the many factories here that hired Chinese laborers after they were too weak to work the docks and other trades. Sago, a starchy staple made from the pith of the rumbia palm, was pounded into balls and dried into "sago pearls" for later use in baking. Sago Lane also became known for its death trade. The ground floors of these shophouses contained businesses catering to those in mourning—funeral parlors, flower wreath and coffin makers, and embalmers. The higher floors were devoted to hospices that served many elderly Chinese who came to this place to die in dignity, and spare their homes from bad spirits and ill fortune associated with death in families' houses.

Once upon a time, the street was home to many tradesmen. Just about the only one you can see today is at #10, **Hong Chaz Repair Antique,** with furniture spilling out into the street and workers sanding away. A few old shops—a couple of old Chinese medical halls and famous bakeries—remain here as well. Where there was once a mask maker and a kite maker, you'll find souvenir shops selling masks and kites with no known craftspeople behind them.

☕ **TAKE A BREAK**   For an incredibly tasty snack now or later, I highly recommend picking up some barbecued pork slices, a Chinese delicacy, at **Hu Zhen Long,** 12 Sago Lane. These dried flat strips of pork are perfectly sweet and salty, and only S$1.50 (US$0.90) each. While you're there, check out their other specialty items, like sesame oil, crispy prawn, and pork floss, plus spice mixtures, durian cake, and other local flavorings.

At the end of Sago Lane, across Trengganu Street, is:

14. **The Chinatown Complex.** This large market packs in row after row of stalls selling souvenirs, luggage, household items, clothing, leather goods, and more. Feel free to bargain. In the back toward the left is a row of stores, a few of which sell large collections of incense, Chinese teapots, antique jade, and carvings. If you're curious, there's a huge wet market (meaning workers there hose down the concrete floor every morning before business) in the basement where you can peruse the exotic fruits and vegetables, dried foodstuffs, and meats, seafood, and poultry. Upstairs, a large hawker center has some good local food on the fast and cheap.

After shopping, eating, or gawking, head back to Trengganu Street, where you came in. Heading away from Sago Street, you'll come to the intersection of:

15. **Trengganu and Smith streets**. At one time, before restoration efforts, Trengganu was peppered with hawkers who laid out their wares on blankets on the sides of the street. The upper floors of many of these houses were brothels. They've been cleaned up for quite some time now, but it's widely known that still today, just nearby on Keong Saik and Teck Lim roads, the trade still thrives.

Primarily a Cantonese area, Trengganu Street, and the intersecting Smith Street, were the center of activity for Chinese opera. The old three-story **Lai Chun Tuen** opera house at the corner is nothing much to see these days. After a severe bombing during the Japanese World War II invasion, it was never restored. Today, it's been thoroughly rebuilt and awaits incoming souvenir shops. However, for a taste of the old craft, there's a small shophouse at 15 Smith St.

(☎ **65/ 323-4862**), which is home to the **Chinese Theater Circle,** one of the few remaining local companies to perform Chinese opera in Singapore. This outfit performs regular snippets of classic tales at Clarke Quay every Wednesday and Friday from 7:30pm to 8:15pm (see chapter 8 for more details) and collaborates with the Singapore Tourism Board for the popular Painted Faces Tour (which I've described in greater detail at the end of this chapter). Inside, you'll find your basic tea shop, but in the afternoons and evenings you can stop in for 3 hours of novice performances during the **Cantonese Opera Karaoke** (2 to 5pm and 7 to 10pm, minimum S$10/US$6 per person food charge). If you can stand it, it's quite a cultural curiosity.

This whole area of Chinatown (Sago Street, Smith Street, and Trengganu Street, plus Temple Street and Pagoda Street, which bisect Trengganu) is being developed by the Urban Redevelopment Authority as a **Chinatown Thematic Zone.** Automobile traffic will eventually be barred from these streets completely, and a promenade for tourists is slowly taking over. Ask any of the local Chinese around here and they'll tell you with sad reminiscence about all the craftsmen—the incense makers, lantern makers, calligraphers, chop cutters, kite makers, and others—who once handcrafted their wares in these shops. In 1983, street hawkers were removed from the streets; and since 1986, when the area was declared a preservation area, almost all tradesmen have disappeared as the newly renovated shops demanded rents far beyond their reach. One look now and you'll see the coming of the future: Most of the artisans' shops have been replaced by souvenir shops.

Despite urban renewal, some of these shops are well worth taking a peek inside. Just outside #01-64 Smith St., you can enjoy a cup of healing Chinese tea poured from huge copper kettles. **Bee's Brand Bird's Nest and Health Product Centre** advertises teas to relieve body ache, cure flu, and relieve fever (from S$.80/US$0.48 to S$3.50/US$2.10). Farther down on Smith, check out **Chinatown Joss Stick and Ceremonial Trading** at #54 or **Nam's Supplies** at #22. Both specialize in joss, the name given to both the temple incense as well as the tablets of thin gold- and silver-leafed paper that are burned in the temples. One of my favorite places is **Kwong Chen** at 16 Smith St. The Chinese proprietor of this 83-year-old tea shop sits behind the counter belting out Cantonese opera through blackened teeth. A most jovial spirit, he'll love to sell you some tea—the tins are gorgeous and his prices are great, but the tea is not the best quality. Still, it's a fabulous gift idea, plus a way to support a fast-disappearing local tradition.

At the end of Smith, you can cross over South Bridge Road to find the:

16. **Eu Yan Seng Medicine Hall.** Since its humble beginnings four generations ago, Eu Yang Seng has grown into an international operation with more than 40 stores in Singapore, Malaysia, and Hong Kong. Founded by Eu Kong, who brought his medical knowledge from China, it was first passed to his son, Eu Tong Sen, a highly respected member of the business community. *Yan Seng,* meaning "caring for mankind," is what this business is all about. The packaged remedies may seem shiny in comparison to the other mom-and-pop medical halls in the neighborhood, but the quality of goods and services here is second to none. Chat up the counter staff, who speak English and is used to curious inquiries, about treatments that are right for you. Or pick up their anthology of Chinese herbs and medicines, with home remedies for nervousness, graying hair, hangovers, and (of course) impotence.

Cross back to the other side of South Bridge Road and go right, walking until you hit:

Go halfway around the world.
Sound like you're halfway around the block.

Global connection with the AT&T Network

AT&T direct service

Calling home from far away? With the world's most powerful network, **AT&T Direct**® Service connects you clear and fast, plus gives you the option of an English-speaking operator. All you need is your AT&T Calling Card or credit card.* Sounds good, especially from the middle of nowhere. FOR A LIST OF **AT&T ACCESS NUMBERS**, TAKE THE ATTACHED WALLET GUIDE.

17. Temple Street. In the earlier part of this century, Temple Street was the place to come for housewares, particularly kitchen items. A few of these old businesses have managed to stay open despite competition from big department stores. **Toh Foong** (at #5) sells the more decorative pieces of pottery, from dining sets to urns, even small Chinese figurines, in traditional patterns and designs. At **Sia Huat** (#9-11) and **Bao Yuan Trading** (#15) you can see how their stock has evolved in keeping with modern needs. If you walk down Temple and cross over Trengganu, look for the peanut seller, **Mei Heong Tuen** at #39, for a bag of fresh steamed or plain nuts scooped up from big glass and tin bins.

Back at the corner of Temple and Trengganu, turn left onto Trengganu and walk to:

18. Pagoda Street. Not all early Chinese immigrants could afford passage to Singapore; many came as indentured servants. Large numbers of the poorest workers were crowded into quarters on the upper floors of these buildings on Pagoda. It was typical for each tiny room to have around 16 bunks, each shared by two laborers—one who worked the night shift and one who worked the day. The stifling heat in these places usually meant that workers, on their free hours, were out and about visiting the opium dens in the area (perpetuating their poverty) or hanging around trying to find work. Thus the name "slave market" was given to this area. Later, just before restorations, this street was visited regularly for its fine tailor shops.

Now, Pagoda and intersecting Trengganu host many touristic gift shops, but I've found the collection of items at **Zhen Lacquer Gallery,** 1 Trengganu St. (with another, larger branch at 256 South Bridge Rd.), of better quality than most of the other knickknack shacks spilling out onto the sidewalk, even though it is a tad more pricey. Above Zhen Lacquer, climb the narrow stairway to the **Tea Village,** 45A-51A Pagoda (☎ **65/221-7825**), for a lesson in the art of traditional Chinese tea making and service—a highly recommended stop to rejuvenate from the heat or rain and appreciate an ancient Chinese tradition at the same time. If you're enchanted by the tea ceremony, Tea Village sells tea sets; however, I've found a much better selection at more reasonable prices around the corner at **D'Art Station** (#65 Pagoda). They sell all sorts of sets, both simple and elaborate, plus all the accompanying accouterments. By the way, they also have a small but nice collection of delicate bamboo birdcages, which are so lovely to look at but make the most impractical gifts. By the time you get the poor thing back home it'll probably look like nothing more than a box of toothpicks. If you're looking for a little modern Singaporean culture, visit **Plastique Kinetic Worms,** #68 Pagoda (☎ **65/324-3221**), a small gallery that showcases contemporary arts.

Pagoda Street is also a nice stop for a rest in one of the many cafes along the pedestrian quarter. If your feeling really overheated, try some fresh barley water, made from boiled and strained barley, with a bit of pandan leaf and sugarcane for flavor; the locals believe this is one of the best ways to cool the body down. At the time of writing, the shophouses at #46 through #50 Pagoda were being converted to make space for a Chinatown Heritage Centre. By press time, it could be up and running.

From this point you can now ask yourself, "Who chose these garish colors to paint these shophouses anyway?"

As you walk down Pagoda Street (heading right from the intersection with Trengganu), approaching on the right-hand corner of Pagoda and South Bridge Road, you can't miss the colorful statuettes on the gopuram (roof) of the:

19. **Sri Mariamman Temple.** The oldest Hindu temple in Singapore, it was originally a small wood-and-thatch shrine founded by Naraina Pillai, an Indian merchant who came to Singapore with Raffles's first expedition. In the main hall of
the temple you can see the small god that Pillai originally placed here.

Turn left on South Bridge and walk 1 block. On your left you'll see the:

20. **Jamae Mosque.** Behind the typical-looking gate, the mosque itself has the neoclassical style that was popular in the 1830s, when it was built. A small shrine
inside memorializes Muhammad Salih Valinva, a local religious leader.

From South Bridge Road, turn left onto Mosque Street to check out **Siong
Moh Paper Products** (#39 Mosque St.). Though they sell joss items similar to
those found in other stores in Chinatown, I thought they had the best selection
of Hell Money and such paper objects as Mercedes Benzes, cellular phones,
radios, televisions, and suits, which are burned for deceased relatives who can
then use them in the afterlife. The 50-year-old **Tai Thong Cake Shop** (#43
Mosque St.) is another local treasure that remained after restoration, Mosque
Street having once been famous for its bakeries and tea houses. Tai Thong's moon
cakes and Chinese pastries still draw regular clients who care about quality and
tradition.

Continue on Mosque Street until it ends at New Bridge Road/Eu Tong Sen
Street, which is a mess as the contractors struggle to dig a new MRT line. Appar-
ently the soil contains too much clay, posing many excavation problems and
enormous delays. Lord only knows when work will be completed. Turn right and
follow New Bridge Road to the intersection with Upper Cross Street. Cross over
New Bridge and Eu Tong Sen to:

21. **Yue Hwa Chinese Emporium.** For all varieties of imported Chinese goods, Yue
Hwa has the best selection—plus, I've managed to pick up quite a few bargains,
from modern silk and embroidered fashions to table linens; ceramics to home
furnishings; musical instruments to arts supplies; ceremonial items, jewelry,
silks—the list goes on. And if you're looking for a formal cheongsam (Mandarin-
style dress) there's no better place for fine work and fabrics than Yue Hwa, which
uses expert tailors from Hong Kong and Shanghai. And I'm sure you gentlemen
will love the ready-made Mandarin-style robes and coolie outfits!

From Yue Hwa, backtrack over Eu Tong Sen and Upper Cross streets to:

22. **Chinatown Point,** which is just catercorner to Yue Hwa at the same intersection. The STB has tried to collect local Chinese artisans in this modern shopping mall, also known as the Singapore Handicraft Centre, to give shoppers
easier access to traditional wares. While many shops here are just modern
souvenir places, there are a few neat things to see and shop for.

The **3 Tunes Music Shop,** #02-61 Chinatown Point (☎ **65/536-1238**), specializes in classical Chinese instruments imported from the mainland. These delicate pieces are gorgeous with inlay and fine detail, and make a beautiful addition
to your home, even if you don't play. However, if you'd like to learn, one of their
resident masters can teach you how to play any one of them. Lessons for the
gu-qin, a flat, seven-stringed, mellow-sounding instrument start at S$100
(US$59.90) for a 45-minute lesson. This is the most ancient of all classical Chi-
nese instruments (3,000 years old), and the best place to begin when learning
Chinese classics. Lessons for the larger 21-stringed gu-zheng are also the same
price. S$60 (US$35.95) will get you a lesson on the pi-pa, the four-stringed
teardrop-shaped lute; the lu-qin, a four-stringed instrument similar to the banjo;
or the zhong-ruan, like the pi-pa only smaller and higher pitched. For S$45
(US$26.95) you can also learn the er-hu, the two-stringed violin-like instrument,

with a hexagonal body covered in snakeskin. They also teach wind instruments for S$35 (US$20.95) per 45-minute session, but for these you have to supply your own instrument. The di-zi is played like a flute, and sounds somewhat similar, while the larger xiao looks and sounds more like a bassoon. They also carry a limited selection of musical theory books and CDs.

If you're keen on feng shui, or Chinese geomancy, step into the **Pu Lin Group** storefront, #02-67 Chinatown Point (☎ **65/294-8338**), for information about upcoming geomancy talks. At the time of writing, master geomancer Koh Pu Lin was giving free evening talks in English and Chinese on the subject at Suntec City's Fountain of Wealth on the 28th of the month, and on the 30th of each month at the shop here at Chinatown Point. Call ahead for the current program schedule.

One level up in Chinatown Point, **Chinatown Seal Carving Souvenir** (#03-72) has a fabulous selection of Chinese seals, or chops, which can be carved with any characters, in English or Chinese (even your name translated) in 1 day's time. The kindly people at **Inherited Arts & Crafts** (#03-69) use their skills not only for chop carving, but also to create beautiful Chinese calligraphy pieces and brush paintings made to order. For another curious souvenir idea, check out **La Belle Collection** (#04-53), selling jewelry crafted from colorful orchids. Gold plate is only used for the edges, so the vivid petals still show through the enamel. The booby prize goes to **B-Love** (#03-68), with the ultimate in odd souvenir items: Imagine all fashions of Chinese characters—the Kuan Yin, the Buddha, mythological dragons, fish, and frogs—carved in huge scale out of yellowish green plastic *that glows in the dark!* Even if you're not in the market, it's great for some laughs.

Walking Tour 3
Little India

Start: Corner of Hastings Road and Serangoon Road.
Finish: Leong San See Temple, Race Course Road.
Time: 2 to 3 hours.
Best Times: Tour buses usually arrive around 10am, so it may be better to get here earlier (and if you arrive at 8 to 8:30am, you can have a local breakfast or coffee in Zhu Jiao Centre). Don't go on a Sunday—it's laborers' only day off, so Serangoon Road gets packed.

Little India did not develop as a community planned by the colonial authorities like Kampong Glam or Chinatown, but came into being because immigrants from India were drawn to business developments here. In the late 1920s, the government established a brick kiln and lime pits here that attracted Indian workers, and the abundance of grass and water made the area attractive to Indian cattle traders. Indigenous bamboo grew on the site of the present Zhu Jiao Centre at the eastern end of Serangoon Road and was used to build fences, while a natural spring provided holy water for religious purposes.

In contrast to Chinatown, Little India still serves as the central focal point for Indian life in Singapore. The Chinese artisans and small businesses of Chinatown may have moved with the population to other areas of the island, but Little India hasn't changed much over the years. Small businesses still occupy their original premises, and shops still spill over into the five-foot ways. In fact, for most of Singapore's Indian community, this area is seen as a vital link to their heritage. It is here that they buy religious trappings for worship, specialty foods and spices for traditional meals, fabrics and accessories for traditional dress, and the imported items from their ancestral homeland that keep them connected to their culture.

Not only is Little India vital, it is also vibrant. Hindi and Tamil hit songs throb from shop fronts, while men stand out of the sun under the five-foot-way chewing betel nuts and gossiping with an old seller. Folks still set up stalls to string colorful flowers together for worshippers to bring to the temple. Beautiful women float by like butterflies resplendent in Punjabi outfits and flowing saris. The smell of incense and spice flows through the streets with the breeze.

The tour begins on the corner of Hastings Road and Serangoon Road, where there's a stone plaque carved with Tamil writing. The animal head on the plaque could be a cow, indicating the cattle industry of the early settlers here. The symbols on the plaque stand for Vishnu, Shiva, and Brahma, the Hindu trinity.

Across Serangoon Road is:

1. **Zhu Jiao Centre.** The hawker stalls in the front part—half designated for Chinese food and the other half for Indian—are a good place to stop for a cup of coffee. The crescent moon and star on some of the signs indicate where food is halal, following the strict dietary laws of Islam. Walk through the stalls to the back, where you'll find a wet market (meaning workers there hose down the concrete floor every morning before business). A walk through the separate sections reveals the strange world of local fruits, Chinese vegetables, local and imported dried fish, mushrooms and chiles, and meats, poultry, and seafood.

At one time they slaughtered the chickens here, but government sanitation laws drove the business to factories. If you're adventurous, hang around early to see if you can meet up with a poultry truck driver who's willing to let you hitch a ride on his delivery route for one of the most unusual tours around the island.

Exit out the side to Buffalo Road and head away from Serangoon Road. **Komala Vilas** (see chapter 4), at #12-14 Buffalo Rd., serves the country's finest dosai (order the paper dosai, a very thin bread pancake) and dal, a mildly spicy lentil sauce for dipping.

At the corner of Buffalo Road and Kerbau Road (Malay for "cow") is:

2. **No. 37 Buffalo Rd.** Here's a little shop that sells batik from Sri Lanka, flowers made into prayer garlands, and betel leaves for red dye. The paan wallah (or betel nut seller) here mixes the slightly narcotic nuts from the acacia tree with lime paste and sometimes other flavors, wraps them in a betel leaf, and sells them to interested chewers. A social tradition, betel is still used to welcome guests in private homes, chewed after dinner to aid digestion, or taken during breaks with friends out on the sidewalk. If you care to try, be prepared for the mixture to turn your whole mouth crimson.

On Kerbau Road, turn right down what looks almost like a back alley, and into an open courtyard. Directly to your right, #37 Kerbau Rd. is called:

3. **Tan House.** This former residence has been restored in perfect Peranakan style, providing a great example of the mixed cultural influences in local architecture. Above the windows in the front, notice the Chinese vents. Called *bienfu,* they're shaped like bats, symbols of good luck. Other Chinese influences include the bamboo engravings on the shutters to symbolize strength and the green tiles above the porch that send rain water running off just outside the front door. This is good feng shui, as water symbolizes money. Keeping the rain close to the door

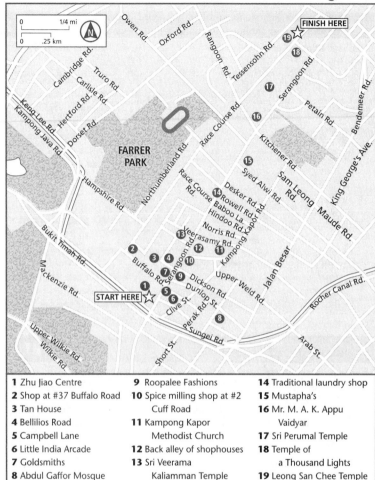

1 Zhu Jiao Centre	**9** Roopalee Fashions	**14** Traditional laundry shop
2 Shop at #37 Buffalo Road	**10** Spice milling shop at #2	**15** Mustapha's
3 Tan House	Cuff Road	**16** Mr. M. A. K. Appu
4 Bellilios Road	**11** Kampong Kapor	Vaidyar
5 Campbell Lane	Methodist Church	**17** Sri Perumal Temple
6 Little India Arcade	**12** Back alley of shophouses	**18** Temple of
7 Goldsmiths	**13** Sri Veerama	a Thousand Lights
8 Abdul Gaffor Mosque	Kaliamman Temple	**19** Leong San Chee Temple

keeps the money close to the home. The green wooden lacelike detail just beneath the eaves shows Malay decorative influence. The columns are European, as are the Edinburgh curved windows.

Continue through the courtyard toward Serangoon Road and you'll hit:

4. Bellilois Road. The street's namesake was a wealthy and influential cattle trader around the turn of the century. (You'll notice many street names in this area reflect the early cattle trade.) The shophouses along this road date back quite early, as evidenced in their short, squat shape and simple ornamentation. These particular houses served as stables, the upstairs housing Indian laborers, most likely too many stuffed into each small room.

From this intersection, Kerbau Road continues to Serangoon Road just ahead. As you make your way toward Serangoon, take a look at some of the shops along this street, outside of which hang hints of a kind of Indian-style feng shui. The *asmi* (a spiritual advisor; the Tamil version of the feng shui master) employ their own superstitions to protect their shops from evil influences. Pumpkins, shells, charcoal, limes, limestone, and even preserved umbilical cords (wrapped in a string like an egg) are hung high, and scary images of gods are placed around the door. These shops always have altars, and before daily business begins, shop owners prepare the altar, burn oil lamps, and offer prayers.

Once you reach Serangoon, cross the street and turn right until, on your left, you find:

5. **Campbell Lane.** Here you'll find shops with Indian arts and crafts, plus souvenirs. You can find feathers from the peacock (the Hindu guardian of the gates of heaven and hell, whose feathers are not plucked but are harvested as they fall out naturally), clay pots that cook the best traditional curries, jugs for water that double as percussion instruments, and pottu—the decorative dot stickers for adorning women's foreheads (by the way, these do not mean that the woman is married). Here you can also find the white powder that's applied to the forehead after prayer, which is made from camphor and cow dung. (Shiva's chariot was drawn by a cow, and the dung symbolizes respect and serves as a reminder that all people will end up as ash. Camphor is a germ killer.)

The best of the souvenir shops is **Kuna's** (#3 Campbell Lane), where you'll find a great variety of handicrafts at fairly reasonable prices. Before you get into any bargaining, it's good to know that when Indians shake their heads from left to right it is affirmative.

Outside Kuna's, stalls adorned with bright flowers provide the Indian community with garlands for religious purposes. Simple jasmine garlands are offered in temples on Tuesdays and Fridays, Hindu holy days (jasmine being a particularly auspicious flower). Other days, especially holidays, you'll find garlands of marigolds and roses as well.

Across the street is:

6. **Little India Arcade.** Its 26 prewar shophouses have been restored to house stalls specializing in Indian imported goods. If you're looking for good gifts and souvenirs, try this arcade for colorful Indian textiles, clothing, ornaments, curio items, incense, costume jewelry, and traditional ceremonial items.

At one of my favorite places here, **Punjab Bazaar** (#01-17 Little India Arcade), women can have their hands painted with henna. If you're interested in trying it out, you can call ahead for an appointment with Ms. Deep at ☎ **65/ 296-0067.** Prices start at around S$15 (US$9) for simple designs.

Back out on Serangoon Road you'll find about a million:

7. **Goldsmiths.** All of these shops operate on the up and up, charging the going rate for gold, plus extra for craftsmanship. Indian gold (more on the orange side than yellow) gets crafted into traditional style bangles, necklaces, rings, and earrings using ancient decorative motifs and designs. Styles are ever changing, and so you'll find many Indian women trading in last year's gold for these craftsman to melt down and re-create into this year's fashion. In these shops you'll also see navarethinam, a man's ring of gold with nine gemstones placed on its face to represent the nine planets. Local fortune-tellers prescribe the order of the setting to harmonize with each wearer's personal astrology for luck and prosperity.

Make a right onto Dunlop Street and follow it until you reach the:

8. **Abdul Gafoor Mosque.** Actually a mosque complex, it consists of the original mosque, a row of shophouses facing Dunlop Street, a prayer hall, and another row of houses facing the mosque. Most of the complex is from the late 19th century.

Backtrack to Serangoon Road or take the parallel Upper Dickson Road for a different view. Shop #84/86 Serangoon Road is:

9. **Roopalee Fashions.** Specializing in salwar kameez, also known as Punjabi dresses, this shop sells the northern Indian style of dress that features a long flowing tunic over long pants, with a long coordinated scarf draped over the shoulders. They also carry accessories, such as delicate sandals and small evening bags to match the outfits.

Back outside, now's a good time to look in the gutter for red paint splashes, which are actually spit marks from betel nut chewers.

When you hit Cuff Road on the right, turn off and look for:

10. **No. 2 Cuff Rd.** It's hard to miss this spice milling shop with its authentic (and very loud) electric Indian spice mill. If you make it inside, be prepared to sneeze from all the spice dust. In addition to grinding spices for local retail, they also prepare special orders—secret blends and family recipes. On the porch at #2 Cuff Rd., if you look up you'll see a square peephole in the ceiling. This was so people sleeping upstairs could see who's at the door during the night. It's very rare to find one of these now that these old places are all being restored.

At the end of Cuff Road is:

11. **Kampong Kapor Methodist Church.** The church is attended almost exclusively by Peranakans.

Backtrack up Cuff Road to the Spice Mill. Across the street, you'll see the:

12. **Back alley of shophouses.** The square patches on the backs of the buildings are where they'd collect the "honey buckets," as some of these places didn't have plumbing until the 1970s. Back alleys like this were introduced in 1915 to provide escape from fires.

Follow the alley to the end. When you reach Veerasamy Road, head left back up to Serangoon, and just across the road you can't miss the:

13. **Sri Veerama Kaliamman Temple.** In front of the temple is a box in which worshippers smash coconuts, a symbolic smashing of the ego to ask to be shown the humble way and for the removal of personal obstacles. The coconuts have two tiny carved "eyes" so the coconut can "see" the obstacle to smash.

TAKE A BREAK   Okay, it's curry break time. Walk northward on Serangoon Road to Race Course Lane, onto which you'll make a left. Follow this to the end, where you'll find Race Course Road and **Muthu's Curry Restaurant,** at #76/78. It ain't elegant, but you can't beat the price, and restaurants don't come much more authentic.

From Sri Veerama Kaliamman Temple, cross Serangoon Road again and keep walking down until you reach the **coffee shop** at the corner of Norris Road, where you can watch chapatis being made.

Farther along at #270 Serangoon Rd. is:

14. **One of Singapore's last remaining traditional laundry shops.** They no longer use charcoal-filled irons, but heavy old electric ones plugged into the ceiling. Catch a glimpse of the Chinese guy who's been working here since 1930. The varicose veins on his legs are one of this walking tour's more edifying sights.

Continue along Serangoon road till you come to **Desker Road,** on the right, famous for its prostitution houses (believe it or not, Singapore does have such a thing). This is a sort of optional side trip, for you curious folk. Male travelers won't have any problems walking in this area, and curious women shouldn't have trouble if accompanied by a man. Women may want to stay away at night. The intersection of Desker and Lembu roads is where transvestites and prostitutes hang around in the evening. Across from Lembu Road, turn off Desker into the alley and at the first walkway intersection, turn left down the narrow alley behind the 2 blocks of buildings. As you walk, if you can peer in the rooms, you can find women waiting for business. Along the way, you'll find stands with people selling pornographic videotapes and displays with everything from aphrodisiacs to enlargement devices, birth control pills, and other related finds. Don't approach unattended displays—rumors have it the authorities plant sting operations here. In the evenings, there's a salesman here with a real sideshow-style sales technique for his wares. Other vendors have displays with Buddhist charms and amulets, and some even have household tools. Go figure. The alley lets out into a street that will let you backtrack to Serangoon Road. Make a right back onto Serangoon.

At the corner of Syed Alwi Road is:

15. **Mustapha's.** This popular department store sells absolutely the largest selection of saris in Singapore. For this southern Indian style, a 6-yard length of cloth is pleated and wrapped around the waist before being draped over one shoulder. In Mustapha's basement (through the entrance off Syed Alwi Road), the row after row of cloth bolts are staggering! Some saris, mostly polyester varieties with simple designs, go for as cheap as S$20 (US$12). Silk versions, kept on the side behind the counter, can run up to S$200 (US$119.75) per piece, especially if there's gold and silver threads running through. At this same counter, inquire about Mustapha's free brochure illustrating how to wrap the sari (truly very helpful). In chapter 7 I've included shops where you can purchase the accompanying blouse, or choli, and the petticoat for underneath.

Mustapha's is also a crazy place to see all the Indian gold styles. Through the main door off Serangoon Road you can't miss the endless display cases of all sorts of solid gold ornamentation. For the curious onlooker, it's basically a museum of Indian jewelry styles—delicate filigrees, intricate collars with matching earrings. Beware, the prices are as staggering as the glitter!

Remain on Serangoon and cross Kitchener Road. The next left is Perumal Road. At #8, on the right, is:

16. **Mr. M. A. K. Appu Vaidyar.** The good doctor prescribes ayurvedic medicines (Sri Lankan mixtures of imported herbs and minerals) such as aphrodisiacs for men and women, immune boosters for children, and ointments for thick hair. Tell him what ails you and he'll find you some goo, with the help of a book to translate to English. Consultation costs vary, but can be as low as S$12 (US$7.20). Don't forget to take off your shoes.

Back out on Serangoon Road, just a half a block on the left is:

17. **Sri Perumal Temple.** The rear building on the temple grounds serves as a wedding hall. If you happen upon a ceremony or party during your visit, ask the attendants if you can watch the proceedings. You'll probably be invited for a meal. If you accept (which is absolutely customary, by the way), give a token gift to the couple—an envelope with money in odd amounts like S$21 or S$31 (never an even amount, for luck reasons) is customary. The best time to find weddings is on Saturdays and Sundays around 6 or 7pm.

To save some time, you can cut through the housing estate apartment complex that neighbors the temple to reach Race Course Road, which runs parallel to Serangoon Road, just behind the temple. You will exit on Race Course Road just next to the Temple of 1,000 Lights. Or, from Sri Perumal Temple, you can backtrack to Perumal Road and follow it until you reach Race Course Road. Take a right on Race Course and follow until you see on your right the:

18. **Temple of a Thousand Lights.** The temple shows influences of Thai architecture, and contains such elements as a replica of a footprint left by the Buddha in Ceylon, statues of baby boddhisattvas for whom worshippers leave candy and toys, and a wheel of fortune that you can spin for S50¢.

Across the street is the small and sleepy:

19. **Leong San Chee Temple or Dragon Mountain Temple.** Many Chinese parents bring their children to this Taoist temple, built in 1926, to pray to its image of Confucius, a practice believed to bring filial piety and good grades.

Walking Tour 4
Arab Street & Kampong Glam

Start: The corner of Arab Street and Beach Road.
Finish: Hajjah Fatimah Mosque on Beach Road.
Time: About 2 hours, but it may stretch to 3 hours or more depending on what kind of shopping frenzy you get into, and how long you want to stop for breaks.
Best Time: Any day but Sunday, when Arab Street is closed.

Kampong Glam is the traditional heart of Singaporean Muslim life. Since early colonial days, the area has attracted Muslims from diverse ethnic backgrounds, fusing them into one community by their common faith and lifestyle.

The name Kampong Glam is a combining of the Malay word for "village" (kampung) and the glam tree, which at one time grew in abundance in the area. Related to the eucalyptus, the glam tree produced an extract that was made into *minyak kaku putih,* an ointment used for treating ailments from earaches to arthritis, and as first aid for dressing wounds.

In 1824, the British made a treaty with Sultan Hussein Shah, then sultan of Singapore, to cede Singapore to the British East India Trading Company. As part of the agreement, the sultan was offered a stipend and given Kampong Glam as a settlement for his palace and subjects. The sultan's original settlement began at Beach Road, which was then at the water's edge, and extended back to the Rochore River, which is now Rochore Canal. From side to side, it stretched from what is now Rochore Road to Jalan Sultan. Sultan Hussein built his palace, Istana Kampong Glam, at the end of Sultan Gate and named the area Kota Raja, Malay for "The King's enclave." Over time, as parcels of land were sold off for burial grounds, schools, mosques, or farms, the area shrunk. Now all that remains of Kota Raja is the Istana itself.

Trade grew in the area as a wave of merchants and tradesmen moved in to serve and provision the large numbers of pilgrims who debarked from here on their journey to Mecca. Blacksmiths set up shops on Sultan Gate and Beach Road and provided ships with anchors, pulleys, and hooks. Tombstone carvers also made a killing in the area, due to the proximity of many local burial grounds.

Although the ethnic Arab population in Singapore has never reached large proportions, their influence is immediately obvious through such Kampong Glam street names as Bussorah Street, Muscat Street, Baghdad Street, Arab Street, and Haji Lane. This walking tour takes you down these streets, where elements of Muslim life still thrive—the regular prayers at the Sultan Mosque, mom-and-pop shops selling Malay and Muslim cultural and religious items, and stalls selling halal food. Unfortunately, some elements of Kampong Glam are slowly disappearing. The Istana, for instance, will soon be transformed into a modern museum (a sad event for many locals, to whom the structure has remained a symbol of Malay glories past), and you'll probably arrive just in time to see the last remains of the blacksmithing and tombstone-carving businesses, whose sad decline is testimony to the growing modernization of Singapore's industrial power.

1. **Arab Street.** From the corner of Arab Street and Beach Road, Arab Street seems like a small place, but the shops on this street are filled with enough cultural curiosities to keep you going for hours. When something piques your interest, feel free to chat up shop workers for snippets of cultural significance or historical explanation. Some of the more interesting shops I've come upon, culturally speaking, are as follows:

At #56 Arab St., **Goodwill Trading** supplies sarongs. Interestingly, while most shops here carry the colorful batik sarongs made for women, Goodwill specializes in pulicat, the light-colored plaid sarongs popularly worn by Malay men.

Contemporary Malay ladies wear an outfit called a sarong kebaya or sarong baju for special occasions. These silk sarongs with long-sleeved tunics allow the lady about town to remain in compliance with Muslim laws for female modesty while also allowing her to sport a little fashion flair in cooling fabrics. Truly, some of the colors are wild. The selection of ready-made sarong baju (the longer top with closed front worn by Malays) and sarong kebaya (the cropped-short top with front opening worn by Peranakans) at **Collezione by Melati** (#55 Arab St.) are quite lovely.

Across the street here, on Baghdad Street, you'll find a few other cultural couture treasures. At **Singalang Jaya** (#9 Baghdad), songkok are still made by hand. These handsome hats, sort of like a cross between a pillbox and a fez, come in all styles, from basic black to models with brocade adornment. Also here, shop for a tudung, the scarf worn by Muslim women to cover the head. For women planning a trip into Malaysia and wishing to visit any of the mosques there, this would be a good time to pick up the appropriate couture.

Campakalal's at #84 Arab St. carries a good selection of Indonesian and Malaysian batik house linens, but I was mostly impressed with their collection of batik wall tapestries, which were quite handsome. Smaller pieces make great little gifts, but the larger ones can run as high as S$75 (US$44.90).

Another Muslim curiosity, alcohol-free perfumes, are carried by a few of these shops, but **Aljuneid Brothers** (#91 Arab St., one of the oldest and best known retailers here) has a nicer selection of scents. According to Islamic law, good Muslims do not consume alcohol, a tradition carried over even to small things like perfume. These oils come in a variety of floral, wood, and copycat designer fragrances. Their selection of lovely cut-glass bottles and atomizers is sweet, too.

The best selection of household batiks such as tablecloths, place mats, napkins, bedcovers, and tapestries can be found at **Maruti Textiles** (#66 Arab St.). The owner has the most stock items to peruse, and a good eye for quality and design. Very traditional and handsome.

While most of the batik shops along this stretch carry very traditional Southeast Asian patterns, one shop **Basharahil Brothers House of Batik** (#99/101 Arab St.), lines its shelves with bolt cottons in thoroughly modern (and sumptuous) designs and colors. A good selection of ikat fabric (woven in Malaysia) and hand-painted batik silks make this place one of my favorite stops for unique fabrics and household linens.

Finally, a stop inside **Kin Lee & Company** (#109 Arab St.) will satisfy any craft person's fix. This place supplies all the necessary items to make delicate

Arab Street & Kampong Glam Walking Tour

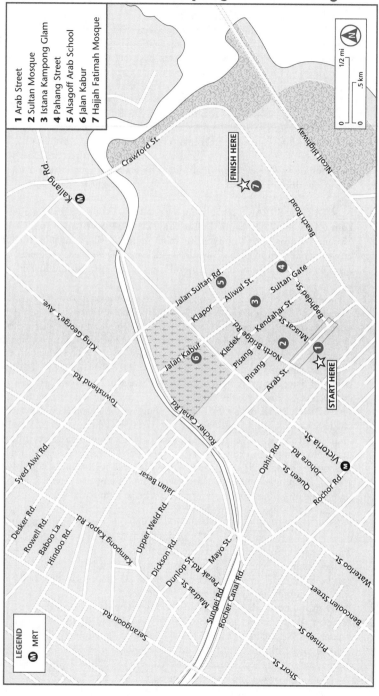

LEGEND
Ⓜ MRT

1 Arab Street
2 Sultan Mosque
3 Istana Kampong Glam
4 Pahang Street
5 Alsagoff Arab School
6 Jalan Kabur
7 Hajjah Fatimah Mosque

FINISH HERE ☆ 7

START HERE ☆ 1

beaded Peranakan slippers. They'll help you pick out a pattern for the uppers (in vivid Peranakan signature florals or geometrics) and get you started with the required beads and notions. Talk to them about having the shoes completed with wooden soles from a local cobbler. You can probably arrange to do this by mail while you're still here, if you care to finish them back at home. You can't find a better conversation piece for your next cocktail party.

Once you've taken in the shopping, the historical portion of the tour begins. Off Arab Street, about midway between Beach Road and North Bridge Road, find Muscat Street. Take it to reach the:

2. **Sultan Mosque.** This is the real center of Singapore's Muslim community. The present mosque was built in 1928 and was funded by donations from the Muslim community. The Saracenic and Mogul flavors of the architecture mask the fact that an Irish guy named Denis Santry actually designed the structure.

🍵 **TAKE A BREAK** If the shopping's got you worn out already, stop in at **Zam Zam's,** 697/699 North Bridge Rd. (☎ **65/298-7011**), behind Sultan Mosque, for a cool drink or a quick meal of murtabak. They stuff this fried flat bread with minced mutton or shredded chicken along with onions, spices, and egg. Dip it in the accompanying bowl of curry for a most delicious lunch.

Continue down Muscat to Kandahar Street. Make a right, then a left as soon as you see an opening in the compound wall to place you on the grounds of the:

3. **Istana Kampong Glam.** It may not look like much now, but this was the family residence of the sultan who once presided over Singapore, and remained the home of his descendants for more than 150 years.

Exit Istana Kampong Glam onto Sultan Gate and follow to the intersection at **Baghdad Street** on your right and **Pahang Street** on your left. Just past this intersection on the right you can still see two remaining foundries at #37 and #39, where there was once a thriving community of metal workers who pounded out hardware for the merchant ships of yesterday. There was also a booming tombstone-carving trade here, a result of the many surrounding graveyards, but that is now completely extinct. Backtrack up Sultan Gate and take a peek around the corner of Baghdad Street to see if any discarded tombstones are still lying around. Interestingly enough, many of the tombstones that were carved here were made by Chinese artisans who had learned to mimic Arabic script.

Next, head across the intersection to:

4. **Pahang Street.** The entire row of refurbished blockhouses to the left have been owned since they were built in 1935 by Arab philanthropist Syed Abdul Rahman Taha Alsagoff. Some small details have been replaced, including the hanging Javanese lamps. As you head down Pahang Street toward Jalan Sultan, keep your eyes peeled for back alleyways, which are great places to see the older buildings, with their crumbling walls and makeshift add-ons.

When you reach Jalan Sultan, turn left. A ways up to the left is the:

5. **Alsagoff Arab School.** Established in 1912, it's the oldest girls' school in Singapore, and was the island's first Muslim school.

Deep in the back alley just beyond the school are street-side barbers. If you want a rare treat, have a shave and a haircut in a back alley. Better than one of those high-style salons you've been going to, don't ya think?

Continue up Jalan Sultan till you reach Victoria Street, and turn left onto it. Not far up Victoria is a road called:

---

6. **Jalan Kabur.** Literally translated as "Cemetery Road," you can find along both its sides a number of ancient royal tombs as well as the graves of Kampong Glam's early settlers. The somewhat serene and peaceful atmosphere of the cemetery, with its shady trees, offers a stark contrast to the rest of Kampong Glam.

Backtrack down Victoria Street and Jalan Sultan until you get to Beach Road. Turn left and follow Beach till, on your left, you see:

7. **Hajjah Fatimah Mosque.** Named for a wealthy businesswoman and socialite from Malacca, the mosque contains a prayer hall, ablution area, gardens and mausoleums, and a few other buildings. Hajjah Fatimah herself is buried in a private room to the side of the main prayer hall, along with her daughter and son-in-law.

2 Organized Tours

Sometimes you don't want to figure out maps, picking and finding your way around to each major attraction. If this is the case, there are many private outfits providing guided tours in English, who can take you around in the comfort of air-conditioned buses. There are also great boat trips that take you up and down the Singapore River or out into the harbor. Some of the vessels are old bumboats (the beat-up water taxis used to take sailors back and forth from ships docked at sea) or replicas of grand Chinese vessels. The views of the city from the sea are magnificent, and, as Singapore is a country built on sea trade, these trips provide a way to experience this important element of Singapore's heritage and work some fun and relaxation into the bargain.

STB THEME TOURS

The Singapore Tourism Board (STB), in partnership with local tour organizers, has developed a number of very creative **thematic tours,** each of which I highly recommend. Of the five currently offered, my favorites are the Flavours of New Asia–Singapore tour, the Painted Faces tour, and the Feng Shui tour.

Flavors of New Asia Tour. Holiday Tours & Travel, 300 Orchard Rd. #07-01/10, The Promenade. ☎ **65/738-2622.**

The 3¹/₂-hour Flavors of New Asia tour begins daily at 8:30am, visiting spice gardens to learn about the origins of familiar Asian flavors; wet markets to see common local ingredients in their natural state; Little India to learn about Indian cuisine's unique spice blends; and Chinatown for a lesson in Chinese herbs and culinary superstitions. Tickets are S$28 (US$16.75) adults, S$15 (US$9) children.

Painted Faces Tour. SH Tours, 100 Kim Seng Rd. #02-02/03, Kim Seng Plaza. ☎ **65/734-9923.**

Due to a growing interest in Cantonese opera, an evening tour has been planned to introduce the curious to this traditional Chinese art form. Beginning at around 5pm (Wednesdays and Fridays only), the Painted Faces tour will escort you to a shop to see elaborate props and costumes used during performances, and to a local clan house for a discussion of the various movements and symbols common to Chinese opera. You'll then head for Clarke Quay to watch actors paint their faces and dress in costume, then stage some of the most popular scenes from traditional Cantonese favorites. Tickets are S$25 (US$14.95) adults, S$15 (US$9) children.

In Harmony With Feng Shui Tour. SH Tours, 100 Kim Seng Rd. #02-02/03, Kim Seng Plaza. ☎ **65/734-9923.**

Join this daily tour for an in-depth look at the ancient art of Chinese geomancy, or placement, at work in the Garden City. The $3^1/2$-hour tour begins at 2:30pm with a discussion of the history and philosophy that dictates feng shui, including topographical influences, the four cardinal points, the basic elements, and the significance of color. Then you'll take a tour of Singapore, stopping to examine places where feng shui is in action, harmonizing buildings to their natural surroundings. Tickets are S$33 (US$19.75) adults, S$17 (US$10.20) children.

Heartlands of New Asia Tour. Holiday Tours & Travel, 300 Orchard Rd. #07-01/10, The Promenade. ☎ **65/738-2622.**

Another recent addition to the tour agenda, the daily, 3-hour Heartlands of New Asia tour may not be a must-see, but is interesting for those who are curious about the way your average Singaporean lives. This tour begins at 1:30pm with a visit to Pulau Ubin, a large island to the northeast of Singapore, where the last kampong villages of Singapore struggle to keep their place in the forests. All of these villages on the main island have disappeared, their inhabitants relocated to Housing Development Board apartments (see the "Kampung Life" box in chapter 2 for more discussion of this phenomenon). Following, you'll be taken to a New Town—a modern residential estate—to learn about how today's Singaporean lives. It's a strange concept for a tour, and definitely more interesting for Singaporephiles. Tickets are S$27 (US$16.15) adults, S$15 (US$9) children.

City Tour. Holiday Tours & Travel, 300 Orchard Rd. #07-01/10, The Promenade. ☎ **65/738-2622.**

For something a bit more traditional, you can always arrange a standard city tour. I only recommend this tour if you're short on time, since the tour is $3^1/2$ hours of packed sightseeing covering all of the city's major ethnic and historic enclaves. Basically, the experience won't be too deep. Tours run twice daily, at 8:30am and 1:30pm. Tickets are S$27 (US$16.15) adults, S$15 (US$9) children.

BUS TOURS

RMG Tours Pte. Ltd. 109C Amoy St. ☎ **65/220-1661.**

RMG's bus tours use guides who are licensed by the Singapore Tourism Board. Tours start daily between 8 and 9am for the morning tours and 2pm for the afternoon tours, and last an average of $3^1/2$ hours. Individual tours cover city attractions, Sentosa, Jurong BirdPark, the Singapore Zoological Gardens, and the Night Safari (starting at 6:30pm). Prices for the tours vary from S$23 to S$48 (US$13.75 to US$28.75) for adults and S$12 to S$38 (US$7.20 to US$22.75) for children.

For an easy trip into **Malaysia,** RMG has a $3^1/2$-hour morning **Johor Bahru tour** at 8am daily for S$25 (US$14.95) for adults and S$12 (US$7.20) for children. Their **Kukup tour** will take you on a full-day tour through rural parts of Malaysia to the small fishing village of Kukup. Departures are at 8am, and cost is S$67 (US$40.10) for adults and S$32 (US$19.15) for children. The full-day **Malacca tour** costs S$75 (US$44.90) for adults and S$37 (US$22.15) for children, with overnight stay packages available for an extra charge.

To find out where to meet tour groups, telephone RMG Tours directly or visit your hotel tour desk.

Singapore Sightseeing Tour East. ☎ **65/332-3755.** www.singnet.com.sg/~sstep.

These people offer unique theme tours for everyone, such as the Cultural Revelations tour through the major historical districts (9:30am to 1pm, S$49/US$29.35 adults,

S$25/US$14.95 children); the Paddle and Peddle tour, with river trips on a bumboat and a trishaw ride through the Historic District (10am to 1pm, S$49/US$29.35) adults, S$25/US$14.95 children), plus other city and island tours. They also offer the standard morning and afternoon trips to major attractions, but at slightly higher prices than the other outfits.

BOAT & FERRY TOURS

These trips are a great way to experience what makes Singapore the second-largest port in the world. From the water, you can get an up-close look at bumboats, sampans, old schooners, cargo ships, and tankers, and sail past all of the river sights—like Raffles landing site and Merlion Park—and, on the longer cruises, head out to surrounding islands.

River tours are conducted in bumboats, small boats once used for unloading cargo from large ships to the "go-downs" (warehouses) along the river. For harbor tours, you'll likely be on a junk, the type of old Chinese vessel used for sailing the seas. For cruises that offer lunch, high tea, or dinner, be aware of cancellation penalties. All boat and ferry trips are subject to tidal and weather conditions.

You can catch the river tours either at the Clarke Quay Festival Village, at Raffles Landing Site on the north bank of the river, or at the Raffles Place jetty in front of the UOB Plaza Raffles Place MRT station. The larger boats depart from Clifford Pier, which can be reached by taking the MRT to Raffles Place and crossing over Change Alley to the pier.

Eastwind Organisation Pte. Ltd. #01-30A Clifford Pier, 70 Collyer Quay. ☎ **65/533-3432** or 65/532-4740.

Eastwind's junks cruise the Singapore River, out into the harbor, and around Singapore's southern islands. The 2¹/₂-hour Emerald Cruise makes a stop at Kusu Island. The boat leaves at 10:30am and 3pm and the tour costs S$20 (US$12) for adults and S$10 (US$5.99) for children. The Sunset Cruise is a 1-hour cruise that leaves at 4pm for S$15 (US$9) for adults and S$10 (US$6) for children, and the Starlite Dinner Cruise lasts 2¹/₂ hours and for S$36 (US$21.55) for adults and S$18 (US$10.80) for children and provides a Singaporean buffet dinner and music. Departures are from Clifford Pier.

Singapore River Boat Pte. Ltd. Cannery Block, River Valley Road, Clarke Quay #02-05/06. ☎ **65/339-6833** or 65/338-9205.

Departing from either the Clarke Quay jetty or the Raffles Place jetty in front of the UOB Plaza, this bumboat tour plies the river to see Singapore's attractions from the water. It's a fun experience and also a pretty great photo opportunity to catch some of the city's interesting angles. Note that after 6pm or so they're required to shut off the prerecorded guided tour—for better or worse. Tickets cost S$7 (US$4.20) for adults and S$3 (US$1.80) for children. Boats leave frequently from 9am to 11pm daily.

Singapore River Cruises and Leisure Pte. Ltd. Boat Quay kiosk. ☎ **65/336-6119** or 65/227-6863.

This half-hour bumboat tour takes you up and down the Singapore River and out into the harbor, past all the waterside attractions. Boats depart from Boat Quay, leaving daily at regular intervals from 9am to 9pm, at a cost of S$10 (US$6) for adults and S$5 (US$3) for children under 10. Singapore River Cruises and Leisure will also make special arrangements for island trips and charter cruises.

Watertours Pte. Ltd. Clifford Pier. ☎ **65/533-9811.**

This outfit offers the Imperial Cruise aboard the *Admiral Cheng Ho,* an exact replica of a famous and very ornate Imperial vessel from the Ming Dynasty, named after an historic Chinese navigator. The Morning Glory cruise starts at 10:30am and lasts 2¹/₂ hours (S$24/US$15.10 adults, S$12/US$7.55 children); the High Tea Cruise departs at 3pm and lasts 2¹/₂ hours (S$29/US$18.25 adults, S$14/US$8.80 children), and the Imperial Dinner Cruise departs at 6:30pm and lasts 2 hours (S$62/US$39 adults, S$30/US$18.90 children). All Imperial Cruises depart from Clifford Pier.

Afternoon catamaran cruises are available at 12:30pm (S$38/US$23.95 adults, S$22/US$13.85 children), high tea cruises at 3pm (S$33/S$20.80 adults, S$19/US$12 children), and dinner cruises at 6pm (S$86/US$54.20 adults, S$48/US$30.25 children).

These cruises all depart from Clifford Pier.

A CABLE CAR TOUR
Singapore Cable Car Pte. Ltd. ☎ **65/270-8855.**

Most people take the ferry as transportation to and from Sentosa Island, but the cable car ride is also a neat way to see some of Singapore, even if you turn around and come straight back. If you depart from Mount Faber Park, the ride is longer, cruising over green forest growth and bungalows before meeting the Cable Car Towers (at the World Trade Centre) and heading out over Keppel Harbour. The view of the container port is pretty fascinating, and you can also see oil refineries and other islands. Be warned, when coming back make sure you get off at the World Trade Centre stop, since it's almost impossible to find ground transportation from the top of Mount Faber. The tours operate from 8:30am to 9pm daily and cost S$6.90 (US$4.15) for adults and S$3.90 (US$2.35) for children round-trip.

3 Personal Tours

For the ultimate in-depth sightseeing experience, you can hire a personal guide to take you to the sights and on walking tours of the city. **The Registered Tourist Guides Association of Singapore** (☎ **65/339-2110**) handles training and licensing of all the official tour guides in Singapore. These people are the experts. They usually handle large groups, but are perfectly willing to take small groups and individuals around the city, and will tailor itineraries to suit your interests. Rates range from S$35 to S$50 (US$20.95 to US$29.95) per hour, depending on the expertise of the tour guide you request.

7

Singapore Shopping

In Singapore, shopping is a sport, and from the practiced glide through haute couture boutiques to skillful back-alley bargaining to win the best prices on Asian treasures, it's always exciting, with something to satiate every pro shopper's appetite.

From its humble beginnings as an operation for the British East India Trading Company, Singapore has always been a trading mecca. When Sir Stamford Raffles first set foot on its shore, he envisioned a free port to serve as a go-between for trade from China in the north and Indonesia in the south to Europe and India in the west. In the early days of maritime trade, the northeast monsoon from November to March would blow in junks from China, Indochina, and Siam, while during the autumn months, the southwest monsoon would usher in Bugis and Indonesian traders. Boat Quay was in its trading glory, with spices, silks, gold, tin, rattan, and, of course, opium.

Today, the focal point of shopping in Singapore is **Orchard Road,** a very long stretch of glitzy shopping malls packed with Western clothing stores, from designer apparel to cheap chic, and many other mostly imported finds. Singaporeans have a love-hate relationship with Orchard Road. As the shopping malls developed, they brought hip styles into the reach of everyday Singaporeans, adding a cosmopolitan sheen to Singapore style. But Orchard Road also ushered in a new culture of obsessive consumerism. One working mother told me about her school-age son who spent a month working at a job for S$200 a week, only to take all his earnings down to Orchard Road and squander it on a pair of S$800 jeans. You can see this kind of blatant image-consciousness in the throngs of teenagers that crowd the malls on weekends and school holidays.

Even to outsiders, Orchard Road is a drug; however, most of the clothing and accessories shops sell Western imports, and while the prices may be bargain-basement for Japanese visitors, the rest of us will find that the prices of Western brand-name fashions are no less expensive than at home. And it's all the same stuff you can get at home, too. I tried to find a unique gift to bring for a Singaporean friend, something she could not get in Singapore, so I went to the gift shop at the Metropolitan Museum of Art in New York City. Sure enough, as soon as I got back to Singapore I found that the Met had opened two outlets on Orchard Road.

In the seventies, before the malls, Singapore was truly a shopping heaven. Local and regional handicrafts were skillfully made by local artisans, who by now have almost all been squeezed out of their quaint shops by rising real estate prices. And who can forget Thieves' Market, a sprawling series of awning-covered back alleys that teemed on weekends with table displays of antique finds from the region; brass and gems from Thailand; jade and ivory from China; batiks from Indonesia; and knock-off luggage, clothing, watches, leather goods, and pirate recordings, all for a bargain. The government shut the place down in the late eighties when drugs started to take the place of other goods sold, and as the government became more aware of copyright violation practices.

Nostalgia aside, there are still some nifty shopping areas around, like the places on **Arab Street,** the night market out at **Bugis Street,** and at the small flea market in **Chinatown,** where you can pick up odd items for bargains. Anybody who's been around Singapore long enough will tell you that most of the really juicy bargains went the way of the dodo when the huge shopping malls came to town, but if you know the prices of certain items that you'd like, some comparison shopping may save you a little money. In this chapter, I'll give you some tips on where to find the better merchandise, competitive prices, and memorable shopping experiences.

1 Singapore Shopping Tips

HOURS   Shopping malls are generally open from 10am to 8pm Monday through Saturday, with some stores keeping shorter Sunday hours. The malls sometimes remain open until 10pm on holidays. Smaller shops are open from around 10am to 5pm Monday through Saturday, but are almost always closed on Sundays. Hours will vary from shop to shop. Arab Street is closed on Sundays.

PRICES   Almost all of the stores in shopping malls have fixed prices. Sometimes these stores will have seasonal sales, especially in July, when they have the monthlong **Great Singapore Sale,** during which prices are marked down, sometimes up to 50% or 75%. In the smaller shops and at street vendors, prices are never marked, and vendors will quote you higher prices than the going rate, in anticipation of the bargaining ritual. These are the places to find good prices, if you negotiate well.

BARGAINING   In Singapore, many shopkeepers cling to the old tradition of not fixing prices on their merchandise, instead making every item's purchase a little performance piece by insisting their customers bargain for it. For Westerners who are unaccustomed to this tradition, bargaining can be embarrassing and frustrating at first—after all, Westerners are accustomed to accepting fixed prices without an argument, and if you don't know the protocol, you can't be sure what to do. All it takes is a little practice, though, and soon you'll be bargaining with the best of 'em. I've seen many travelers go into their first market like lambs to the slaughter, only to loosen up after a few encounters and begin to enjoy the process for the sport it really is.

The most important thing to remember when bargaining is to keep a friendly, good-natured banter between you and the seller. Getting him or her mad won't save you a dime, and if you get 'em really riled up, they won't sell you anything at any price and will just throw you out. But don't let that scare you; just be nice and patient, and you'll get where you want to go.

One important tip for bargaining is to first have an idea of the value of what you're buying. This can be difficult for unusual items, but a little comparison shopping here may help you out. Try to look like you live in Singapore. A lot of the local European and North American residents shop at these places, so you won't look out of place. If a salesperson asks you where you are from, don't smile and say London or San Francisco, but toss out a blasé "Katong" or "Holland Village" without even looking up. If they think you're a local, they'll try to get away with less.

A simple "How much?" is the place to start, to which they'll reply with their top price. Let the bidding begin! It's always good to come back with a little smile and ask "Is that your best price?" They'll probably come down a bit, but if it's obvious they're trying to soak you, tell them you'll pay a price that's about half of what they had originally offered; otherwise, just knock about 30% or 40% off. The standard reaction from them will always be to look at you like you're a crazy person for even suggesting such a discount—but don't falter! This is standard technique. For each little bit their price comes down, bring yours up just a bit until you reach a price you like. If you're having trouble talking them down, try these strategies: When buying more than one item, ask for a generous discount on the less expensive item. If you've seen it cheaper elsewhere, tell them. Or you can pull the old, "But I only have $20" ploy. (Just make sure you don't turn around and ask them to change a $50!) Try anything, even if it's just a wink and a little, "Don't you have any special discounts for ladies shopping on Wednesdays?"

Some people have said that once you start the bargaining ritual, it's rude to walk away and not purchase the item. Well, I see it this way: It's my money, and if I still don't feel comfortable shelling it out, then I won't do it under any feeling of obligation. (However, if you've spent hours negotiating over a high-priced item, and the owner agrees to your offer, it may be considered harsh to walk away after going through all that trouble). Besides, the final bargaining strategy is to just politely say, "No, thank-you" and walk away. You'll be surprised at how fast prices can come down as you're walking out the door.

GST TOURIST REFUND SCHEME   When you shop in stores that display the blue "Tax Free Shopping" logo, the government will refund the goods and services tax (GST) you pay on purchases totaling S$300 (US$179.65) or more. Upon request, the sales clerk will fill out a Tax Free Shopping Cheque, which you retain with your receipt. If you've purchased up to S$300 at the same store, but on different dates, you can still claim the refund for all of the items. When you leave Singapore, present your checks at Customs along with your passport, and let them see the goods you've purchased to show that you're taking them out of the country with you. Customs will stamp the forms, which you then present at any of the Global Refund Counters in the airport for an on-the-spot cash refund—or, if you like, you can mail in the stamped form to receive a check or a direct transfer of the amount to your bank account. Certain restrictions apply—if you've been working in Singapore, for instance, or fail to take the items out of the country within 2 months of the purchase date. For complete details, call STB at ☎ **1800/736-2000.**

DUTY-FREE ITEMS   Changi International Airport has a large duty-free shop that carries cigarettes, liquor, wine, perfumes, cosmetics, watches, jewelry, and other designer accessories. There's also a chain of duty-free stores in Singapore called DFS. Their main branch is at Millennia Walk, next to the Pan Pacific Hotel down by Marina Square (Millennia Walk, ☎ **65/332-2118**). The store is huge and impressive, but unfortunately, the only truly duty-free items are liquor and cigarettes, which you can arrange to pick up at the airport before you depart—everything else carries the standard 3% GST. Feel free to apply for the Tourist Refund Scheme here, though.

CLOTHING SIZES   Those of you used to shopping in big-and-tall stores will unfortunately find little ready-to-wear clothing in Singapore that'll fit you—but that doesn't mean you can't take advantage of the many excellent tailors around town. If you wear a standard size, however, this chart will help you convert your size to local measures.

Urban Singapore Shopping

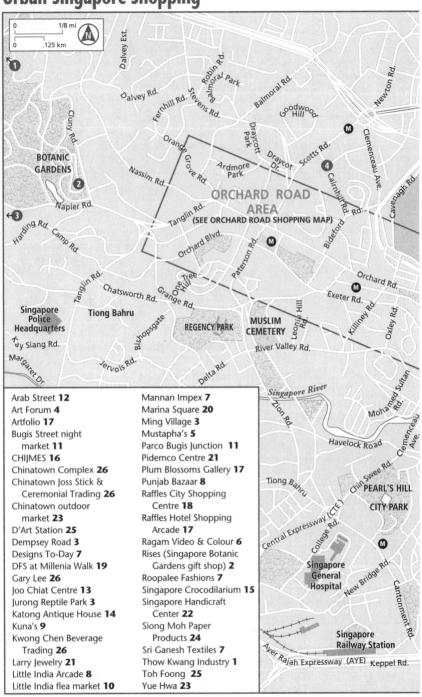

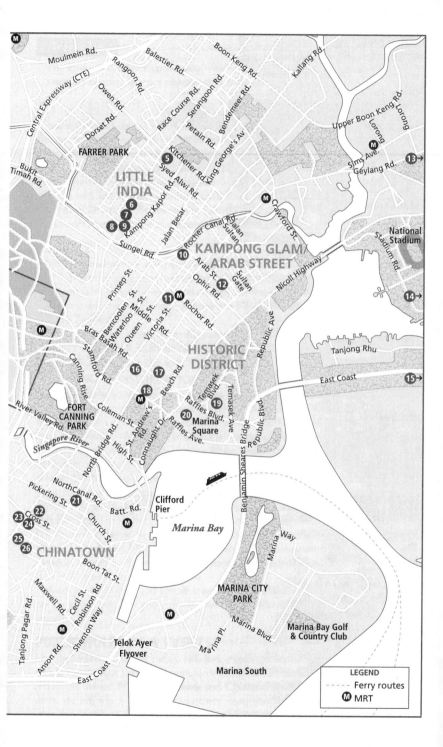

Ladies' Dress Sizes

U.S.	8	10	12	14	16	18
U.K.	30	32	34	36	38	40
Continental	36	38	40	42	44	46

Ladies' Shoes

U.S.	5	$5^1/_2$	6	$6^1/_2$	7	$7^1/_2$	8	$8^1/_2$	9
U.K.	$3^1/_2$	4	$4^1/_2$	5	$5^1/_2$	6	$6^1/_2$	7	$7^1/_2$
Continental	35	35	36	37	38	38	38	39	40

Men's Suits

U.S. & U.K.	34	36	38	40	42	44	46	48
Continental	44	46	48	50	52	54	56	58

Men's Shirts

U.S. & U.K.	14	$14^1/_2$	15	$15^1/_2$	16	$16^1/_2$	17	$17^1/_2$
Continental	36	37	38	39	40	41	42	43

Men's Shoes

U.S.	7	$7^1/_2$	8	$8^1/_2$	9	$9^1/_2$	10	$10^1/_2$	11	$11^1/_2$
U.K.	$6^1/_2$	7	$7^1/_2$	8	$8^1/_2$	9	$9^1/_2$	10	$10^1/_2$	11
Continental	39	40	41	42	43	43	44	44	45	45

Children's Clothes

U.S.	2	4	6	8	10	13	15
U.K.	1	2	5	7	9	10	12
Continental	1	2	5	7	9	10	12

2 The Shopping Scene, Part 1: Western-Style Malls

Orchard Road is the biggie, as I've said, but other good mall spots are at Marina Bay, Bugis Junction, Raffles City, and at Raffles Hotel. In this section, I'll give you the low-down on the hot spots.

ORCHARD ROAD AREA

The malls on Orchard Road are a tourist attraction in their own right, with smaller boutiques and specialty shops intermingled with huge department stores. **Takashimaya** and **Isetan** have been imported from Japan. **Lane Crawford** comes out of the West, as does **Kmart. John Little Pte. Ltd.** is one of the oldest department stores in Singapore, followed by **Robinson's. Tang's** is historic, having grown from a cart-full of merchandise nurtured by the business savvy of local entrepreneur C. K. Tang. Boutiques range from the younger styles of **Stussy** and **Guess?** to the sophisticated fashions of **Chanel** and **Salvatore Ferragamo.** You'll also find antiques, oriental carpets, art galleries and curio shops, Tower Records and HMV music stores, Kinokuniya and Borders bookstores, video arcades, and scores of restaurants, local food

Orchard Road Area Shopping

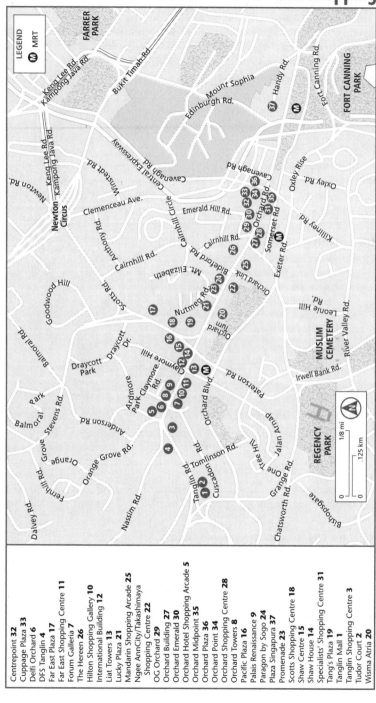

LEGEND
Ⓜ MRT

Centrepoint **32**
Cuppage Plaza **33**
Delfi Orchard **6**
DFS Tanglin **4**
Far East Plaza **17**
Far East Shopping Centre **11**
Forum Galleria **7**
The Heeren **26**
Hilton Shopping Gallery **10**
International Building **12**
Liat Towers **13**
Lucky Plaza **21**
Mandarin Shopping Arcade **25**
Ngee AnnCity/Takashimaya
  Shopping Centre **22**
OG Orchard **29**
Orchard Building **27**
Orchard Emerald **30**
Orchard Hotel Shopping Arcade **5**
Orchard Midpoint **35**
Orchard Plaza **36**
Orchard Point **34**
Orchard Shopping Centre **28**
Orchard Towers **8**
Pacific Plaza **16**
Palais Renaissance **9**
Paragon by Sogo **24**
Plaza Singapura **37**
Promenade **23**
Scotts Shopping Centre **18**
Shaw Centre **15**
Shaw House **14**
Specialists' Shopping Centre **31**
Tang's Plaza **19**
Tanglin Mall **1**
Tanglin Shopping Centre **3**
Tudor Court **2**
Wisma Atria **20**

courts, fast-food joints, and coffeehouses—even a few discos, which open in the evenings (see chapter 8). It's hard to say when Orchard Road is not crowded, but it's definitely a mob scene on weekends, when folks have the free time to come and hang around, looking for fun.

Centrepoint. 176 Orchard Rd.

Centrepoint is home to Robinson's department store, which first opened in Singapore in 1858. Here you'll find about 150 other shops, plus fast-food outlets, and on the fourth level are two large English bookstores, Times and MPH.

Far East Plaza. 14 Scotts Rd.

At this crowded mall, the bustle of little shops will sell everything from CDs to punk fashions, luggage to camera equipment, eyewear to souvenirs. Mind yourself here: Most of these shops do not display prices, but rather gauge the price depending on how wealthy the customer appears. If you must shop here, use your shrewdest bargaining powers. It may pay off to wear an outfit that's seen better days.

The Heeren. Orchard Rd.

Thanks to the opening of a Singapore branch of Britain's HMV music stores, the Heeren is the latest hangout joint for teens. The front entrance of the mall hums with towers of video monitors flashing and blaring the latest in American and British chart toppers. There is also a nice cafe to the side, with a garden for enjoying a cup of coffee, tea, or a snack. At the midway point along the Orchard Road stretch, it's a recommended stop for a break.

Hilton Shopping Gallery. 581 Orchard Rd.

The shopping arcade at the Hilton International Hotel is the most exclusive shopping in Singapore. Gucci, Donna Karan, Missoni, and Luis Vuitton are just a few of the international design houses that have made this their Singapore home.

Lucky Plaza. 304 Orchard Plaza.

The map of this place will take hours to decipher, as there are more than 400 stores here. (No kidding.) It's basically known for sportswear, camera equipment, watches, and luggage. If you buy electronics, please make sure you get an international warranty with your purchase. Also, like Far East Plaza, Lucky Plaza is a notorious rip-off problem for travelers. Make sure you come here prepared to fend off slick sales techniques. It may also help to take the government's advice and avoid touts and offers that sound too good to be true.

Ngee Ann City/Takashimaya Shopping Centre. 391 Orchard Rd.

Takashimaya, a major Japanese department store import, anchors Ngee Ann City's many smaller boutiques. Alfred Dunhill, Chanel, Coach, Tiffany & Co., Royal Copenhagen, and a Waterford and Wedgwood boutique are found here, along with many other local and international fashion shops.

Orchard Towers. 400 Orchard Rd.

This mall is a mix of smaller shops dealing in cheap chic clothing, jewelry, eyewear, tailoring, books, and more. There's a 7-Eleven on the ground floor for Americans experiencing screwy homesickness, and a Jason's Supermarket at the back, specializing in imported foods.

Palais Renaissance. 390 Orchard Rd.

Shops here include upmarket boutiques like Krizia and Guerlain. More shops are expected to move in soon.

Paragon by Sogo. 290 Orchard Rd.

Another upmarket shopping mall, Paragon houses Emanuel Ungaro, Escada, Van Cleef and Arpels, and the Paloma Picasso Boutique.

Shaw House. 350 Orchard Rd.

The main floors of Shaw House are taken up by Isetan, a large Japanese department store with designer boutiques for men's and women's fashions, accessories, and cosmetics. On the fifth level, the Lido Theatre screens new releases from Hollywood and around the world.

Specialists' Shopping Centre. 277 Orchard Rd.

The anchor store in this smaller shopping mall is John Little, Singapore's oldest department store, which opened in 1845. The prices, however, are very up-to-date.

Tanglin Shopping Centre. Tanglin Rd.

Tanglin Shopping Centre is unique and fun. You won't find many clothing stores here, but you'll find shop after shop selling antiques, art, and collectibles—from curios to carpets.

Tang's Plaza. 320 Orchard Rd.

Once upon a time, C. K. Tang peddled goods from an old cart in the streets of Singapore. An industrious fellow, he parlayed his business into a small department store. A hit from the start, Tang's has grown exponentially over the decades, and now competes with all the other international megastores that have moved in. The beauty is that Tang's is truly Singaporean, and its history is a local legend.

Wisma Atria. 435 Orchard Rd.

Wisma Atria caters to the younger set. Here you'll find everything from Nine West to a Levi's store mixed in with numerous eyewear, cosmetics, and high- and low-fashion boutiques, all under one roof.

MARINA BAY

The Marina Bay area arose from a plot of reclaimed land, and now boasts the giant Suntec City convention center and all the hotels, restaurants, and shopping malls that have grown up around it. Shopping in the Marina Bay area is popular for everyone because of its convenience, with the major malls and hotels all interconnected by covered walkways and pedestrian bridges, making it easy to get around with minimal exposure to the elements.

Marina Square. 6 Raffles Blvd.

Marina Square is a huge complex that, in addition to a wide variety of shops, has a cinema, fast-food outlets and cafes, pharmacies, and convenience stores.

Millenia Walk. 9 Raffles Blvd.

Smaller than Marina Square, Millenia Walk has more upmarket boutiques like Fendi, Guess?, and Liz Claiborne, to name a few.

AROUND THE CITY CENTER

While the Historic District doesn't have as many malls as the Orchard Road area, it still has some good shopping. Raffles City can be overwhelming in its size, but convenient because it sits right atop the City Hall MRT stop. One of my favorite places to go, however, is the very upmarket Raffles Hotel Shopping Arcade, where I like to window-shop and dream about actually being able to afford some of the stuff on display.

Parco Bugis Junction. Victoria St.

Here you'll find restaurants—both fast food and fine dining—mixed in with clothing retailers, most of which sell fun fashions for younger tastes.

Raffles City Shopping Centre. 252 North Bridge Rd.

Raffles City sits right on top of the City Hall MRT station, which makes it a very well visited mall. Men's and women's fashions, books, cosmetics, and accessories are sold in shops here, along with gifts.

Raffles Hotel Shopping Arcade. 328 North Bridge Rd.

These shops are mostly haute couture; however, there is the Raffles Hotel gift shop for interesting souvenirs. For golfers, there's a Jack Nicklaus signature store.

3 The Shopping Scene, Part 2: Multicultural Shopping

The most exciting shopping has got to be in all the ethnic enclaves throughout the city. Down narrow streets, bargains are to be had on all sorts of unusual items—many of which are perfect for gifts to take back home. If you're stuck for a gift idea, read on. Chances are I'll mention something for even the most difficult person on your list.

CHINATOWN

In Chinatown, I've stumbled on some of my most precious treasures. My all-time favorite gift idea? Spend an afternoon learning the traditional Chinese tea ceremony at either **The Tea Village,** 45A-51A Pagoda St. (☎ 65/221-7825), or **The Tea Chapter,** 9A Neil Rd. (☎ 65/226-1175), then head down to **D'Art Station,** 65 Pagoda St. (☎ 65/225-8307), to pick up a good quality tea set and accessories. After a stop at **Kwong Chen Beverage Trading,** 16 Smith St. (☎ 65/223-6927), for some Chinese teas in handsome tins, you'll be ready to give a fabulous gift—not just a tea set, but your own cultural performance as well, as you teach your friends a new art. While the teas are really inexpensive, they're packed in lovely tins—great to buy lots to bring back as smaller gifts.

Another neat place, **Gary Lee**, 20 Smith St. (☎ 65/221-8129), carries a fantastic selection of linens imported from China. These hand-embroidered gems include bedding, dining linens, tea towels and handkerchiefs, and other decorative items for the home. They're priced right, and won't break on the trip back home. For something a little more unusual, check out **Chinatown Joss Stick & Ceremonial Trading,** 54 Smith St. (☎ 65/227-6821), or **Siong Moh Paper Products,** 39 Mosque St. (☎ 65/ 224-3125), both of which carry a full line of ceremonial items. Pick up some joss sticks (temple incense) or joss paper (books of thin sheets of paper, stamped in reds and yellows with bits of gold and silver leaf). Definitely a conversation piece, as is the Hell Money, stacks of "money" that believers burn at the temple for their ancestors to use in the afterlife. Perfect for that friend who has everything? Also, if you duck over to **Sago Lane** while you're in the neighborhood, there are a few souvenir shops that sell Chinese kites and Cantonese Opera masks—cool for kids.

For one-stop souvenir shopping, you can tick off half your shopping list at Chinatown Point, aka the **Singapore Handicraft Center,** 133 New Bridge Rd. The best gifts there include hand-carved chops, or Chinese seals. **Chinatown Seal Carving**

Souvenir, #03-72 (☎ 65/534-0761), has an absolutely enormous selection of carved stone, wood, bone, glass, and ivory chops ready to be carved to your specifications. Simple designs are really quite affordable, while some of the more elaborate chops and carvings fetch a handsome sum. At **Inherited Arts & Crafts,** #03-69 (☎ 65/534-1197), you can commission a personalized Chinese scroll painting or calligraphy piece. The handiwork is quite beautiful. Amid the many jade and gold shops at Chinatown Point, **La Belle Collection,** #04-53 (☎ 534-0231), stands out for its jewelry crafted from orchids. The coating lets the flowers' natural colors show, while delicate gold touches add a little extra sparkle.

For Chinese goods, however, nothing beats **Yue Hwa,** 70 Eu Tong Sen St. (☎ 65/538-4222). This five-story Chinese Emporium is an attraction in its own right. The superb inventory includes all manner of silk wear (robes, underwear, blouses); embroidery and house linens, bolt silks, tailoring services (for perfect mandarin dresses!), cloisonne jewelry and gifts, lacquerware, pottery, musical instruments, traditional Chinese clothing for men and women (from scholars' robes to coolie duds!), jade and gold, cashmere, traditional items, art supplies, herbs, home furnishings—I could go on and on. Plan to spend some time here.

ARAB STREET

Over on ✪ **Arab Street,** shop for handicrafts from Malaysia and Indonesia. I go for sarongs at **Hadjee Textiles,** 75 Arab St. (☎ 65/298-1943), for their stacks of folded sarongs in beautiful colors and traditional patterns. They're perfect for traveling, as they're lightweight, but can serve you well as a dressy skirt, a bedsheet, beach blanket, window shade, bath towel, or whatever you need—when I'm on the road I can't live without mine. Buy a few here and the prices really drop. If you're in the market for a more masculine sarong, **Goodwill Trading,** 56 Arab St. (☎ 298-3205), specializes in pulicat, or the plaid sarongs worn by Malay men. For modern styles of batik, check out **Basharahil Brothers,** 99-101 Arab St. (☎ 65/296-0432), for their very interesting designs, but don't forget to see their collection of fine silk batiks in the back. For batik household linens, you can't beat **Maruti Textiles,** 93 Arab St. (☎ 65/392-0253), where you'll find high quality place mats and napkins, tablecloths, pillow covers, and quilts. The buyer for this shop has a good eye for style.

I've also found a few shops on Arab Street that carry handicrafts from other countries in Southeast Asia. **Memoirs,** 18 Baghdad St. (☎ 65/294-5900), sells mostly Indonesian crafts, from carved and hand-painted decorative items to scored leather shadow puppets and unusual teak gifts. **Ahn Yeu Em De Paris,** 15 Baghdad St. (☎ 65/292-1523), carries boxes of velvet hand-beaded evening shoes, made in Vietnam. So inexpensive! For antiques and curios, try **Gim Joo Trading,** 16 Baghdad St. (☎ 65/293-5638), a jumble of the unusual, some of it old. A departure from the more packed and dusty places here, **Suraya Betawj,** 67 Arab St. (☎ 65/398-1607), carries gorgeous Indonesian and Malaysian crafted housewares in contemporary design—the type you normally find for huge prices in shopping catalogues back home.

Other unique treasures include the large assortment of fragrance oils at **Aljunied Brothers,** 91 Arab St. (☎ 65/291-8368). Muslims are forbidden from consuming alcohol in any form (a proscription that includes the wearing of alcohol-based perfumes as well), so these oil-based perfumes re-create designer scents plus other floral and wood creations. Check out their delicate cut-glass bottles and atomizers as well. Finally, for the crafter in your life, **Kin Lee & Co.,** 109 Arab St. (☎ 65/291-1411), carries a complete line of patterns and accessories to make local Peranakan beaded slippers. In vivid colors and floral designs, these traditional slippers were always made by hand, to be attached later to a wooden sole. The finished versions are exquisite, plus they're fun to make.

LITTLE INDIA

I have a ball shopping the crowded streets of Little India. The best shopping is on Serangoon Road, where Singapore's Indian community shops for Indian imports and cultural items. If you fancy casual lightweight cottons, many ready-to-wear outfits are on hand at **Designs To-Day,** 81 Serangoon Rd. (☎ 65/292-1641), from dresses and skirts to blouses and shirts. Vegetable-dyed cotton prints feature embroidery and other Indian-style adornment. Prices are just right, too.

For something more traditional, you can pick up a sari or a Punjabi suit. **Punjab Bazaar,** #01-07 Little India Arcade, 48 Serangoon Rd. (☎ 65/296-0067), carries a larger choice of salwar kameez, also called Punjabi suits, in many styles and fabrics. These graceful three-piece outfits, consisting of a pair of drawstring pants worn under a flowing dress with a long coordinated scarf wrapped over the shoulders, translate elegantly in any culture. If nothing strikes your fancy at Punjab Bazaar, try **Roopalee Fashions,** a little farther down at 84 Serangoon Rd. (☎ 65/298-0558). Their selection is a bit smaller, but you may find something there you like. Both shops carry sandals, bags, and other accessories to compliment your new outfit.

Of the multitude of shops that sell saris, I like the selection at **Sri Ganesh Textiles,** 100 Serangoon Rd. (☎ 65/298-2029). Choose your favorite colors and patterns from the many bolts stacked on the counters, and the staff will cut the required 6-meter length for you. They keep the less expensive polyesters in the front of the shop, but wander to the back to find the gorgeous silk ones. A sari is worn over a choli (a tiny tight-fitting blouse) and a cotton petticoat. These can also be purchased at Sri Ganesh for a very small sum. The absolute largest selection of saris, however, has to be at Mohamed Mustapha & Samsuddin Co., locally known simply as **Mustapha's,** 320 Serangoon Rd./145 Syed Alwi Rd., at the corner of Serangoon and Syed Alwi (☎ 65/299-2603). Down in the basement, the piles of sari fabric bolts go as far as the eye can see. The best part about buying your sari at Mustapha's is their free pamphlet on how to tie the things! It's pretty easy to follow (I actually didn't do too bad with mine!)

Little India offers all sorts of small finds, especially throughout Little India Arcade (48 Serangoon Rd.) and just across the street on Campbell Lane at **Kuna's,** #3 Campbell Lane (☎ 65/294-2700). Here you can buy inexpensive Indian costume jewelry like bangles, earrings, and necklaces in exotic designs, and a wide assortment of decorative dots (called *pottu* in Tamil) to grace your forehead. Indian handicrafts include brass work, wood carvings, dyed tapestries, woven cotton household linens, small curio items, very inexpensive incense, colorful pictures of Hindu gods, and other ceremonial items. Look here also for Indian cooking pots and household items. If after you pick up these items you care to try your hand at making your own curry, head for **Mannan Impex,** 118 Serangoon (☎ 65/299-8424), to peruse all the necessary spices.

Oh, and if you've never seen a Bollywood production, now's your chance. These Indian megahit movies feature amazingly huge music and dance numbers, fabulous costumes, and time-honored stories of danger and romance. At **Ragam Video & Colour,** 124 Serangoon Rd. (☎ 65/291-5760), shop for the latest releases and old favorites on video CD with English subtitles. (*Note:* Video CDs—or VCDs—are not technically DVDs, but you can play them on a DVD player.)

OUTDOOR MARKETS

A few outdoor markets still exist in Singapore, though it ain't like the old days. At the Bugis MRT station, across from Parco Bugis Junction, a well-established

night market (which is also open during the day) delivers overpriced cheap chic, some curio items, accessories, and video compact discs (VCDs) to tourists. In **Chinatown,** on the corner of South Bridge Road and Cross Street look for the old guys who come out with blankets full of odd merchandise—old watches, coins, jewelry, Mao paraphernalia, Peranakan pottery, and local artifacts from decades past. There's not many of these guys there, but for impromptu markets, I thought their merchandise was far more imaginative than at Bugis. If you're really desperate for a **flea market,** you can always head for the field between Little India and Arab Street (just behind the Johor bus terminal), where you'll find about five times more vendors than at Chinatown, but be warned: The goods are weird. Old nasty shoes, Barry Gibb records, broken radios—the same crap you'd see at garage sales back home, only local style. It could be interesting culturally. If you're in the mood.

4 Best Buys A to Z

Basically, you can buy most things in Singapore that you can buy at home for a comparable price. There are, however, some items available here that are real steals. Following is a list of some of your better buys in Singapore.

ANTIQUES   At the northern tip of Orchard Road is the mellow **Tanglin Shopping Centre** (Tanglin Road), whose quiet halls are just packed with little antiques boutiques. Tanglin is a quiet place, which adds to the museum feel as you stroll past window displays of paintings, pottery, tapestries, and curios made of jade or brass—all kinds of excellent, quality collectibles and gifts. A couple of good shops to visit are **Tzen Gallery,** Basement 1 (☎ 65/734-4339), and **Ling Antique House,** Level 3 (☎ 65/732-1422). There are many, many more, though. This is a place to really explore.

Just next to Tanglin Shopping Centre you'll find Tudor Court, with many gallery-quality shops. I can browse forever in **Lopoburi Arts & Antiques** (☎ 65/735-2579), which features a large selection of beautiful Buddha sculptures from around the world, but most particularly Thailand.

To get an eyeful of some local furnishings in antique Indonesian, Chinese, and Peranakan styles, take a taxi out to **Dempsey Road** and walk up the hill to the warehouses. Inside each warehouse are dealers with enticing names like **Vintage Palace Pte. Ltd.,** Blk. 7 #01-03/04 (☎ 65/479-2181), **Asia Passion,** Blk. 13 #01-02 (☎ 65/473-1339), **Yesterdays Antiques & Curios,** Blk. 13 #01-05 (☎ 65/476-4831), **Journey East Pte. Ltd.,** Blk. 13 #01-04 (☎ 65/473-1693), and **Eastern Discoveries,** Blk. 26 #01-04 (☎ 65/475-1814). There are more than a dozen places here, each specializing in different wares. Some have large furniture pieces, from carved teak Indonesian-style reproduction furniture to authentic pieces from mainland China. Some have smaller collectible items, like antique baskets, carved scale weights from the old opium trade, or collections of Buddha images. There are also oriental carpet shops mixed in. The stores on Dempsey Road are all open daily from around 10:30am to 6:30pm, though they close for a short lunch break at midday. As with all of the antiques shops in Singapore, they'll help you locate a reliable shipper to send your purchases home.

I always recommend a special trip out to **Geylang** to visit the **Katong Antique House,** 208 East Coast Rd. (☎ 65/345-8544). Carrying a unique collection of old items from Peranakan homes and closets, including the exquisitely embroidered kebayas (blouses) and fine Peranakan beaded slippers, this shop has made my Peranakan friends get misty-eyed from nostalgia. Call the proprietor beforehand to schedule an appointment.

EYEGLASSES   Eyeglasses? Why would anyone want to buy eyeglasses on his vacation? Because in Singapore they're dirt cheap, that's why. For the price of one pair of frames with prescription lenses in the United States, I can get a pair of prescription glasses, a pair of prescription sunglasses, contact lenses, and even have my old frames relensed. If you can beat that at home, do it. If not, take advantage while you can.

They're so inexpensive because the government does not have as strict regulations on optometry as do countries in the West. However, I assure you the larger prescription firms are very good at what they do, and many shops carry the latest frames from international designers. At **Capitol Optical** you'll get the best price on generic frames, but not cheap quality in the lenses. Centrally located branches are at #03-132 Far East Plaza (☎ **65/736-0365**); #01-77 Lucky Plaza (☎ **65/734-4166**); and 435 Orchard Rd. #03-39 Wisma Atria (☎ **65/732-2401**).

FABRICS   Exquisite fabrics like Chinese silk, Thai silk, batiks, and inexpensive gingham are very affordable and the selections are extensive. If you have time, see if you can have something tailored. There are many fine men's tailors for suits and slacks made to fit. For women, the ultimate souvenir is to order a **cheongsam,** the Chinese dress with the Mandarin collar, frog clasps, and high slits up the side. Ready-made ones of lesser-quality silk and sateens are really cheap and kitsch, but a tailored full-length dress from rich Chinese silk makes for an elegant addition to your formal wardrobe.

On another note, if you've ever dreamed of owning a sarong or sari, you can get them in Singapore for great prices. A suggestion: I buy the traditional Asian prints and have them tailored into Western designs for my own East-meets-West styles.

Most fabrics are sold by the meter and there is no standard width, so make sure you inquire when you're purchasing off the bolt. **Chinese silks** are found at places like the **China Silk House,** Tanglin Shopping Centre, Level 2, Tanglin Road (☎ **65/235-5020**), or in **Centrepoint,** 176 Orchard Rd. (☎ **65/733-0555**), which has one of the largest selections on the island. High-quality Chinese silks are also at **Yue Hua** in the People's Park Centre (see above), which also has exceptional tailoring services for cheongsams (see above), as well as ready-made silk fashions. Other silk dealers are in almost every mall in the Orchard Road area.

You should also check out **Arab Street.** I love the selection of modern batik fabrics at **Basharahil Bros.,** 101 Arab St. (☎ **65/296-0432**), and be sure to take a peek at their batik silks in the back—just gorgeous! For bolt batik cottons in traditional patterns, the following shops have good selections: **Hadjee Textiles,** 75 Arab St. (☎ **65/298-1943**); **Bian Swee Hin & Co.,** 107 Arab St. (☎ **65/293-4763**); and **Aik Joo Textiles,** 68 Arab St. (☎ **65/293-7580**). Large selections of silks at **Sing Tung,** 47 Arab St. (☎ **65/298-1744**), and **Teng Joo Textile Company,** 102 Arab St. (☎ **65/293-1678**), can be bargained for and bought for a song. For nice cottons, especially Western-style shirting, see the numerous offerings at **Aik Bee Textile Company,** 69/73 Arab St. (☎ **65/298-1752**).

For other finds, a few shops along Serangoon Road in Little India have some fine **Indian silks.** The largest selection is at Mohd Mustapha & Samsuddin Co., Pte. Ltd., more commonly known as **Mustapha's,** 320 Serangoon Rd. (☎ **65/299-2603**). If you're heading out to Geylang to see the Malay Village, **Joo Chiat Centre** (at the corner of Geylang Road and Joo Chiat Road, across from Malay Village) has many, many small to midsize fabric shops. You can find mostly polyesters, with some selections of silks, batiks, and cottons at unbeatable prices.

FINE ART   As Singaporeans' wealth increases, so does appreciation of the arts, so you'll get to see a multitude of successful galleries cropping up, many of which feature

the works of local and regional artists. Late 19th-century Chinese oil paintings, watercolors, and brush paintings blend agreeably with contemporary artworks by well-known and new-to-the-scene artists from ASEAN countries as well as the United States and Europe. Rich antique embroideries, carved jade and wooden pieces, and calligraphy (an art unto itself) beg to be admired for their excellent craftsmanship.

Artfolio's exhibits at #02-25 Raffles Hotel Arcade, 328 North Bridge Rd. (☎ 65/334-4677), always make me wish I were rich enough to collect. **Art Forum,** 82 Cairnhill Rd. (☎ 65/737-3448), operated by a diva of the local scene, also features contemporary Singaporean and ASEAN artworks. If you're in the market for fine arts from the mainland (China, that is), **Plum Blossoms,** #02-37 Raffles Hotel Shopping Arcade, 328 North Bridge Rd. (☎ 65/334-1198), showcases contemporary works.

With the burgeoning collecting mania for oriental artifacts, paintings, sculpture, calligraphy, and antique furniture, prominent international auction houses **Christie's,** Goodwood Park Hotel, 22 Scotts Rd. (☎ 65/235-3828), and **Sotheby's,** The Regent Singapore, 1 Cuscaden Rd. (☎ 65/732-8239), have established themselves in Singapore.

JEWELRY & ACCESSORIES Crocodile skin products are well made and affordable at **Jurong Reptile Park,** 241 Jalan Ahmad Ibrahim (☎ 65/261-8866), and **The Singapore Crocodilarium,** 730 East Coast Pkwy., running along East Coast Park (☎ 65/447-3722). They both have showrooms filled with crocodile goods, as well as pelts from other exotic beasts. Jewelry is also a bargain. Gold, which is sold at the day's rate, is fashioned into modern Western styles and into styles that suit Chinese and Indian tastes. Loose stones, either precious or semiprecious, are abundant in many reputable shops, and can be set for you during your stay.

For upmarket jewels and settings, the most trusted dealer in Singapore is **Larry Jewelry (S) Pte. Ltd.,** 400 Orchard Rd., #01-10 Orchard Towers (☎ 65/732-3222), but be prepared to drop some serious cash.

For gold jewelry, the place to go is **Pidemco Centre,** 95 South Bridge Rd. With 20 or so goldsmiths who also carry jade and precious stones, this is a great starting point for good prices and reputable salespeople.

Peek in the window displays of the **gold shops along Serangoon Road** and you'll see all kinds of Indian-style gold necklaces and bangles. Each Indian ethnic group has its own traditional patterns, all of them featuring intricate filigree. Indian gold is more reddish in color, and the delicate designs are brilliant and very unusual. The selection at Mustapha's, 320 Serangoon Rd. (☎ 65/299-2603), is absolutely mind-blowing. I can't imagine the staggering value of all their merchandise. Enter from the Serangoon Road entrance, which will put you in the jewelry department.

ORIENTAL RUGS Once you've walked on a hand-knotted Turkoman in your bare feet, trailed your fingers along the pile of an antique Heriz, or admired the sensuous colors of a Daghostani, you'll never look at broadloom again with the same forbearance. And best yet, they come in a range of sizes and prices to suit most any room and wallet. Think of your purchase as an investment—even the new carpets coming out of Turkey and other Middle Eastern countries increase in value. (Ask that of your wall-to-wall.) Still don't want to splurge? Check out the "minirugs," which measure about a foot square. They're very inexpensive, fit in your luggage, and, once home, drape nicely over the arm of a sofa or look elegant on the hall table.

Many shops also carry **kilims** (woven carpets). These tribals lend a primitive elegant ambience to most any decorating scheme. Antique camel bags, tent door hangings (how did you think the nomads maintain their privacy?), and other colorful pieces are offered at reasonable prices.

Ask anyone in Singapore where to shop for carpets, and he'll send you to **Hassan's Carpets,** #03-01/06 Tanglin Shopping Centre (☎ 65/737-5626), which has been a fixture in Singapore for generations with a stock of more than US$5 million worth of museum-quality carpets. Proprietor Suliman Hamid is the local authority on carpets, having advised on and supplied the carpets for the restoration of Raffles Hotel. He and his staff know the background of every rug and have wonderful stories to tell. They forego the hard sales pitch for more civilized discourse on carpet appreciation. It's an afternoon well spent.

If you still want to see more carpets, you can take a taxi out to Dempsey Road to **Kashmir Carpet House,** Blk. 6E (☎ 65/732-0969), **Jehan Gallery,** Blk. 26 #01-01/02 (☎ 65/475-0003), or **Tandis Gallery,** Blk. 26 #01-05 (☎ 65/475-7220).

PEWTER   Royal Selangor, the famous Malaysian pewter manufacturer since 1885, rode high on the Malaysian tin business at the turn of the century, pewter being a tin alloy. This firm is based in Kuala Lumpur and has eight showrooms in Singapore. The most centrally located are at #02-38 Raffles City Shopping Centre (☎ 65/339-3958), #02-40 Paragon by Sogo, 290 Orchard Rd. (☎ 65/235-6633), and #02-127 Marina Square (☎ 65/339-3115).

POTTERY   Antique porcelain items can be found in the many small shops along Pagoda and Trenagganu streets in Chinatown. Beautiful examples of antique reproductions are to be had at the showroom at **Ming Village,** 32 Pandan Rd. (☎ 65/265-7711), which is also written up in chapter 5. For modern table settings in traditional Chinese designs, plus numerous curios, check out **Toh Foong,** 5 Temple St. (☎ 65/223-1343).

The ultimate in pottery shopping, however, is a place the locals refer to as the "pottery jungle." **Thow Kwang Industry Pte. Ltd.** is a taxi ride away at 85 Lorong Tawas off Jalan Bahar (☎ 65/265-5808). This backwoods place has row after row of pots, lamps, umbrella stands—you name it. There's even a room with antique pieces.

SOUTHEAST ASIAN HANDICRAFTS   Naturally, Southeast Asian handicrafts are all cheaper here than as imports available in the West. I've covered a lot of ground with regard to local and regional handicrafts in "The Shopping Scene: Part 2" section above. I've found the best shopping for local treasures is within Chinatown, Kampong Glam, and Little India. My walking tours in chapter 6 take you past many of these places, so leave time for shopping while you take in the sights. Outside of the ethnic quarters, there are a few other interesting places to note. Note, though, that if you'll be traveling to other countries in Southeast Asia, you should probably wait to do your shopping there. The downside of doing this, however, is that sometimes these countries export the finest quality merchandise, saving only the shoddier varieties for domestic sales.

A gold-plated orchid is something you don't find every day, but you do find them every day at **Rises,** Singapore Botanic Gardens gift shop, Cluny Road (☎ 65/475-5104; see "Attractions Outside the Urban Area" in chapter 5 for full gardens information). The process was developed in the 1970s and is exclusive to Singapore. Different orchid species make up the pins, earrings, and pendants, and the choices are extensive.

If unique and comfortable batik fashions sound good to you, head for local clothing designer **Peter Hoe's** boutique, at 30 Victoria St., #01-05 CHIJMES (☎ 65/339-6880). This Malaysian fabric and clothing designer fashions very handsome individual fabric patterns pieced together in styles to suit Western wardrobes. His collection of regional silver jewelry is also worth noting.

Singapore After Dark

What do you want to do tonight? Do you want to go out for a cultural experience and find a traditional dance or music performance or a Chinese opera, or do you want to put on your finery and rub elbows with society at the symphony? If it's live performance you're looking for, you have your choice not only of the local dance and theater troupes but of the many West End and Broadway shows that come through on international tours. Or you may want to try a local performance—smaller theater groups have lately been hitting nerves and funny bones through stage portrayals of life in the Garden City. Singapore has been transforming itself into a center for the arts in this part of the world, and is beginning to achieve the level of sophistication you'd come to expect from a Western city.

If partying it up is more your speed, there's all kinds of nighttime revelry going on. Society may seem puritanical during the daylight hours, but once the night comes, the clubs get crazy.

Start at **Boat Quay.** This strip of renovated shophouses turns into a veritable parade of bars, karaoke lounges, discos, and cafes after 9 or 10pm in the evening. As you stroll along the river, you can hear the hip-hop, reggae, jazz, blues, rap, techno, disco—you name it—pouring from each door. It seems like there's a million places here, and you're bound to find at least some of them appealing.

A newer place with a bizarre collection of clubs is **Mohamed Sultan Road.** A few of these places try to speak to a smaller, trendier audience, but for a fun bar, I recommend trying the Next Page (reviewed later in this chapter).

Then there's **Orchard Road.** The area around the Scotts Road and Orchard Road intersection has a tremendous number of nightclubs, each with its own favorite clientele and all with high prices of admission. This area is the hub of the wealthier Singaporean club-hoppers, who buy VIP memberships that let them sit in special quarters. Half the fun of Orchard Road at night is watching all these people. On weekends, between the jet-setters and the wannabes, the area is sometimes more crowded at midnight than it is at noon.

Orchard Towers is an intriguing place. There are a number of clubs inside, each of which has a reputation as a place to meet women of the world. One place is frequented by Filipino ladies, another by Indonesian ladies, and so on. These discos are about as sleazy as Singapore gets, so I've only listed one of them, Top Ten, in this book.

Urban Singapore Nightlife

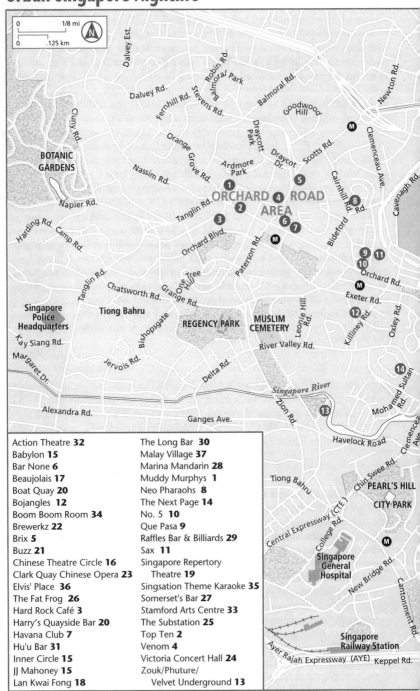

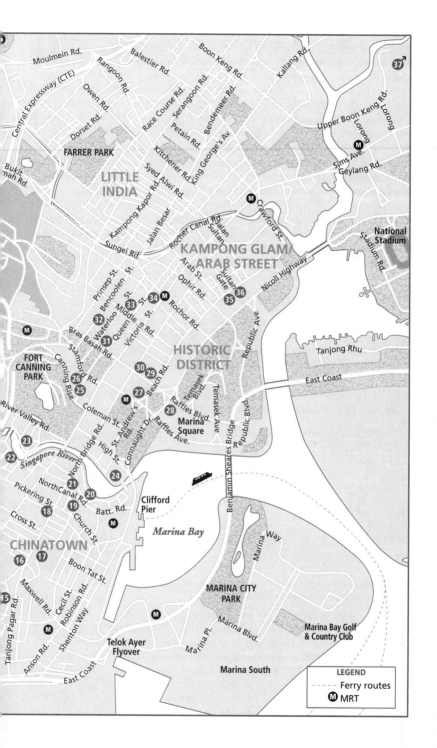

Moulmein Rd.
Rangoon Rd.
Balestier Rd.
Boon Keng Rd.
Kallang Rd.

Central Expressway (CTE)
Owen Rd.
Dorset Rd.
Race Course Rd.
Serangoon Rd.
Petain Rd.
Bendemeer Rd.
Kitchener Rd.
King George's Av.
Upper Boon Keng Rd.
Lorong
Lorong
Sims Ave.
Geylang Rd.

Bukit nah Rd.

FARRER PARK

LITTLE
INDIA

Syed Alwi Rd.
Kampong Kapor Rd.
Jalan Besar
Rochor Canal Rd.
Jalan Sultan
Crawford St.

Sungei Rd.

KAMPONG GLAM/
ARAB STREET

Arab St.
Sultan Gate
Ophir Rd.
Nicoll Highway

National
Stadium
Stadium Rd.

Prinsep St.
Bencoolen St.
Middle St.
Waterloo St.
Queen St.
Victoria St.
33
34
Rochor Rd.
36
35

Bras Basah Rd.
32
31

Tanjong Rhu

FORT
CANNING
PARK
M

Stamford Rd.
Canning Rise
26
25
Coleman St.
30 **29** Beach Rd.
HISTORIC
DISTRICT
Republic Ave.
East Coast

River Valley Rd.

23

22
Singapore River
NorthCanal Rd.
21
20
24
27
St. Andrew's Rd.
Connaught Dr.
Raffles Ave.
28
Marina
Square
Raffles Blvd.
Temasek Blvd.
Temasek Ave.
Republic Blvd.

Pickering St.
19
18
Cross St.
Church St.
Batt. Rd.
M
Clifford
Pier

Benjamin Sheares Bridge

CHINATOWN
16 **17**
Boon Tat St.

Marina Bay

Maxwell Rd.
15
Cecil St.
Robinson Rd.
Robinson Way
Shenton Way
Anson Rd.
East Coast
M
Tanjong Pagar Rd.

Telok Ayer
Flyover

M

Marina Pl.
Marina Blvd.
Marina Way

MARINA CITY
PARK

Marina Bay Golf
& Country Club

Marina South

LEGEND
- - - Ferry routes
M MRT

217

1 Tips on Singapore Nightlife

INFORMATION   Major cultural festivals are highly publicized by the Singapore Tourism Board (STB), so one stop by their office will probably provide enough info to fill your evening agenda for your whole trip. Another source is the *Straits Times,* which lists events around town, as well as the *New Paper,* which also lists musical events like local bands and international rock and pop tours. Both of these papers also provide cinema listings and theater reviews.

TICKETS   Two ticket agents, TicketCharge and Sistic, handle bookings for almost all theater performances, concert dates, and special events. You can find out about schedules before your visit through their Web sites: www.ticketcharge.net and www.sistic.com.sg. When in Singapore, stop by one of their centrally located outlets to pick up a schedule, or call them for more information. Call **TicketCharge** at ☎ **65/296-2929** or head for Centrepoint, Forum–The Shopping Mall, Funan–The IT Mall, Marina Square Shopping Centre, Tanglin Mall, or the Substation. For **Sistic** bookings call ☎ **65/348-5555,** or see them at the Victoria Concert Hall Box Office, Bugis Junction, Raffles Shopping Centre, Scotts, Specialists' Shopping Center, Suntec Mall, Takashimaya Shopping Centre, or Wisma Atria. The STB also carries information about current and coming events.

HOURS   Theater and dance performances can begin anywhere between 7:30 and 9pm. Be sure to call for the exact time. Many bars open in the late afternoon, a few as early as lunchtime. Disco and entertainment clubs usually open around 6pm, but generally don't get lively until 10 or 11pm. Closing time for bars and clubs is at 1 or 2am on weekdays, 3am on weekends.

DRINK PRICES   Because of the government's added tariff, alcoholic beverage prices are high everywhere, whether in a hotel bar or a neighborhood pub. "House pour" drinks (generics) are between S$10 and S$13 (US$6 and US$7.80). A glass of house wine will cost between S$10 and S$15 (US$6 and US$9), depending if it's a red or a white. Local draft beer (Tiger), brewed in Singapore, is on average S$10 (US$6). Almost every bar and club has a happy hour before 7:30pm and discounts can be up to 50% off for house pours and drafts. Most of the disco and entertainment clubs charge steep covers, but they will usually include one drink. Hooray for ladies' nights—at least 1 night during the week—when those of the feminine persuasion get in for free.

DRESS CODE   Many clubs will require smart casual attire. Feel free to be trendy, but stay away from shorts, T-shirts, sneakers, and torn jeans. Be forewarned that you may be turned away if not properly dressed. Many locals dress up for their night on the town, either in elegant garb or trend-setting threads, although a certain amount of respectability is always expected.

SAFETY   You'll be fairly safe out during the wee hours in most parts of the city, and even a single woman alone has little to worry about. Occasionally, groups of young men may cat call, but by and large those groups are not hanging out in the more cosmopolitan areas. On the weekends, police set up barricades around the city to pick up drunk drivers, so if you rent a car, be careful about your alcohol intake, or appoint a designated driver. Otherwise, you can get home safely in a taxi, which fortunately isn't too hard to find even late at night, with one exception: When Boat Quay clubs close, there's usually a mob of revelers scrambling for cabs. (Note that after midnight, a 50% surcharge is added to the fare, so make sure you don't drink away your ride home!)

2 Best Bets

Reviews and address information on all the places listed here can be found later in this chapter.

- **Wildest Party:** At **Elvis' Place** they had to put banisters on the bar to keep the crazy weekend people from tumbling behind into the sink.
- **Best Arty Hangout:** At **The Fat Frog** you can meet folks from the Substation arts center next door, and plenty of others interested in the scene.
- **Best Chinois Kitsch:** Chairman Mao always has a smile at the **Next Page.** Don't let the authentic Chinese decor at **Lan Kwai Fong** fool you: The disco, pub, and wine bar are definitely circa 2000.
- **Best Place for an Afternoon Beer: No. 5** is cool and dark—a refreshing contrast to the scorching heat outside. In the afternoons it's so quiet that you'd never know there's madness going on just outside on Orchard Road.
- **Most Hopping Dance Club: Buzz** hasn't the glitzy freak show of Zouk, but I'll bet you'll hear 100 songs that are all favorites.
- **Best Use of Day-Glo Decor: Zouk.** Period.
- **Best Show:** The drag queens at **Boom Boom Room** win the prize here. The club is all that remains of the once-thriving sex industry on Bugis Street.
- **Best Live Music:** For real music appreciation, head for one of Singapore's Jazz venues: **Sax, Somerset's,** or **Harry's Quayside** always feature excellent musicians in their nightly sessions.

3 The Bar & Club Scene

Singaporeans love to go out at night, whether it's to lounge around in a cozy wine bar or to jump around on a dance floor until 3 in the morning. And this city has become pretty eclectic in its entertainment choices, so you'll find everything from live jazz to Elvis, from garage rock to techno, world beat, or just plain rock. The truth is, the nightlife is happening. Local celebrities and the young, wealthy, and beautiful are the heroes of the scene, and their quest for the "coolest" spot keeps the club scene on its toes. The listings here are keyed in to help you find the latest or most interesting place. *A tip:* At press time, the most happening bars and clubs were anything on Mohamed Sultan Road and the new Chinese-chic Lan Kwai Fong. Start from there.

BARS

Bojangles. 174 Killiney Rd. ☎ **65/734-5446.** No cover. Draft beer around S$9 (US$5.40). Sun–Thurs 3pm–1am; Fri–Sat 3pm–2am. Happy hour 3–8pm.

I like to recommend Bojangles because it's got a great location, but manages to stay off tourist agendas. The happy hour specials are some of the best in Singapore. I especially appreciate the relaxed and casual atmosphere. The staff serves with a smile (a *real* smile), and patrons tend to be more down-to-earth than at the more trendy places—most are regulars. It's warm and welcoming, and far from the madding crowds.

Brix. Grand Hyatt Singapore, 10–12 Scotts Rd. ☎ **65/738-1234.** No cover. Draft beer and house-pours around S$10 (US$6). Sun–Thurs 5pm–2am; Fri–Sat 5pm–3am. Nightly happy hour 5–8pm.

In the basement of the Grand Hyatt Regency, Brix has inherited the spot once reserved for Brannigan's, a rowdy up-market watering hole and pickup joint. Grand Hyatt decided to clean up its act, and had Brix move in instead. Decidedly more sophisticated than its predecessor, Brix has a new air of class, but somehow lacks a certain seedy spontaneity. Still, it's a nice new place on the scene for those who prefer a more discriminating kind of fun. The Music Bar features live jazz and R&B, while the Wine & Whiskey Bar serves up a fine selection of wines, scotch, and cognacs.

✪ **Elvis' Place.** #B1-13 The Concourse Shopping Mall, 298 Beach Rd. ☎ **65/299-8403.** No cover. Draft beer and house-pours from S$9 (US$5.40). Mon–Thurs 4pm–1am; Fri–Sat 4pm–3am. Happy hour nightly 4–8:30pm with half-price drafts.

Welcome to the delightful world of Elvis Wee, Singapore's resident Elvis Presley tribute artist. Elvis (Mr. Wee) is a local celebrity, known for his impersonations and large collection of memorabilia. He hangs out at the bar and loves to talk about Elvis, life, and the world, and is very gracious when you ask for a photo or autograph. As for the bar, it's no bigger than a postage stamp, but on Friday and Saturday nights the place rocks so hard, Elvis and his crew had to put railings on the bar to keep folks from falling into the sink. It's truly a United Nations crowd here, and even though Mr. Wee hung up his cape a few years ago, the crowd is more than happy to fill in where he left off. Whether you love The King or not, you've got to love a place that gets down like this.

✪ **The Fat Frog.** 45 Armenian St. (behind the Substation). ☎ **65/338-6201.** No cover. Limited menu. Draft beer around S$9 (US$5.40). Sun–Thurs 11:30am–midnight; Fri–Sat 11:30am–1am.

More a cafe than a bar, Fat Frog draws folks who prefer conversation without intrusive music. The patio at the back of this place stays quiet in the afternoons, and at night fills up, but rarely becomes overcrowded. The main attraction is its location— behind the Substation, a hub for Singapore's visual and performing-arts scene, making this place a good stop after a show. Sometimes you can even run into performers and other majors from the local scene. Inside you'll find a bulletin board promoting current shows, performances, and openings. Around the patio courtyard walls local painters contribute mural work to the decor.

Hard Rock Cafe. #02-01 HPL House, 50 Cuscaden Rd. ☎ **65/235-5232.** Cover S$20 (US$12) Fri–Sat only. Cover includes first drink. Draft beer from S$10 (US$6). Sun–Thurs 11am–2am; Fri–Sat 11am–3am.

The Hard Rock Cafe in Singapore is like the Hard Rock Cafe in your hometown. You probably don't go to that one, so don't bother spending your vacation time in this one either. Not that it's all bad—the Filipino bands are usually pretty good and, of course, so are the burgers. Other than that it's not much more than a tourist pickup joint. Bring mace.

✪ **Harry's Quayside Bar.** 28 Boat Quay. ☎ **65/538-3029.** No cover. Draft beer from S$9 (US$5.40). Sun–Thurs 11am–1am; Fri–Sat 11am–2am. Happy hour daily 11am–9pm.

The official after-work drink stop for finance professionals from nearby Shenton Way, Harry's biggest claim to fame is that it was bank-buster Nick Leeson's favorite bar. But don't let the power ties put you off. Harry's is a cool place, from airy riverside seating, to cozy tables next to the stage. Harry's is known for it's live jazz and R&B music, which is always good. Of all the choices along Boat Quay, Harry's remains the most classy; and even though it's also the most popular, you can usually get a seat.

Hu'u Bar. Singapore Art Museum, 71 Bras Basah Rd. ☎ **65/338-6828.** No cover. Sun–Thurs 6pm–2am; Fri–Sat 6pm–3am.

Opened by seasoned Singaporean clubbers, Hu'u Bar presents their vision of how a great bar should be. I'd say the best part of the place is the music, a smooth mix of acid jazz that's both sophisticated and funky. Decor follows an Indonesian theme, but the club is still distinctly modern. Its location in the Singapore Art Museum adds another classy element—very urban, very progressive. A nice change from the usual Singaporean nightclub scene.

JJ Mahoney. 58 Duxton Rd. ☎ **65/225-6225.** No cover. Draft beer from S$8 (US$4.80), with house-pours just slightly more. Sun–Thurs 5pm–1am; Fri–Sat and the eve of public holidays 5pm–2am. Happy hour nightly 5–8pm.

If you're looking for a real bar–type bar, JJ Mahoney comes pretty close. You have the tile floor, the dark wood bar and paneling, stools lining the sides, and everyday people sidling up for another round. The first floor is a nice place to hang out and meet people (until about 10:30, when the band kicks in with contemporary but rather loud music), and will broadcast soccer games from time to time. The second floor, up a wide hardwood staircase, has small tables where you can order drinks and play games like Scrabble, Yahtzee, chess, and checkers. The third floor is reserved for KTV, a karaoke lounge where you can sing without worrying about con-women hitting you up for overpriced and watered-down drinks.

✪ **The Long Bar.** Raffles Hotel Arcade, Raffles Hotel, 1 Beach Rd. ☎ **65/337-1886.** No cover. Draft beer S$9 (US$5.40), Singapore Sling S$16 (US$9.60), Sling with souvenir glass S$25 (US$14.95). Sun–Thurs 11am–1am; Fri–Sat 11am–2am. Happy hour nightly 6–9pm, with special deals on pitchers of beer and mixed drinks.

Here's a nice little gem of a bar, even if it is touristy and expensive. With tiled mosaic floors, large shuttered windows, electric fans, and punkah fans moving in waves above, Raffles Hotel has tried to retain much of the charm of yesteryear, so you can enjoy a Singapore Sling in its birthplace and take yourself back to when history was made. And truly, the thrill at the Long Bar is tossing back one of these sweet juicy drinks while pondering the Singapore adventures of all the famous actors, writers, and artists who came through here in the first decades of the century. If you're not inspired by the poetry of the moment, stick around and get juiced for the pop/reggae band at 9pm, which is quite good.

Muddy Murphys. #B1-01/01-06 Orchard Hotel Shopping Arcade, 442 Orchard Rd. ☎ **65/735-0400.** No cover. Draft beer and house-pours around S$12.50 (US$7.50). Sun–Thurs 11am–1am; Fri–Sat 11am–3am. Happy hour daily 11am–7:30pm (happy hour begins earlier, but the discount is not as great as other places).

This is one of a few Irish bars in Singapore. Located on two levels in the shopping mall, on the upper level you have the more conservative business set having drinks after their 9-to-5 gigs, while downstairs the party lasts a little longer and gets a little more lively. Irish music rounds out the ambience created by the mostly Irish imported trappings around the place. Occasionally they'll even have an Irish band. There is a limited menu for lunch, dinner, and snacks.

✪ **The Next Page.** 17 Mohamed Sultan Rd. ☎ **65/235-6967.** No cover. Small snack menu available. Draft beer S$9 (US$5.40). Daily 3pm–3am. Happy hour daily 3–9pm.

Few bars stand out for ambience like The Next Page, which is a freaky Chinese dream in an old Singaporean shophouse. Creep through the pintu pagar front door and pass the opium bed in the front hall into the main room, its old walls of crumbling stucco washed in sexy Chinese red, and lanterns glowing crimson in the air shaft rising above the island bar, to the left of which is a giant portrait of a smiling Mao Zedong. It's a delightfully sick twist of Chinese decadence. Far out. The crowd is mainly young professionals who by late night have been known to dance on the bar (and not only on weekends). The back has a bit more space for seating, darts, and a pool table.

✪ **No. 5.** 5 Emerald Hill. ☎ **65/732-0818.** No cover. Draft beer and house-pours S$9 (US$5.40). Mon–Thurs noon–2am, Fri–Sat noon–3am, Sun 5pm–2am. Happy hour daily noon–9pm, including S$5 (US$3) drafts, house-pours, and house wine.

Down Peranakan Place there are a few bars, one of which is No. 5, a cool, dark place just dripping with Southeast Asian ambience, from its old shophouse exterior to its partially crumbling interior walls hung with rich wood carvings. The hardwood floors and beamed ceilings are complemented by seating areas cozied with Oriental carpets and kilim throw pillows. Upstairs is more conventional table-and-chair seating. The glow of the skylighted air shaft and the whirring fans above make this an ideal place to stop for a cool drink on a hot afternoon. In the evenings, be prepared for a lively mix of people.

MICROBREWERIES

Brewerkz. #01-05 Riverside Point, 30 Merchant Rd. ☎ **65/438-7438.** No cover. Sun–Thurs 5pm–1am; Fri–Sat 5pm–3am. Happy hour daily 3–9pm with 2-for-1 beers.

Brewerks, with outside seating along the river and an airy contemporary style inside—like a giant IKEA room built around brewing kettles and copper pipes—brews the best house beer in Singapore. The bar menu features five tasty brew selections from recipes created by their English brew master: Nut Brown Ale, Red Ale, Wiesen, Bitter, and Indian Pale Ale (which, by the way, has the highest alcohol content). A pint will set you back about S$12 (US$7.20), while the sampler set of 2-ounce portions of each beer is S$13 (US$7.80). Their American cuisine lunch, dinner, and snack menu is also very good—I recommend planning a meal here as well.

JAZZ BARS

Raffles Bar & Billiards. Raffles Hotel, 1 Beach Rd. ☎ **65/331-1746.** No cover. Daily 11:30am–12:30am.

Talk about a place rich with the kind of elegance only history can provide. Raffles Bar & Billiards began as a bar in 1896 and over the decades has been transformed to perform various functions as the hotel's needs dictated. In its early days, legend has it that a patron shot the last tiger in Singapore under a pool table here. Whether or not the tiger part is true, one of its two billiards tables is an original piece, still in use after 100 years. In fact, many of the fixtures and furniture here are original Raffles antiques, including the lights above the billiards tables and the scoreboards, and are marked with small brass placards. In the evenings, a jazzy little trio shakes the ghosts out of the rafters, while from 6pm to 1am nightly people lounge around enjoying single malts, cognacs, coffee, port, Champagne, chocolates, and imported cigars. Expect to drop a small fortune. From 11:30am to 2:30pm, they serve a S$40 (US$23.95) per person seafood buffet; from 3:30 to 6pm, stop by for high tea.

✪ **Sax.** 23 Cuppage Terrace. ☎ **65/835-3090.** No cover. Draft beer and house-pours from S$9 (US$5.40). Sun–Thurs 6pm–2am; Fri–Sat 6pm–3am. Happy hour daily 4–9pm, including half-price drafts (not honored on the patio).

For a not-so-highbrow jazz evening, try Saxophone, a hole-in-the-wall place with great live jazz and blues every day except Monday from about 9:45pm till around 12:30am. Inside seems tiny, but you can still hear the music from the outside patio. Sax also has some interesting local pieces of art hung here and there. Above the bar, check out the old poster from the seventies, displaying how Singaporean men are supposed to wear their hair.

✪ **Somerset's Bar.** The Westin Stamford and Westin Plaza hotels, 2 Stamford Rd. ☎ **65/431-5332.** No cover. Draft beer from S$11 (US$6.60), cocktails from S$14 (US$8.40). Daily 5pm–2am. Happy hour 5–8:30pm daily.

This huge hotel lounge can accommodate large crowds very comfortably. Good thing, as the place serves quite a lot of patrons, mostly jazz lovers who come for the best live jazz in the city. They feature at least two sets of live music every night: country, pop, and rock from 6:15 to 8:15pm except Saturday, and a jazz set from 9pm to around 1am every night. From time to time they've hosted internationally renowned performers like bassist Eldee Young, pianist Judy Roberts, and vocalist Nancy Kelly. Call ahead to find out their schedule of performances, and plan some time here for a nice evening in their relaxing environment.

DISCOS

✪ **Buzz.** 88 Circular Rd. ☎ **65/536-9557.** No cover. Selected bottled beers from S$8 (US$4.80). Mon–Thurs 6pm–1am; Fri 6pm–2am; Sat 7pm–2am; Sun 7pm–1am. Happy hour Mon–Fri 6–9pm; Sat 7–9pm.

Buzz isn't as glitzy and high profile as some of the other dance clubs in Singapore, but everyone who goes out at night knows about it. Its many regulars come back again and again to dance to eighties music, which sometimes includes a tune or two you'd never thought you'd hear again. The crowd here is always unusual—you'll find everything from businessmen to college students, and the attitude is far more casual than the other Cooler-Than-Thou discos. A great choice if you just want to party without all the aftertaste.

✪ **Lan Kwai Fong.** 50 Eu Tong Sen St. ☎ **65/534-3233.** Cover Sun–Thurs S$10 (US$6); Fri–Sat S$15 (US$9). Draft beers and house-pours from S$9 (US$5.40). Daily 6pm–3am. Happy hour daily 6–9pm.

These Singaporeans just can't get enough Chinese kitsch. One of the most talked about newcomers on the scene, Lan Kwai Fong, occupies a traditional medical hall in Chinatown. The restored building and its contents are so completely authentic that you'd think it was a stop on the Chinatown walking tour. The music in the downstairs bar and disco, however, is completely modern. Don't forget to find the wine bar on the top floor.

Top Ten. #05-18A Orchard Towers, 400 Orchard Rd. ☎ **65/732-3077.** Cover Sun–Thurs S$17.15 (US$10.25); Fri S$22.90 (US$13.70); Sat and eve of public holidays S$28.60 (US$17.15). Daily 5pm–3am. Happy hour daily 9–11pm.

Even though it's one of the sleazier joints in Singapore, Top Ten has one of the highest cover charges. The huge space is like an auditorium, with a stage and dance floor at one end, seating areas on levels grading up to the top of the other end, and a lighted cityscape scene surrounding the whole thing. A cover band plays three sets of pop 7 days a week, but people don't come here for the decor or even the music: Top Ten is a notorious pickup joint for Asian women (men, bring your wallet, if you get my meaning). Tuesday night is ladies' night and women don't have to pay the cover, but no doubt you'll be buying drinks all night.

Venom. Pacific Plaza Penthouse, 9 Scotts Rd. ☎ **65/734-7677.** Cover charge Tues–Thurs S$20 (ladies free Wed); Fri–Sat S$18 (US$10.80) before 10pm and S$25 after 10pm. Tues–Thurs 6pm–3am; Fri–Sun 8pm–3am; closed Mon.

Trendy and slick, Venom captures the spirit of a London-style dance club with futuristic decor in industrial metallics. Known as the latest spot for Singapore's beautiful, fashionable, and famous, it gets pretty full on weekends with a mixed crowd of young and old, locals, expatriates, and travelers. The dance floor throbs with guest DJs spinning the latest international house, garage, and techno rhythms, while from the upstairs bar you can view the wild dance party from behind the safety of glass panels.

If you fancy a bite, there's a sushi bar. Even more unique, look for the small screening room where they show full-length films and music videos.

✪ **Zouk/Phuture/Velvet Underground.** Jiak Kim St. ☎ **65/738-2988.** Zouk open Wed (cover S$20), Fri–Sat (cover S$20/US$12 women, S$25/US$14.95 men); Phuture open Wed (cover S$23/US$13.75), Thurs (cover S$10/US$6), Fri–Sat (cover S$20/US$12 women, S$25/US$14.95 men); Velvet Underground open Tues and Thurs (cover S$20/US$12), Wed (cover S$25/US$14.95), Fri–Sat (cover S$20/US$12 women, S$25/US$14.95 men). Payment of highest cover charge among the three clubs in the complex allows admission to the other clubs as well; otherwise, additional charges will incur when moving between clubs. All open 6pm–3am.

Singapore's first innovative danceteria, Zouk introduced the city to house music, which throbs nightly in its cavernous disco, comprised of three warehouses joined together. They play the best in modern music, so even if you're not much of a groover you can still have fun watching the party from the many levels that tower above the dance floor. If you need a bit more intimacy in your nightlife, Velvet Underground, within the Zouk complex, drips in red velvet and soft lighting—a good complement to the more soulful sounds spinning here. The newer addition to Zouk, Phuture, draws a younger, more hip-hop-loving crowd than VU. Including the wine bar outside, Zouk is basically your one-stop shopping for a party; and in Singapore, this place is legendary.

CABARET

✪ **Boom Boom Room.** #02-04 Bugis Village, 3 New Bridge Rd. ☎ **65/339-8187.** Cover Wed–Thurs S$17 (US$10.20); Fri–Sat S$23 (US$13.75); no cover Mon–Tues. Sun–Thurs 8pm–2am; Fri–Sat 8pm–3am.

Bugis Street, once a seedy nightspot teeming with drag queens, transvestites, and sex performers (à la Bangkok), changed its tune in the 1980s when the government cleaned up the area and opened a night market. Just about the only reminder is the Boom Boom Room, a rather antiseptic version of the shenanigans of days gone by, but still a fun night out with female impersonators and somewhat bawdy vaudeville acts. Local TV stars Kumar and Leena perform regularly, while Monday and Tuesday are reserved for new acts, to give stage experience to up-and-coming impersonators. Shows start daily at 10:45pm and midnight, with additional weekend shows at 1:45am. Drinks are moderately priced.

GAY & LESBIAN NIGHTSPOTS

It seems a few of Singapore's better known gay and lesbian spots have closed down in the past couple of years, but new places are popping up regularly. The Web has listings at www2.best.com/~utopia/tipsing.htm, but I've found some of these to be outdated. For the latest info, I'd recommend one of the chat rooms suggested at the address above, and talk to the experts. Recent word has it that Velvet Underground, part of the Zouk complex (see above), welcomes a mixed clientele of gays, lesbians, and straight folks. In addition to the places I've listed below, there are a couple of gay bars that have asked to remain unlisted in this book, so ask around for a better sense of the scene in Singapore.

Babylon. 52 Tanjong Pagar Rd. ☎ **65/227-7466.** No cover. Draft beer from S$9.50 (US$5.70). Mon–Thurs 7pm–2am; Fri–Sat and the eve of public holidays 7pm–3am; Sun 7pm–midnight. Happy hour daily 7–8:30pm.

Babylon is a small, gay karaoke club, comparable in size to Inner Circle (see below), though with a slightly nicer atmosphere. The crowd at this bar is younger and might not be as open as at Inner Circle, but try it out anyway.

Inner Circle. 78 Tanjong Pagar Rd. ☎ **65/222-8462.** No cover. Mon–Thurs 7pm–midnight; Fri 7pm–1am; Sat 7pm–2am. Happy hour Sun–Thurs 7–8:30pm.

In researching this guidebook, I have yet to chat up the people at Inner Circle and get anything but nice. The place is pretty small and dark, with a tiny bar, a large karaoke screen, and not much more to write home about. Most of the clientele are Singaporeans, but the staff is very friendly and open, and assure me that Westerners, although not frequent guests, are very welcome and will definitely have a good time.

KARAOKE

JJ Mahoney. 58 Duxton Rd. ☎ **65/225-6225.** No cover. Draft beer from S$9 (US$5.40), with house-pours just slightly more. Sun–Thurs 5pm–1am; Fri–Sat and the eve of public holidays 5pm–2am. Happy hour 5–8pm.

JJ Mahoney is also listed under bars, but if you're looking for a nice place for karaoke, up on the third floor there's an intimate little lounge with friendly staff who'll spin from many books filled with all the tunes you could ever want to squeak out.

Singsation Theme Karaoke. The Plaza Hotel, 7500A Beach Rd. ☎ **65/298-0011.** No cover. Drinks from S$10 (US$6). Daily 6pm–1am.

Singsation has 18 theme rooms, from cozy log cabins to a drive-in movie setting to the interior of an airplane, complete with seats and an aisle. There's also a large room for those who like to croon to a bigger crowd.

WINE BARS

Beaujolais. 1 Ann Siang Hill. ☎ **65/224-2227.** No cover. Mon–Thurs 11am–midnight; Fri 11am–2am; Sat 6pm–2am. Happy hour opening until 9pm.

This little gem of a place, in a shophouse built on a hill, is smaller than small, but its charm makes it a favorite for loyal regulars. Two tables outside (on the five-foot-way, which serves more as a patio than a sidewalk) and two tables inside doesn't seem like much room, but there's more seating upstairs. They believe that wine should be affordable, and so their many labels tend to be more moderately priced per glass and bottle.

Que Pasa. 7 Emerald Hill. ☎ **65/235-6626.** No cover. Sun–Thurs 6pm–2am; Fri–Sat 6pm–3am.

One of the more mellow stops along Peranakan Place, this little wine bar serves up a collection of some 70 to 100 labels with plenty of atmosphere and a nice central location. It's another bar in a shophouse, but this one has as its centerpiece a very unusual winding stairway up the air shaft to the level above. Wine bottles and artwork line the walls. In the front you can order Spanish-style finger food—tapas, anyone?—and cigars. The VIP club on the upper floor has the look and feel of a formal living room, complete with wing chairs and board games. Wines from France, Australia, Chile, California, New Zealand, and Germany are priced at S$40 (US$24) and up, while white and red wines sold by the glass will only set you back between S$8 and S$10 (US$4.80 and US$6).

A CIGAR BAR

Havana Club. Lobby level Marriott Hotel, 320 Orchard Rd. ☎ **65/834-1088.** Daily 10am–12:30am.

In a tiny living-room setting in the corner of the Marriott lobby, you can sit and gnaw your stogie or take it away. They have more than 200 kinds of cigars, including Cubanos, ranging from S$4 to S$80. They also serve a small selection of cognacs.

4 The Performing Arts

Singapore is not a cultural backwater. Professional and amateur theater companies, dance troupes, opera companies, and musical groups offer a wide variety of not only Asian performances, but Western as well. Broadway road shows don't stop in San Francisco, where the road ends, but continue on to include Singapore in their itineraries, and international stars like Domingo, Pavarotti, Yo Yo Ma, Winston Marsalis, Tito Puente, and Michael Jackson have come to town. International stars make up only a small portion of the performance scene, though. Singapore theater comprises four distinct language groups—English, Chinese, Malay, and Indian—and each maintains its own voice and culture.

The Singapore Symphony Orchestra, just 18 years old, gives concerts any jaded New Yorker or Londoner would find inspiring. Singapore's own artists, such as U.S.-based violinist Siow Lee Chin and former Air Supply lead guitarist Rex Goh, to name just two, have garnered critical acclaim worldwide.

Around town, impromptu stages feature irregularly scheduled performances of traditional entertainments. **Wayang (Chinese opera)** is loud, gaudy, and much fun to watch. Gongs and drums herald the lavishly costumed, heavily made-up actors, who perform favorite Chinese tales in the original language. Don't worry about trying to follow the story line, since the actions more than make up for any language barrier. Performances are especially numerous during the Festival of the Hungry Ghosts in August (see chapter 2).

You also might be fortunate enough to happen upon a production as simple as one I saw, in which two "old Chinese gents" sat on a park bench talking about ancient times. The performance was so realistic that an elderly bystander, overjoyed to find compatriots, sat himself down between the two and joined the conversation. The two actors carried on in true showbiz fashion and included the old man, much to the delight of the audience.

CLASSICAL PERFORMANCES

The **Singapore Symphony Orchestra,** 11 Empress Place, 2nd Storey, Victoria Hall (☎ 65/338-1230; www.sso.org.sg), performs every weekend at the Victoria Concert Hall, with regular special guest appearances by international celebrities. Concerts begin at 8:15pm on Fridays and Saturdays, and tickets range from S$8 to S$50 (US$4.80 to US$29.95). Sistic handles bookings for SSO performances, so call their hot line at ☎ 65/348-5555, or visit their main office at the Victoria Concert Hall Box Office or one of their other locations listed above in this chapter.

Singapore also hosts the Malaysian Philharmonic Orchestra, plus events such as the International Piano Festival.

The **Singapore Lyric Opera,** Stamford Arts Centre, 155 Waterloo St. #03-06 (☎ 65/336-1929), also appears at the Victoria Concert Hall regularly. For the millennium, they staged the ever-popular *Die Fledermaus* with local talents. Call them for upcoming schedules, or call Sistic at the Victoria Concert Hall Box Office (☎ 65/348-5555).

The **Singapore Chinese Orchestra,** the only professional Chinese orchestra in Singapore, has won several awards for its classic Chinese interpretations. They perform every 2 weeks at a variety of venues (including outdoor concerts at the Botanic Gardens). Ticket prices vary from S$8 to S$20 (US$4.80 to US$12). Contact them c/o People's Association, Block B, Room 5, No. 9 Stadium Link (☎ **65/440-3839;** www.sco-music.org.sg). Ticket sales are handled by Sistic.

THEATER

Most international companies will perform at the **Victoria Concert Hall,** with bookings handled by Sistic (☎ **65/348-5555**).

A few local companies are quite noteworthy. Granted, theater is new to Singaporeans; however, many local playwrights have emerged to capture life here (with some hilarious interpretations), using local stage talents. **Action Theatre,** 42 Waterloo St. (☎ **65/837-0842**), with tickets between S$35 and S$42 (US$20.95 and US$25.15), is one of the best companies to capture poignant and funny social themes, many of which cross cultural barriers. The **Necessary Stage,** 126 Cairnhill Arts Centre, Cairnhill Road (☎ **65/738-6355**), blazed trails for the local performing arts scene after staging productions that touched tender nerves for the community, including a startlingly frank monologue by the first Singaporean to publicly declare his struggle with AIDS. Tickets are handled by Sistic, at prices ranging from S$20 to S$30 (US$12 to $18). The **Singapore Repertory Theatre,** Far East Square, 130-132 Amoy St. (☎ **65/221-5585**), invites theatergoers to *Ah Kong's Birthday Party,* a banquet to celebrate Grandfather's 71st birthday. Actors and audience combine as the fourth wall breaks down, and guests are lured into family scandals and the odd antics of poor Grandfather's crazy family. Sistic (☎ 65/348-5555) handles the tickets, which are S$75 (US$44.90), including buffet dinner. Also check out the many events at **The Substation,** 45 Armenian St. (☎ **65/337-7800;** www.substation.org), which offers its space to many smaller troupes, plus performance artists.

CULTURAL SHOWS

Once upon a time, Cantonese opera could be seen under tents on street corners throughout the city. These days, local and visiting companies still perform, but very sporadically. For a performance you can count on, the **Chinese Theatre Circle,** #15 Smith St. (☎ **65/323-4862**), sets up shop every Wednesday and Friday at Clarke Quay. While you won't catch a full story (thank goodness—each opera is about 3¹/₂ hours long!), you will see excerpts from the most famous and beloved tales, with monitors carrying English and Chinese subtitles. Come at 7:45pm for the 45-minute show, or get there at 6:30pm for an extra treat: Actors welcome curious observers to watch them don costumes and apply makeup before the performance. Admission is free.

If you're looking for something with a little Malay flavor, head for **Malay Village,** 39 Geylang Serai (☎ **65/748-4700**), on weekends. Every Saturday and Sunday at 5pm (except during the fasting month of Ramadan), you can enjoy Indo-Malay dancers performing in traditional costume accompanied by a live gamelan orchestra. Come on Saturdays for the Kuda Kepang, a traditional dance from Johor in southern Malaysia. Featuring male dancers on wooden horses, this long performance is well worth the wait. During the grand finale, the dancers walk on glass, eat glass, and tear coconuts with their teeth. It's all real, and highly recommended.

For a bit of cultural theater, **Marina Mandarin's** "Heritage Night" introduces dance and costumes from some of Singapore and Southeast Asia's prominent ethnic groups. Each night, they serve an international buffet starting at 6:30pm, followed by the performance at 7:30pm. The 45-minute show includes a Chinese lion dance, bamboo dance from the Philippines, Indian dance, a Chinese fan dance, and a traditional Malay wedding dance. Advance reservations are advisable; call ☎ **65/338-3388.** Tickets cost S$38 (US$22.75), including dinner.

9

Planning a Trip to Malaysia

Compared with spicy Thailand to the north and cosmopolitan Singapore to the south, Malaysia is a relative secret to many from the West, and most travelers to Southeast Asia skip over it, opting for more heavily traversed routes.

Boy, are they missing out. Those who venture here wander through streets awash with international influences from colonial times and trek through mysterious rain forests and caves, often without another tourist in sight. They relax peacefully under palms on lazy white beaches that fade into blue, blue waters. They spy the bright colors of batik sarongs hanging to dry in the breeze. They hear the melodic drone of the Muslim call to prayer seeping from exotic mosques. They taste culinary masterpieces served in modest local shops—from Malay with its deep mellow spices to succulent seafood punctuated by brilliant chile sauces. In Malaysia I'm always thrilled to witness life without the distracting glare of the tourism industry, and I leave impressed by how accessible Malaysia is to outsiders while remaining true to its heritage.

Malaysia just doesn't get the tourism press it deserves, but it's not because foreign travelers aren't welcome. True, the Malaysian Tourism Board has almost no international advertising campaign—and you'll be hard-pressed to get any useful information out of them—but everyone from government officials in Kuala Lumpur to boat hands in Penang seems delighted to see the smiling face of a traveler who has discovered just how beautiful their country is.

Chapter 10 covers the major destinations of peninsular Malaysia. We begin with the country's capital, **Kuala Lumpur,** then tour the peninsula's west coast—the cities of **Johor Bahru, Malacca** (Melaka), the hill resorts at **Cameron** and **Genting Highlands,** plus islands like the popular **Penang** and the luxurious **Langkawi.** Chapter 11 takes you up the east coast of the peninsula, through resort areas such as **Desaru, Mersing, Kuantan, Cherating,** and the small and charming **Tioman Island,** all the way north to the culturally stimulating cities of **Kuala Terengganu** and **Kota Bharu.** My coverage will also include **Taman Negara National Park,** peninsular Malaysia's largest national forest. Finally, in chapter 12, we cross the South China Sea to the island of Borneo, where the Malaysian states of **Sarawak** and **Sabah** feature Malaysia's most impressive forests as well as unique and diverse cultures.

Malaysia is easily accessible to the rest of the world through its international airport in Kuala Lumpur. Or if you want to hop from another country in the region, daily flights to Malaysia's many smaller airports give you access to all parts of the country, and you can also travel by car, bus, or train from Singapore or Thailand. In this section I'll run through your options and get you started.

1 Malaysia's Regions in Brief

Malaysia's territory covers peninsular Malaysia—bordering Thailand in the north just across from Singapore in the south—and two states on the island of Borneo, Sabah and Sarawak, approximately 240 kilometers (150 miles) east across the South China Sea. All thirteen of its states total 336,700 square kilometers (202,020 sq. miles) of land. Of this area, **Peninsular Malaysia** makes up about 465,000 square kilometers (134,680 sq. miles) and contains 11 of Malaysia's 13 states: Kedah, Perlis, Penang, and Perak are in the northwest; Kelantan and Terengganu are in the northeast; Selangor, Negeri Sembilan, and Melaka are about midway down the peninsula on the western side; Pahang, along the east coast, sprawls inward to cover most of the central area (which is mostly forest preserve); and Johor covers the entire southern tip from east to west, with two vehicular causeways linking it to Singapore, just over the Strait of Johor. Kuala Lumpur, the nation's capital, appears on a map to be located in the center of the state of Selangor, but it is actually a federal district similar to Washington, D.C., in the United States.

On **Borneo,** Sarawak and Sabah share the landmass with Indonesia's Kalimantan. Also sharing the island, in a tiny nook on the Sarawak coast, is the tiny oil-rich Sultanate of Brunei Darussalam.

Back on the peninsula, the major cities can be found closer to the coastline, many having built on old trade or mining settlements, usually near one of Malaysia's many rivers.

Tropical evergreen forests, estimated to be some of the oldest in the world, cover more than 70% of Malaysia. The country's diverse terrain allows for a range of forest types, such as montane forests, sparsely wooded tangles at higher elevations; lowland forests, the dense tropical jungle type; mangrove forests along the waters' edge; and peat swamp forests along the waterways. On the peninsula, three national forests—Taman Negara (or "National Forest") and Kenong Rimba Park, both inland, and Endau Rompin National Park, located toward the southern end of the peninsula—welcome visitors regularly, for quiet nature walks to observe wildlife or hearty adventures like white-water rafting, mountain climbing, caving, and jungle trekking. Similarly, the many national forests of Sabah and Sarawak provide a multitude of memorable experiences, which can include brushes with the indigenous peoples of the forests.

Surrounded by the South China Sea on the east coast and the Strait of Malacca on the west, the waters off the peninsula vary in terms of sea life (and beach life). The

Abbreviating Malaysia

The first tip here is that people are always abbreviating Kuala Lumpur to KL. Okay, that's pretty obvious. But these people will abbreviate everything else they can get away with. So, Johor Bahru becomes JB, Kota Bharu KB, Kota Kinabalu, KK—you get the picture. Malaysia itself is often shortened to M'sia and Singapore to S'pore. To make it easier for you, the only shortened version I've used in this book is KL.

Peninsular Malaysia

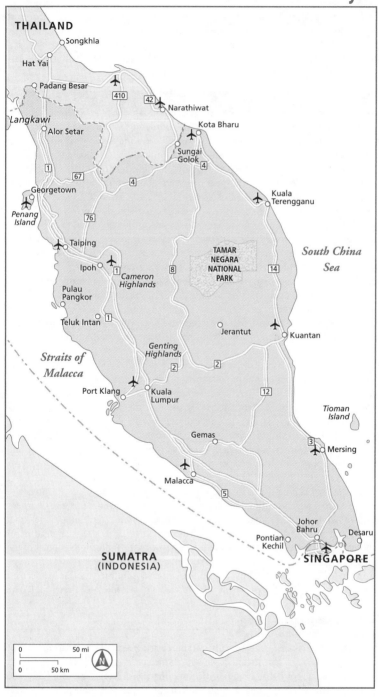

THAILAND

Songkhla

Hat Yai

Padang Besar

410

42 Narathiwat

Langkawi

Alor Setar

Kota Bharu

Sungai
Golok

4

1

67

4

Georgetown

76

Penang
Island

Taiping

Ipoh

1

Cameron
Highlands

8

TAMAR
NEGARA
NATIONAL
PARK

Kuala
Terengganu

South China
Sea

14

Pulau
Pangkor

Teluk Intan

1

Jerantut

Kuantan

Genting
Highlands

2

2

Straits of
Malacca

Port Klang

Kuala
Lumpur

12

Tioman
Island

Gemas

3 Mersing

Malacca

5

Johor
Bahru

Pontian
Kechil

Desaru

SUMATRA
(INDONESIA)

SINGAPORE

0   50 mi

0   50 km

N

waters off the east coast house a living coral reef, good waters, and gorgeous tropical beaches, while more southerly parts host beach resort areas. By way of contrast, the surf in southern portions of the Strait of Malacca is choppy and cloudy from shipping traffic—hardly ideal for diving or for the perfect Bali Hai vacation. But once you get as far north as Penang, the waters become beautiful again. Meanwhile, the sea coast of Sabah and Sarawak count numerous resort areas that are ideal for beach vacationing and scuba diving. In fact, one of the world's top 10 dive sites is located at Sipadan in Sabah.

2 Visitor Information

The **Malaysia Tourism Board (MTB)** can provide some information by way of pamphlets and advice before your trip, but keep in mind they are not yet as sophisticated as the Singapore Tourism Board. Much of the information they provide is vague, broad-stroke descriptions with few concrete details that are useful for the traveler. Overseas offices are located as follows.

IN THE UNITED STATES

- **New York:** 595 Madison Ave., Suite 1800, New York, NY 10022 (☎ **212/754-1113;** fax 212/754-1116)
- **Los Angeles:** 818 W. 7th St., Suite 804, Los Angeles, CA 90017 (☎ **213/689-9702;** fax 213/689-1530)

In Canada

- **Vancouver:** 830 Burrard St., Vancouver, B.C., Canada V6Z 2K4 (☎ **604/ 689-8899;** fax 604/689-8804)

In Australia

- **Sydney:** 65 York St., Sydney, NSW 2000, Australia (☎ **02/9299-4441;** fax 02/ 9262-2026)
- **Perth:** 56 William St., Perth, WA 6000, Australia (☎ **08/9481-0400;** fax 08/ 9321-1421).

In the United Kingdom

- **London:** 57 Trafalgar Square, London, WC2N 5DU, UK (☎ **071/930-7932;** fax 071/930-9015)
- **In Malaysia:** 17th Floor, Menara Dato' Onn, Putra World Trade Centre, 45 Jalan Tun Ismail, 50480 Kuala Lumpur (☎ **03/293-5188,** fax 03/293-5884).

For MTB offices in other cities, refer to individual city listings. The official Web site of the Malaysia Tourism Board is http://tourism.gov.my.

3 Entry Requirements

To enter the country you must have a valid passport. Citizens of the United States do not need visas for tourism and business visits, and upon entry are granted a Social/Business Visit Pass good for up to 3 months. Citizens of Canada, Australia, New Zealand, and the United Kingdom can also enter the country without a visa, and will be granted up to 30 days pass upon entry. For other countries, please consult the nearest Malaysian consulate before your trip for visa regulations. *Also note:* Travelers holding Israeli passports are not permitted to travel within Malaysia (likewise, Malaysians are forbidden from traveling to Israel).

While in Malaysia, should you need to contact an official representative from your home country, the following contact information in Kuala Lumpur can help you out: **United States Embassy** ☎ 03/2168-5000; **Canadian High Commission** ☎ 03/ 243-9499; **Australian High Commission** ☎ 03/240-6642; **New Zealand High Commission** ☎ 03/201-0846; and the **British High Commission** ☎ 03/ 248-2122.

If you are arriving from an area in which yellow fever has been reported, you will be required to show proof of yellow fever vaccination. Contact your nearest MTB office to research the specific areas that fall into this category.

CUSTOMS REGULATIONS

With regard to currency, you can bring into the country as many foreign currency notes or traveler's checks as you please, but you are not allowed to leave the country with more foreign currency or traveler's checks than you had when you arrived. Due to controls on currency speculation in recent years, the government is keeping an eye on every ringgit. Regarding Malaysian currency, you are not permitted to carry in or take out more than RM1,000 per person. Upon entry, you'll be asked to complete a form issued by the Central Bank of Malaysia (Bank Negara Malaysia) stating the value of all currencies carried. This form is to be held with your passport until, on departure, you'll be asked to retally your cash on hand and submit the form to Customs personnel.

Social visitors can enter Malaysia with 1 liter of hard alcohol and one carton of cigarettes without paying duty—anything over that amount is subject to local taxes.

Prohibited items include firearms and ammunition, daggers and knives, and pornographic materials. Be advised that, similar to Singapore, Malaysia enforces a very strict drug abuse policy that includes the death sentence for convicted drug traffickers.

4 Money

Malaysia's currency is the **Malaysian ringgit.** It's also commonly referred to as the Malaysian dollar, but prices are marked as RM (a designation I've used throughout this book). Notes are issued in denominations of RM2, RM5, RM10, RM20, RM50, RM100, RM500, and RM1000. One ringgit is equal to 100 sen. Coins come in denominations of 1, 5, 10, 20, and 50 sen, and there's also a 1-ringgit coin.

Following the dramatic decline in the value of its currency during the Southeast Asian economic crisis, the Malaysian government has sought to stabilize the ringgit to ward off currency speculation by pegging the ringgit at an artificial exchange rate. At the time of writing, exchange rates were RM3.79 to US$1.

CURRENCY EXCHANGE   Currency can be changed at banks and hotels, but you'll get a more favorable rate if you go to one of the money changers that seem to be everywhere; in shopping centers, in little lanes, and in small stores—just look for signs. They are often men in tiny booths with a lit display on the wall behind them showing the exchange rate. All major currencies are generally accepted, and there is never a problem with the U.S. dollar.

AUTOMATED TELLER MACHINES   Kuala Lumpur, Penang, and Johor Bahru have quite a few automated teller machines (ATMs) scattered around, but they are few and far between in the smaller towns. In addition, some ATMs do not accept credit cards or debit cards from your home bank. I have found that debit cards on the MasterCard/Cirrus or VISA/PLUS networks are almost always accepted at **Maybank,** with at least one location in every major town. Cash is dispensed in ringgit deducted from your account at the day's rate.

TRAVELER'S CHECKS   Generally, travelers to Malaysia will never go wrong with American Express and Thomas Cook traveler's checks, which can be cashed at banks,

Malaysian Ringgit Conversion Chart

RM	U.S.$	Can$	A$	NZ$	U.K.£
.10	.03	.04	.04	.05	.01
.20	.05	.08	.08	.11	.03
.50	.13	.19	.20	.27	.08
1.00	.26	.38	.41	.54	.16
2.00	.53	.76	.83	1.05	.33
5.00	1.30	1.90	2.05	2.70	.82
10.00	2.65	3.80	4.15	5.35	1.65
20.00	5.25	7.60	8.25	10.75	3.30
50.00	13.15	19.00	20.70	26.85	8.20
100.00	26.30	38.00	41.40	53.75	16.40
500.00	131.65	189.90	206.95	268.70	81.95
1000.00	263.30	379.85	413.95	537.40	163.90

What Things Cost in Kuala Lumpur

Taxi from the airport to city center (coach service; no taxis permitted)	RM18–RM25 (US$4.75–$6.60)
Local telephone call (3 min.)	RM.20 (US$0.05)
Double room at an expensive hotel (J. W. Marriott)	RM500 (US$131.60)
Double room at a moderate hotel (Concorde Hotel)	RM320 (US$84.20)
Double room at an inexpensive hotel (Swiss-Inn)	RM150 (US$39.45)
Dinner for one at an expensive restaurant (Ching Yuen Lai)	RM70–RM100 (US$18.40–$26.30)
Dinner for one at a moderate restaurant (Legends Natural Cuisine)	RM50–RM70 (US$13.15–$18.40)
Dinner for one at an inexpensive restaurant (Benson & Hedges Bistro)	RM25 (US$6.60)
Glass of beer	RM15–RM20 (US$3.95–$5.25)
Coca-Cola	RM2–RM6 (US$0.53–$1.60)
Cup of coffee at common coffee shop	RM1.50 (US$0.39)
Cup of coffee in a hotel	RM4 (US$1.05)
Roll of 36-exposure color film	RM15 (US$3.95)
Admission to the Museum Negara	RM1 (US$0.26)
Movie ticket	RM10(US$2.65)

hotels, and licensed money changers. Unfortunately, they are often not accepted at smaller shops. Even in some big restaurants and department stores, many cashiers don't know how to process these checks, which might lead to a long and frustrating wait.

CREDIT CARDS   Credit cards are widely accepted at hotels and restaurants, and at many shops as well. Most popular are American Express, MasterCard, and Visa. Some banks may also be willing to advance cash against your credit card, but you have to ask around because this service is not available everywhere.

In Malaysia, to report a **lost or stolen card,** call American Express via the nearest **American Express** representative office (see individual city listings), or the head office in Kuala Lumpur (☎ 603/213-0000); for **MasterCard** Emergency Assistance for International Visitors call ☎ 1-800/88-4594; and for **Visa** Emergency Assistance call ☎ 1-800/80-1066. Both numbers are toll-free from anywhere in the country.

5 When to Go

There are two **peak seasons** in Malaysia, one in winter and another in summer. The peak winter tourist season falls roughly from the beginning of December to the end of January, covering the major winter holidays—Christmas, New Year's Day, Chinese New Year, and Hari Raya. These dates can change according to the full moon, which

Travel Tip

For up-to-date money conversion, visit CNN's Web site at **www.cnn.com/travel/currency**, or the currency chart at **www.xe.net/ict**.

dictates the exact dates of the Chinese New year and Hari Raya holidays. Note that due to the monsoon at this time (November through March), the east coast of peninsular Malaysia is rainy and the waters are rough. Resort areas, especially Tioman, are deserted and oftentimes closed. Tourist traffic slows down from February through the end of May, then picks up again in June. The peak summer season falls in the months of June, July, and August, and can last into mid-September. After September it's quiet again until December. Both seasons experience approximately equal tourist traffic, but in summer months that traffic may ebb and flow.

CLIMATE

Climate considerations will play a role in your plans. If you plan to visit any of the east coast resort areas, the low season is between November and March, when the monsoon tides make the water too choppy for water sports and beach activities. On the west coast, the rainy season is from April through May, and again from October through November.

The temperature is basically static year-round. Daily averages are between 67°F and 90°F (21°C and 32°C). Temperatures in the hill resorts get a little cooler, averaging 67°F (21°C) during the day and 50°F (10°C) at night.

CLOTHING CONSIDERATIONS   You will want to pack light, loose-fitting clothes, sticking mostly to natural fibers. Women have additional clothing requirements, as it can sometimes be uncomfortable walking through Muslim streets wearing short shorts or a sleeveless top—in many areas people *will* stare. The traditional dress for Good Muslim Women in Malaysia is that which covers the body, including the legs, arms, and head. And while many Malay women chose to continue this tradition (and with color and pizzazz, I might add), those who do not are still perfectly acceptable within Malaysia's contemporary society. As a female traveler I pack slacks and jeans, long skirts and dresses (below the knee is fine), and loose-fitting, short-sleeved cotton tops. In modern cities such as Kuala Lumpur, Johor Bahru, Malacca, Penang, and Kuching, I don't feel conspicuous in modest walking shorts, and at beach resorts I'm the first to throw on my bikini and head for the water. I always bring one lightweight long-sleeved blouse and a scarf large enough to cover my head—visits to mosques require it. If you get worried about what's appropriate, the best thing to do is to look around you and follow suit.

A tip for both male and female travelers is to wear shoes that are easily removed. Local custom asks that you remove your shoes before entering any home or place of worship

PUBLIC HOLIDAYS & EVENTS

During Malaysia's official public holidays, expect government offices to be closed, as well as some shops and restaurants, depending on the ethnicity of the shop owner or restaurant owner. **Hari Raya Puasa** and **Chinese New Year** fall close to the same dates, during which time you can expect many shop and restaurant closings. However, during these holidays, look out for special sales and celebrations. Also count on public parks, shopping malls, and beaches to be more crowded during public holidays, as locals will be taking advantage of their time off.

Official public holidays fall as follows: Hari Raya Aidil Fitri (December or January), New Year's Day (January 1), Chinese New Year (January or February), Hari-Raya Aidil-Adha (March or April), Wesak Day (May), Prophet Mohammed's Birthday (June 26), National Day (August 31), and Christmas (December 25). Where general dates are given above, expect these holidays to shift from year to year depending on the lunar calendar. The MTB can help you with exact dates as you plan your trip. In addition, each state has a public holiday to celebrate the birthday of the state Sultan.

6 Health & Insurance

The **tap water** in Kuala Lumpur is supposedly potable, but I don't recommend drinking it—in fact, I don't recommend drinking tap water anywhere in Malaysia. Bottled water is inexpensive enough and readily available at convenience stores and food stalls. **Food** prepared in hawker centers is generally safe—I have yet to experience trouble and I'll eat almost anywhere. If you buy fresh fruit, wash it well with bottled water and carefully peel the skin off before eating it.

Malaria has not been a major threat in most parts of Malaysia, even Malaysian Borneo. **Dengue fever,** on the other hand, which is also carried by mosquitoes, remains a constant threat in most areas, especially rural parts. Dengue, if left untreated, can cause fatal internal hemorrhaging, so if you come down with a sudden fever or skin rash, consult a physician immediately. There are no prophylactic treatments for dengue; the best protection is to wear plenty of insect repellent. Choose a product that contains DEET or is specifically formulated to be effective in the tropics.

For further health and insurance information, see chapter 2.

7 Getting There

BY PLANE

Malaysia has five international airports—at Kuala Lumpur, Penang, Langkawi, Kota Kinabalu and Kuching—and 14 domestic airports at locations that include Johor Bahru, Kota Bharu, Kuantan, and Kuala Terengganu. Specific airport information is listed with coverage of each city.

A passenger service charge, or **airport departure tax,** is levied on all flights. A tax of RM5 (US$1.30) for domestic flights and RM40 (US$10.50) for international flights is usually included when you pay for your ticket.

Few Western carriers fly directly to Malaysia. If Malaysian Airlines does not have suitable routes directly from your home country, you'll have to contact another airline to work out a route that connects to one of Malaysia Airline's routes.

FROM THE UNITED STATES   Malaysia Airlines (☎ 800/552-9264) flies at least once daily from Los Angeles to Kuala Lumpur, and three times a week from New York.

FROM CANADA   North American carriers will have to connect with a Malaysian Airlines flight, either in East Asia or in Europe.

FROM THE UNITED KINGDOM   Malaysia Airlines (☎ 0171/341-2020) has two daily nonstop flights from London Heathrow airport, operating domestic connections from Glasgow, Edinburgh, Teesside, Leeds Bradford, and Manchester. **British Airways** (☎ 0345/222111, a local call from anywhere within the U.K.) departs London to KL daily, except on Mondays and Fridays.

FROM AUSTRALIA   Malaysia Airlines (☎ 02/132627) flies directly to Kuala Lumpur from Perth, Adelaide, Brisbane, Darwin, Sydney and Melbourne, and flies connecting routes via one of these airports from Cairns, Coolangatta, Canberra, and Hobart. **Quantas Airlines** (☎ **02/131211**) provides service from Sydney to KL on Tuesday, Friday, and Saturday.

FROM NEW ZEALAND   **Malaysia Airlines** (☎ **09/373-2741** or 0800/657-472) flies a direct route from Auckland with connecting service from Wellington, Christchurch, Dunedin, and Palmeston.

BY TRAIN

FROM SINGAPORE   The Keretapi Tanah Melayu Berhad (KTM), Malaysia's rail system, runs express and local trains that connect the cities along the west coast of Malaysia with Singapore to the south and Thailand to the north. Trains depart three times daily from the **Singapore Railway Station** (☎ **65/222-5165**), on Keppel Road in Tanjong Pagar, not far from the city center. About five daily trains to Johor Bahru cost S$4.20 (US$2.50) for first-class passage, S$1.90 (US$1.15) for second class, and S$1.10 (US$.65) for third class for the half-hour journey. **Johor Bahru's train station** is very centrally located at Jalan Campbell (☎ **07/223-4727**), and taxis are easy to find. Trains to Kuala Lumpur depart five times daily for fares from S$60 (US$36) for first class, S$26 (US$15.60) for second class, and S$14.80 (US$8.90) for third. The trip takes around 6 hours. The Kuala Lumpur Central Railway Station is on Jalan Hishamuddin (☎ **03/273-8000**), also centrally located, with a taxi line. For Butterworth (Penang), the fare is S$118.50 (US$71.10) first class, S$51.40 (US$30.85) second class, and S$29.20 (US$17.50) third class. You will have to change trains in Kuala Lumpur. Please refer to the section on Penang for specific coverage about "getting there" options.

FROM THAILAND   KTM's international service departs from the **Hua Lamphong Railway Station** (☎ **662/223-7010** or 662/223-7020) in Bangkok, with operations to Hua Hin, Surat Thani, Nakhon Si Thammarat, and Hat Yai in Thailand's southern peninsula. The final stop in Malaysia is at Butterworth (Penang), so passage to KL will require you to catch a connecting train onward. The daily service departs at 3:15pm and takes approximately 22 hours from Bangkok to Butterworth. There is no first- or third-class service on this train, only air-conditioned second class; upper birth goes for 940B (US$25.40), and lower is 1,010B (US$27.30).

For a fascinating journey from Thailand, you can catch the **Eastern & Orient Express (E&O),** which operates a route between Bangkok, Kuala Lumpur, and Singapore. Traveling in the luxurious style for which the Orient Express is renowned, you'll finish the entire journey in about 42 hours. Compartments are classed as Sleeper (approximately US$1,248 per person double occupancy), State (US$1,758 per person double occupancy), and Presidential (US$3,270 per person double occupancy). All fares include meals on the train. Overseas reservations for the E&O Express can be made through a travel agent or, from the United States and Canada call ☎ **800/ 524-2420,** from Australia ☎ 3/9699-9766, from New Zealand ☎ 9/379-3708, and from the United Kingdom ☎ 171/805-5100. From Singapore, Malaysia, and Thailand contact the E&O office in Singapore at ☎ **65/392-3500.**

BY BUS

From Singapore, there are many bus routes to Malaysia. The easiest depart from the Johor-Singapore bus terminal at the corner of Queen and Arab streets. Buses to Kuala Lumpur leave three times daily and cost S$25 (US$6.60). Contact **The Singapore-KL bus service** at ☎ **65/292-8254.** You'll be dropped at a field outside of the city—thank goodness there's a regular shuttle to Puduraya Bus Terminal in central Kuala Lumpur for only RM1, but be prepared to line up (and try to have an RM1 coin handy). Buses to Johor Bahru and Malacca can also be picked up at this terminal, leaving at regular intervals throughout the day. Call ☎ 65/292-8149 for buses to Johor Bahru (S$2.10/US$0.55) and ☎ 65/293-5915 for buses to Malacca (S$11/US$2.90). If you wish to travel by bus to a smaller destination, the best way is to hop a bus to Johor Bahru and then transfer to a bus to your final stop.

From Thailand, you can grab a bus in either Bangkok or Hat Yai (in the Southern part of the country) heading for Malaysia. I don't recommend the bus trip from Bangkok. It's just far too long a journey to be confined to a bus. You're better off taking the train. From Hat Yai, many buses leave regularly to northern Malaysian destinations, particularly Butterworth (Penang).

BY TAXI (FROM SINGAPORE)
From the Johor-Singapore bus terminal at Queen and Arab streets, the **Singapore Johor Taxi Operators Association** (☎ **65/296-7054**) can drive you to Johor Bahru for S$28 (US$16.80) if you get to the terminal yourself, or S$40 (US$24) if you ask to be picked up at your hotel.

BY FERRY
Ferries are really only convenient for travel to Desaru and Tioman Island in Malaysia. For specific information, please refer to chapter 11.

BY CAR
For convenience, driving to Malaysia from Singapore can't be beat. You can go where you want to go, when you want to go, and without the hassle of public transportation—but it is quite expensive. Cars can be rented in Singapore (see chapter 2 for details), then driven to and even dropped off in Malaysia. A slightly cheaper option is taking the ferry from Singapore to Johor and renting there.

8 Getting Around

The modernization of Malaysia has made travel here—whether it's by plane, train, bus, taxi, or self-driven car—easier and more convenient than ever. Malaysia Airlines has service to every major destination within the peninsula and East Malaysia. Buses have a massive web of routes between every city and town. Train service up the western coast and out to the east provides even more options. And a unique travel offering—the **outstation taxi**—is available to and from every city on the peninsula. All the options make it convenient enough for you to plan to hop from city to city and not waste too much precious vacation time.

By and large, all the modes of transportation between cities are reasonably comfortable. Air travel can be the most costly of the alternatives, followed by outstation taxis, then buses and trains.

BY PLANE
Malaysia Airlines links from its hub in Kuala Lumpur (☎ **03/746-3000**) to the cities of Johor Bahru (☎ **607/334-1001**), Kota Bharu (☎ **609/744-7000**), Kota Kinabalu (☎ **6088/213-555**), Kuala Terengganu (☎ **609/622-1415**), Kuantan (☎ **609/515-7055**), Kuching (☎ **6082/246-622**), Langkawi (☎ **604/966-6622**), Penang (☎ **604/262-0011**), and other smaller cities not covered in this volume. These listed phone numbers are for Malaysia Airlines reservations offices in each city. Individual airport information is provided in sections for each city that follows. One-way domestic fares can average RM75 (US$19.75) to RM200 (US$52.65).

BY TRAIN

The Keretapi Tanah Melayu Berhad (KTM) provides train service throughout peninsular Malaysia. Trains run from north to south between the Thai border and Singapore, with stops between including Butterworth (Penang), Kuala Lumpur, and Johor Bahru. There is a second line that branches off this line at Gemas, midway between Johor Bahru and KL, and heads northeast to Tempas near Kota Bharu. Fares range from RM55.50 (US$14.60) for first-class between Johor Bahru and KL, to RM114 (US$30) for first-class passage between Johor Bahru and Butterworth. Train station information is provided for each city in individual city headings in the following chapters.

KTM has a **good deal for students.** For US$38, the ISSA Explorer Pass will get you anywhere in Malaysia for a week (US$50 for 2 weeks, US$60 for 3 weeks). The deal applies only to students under 30 who carry an ISIC International Student Identity Card, Go Card, or Youth Hostel Card. It's good for travel on second class only. Call Kuala Lumpur (☎ **03/442-4722** or fax 03/443-3707) for more information. You can also obtain a similar deal for rail travel in neighboring Thailand as well.

BY BUS

Malaysia's intercity coach system is extensive, reliable, and inexpensive. Buses depart several times daily for many destinations on the peninsula, and fares are charged according to the distance you travel. Air-conditioned express bus service (called Executive Coach service or Business Class) will cost you more, but since the fares are so inexpensive, it's well worth your while to spend the couple of extra dollars for the comfort. For an idea of price, it costs about RM16.30 (US$4.35) for service from KL to Johor Bahru, and RM18 (US$4.75) from KL to Penang. While there are more than a few independent bus companies around, for this book I've stuck to only the two major route providers, **Transnasional** and **Park May** (which operate the NiCE and Plusliner buses). I've found these companies to be more reliable and comfortable than the others. For each city covered, I've listed bus terminal locations, but scheduling information must be obtained from the bus company itself.

BY TAXI

You can take special hired cars, called **outstation taxis,** between every city and state on the peninsula. Rates depend on the distance you plan to travel. They are fixed, and stated at the beginning of the trip, but many times can be bargained down. In Kuala Lumpur, go to the second level of the Puduraya Bus Terminal to find cabs that will take you outside the city or call the Kuala Lumpur Outstation Taxi Service Station, 123 Jalan Sultan, Kuala Lumpur (☎ **03/238-3525**). A taxi from KL to Malacca will cost you approximately RM120 (US$31.60), KL to Cameron Highlands RM180 (US$47.40), KL to Butterworth or Johor Bahru RM220 (US$57.90). Outstation taxi stand locations are included under each individual city heading.

Also, within each of the smaller cities, feel free to negotiate with unmetered taxis for hourly, half-day, or daily rates. It's an excellent way to get around for sightseeing and shopping without transportation hassles. Hourly rates are anywhere from RM15 (US$3.95) to RM25 (US$6.60).

BY CAR

As recently as the 1970s, there was trouble with roadside crime—bandits stopping cars and holding up the travelers inside. Fortunately for drivers in Malaysia, this is a thing of the past. In the mid-1990s, Malaysia opened the North-South Highway, running from Bukit Kayu Hitam in the north on the Thai border to Johor Bahru at the southern tip of the peninsula. The highway (and the lack of bandits) has made travel along the west coast of Malaysia easy. There are rest areas with toilets, food outlets, and emergency telephones at intervals along the way. There is also a toll that varies depending on the distance you're traveling.

Driving along the east coast of Malaysia is actually much more pleasant than driving along the west coast. The highway is narrower and older, but it takes you through oil palm and rubber plantations, and the essence of kampung Malaysia permeates throughout. As you near villages you'll often have to slow down and swerve past cows and goats, which are really quite oblivious to oncoming traffic. You have to get very close to honk at them before they move.

The speed limit on highways is 110 kilometers per hour. On the minor highways the limit ranges from 70 to 90 kilometers per hour. Do not speed, as there are traffic police strategically situated around certain bends.

Distances between major towns are: From KL to Johor Bahru, 368 kilometers (221 miles); from KL to Malacca, 144 kilometers (86 miles); from KL to Kuantan, 259 kilometers (155 miles); from KL to Butterworth, 369 kilometers (221 miles); from Johor Bahru to Malacca, 224 kilometers (134 mi.); from Johor Bahru to Kuantan, 325 kilometers (195 miles); from Johor Bahru to Mersing, 134 kilometers (80 miles); from Johor Bahru to Butterworth, 737 kilometers (442 miles).

To rent a car in Malaysia, you must produce a driver's license from your home country that shows you have been driving at least 2 years. There are desks for major car-rental services at the international airports in Kuala Lumpur and Penang, and additional outlets throughout the country (see individual city sections for this information).

Hitchhiking is not common among locals and I don't really think it's advisable for you either. The buses between cities are very affordable, so it's a much better idea to opt for those instead.

9 Suggested Itineraries

Planning a trip to Malaysia requires a few considerations. It's important to consider the time required for traveling around the country. The trip overland from Singapore to Penang, for instance, takes up a whole day. Similarly, flying from, say, Langkawi Island to Kota Kinabalu can also take up a whole day. If your time is limited, your best bet is to narrow down your destinations within Malaysia depending on the activities that are important to you.

While Kuala Lumpur presents the most obvious choice of destinations, if you have only 3 days I'd recommend **Malacca** for its cultural charm, **Penang** for its British colonial history and good food, **Langakwi** for its luxurious beach resorts, or **Tioman Island** for laid-back beach bumming. Each are easily accessible by air, bus, or ferry from Singapore, and your travel time will be minimal. If you have a week, you can add **Kuala Lumpur** to your itinerary, or maybe a 3 day trip to **Taman Negara,** peninsular Malaysia's most exciting national park.

The most ideal itinerary would be 10 days to 2 weeks. If you're free, I'd recommend traveling north from Singapore, stopping in Malacca, Kuala Lumpur, Penang, and Langkawi. A nice trip up the east coast of the peninsula would also require at least 10 days to visit Tioman Island, Kuantan, Kuala Terengganu, and Kota Bahru.

Planning trips to **Sabah and Sarawak** usually require more time because most of the more fascinating activities here involve wildlife tours, outdoor adventure, and visits to indigenous villages, all of which require travel to the interior—quite a time-consuming proposition, but well worth the investment. Try to budget at least 10 days to enjoy any of these activities.

10 Malaysia's People, Etiquette & Customs

The mix of cultural influences in Malaysia is the result of centuries of immigration and trade with the outside world, particularly with Arab nations, China, and India. Early groups of incoming foreigners brought wealth from around the world, plus their own unique cultural heritages and religions. Further, once imported, each culture remained largely intact; that is, none have truly been homogenized. Traditional temples and churches exist side by side with mosques.

Likewise, **traditional art forms** of various cultures are still practiced in Malaysia, most notably in the areas of dance and performance art. Chinese opera, Indian dance, and Malay martial arts are all very popular cultural activities. Silat, originating from a martial arts form (and still practiced as such by many), is a dance performed by men and women. Religious and cultural festivals are open for everyone to appreciate and enjoy. Unique arts and traditions of indigenous people distinguish Sabah and Sarawak from the rest of the country.

Traditional **Malaysian music** is very similar to Indonesian music. Heavy on rhythms, its constant drum beats underneath the light repetitive melodies of the stringed gamelan (no relation at all to the Indonesian metallophone gamelan, with its gongs and xylophones), will entrance you with its simple beauty.

Questions of etiquette in Malaysia are very similar to those in Singapore, so see chapter 2 for more information.

11 Tips on Accommodations

Peak months of the year for hotels in western peninsular Malaysia are December through February and July through September. For the east coast the busy times are July through September. You will need to make reservations well in advance to secure your room during these months.

TAXES & SERVICE CHARGES   All the nonbudget hotels charge 10% service charge and 5% government tax. As such, there is no need to tip. But bellhops still tend to be tipped at least RM2 per bag and car jockeys or valets should be tipped at least RM4 or more.

12 Tips on Dining

Malaysian food seems to get its origins from India's rich curries influenced by Thailand's herbs and spices. You'll find delicious blends of coconut milk and curry, shrimp paste and chiles, accented by exotic flavors of galangal (similar to turmeric), lime, and lemongrass. Sometimes pungent, a few of the dishes have a deep flavor from fermented shrimp paste that is an acquired taste for Western palates. By and large, Malaysian food is delicious, but in multicultural Malaysia, so is the Chinese food, the Peranakan food, the Indian food—the list goes on. The Chinese brought their own flavors from their points of origin in the regions of Southern China. Teochew, Cantonese, and Szechuan are all styles of Chinese cuisine you'll find throughout the country. Peranakan food is unique to Malacca, Penang, and Singapore. The Peranakans or "Straits Chinese" combined local ingredients with some traditional Chinese dishes to create an entirely new culinary form. And Indian food, both Northern and Southern, can be found in most every city, particularly in the western part of the peninsula. And, of course you'll find gorgeous fresh seafood almost everywhere. For a more detailed description of each cuisine, see chapter 4.

I strongly recommend eating in a hawker stall when you can, especially in Penang, which is famous for its local cuisine. Also, many Malaysians eat with their hands off of banana leaves when they are having nasi padang or nasi kandar (rice with mixed dishes). This is absolutely acceptable. If you choose to follow suit, wash your hands first and try to use your right hand, as the left is considered unclean (traditionally, it's the hand used to wash after a visit to the toilet). While almost all of the food you encounter in a hawker center will be safe for eating, it is advisable to go for freshly cooked hot or soupy dishes. Don't risk the precooked items. Also, avoid having ice in your drink in the smaller towns, as it may come from a dubious water supply. If you ask for water, either make sure it's boiled or buy mineral water.

TAXES & SERVICE CHARGES   A 10% service charge and 5% government tax are levied in proper restaurants, but hawkers charge a flat price.

13 Tips on Shopping

Shopping is a huge attraction for tourists in Malaysia. In addition to modern fashions and electronics, there are great local handicrafts. In each city section, I've listed some places to go for local shopping.

For **handicrafts,** prices can vary. There are many handicraft centers, such as Karyaneka, with outlets in cities all over the country, where goods can be priced a bit higher but where you are assured of good quality. Alternatively, you could hunt out bargains in markets and at roadside stores in little towns, which can be much more fun.

Batik is one of the most popular arts in Malaysia, and the fabric can be purchased just about anywhere in the country. Batik can be fashioned into outfits and scarves or purchased as sarongs. Another beautiful Malaysian textile craft is songket weaving. These beautiful cloths are woven with metallic threads. Sometimes songket cloth is patterned into modern clothing, but usually it is sold as sarongs.

Traditional wood carvings have become popular collectors' items. Carvings by *orang asli* groups in peninsular Malaysia and by the indigenous tribes of Sabah and Sarawak have traditional uses in households or are employed for ceremonial purposes to cast off evil spirits and cure illness. They've have become much sought after by tourists.

Malaysia's **pewter products** are famous. Selangor Pewter is the brand that seems to have the most outlets and representation. You can get anything from a picture frame to dinner sets.

Silver designs are very refined, and jewelry and fine home items are still made by local artisans, especially in the northern parts of the peninsula. In addition, craft items such as wayang kulit (shadow puppets) and wau (colorful Malay kites) make great gifts and souvenirs.

Fast Facts: Malaysia

American Express   See individual city sections for offices.

Business Hours   **Banks** are open from 10am to 3pm Monday through Friday and 9:30 to 11:30am on Saturday. **Government offices** are open from 8am to

12:45pm and 2 to 4:15pm Monday through Friday and from 8am to 12:45pm on Saturday. **Smaller shops** like provision stores may open as early as 6 or 6:30am and close as late as 9pm, especially those near the wet markets. Many such stores are closed on Saturday evenings and Sunday afternoons and are busiest before lunch. Other shops are open 9:30am to 7pm. **Department stores and shops in malls** tend to open later, about 10:30am or 11am till 8:30pm or 9pm throughout the week. Bars, except for those in Penang and the seedier bars in Johor Bahru, must close at 1am. Note that in Kuala Terengganu and Kota Bharu the weekday runs from Saturday to Wednesday. The above hours generally apply to that part of the country too.

Dentists & Doctors   Consultation and treatment fees vary greatly depending on whether the practitioner you have visited operates from a private or public clinic. Your best bet is at a private medical center if your ailment appears serious. These are often expensive but, being virtual minihospitals, they have the latest equipment. If you just have a flu, it's quite safe to go to a normal M.D.—most doctors have been trained overseas, and will display diplomas on their walls. The fee at a private center ranges from RM20 to RM45 (US$5.25 to $11.85). Call ☎ **999** for emergencies.

Drug Laws   As in Singapore, the death sentence is mandatory for drug trafficking (defined as being in possession of more than 15 grams of heroin or morphine, 200 grams of marijuana or hashish, or 40 grams of cocaine). For lesser quantities you'll be thrown in jail for a very long time and flogged with a cane.

Electricity   The voltage used in Malaysia is 220–240 volts AC (50 cycles). The three-point square plugs are used, so buy an adapter if you plan to bring any appliances. Also, many larger hotels can provide adapters upon request.

Internet   Service is available to almost all of the nation, and I have found Internet cafes in the most surprisingly remote places. While the major international hotels will have access for their guests in the business center, charges can be very steep. Still, most locally operated hotels do not offer this service for their guests. For each city I have listed at least one alternative, usually for a very inexpensive hourly cost of RM5 to RM10 (US$1.30 to $2.65).

Language   The national language is Bahasa Malaysia, although English is widely spoken. Chinese dialects and Tamil are also spoken.

Liquor Laws   Liquor is sold in pubs and supermarkets in all big cities, or in provision stores. You'll hardly find any sold at Tioman though, so bring your own if you're headed there and wish to imbibe. A recent ruling requires pubs and other nightspots to officially close by 1am.

Newspapers & Magazines   English-language papers the *New Straits Times, The Star, The Sun,* and *The Edge* can be bought in hotel lobbies and magazine stands. Of the local KL magazines, *Day & Night* has great listings and local "what's happening" information for travelers.

Postal Services   Post office locations in each city covered are provided in each section. Overseas airmail postage rates are as follows: RM.50 (US$.13) for postcards and RM1.50 (US$.39) for a 100-gram letter.

Safety/Crime   While you'll find occasional news reports about robberies in the countryside, there's not a whole lot of crime going on, especially crime that would impact your trip. There's very little crime against tourists like pickpocketing and purse slashing. Still, hotels without in-room safes will keep valuables in

Telephone Dialing Info at a Glance

- **To place a call from your home country to Malaysia:** Dial the international access code (011 in the U.S., 0011 in Australia, or 00 in the U.K., Ireland, and New Zealand), plus the country code (60), plus the Malaysia area code (Cameron Highlands 5, Desaru 7, Genting Highlands 9, Johor Bahru 7, Kuala Lumpur 3, Kuala Terengganu 9, Kota Bharu 9, Kota Kinabalu 88, Kuantan 9, Kuching 82, Langkawi 4, Malacca 6, Mersing 7, Penang 4, Tioman 9), followed by the six-, seven-, or eight-digit phone number (for example, from the U.S. to Kuala Lumpur, you'd dial 011-60-3/000-0000).
- **To call Malaysia from Singapore:** dial the access code for Malaysia (02) then the city code and the number (for example, to call Kuala Lumpur, you'd dial 02 + 3 + 000-0000).
- **To call Singapore from Malaysia:** Dial the Singapore access code (02) then the number (for example, 02/000-0000). There is no need to dial the country code for calls to Singapore.
- **To place a direct international call from Malaysia:** Dial the international access code (00), plus the country code of the place you are dialing (U.S. and Canada 1, Australia 61, Republic of Ireland 353, New Zealand 64, U.K. 44), plus the area/city code and the residential number.
- **To reach the international operator:** Dial 108.
- **To place a call within Malaysia:** You must use area codes if calling between states. Note that for calls within the country, area codes are preceded by a zero (Cameron Highlands 05, Desaru 07, Genting Highlands 09, Johor Bahru 07, Kuala Lumpur 03, Kuala Terengganu 09, Kota Bharu 09, Kota Kinabalu 088, Kuantan 09, Kuching 082, Langkawi 04, Malacca 06, Mersing 07, Penang 04, Tioman 09).

the hotel safe for you. Be careful when traveling on overnight trains and buses where there are great opportunities for theft (many times by fellow tourists, believe it or not). Keep your valuables close to you as you sleep.

Taxes Hotels add a 5% government tax to all hotel rates, plus an additional 10% service charge. Larger restaurants also figure the same 5% tax into your bill, plus a 10% service charge, whereas small coffee shops and hawker stalls don't charge anything above the cost of the meal. While most tourist goods (such as crafts, camera equipment, sports equipment, and cosmetics, and select small electronic items) are tax-free, a small, scaled tax is issued on various other goods such as clothing, shoes, and accessories that you'd buy in the larger shopping malls and department stores.

Telephones & Faxes Most hotels have **international direct dialing** service and will charge extra for calls made using the service. **Local calls** can be made from public phones using coins or phone cards. Half the public phones (the coin ones) don't seem to work in Malaysia, though they'll happily eat your money. Among those that do work, one point of confusion stems from the fact that some phones take only 20 sen or 50 sen coins while others take 10 sen coins. Those that take the larger coins usually have an option for follow-on calls. If you've only spoken a short time and need to make another call, don't hang up after the first call; instead, just press the follow-on button, and you can make another local call. Otherwise, you lose your credit.

Phone cards can be purchased at convenience stores for stored value amounts. While these cards are much more handy than coins, there are three companies providing coin phone service in Malaysia, and each of them only accepts their own phone cards. Telekom, represented by blue phone boxes, is the most reliable one I've found, and locations are more abundant than the two others.

International calls can be made from phones that use cards, or from a telecom office.

Television   Guests in larger hotels will sometimes get satellite channels such as HBO, Star TV, or CNN. Another in-house movie alternative, Vision Four, pre-programs videos throughout the day. Local TV stations TV2, TV5, and TV7 show English-language comedies, movies, and documentaries.

Time   Malaysia is 8 hours ahead of Greenwich mean time, 16 hours ahead of U.S. Pacific standard time, 13 ahead of eastern standard time, and 2 hours behind Sydney. It is in the same zone as Singapore. There is no daylight saving time.

Tipping   People don't tip, except to bellhops and car jockeys. For these, an amount not less than RM4 is okay.

Toilets   To find a public toilet, ask for the *tandas*. In Malay, lelaki is male and perempuan is female. Be prepared for pay toilets. Coin collectors sit outside almost every public facility, taking RM20 per person, RM30 if you want paper. Once inside, you'll find it obvious that the money doesn't go for cleaning crews.

Water   Water in Kuala Lumpur is supposed to be potable, but most locals boil the water before drinking it—and if that's not a tip-off, I don't know what is. I advise against drinking the tap water anywhere in Malaysia. Hotels will supply bottled water in your room. If they charge you for it, expect inflated prices. A 1.5-liter bottle goes for RM7 in a hotel minibar, but RM2 at 7-Eleven.

10 Peninsular Malaysia: Kuala Lumpur & the West Coast

The most popular destinations in Malaysia dot the west coast of the peninsula where the main rail line passes through, connecting Singapore with Kuala Lumpur and on to Bangkok.

The convenience of train travel isn't the only draw of this part of the country; it also holds some of Malaysia's most significant historical towns. As you travel north from Singapore, **Johor Bahru** makes for a great day trip for those with only a short time to experience Malaysia. Three hours north of Johor Bahru, the sleepy town of **Malacca** reveals the evidence of hundreds of years of Western conquest and rule. Three hours north of Malacca, and you're in **Kuala Lumpur,** the cosmopolitan capital of the country, full of shopping, culture, history, and nightlife. Close by, **Genting Highlands** draws tourists from all over the region for the casino excitement, while the more relaxed **Cameron Highlands** offers a cool and charming respite from Southeast Asia's blaring heat. Still farther north, **Penang,** possibly Malaysia's most popular destination, retains all the charm of an old-time Southeast Asian waterfront town, full of romance (and great food!), with the added advantage of beach resorts nearby. Still farther north, just before you reach the Thai border, **Langkawi** proves that there are still a few tropical paradise islands left on the planet that are not swarming with tourists.

1 Kuala Lumpur

Kuala Lumpur (or KL as it is commonly known) is more often than not a traveler's point of entry to Malaysia. As the capital it is the most modern and developed city in the country, with contemporary highrises and world-class hotels, glitzy shopping malls and international cuisine.

The city began sometime around 1857 as a small mining town at the spot where the Gombak and Klang rivers meet, at the spot where the Masjid Jame sits in the center of the city. Fueled by tin mining in the nearby Klang River valley, the town grew under the business interests of three officials: a local Malay raja Abdullah, a British resident, and a Chinese headman (Kapitan China). The industry and village attracted Chinese laborers, Malays from nearby villages, and Indian immigrants who followed the British, and as the town grew, colonial buildings that housed local administrative offices were erected around

Kuala Lumpur

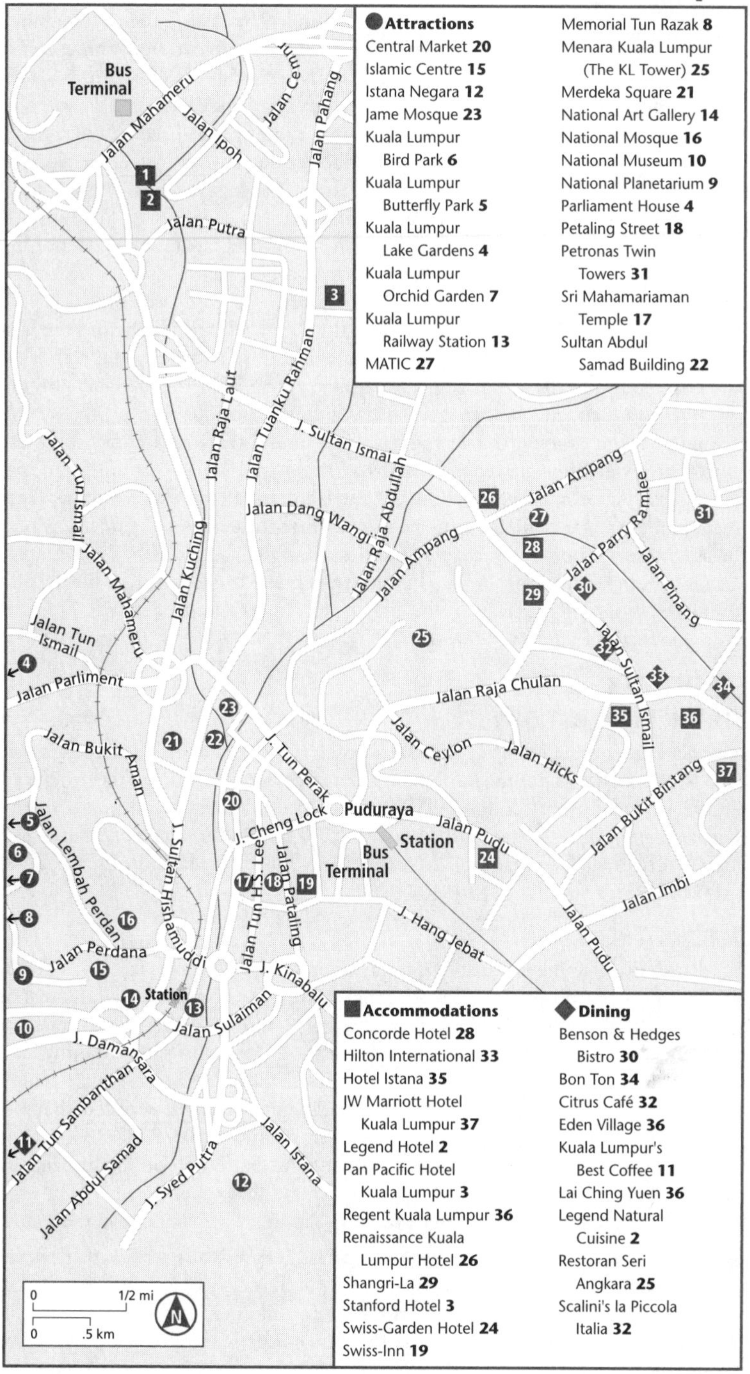
Attractions
Central Market 20
Islamic Centre 15
Istana Negara 12
Jame Mosque 23
Kuala Lumpur Bird Park 6
Kuala Lumpur Butterfly Park 5
Kuala Lumpur Lake Gardens 4
Kuala Lumpur Orchid Garden 7
Kuala Lumpur Railway Station 13
MATIC 27
Memorial Tun Razak 8
Menara Kuala Lumpur (The KL Tower) 25
Merdeka Square 21
National Art Gallery 14
National Mosque 16
National Museum 10
National Planetarium 9
Parliament House 4
Petaling Street 18
Petronas Twin Towers 31
Sri Mahamariaman Temple 17
Sultan Abdul Samad Building 22
Accommodations
Concorde Hotel 28
Hilton International 33
Hotel Istana 35
JW Marriott Hotel Kuala Lumpur 37
Legend Hotel 2
Pan Pacific Hotel Kuala Lumpur 3
Regent Kuala Lumpur 36
Renaissance Kuala Lumpur Hotel 26
Shangri-La 29
Stanford Hotel 3
Swiss-Garden Hotel 24
Swiss-Inn 19
Dining
Benson & Hedges Bistro 30
Bon Ton 34
Citrus Café 32
Eden Village 36
Kuala Lumpur's Best Coffee 11
Lai Ching Yuen 36
Legend Natural Cuisine 2
Restoran Seri Angkara 25
Scalini's la Piccola Italia 32
Bus Terminal
Jalan Mahameru
Jalan Ipoh
Jalan Cemur
Jalan Pahang
Jalan Putra
Jalan Tuanku Rahman
Jalan Raja Laut
J. Sultan Ismai
Jalan Tun Ismail
Jalan Kuching
Jalan Dang Wangi
Jalan Raja Abdullah
Jalan Ampang
Jalan Parry Ramlee
Jalan Pinang
Jalan Sultan Ismail
Jalan Parliment
Jalan Bukit Aman
Jalan Raja Chulan
Jalan Ceylon
Jalan Hicks
J. Tun Perak
Puduraya Station
Bus Terminal
Jalan Pudu
J. Cheng Lock
Jalan Tun H.S. Lee
Jalan Petaling
Jalan Bukit Bintang
Jalan Imbi
J. Hang Jebat
Jalan Lembah Perdana
J. Sultan Hishamuddi
Jalan Perdana
Station
J. Kinabalu
Jalan Sulaiman
J. Damansara
Jalan Tun Sambanthan
Jalan Abdul Samad
J. Syed Putra
Jalan Istana
0 1/2 mi
0 .5 km
N

Merdeka Square, close to Masjid Jame and bounded by Jalan Sultan Hishamuddin and Jalan Kuching. The town, and later the city, spread outward from this center.

Life in KL had many difficult starts and stops then—tin was subject to price fluctuations, the Chinese were involved in clan "wars," but worst of all, malaria was killing thousands. Still, in the late 1800s KL overcame its hurdles to become the capital of the State of Selangor, and later the capital of the Federated Malay States (Perak, Selangor, Negeri Sembilan, and Pahang) and got its big break as the hub of the Malayan network of rail lines. Its development continued to accelerate, save for during the Japanese occupation (1942–45), and in 1957, with newly won independence from Britain, Malaysia declared Kuala Lumpur its national capital.

Today the original city center at **Merdeka Square** is the core of KL's history. Buildings like the Sultan Abdul Samad Building, the Royal Selangor Club, and the Kuala Lumpur Railway Station are gorgeous examples of British style peppered with Moorish flavor. South of this area is KL's **Chinatown.** Along Jalan Petaling and surrounding areas are markets, shops, food stalls, and the bustling life of the Chinese community. There's also a **Little India** in KL, around the area occupied by Masjid Jame, where you'll find flower stalls, Indian Muslim and Malay costumes, and traditional items. Across the river you'll find **Lake Gardens,** a large sanctuary that houses Kuala Lumpur's bird park, butterfly park, and other attractions and gardens. Modern Kuala Lumpur is rooted in the city's **"Golden Triangle,"** bounded by Jalan Ampang, Jalan Tun Razak, and Jalan Imbi. This section is home to most of KL's hotels, office complexes, shopping malls, and sights like the KL Tower and the Petronas Twin Towers, the tallest buildings in the world.

ESSENTIALS
VISITOR INFORMATION

In Kuala Lumpur, the Malaysia Tourism Board has several offices. The largest is at the MATIC, the Malaysia Tourist Information Complex (see "Attractions," below), located on 109 Jalan Ampang (☎ 03/254-3929); another is located at the Kuala Lumpur Railway Station, Jalan Sultan Hishamuddin (☎ 03/274-6063); and another is at the Putra World Trade Centre, Level 2, Menara Dato 'Onn, 45 Jalan Tun Ismail (☎ 03/441-1295).

GETTING THERE

BY PLANE   The new Kuala Lumpur International Airport (KLIA) (☎ 03/8776-0259) opened in June 1998. Although its first 2 or 3 months had quite a few operational problems (such as misdirected baggage and confusing sign boards), the government has worked hard to fix the problems and the airport runs smoothly today. Located in Sepang, 53 kilometers (32 miles) outside the city, KLIA is a huge complex with business centers, dining facilities, a fitness center, medical services, shopping, post offices, and an airport hotel operated by Pan Pacific (☎ 03/8787-3333). While there are money changers, they are few and far between, so hop on the first line you see, and don't assume there's another one just around the corner.

From KLIA, domestic flights can be taken to almost every major city in the country.

Getting into Town from the Airport   There's an **express bus service** that operates until midnight daily that takes you as far as the Tun Razak Hockey Stadium. The Luxury Coach (RM25/US$6.60) departs every 15 minutes, and the Semi Luxury (RM18/US$4.75) every half hour. City **taxis** are not permitted to pick up fares from the airport, but from the stadium you can take a taxi to the city. **Airport Limousines** (☎ 03/8787-3678) operates round the clock. Coupons must be purchased at the arrival concourse for Premier Service (Mercedes, RM91.70/US$24.15) or Budget Service (Malaysian-built Proton, RM66.70/US$17.55).

BY BUS   There's more than one bus terminal in Kuala Lumpur, and it can be somewhat confusing. The main bus terminal, **Puduraya Bus Terminal,** is on Jalan Pudu right in the center of town—literally. Buses heading in and out of the station block traffic along already congested city streets, spewing noxious gasses. The terminal itself is hot, filthy, and noisy; the heavy-metal boom box wars between the provision shops is amusing for about 30 seconds. This terminal handles bus routes to all over the country, but more specifically to areas on the west coast from north to south. Buses to Penang or Malacca will leave from here. I think Puduraya is a mess to be avoided at all costs. It is a well-kept secret that many business-class and executive coaches to Penang, Johor Bahru, and Singapore depart peacefully from the **KL Railway Station,** which is a far saner alternative.

The other main terminals are the **Putra Bus Terminal** on Jalan Tun Ismail just across from the Putra World Trade Centre and the **Pekililing terminal** on Jalan Ipoh, also not far from Putra WTC. Both terminals deal primarily with buses to east coast cities such as Kota Bharu, Kuala Terengganu, and Kuantan.

The bus terminals have no telephone numbers in their own right. Inquiries must be made directly to individual bus companies.

BY TAXI   The outstation taxi stand in Kuala Lumpur is located at **Puduraya Bus Terminal** on Jalan Pudu. Call ☎ **03/238-3525** for booking to any city on the peninsula. Fares will run you about RM180 (US$47.35) to Cameron Highlands, RM120 (US$31.60) to Malacca, RM220 (US$57.90) to Johor Bahru, and RM220 (US$57.90) to Penang and to Kuantan. These taxis can pick you up at your hotel for an additional RM10 (US$2.65) upon request.

GETTING AROUND

Kuala Lumpur is a prime example of a city that was not planned, per se, from a master graph of streets. Rather, because of its beginnings as an outpost, it grew as it needed to, expanding outward and swallowing up suburbs. The result is a tangled web of streets too narrow to support the traffic of a capital city. Cars and buses weave through one-way lanes, with countless motorbikes sneaking in and out, sometimes in the opposite direction of traffic or up on the sidewalks. Expect traffic jams in the morning rush between 6 and 9am, and again between 4 and 7pm. At other times, taxis are a convenient way of getting around, as the LRT (commuter railway) doesn't hit areas most frequented by tourists, and buses are hot and crowded with some very confusing routes. Walking can also be frustrating. Many sidewalks are in poor condition, with buckled tiles and gaping gutters. The heat can be prohibitive as well. However, areas within the colonial heart of the city, Chinatown, Little India, and some areas in the Golden Triangle are within walking distance of each other.

BY TAXI   Taxis around town can be waved down by the side of the road, or can be caught at taxi stands outside shopping complexes or hotels. The metered fare is RM2 (US$0.55) for the first kilometer and an additional 10 sen for each 200 meters after that. Between midnight and 6am you'll be charged an extra 50% of the total fare. If you call ahead for a cab, there's an extra charge of RM1 (US$0.25). Government regulations have made it compulsory for cabbies to charge the metered fare, but some still try to fix a price, which is invariably higher than what the metered fare would be.

To request a cab pickup, call **KL Hotline Cab** at ☎ **03/255-3399.**

BY BUS   There are regular city buses and minibuses to take you around the city. The fare is 20 sen for the first kilometer and 5 sen for each additional kilometer. Know, however, that the buses in Kuala Lumpur are not dependable. You can wait at a stop for a long time only to find when the bus arrives that it's hot and packed so full that passengers seem to be hanging out every window. It's not the most relaxing way to get around.

BY RAIL   The **LRT,** or Light Rail Transit, has opened its first phase in Kuala Lumpur. It covers a 12-kilometer (7.4 miles) circuit, with 13 stops between Jalan Sultan Ismail and Jalan Ampang. The cost is 75 sen between stations, the longest ride costing RM2.95 (US$0.78). Tickets are purchased at LRT stations. Stored-value cards can be purchased in increments of RM20 and RM50 (US$5.25 and US$13.15). The system operates from 6am to midnight daily, with trains coming around every 5 to 10 minutes.

ON FOOT   The heat and humidity can make walking between attractions pretty uncomfortable. However, sometimes the traffic is so unbearable that you'll get where you're going much faster by strapping on your tennis shoes and hiking it.

FAST FACTS: KUALA LUMPUR

The main office for **American Express** is located in KL at The Weld, 18th floor, Jalan Raja Chulan (☎ **03/2163-5000**). You'll also find headquarters for all Malaysian and many international **banks,** most of which have outlets along Jalan Sultan Ismail plus ATMs at countless locations thought the city. Look for **money changers** in just about every shopping mall, they're a better bargain than banks or hotel cashiers.

KL's **General Post Office,** on Jalan Sultan Hishamuddin (☎ **03/2274-1122**) can be pretty overwhelming. If you can, try to use your hotel's mail service for a much easier time. **Internet service** in KL will run about RM6 (US$1.60) per hour for usage. I like **Master-World SurfNet Café,** 23 Jalan Petaling, M floor (technically it's on Jalan Cheng Lock around the corner) (☎ **03/201-0133**), which charges RM6 (US$1.60) per hour. For convenience, you can also try the **Travelers Network Station Cyber Café** on the second floor at the KL train station (☎ **03/2272-2237**), with rates of RM6 (US$1.60 per hour. If you're near the KL City Centre, try **Café Caravali,** Lot 346, third floor next to the cinema (☎ **03/382-9033**). It's a bit more expensive (RM10/US$2.65 per hour), but is a nice setting.

If you have a **medical emergency,** the number to dial is ☎ **999.** This is the same number for **police and fire emergencies** as well.

ACCOMMODATIONS

There are dozens of hotels in Kuala Lumpur, most of them within city limits; an especially large number of them are in the Golden Triangle area. Other hotels listed in this chapter are located in the Chinatown area, within walking distance of plenty of shopping attractions and nightlife.

VERY EXPENSIVE

✪ **The Regent Kuala Lumpur.** 160 Jalan Bukit Bintang, 55100 Kuala Lumpur. ☎ **800/545-4000** in the U.S. and Canada, 800/022-800 in Australia, 0800/440-800 in New Zealand, 0800/282-245 in the U.K., or 03/241-8000. Fax 03/242-1441. 468 units. A/C MINIBAR TV TEL. RM575 (US$151.30) double; RM748–RM2,070 (US$196.85–US$544.75) suite. AE, DC, JCB, MC, V.

Of the five-star properties in Kuala Lumpur, nobody delivers first-class accommodations with the finesse of The Regent. The lobby and guest rooms are contemporary and elegant, without a single sacrifice to comfort. Touches like soft armchairs and cozy comforters in each room will make you want to check in and never leave, and the large marble bathrooms will make you feel like a million bucks even on a bad-hair day. The outdoor pool is a palm-lined free-form escape, and the fitness center is state-of-the-art, with sauna, steam, spa, and Jacuzzi.

Dining: The Grill serves the best Continental fare in town in an elegant deep-wood setting, while Lai Ching Yuen (reviewed later in this chapter) remains one of KL's top-rated Chinese restaurants. There's also the handsome Terrace cafe, Edo Kirin Japanese restaurant, and the informal Brasserie cafe.

Amenities: A all rooms have voice mail and data port, with in-room fax available. There's also 24-hour room service; beauty salon; business center; fitness center; and full spa with steam, sauna, Jacuzzi, and massage; plus an outdoor pool and squash courts.

Renaissance Kuala Lumpur Hotel. Corner of Jalan Sultan Ismail and Jalan Ampang, 50450 Kuala Lumpur. ☎ **800/HOTELS-1** in the U.S. and Canada, 800/222-431 in Australia (Sydney 02/251-8484), 0800/441-111 in New Zealand, 0800/181-738 in the U.K., 800/7272 toll free in Malaysia, or 03/262-2233. Fax 03/263-1122. 400 units. A/C MINIBAR TV TEL. RM535 (US$140.80) double, RM755 (US$198.70) executive double; from RM955 (US$251.30) suite. AE, DC, JCB, MC, V.

The Renaissance is definitely geared to satisfying the needs of very discriminating travelers, and has become a very elegant address in KL. The lobby is a huge oval colonnade with a domed ceiling and massive marble columns rising from the sides of a geometric starburst on the floor. You could be walking into a futuristic version of Washington, D.C.'s Capitol Building. The guest rooms have an equally "official" feel to them—very bold and impressive, and completely European in style. In fact, you'll never know you're in Malaysia. Facilities include a very large free-form outdoor pool with beautiful landscaped terraces. The fitness center is one of the largest I've seen—and one of the most active, attracting private members from outside the hotel. It also has Jacuzzi and sauna. Other facilities include two outdoor tennis courts, a launderette, and a shopping arcade.

Dining/Diversions: Six restaurants provide excellent in-house fare: Sagano for fine Japanese dining, Marche for elegant Mediterranean, Vogue Café & Patisserie for light cuisine and baked goods, plus a poolside grill and nightly music at the Mezzo Bar & Lounge.

Amenities: Guest rooms feature three phones with voice mail plus data port, and in-house movies. Their huge, gorgeous free-form pool, set in a lovely landscaped terrace garden, is my favorite in KL, while the adjacent fitness center includes sauna and a steam bath. You can also take advantage of their concierge, tour desk, beauty salon, business center, and shops.

EXPENSIVE

Hotel Istana. 73 Jalan Raja Chulan, 50200 Kuala Lumpur. ☎ **03/241-9988.** Fax 03/244-0111. 593 units. A/C MINIBAR TV TEL. RM495–RM530 (US$130.25–US$139.45) double; RM625 (US$164.45) executive club; RM1,095 (US$288.15) suite. AE, DC, JCB, MC, V.

Fashioned after a Malay palace, Hotel Istana is rich with Moorish architectural elements, and songket weaving patterns are featured in decor elements throughout. The guest rooms have Malaysian touches like handwoven carpets and upholstery in local fabric designs, capturing the exotic flavor of the culture without sacrificing modern comfort and convenience. Located on Jalan Raja Chulan, Istana is in a favorable Golden Triangle location, within walking distance to shopping and some of the sights in that area. Ask about big rate discounts in the summer months.

Dining: Fine dining is provided by Kyoka Restaurant, with Japanese sushi, tatmi, and teppanyaki; Ristorante Bologna, serving gourmet Italian fare; and Fu Gui, a lovely rosewood tones Cantonese restaurant specializing in dim sum, seafood, and steamboat.

Amenities: Facilities include a large outdoor pool in a landscaped courtyard, a fitness center with Jacuzzi and sauna, two outdoor tennis courts, a launderette, and a shopping arcade.

JW Marriott Hotel Kuala Lumpur. 183 Jalan Bukit Bintang, 55100 Kuala Lumpur. ☎ **800/228-9290** in the U.S. and Canada, 800/251-259 in Australia (Sydney 02/299-1614), 0800/221-222 in the U.K., or 03/925-9000. Fax 03/925-7000. 552 units. A/C MINIBAR TV TEL. RM500 (US$131.60) double, RM600 (US$157.90) executive double; RM1,000 (US$263.15) suite. AE, DC, JCB, MC, V.

Opened in July 1997, the Marriott is one of the newer hotels in town. The smallish lobby area still allows for a very dramatic entrance, complete with wrought-iron filigree and marble. The modern guest rooms have a sleek, European flavor, decorated in deep greens and reds with plush carpeting, large desks, and a leather executive chair for great work space. The staff is very motivated and enthusiastic. Another great plus: The hotel is next door to some of the most upmarket and trendy shopping complexes in the city.

Dining: JW's California Grill draws regular customers daily for its light contemporary cuisine. In addition, you can have sandwiches and snacks at the Marriott Café or the poolside terrace.

Amenities: Facilities include a large outdoor pool, a very modern fitness center with Jacuzzi, sauna and spa, one outdoor tennis court, use of a nearby golf course and a shopping arcade.

☉ Kuala Lumpur Hilton International. Jalan Sultan Ismail, 50250 Kuala Lumpur. ☎ **800/445-8667** in the U.S. Fax 03/244-2157. www.hilton.com. 577 units. A/C MINIBAR TV TEL. RM483 (US$127.10) double; RM860–RM5,080 (US$226.30–US$1,336.85) suite. AE, DC, JCB, MC, V.

The Hilton opened in 1973, making it the first world-class hotel in Kuala Lumpur. Situated on Jalan Sultan Ismail, it's in the middle of the business and shopping heart of the city. The hotel is set back from the road, stately and quiet, giving guests a bit of peace and quiet. The guest rooms are very spacious, with separate dressing areas, a sitting area, and nice desk space. City view rooms deliver fantastically on what they promise.

Dining/Diversions: Hilton's Tsui Yuen Cantonese restaurant serves a daily dim sum lunch, with weekday all-you-can-eat specials. FIC's Restaurant & Bar has mixed East and West cuisine in a contemporary setting, while the Planter's Inn serves local and Western food in a more casual setting. There's also Gourmet House delicatessen, plus TM2 Fun Bar (with live music nightly) and the Churchill Cigar Salon.

Amenities: Shopping arcade, small outdoor pool (with a view of the Petronas Twin Towers), and a popular fitness center with massage, sauna, steam, and facials.

The Pan Pacific Hotel Kuala Lumpur. Jalan Putra, P.O. Box 11468, 50746 Kuala Lumpur. ☎ **800/327-8585** in the U.S. and Canada, 800/625-959 in Australia (Sydney 02/923-37888), or 03/442-5555. Fax 03/441-7236. 565 units. A/C MINIBAR TV TEL. RM520–RM650 (US$136.85–US$171.05) double; from RM960 (US$252.65) suite. AE, DC, JCB, MC, V.

One thing you'll love about staying at the Pan Pacific is the view from the glass elevator as you drift up to your floor. The atrium lobby inside is bright and airy and filled with the scent of jasmine, and the hotel staff handles the demands of its international clientele with courtesy and professionalism. The rooms are spacious and stately. Sunken windows with lattice work frame each view.

Dining: The centerpiece here is Keyaki, a Japanese restaurant featuring a host of delicacies hard to find elsewhere. There's also the Hai Tien Lo Cantonese restaurant and the brasserie-style Selera Restaurant.

Amenities: Facilities include a midsized outdoor pool, fitness center with Jacuzzi and sauna, and squash and tennis courts.

✪ **The Shangri-La Hotel Kuala Lumpur.** 11 Jalan Sultan Ismail, 50250 Kuala Lumpur. ☎ 800/942-5050 in the U.S. and Canada, 800/222-448 in Australia, 0800/442-179 in New Zealand, or 03/232-2388. Fax 03/202-1245. 681 units. A/C MINIBAR TV TEL. RM420–RM505 (US$110.55–US$132.90) double; RM575 (US$151.30) executive club room; RM1,300 (US$342.10) suite. AE, DC, JCB, MC, V.

I don't know how they do it, but Shangri-La can always take what could easily be a dull building in a busy city and turn it into a resort-style garden oasis. Their property in KL is no different. With attention paid to landscaping and greenery, the hotel is one of the more attractive places to stay in town. The guest rooms are large with cooling colors and nice views of the city.

Dining/Diversions: Shangri-La hotels always have great choices for dining. This one offers Restaurant Lafite for classic French cuisine, Nadaman Japanese restaurant, Shang Palace Cantonese restaurant, and a coffee garden and pool cafe. Also check out their pub, cigar bar, and wine shop.

Amenities: The outdoor pool area was recently renovated, as was the fitness center (with totally new equipment). Other facilities include a travel office and a shopping arcade.

MODERATE

✪ **Concorde Hotel Kuala Lumpur.** 2 Jalan Sultan Ismail, 50250 Kuala Lumpur. ☎ 03/244-2200. Fax 03/244-1628. 610 units. A/C MINIBAR TV TEL. RM320 (US$84.20) double; RM530–RM1,880 (US$139.45–US$494.75) suite. AE, DC, JCB, MC, V.

Jalan Sultan Ismail is the address for the big names in hotels, like Shangri-La and Hilton, but tucked alongside the giants is the Concorde, a very reasonably priced choice. What's best about staying here is that you don't sacrifice amenities and services for the lower cost. Although rooms are not as large as those in the major hotels, they're well outfitted in an up-to-date style that can compete with the best of them. Choose Concorde if you'd like location and comfort for less. It also has a small outdoor pool facing a fitness center. A well-equipped business center adds additional value.

The Legend Hotel. Putra Place, 100 Jalan Putra, 50350 Kuala Lumpur. ☎ 800/637-7200 in the U.S., 1800/655-147 in Australia, 0800/25-28-40 in the U.K., or 03/442-9888. Fax 03/443-0700. 400 units. A/C MINIBAR TV TEL. RM380–RM530 (US$100–US$139.45) double; RM630 (US$165.80) Legend Crest; RM830 (US$218.40) executive suite. AE, DC, JCB, MC, V.

Lovely marble in earthy tones creates a luxurious atmosphere in the Legend's public space, which is enhanced with Chinese touches such as carved wood furniture and terra-cotta warrior statues—and since the lobby is located nine stories above street level, there's not the usual commotion in it. Guest rooms are spacious, and all overlook the city, but ask to face the Twin Towers for the best view. Also, the less expensive rooms seem to have the nicest decor, with soft tones and modern touches. The Crest rooms are rather strange—mine had a bright pink frilly bedcover. Facilities include an outdoor pool, fitness center with Jacuzzi and sauna, squash courts, a launderette, and a shopping arcade.

✪ **Swiss-Garden Hotel.** 117 Jalan Pudu, 55100 Kuala Lumpur. ☎ **03/241-3333,** or 800/3093 toll-free in Malaysia. Fax 03/241-5555. www.sgihotels.com.my. 326 units. A/C MINIBAR TV TEL. RM320–RM390 (US$84.20–US$102.65) double; RM430–RM600 (US$113.15–US$157.90) suite. AE, DC, JCB, MC, V.

For mid-range prices, Swiss-Garden offers reliable comfort, good location, and affordability that attracts many leisure travelers to its doors. It also knows how to make you feel right at home, with a friendly staff (the concierge is on the ball) and a hotel lobby bar that actually gets patronized (by travelers having cool cocktails at the end of a busy day of sightseeing). The guest rooms are simply furnished, but are neat and comfortable. Swiss-Garden is just walking distance from KL's lively Chinatown district, and close to the Puduraya bus station. Facilities include an outdoor pool and a fitness center.

INEXPENSIVE

Stanford Hotel. 449 Jalan Tuanku Abdul Rahman, 50100 Kuala Lumpur. ☎ **03/291-9833.** Fax 03/291-3103. 168 units. A/C TV TEL. RM166–RM235 (US$43.70–US$61.85) double. AE, MC, V.

The Stanford Hotel is a good alternative for the budget-conscious traveler. The lobby feels like a miniversion of a more upmarket hotel, and with new carpeting in the corridors and guest rooms, fresh paint, and refurbished furnishings and bathrooms, the place provides accommodations that are good value for your money. And some of the rooms even have lovely views of the Petronas Twin Towers. Discounted rates as low as RM100 (US$26.30) can be had if you ask about promotions. Facilities are thin, with only a small business center and a coffeehouse serving up decent local dishes.

✪ **Swiss-Inn.** 62 Jalan Sultan, 50000 Kuala Lumpur. ☎ **03/232-3333.** Fax 03/201-6699. www.sgihotels.com.my. 110 units. A/C TV TEL. RM150–RM184 (US$39.45–$48.40) double. AE, DC, JCB, MC, V.

You can't beat the Swiss-Inn for comfortable and modern accommodations in Kuala Lumpur. Tucked away in the heart of Chinatown, just beyond this hotel's small lobby is the action of the street markets and hawkers. The place is small, and offers almost no facilities, but the compact rooms are clean and adequate. Best yet, discounts here can bring the rates down under RM100 (US$26.30) (*beware:* lower-category rooms have no windows). Make sure you reserve your room early, because this place runs at high occupancy year round. The hotel offers in-house movies, and has a 24-hour sidewalk coffeehouse. Guests have access to the Swiss-Garden Hotel's fitness center.

DINING

Kuala Lumpur, like Singapore, is very cosmopolitan. Here you'll not only find delicious and exotic cuisine, but you'll find it served in some pretty trendy settings.

Benson & Hedges Bistro. Ground floor, Life Centre, Jalan Sultan Ismail. ☎ **03/ 2164-4426.** Reservations not accepted. Entrees RM13.50–RM35 (US$3.55–US$9.20). AE, DC, MC, V. Daily 7–10am breakfast, 11am–3pm lunch; Sun–Thurs dinner from 6pm–midnight, Fri–Sat from 6pm–2am. TEX-MEX/AMERICAN.

The latest in trendy hangouts, this bistro is part coffee bar and part restaurant, decorated in contemporary style, with mood lighting glistening off bronze coffee bean dispensers. While it's not a place for a special night out, it is an excellent choice for a quick and easy bite in a fun and laid-back atmosphere. Staff is dressed in black, with casual and hip attitudes. Good entrees are the chicken piccata, roast duck lasagna, or the blackened rack of lamb. Reservations are not accepted, and on the weekends the wait can be long, partly because no one will ever rush you to get you out. In short, be there early.

✪ **Bon Ton.** No.7 Jalan Kia Peng. ☎ **03/241-3611.** Reservations recommended. Entrees RM20–RM55 (US$5.25–US$14.45). Set meals RM40–RM101 (US$10.55–US$26.60). AE, DC, MC, V. Lunch Mon–Fri noon–2:30pm. Dinner daily 6–10:30pm. ASIAN MIX.

Let me tell you about my favorite restaurant in Kuala Lumpur. First, Bon Ton has an incredible atmosphere. In a 1930s bungalow that was once a school, the place winds through room after room, its walls painted in bright hues and furnished with an assortment of mix-and-matched teak tables, chairs, and antiques. Second, the menu is fabulous. While à la carte is available, Bon Ton puts together theme set meals. You have 12 to chose from, including Nonya, Malacca Portuguese, Traditional Malay, even vegetarian. They're all brilliant.

Citrus Café. 19 Jalan Sultan Ismail. ☎ **03/242-5188.** Entrees RM24–RM46 (US$6.30–US$12.10). AE, DC, JCB, MC, V. Daily noon–2:30pm lunch; 6–10:30pm dinner. ASIAN MIX.

This place has become very popular with the yuppie international set—locals, expatriates, and tourists alike. The theme is Asia, contemporary style, and is reflected in the decor, music, and cuisine, which ranges from Malay to Thai to Japanese, with some Western elements thrown in too. The dining room, sushi bar, and terrace cafe are sparse and minimal. Dishes like the rotisserie chicken and the special sushi rolls are served in portions to share at your table.

✪ **Eden Village.** 260 Jalan Raja Chulan. ☎ **03/241-4027.** Reservations recommended. Entrees RM18–RM100 and up (US$4.75–US$26.30). AE, MC, V. Daily noon–3pm and 7pm–midnight, closed for lunch on Sun. SEAFOOD.

Uniquely designed inside and out to resemble a Malay house, Eden Village has great local atmosphere. Waitresses are clad in traditional *sarong kebaya,* and serve up popular dishes like braised shark's fin in a clay pot with crabmeat and roe, and the Kingdom of the Sea (a half lobster baked with prawns, crab, and cuttlefish). The terrace seating is the best in the house.

✪ **Lai Ching Yuen.** The Regent Kuala Lumpur, 160 Jalan Bukit Bintang. ☎ **03/249-4250.** Reservations recommended. Entrees RM26–RM58 (US$6.85–US$15.25). AE, DC, JCB, MC, V. Daily noon–2:30pm lunch; 6:30–10:30pm dinner. CANTONESE.

In the Regent's signature elegant style, dining is truly fine at Lai Ching Yuen. With delicacies like shark's fin, bird's nest, abalone, and barbecue specialties, the menu is extensive. A lunchtime dim sum and set lunch menu are also excellent. Each dish is presented as a piece of art. The restaurant is large and sectioned with etched glass panels. Gorgeous accents are added with modern Chinese art and silver and jade table settings.

Legend Natural Cuisine. The Legend Hotel and Apartments, 100 Jalan Putra. ☎ **03/442-9888.** Reservations recommended for lunch and dinner; required for high tea. Entrees RM38–RM55 (US$10–US$14.45). AE, DC, JCB, MC, V. Daily 6:30am–1am. INTERNATIONAL.

Legend Natural Cuisine's menu is selected by dieticians, its dishes incorporating organically grown produce and calorie-conscious recipes with a mind toward health awareness. Off the Legend Hotel's lobby, the restaurant is spacious and cozy, and the food is so good you'll never know it's healthy. It's easy to forget about dieting when you're traveling, but Legend Natural Cuisine makes it incredibly easy to stick to one. Try the rack of lamb, and the forest mushroom soup is an unbelievably good appetizer.

Restoran Seri Angkasa. Jalan Punchak, off Jalan P. Ramlee. ☎ **03/208-5055.** Reservations recommended. Lunch buffet RM55 (US$14.45); dinner buffet RM75 (US$19.75). AE, DC, MC, V. Daily noon–2:30pm lunch; 3:30–5:30pm high tea; 6:30–11pm dinner. MALAYSIAN.

At the top of the Menara KL (KL Tower) is Restoran Seri Angkasa, a revolving restaurant with the best view in the city. Better still, it's a great way to try all the Malay-, Chinese-, and Indian-inspired local dishes at a convenient buffet, with a chance to taste just about everything you have room for—like nasi goreng, clay-pot noodles, or beef rendang.

✪ **Scalini's la Piccola Italia.** 19 Jalan Sultan Ismail. ☎ **03/245-3211.** Reservations recommended. Entrees RM26–RM58 (US$6.85–US$15.25). AE, DC, MC, V. Sun–Thurs noon–2:30pm and 6–10:30pm, Fri noon–2:30pm and 6–11pm, Sat 6–11pm. ITALIAN.

Four chefs from Italy create the dishes that make Scalini's a favorite among KL locals and expatriates. From a very extensive menu you can select pasta, fish, and meat, as well as a large selection of pizzas. The specials are superb and change all the time. Some of the best dishes are salmon with creamed asparagus sauce and ravioli with goat cheese and zucchini. Scalini's has a large wine selection (that is actually part of the romantic decor) with labels from California, Australia, New Zealand, France, and, of course, Italy.

ATTRACTIONS

Most of Kuala Lumpur's historic sights are located in the area around Merdeka Square/Jalan Hishamuddin area, while many of the gardens, parks, and museums are out at Lake Gardens. Taxi fare between the two areas will run you about RM5 (US$1.30).

✪ **Central Market.** Jalan Benteng. ☎ **03/2274-6542.** Daily 10am–10pm. Shops until 8pm.

The original Central Market, built in 1936, used to be a wet market, but the place is now a cultural center (air-conditioned!) for local artists and craftspeople selling antiques, crafts, and curios. It is a fantastic place for buying Malaysian crafts and souvenirs, with two floors of shops to chose from. The Central Market also stages evening performances (at 8:15pm) of Malay martial arts, Indian classical dance, or Chinese orchestra. Call the number above for performance information.

Kuala Lumpur Railway Station. Jalan Sultan Hishamuddin. ☎ **03/274-9422.** Daily 7:30am–10:30pm.

Built in 1910, the KL Railway Station is a beautiful example of Moorish architecture.

✪ **National Museum (Muzim Negara).** Jalan Damansara. ☎ **03/282-6255.** Admission RM1 (US$0.26), children under 10 free. Sat–Thurs 9am–6pm, Fri 9am–noon and 3–6pm.

Located at Lake Gardens, the museum has more than 1,000 items of historic, cultural, and traditional significance, including art, weapons, musical instruments, and costumes.

National Art Gallery. Jalan Sultan Hishamuddin (across in the KL Railway Station). ☎ **03/4025-4990.** Free admission. Sat–Thurs 10am–6pm, Fri 10am–noon and 3–6pm.

The building that now houses the National Art Gallery was built as the Majestic Hotel in 1932 and has been restored to display contemporary works by Malaysian artists. There are international exhibits as well.

National Mosque (Masjid Negara). Jalan Sultan Hishamuddin (near the KL Railway Station). No phone.

Built in a modern design, the most distinguishing features of the mosque are its 73-meter (243-ft.) minaret and the umbrella-shaped roof, which is said to symbolize a newly independent Malaysia's aspirations for the future. Could be true, as the place was built in 1965, the year Singapore split from Malaysia.

Sultan Abdul Samad Building. Jalan Raja. No phone.

In 1897 this exotic building was designed by Regent Alfred John Bidwell, a colonial architect responsible for many of the buildings in Singapore. He chose a style called "Muhammadan" or "Neo-saracenic," which combines Indian Muslim architecture with Gothic and other Western elements. Built to house government administrative offices, today it is the home of Malaysia's Supreme and High Courts.

Merdeka Square. Jalan Raja.

Surrounded by colonial architecture with an exotic local flair, the square is a large field that was once the site of British social and sporting events. These days, Malaysia holds its spectacular Independence Day celebrations on the field, which is home to the world's tallest flagpole, standing at 100 meters (330 ft.).

National Planetarium. Lake Gardens. ☎ **03/2273-5484.** Admission to exhibition hall RM1 (US$0.26), children under 10 free; extra charges for screenings. Sat–Thurs 10am–7pm, Fri 10am–noon and 2:30–7pm.

The National Planetarium has a Space Hall with touch-screen interactive computers and hands-on experiments, a Viewing Gallery with binoculars for a panoramic view of the city, and an Ancient Observatory Park with models of Chinese and Indian astronomy systems. The Space Theatre has two different outer-space shows.

✪ **Jame Mosque (Masjid Jame).** Jalan Tun Terak. No phone.

The first settlers landed in Kuala Lumpur at the spot where the Gombak and Klang rivers meet, and in 1909 a mosque was built here. Styled after an Indian Muslim design, it is one of the oldest mosques in the city.

Petronas Twin Towers. Kuala Lumpur City Centre. No phone.

After 5 years of planning and building, Petronas Twin Towers has been completed. Standing at a whopping 451.9 meters (1,482 ft.) above street level, the towers are the tallest buildings in the world. From the outside, the structures are designed with the kind of geometric patterns common to Islamic architecture, and on levels 41 and 42 the two towers are linked by a bridge. Opened just after the regional economic crisis, the 88 floors of each tower are half empty—not because tourists aren't allowed in to look around, but because they can't rent the space.

Islamic Centre. Jalan Perdana. ☎ **03/2274-9333.** Sat–Thurs 7:30am–4:45pm; Fri 7:30am–12:15pm and 2:30–4:45pm.

The seat of Islamic learning in Kuala Lumpur, the center has displays of Islamic texts, artifacts, porcelain, and weaponry.

Istana Negara. Jalan Negara. No phone.

Closed to the public, this is the official residence of the king. You can peek through the gates at the istana (palace) and its lovely grounds.

✪ **Menara Kuala Lumpur (The KL Tower).** Bukit Nanas. ☎ **03/208-5448.** Adults RM8 (US$2.10); children RM3 (US$0.79). Daily 10am–10pm.

Standing 421 meters (1,389 ft.) tall, this concrete structure is the third tallest tower in the world, and the views from the top reach to the far corners of the city and beyond. At the top, the glass windows are fashioned after the Shah Mosque in Isfahan, Iran.

MATIC (Malaysia Tourist Information Complex). Jalan Ampang. ☎ **03/2164-3929.** Daily 9am–6pm.

At MATIC you'll find an exhibit hall, tourist information services for Kuala Lumpur and Malaysia, and other travel-planning services. On Tuesdays, Thursdays, Saturdays, and Sundays, there are cultural shows at 2pm. Shows are RM2 (US$0.53) for adults, RM1 (US$0.26) for children.

Kuala Lumpur Lake Gardens (Taman Tasik Perdana). Enter via Jalan Parliament. Free admission. Daily 9am–6pm. No phone.

Built around an artificial lake, the 91.6-hectare (229-acre) park has plenty of space for jogging and rowing, and has a playground for the kids. It's the most popular park in Kuala Lumpur.

Kuala Lumpur Orchid Garden. Jalan Perdana. ☎ **03/293-0191.** Adults RM1 (US$0.26), children RM.50 (US$0.13). Daily 9am–6pm.

This garden has a collection of over 800 orchid species from Malaysia, and also contains thousands of international varieties.

Kuala Lumpur Bird Park. Jalan Perdana. ☎ **03/274-2042.** Adults RM3 (US$0.79), children RM1 (US$0.26). Daily 9am–5pm.

Nestled in beautifully landscaped gardens, the bird park has over 2,000 birds within its 3.2 hectares (8 acres).

Kuala Lumpur Butterfly Park. Jalan Cenderasari. ☎ **03/293-4799.** Adults RM4 (US$1.05), children RM2 (US$0.53). Daily 9am–6pm.

Over 6,000 butterflies belonging to 120 species make their home in this park, which has been landscaped with more than 15,000 plants to simulate the butterflies' natural rain forest environment. There are also other small animals and an insect museum.

Memorial Tun Razak. Jalan Perdana. ☎ **03/291-2111.** Free admission. Tues–Thurs and Sat–Sun 9am–6pm, Fri 9am–noon and 3–6pm.

Tun Razak was Malaysia's second prime minister, and this museum is filled with his personal and official memorabilia.

Parliament House. Jalan Parliament. Parliament sessions are not open to the public. No phone.

In the Lake Gardens area, the Parliament House is a modern building housing the country's administrative offices, which were once in the Sultan Abdul Samad Building at Merdeka Square.

Sri Mahamariaman Temple. Jalan Bandar. No phone.

With a recent face-lift (Hindu temples must renovate every 12 years), this bright temple livens the gray street scene around. It's a beautiful temple tucked away in a narrow street in KL's Chinatown area, which was built by Thambusamy Pillai, a pillar of old KL's Indian community.

✪ Petaling Street.

This is the center of KL's Chinatown district. By day, stroll past hawker stalls, dim sum shops, wet markets, and all sorts of shops, from pawn shops to coffin makers. At night, a crazy bazaar (which is terribly crowded) pops up—look for designer knockoffs, fake watches, and pirate VCDs (Video CDs) here.

GOLF

People from all over Asia flock to Malaysia for its golf courses, many of which are excellent standard courses designed by pros. The **Bangi Golf Resort,** No. 1 Persiaran Bandar, Bandar Baru Bangi, 43650 Selangor (☎ 03/825-3728; fax 03/825-3726), has 18 holes, par 72, designed by Ronald Fream, with greens fees of RM100 (US$26.30) weekdays, RM170 (US$44.75) weekends and holidays. **The Mines**

Resort & Golf Club, 10¹/₅ mile, Jalan Sungei Besi, 43300 Seri Kembangan, Selangor (☎ 03/943-2288), features 18 holes, par 71, designed by Robert Trent Jones, Jr., with greens fees of RM280 (US$73.70) weekdays, RM350 (US$92.10) weekend and holidays. **Suajana Golf & Country Club,** km 3, Jalan Lapangan Terbang Sultan Abdul Aziz Shah, 46783 Subang Selangor (☎ 03/746-1466; fax 03/746-7818), has two 18-hole courses, each par 72, deigned by Robert Trent Jones, Jr., with greens fees of RM170 (US$44.75) weekdays, RM290 (US$76.30) weekends and holidays.

SHOPPING

Kuala Lumpur is a truly great place to shop. In recent years, mall after mall has risen from city lots, filled with hundreds of retail outlets selling everything from haute couture to cheap chic clothing, electronic goods, jewelry, and arts and crafts. The major **shopping malls** are located in the area around Jalan Bukit Bintang and Jalan Sultan Ismail. There are also a few malls along Jalan Ampang. **Suria KLCC,** located just beneath the Petronas Twin Towers, has to be KLs best and brightest mall, and its largest. If you purchase electronics, make sure you get an international warranty.

Still the best place for Malaysian handicrafts, the huge **Central Market** on Jalan Benteng (☎ 03/2274-6542) keeps any shopper saturated for hours. There you'll find a jumble of local artists and craftspeople selling their wares in the heart of town. It's also a good place to find Malaysian handicrafts from other regions of the country. One specific shop I like to recommend for Malaysian handicrafts is **Karyaneka,** Lot B, Kompleks Budaya Kraf (☎ 03/264-4344), with a warehouse selection of assorted goods from around the country, all of it fine quality.

Another favorite shopping haunt in KL is **Chinatown,** along Petaling Street. Day and night, it's a great place to wander and bargain for knockoff designer clothing and accessories, sunglasses, T-shirts, souvenirs, fake watches, and pirated videos.

Pasar malam (night markets) are very popular evening activities in KL. Whole blocks are taken up with these brightly lit and bustling markets packed with stalls selling everything you can dream of. They are likely to pop up anywhere in the city. Two good bets for catching one: Go to Jalan Haji Taib after dark until 10pm. On Saturday nights, head for Jalan Tuanku Abdul Rahman.

NIGHTLIFE

There's nightlife to spare in KL, from fashionable lounges to sprawling discos to pubs perfect for lounging. Basically, you can expect to pay about RM11 to RM20 (US$2.90 to US$5.25) for a pint of beer, depending on what and where you order. While quite a few pubs are open for lunch, most clubs won't open until about 6 or 7pm. These places must all close by 1am, so don't plan on staying out too late. Nearly all have a happy hour, usually between 5 and 7pm, when drink discounts apply on draft beers and "house-pour" (lower shelf) mixed drinks. Generally, you're expected to wear dress casual clothing for these places, but avoid old jeans, tennis shoes, and very revealing outfits.

While there are some very good places in Kuala Lumpur, the true nightlife spot is in a place called ✪ **Bangsar,** just outside the city limits. It's 2 or 3 blocks of bars, cafes, and restaurants that cater to a variety of tastes (in fact, so many expatriates hang out there, they call it Kweiloh Lumpur, "Foreigner Lumpur" in Mandarin). Every taxi driver knows where it is. Get in and ask to go to Jalan Telawi Tiga in Bangsar (fare should be no more than RM5 or RM6), and once there it's very easy to catch a cab back to town. Begin at **The Roof** (☎ 03/282-7168), a three-story open-air cafe/bar that looks like a crazy Louisiana cathouse (you really can't miss it). From there you can try **Echo** (☎ 03/248-3022) for some funky dance music; **Grappa** (☎ 03/287-0080), a sophisticated wine bar; or **Finnegan's** (☎ 03/284-0187), a very rowdy Irish bar. And that's only the beginning.

Back in Kuala Lumpur, there are some very good bars and pubs that I'd recommend. **Bier Keller,** on the ground floor, Menara Haw Par, Jalan Sultan Ismail (☎ 03/201-3313), serves German beers in tankards and traditional German cuisine such as sauerkraut and beer bread. **Delaney's,** ground floor, Park Royal Hotel, Jalan Sultan Ismail (☎ 03/241-5195), has a good selection of draft beers.

For a little live music with your drinks, the **Hard Rock Cafe,** Wisma Concorde, Jalan Sultan Ismail next to Concorde Hotel (☎ 03/244-4152), hosts the best of the regional bands, which play nightly for a crowd of locals, tourists, and expatriates who take their parties very seriously.

While many of the larger dance clubs in the city cater to young clientele, a good choice for a more upscale dance party is **Modesto's,** Rohas Berkasa, Jalan P. Ramlee (☎ 03/381-1998).

2 Johor Bahru

Johor Bahru, the capital of the state of Johor, is at the southern tip of the Malaysian peninsula, where Malaysia's north-south Highway comes to its southern terminus. Since it's just over the causeway from Singapore, a very short jump by car, bus, or train, it's a popular point of entry to Malaysia. Johor Bahru, or "JB," is not the most fascinating destination in Malaysia, but for a quick day visit from Singapore or as a stopover en route to other Malaysian destinations, it offers some good shopping, sightseeing, and dining.

Johor's early beginnings were very closely entwined with nearby Malacca's. The Portuguese and Dutch, who each had their eye on the successful city-port, used Johor as a stepping-stone—the Portuguese pummeled the place to get to Malacca in 1511, and in 1641 the Dutch formed a strategic alliance with Johor to overthrow the Portuguese. In an ironic twist, Malacca's success did not continue under the Portuguese or the Dutch. In fact, by the 1700s, favorable rights bestowed upon Johor turned the state into a powerful threat to Malacca's trade. Eventually the envious Dutch attacked Johor, driving its leaders to establish a capital on the island of Riau, just south of the peninsula.

Under the successful administration of the Temenggong and Bendahara families (ministerial agents for the Sultanate), Riau grew into a very successful entry port. But conflict between the two families led to the assassination of the Sultan. The city was weakened, as the Malays believed the Sultan to be the last direct descendent of Raja Iskander Zul-karnain, Alexander the Great, and his passing left a great void. This fragile state left the city vulnerable to the Bugis, who came to settle to escape conflict in their home in southern Sulawesi. The Bugis, master navigators and skilled traders with countless allies, catapulted Riau's status ever higher, but in meddling with affairs of the leadership won few supporters among the local Malays. By 1721, the Bugis were ruling under a puppet sultan, yet intermarriage secured the Bugis bloodline that many Malays carry with them to this day.

In 1757 the Malays once again aligned themselves with the Dutch to overthrow the Bugis, and by 1760 all foreign-born Bugis were expelled. However, the economic success of Riau waned in the decades to follow. The Bugis-controlled sultan was deposed, and the Dutch appointed one of his sons, Abdul Rahman, as his successor.

It was Temmenggong Ibrahim, under that Sultan Abdul Rahman, who signed a treaty in 1819 with Sir Stamford Raffles, allowing the British East India Company to set up shop on Singapore. During the 1800s Singapore's success greatly overshadowed Riau's former glory. In the mid-1800s under Sultan Abu Bakar (who was raised and educated in Singapore), Johor became an administerial extension of Singapore. In 1866 Johor Bahru was named the state capital, and it was developed with a Western-style government. Hence, today Abu Bakar is known as "The Father of Modern Johor." Finally, in 1914 Johor was placed under the Federated States of Malaya. The sultan lost his power, except to perform ceremonial duties—for example, his successors could retain the official yellow costume of the sultanate. To this day no one (including you) is permitted to wear yellow at the sultan's favorite golf courses (especially at the Royal Johor Golf Club). The present sultan is His Majesty Sultan Iskander, who has held the title since 1981.

ESSENTIALS
VISITOR INFORMATION
The Malaysia Tourism Board office in Johor Bahru is at the **Johor Tourist Information Centre** (JOTIC), centrally located on Jalan Ayer Molek, on the second floor (☎ **07/224-2000**). Information is available not only for Johor Bahru, but for the state of Johor as well.

GETTING THERE
BY CAR   If you arrive by car via the causeway you will clear the immigration checkpoint (☎ **07/223-5007**) upon entering the Malaysia side.

BY BUS   Buses to and from other parts of Malaysia are based at the Larkin Bus Terminal off Jalan Garuda in the northern part of the city. Taxis are available at the terminal to take you to the city. The easiest way to catch a bus from KL is at the KL Railway Station. **Plusliner** (☎ **03/227-2760**) runs service 10 times daily for RM16.30 (US$4.30). The trip takes just under 6 hours. Most all other cities in Malaysia have service to Johor Bahru. Consult each city section for bus terminal information. From Singapore, the **Singapore-Johor Express** (☎ **65/292-8149**) operates every 10 minutes between 6:30am and midnight from the Ban Sen Terminal at Queen Street near Arab Street, Singapore. The cost for the half-hour trip is S$2.10 (US$1.25).

If you're looking to depart Johor Bahru via bus, contact one of the following companies at Larkin for route information: **Transnasional** (☎ **07/224-5182**) or **Plusliner/ NICE** (☎ **07/222-3317**).

BY TRAIN   The **Keretapi Tanah Melayu Berhad** (KTM) trains arrive and depart from the Johor Bahru Railway Station at Jalan Tun Abdul Razak, opposite Merlin Tower (☎ **07/223-4727**). Catch trains from KL's Railway Station (☎ **03/274-7434**) four times daily for a cost between RM13.70 and RM55.50 (US$3.60 and US$14.60), depending on the class you travel. From the **Singapore Railway Station** (☎ **65/222-5165**), on Keppel Road in Tanjong Pagar, the short trip is between S$1.10 and S$4.20 (US$0.66 and US$2.50).

BY PLANE   The **Sultan Ismail Airport,** 30 to 40 minutes outside the city (☎ **07/599-4737**), has regular flights to and from major cities in Malaysia and also from Singapore. The airport tax is RM20 (US$5.25) for international flights and RM5 (US$1.30) for domestic, but this is usually reflected in the price of the ticket.

For reservations on **Malaysian Airlines** flights call ☎ **07/334-1001** in Johor Bahru. A taxi from the airport to the city center will run you RM20 to RM25 (US$5.25 to US$6.60) per person. There's also a **Hertz** counter, but to make your reservation you must call their downtown office at ☎ **07/223-7520.** A RM4 (US$1.05) coach service runs between the airport and the JOTIC tourist information center in town. If you use this service for departures, make sure you catch the coach at least 2 hours before departure time. Call ☎ **07/221-7481** for more information.

BY TAXI   Outstation taxis can bring you to Johor Bahru from any major city on the peninsula. From KL's Puduraya Bus Terminal (☎ **03/238-3525** Outstation Taxi) the cost is about RM220 (US$57.90). For taxi stands in other cities please refer to each city's section. For taxi hiring from Johor Bahru call ☎ **07/223-4494.** The outstation taxi stand is located at Larkin Bus Terminal, but for an extra RM10 (US$2.65) they'll pick you up at your hotel.

GETTING AROUND

As in Kuala Lumpur, taxis charge a metered fare, RM2.05 (US$0.54) for the first kilometer and an additional 10 sen for each 200 meters after that. Between midnight and 6am you'll be charged an extra 50% of the total fare. For taxi pickup there's an extra RM1 (US$0.26) charge. Call **Citycab** at ☎ **07/354-0007.**

FAST FACTS: JOHOR BAHRU

The **American Express** office is located at Mansfield Travel, ground floor, New Orchid Plaza, Jalan Wong Ah Fook (☎ **07/224-9511**). **Major banks** are located in the city center, and **money changers** at shopping malls and at JOTIC.

The main **post office** is on Jalan Dato Onn (☎ **07/223-2555**), just around the corner from JOTIC. For **Internet** connection, I recommend the conveniently located **Weblinks Connexions** in the JOTIC center on Jalan Ayer Molek, L1-2 (☎ **07/ 225-1287**). They charge RM2.50 (US$0.66) per hour.

ACCOMMODATIONS

Several international chains have accommodations in JB. Most are intended for the business set, but holiday travelers will find the accommodations very comfortable.

The Holiday Inn Crowne Plaza. Jalan Dato Sulaiman, Century Garden, 80990 Johor Bahru, Johor. ☎ **800/465-4329** in the U.S. and Canada, 800/221-066 in Australia, 0800/442-222 in New Zealand, 0800/987-121 in the U.K., or 07/332-3800. Fax 07/331-8884. 350 units. A/C MINIBAR TV TEL. RM370 (US$97.35) double; RM550 (US$144.75) suite. AE, DC, JCB, MC, V.

While this hotel is not walking distance from the city center, it was the first five-star business-class hotel in Johor Bahru, and is larger than the other hotels in the city. It's comfortable and not overly formal, with furniture in traditional fabrics, wood paneling details, and marble floors in the lobby. VCRs are available upon request, with RM15 (US$3.90) video rentals. Services include airport shuttle and valet service. Facilities include a business center, a midsize outdoor pool, one squash court, and a fitness center with sauna, steam bath, and massage; there is also a shopping complex attached. Recent deals offered by the hotel include a 50% discount off the suite rate.

✪ **The Hyatt Regency.** Jalan Sungai Chat, P.O. Box 222, 80720 Johor Bahru, Johor. ☎ **800/233-1234** or 07/222-1234. Fax 07/223-2718. 400 units. A/C MINIBAR TV TEL. RM420–RM480 (US$110.55–US$126.30) double; RM500–RM600 (US$131.60–US$157.90) Executive Floor; from RM800 (US$210.55) suite. AE, DC, JCB, MC, V.

The Hyatt is near the City Square, but likes to fancy itself as a city resort, focusing on landscaped gardens and greenery around the premises—the private lagoon-style pool,

Johor Bahru

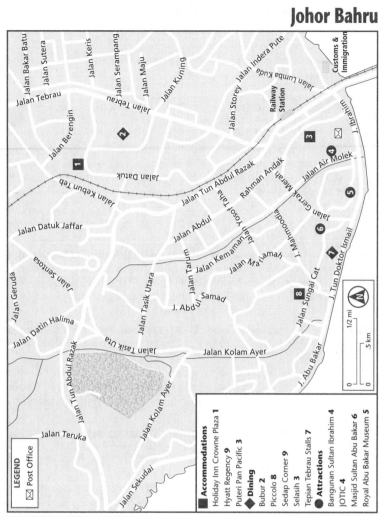

LEGEND
⊠ Post Office

Accommodations
Holiday Inn Crowne Plaza **1**
Hyatt Regency **9**
Puteri Pan Pacific **3**

◆ Dining
Bubur **2**
Piccolo **8**
Sedap Corner **9**
Selasih **3**
Tepian Tebrau Stalls **7**

● Attractions
Bangunan Sultan Ibrahim **4**
JOTIC **4**
Masjid Sultan Abu Bakar **6**
Royal Abu Bakar Museum **5**

with gardens seen from the glass windows of the main lobby, is surely spectacular. The deluxe rooms are located better than the others, with views of Singapore and fabulous sunsets. Facilities include a business center, two tennis courts, and a fitness center with sauna, Jacuzzi, and massage. Discount packages are available.

The Puteri Pan Pacific. "The Kotaraya," P.O. Box 293, 80730 Johor Bahru, Johor. ☎ **07/ 223-3333,** or 800/8533 toll-free in Malaysia. Fax 07/223-6622. 460 units. A/C MINIBAR TV TEL. RM330–RM400 (US$86.85–US$105.25) double; RM450–RM2,000 (US$118.40– US$526.30) suite. AE, DC, JCB, MC, V.

The good news about the Puteri is it's located in the heart of the city, near attractions and shopping. The bad news is it is a very busy hotel and human traffic makes it noisy and somewhat on the run-down side. Nevertheless, little traditional touches to the decor make the Pan Pacific unique. Be sure to ask about special discounts, which can bring the price down by as much as half! Facilities include an outdoor pool, tennis and squash courts, fitness center, saunas, steam room, and business center.

DINING

The majority of fine dining in Johor Bahru is in the hotels. Outside the hotels you can sample some great local cuisine, both Malay and Chinese, and wonderful seafood from the city's hawker stalls.

Bubur. 191 Jalan Harimau, Century Garden. ☎ **07/335-5891.** Reservations held for a half hour only. Entrees RM7–RM12 (US$1.85–US$3.15). AE, MC, V. Daily 11am–5am except 4 days into the Chinese New Year. TAIWAN CHINESE.

For fast, inexpensive eats you can even order for takeout, try this place. It's a family restaurant, so it can get pretty lively. The staff is quick and attentive without being imposing. Best dishes are the traditional braised pork in soy sauce and the grilled butterfish in black-bean sauce.

✪ **Piccolo.** Hyatt Regency, Jalan Sungai Chat. ☎ **07/222-1234.** Entrees RM20–RM58 (US$5.25–US$15.25). AE, DC, JCB, MC, V. Daily 11:30am–2:30pm and 6:30–10:30pm. ITALIAN.

Perhaps the most popular restaurant for the expatriate community in Johor Bahru, Piccolo's lush lagoon-style poolside ambience has a very tropical and relaxed feel. Under the timber awning, the high ceiling and bamboo chick blinds make for romantic terrace dining. The antipasto is wonderful, as are dishes like chicken with shrimp and spinach. The grilled seafood is outstanding.

Sedap Corner. 11 Jalan Abdul Samad. ☎ **07/224-6566.** Reservations recommended. Entrees RM4.50–RM24 (US$1.20–US$6.30), though most dishes no more than RM6 (US$1.60). No credit cards. Daily 9am–9:45pm. THAI/CHINESE/MALAY.

Sedap Corner is very popular with the locals. It's dressed down in metal chairs and Formica-top tables, with a coffee shop feel. Local dishes like sambal sabah, otak-otak, and fish head curry are house specials, and you don't have to worry about them being too spicy.

✪ **Selasih.** The Puteri Pan Pacific, "The Kotaraya." ☎ **07/223-3333,** ext. 3151. Reservations recommended. Buffet lunch RM28 (US$7.35); buffet dinner RM40 (US$10.55). AE, DC, JCB, MC, V. Daily 11:30am–2:30pm and Fri–Sat 6:30–10:30pm (no dinner on weekdays). MALAY.

For a broad-range sampling of Malaysian cuisine, try Selasih, which has a daily buffet spread of more than 70 items featuring regional dishes from all over the country. Each night, the dinner buffet is accompanied by traditional Malay music and dance performances. Children and seniors receive a 50% discount.

HAWKER CENTERS

The ✪ **Tepian Tebrau Stalls** in Jalan Skudai (along the seafront) and the stalls near the **Central Market** offer cheap local eats in hawker-center style. The dish that puts Johor Bahru on the map, ikan bakar (barbecued fish with chiles), is out of this world at the Tepian Tebrau stalls.

ATTRACTIONS

The sights in Johor Bahru are few, but there are some interesting museums and a beautiful istana and mosque. It's a fabulous place to stay for a day, especially if it's a day trip from Singapore, but to stay for longer may be stretching the point.

✪ **Royal Abu Bakar Museum.** Grand Palace, Johor. Jalan Tun Dr Ismail. ☎ **07/ 223-0555.** Adults RM26.60 (US$7); children under 12 RM11.40 (US$3). Sat–Thurs 9am–5pm.

Also called the Istana Bakar, this gorgeous royal palace was built by Sultan Abu Bakar in 1866. Today it houses the royal collection of international treasures, costumes, historical documents, fine art from the family collection, and relics of the Sultanate.

Bangunan Sultan Ibrahim (State Secretariat Building). Jalan Abdul Ibrahim. No phone.

The saracenic flavor of this building makes it feel older than it truly is. Built in 1940, today it houses the State Secretariat.

Masjid Sultan Abu Bakar. Jalan Masjid. No phone.

This mosque was commissioned by Sultan Ibrahim in 1890 after the death of his father, Sultan Abu Bakar. It took 8 years and RM400,000 to build, and is one of the most beautiful mosques in Malaysia—at least from the outside. The inside? I can't tell you. I showed up in "good Muslim woman" clothing, took off my shoes, and crept up to the outer area (where I know women are allowed), and a Haji flew out of an office and shooed me off in a flurry. He asked if I was Muslim, I said no, and he said I wasn't allowed in. When I reported this to the tourism office at JOTIC, they thought I was nuts, and said anyone with proper attire could enter the appropriate sections. Let me know if you get in.

SPORTS & THE OUTDOORS

In addition to its cities and towns, Johor also has some beautiful nature to take in, which is doubly good if you have only a short time to see Malaysia and can't afford to travel north to some of the larger national parks.

Johor Endau Rompin National Park is about 488 square kilometers (293 sq. miles) of lowland forest. There's jungle trekking through 26 kilometers (16 miles) of trails and over rivers to see diverse tropical plant species, colorful birds, and wild animals. Unfortunately, you'll have to be a camper to really enjoy the park, as this is the only accommodation you'll get. Still, for those who love the great outdoors, first contact the National Parks (Johor) Corporation, JKR 475, Bukit Timbalan, Johor Bahru (☎ 07/ 223-7471), for entry permission. You'll have to take an outstation taxi from Johor Bahru (cost: RM60/US$15.80); for booking, call ☎ 07/223-4494 to Kluang. The taxi driver will drop you at the shuttle to the park entrance. Take this shuttle (which you'll prearrange through the National Parks Board) to the park entrance at Kahang. The 3-hour trip costs RM350 (US$92.10) for two people, then you'll have to pay the RM20 (US$5.25) per-person entrance fee to the park. They can rent you all the gear you'll need, but you must bring your own food, and remember to boil your drinking water at least 10 minutes to get it into a potable condition.

The **Waterfalls at Lombong,** near Kota Tinggi, measuring about 34 meters (112 ft.) high, are about 56 kilometers (34 miles) northeast of Johor Bahru. You can cool off in the pools below the falls and enjoy the area's chalets, camping facilities, restaurant, and food stalls. An outstation taxi will also take you to the falls, which are a little off the track on your way east to Desaru. The cost would also be around RM60 (US$15.80).

Johor is a favorite destination for **golf** enthusiasts. The Royal Johor Country Club and Pulai Springs Country Club are just outside Johor Bahru and offer a range of country club facilities, while other courses require a bit more traveling time, but offer resort-style accommodations. *One note of caution:* If you play in Johor, especially at the Royal Johor Country Club, don't wear yellow. It is the official color of the Sultan, and is worn only by him when he visits the courses.

The most famous course has to be the **Royal Johor Country Club,** 3211 Jalan Larkin, 80200 Johor Bahru, Johor (☎ 07/223-3322; fax 07/224-0729). This

18-hole, par-72 course provides the favored game of the Sultan of Johor, so they don't accept walk-ins. You must contact the club manager beforehand to obtain admission. Once you've received his okay, expect to pay RM105 (US$27.65) for weekday play and RM210 (US$55.25) for weekends. Other courses to try include **Palm Resort Golf & Country Club,** Jalan Persiaran Golf, off Jalan Jumbo, 81250 Senai, Johor (☎ 07/599-6222; fax 07/599-6001), with two 18-hole courses, par 72 and 74, and greens fees RM150 (US$39.45) weekdays, RM250 to RM325 (US$65.80 to US$85.55) weekends; **Pulai Springs Country Club,** km 20 Jalan Pontian Lama, 81110 Pulai, Johor (☎ 07/521-2121; fax 07/521-1818), with two 18-hole courses (both par 72) and greens fees of RM80 to RM100 (US$21.05 to US$26.30) weekdays, RM180 to RM200 (US$47.35 to US$52.65) weekends); or the **Ponderosa Golf & Country Club,** 10-C Jalan Bumi Hijau 3, Taman Molek, 81100 Johor Bahru, Johor (☎ 07/354-9999; fax 07/355-7400), with 18 holes, par 72, and greens fees of RM80 (US$21.05) weekdays, RM150 (US$39.45 weekends).

SHOPPING

The **Johor Craftown Handicraft Centre,** 36 Jalan Skudai, off Jalan Abu Bakar (☎ 07/236-7346), has, in addition to a collection of local crafts, demonstration performances of handicrafts techniques. **JOTIC,** 2 Jalan Ayer Molek (☎ 07/224-2000), is a shopping mall with tourist information, cultural performances, exhibits, demonstrations of crafts, and restaurants.

3 Malacca

While the destinations on the east coast are ideal for resort-style beach getaways, the cities on the west coast are perfect for vacations filled with culture and history, and Malacca is one of the best places to start. The attraction here is the city's cultural heritage, around which a substantial tourism industry has grown. If you're visiting, a little knowledge of this history will help you understand and appreciate all there is to see.

Malacca was founded around 1400 by Parameswara, called **Iskander Shah** in the Malay Annals. After he was chased from Palembang in southern Sumatra by invading Javanese, he set up a kingdom in Singapore (Temasek), and after being overthrown by invaders there, ran up the west coast of the Malay peninsula to Malacca, where he settled and established a port city. The site was an ideal midpoint in the east-west trade route and was in a favorable spot to take advantage of the two monsoons that dominated shipping routes. Malacca soon drew the attention of the Chinese, and the city maintained very close relations with the mainland as a trading partner and a political ally. The Japanese were also eager to trade in Malacca, as were Muslim merchants. After Parameswara's death in 1414, his son, Mahkota Iskander Shah, converted to Islam and became the first sultan of Malacca. The word of Islam quickly spread throughout the local population.

During the 15th century, Malacca was ruled by a succession of wise sultans who expanded the wealth and stability of the economy, built up the administration's coffers, extended the sultanate to the far reaches of the Malay peninsula, Singapore, and parts of northern Sumatra, and thwarted repeated attacks by the Siamese. The success of the empire was drawing international attention.

The Portuguese were one of the powers eyeing the port and formulating plans to dominate the east-west trade route, establish the naval supremacy of Portugal, and promote Christianity in the region. They struck in 1511 and conquered Malacca in a battle that lasted only a month. It is believed the local Malaccans had become accustomed to the comforts of affluence and turned soft and vulnerable. After the defeat, the sultanate fled to Johor, where it reestablished the seat of Malay power. Malacca would never again be ruled by a sultan. The Portuguese looted the city and sent its riches off to Lisbon.

The Portuguese were also the first of a chain of ruling foreign powers who would struggle in vain to retain the early economic success of the city. The foreign conquerors had a major strike against them: Their Christianity alienated the locals and repelled Muslim traders. The city quickly became nothing more than a sleepy outpost.

In 1641, the Dutch, with the help of Johor, conquered Malacca and controlled the city until 1795. Again, the Dutch were unsuccessful in rebuilding the glory of past prosperity in Malacca, and the city continued to sleep.

In 1795, the Dutch traded Malacca to the British in return for Bencoolen in Sumatra, being far more concerned with their Indonesian interests anyway. Malacca became a permanent British settlement in 1811, but by this time had become so poor and alienated that it was impossible to bring it back to life.

The final blow came in 1941, when the city fell under Japanese occupation for four years. It wasn't until 1957 that Malacca, along with the rest of Malaysia, gained full independence.

ESSENTIALS
VISITOR INFORMATION
Surprisingly, there is no Malaysia Tourism Board office in Malacca, but there is a locally operated **Malacca Tourism Centre** in the Town Square (☎ **06/283-6538**).

GETTING THERE
While there is an airport in Malacca, it's not open for any flights due to lack of demand. And while Malacca doesn't have a proper train station, the KTM stops at Tampin (☎ **06/441-1034**), 38 kilometers (23.75 miles.) north of the city. It's not the most convenient way in and out of Malacca, but if you decide to stop en route between Kuala Lumpur and Johor Bahru, you can easily catch a waiting taxi to your hotel in town for between RM35 and RM40 (US$9.20 and US$10.55).

BY BUS   From Singapore, contact **Malacca-Singapore Express** at ☎ **65/ 293-5915.** Buses depart seven times daily for the $4^{1}/_{2}$-hour trip (S$11/US$6.60). From Johor Bahru's Larkin Bus Terminal, **Jebat Ekspress** (☎ **07/223-3712**) has five daily buses at a cost of RM9 (US$2.35). From KL's Puduraya Bus Terminal on Jalan Pudu, **Transnasional** (☎ **03/230-5044**) has hourly buses between 8am and 10pm for RM6.80 (US$1.80).

The bus station in Malacca is at Jalan Kilang, within the city. Taxis are easy to find from here.

BY TAXI   Outstation taxis can bring you here from any major city, including Johor Bahru (about RM120/US$31.60) and Kuala Lumpur (RM120/US$31.60). Taxi reservation numbers are listed in each city's section. The outstation taxi stand in Malacca is at the bus terminal on Jalan Kilang. There's no number for reservations.

GETTING AROUND
Most of the historic sights around the town square are well within walking distance. For other trips **taxis** are the most convenient way around, but are at times difficult to find. They're also not as clearly marked as in KL or Johor Bahru. They are also not

metered, so be prepared to bargain. Basically, no matter what you do, you'll always be charged a higher rate than a local. Tourists are almost always quoted at RM10 (US$2.65) for local trips. Malaysians pay RM5 (US$1.30). You should try to bargain for a price somewhere in between. Trips to Ayer Keroh will cost about RM20 (US$5.25).

Trishaws (bicycle rikshaws) are all over the historic areas of town, and in Malacca they're renowned for being very, very garishly decorated (which adds to the fun!). Negotiate for hourly rates of about RM15 (US$3.95).

FAST FACTS: MALACCA

Major **Banks** are located in the historic center of town, with a couple along Jalan Putra. The most convenient **post office** location is on Jalan Laksamana (☎ 06/ 284-8440), while the most centrally located **Internet** is E-netlink Cyber Café, 54 Jalan Parameswara (☎ 06/292-1969), for RM3 (US$0.79) per hour.

ACCOMMODATIONS

Malacca is not very large, and most of the places to stay are well within walking distance of attractions, shopping, and restaurants.

Century Mahkota Hotel Melaka. Jalan Merdeka, 75000 Malacca. ☎ **800/536-7361** in the U.S., or 06/281-2828. Fax 06/281-2323. 617 units. A/C MINIBAR TV TEL. RM350 (US$92.10) double; RM350–RM650 (US$92.10–US$171.05) 1- to 3-bedroom apt. AE, DC, JCB, MC, V.

Located along the waterfront, the hotel is walking distance from sightseeing, historical areas, shopping, and commercial centers. It's a suite hotel and while it's not luxurious, its rooms are more like holiday apartments, making it a good choice for families. The views are of either the pools, the shopping mall across the street, or the muddy reclaimed seafront. Facilities include two outdoor pools, a fitness center with sauna and massage, tennis and squash courts, a children's playground, a game room, minigolf and access to nearby golf, and a business center. It's across the street from the largest shopping mall in Malacca.

✪ **Heeren House.** 1 Jalan Tun Tan Cheng Lock, 75200 Malacca. ☎ **06/281-4241**. Fax 06/281-4239. 7 units. A/C TV TEL. Sun–Thurs RM129–RM139 (US$33.95–US$36.60) double; RM239 (US$62.90) family suite. No credit cards.

This is the place to stay in Malacca for a taste of the local culture. Started by a local family, the guest house is a renovated 100-year-old building furnished in traditional Peranakan and colonial style and located right in the heart of historical European Malacca. All the bedrooms have views of the Malacca River, and outside the front door of the hotel is a winding stretch of old buildings housing antique shops. Just walk out and wander. The rooms on the higher floors are somewhat larger. Laundry service is available, and there's a cafe and gift shop on the premises.

Hotel Puri. 118 Jalan Tun Tan Cheng Lock, 75200 Malacca. ☎ **06/282-5588**. Fax 06/281-5588. 50 units. A/C TV TEL. RM150 (US$39.45) double; RM245 (US$64.45) suite. Rates include breakfast. AE, MC, V.

In the olden days, Jalan Tun Tan Cheng Lock was known as "Millionaire Row" for all the wealthy families that lived here. This old "mansion" has been converted into a guest house, its tiled parlor has become a lobby, and the courtyard is where breakfast is served each morning. While Hotel Puri isn't big on space, it is big on value (discount rates can be pretty low). Rooms are very clean, and while not overly stylish, are comfortable enough for any weary traveler. Friendly and responsive staff add to the appeal.

Malacca

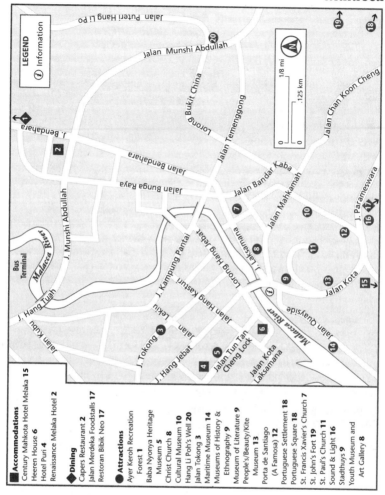

LEGEND
i Information

0 1/8 mi

0 .125 km

Accommodations
Century Mahkota Hotel Melaka **15**
Heeren House **6**
Hotel Puri **4**
Renaissance Melaka Hotel **2**

Dining
Capers Restaurant **2**
Jalan Merdeka Foodstalls **17**
Restoran Bibik Neo **17**

Attractions
Ayer Keroh Recreation
Forest **1**
Baba Nyonya Heritage
Museum **5**
Christ Church **8**
Cultural Museum **10**
Hang Li Poh's Well **20**
Jalan Tokong **3**
Maritime Museum **14**
Museums of History &
Ethnography **9**
Museum of Literature **9**
People's/Beauty/Kite
Museum **13**
Porta de Santiago
(A Famosa) **12**
Portuguese Settlement **18**
Portuguese Square **18**
St. Francis Xavier's Church **7**
St. John's Fort **19**
St. Paul's Church **11**
Sound & Light **16**
Stadthuys **9**
Youth Museum and
Art Gallery **8**

✪ **Renaissance Melaka Hotel.** Jalan Bendahara, 75100 Malacca. ☎ **06/284-8888** in Malaysia, or 800/601-1882 in Singapore. Fax 06/284-9269. 316 units. A/C MINIBAR TV TEL. RM437 (US$115) double; RM495–RM4,025 (US$130.25–US$1,059.20) suite. AE, JCB, MC, V.

Renaissance is one of the more posh hotels in Malacca, and, according to business travelers, is the most reliable place for quality accommodations—but aside from the pieces of Peranakan porcelain and art in the public areas, you could almost believe you weren't in Malacca at all. The hotel is, however, situated in a good location, though you'll still need a taxi to most of the sights. Renovations were completed 2 years ago to upgrade the guest rooms, which are fairly large and filled with Western comforts. Don't expect much from the views, as the hotel is in a more business-minded part of the city. No historical landmarks to gaze upon here. Facilities include an outdoor pool, fitness center with massage, sauna, and steam, two indoor squash courts, a tour operator desk, and a beauty salon. Golf is located nearby.

DINING

In Malacca you'll find the typical mix of authentic Malay and Chinese food, and as the city was the major settling place for the Peranakans in Malaysia, their unique style of food is featured in many of the local restaurants.

A good recommendation for a quick bite at lunch or dinner if you're strolling in the historical area is the long string of **open-air food stalls** along Jalan Merdeka, just between Mahkota Plaza Shopping and Warrior Square. **Mama Fatso's** is especially good for Chinese style seafood and Malay sambal curry. A good meal will run you about RM35 to RM40 (US$9.20 to US$10.55) per person. And believe me, it's a good meal.

✪ **Capers Restaurant.** Renaissance Melaka Hotel, Jalan Bendahara. ☎ **06/284-8888.** Reservations recommended. Entrees RM20–RM48 (US$5.25–US$12.65). AE, DC, MC, V. Mon–Sat 6:30–10:30pm. CONTINENTAL.

This is the only fine-dining establishment in Malacca at the moment, which means it is quite formal and pricey. Warm lighting and crystal and silver flatware are only a few of the many details that add to the elegant and romantic atmosphere. The signature dishes, like grilled tenderloin, come from the charcoal grill. The panfried sea bass is served quite artfully in a ginger and dill sauce over bok choy and potatoes. Their wine list is large and international (including Portuguese selections, in keeping with the Malacca theme).

Portuguese Settlement. Jalan d'Albuquerque off Jalan Ujon Pasir. No phone. Dinner from RM15–RM20 (US$3.95–5.25) per person. No credit cards. Open nightly from 6pm onwards.

For a taste of Portuguese Malacca head down to the Portuguese Settlement where open-air food stalls by the water sell an assortment of dishes inspired by these former colonial rulers, including many fresh seafood offerings. Saturday nights are best when, at 8pm, there's a cultural show with music and dancing.

✪ **Restoran Bibik Neo.** No. 6, ground floor, Jalan Merdeka, Taman Melaka Raya. ☎ **06/ 281-7054.** Reservations recommended. Entrees RM5–RM15 (US$1.30–US$3.95). AE, DC, MC, V. Daily 11am–3pm and 6–10pm. PERANAKAN.

For a taste of the local cuisine, the traditional Nyonya food here is delicious and very reasonably priced. And while the restaurant isn't exactly tops in terms of decor, be assured that the food here is excellent and authentic. Ikan assam with eggplant is a tasty mild fish curry that's very rich and tasty, but I always go for the otak-otak (pounded fish and spices baked in a banana leaf).

ATTRACTIONS

To really understand what you're seeing in Malacca you have to understand a bit about the history, so be sure to read the introduction at the beginning of this section. Most of the really great historical places are on either side of the Malacca River. Start at Stadthuys (the old town hall) and you'll see most of Malacca pretty quickly.

MUSEUMS

✪ **The Museums of History & Ethnography and the Museum of Literature.** Stadthuys. Located at the circle intersection of Jalan Quayside, Jalan Laksamana, and Jalan Chan Koon Cheng. ☎ **06/282-6526.** Admission RM2.50 (US$0.66) adults, RM.50 (US$0.13) children. Sat–Thurs 9am–6pm, Fri 9am–12:45pm and 2:45–6pm.

The Stadthuys Town Hall was built by the Dutch in 1650, and it's now home to the Malacca Ethnographical and Historical Museum, which displays customs and traditions of all the peoples of Malacca, and takes you through the rich history of this city.

Behind Stadthuys, the Museum of Literature includes old historical accounts and local legends. Admission price is for both exhibits.

The Peoples Museum, the Museum of Beauty, the Kite Museum, and the Governor of Melaka's Gallery. Kota Rd. ☎ **06/282-6526**. Admission RM2.50 (US$0.66) adults, RM.50 (US$0.13) children. Sat–Thurs 9am–6pm, Fri 9am–12:45pm and 2:45–6pm.

This strange collection of displays is housed under one roof. The Peoples Museum is the story of development in Malacca. The Museum of Beauty is a look at cultural differences of beauty throughout time and around the world. The Kite Museum features the traditions of making and flying *wau* (kites) in Malaysia, and the governor's personal collection is on exhibit at the Governor's Gallery.

The Maritime Museum and the Royal Malaysian Navy Museum. Quayside Rd. ☎ **06/282-6526**. Admission RM2.50 (US$0.66) adults, RM.50 (US$0.13) children. Sat–Thurs 9am–6pm, Fri 9am–12:45pm and 2:45–6pm.

These two museums are located across the street from one another but share admission fees. The Maritime Museum is in a restored 16th-century Portuguese ship, with exhibits dedicated to Malacca's history with the sea. The Navy Museum is a modern display of Malaysia's less-pleasant relationship with the sea.

The Youth Museums and Art Gallery. Laksamana Rd. ☎ **06/282-6526**. Admission RM1 (US$0.26) adults, RM.50 (US$0.13) children. Sat–Thurs 9am–6pm, Fri 9am–12:45pm and 2:45–6pm.

In the old General Post office are these displays dedicated to Malaysia's youth organizations and to the nation's finest artists. An unusual combination.

✪ **The Cultural Museum.** Kota Rd., next to Porta de Santiago. ☎ **06/282-6526**. Admission RM1.50 (US$0.39) adults, RM.50 (US$0.13) children. Sat–Thurs 9am–6pm, Fri 9am–12:45pm and 2:45–6pm.

A replica of the former palace of Sultan Mansur Syah (1456–77), this museum was rebuilt according to historical descriptions to house a fine collection of cultural artifacts such as clothing, weaponry, and royal items.

✪ **Baba Nyonya Heritage Museum.** 48/50 Jalan Tun Tan Cheng Lock. ☎ **06/283-1273**. Admission RM8 (US$2.10) adults, RM 4 (US$1.05) children. Daily 10am–12:30pm and 2–4:30pm.

Called Millionaire's Row, Jalan Tun Ten Cheng Lock is lined with row houses that were built by the Dutch and later bought by wealthy Peranakans; the architectural style reflects their East-meets-West lifestyle. The Baba Nyonya Heritage Museum sits at nos. 48 and 50 as a museum of Peranakan heritage. The entrance fee includes a guided tour.

HISTORICAL SITES

Sound & Light. Warrior Sq., Jalan Kota. ☎ **06/282-6526**. Admission RM5 (US$1.30) adults, RM2 (US$0.53) children. Shows nightly at 9:30pm.

The Museums Department has developed a sound-and-light show at the Warrior Square, the large field in the historical center of the city, which narrates the story of Malacca's early history, lighting up the historical buildings in the area for added punch. This is a good activity when you first arrive to help you get your historical bearings.

✪ **Porta de Santiago (A Famosa).** Located on Jalan Kota, at the intersection of Jalan Parameswara. No phone.

Once the site of a Portuguese fortress called A Famosa, all that remains today of the fortress is the entrance gate, which was saved from demolition by Sir Stamford

Raffles. When the British East India Company demolished the place, Raffles realized the arch's historical value and saved it. The fort was built in 1512, but the inscription above the arch, "Anno 1607," marks the date when the Dutch overthrew the Portuguese.

Hang Li Poh's Well. Located off Jalan Laksamana Cheng Ho (Jalan Panjang). No phone.

Also called "Sultan's Well," Hang Li Poh's Well was built in 1495 to commemorate the marriage of Chinese Princess Hang Li Poh to Sultan Mansor Shah. It is now a wishing well, and folks say that if you toss a coin in, you'll someday return to Malacca.

St. John's Fort. Located off Lorong Bukit Senjuang. No phone.

The fort, built by the Dutch in the late 18th century, sits on top of St. John's Hill. Funny how the cannons point inland, huh? At the time, threats to the city came from land. It was named after a Portuguese church to St. John the Baptist, which originally occupied the site.

St. Paul's Church. Located behind Porta de Santiago. No phone.

The church was built by the Portuguese in 1521, but when the Dutch came in, they made it part of A Famosa, converting the altar into a cannon mount. The open tomb inside was once the resting place of St. Francis Xavier, a missionary who spread Catholicism throughout Southeast Asia, and whose remains were later moved to Goa.

St. Francis Xavier's Church. Located on Jalan Laksamana. No phone.

This church was built in 1849 and dedicated to St. Francis Xavier, a Jesuit who brought Catholicism to Malacca and other parts of Southeast Asia.

Christ Church. Located on Jalan Laksamana. No phone.

The Dutch built this place in 1753 as a Dutch Reform Church, and its architectural details include such wonders as ceiling beams cut from a single tree and a Last Supper glazed tile motif above the altar. It was later consecrated as an Anglican church, and mass is still performed today in English, Chinese, and Tamil.

Portuguese Settlement and Portuguese Square. Located down Jalan d'Albuquerque off of Jalan Ujon Pasir in the southern part of the city.

The Portuguese Settlement is an enclave once designated for Portuguese settlers after they conquered Malacca in 1511. Some elements of their presence remain in the Lisbon-style architecture. Later, in 1920, the area was a Eurasian neighborhood. In the center of the settlement, Portuguese Square is a modern attraction with Portuguese restaurants, handicrafts, souvenirs, and cultural shows. It was built in 1985 in an architectural style to reflect the surrounding flavor of Portugal.

✪ **Jalan Tokong.**

Not far from Jalan Tun Tan Cheng Lock is Jalan Tokong, called the "Street of Harmony" by the locals because it has three coexisting places of worship: the Kampong Kling Mosque, the Cheng Hoon Teng Temple, and the Sri Poyyatha Vinayar Moorthi Temple.

OTHER ATTRACTIONS

Outside of Malacca is the 202 hectares (500 acres) of forest that make up **Ayer Keroh Recreational Forest,** where many attractions have been built. A taxi from Malacca will run you about RM20 (US$5.25). See the **Reptile Park** (☎ 06/231-9136), admission RM4 (US$1.05) adults, RM2 (US$0.53) children, open daily 9am to 6pm; the **Butterfly & Reptile Sanctuary** (☎ 06/232-0033), admission RM5 (US$1.30)

adults, RM3 (US$0.79) children, open daily 8:30am to 5:30pm; the **Malacca Zoo**
(☎ 06/232-4053), admission RM3 (US$0.79) adults, RM1 (US$0.26) children, open
daily 9am to 6pm; and the **Taman Mini Malaysia/Mini ASEAN** (☎ 06/231-6087),
admission RM5 (US$1.30) adults, RM2 (US$0.53) children, open 9am to 5pm daily.

SHOPPING

Antique hunting has been a major draw to Malacca for decades. Distinct Peranakan
and teak furniture, porcelain, and household items fetch quite a price these days, due
to a steady increase in demand for these rare treasures. The area down and around
Jalan Tun Tan Cheng Lok sports many little antique shops that are filled with as
many gorgeous items as any local museum. Whether you're buying or just looking, it's
a fun way to spend an afternoon.

Modern shopping malls are sprouting up in Malacca, the biggest being the
Mahkota Parade on Jalan Merdeka, just south of the field (Warrior Square) in the
historic district. Two hundred retail stores sell everything from books to clothing.

For crafts, start at **Karyaneka** (☎ 06/284-3270) on Jalan Laksamana close to the
Town Square. If you travel down Laksamana you'll find all sorts of small crafts and
souvenir shops.

There's also a daily **flea market** on the north end of the field (Warrior Square) just
in the historic district. Try your bargaining skills here for batiks, baskets, regional
crafts, and souvenirs.

4 Genting Highlands

Genting Highlands, the "City of Entertainment," serves as Malaysia's answer to Las
Vegas, complete with bright lights (that can be seen from Kuala Lumpur) and gambling. And while most people come here to gamble, there's a wide range of other activities, although most of them seem to serve the purpose of entertaining the kids while
you bet their college funds at the roulette wheel. Still, nestled in the cool mountains
above the capital city, it's a hop from town and a fun diversion from all that *culture!*

ESSENTIALS

VISITOR INFORMATION   The Genting Highlands Resort is owned and operated
by Resorts World Berhad, who'll be glad to provide you with any further information.
For hotel reservations call ☎ 03/262-3555 or fax 03/261-6611. You can also visit
their central office at Wisma Genting on Jalan Sultan Ismail in KL.

GETTING THERE   For buses from Kuala Lumpur, call **Genting Highlands
Transport,** operating buses every half hour from 6:30am to 9pm daily from the Peke-
liling Bus Terminal on Jalan Ipoh. The cost for one way is RM2.60 (US$0.68) and the
trip takes 1 hour. The bus lets you off at the foot of the hill, where you take the cable
car to the top for RM3 (US$0.79). For bus information, call ☎ 03/441-0173.

You can also get there by hiring an outstation taxi. The cost is RM40 (US$10.55)
and can be arranged by calling the Puduraya outstation taxi stand at ☎ 03/
238-3525.

ACCOMMODATIONS

There are four hotels of varying prices within the resort. Rates vary depending on
whether it's the low season, shoulder season, peak season, or super peak. The calendar changes each year, but basically weekends are peak, as well as the last week in
November through the end of December. Super peak times are around Christmas,

the calendar New Year, and Chinese New Year, with a few other days dotted over the summer. With the above exceptions, weekdays are generally low season.

Genting Hotel. Genting Highlands 69000, Pahang Darul Makmur. ☎ **03/211-1118.** Fax 03/211-1888. 700 units. A/C MINIBAR TV TEL. Low RM190 (US$50); shoulder RM230 (US$60.55); peak RM280 (US$73.70); super peak RM350 (US$92.10) double. AE, MC, V.

Genting Hotel is a newer property in the resort complex, and is linked directly to the casino. Promotional rates can be as low as RM97 (US$25.60) for low period weekdays.

Highlands Hotel. Genting Highlands 69000, Pahang Darul Makmur. ☎ **03/211-1118.** Fax 03/211-1888. 875 units. A/C MINIBAR TV TEL. Low RM210 (US$55.25); shoulder RM250 (US$65.80); peak RM300 (US$78.95); super peak RM370 (US$97.35) double. AE, MC, V.

Highlands Hotel's main attraction is its direct link to the casino. You'll pay the highest rate here, as promotional rates in this hotel are very rare.

Resort Hotel. Genting Highlands 69000, Pahang Darul Makmur. ☎ **03/211-1118.** Fax 03/211-1888. 800 units. A/C MINIBAR TV TEL. Low RM160 (US$42.10); shoulder RM190 (US$50); peak RM230 (US$60.55); super peak RM 290 (US$76.30) double. AE, MC, V.

Resort Hotel is comparable to the Theme Park Hotel below, but it's a little newer and the double occupancy rooms all have two double beds and standing showers only.

Theme Park Hotel. Genting Highlands 69000, Pahang Darul Makmur. ☎ **03/211-1118.** Fax 03/211-1888. 440 units. A/C MINIBAR TV TEL. Low RM120 (US$31.60); shoulder RM 160 (US$42.10); peak RM200 (US$52.65); super peak RM220 (US$57.90) double. AE, MC, V.

The Theme Park Hotel is a little less expensive than the others, primarily because it's a little older and you must walk outside to reach the casino. Promotional rates during the week can be as low as RM62 for up to three people in one room.

DINING & ENTERTAINMENT

Genting doesn't stop at the casinos when it comes to nightlife. International entertainers perform pop concerts, and the theaters put on everything from lion dance competitions to Wild West shows to magic extravaganzas. The **Genting International Showroom,** on the second floor of the Genting Hotel, hosts a show package, with theater-seating tickets starting from RM40 (US$10.55) and cocktail seats starting at RM50 (US$13.15), drinks not included. For dining, the most highly recommended place is **The Peak Restaurant & Lounge,** Genting's fine-dining restaurant on the 17th floor of the Genting Hotel. Ask about special one-price combination dinner and show tickets.

ATTRACTIONS

Gambling, gambling, and more gambling. The **resort casino** is open 24 hours. Entry is a refundable deposit of RM200 (US$52.65) whether you're a guest at the resort or just visiting for the day. By the way, you must be at least 21 years old to enter the casino. Inside it's a gambler's paradise, with all the games you'd care to wager a bet on, including blackjack, roulette, and baccarat.

For outdoor excitement, the resort has an **outdoor pond** with boats and a **horse ranch** with riding for all levels of experience. For somewhat less excitement (but better photo ops) the **cable car ride** down the mountain from the resort offers aerial views of the Malaysian jungle. A one-way fare is RM3 (US$0.79) for adults and children; Sunday to Thursday 8am to 7:30pm and Friday and Saturday 8am to 8:30pm. Additional facilities include a bowling alley and an indoor heated pool. The **Awana Golf and Country Club** (☎ 03/211-3025; fax 03/211-3535) is the premier golf course in Genting.

For children, there's the huge **Genting Theme Park** (☎ 03/211-1118; ext. 58240), covering 100,000 square feet and mostly filled with rides, plus many Western fast-food eating outlets, games, and other attractions. The Outdoor Theme Park has four roller coasters, flume rides, and a balloon ride, while the Indoor Theme Park has a Space Odyssey roller coaster and a motion simulator. Don't miss the Disco Bumper Cars! Admission to both parks is free, but to ride the rides you'll have to buy a 1-day unlimited ride pass, which will set you back RM30 (US$7.90) for adults and RM18 (US$4.75) for children. The Outdoor Theme Park is open Monday to Friday 10am to 6:45pm, Saturday and Sunday 8am to 7:45pm; Indoor Theme Park daily 9am to 2am.

5 Cameron Highlands

Although Cameron Highlands is in Pahang, it is most often accessed via Kuala Lumpur. Located in the hills, Cameron Highlands has a cool climate, which makes it the perfect place for luxury resorts tailored to weekend getaways by Malaysians, Singaporeans, and international travelers.

The climate is also very conducive to agriculture. After the area's discovery by British surveyor William Cameron in 1885, the major crop here became tea, which is still grown today. There is even a tea factory you can visit to see how tea leaves are processed. The area's lovely gardens supply cities from KL to Singapore with vegetables, flowers, and fruit year-round. As you go up into the highlands, you can see the farmland on terraces in beautiful patterns along the sides of the hills. Among the favorites here are the strawberries, which can be eaten fresh or transformed into yummy desserts in the local restaurants. At the many commercial flower nurseries you can see chrysanthemums, fuchsias, and roses growing on the terraces. Rose gardens are prominent here.

Ringlet is the first town you see as you travel up the highlands. It is the main agricultural center. Travel farther up the elevation to **Tanah Rata,** the major tourism town in the Highlands, where you'll find chalets, cottages, and bungalows. The town basically consists of shops along one side of the main street (Jalan Sultan Ahmad Shah) and food stalls and the bus terminal on the other. **Brinchang,** at 1,524 meters (5,029 ft.) above sea level, is the highest town, surrounding a market square where there are shops, Tudor inns, rose gardens, and a Buddhist temple.

Temperatures in the Cameron Highlands average 70°F (21°C) during the day and 50°F (10°C) at night. There are paths for lovely treks though the countryside and to peaks of surrounding mountains. Two waterfalls, the Robinson Falls and Parit Falls, have pools at their feet where you can have a swim.

ESSENTIALS

VISITOR INFORMATION   There are no visitor information services here. They've been closed for a very long time, and have no immediate plans for reopening.

GETTING THERE   **Kurnia Bistari Express Bus** (☎ 05/491-2978) operates between Kuala Lumpur and Tanah Rata four times daily for RM10.10 (US$2.65) one way. They don't accept bookings in Kuala Lumpur, asking you to just show up at Puduraya bus terminal to buy your ticket and board the next bus. Kurnia Bistari also provides service to and from Penang two times daily for RM14.10 (US$3.70). The bus terminal is in the center of town along the main drag. Just next to it is the taxi stand. It's a two-horse town; you can't miss either of them. **Outstation taxis** from KL will cost RM180 (US$47.35) for the trip. Call ☎ 03/238-3525 for booking. For trips from Cameron Highlands call ☎ 05/491-2355. Taxis are cheaper on the way back because they don't have to climb the mountains.

GETTING AROUND   Walking in each town is a snap because the places are so small, but the towns are far apart, so a walk between them could take up much time. There are local buses that ply at odd times between them for around RM3 (US$0.79), or you could pick up one of the ancient, unmarked taxis and cruise between towns for RM4 (US$1.05).

FAST FACTS   You'll find **banks** with ATMs and money-changing services along the main road in Tanah Rata. The local **post office** is also in Tanah Rata (☎ 05/491-1051).

ACCOMMODATIONS

✪ **The Cool Point Hotel.** 891 Persiaran Dayang Endah, 39000 Tanah Rata, Cameron Highlands, Pahang Darul Makmur. ☎ **05/491-4914.** Fax 05/491-4070. 47 units. A/C TV TEL. Off-season RM90–RM140 (US$23.70–US$36.85) double. Peak season RM125–RM180 (US$32.90–US$47.35) double. MC, V.

Cool Point has an outstanding location, a 2-minute walk to Tanah Rata. While the modern building has some Tudor-like styling on the outside, the rooms inside are pretty standard, but the place is very clean. Make sure you book your room early. This place is always a sellout. Cool Point also has a restaurant serving local and Western dishes.

✪ **The Smokehouse Hotel.** Tanah Rata, Cameron Highlands, Pahang Darul Makmur. ☎ **05/491-1215.** Fax 05/491-1214. 13 units. TEL. RM440–RM680 (US$115.80–US$178.95) suite. AE, DC, MC, V.

Situated between Tanah Rata and Brinchang is a gorgeous Tudor mansion with lush gardens outside and a stunning old-world ambience inside. Built in 1937 as a country house in the heyday of colonial British getaways, the conversion into a hotel has kept the place happily in the 1930s. Guest suites have four-poster beds and antique furnishings, and are stocked with plush amenities. The hotel encourages guests to play golf at the neighboring course, sit for afternoon tea with strawberry confections, or trek along nearby paths (for which they'll provide a picnic basket). It's all a bizarre escape from Malaysia, but an extremely charming one.

DINING

For fine dining in a restaurant, the continental cuisine at the **Smokehouse Hotel** (☎ 05/491-1215) is really your only option. And although it's pricey, it's top rate. As for a more local experience, there's an al fresco **food court** along the Main Street in Tanah Rata that serves excellent Indo-Malay and Western dishes for breakfast, lunch, and dinner at unbeatable prices. Also along Main Street are **cafes** that are good for dinner but seem even more popular for a cold afternoon beer.

ATTRACTIONS

Most of the sights can be seen in a day, but it's difficult to plan your time well. In Cameron Highlands I recommend trying one of the sightseeing outfits in either Brinchang or Tanah Rata as getting around on your own can be quite difficult. **C. S. Travel & Tours,** 47 Main Rd., Tanah Rata (☎ 05/491-1200; fax 05/491-2390), is a highly reputable agency that will plan half-day tours for RM15 (US$3.95) or full days starting from RM80 (US$21.05). On your average tour you'll see the Boh tea plantation and factory, flower nurseries, rose gardens, strawberry farms, butterfly farms and the Sam Poh Buddhist Temple. You're required to pay admission to each attraction yourself. They also provide **trekking and overnight camping tours** in the surrounding hills with local trail guides. Treks are RM30 (US$7.90), camping RM150 (US$39.45) for 2 days/1 night. Bookings are requested at least 1 day in advance. Also, pretty much every hotel can arrange these services for you.

GOLF

If you want to hit around some balls, **Padang Golf,** Main Road between Tanah Rata and Brinchang (☎ **05/491-1126**), has 18 holes at par 71, with greens fees around RM42 (US$11.05) on weekdays and RM63 (US$16.60) on weekends. They also provide club rentals, caddies, shoes, and carts.

6 Penang

Penang is unique in Malaysia because, for all intents and purposes, Penang has it all. Tioman Island (see chapter 11) may have beaches and nature, but it has no shopping or historical sights to speak of. And while Malacca has historical sights and museums, it hasn't a good beach for miles. Similarly, while KL has shopping, nightlife, and attractions, it also has no beach resorts. Penang has all of it: beaches, history, diverse culture, shopping, food—you name it, it has it. If you only have a short time to visit Malaysia but want to take in as wide an experience as you can, Penang is your place.

Penang gets its name from the Malay word "pinang," in reference to the areca plant, which grew on the island in abundance. The nut of the tree, commonly called "betel," was chewed habitually in the East. In the 15th century it was a quiet place populated by small Malay communities, attracting the interest of some southern Indian betel merchants. By the time Francis Light, an agent for the British East India Company, arrived in 1786, the island was already on the maps of European, Indian, and Chinese traders. Light landed on the northeast part of the island, where he began a settlement after an agreement with the Sultan of Kedah, on the mainland. He called the town **Georgetown,** after George III. To gain the help of local inhabitants for clearing the spot, he shot a cannon-load of coins into the jungle.

Georgetown became Britain's principle post in Malaya, attracting traders and settlers from all over the world. Europeans, Arabs, northern and southern Indians, southern Chinese, and Malays from the mainland and Sumatra flocked to the port. But it was never extremely profitable for England, especially when in 1819 Sir Stamford Raffles founded a new trading post in Singapore. Penang couldn't keep up with the new port's success.

In 1826 Penang, along with Malacca and Singapore, formed a unit called the Straits Settlements, and Penang was narrowly declared the seat of government over the other two. Finally in 1832, Singapore stole its thunder when authority shifted there. In the late 1800s Penang got a big break. Tin mines and rubber plantations on mainland Malaya were booming, and with the opening of the railway between KL and **Butterworth** (the town on the mainland just opposite the island), Penang once again thrived. Singapore firms scrambled to open offices in Butterworth.

The Great Depression hit Penang hard. So did the Japanese occupation from 1941 to 1945. The island had been badly bombed. But since Malaysia's independence in 1957, Penang has had relatively good financial success. Today the state of Penang is made up of the island and a small strip of land on the Malaysian mainland. Georgetown is the seat of government for the state. Penang Island is 285 square kilometers (171 sq. miles) and has a population of a little more than one million. Surprisingly, the population is mostly Chinese (59%), followed by Malays (32%) and Indians (7%).

ESSENTIALS
VISITOR INFORMATION

The main **Malaysia Tourism Board (MTB)** office is located at No. 10 Jalan Tun Syed Sheh Barakbah (☎ 04/261-9067), just across from the clock tower by Fort Cornwallis. There's another information center at **Penang International Airport** (☎ 04/643-0501) and a branch on the third level at **KOMTAR (Kompleks Tun Abdul Razak)** on Jalan Penang (☎ 04/261-4461).

GETTING THERE

BY PLANE   **Penang International Airport** (☎ 04/643-0811) has direct flights from Singapore about seven times daily (Singapore Airlines toll-free in Singapore ☎ 1800/223-8888; Malaysia Airlines ☎ 65/336-6777). From KL, Malaysia Airlines has two flights daily (☎ 03/746-3000). The airport is 20 kilometers (12 miles) from the city. To get into town, you must purchase fixed-rate coupons for taxis (RM23/US$6.05 to Georgetown; RM35/US$9.20 to Batu Feringgi). There's also the **Penang Yellow Bus Company** bus no. 83, which will take you to Weld Quay in Georgetown.

There are also car rentals at the airport. Talk to **Hertz** (☎ 04/643-0208) or **Budget** (☎ 04/643-6025).

BY TRAIN   By rail, the trip from KL to Butterworth takes 6 hours and costs RM58.50 (US$15.40) first-class passage, RM25.40 (US$6.70) for second class, and RM14.40 (US$3.80) for third class. Three trains leave daily. Call the **KL Railway Station** (☎ 03/274-7434) for schedule information.

The train will let you off at the **Butterworth Railway Station** (☎ 04/334-7962), on Jalan Bagan Dalam (near the ferry terminal) in Butterworth, on the Malaysian mainland. From there, you can take a taxi to the island or head for the ferry close by.

BY BUS   Many buses will bring you only to Butterworth, so if you want the trip to take you all the way onto the island, make sure you buy a ticket that specifically says Penang. These buses will let you out at **KOMTAR** on Jalan Gladstone across from the Shangri-La Hotel. If you're dropped in Butterworth at the bus terminal on Jalan Bagan Dalam (next to the ferry terminal), you'll need to grab a taxi or take the ferry to the island.

In KL, **Plusliner/NICE** (☎ 03/272-2760) departs from the KL Train Station regularly. The NICE Executive Express coaches leave four times daily, costing RM45 (US$11.85), while the Plusliner standard coaches head for Butterworth three times daily (RM16.50/US$4.35) and Penang Island eight times daily (RM18/US$4.75). The trip takes about 4¹/₂ hours.

For buses back to KL call the **S. E. Bus Line** (☎ 04/262-8723) at the main bus terminal in the basement at KOMTAR.

BY FERRY   The ferry to Penang is nestled between the Butterworth Railway Station and the Butterworth bus terminal. It operates 24 hours a day and takes 20 minutes from pier to pier. From 6am to midnight ferries leave every 10 minutes. From midnight to 1:20am boats run every half hour, and from 1:20 to 6am they run hourly. Purchase your passage by dropping 60 sen (US$0.16) exact change in the turnstile (there's a change booth if you don't have it). Fare is paid only on the trip to Penang. The return is free. The ferry lets you off at **Pengalan Raja Tun Udah,** Weld Quay (☎ 04/ 210-2363).

The ferry will also take cars for a fee of RM7 (US$1.85), which includes passenger fees.

Penang Island

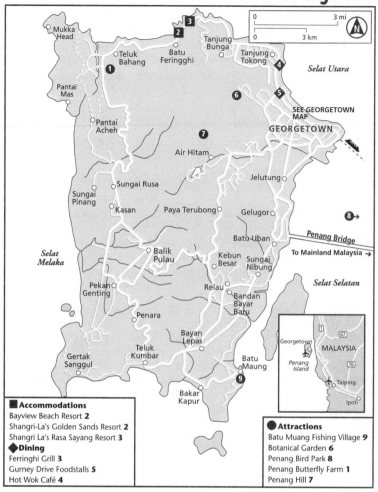

BY TAXI   The outstation taxi stand is in Butterworth (☎ **04/323-2045**). Fares to Butterworth from KL will be about RM240 (US$63.15).

BY CAR   If you're driving you can cross over the 13$\frac{1}{2}$-kilometer (8-mile) Penang Bridge, the longest bridge in Southeast Asia. All cars are charged RM7 (US$1.85) for the trip to Penang. It's free on the return.

GETTING AROUND

BY TAXI   Taxis are abundant, but be warned they do not use meters, so you must agree on the price before you ride. Most trips within the city are between RM3 and RM6. If you're staying out at the Batu Feringgi beach resort area, expect taxis to town to run RM20 (US$5.25); RM30 (US$7.90) at night. The ride is about 15 or 20 minutes, but can take 30 during rush hour.

BY BUS   Buses also run all over the island, and are well used by tourists, who don't want to spring RM20 every time they want to go to the beach. The most popular route is the **Hin Bus Co. (Blue Bus) no. 93,** which operates every 10 minutes between Pengkalan Weld (Weld Quay) in Georgetown and the beach resorts at Batu Feringgi. It makes stops at KOMTAR Shopping Plaza and also at the ferry terminal. Fare is RM1 (US$0.26). Give your money to the nice ticket person on board.

CAR RENTAL   Hertz has an office in Georgetown at 38 Farquhar St. (☎ 04/ 263-5914).

BY BICYCLE & MOTORCYCLE   Along Batu Feringgi there are bicycles and motorcycles available for rent.

BY TRISHAW   In Georgetown it's possible to find some trishaw action for about RM15 (US$3.95) an hour. It's fun and I recommend it for traveling between sights, at least for an hour or two.

ON FOOT   I think everyone should walk at least part of the time to see the sights of Georgetown, because in between each landmark and exhibit there's so much more to see. A taxi, even a trishaw, will whisk you right by back alleys where elderly hair-cutters set up al fresco shops, bicycle repairmen sit fixing tubes in front of their stores, and Chinese grannies fan themselves in the shade. The streets of Georgetown are stimulating, with the sights of old trades still being plied on these living streets, the noise of everyday life, and the exotic smells of an old Southeast Asian port. Give yourself at least a day here.

FAST FACTS: PENANG

American Express has an office in Georgetown at Mayflower Acme Tours, Tan Chong Building, 274 Victoria St. (☎ 04/262-6196). The **banking center** of Georgetown is in the downtown area (close to Fort Cornwallis) on Leboh Pantai, Leboh Union and Leboh Downing. For **Internet service** in town, try sTc Net Café, 221 Chulia St. (☎ 04/264-3378), which charges RM6 (US$1.60) per hour. Out on Batu Feringgi head for **Cyber By the Beach,** Golden Sands Resort (☎ 04/ 881-2096), with fees of RM5 (US$1.30) per hour.

   The main **post office** in Georgetown is on Leboh Downing (☎ 04/261-9222). Another convenient location is out on Jalan Batu Feringgi (☎ 04/881-2555).

ACCOMMODATIONS

While Georgetown has many hotels right in the city for convenient sightseeing, many visitors choose to stay at one of the beach resorts 30 minutes away at Batu Feringgi. Trips back and forth can be a bother (regardless of the resorts' free shuttle services), but if you're not staying in a resort, most of the finer beaches are off limits.

The Bayview Beach Resort. Batu Feringgi Beach, 11100 Penang. ☎ 04/881-2123. Fax 04/881-2140. 366 units. A/C MINIBAR TV TEL. RM402.50 (US$105.90) hill-view double, RM483 (US$127.10) sea-view double; RM655.50 (US$172.50) hill-view suite, RM862.50 (US$226.95) sea-view suite. AE, DC, JCB, MC, V.

Located right on Batu Feringgi Beach, the Bayview is a relaxing resort with all the conveniences you look for in a large international hotel. The feel of the place is spacious and airy, an ambience carried over into the rooms—the standard double room, for instance, is quite large. Rooms facing the road have views of the neighboring condominium complex, and can be noisy. Get the sea view so you can take advantage of your balcony. Facilities include an outdoor pool, squash and tennis courts, billiards, table tennis, and a fitness center with Jacuzzi, sauna, and steam. Cycling, parasailing, water-skiing, sailing, windsurfing, canoeing, and boat trips to beachside barbecues and fishing spots are all available. Recent discount packages offer 50% discounts off all categories of rooms.

Georgetown

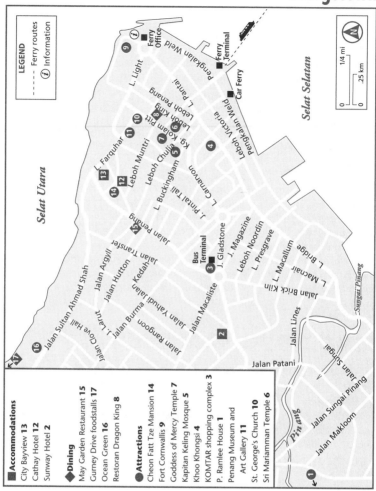

LEGEND
---- Ferry routes
(i) Information

Selat Utara

Selat Selatan

Sungai Pinang

Accommodations
City Bayview **13**
Cathay Hotel **12**
Sunway Hotel **2**

◆**Dining**
May Garden Restaurant **15**
Gurney Drive foodstalls **17**
Ocean Green **16**
Restoran Dragon King **8**

●**Attractions**
Cheon Fatt Tze Mansion **14**
Fort Cornwallis **9**
Goddess of Mercy Temple **7**
Kapitan Keling Mosque **5**
Khoo Khongsi **4**
KOMTAR shopping complex **3**
P. Ramlee House **1**
Penang Museum and
   Art Gallery **11**
St. George's Church **10**
Sri Mariamman Temple **6**

Cathay Hotel. No. 15 Leith St., Georgetown 10200, Penang. ☎ **04/262-6271.** Fax 04/263-9300. 37 units. TV. Double RM59.80 (US$15.75) without A/C, RM69 (US$18.15) with A/C. No credit cards.

Cathay is highly recommended for its location and price. Within walking distance of the city attractions, it's definitely a budget place, but it has a charming faded elegance. Housed in a traditional Chinese prewar mansion, nice touches include high ceilings, mosaic tile and wood floors, and whitewashed walls. The decor features Chinese lanterns and ceiling fans. You won't find a budget hotel with more style and respectability. The only real faults are the small, old bathrooms and the lack of room service or laundry services.

✪ **The City Bayview Hotel, Penang.** 25-A Farquhar St., Georgetown 10200 Penang. ☎ **04/263-3161.** Fax 04/263-4124. 176 units. A/C MINIBAR TV TEL. RM300–RM350 (US$78.95–US$92.10) double. AE, DC, MC, V.

Situated on Farquhar Street, City Bayview has a convenient location for visitors who want to take in the historic and cultural sights of Georgetown. A new wing opened last year featuring large guest rooms that have style and amenities that bring the hotel up to date (before this it hadn't seen renovation since 1975!). Newly renovated suites in the old wing have been completely updated with new furnishings and amenities.

✪ **Shangri-La's Rasa Sayang Resort.** Batu Feringgi Beach, 11100 Penang. ☎ **800/ 942-5050** in the U.S. and Canada, 800/222448 in Australia, 0800/442179 in New Zealand, or 04/881-1811. Fax 04/881-1984. www.shangri-la.com. 515 units. A/C MINIBAR TV TEL. RM580–RM680 (US$152.65–US$178.95) double, RM780 (US$205.25) deluxe sea-facing double; RM740 (US$194.75) deluxe garden/patio rm; from RM1,000 (US$263.15) suite. AE, DC, JCB, MC, V.

Of all the beachfront resorts on Penang, Rasa Sayang is the finest. It has been here the longest, celebrating its 25-year anniversary in 1998, so it had the first pick of beach-front property and plenty of space to create lush gardens and pool areas. Get a room looking over the pool area, and your private balcony will be facing the picturesque palm-lined beach. The free-form pool is sprawled amid tropical landscaping and cafes, and the rest of the grounds have strolling gardens that are romantically illuminated in the evenings. The hotel is both elegant and relaxed, with Malay-style decor in the pub-lic areas and rooms. You'll also appreciate the good seafood restaurants nearby. Facili-ties include an outdoor pool, fitness center, small putting green, and table tennis. Guests have access to nearby tennis courts, sailing, boating, and waterskiing. Make sure to ask about the incredible bargain packages.

Shangri-La's Golden Sands Resort. Batu Feringgi Beach, 11100 Penang. ☎ **800/ 942-5050** in the U.S. and Canada, 800/222448 in Australia, 0800/442179 in New Zealand, or 04/881-1911. Fax 04/881-1880. www.shangri-la.com. 395 units. A/C MINIBAR TV TEL. RM430–RM610 (US$113.15–US$160.55) double; RM1,250 (US$328.95) suite. AE, DC, JCB, MC, V.

Rasa Sayang's little sister property is located just next door. A newer resort, it is priced lower than the Rasa Sayang, so it attracts more families. The beach, pool area, and public spaces fill up fast in the morning, and folks are occupied all day with beach sports like parasailing and jet skiing, and pool games. For the younger set, a kids' club keeps small ones busy while mom and dad do "boring stuff." Rooms are large with full amenities, and the higher priced categories have views of the pool and sea. Better still, guests here can use the facilities at Rasa Sayang.

Sunway Hotel. 33 New Lane, Georgetown, 10400 Penang. ☎ **04/229-9988.** Fax 04/228-8899. 262 units. A/C MINIBAR TV TEL. RM330 (US$86.85) double; RM600 (US$157.90) suite. Ask about discounts as low as 165RM (US$43.40) for a double, including American breakfast. AE, DC, MC, V.

The Sunway is centrally located in Georgetown, near the KOMTAR shopping com-plex and the Penang Museum. Built in 1994, the hotel is warm and elegant, with mar-ble details and a new and modern feel to the open spaces. The rooms are fresh and spacious, and rooms on all sides have views of the city. Facilities include an outdoor pool and a fitness center with Jacuzzi. The hotel can arrange tennis, squash, and sauna at nearby facilities.

DINING

✪ **Feringgi Grill.** Shangri-La's Rasa Sayang Resort, Batu Feringgi Beach. ☎ **04/881-1811.** Reservations recommended. Entrees RM49.50–RM68 (US$13.05–US$17.90). Daily 7–10:30pm. CONTINENTAL.

The Feringgi Grill is comparable to any five-star hotel grill anywhere. From the dreamy lobster bisque to the carving cart of perfectly grilled top-quality meats flown in from all over the world, you'll be living the good life with each bite. A good wine selection will help revive you when you think you've died and gone to heaven. And don't even mention the desserts—the whole cart is a sore temptation sent straight from hell. Feringgi is perfect for a romantic dinner, or a change from all that char koay teow you've been eating in town.

✪ **Hot Wok Café.** 125-D Desa Tanjung, Jalan Tanjung. ☎ **04/899-0858.** Reservations recommended for weekends. Entrees RM9–RM15 (US$2.35–US$3.95). AE, DC, MC, V. Daily 11am– 3pm and 6–11pm. PERANAKAN.

This place is the number one recommended Peranakan restaurant in the city, and small wonder: The food is great and the atmosphere is fabulous. Filled with local treasures such as wooden lattice work, wooden lanterns, carved Peranakan cabinets, tapestries, and carved wood panels, the decor will make you want to just sit back, relax, and take in sights you'd only ever see in a Peranakan home. Their curry capitan, a famous local dish, is curry chicken stuffed with potatoes, with a thick delicious coconut-based gravy. The house specialty is a mean perut ikan (fish intestine with roe and vegetable).

✪ **May Garden Restaurant.** 70 Jalan Penang. ☎ **04/261-6806.** Reservations recommended. Entrees start at RM8 (US$2.10). Seafood is priced by weight in kilograms. AE, DC, MC, V. Noon–3pm and 6–10:30pm. CANTONESE.

This is a top Cantonese restaurant in Georgetown, and while it's noisy and not too big on ambience, it has excellent food. But how many Chinese do *you* know who go to places for ambience? It's the food that counts! Outstanding dishes include the tofu and broccoli topped with sea snail slices or the fresh steamed live prawns. They also have suckling pig and Peking duck. Don't agree to all the daily specials or you'll be paying a fortune.

✪ **Ocean Green.** 48F Jalan Sultan Ahmad Shah. ☎ **04/226-2681.** Reservations recommended. Entrees starting from RM12 (US$3.15); seafood priced according to market value. Open daily 9am–11pm. AE, MC, V. SEAFOOD.

I can't rave enough about Ocean Green. If the beautiful sea view and ocean breezes don't make you weep with joy, the food certainly will. A long list of fresh seafood is prepared steamed or fried, with your choice of chile, black-bean, sweet-and-sour, or curry sauces. On the advice of a local food expert, I tried the lobster thermidor, expensive but divine, and the chicken wings stuffed with minced chicken, prawns, and gravy.

Restoran Dragon King. 99 Leboh Bishop. ☎ **04/261-8035.** Entrees RM8–RM20 (US$2.10–US$5.25). No credit cards. Daily 11am–3pm and 6–10pm. PERANAKAN.

Penang is famous around the world for delicious local Peranakan dishes, and Dragon King is a good place to sample the local cuisine at its finest. It was opened 20 years ago by a group of local teachers who wanted to revive the traditional dishes cooked by their mothers. In terms of decor, the place is nothing to shout about—just a coffee shop with tile floors and folding chairs—but all the curries are hand blended to perfection. Their curry capitan will make you weep with joy, it's so rich. But come early for the otak-otak, or it might sell out. While Dragon King is hopping at lunchtime, dinner is quiet.

FOOD STALL DINING

No section on Penang dining would be complete without full coverage of the local food stall scene, which is famous. Penang hawkers can make any dish you've had in Malaysia, Singapore, or even southern Thailand better. I had slimy char koay teow in

Singapore and swore off the stuff forever. After being forced to try it in Penang (where the fried flat noodles and seafood are a specialty dish), I was completely addicted. Penang may be attractive for many things—history, culture, nature—but it is loved for its food.

Gurney Drive Foodstalls, toward the water just down from the intersection with Jalan Kelawai, is the biggest and most popular hawker center. It has all kinds of food, including local dishes with every influence: Chinese, Malay, Indian. In addition to the above-mentioned char koay teow, there's char bee hoon (a fried thin rice noodle), laksa (fish soup with noodles), murtabak (a sort of curry mutton burrito), oh chien (oyster omelette with chile dip), and rojak (a spicy fruit and seafood salad). After you've eaten your way through Gurney Drive, you can try the stalls on **Jalan Burmah** near the Lai Lai Supermarket.

ATTRACTIONS
IN GEORGETOWN

✪ **Fort Cornwallis.** Lebuhraya Light. No phone. Admission RM1 (US$0.26) adults, RM.50 (US$0.13) children. Daily 8am–7pm.

Fort Cornwallis is built on the site where Capt. Francis Light, founder of Penang, first landed in 1786. The fort was first built in 1793, but this site was an unlikely spot to defend the city from invasion. In 1810 it was rebuilt in an attempt to make up for initial strategic planning errors. In the shape of a star, the only actual buildings still standing are the outer walls, a gunpowder magazine, and a small Christian chapel. The magazine houses an exhibit of old photos and historical accounts of the old fort.

✪ **Cheong Fatt Tze Mansion.** Lebuhraya Leith. No phone. Admission RM12 (US$3.15) adults and children. Open for guided tours only Thurs–Fri at 9am.

Cheong Fatt Tze (1840–1917), once dubbed as "China's Rockefeller" by *The New York Times,* built a vast commercial empire in Southeast Asia, first in Indonesia, then in Singapore. He came to Penang in 1890 and continued his success, giving some of his spoils to build schools throughout the region. His mansion, where he lived with his eight wives, was built between 1896 and 1904. Inside are lavish adornments—stained glass, crown moldings, gilded wood-carved doors, ceramic ornaments, and seven staircases.

✪ **Khoo Khongsi.** Leburaya Cannon. ☎ **604/261-4609.** Free admission. Daily 9am–5pm.

The Chinese who migrated to Southeast Asia created clan associations in their new homes. Based on common heritage, these social groups formed the core of Chinese life in the new homelands. The Khoo clan, who immigrated from Hokkien province in China, acquired this spot in 1851 and set to work building row houses, administrative buildings, and a clan temple around a large square. The temple here now was actually built in 1906 after a fire destroyed its predecessor. It was believed the original was too ornate, provoking the wrath of the gods. One look at the current temple, a Chinese baroque masterpiece, and you'll wonder how that could possibly be. Come here in August for Chinese operas.

P. Ramlee House. Jalan P. Ramlee. No phone. Free admission. Daily 9am–5pm.

This is the house where legendary Malaysian actor, director, singer, composer, and prominent figurehead of the Malaysian film industry P. Ramlee (1928–73) was born and raised. A gallery of photos from his life and personal memorabilia offer a glimpse of local culture even those who've never heard of him can appreciate.

☼ Penang Museum and Art Gallery. Leburaya Farquhar. ☎ **04/261-3144.** Free admission. Open Sat–Thurs 9am–5pm.

The historical society has put together this marvelous collection of ethnological and historical findings from Penang, tracing the port's history and diverse cultures through time. It's filled with paintings, photos, costumes, and antiques among much more, all presented with fascinating facts and trivia. Upstairs is an art gallery. Originally the Penang Free School, the building was built in two phases, the first half in 1896 and the second in 1906. Only half of the building remains; the other was bombed to the ground in World War II. It's a favorite stop on a sightseeing itinerary because it's *air-conditioned!*

Kapitan Keling Mosque. Jalan Masjid Kapitan Keling (Leboh Pitt). No phone.

Captain Light donated a large parcel of land on this spot for the settlement's sizable Indian Muslim community to build a mosque and graveyard. The leader of the community, known as Kapitan Keling (or Kling, which ironically was once a racial slur against Indians in the region), built a brick mosque here. Later, in 1801, he imported builders and materials from India for a new, brilliant mosque. Expansions in the 1900s topped the mosque with stunning domes and turrets, adding extensions and new roofs.

Goddess of Mercy Temple. Leboh Pitt. No phone.

Dedicated jointly to Kuan Yin, the goddess of mercy, and Ma Po Cho, the patron saint of sea travelers, this is the oldest Chinese temple in Penang. On the 19th of each second, sixth, and ninth month of the lunar calendar, Kuan Yin is celebrated with Chinese operas and puppet shows.

St. George's Church. Farquhar St. No phone.

Built by Rev. R. S. Hutchins (who was also responsible for the Free School next door, home of the Penang Museum) and Capt. Robert N. Smith, whose paintings hang in the museum, this church was completed in 1818. While the outside is almost as it was then, the contents were completely looted during World War II. All that remains are the font and the bishop's chair.

Sri Mariamman Temple. Leburaya Queen. No phone.

This Hindu temple was built in 1833 by a Chettiar, a group of Southern Indian Muslims, and received a major face-lift in 1978 with the help of Madras sculptors. The Hindu Navarithri festival is held here, whereby devotees parade Sri Mariamman, a Hindu goddess worshipped for her powers to cure disease, through the streets in a night procession. It is also the starting point of the Thaipusam Festival, which leads to a temple on Jalan Waterfall.

OUTSIDE GEORGETOWN

Batu Muang Fishing Village. Southeast tip of Penang. No central phone.

If it's a local fishing village you'd like to see, here's a good one. This village is special for its shrine to Admiral Cheng Ho, the early Chinese sea adventurer.

☼ Botanical Garden. About a 5- or 10-min. drive west of Georgetown. ☎ **604/228-6248.** Free admission. Daily 5am–8pm.

Covering 30 hectares (70 acres) of landscaped grounds, this botanical garden was established by the British in 1884, with grounds that are perfect for a shady walk and a ton of fun if you love monkeys. They're crawling all over the place and will think nothing of stepping forward for a peanut (which you can buy beneath the "do not feed the monkeys" sign). Also in the gardens is a jogging track and kiddie park.

Penang Butterfly Farm. Jalan Teluk Bahang. ☎ **04/881-1253.** Admission RM5 (US$1.30) adult, RM2 (US$0.53) child over 5; free for children under 4. Mon–Fri 9am–5pm, Sat–Sun 9am–6pm.

The Penang Butterfly Farm, located toward the northwest corner of the island, is the largest in the world. On its 0.8-hectare (2-acre) landscaped grounds there are more than 4,000 flying butterflies from 120 species. At 10am and 3pm there are informative butterfly shows. Don't forget the insect exhibit—there are about 2,000 or so bugs.

✪ **Penang Hill.** A 20- to 30-min. drive southwest from Georgetown. The funicular station is on Jalan Stesen Keretapi Bukit.

Covered with jungle growth and 20 nature trails, the hill is great for trekking. Or, you can go to Ayer Hitam, a town in the central part of Penang, and take the **Keretapi Bukit Bendera** funicular railway to the top. It sends trains up and down the hill every half hour from 6:30am to 10:30pm weekdays and until midnight on weekends, and costs RM4 (US$1.05) for adults and RM2 (US$0.53) for children. If you prefer to make the trek on foot, go to the "Moon Gate" at the entrance to the Botanical Garden for a 5.5-kilometer (9-miles), 3-hour hike to the summit.

Penang Bird Park. Jalan Teluk, Seberang Jaya. ☎ **04/399-1899.** Admission RM10 (US$2.65) adult, RM5 (US$1.30) child. Daily 9am–7pm.

The Bird Park is not on Penang Island, but on the mainland part of Penang state. The 2-hectare (5-acre) park is home to some 200 bird species from Malaysia and around the world.

SHOPPING

The first place anyone here will recommend you to go for shopping is **KOMTAR.** Short for "Kompleks Tun Abdul Razak," it is the largest shopping complex in Penang, a full 65 stories of clothing shops, restaurants, and a couple of large department stores. There's a **duty-free shop** on the 57th floor. On the third floor is a **tourist information center.**

Good shopping finds in Penang are batik, pewter products, locally produced curios, paintings, antiques, pottery, and jewelry. If you care to walk around in search of finds, there are a few streets in Georgetown that are the hub of shopping activity. In the city center, the area around Jalan Penang, Leburhaya Campbell, Lebuhraya Kapitan Keling, Lebuhraya Chulia, and Lebuhraya Pantai is near the Sri Mariamman Temple, the Penang Museum, the Kapitan Keling Mosque, and other sites of historic interest. Here you'll find everything from local crafts to souvenirs and fashion, and maybe even a bargain or two. Most of these shops are open from 10am to 10pm daily.

Out at Batu Feringgi, the main road turns into a fun **night bazaar** every evening just at dark. During the day, there are also some good shops for batik and souvenirs.

NIGHTLIFE

Clubs in Penang stay open a little later than in the rest of Malaysia, and some even stay open until 3am on the weekends.

If you're looking for a bar that's a little out of the ordinary, visit **20 Leith Street,** 11-A Lebuh Leith (☎ **04/261-6301**). Located in an old 1930s house, the place has seating areas fitted with traditional antique furniture in each room of the house. Possibly the most notorious bar in Penang is the **Hong Kong Bar,** 371 Lebuh Chulia (☎ **04/261-9796**), which opened in 1920 and was a regular hangout for military personnel based in Butterworth. It has an extraordinary archive of photos of the servicemen who have patronized the place throughout the years, plus a collection of medals, plaques, and buoys from ships.

For dancing, the resorts in Batu Feringgi have the better discos. **Borsalino,** Penang Park Royal, 1 Batu Ferringhi Beach (☎ 04/881-1133, ext. 8844), is popular, with upbeat dance music and slick disco decor. Much of the clientele seems to remember when disco meant doing the hustle. **Zulu's Seaside Paradise,** Paradise Tanjung Bungah (☎ 04/890-8808), is a world-beat dance club, spinning African, reggae, and other danceable international music.

Hard Life Café, 363 Lebuh Chulia (☎ 04/262-1740), is an interesting alternative hangout. Decorated with Rastafarian paraphernalia, the place fills up with backpackers, who sometimes aren't as laid-back as Mr. Marley would hope they'd be. Still, it's fun to check out the books where guests comment on their favorite (or least favorite) travel haunts in Southeast Asia.

7 Langkawi

Where the beautiful Andaman Sea meets the Strait of Malacca, Langkawi Island positions itself as one of the best emerging island paradise destinations in the region. Since 1990, the Malaysian Tourism Board has dedicated itself to promoting the island and developing it as an ideal travel spot. Now, after a decade of work, the island has proven itself as one of this country's holiday gems.

Its biggest competition comes from Phuket, Thailand's beach-lover fantasy to the north. But, day for day and dollar for dollar, I'd take Langkawi over Phuket hands down. Why? Well, despite being pumped up by government money and promotional campaigns, Langkawi remains relatively unheard of on the travel scene. So, while you get the same balmy weather, gorgeous beaches, fun water sports, and great seafood, you also avoid the horrible effects of tourism gone awry—inflated prices, annoying touts, and overcrowding. Besides, I've stayed in almost every luxury property on Phuket, and can testify that Langkawi's finest resorts can compete with pride.

This small island also claims a Hollywood credit, starring in the 1999 film *Anna and the King*. Langkawi played the part of Thailand to Jodie Foster's Anna Leonowens and Chow Young Fatt's King Mongkut (Rama IV). The Thais wouldn't allow the filmmakers to shoot on location in their kingdom (and rightly so, as King Mongkut, their revered Father of Modern Thailand, has been continuously portrayed in the West as a stubborn, immature fop who got all his great ideas from a common English tutor—indeed, historians agree that according to many well-documented sources, Anna Leonowens's famous account of her time at the Royal Palace had more basis in her imagination than in reality), so Hollywood turned to neighboring Malaysia for location filming. The palatial Thai-style buildings constructed for the set have never been torn down, and you can still hear all kinds of local gossip about the film's stars.

Technically, Langkawi is a cluster of islands, the largest of which serves as the main focal point. Ask how many islands actually make up Langkawi and you'll hear either 104 or 99. The official MTB response? "Both are correct. It depends on the tide!" On Langkawi Island itself, the main town, **Kuah,** provides the island's administrative needs, while on the western and northern shores, the beaches have been developed with resorts. The west-coast beaches of **Pantai Cenang** and **Pantai Tengah** are the most developed; however, the concept of development here should be taken in relative terms. To the north, **Datai Bay** and **Tanjung Rhu** host the island's two finest, and most secluded, resorts.

One final note: Malaysia has declared Langkawi a duty-free zone, so take a peek at some of the shopping in town, and enjoy RM4 (US$1.05) beers!

ESSENTIALS
GETTING THERE
BY PLANE   Malaysia Airways makes Langkawi very convenient from either mainland Malaysia or Singapore. From KL, two daily flights depart for Langkawi's International Airport (☎ 04/955-1322). Call Malaysia Airline's ticketing office in KL (☎ 03/746-300) or their reservations line on Langkawi (☎ 04/966-6622). From Singapore, Malaysian Airlines flies direct daily, but has numerous other flights with stops in either KL or Penang. For Singapore reservations call ☎ 65/336-6777.

The best thing to do is prearrange a **shuttle pickup** from your resort, otherwise you can just grab a taxi out in front of the airport. To Pantai Cenang or Pantai Tengah, the fare should be about RM25 (US$6.60), while to the farther resorts at Tanjung Rhu and Datai Bay it will be as high as RM40 (US$10.55). To call for a pickup from the airport dial ☎ 04/955-1800.

BY TRAIN   Taking the train can be a bit of a hassle, because the nearest stop (in Alor Setar) is quite far from the jetty to the island, requiring a cab transfer. Still, if you prefer rail, hop on the overnight train from KL (the only train), which will put you in to Alor Setar at around 6am. Just outside the train station you can find the taxi stand, with cabs to take you to the Kuala Kedah jetty for RM10 (US$2.65). Call the KL Railway Station at ☎ 03/274-7434 or the Alor Setar Railway Station at ☎ 04/731-4045 for further details.

BY BUS   To be honest, I don't really recommend using this route. If you're coming from KL, the bus ride is long and uncomfortable, catching the taxi transfer to the jetty can be problematic, and by the time you reach the island you'll need a vacation from your vacation. Fly or use the train. If you're coming from Penang, the direct ferry is wonderfully convenient.

BY FERRY   From the jetty at Kuala Kedah, there are about five companies that provide ferry service to the island (trip time: about 1 hr. and 45 min.; cost: RM15/US$3.95). Contact **LADA Holdings** at ☎ 04/762-3823 in Kuala Kedah or 04/966-8823 in Langkawi; Langkawi Ferry Services at ☎ 04/762-4524 in Kuala Kedah or 04/966-9439; or Nautica Ferries at ☎ 04/762-1201 in Kuala Kedah or 04/966-7868 in Langkawi. Ferries let you off at the main ferry terminal in Kuah, where you can hop a taxi to your resort for between RM30 and RM40 (US$7.90 and US$10.55).

If you're coming from Penang, the ferry is the way to go. **Bahagia Express** has a morning and afternoon speedboat from Weld Quay in Georgetown for RM35 (US$9.20). Call them in Penang at ☎ 04/263-1943 or visit their office across from the clock tower, just next to the main tourism board office. If you're heading from Langkawi to Penang, you can call Bahagia in Langkawi at ☎ 04/966-5784.

VISITOR INFORMATION
The MTB office is unfortunately situated in Kuah town on Jalan Persiaran Putra, so most travelers miss it completely, instead heading straight for the beach areas. If you'd like to pick up some of their information, ask your taxi driver to stop on the way to your resort. For specific queries, you can also call them at ☎ 04/966-7789. If you're arriving by plane, there's another MTB office at the airport (☎ 04/955-7155).

Langkawi

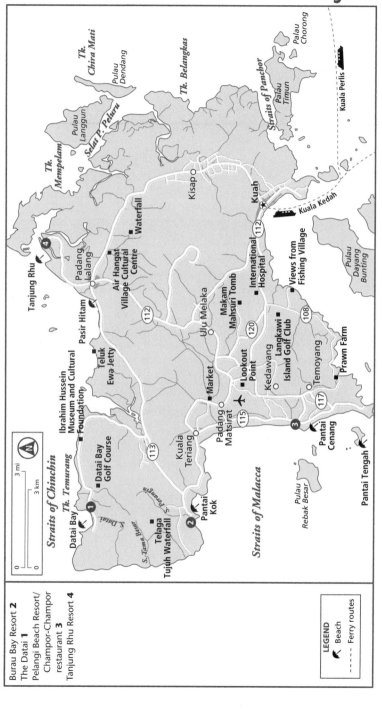

Burau Bay Resort **2**
The Datai **1**
Pelangi Beach Resort/
Champor-Champor
restaurant **3**
Tanjung Rhu Resort **4**

LEGEND
Beach
- - - - Ferry routes

Tk. Chira Mati

Pulau Dendang

Pulau Langgun

Tk. Belangkas

Straits of Panchor

Pulau Chorong

Pulau Timun

Kuala Perlis

Tk. Mempelam

Selat T. Pelaru

Kisap

Kuah

Kuala Kedah

Waterfall

Padang Lalang

Pulau Dayang Bunting

Tanjung Rhu

Air Hangat Village Cultural Centre

Pasir Hitam

International Hospital

Views from Fishing Village

Ulu Melaka

Makam Mahsuri Tomb

Teluk Ewa Jetty

Langkawi Island Golf Club

Market

Lookout Point

Kedawang

Temoyang

Prawn Farm

Ibrahim Hussein Museum and Cultural Foundation

Datai Bay Golf Course

Padang Matsirat

Pantai Cenang

Straits of Chinchin

Tk. Temurang

Datai Bay

Kuala Teriang

Pantai Tengah

Pulau Rebak Besar

Telaga Tujuh Waterfall

Pantai Kok

Straits of Malacca

N

3 mi

3 km

112

112

120

115

117

108

113

GETTING AROUND

BY TAXI   Taxis generally hang around at the airport, the main jetty, the taxi stand in Kuah, and at some major hotels. From anywhere in between, your best bet is to call the taxi stand for a pickup (☎ **04/966-5249**). Keep in mind, if you're going as far as one side of the island to the other, your fare can go as high as RM40 (US$10.55).

CAR & MOTORCYCLE RENTAL   At the airport and from agents in the complex behind the main jetty, car rentals can be arranged starting at RM60 (US$15.80) per day. This is for the standard, no-frills model—actually, mine was more reminiscent of some of the junkers I drove throughout college, but it still got me around. Insurance policies are lax, as are rental regulations. My rental guys seemed more concerned with my passport documents than with my driver's license. If you're out on the beach at Cenang or Tengah, a few places rent Jeeps and motorcycles from RM80 (US$21.05) per day and RM30 (US$7.90) per day, respectively. Pick a good helmet.

BY FOOT   The main beaches at Cenang and Tengah can be walked quite nicely; however, don't expect to be able to walk around to other parts of the island.

FAST FACTS: LANGKAWI

The only major **bank** branches seem sadly located far from the beach areas, in Kuah town, mostly around the blocks across the street from the Night Hawker Center (off Jalan Persiaran Putra). **Money changers** keep long hours out at Pantai Cenang and Pantai Tengah, but for other resorts you'll have to change your money at the resort itself. The main **post office** is in Kuah town at the LADA Kompleks on Jalan Persiaran Putra (☎ **04/966-7271**). Otherwise, use your resort's mail services. Along the Pantai Cenang and Pantai Tengah main road, you'll find at least a half dozen small **Internet** places. **The Shop,** a small convenience store along the strip, provides service for RM6 (US$1.60) per hour.

ACCOMMODATIONS

Burau Bay Resort. Teluk Burau, 07000 Langkawi, Kedah. ☎ **04/959-1061.** Fax 04/959-1172. 150 units. A/C MINIBAR TV TEL. RM250 (US$65.80) garden-view chalet; RM280 (US$73.70) sea-view chalet; RM370 (US$97.35) family chalet; RM735 (US$193.40) royal chalet. AE, DC, JCB, MC, V.

Pelangi's little-sister property, Burau offers beachside resort accommodations for less money than its upscale sibling. Not nearly as ritzy, this place feels more like summer camp than a resort. All guest rooms are contained in cabanas, with simple decor that's a bit on the older side. For the price, though, they offer value for money. The only restaurant serves local cuisine and Western elections al fresco. All rooms have in-house movies. Burau also organizes golf, massage, Jeep treks, jungle treks, mountain biking, tennis, canoeing, catamaran sailing, jet skiing, scuba diving, snorkeling, fishing, water-skiing, windsurfing, and yachting. Facilities include an outdoor pool, daily shuttle to town, overnight room service, games pavilion, and provision shop.

✪ **The Datai.** Jalan Teluk Datai, Langkawi, Kedah. ☎ **04/959-2500.** A/C MINIBAR TV TEL. RM1057 (US$279) double; RM1213–RM1781 (US$320–US$470) villa; US$470–US$1,380 suite. Prices jump about 50% from Dec–Jan. AE, DC, MC, V.

Aesthetically speaking, this is one of my favorite resorts in Southeast Asia, coming damn close to heaven. It is simply elegant and elegantly simple. I love how the resort blends with its natural jungle surroundings. There's literally nothing to distract you from the beauty of this place. The rooms delight, with lovely daybeds looking out to your private balcony. Minimalist in design, the decor's color schemes stick close to natural, with rosewood tones, deep local tapestries, and regal celadon upholstery.

Designer body-care products make an evening in the oversized bathrooms pure joy. Villas carry through the same theme, but ensure additional privacy. My one complaint? The beach is inferior to others on the island—the narrow strip of sand flanks a bay that's full of rocks.

Dining/Diversions: The Pavilion serves exquisite Thai fare al fresco, while the dining room serves Malaysian and Western cuisine. The Beach Club, near the large pool, serves snacks and light meals. The bar off the lobby can't be beat, with its spectacular view—perfect for lazing about with cocktails to watch the sunset.

Amenities: They provide in-house movies, nature walks, and all sorts of other diversions: massage and spa facilities, fitness center, sailing, tennis, water sports, car rental, and a tour desk. There's also a golf course nearby.

✪ **Tanjung Rhu Resort.** Tanjung Rhu, Mukim Ayer Hangat, Langkawi, Kedah. 138 units. A/C MINIBAR TV TEL. RM777–RM1666 (US$205–US$440) double. AE, DC, JCB, MC, V.

Everyone on the island will agree that the beach at Tanjung Rhu—a wide crescent wrapped around a perfect bay—wins first prize, no contest. It's spectacular. This resort claims 1,100 acres, monopolizing the scene for extra privacy, but it has its pros and cons. The pros? Guest rooms are enormous and decorated with a sensitivity to the environment, from natural materials to organic recycled-paper wrapped toiletries. The cons? Make sure you don't book your vacation during a Malaysian or Singaporean school vacation, since the place draws families like flies, and believe me the kids will buzz all over the place. Still, during between-holiday downtime, I love this resort's friendly and casual atmosphere—and, of course, the beach.

Dining/Diversions: Their Mediterranean fine-dining establishment and a poolside restaurant serving casual fare provide all meals. The beachside bar makes for a really happy hour, while things get more lively at the disco (but only when the resort is full).

Amenities: In-room VCRs can be used with the resort's large collection of videos. A fitness center with sauna and massage, large outdoor pool, tennis, water sports, and 40-foot yacht (for rental) round out the facilities. They also plan regular rain forest tours, mangrove river boat rides, cave explorations, and nature walks.

✪ **Pelangi Beach Resort.** Pantai Cenang, 07000 Langkawi, Kedah ☎ 04/ 955-1001. Fax 04/955-1122. 350 units. A/C MINIBAR TV TEL. RM513–RM563 (US$135–US$148.15) double; RM820–RM1,520 (US$215.80–US$400) suite. AE, DC, JCB, MC, V.

For those who prefer a more active vacation, I recommend Pelangi. A top-quality resort, this place stands out from neighboring five-star resorts for it's sheer fun. A long list of organized sports and leisure pastimes make it especially attractive for families, but surprisingly I never found children to be a distraction here. Pelangi's 51 ethnic wooden chalets are huge inside, and are divided into either one, two, or four guest rooms. You'll be welcomed by vaulted ceilings, modern bathrooms, and large living spaces. But it's the little things you'll love—I didn't want to get out of bed and leave my squishy down pillows and snuggly bedding! In addition, Pelangi's location, near the central beach strip for island life, means you're not cloistered away from the rest of civilization.

Dining/Diversions: While the Niyom Thai restaurant does a fine job with Thai cuisine, the Spice Market proves the resort's premier restaurant with local and Western cuisine, featuring an international buffet nightly. The Cenang Beach Bar is the nicest dinner, serving barbecue seafood feasts by the sea.

Amenities: Recreation facilities include a fitness center with steam and sauna; two large outdoor pools; a children's center; tennis and squash courts; a water-sports center for arranging boat trips, snorkeling, and diving; plus a tour desk for booking treks.

DINING

If you're out at one of the more secluded resorts, chances are you'll stay there for most of your meals. However, if you're at Pantai Cenang or Pantai Tengah, I strongly recommend taking a stroll down to **Champor-Champor**, just across the road in the Pelangi Resort (☎ 04/955-1449), which serves magnificently creative dishes at lunch and dinner—a local roti canai served like a pizza, and local fish catches doused in sweet sauces. Everything is incredibly fresh, wildly delicious, and amazingly inexpensive. As for decor, the imaginative catchall beach shack atmosphere really relaxes. After dinner, hang around the bar for the best fun on the island. Since Langkawi is an official duty-free port, one beer costs a wee RM4 (US$1.05)! If you're in Kuah town looking for something good to eat, the best local dining experience can be found at the evening **hawker stalls** just along the waterfront near the taxi stand. A long row of hawkers cook up every kind of local favorite, including seafood dishes. You can't get any cheaper or more laid-back. After dinner, from here it's easy to flag down a taxi back to your resort.

Finally, I'm not one to bash places, but I got suckered by a glossy brochure for **Barn Thai**—a Thai restaurant on the eastern side of the island built deep inside a thick mangrove forest. Sound interesting? The food was terrible and overpriced while the atmosphere was destroyed by busloads of tourists. Stay away.

ATTRACTIONS

Most visitors will come for the **beaches.** All resorts are pretty much self-contained units, planning numerous water-sports activities, trekking, sports, and tours.

For a fun day trip I recommend taking one of the local boat trips to some of Langkawi's other islands. Most diving trips take you out to **Payar Marine Park** for two dives per day. Off Payar Island, a floating platform drifts above a stunning coral reef, where dive operators and snorkel gear rentals are available (there's also a glass-bottom boat if you don't want to get wet). Day trips to other **surrounding islands** such as Pulau Singa Besar, Pulau Langgun, Pulau Rebak, or Pulau Beras Basah give you a day of peaceful sun-soaking and swimming. The full day trip to Payar Island floating reef platform costs RM170 (US$44.75), but dives and rental of snorkel gear cost extra. If you want to hop around to nice secluded island beaches, the half-day **island hopping tour** costs RM45 (US$11.85). The half-day **round-island tour** also stops at a few attractions, including the Batik Art Village (RM30/US$7.90). In Langkawi call Asian Overland at ☎ 04/955-2002, or talk to your hotel tour desk operator.

Perhaps one of the loveliest additions to Langkawi's attractions is the **Ibrahim Hussein Museum and Cultural Foundation,** Pasir Tengkorak, Jalan Datai (☎ 04/959-4669). The artistic devotion of the foundation's namesake fueled the creation of this enchanting modern space designed to showcase Malaysia's contribution to the international fine-arts scene. If you can pull yourself from the beach for any one activity in Langkawi, this is the one I recommend. Mr. Hussein has created a museum worthy of international attention. Truly a gem. It's open daily from 10am to 5pm; adults RM7 (US$1.85), children free.

SHOPPING

Langkawi's designated Duty Free Port status makes shopping here quite fun and very popular. In Kuah town, the Sime Darby Duty Free Shop, **Langkawi Duty Free,** 64 Persiaran Putra, Pekan Kuah (☎ 04/966-6052), carries the largest selection.

Peninsular Malaysia: The East Coast

Over the past 200 years, while the cities on the western coast of peninsular Malaysia preoccupied themselves with waves of foreign domination, those on the eastern coast developed in relative seclusion. Today, this part of the country remains true to its Malay heritage, from the small fishing kampungs in the south to the Islamic strongholds of the north. The southern parts of the coastline see quite a few visitors each year, mostly Singaporeans who come to unwind on the long palm-fringed beaches of **Desaru, Tioman Island,** and **Kuantan,** lapped by the South China Sea. However, few travelers venture to the northern parts, the cities of **Kuala Terengganu** and **Kota Bharu,** where you'll find some of the most developed cottage industries producing Malaysia handicrafts, plus an orthodox Muslim history and way of life. For visitors who prefer a less plodded path, these areas prove quite a joy.

One note before you plan your trip: If you're looking for beach fun, the monsoon from November through February makes the waters too choppy, so avoid the southern resorts. Meanwhile in the north, with the exception of a few beach resorts, Muslim modesty will probably make you uncomfortable wearing a Western-style bathing suit at a public beach (the locals swim fully clothed).

1 Desaru

Desaru is an odd place. If it weren't for the resorts here, it probably wouldn't be a place at all. A large arch appears over the road as you approach, welcoming you to the resort town, while just outside there's not much to speak of. Situated along 17 kilometers (10 miles) of sandy beach on the South China Sea, this collection of six resorts and campgrounds has become a very popular vacation spot. Its claim to fame? It's close to Singapore, which means the great majority (up to 90%) of folks who come are Singaporeans or expatriates on weekend getaways for beaches and golf. Desaru gets jam-packed on these days, and is not very conducive to relaxation. With this in mind, plan on a trip to Desaru from Monday through Thursday (and not during a public holiday). Still, in all, Desaru has a far way to go before it's overdeveloped.

Once in Desaru, you'll probably be staying within your resort most of the time. All have pools and beachfronts with a variety of water sports. The staff at the front desks can arrange golf for you at the local course.

ESSENTIALS

GETTING THERE   You can reach Desaru over well-laid roads by **car** from Johor Bahru, or **outstation taxis** from Johor can deliver you to Desaru for about RM100 (US$26.30). For booking call ☎ **07/223-4494.** The number to call for outstation taxis from Desaru is ☎ **07/823-6916.** They can take you to Kota Tinggi (see Johor's "Sports & the Outdoors" section in chapter 10) for RM50 (US$13.15) or to Mersing for RM130 (US$34.20).

From the Changi Ferry Terminal on the east coast of Singapore, **FerryLink** (☎ **65/545-3600**) departs daily at 8:15am, 11:15am, 2:15pm, and 5:15pm. The trip is S$19 (US$11.40) one-way and S$26 (US$15.55) round-trip. Children cost S$11.50 (US$6.90) and S$16 (US$9.60) respectively. The trip is a slow and peaceful 45 minutes to the jetty at Tanjong Belungkor (☎ **07/251-7404**). From here you can prearrange shuttle service with your resort, or you can go it alone with one of the outstation taxis that wait outside the jetty building (RM40/US$10.55 with air-conditioning, RM25/US$6.60 without). The ride takes a half hour.

GETTING AROUND   The resorts at Desaru are self-contained, with restaurants and activities, including golf, water sports and nature treks. Should you require other services, the front desk of any resort can help you out.

ACCOMMODATIONS

✪ **Desaru Golden Beach Hotel.** P.O. Box 50, Tanjung Penawar, 81907 Kota Tinggi, Johor. ☎ **07/822-1101.** Fax 07/822-1480. Singapore reservations ☎ 65/235-5476. 57 units, 115 villas. A/C MINIBAR TV TEL. Weekdays RM170 (US$44.75) double; RM190 (US$50) villa. Weekends RM240 (US$63.15) double; RM260 (US$68.40) villa. AE, DC, JCB, MC, V.

Desaru Golden Beach Resort is casual and comfortable, with a tropical open-air lobby with a high timbered ceiling to allow for cool breezes. The standard rooms face the parking area and garden, while the superior rooms face the sea, and are assigned on a first-come, first-served basis. The villas are like small apartments, and their balconies have plenty of space for sitting with a cool drink. And while their privacy is nice, one feature I don't like is that the villas have carpeting, which makes the rooms feel warm. The double rooms off the lobby feel cooler and fresher with clean tiled floors. Dining options are a seafood restaurant and another offering local dishes. Facilities include a large outdoor lagoon pool, access to the fitness center at Desaru Perdana Beach Resort, a Jacuzzi, two outdoor tennis courts, water-sports equipment, and bicycle rental.

The main attraction here besides the beach is **golfing,** which the resort is happy to arrange for you. See below for course details.

Desaru Perdana Beach Resort. P.O. Box 29, Bandar Penawar, 81900 Kota Tinggi, Johor. ☎ **07/822-2222.** Fax 07/822-2223. Singapore reservations ☎ 65/223-2157 (for reservations from Singapore, rates are quoted in S$). 229 units. Weekdays RM330 (US$86.85) garden-view double, RM340 (US$89.45) sea-view double; RM500 (US$131.60) suite. Weekends RM350 (US$92.10) garden-view double, RM360 (US$94.75) sea-view double; RM600 (US$157.90) suite. AE, DC, MC, V.

An upmarket resort, this property attracts a more varied group of international guests (especially Japanese). It's newer than the others, so the architectural styling has a more modern distinction. The Bali-style open-air lobby features a paneled ceiling and high wooden beams. Guest rooms are also very up-to-date, with new furnishings in Western styles and all the amenities. Perdana fills huge blocks of buildings, which on the outside look like condominiums, while Golden Beach (above) is smaller and a little more spread out.

Perdana has three restaurants: Japanese, Chinese and Continental, and a bar with live entertainment nightly. Facilities include a large outdoor pool, a small fitness center, Jacuzzi, sauna, tennis courts, water-sports equipment, and a souvenir shop.

DESARU OUTDOORS

It goes without saying that many visitors come for the **golf.** Guests at any of the resorts can arrange golf through their resort's front desk. The **Desaru Golf & Country Club,** P.O. Box 57, Tanjung Penawar, 81907 Kota Tinggi, Johor (☎ 07/822-2333; fax 07/822-1855), has 45 holes and an 18-hole Robert Trent Jones Jr. course. Greens fees for 18 holes on weekends and public holidays are RM150 (US$39.45) and RM90 (US$23.70) Monday through Friday. Club rentals, shoes, carts, and buggies are available for rent, and caddy fees run about RM30 (US$7.90). Be sure to confirm your reservation 2 weeks beforehand.

Beach activities include parasailing and windsurfing (with instruction), canoeing, jet skiing, waterskiing, fishing (including night fishing), snorkeling, and speedboat rides. The resorts can also arrange hikes in the nearby jungle, horseback riding, go-carts, tennis, volleyball, and other activities.

2 Mersing

Mersing is not so much a destination in itself but more a jump-off point for ferries to the islands on the East Coast of Malaysia, such as Tioman. Nobody really stays in Mersing unless he's missed the boat—literally. There are a couple of good seafood restaurants in town, but otherwise it's just a small, relaxed fishing town.

GETTING THERE

The main focal point of the town is the **R&R Plaza,** by the main jetty to Tioman. Here you'll find the bus terminal just behind the food stalls (which are great to graze at as you wait for a ferry or bus). In front of these are the offices where you book the ferry or speedboats to Tioman. Outside of R&R are taxis—some local, some outstation, none metered. Local trips are about RM5 (US$1.30). You can also hire outstation taxis to other cities from R&R Plaza. Expect to pay RM140 (US$36.85) to Kuantan, and RM120 (US$31.60) to Johor Bahru.

SPM Ekspress operates daily **bus** service from KL's Puduraya Bus Terminal to Mersing (☎ 03/202-5255 in KL). From Johor Bahru take Johora Express from the Larkin Terminal (☎ 07/224-8280). They have a daily bus costing RM7 (US$1.85) for the trip. For outgoing bus information from Mersing, call **Johora Express** at (☎ 07/799-5227).

ACCOMMODATIONS

While Mersing has no world-class accommodations or resorts, you will find basic accommodations suitable for those just passin' through.

Mersing Inn. 38 Jalan Ismail, next to the Parkson supermarket, 86800, Mersing, Johor. ☎ 07/799-2288. Fax 07/799-1919. 40 units. RM65 (US$17.10) double. MC.

The rooms here are small but clean, but some do not have air-conditioning, so be sure to specify. Others don't have televisions or telephones. There are private bathrooms for each room, however.

✪ **Timotel.** 839 Jalan Endau, 86800, Mersing, Johor. ☎ 07/799-5888. Fax 07/799-5333. 50 units. A/C MINIBAR TV TEL. RM98–RM126 (US$25.80–US$33.15) double; RM189–RM210 (US$49.75–US$55.25) suite. AE, MC.

This hotel, one of the newest and most pleasant in Mersing, has clean and neat rooms and modern conveniences like room service and laundry services. The hotel provides free transfers to and from the jetty. There's a fitness center, and bicycle rental can be arranged.

DINING

Just as with the hotels in Mersing, none of the restaurants are particularly "fine." There is, however, some pretty good seafood to be eaten here, if you don't mind a really low-key and colloquial dining experience. Neither of the places below has a phone, and if they, did they probably wouldn't use them for silly things like taking reservations. Just head on down and find a table.

Ee lo Restoran. Jalan Abu Bakar, next to the roundabout beside the newspaper shop. No phone. Meals from RM5–RM10 (US$1.30–US$2.65). No credit cards. Daily 9am–10pm.

Here is the best place to eat while waiting for your boat. About a 5-minute walk from R&R Plaza, this coffee shop has menu items like mee hoon and kuay teow, Hainan chicken rice, and all sorts of seafood and vegetable dishes. The steamed prawns are succulent, and Ee lo serves an unusual dish—stir-fried vegetables in milk—which is quite tasty.

Mersing Seafood Restaurant. Jalan Ismail, next to the Shell station. No phone. Noodle dishes RM3 (US$0.79) and up; other dishes RM10 (US$2.65) and up. MC. Daily 12:30pm–midnight. CHINESE/SEAFOOD.

You won't need a reservation here, even though it gets crowded on weekends. The service is lousy and the place is a little grubby, but the food is so good nobody seems to care. It's also air-conditioned. Prices will range according to season. Some great dishes to try are the deep-fried squid stuffed with salted egg yolk, the bamboo or asparagus clams fried in chile sauce, or the sautéed garlic prawns.

3 Tioman Island

Tioman Island is by far the most popular destination on Malaysia's east coast. It's in the state of Pahang, Tioman's mainland gateway; Mersing (above), is in Johor. The island is only 39 kilometers (23.4 miles) long and 12 kilometers (7.2 miles) wide, with sandy beaches, clear water with sea life and coral reefs, and jungle mountain-trekking trails with streams and waterfalls. So idyllic is the setting that Tioman was the location for the 1950s Hollywood film *South Pacific.*

Despite heavy tourist traffic, Tioman has retained much of its tropical island charm, perhaps by virtue of the fact that few large hotels have been built on it. However, some parts are becoming very commercial, particularly **Kampung Tekek,** which is where you arrive at either the main jetty or the airport. A paved stretch of road runs up the west coast, between Tekek and Berjaya Tioman Beach Resort (the only true resort on the island), and this area is more built up than the rest of the island. *Built up* is really a relative term; trust me, it's a one-horse town. If you trek overland from Tekek to the east coast, you'll find beaches that are more peaceful and serene.

There is a small local population on the island living in the kampungs (villages), but at almost any given time there are fewer locals than tourists, most of whom come from Singapore and other parts of Malaysia. Most are there for the scuba and beaches, but from November through February you won't find many tourists. Monsoon tides make Tioman inaccessible by ferry, and not the most perfect vacation in the tropics.

Activity is spread throughout the kampungs along the shores of the island. Each of these places has some sort of accommodation facilities, most of them very basic

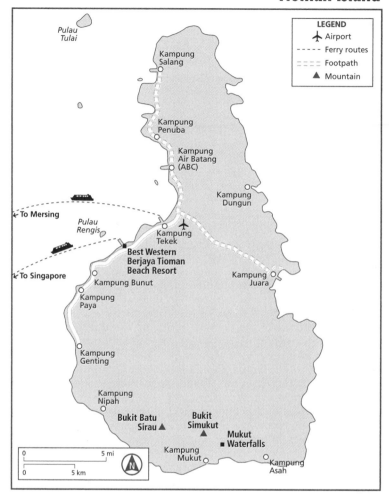

Tioman Island

LEGEND
- ✈ Airport
- --- Ferry routes
- ≡ Footpath
- ▲ Mountain

Pulau Tulai

Kampung Salang

Kampung Penuba

Kampung Air Batang (ABC)

Kampung Dungun

← To Mersing

Pulau Rengis

Kampung Tekek

Best Western Berjaya Tioman Beach Resort

← To Singapore

Kampung Bunut

Kampung Paya

Kampung Juara

Kampung Genting

Kampung Nipah

Bukit Batu Sirau ▲

Bukit Simukut ▲

Mukut ■ Waterfalls

Kampung Mukut

Kampung Asah

0 ___ 5 mi
0 ___ 5 km
N

chalets, with some access to canteens or restaurants. The lay of the land looks like this: On the west side of the island are most of the kampungs. **Tekek** is about midway from north to south. It's the only kampung with a paved road, which is only a few kilometers long. North of Tekek is **Kampuung Air Batang** (also called ABC), and north of that is **Salang.** Both of these kampungs have paved walking paths connecting them with Tekek and with each other. The path from ABC to Tekek is lighted at night. A hike between kampungs takes about 30 to 40 minutes.

South of Tekek is the **Berjaya Tioman Resort,** and south of that is **Kampung Paya** and **Kampung Genting.** Neither Paya nor Genting is accessible via a walking path. I haven't covered either of them in this section because, frankly, I don't recommend you stay there. The main snorkel, dive, and fishing operators, as well as the better places to eat, are in other kampungs, and while Paya and Genting are secluded, their beaches are not particularly good. So while most of the touting in Mersing is for accommodations in Paya and Genting, beware. I've seen plenty of travelers take up these offers, only to change kampungs within a day or two.

If you really want seclusion, head for **Juara,** the only kampung on the eastern side of the island. The beach is also the island's finest, but be prepared for provision of only the most minimal of human necessities. Juara is connected with Tekek by a hiking trail over the hills in the center of the island, and while the locals can make the trip in just over an hour, most of us will need two. If you're making the hike, be sure to leave no later than 4pm to allow time to make it before dark.

ESSENTIALS

GETTING THERE   Flights to Tioman originate from Kuala Lumpur, operated by a private airline, **Berjaya Air,** and coordinated by the folks at the Best Western Berjaya Tioman Beach Resort on Tioman. However, you need not stay at the resort to book passage on these flights. When considering travel to Tioman, keep in mind the monsoon. Berjaya Air does operate a daily flight during low season, but many times flights are cancelled due to inclement weather conditions. (In fact, during the 1999/2000 monsoon season, the island was closed off from the mainland for an entire week and supplies had to be dropped down from military craft!) During the lovely months of March through October, Berjaya flies twice daily. Call their KL office for reservations at ☎ **03/746-8228.** Their office in Tioman is at the Berjaya Resort (☎ 09/ 419-1000). The airport in Tioman is in Kampung Tekek, just across from the main jetty. If you're staying at Berjaya Tioman, a shuttle will fetch you; however, if you plan to stay elsewhere, you're on your own. See "Getting Around," below.

Aside from air travel, your other option is to travel by one of the ten **speedboats** that depart from Mersing each day. Book passage on one of them from the many booking agents huddled around the dock near Mersing's R&R Plaza. They're basically all the same, each reserving trips on the same boats. Boats leave Mersing Jetty at intervals that depend on the tide. The trip takes around $1^1/2$ hours and can cost between RM20 and RM25 (US$5.25 and US$6.60), depending on the power of the boat you hire. The last boat leaves for Tioman between 5 and 6pm every evening. If you miss this boat, you're stuck in Mersing for the night. If you're not sure when you want to leave Tioman, you can purchase a one-way trip; then when you're ready to return, just show up at the jetty in Tekek before 8am. You can buy a ticket then and catch the morning boat back.

From Singapore, **Auto Batam Ferries & Tours** (☎ **65/524-7105**) operates a daily ferry at 8:30am from the Tanah Merah Ferry Terminal for S$148 to S$168 (US$88.60 to US$100.60) adults and S$58 to S$93 (US$34.75 to US$55.70) for children. The ferry takes 4 hours to reach the Berjaya resort, which is also where you catch the ferry back to Singapore at 2:30pm each day.

GETTING AROUND   Aside from walking the trails between kampungs (see above), the most popular mode of transport is **water taxi.** Each village has a jetty; you can pay your fare either at tour offices located near the foot of the pier, or pay the captain directly. The taxis stop operating past nightfall, so make sure you get home before six or seven. A few sample fares: from Tekek to ABC is RM12 (US$3.15) per person, to Salang RM20 (US$5.25), to Juara RM60 (US$15.80). Also, these guys don't like to shuttle around only one person, so if there's only one of you, be prepared to pay double.

Note that water taxis usually don't hang around Juara. If you're looking to get back to civilization by boat, you either have to get lucky with a supplies-delivery boat or wait for a taxi to make a drop-off (which can be days). Otherwise, there's a daily **sea bus** at 3pm that can take you to the other kampungs.

Tioman Travel Tips

If you have not already acquired a good **mosquito repellent,** do so before heading to Tioman. You'll need something with DEET. Tioman mosquitoes are hungry. If you plan to stay in one of the smaller chalet places, you might want to invest in a mosquito net. Also, bring a **flashlight to** help you get around after sunset.

In Tekek, where paved roads allow, many locals have motorbikes, and some will scoot you someplace for anywhere between RM5 and RM10 (US$1.30 and US$2.65).

FAST FACTS   You'll find **money changers** who accept traveler's checks in Tekek at the airport, by the jetty, and at Berjaya Tioman Resort. Other places will take traveler's checks, and some of the smaller accommodations now accept them as payment. The best idea for a better rate is to cash them at a bank on the mainland before you go.

There are **public phones** at Tekek, ABC, and Salang, which you can use with Telekom phone cards bought on the island. Most guest houses have nothing more than cellular phones that they will allow guests to use—at a price. These days you can find reliable **Internet access** in Tekek or from the couple of small shops in Salang. Rates run between RM5 and RM10 (US$1.30 and US$2.65) per hour.

ACCOMMODATIONS

Unless you stay at the Best Western Berjaya Tioman Beach Resort, expect to be roughing it. For some travelers, the Berjaya Tioman, with its wonderful modern conveniences, is what it takes to make a tropical island experience relaxing. Your shower is always warm, you can order food to your room, and you can arrange any activity through the concierge in the lobby. For others, though, real relaxation comes from an escape from modern distractions. The small **chalets in the kampungs** have very minimal facilities and few or no conveniences such as hot showers and telephones. Why would you want to stay in them? Because they're simple, quiet, close to the beach, and less touristy than the resort. You will also have to trek around to find dining options, as few of these places have canteens. Yes, you sacrifice a lot, but the peaceful nature of the island is a more idyllic experience when you stay at a chalet. Be warned, however, that touts at the jetty in Mersing will offer you all sorts of really, really cheap accommodations, many of which are so rustic they're beyond Robinson Crusoe. Those I've listed under "The Kampungs," below, are all on the habitable side of rustic.

✪ **Best Western Berjaya Tioman Beach Resort.** Tioman Island, Pahang Darul Makmur. ☎ **09/419-1000.** Fax 09/419-1718. 380 units. A/C MINIBAR TV TEL. Mar–Oct RM260 (US$68.40) double; RM360 (US$94.75) chalet; RM430–RM975 (US$113.15–US$256.60) suite. Nov–Feb rates discounted 50%. AE, DC, MC, V.

Berjaya Tioman is the only true Western-style resort on the island, and provides all the conveniences you'd expect from a chain hotel. For modern comforts and golf, this is the place to be, but be prepared to be in the middle of Tourist Central. A range of sports opportunities and facilities are offered, including scuba diving, windsurfing, sailing, fishing, snorkeling, canoeing, glass-bottom boat rides, horseback riding, four tennis courts, swimming pools, spa pool, waterslide, children's playground, 18-hole international championship standard golf course with pro shop, jungle treks, slot machines and video games, billiards, and boat trips to nearby islands. Four restaurants provide perhaps the best dining on the island, including a nightly beachside seafood buffet. Services include complimentary airport transfers, foreign currency exchange, and laundry services. Berjaya carries a full line of water-sports equipment for guests, a PADI dive operator on the premises, plus a nine-hole golf course (which is really not too spectacular).

DINING

You won't find fantastic food on the island. Most cuisine consists of simple sandwiches and local food, unless you dine at Berjaya Resort, where the choices are much more extensive. There are inexpensive provision shops here and there. Beer is available in Tekek and Salang, and at Nazri's Place, a restaurant in the very southern part of ABC.

THE KAMPUNGS

KAMPUNG TEKEK

Kampung Tekek is the center of life on Tioman, which means it's the busiest spot, and while there are small accommodations here—as well as some convenience stores (open from 7am to 11pm), souvenir shops, and restaurants—you're better off in one of the other kampungs. The best dining is to the side of the main jetty, where you'll find open-air seafood stalls selling soups, noodle dishes, and seafood and vegetable dishes, at very inexpensive prices.

Just beyond the stalls is the office for **Dive Asia** (☎ **09/419-1337**). Daily dives usually hit two or three spots: Chebeh Island, Malang rocks, and Labas Island. With equipment rentals an excursion costs about RM150 (US$39.45). Night dives to Pirate Reef run about RM80 (US$21.05). You can also enroll for a PADI open-water course starting at RM745 (US$196.05). Dive Asia accepts MasterCard and Visa. Mask and snorkel equipment rentals go for RM20 (US$5.25) per day. There is also a Dive Asia branch at Salang. For bookings feel free to e-mail them at diveasia@tm.net.my.

KAMPUNG ABC

This village lines a long rocky beach that is not the best for swimming in spots, but ABC is very laid-back and comfortable in other ways. Chalets line the pathway along the beach, where you'll find small shady picnic areas and hammocks to swing in. While ABC is well populated by travelers, the people here tend to be more relaxed.

The nicest place to stay is **Air Batang Beach Cabanas,** Kampung Air Batang, 86800 Mersing (no phone). Creeping up the side of the hill, these chalets, many with views of the sea, are the largest and newest in the kampung. Rates go from RM120 (US$31.60) for units with air-conditioning and RM70 (US$18.40) for those without. All cabins have private toilets with cold shower. Cash is accepted, but not credit cards or traveler's checks.

Really the only place to eat here is **Nazri's place** in the south end of the beach, which serves breakfast, lunch, and fish or chicken barbecue dinner daily.

B&J Diving Centre (☎ **09/419-1218**) has a branch along the path. They charge RM150 (US$39.45) for two dives in one day, usually to nearby Chebeh and Sapoy Islands. They also have PADI courses and accept MasterCard and Visa. Daily snorkeling rentals are RM20 (US$5.25).

KAMPUNG SALANG

This kampung is a happening spot. Snuggled in a big cove of lovely beach and blue water, the village has relatively more conveniences for visitors, such as a choice of eating places serving continental and local seafood dishes for a song, a few bars, money changers, convenience stores, and places to make international calls. It is not a metropolis by any standard, though, and accommodations remain basic.

A good place to stay is at **Salang Indah Resorts,** Kampung Salang, Tioman (☎ **09/419-5015;** fax 09/419-5024). Choices of rooms vary from fan-cooled hillside chalets at RM25 (US$6.55), to air-conditioned hillside chalets at RM90 (US$23.70) and sea-view chalets for between RM130 (US$34.20) and RM150 (US$39.45). Air-conditioned chalets also feature hot-water showers.

Both **B&J** (☎ **09/419-5555**) and **Dive Asia** (☎ **09/419-5017**) have offices in Salang. See above locations for prices and services.

✪ KAMPUNG JUARA

Juara is where to go if you really want to get away from it all. A gorgeous cove of crystal blue waters and wide clean sand make for the best beach on the island. Come here expecting to rough it, though. Most of the chalets here are terrible, some only slightly more accommodating than dog houses. There are no phones, only one TV, one place to eat (**The Happy Café,** which has the one TV and a few small convenience store items), and no air-conditioning anywhere. But I still found a quite decent place to stay. On the north end of the beach is **Juara Bay Village Resort,** with 20 rooms that go for RM30 (US$7.90) for hill views and RM40 (US$10.55) for sea views. Credit cards aren't accepted here. Each room has a fan and private bathroom, and they're all good-size and clean. Communications services to this side of the island have yet to be developed, making reservations impossible, so you'll just have to show up and try your luck. If no rooms are available (hardly likely), there are other choices around.

TIOMAN OUTDOORS

After you're waterlogged, you can trek the trail from Tekek to Juara, and some of the paths along the west coast. The hike across the island will take around 2 hours. Bring water and mosquito repellent, and don't try it unless you are reasonably fit.

At the southern part of the island are Bukit Batu Sirau and Bukit Simukut, **"The Famous Twin Peaks,"** and closer to the water near Kampung Mukut are the **Mukut Waterfalls.** There are two smallish pools for taking a dip. Some regular trails exist, but it's inadvisable to venture too far from them because the forest gets dense and it can be tough to find your way back. Negotiate with water taxis to bring you down and pick you up.

4 Kuantan

Kuantan is the capital of Pahang Darul Makmur, the largest state in Malaysia, covering about 35,960 square kilometers (22,475 sq. miles). Travelers come to Pahang for the beautiful beaches, which stretch all the way up the east coast, and for inland jungle forests that promise adventures in trekking, climbing, and river rafting. Much of **Taman Negara,** Malaysia's national forest preserve, is in this state, although most people access the forest via Kuala Lumpur. Kuantan, although it's the capital, doesn't have the feel of a big city. If you're staying at the beach at **Telok Chempedak,** 5 kilometers (3.1 miles) north of Kuantan, the atmosphere is even more relaxed.

ESSENTIALS
VISITOR INFORMATION

There is a **Tourist Information Centre** (☎ **09/517-1624**) located on Jalan Penjara in the center of town. Staff here are exceptionally helpful and good at answering specific inquiries.

GETTING THERE

BY AIR   Malaysia Airlines has a daily flight from KL. For reservations call (☎ 03/746-3000). Flights arrive at the Sultan Ahmad Shah Airport (☎ 09/538-1291). Just outside the airport is a taxi stand where you can get a cab to Kuantan for RM25 (US$6.60) or to Cherating for RM60 (US$15.80).

BY BUS   Bus routes service Kuantan from all parts of the peninsula. If you're coming from KL, **Plusliner** (☎ 03/442-1256) departs from the Putra Bus Terminal, opposite from the Putra World Trade Centre. Seven daily buses make the trip for RM11.70 (US$3.10). From Mersing, **Transnasional/Naelia** (☎ 07/799-3155) has two daily coaches to Kuantan for RM10.40 (US$2.75). The bus terminal in Kuantan is in **Kompleks Makmur**. Taxis at the stand just outside the terminal can take you to town for RM10 (US$2.65).

For buses from Kuantan to other destinations call **Plusliner** at ☎ 09/515-0991 or **Transnasional** at ☎ 09/515-6740.

BY TAXI   Outstation taxis from KL (☎ 03/238-3525) will cost RM220 (US$57.90). From Johor Bahru the fare will be about RM150 (US$39.45), and from Mersing RM100 (US$26.30). For outstation taxi booking from Kuantan call ☎ 09/513-6950. The stand is at the bus terminal.

GETTING AROUND

The areas in the town's center are nice for walking. Otherwise stick with **taxis,** which can be waved down on any street. If you need to arrange for a pickup, call the taxi stand at the bus terminal at ☎ 09/513-4478. There's also a stand behind the Tourist Information Centre where you'll be sure to find a cab in a pinch. Taxis here are not metered, so you must negotiate the fare before you set out. This is a good deal when you want to hire someone for a few hours to take you around the city. Rates are from RM15 (US$3.95) per hour. Use taxis to travel to areas of interest outside the city that are covered later in this section.

FAST FACTS

The **American Express** office is at Mayflower Acme Tours, Ground Floor, Sultan Ahmad Shah Airport (☎ 09/538-3490). Most major **banks** are located appropriately along Jalan Bank, near the State Mosque.

The central **post office** (☎ 09/552-1078) is near the State Mosque on Jln. Haji Abdul Aziz. **Internet service** is available from a couple of cafes at the Kompleks Makmur; check the shopping mall adjacent to the bus terminal.

ACCOMMODATIONS

Kuantan is not a very large place, and most of those who vacation here prefer to stay just a little farther north, in **Cherating,** which is more established as a resort destination. If staying in Kuantan is important to you, though, the Hotel Grand Continental is a fine, centrally located place. Near the beach at Telok Chempedak, the Hyatt Regency is as romantic and relaxing as any place at Cherating.

Hotel Grand Continental. Jalan Gambut, 25000 Kuantan, Pahang Darul Makmur. ☎ 09/515-8888. Fax 09/515-9999. 202 units. A/C MINIBAR TV TEL. RM222 (US$58.40) double; RM360 (US$94.75) suite. AE, DC, JCB, MC, V.

Located in the heart of Kuantan, this hotel is near the central mosque. It's a simple three-star hotel, with new and adequate facilities that are somewhat reminiscent of the 1970s. The front view of the bridge and river is more pleasant than the view in the rear rooms. There's a fitness center, pool, and shops on the premises.

Kuantan

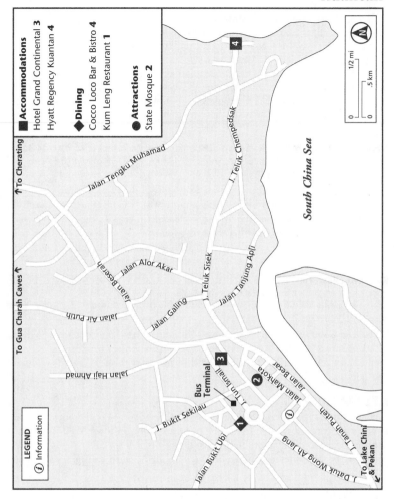

LEGEND
ⓘ Information

Accommodations
Hotel Grand Continental **3**
Hyatt Regency Kuantan **4**

◆**Dining**
Cocco Loco Bar & Bistro **4**
Kum Leng Restaurant **1**

●**Attractions**
State Mosque **2**

To Cherating
To Gua Charah Caves
Jalan Tengku Muhamad
Jalan Alor Akar
Jalan Beserah
Jalan Air Putih
Jalan Galing
Jalan Haji Ahmad
J. Bukit Sekilau
Jalan Bukit Ubi
J. Tun Ismail
Bus Terminal
J. Teluk Sisek
J. Teluk Chempedsak
Jalan Tanjung Apli
Jalan Mahkota
Jalan Besar
J. Tanah Puteh
J. Datuk Wong Ah Jang
To Lake Chini & Pekan
South China Sea

0   1/2 mi
0   .5 km

✪ **Hyatt Regency Kuantan.** Telok Chempedak, 25050 Kuantan, Pahang. ☎ **800/233-1234** from the U.S., or 09/566-1234. Fax 09/567-7577. 336 units. A/C MINIBAR TV TEL. RM391–RM450 (US$102.90–US$118.40) double; RM841–RM956 (US$221.30–US$251.60) suite. AE, DC, JCB, MC, V.

The Hyatt Regency is located on the beach at Telok Chempedak, about 10 minutes outside of Kuantan proper. The long stretch of sandy beach bordering it is perfect for relaxation and fun, and in the evening the crashing waves are the perfect romantic backdrop. Hyatt has built a five-star resort here, and it is five-star in every sense, from outstanding facilities to large well-appointed rooms. Higher prices are of course for rooms with sea views. Facilities include two outdoor swimming pools (one a more active family frolic spot, while the other is quiet and calm), three lighted tennis courts, two squash courts, table tennis, darts, volleyball, and a water-sports center with windsurfing, sailing, waterskiing, and jet skis. The hotel is near locations for golf, jogging, and jungle hikes.

Hyatt has **the best bar in Kuantan,** oftentimes with a live band nightly. They also offer a few dining choices, including a great coffee shop for local and Western fare, plus the Coco Loco Bistro & Bar, a good choice for Italian.

DINING

You can find both seafood and local food in Kuantan, but like the other smaller destinations in Malaysia, you'll be hard-pressed to find fine dining outside of the larger hotels. The best evening activities are centered around the beach area at Telok Chempedak.

Cocco Loco Bistro & Bar. Hyatt Regency Kuantan, Telok Chempedak. ☎ **09/566-1234,** ext. 7700. Reservations recommended. Entrees RM20–RM48 (US$5.25–US$12.65). AE, DC, JCB, MC, V. Daily noon–2:30pm and 6–10:30pm. ITALIAN.

For a little fine dining in Kuantan, your best bet is at the Hyatt's Italian restaurant, Cocco Loco. Local seafood like sea bass and prawns is transformed into beautiful entrees, with light sauces and the freshest ingredients. There is a good wine list with many international labels. If you arrive early, you can still see the ocean from huge glass windows. However, even after dark, Cocco Loco has a beautiful atmosphere enhanced by romantic lights, terra-cotta floors, and bright table linens.

Kum Leng Restoran. E-897/899/901 Jalan Bukit Ubi, Kuantan. ☎ **09/513-4446.** Seafood priced according to seasonal availability; other dishes can be as low as RM5 (US$1.30) for fried tofu or as high as RM100 (US$26.30) for shark's fin. No credit cards. Daily 11:30am–2:30pm and 5:30–10:30pm. CANTONESE.

Kum Leng is one of the top restaurants in Kuantan. A bit cramped, it's always doing a good business but there's rarely a wait. Try the fried chicken with dry chile topped with onions and cashew nuts, or the fried chile prawns with shells. They're very fresh and not too spicy.

ATTRACTIONS

Kuantan can really be seen in a day. While there are a few fun crafts shops, the place is not exactly a hotbed of culture. The main attraction in town is the huge **State Mosque,** which is quite beautiful inside and out, with a distinct dome, minarets, and stained glass. Late afternoon is the best time to see it, when the light really shines through the glass.

SHOPPING

You can have a nice walk down **Jalan Besar,** sampling local delicacies sold on the street and shopping in the smaller craft and souvenir shops. Visit **HM Batik & Handicraft,** 45 N-1, Bangunan LKNP, Jalan Besar (☎ **09/552-8477**), and **Kedai Mat Jais B. Talib,** 45N-8, Bangunan LKNP, Jalan Besar (☎ **09/555-2860**), for good selections of batiks and crafts. **Batik RM** has a showroom on Jalan Besar (2-C Medan Pelan-cung, ☎ **09/514-2008**), but the showroom out on Jalan Tanah Puteh (☎ **09/ 513-9631**) is much more fun. Tours around the back allow you to watch the waxing and dyeing processes. Their showroom has some great batik fashions—more stylish than so much of the batik clothing that you find in the markets.

ATTRACTIONS OUTSIDE KUANTAN

Pahang is home to peninsular Malaysia's most stunning forests. With Kuantan as your starting point, it's easy jump out to these spots for a day or half-day trip.

Gua Charah caves are about 25 kilometers (15.6 mi.) outside of Kuantan. Also called Pancing caves (they're located in a town called Pancing), one of the caves in the network is a temple, home to a huge reclining Buddha. It is said that the monk care-taker, who has grown very old, is having difficulty finding another monk who will take over his duties at the caves. An outstation taxi can take you there for RM80 (US$21.05).

Also fun is **Lake Chini,** 12 freshwater lakes that have local legends that rival Loch Ness. They say that there once was an ancient Khmer city at the site of the lakes, but it is now buried deep under the water, protected by monsters. Some have tried to find both city and monsters, but have come up with nothing. Boats are there to take you across the lake to an *orang asli* (indigenous peoples) kampung to see the native way of life. Lake Chini is 60 kilometers (38 mi.) southwest of Kuantan, and an outstation taxi can take you there for RM80 (US$21.05).

Just south of Kuantan is **Pekan,** which for history and culture buffs is far more interesting then Kuantan. Pekan is called "the Royal City" because it is where the Sultan of Pahang resides in a beautiful Malay-style istana. The **State Museum** on Jalan Sultan Ahmad has displays depicting the history of Pahang and its royal family, as well as sunken treasures from old Chinese junks. Outstation taxis to Pekan are RM20 (US$5.25).

GOLF

The **Royal Pahang Golf Club** is near Kuantan's beach resort area on Jalan Teluk Chempedak (☎ **09/567-5811;** fax 09/567-1170). Your hotel will be happy to make all necessary reservations for you.

5 Cherating

Because Kuantan is such a small town, some travelers coming through these parts choose to stay 47 kilometers (28 miles) north in ✪ Cherating. This area supports a few international-class resorts along the beautiful beachfront of the South China Sea. Funny thing: Compared to Kuantan, the town of Cherating has even fewer things to do, and guests tend not to stray too far from their resort. Self-contained units, they each offer a few dining choices, arrange all the water-sports facilities and outdoor activities you have time for, and can even provide transport to and from Kuantan if you need to see a little "big city life." Windsurfers take note: Cherating is world famous for excellent conditions, and the home of a few international competitions and exhibitions. Resorts can also arrange trips through the mangroves up the Cherating River in a hired bumboat, and trips to crafts shops and cultural shows. A little more than 11 kilometers (6.8 miles) north of Cherating is Chendor Beach, one of the peninsula's special beaches where giant Leatherback turtles lay their eggs from May to October.

ACCOMMODATIONS

Club Med. Correspondence through KL office only via Vacances, Suite 1.1, 1st Floor Bangu-nan MAS, Jalan Sultan Ismail, 50250 Kuala Lumpur. ☎ **03/261-4599.** Fax 03/261-7229. www.clubmed.com. E-mail: cmkul@po.jaring.my. 315 units. A/C MINIBAR TEL. Weekdays (Sun–Fri) RM300 (US$78.95) per adult, RM30–RM180 (US$7.90–US$47.35) per child; week-ends (Sat) RM350 (US$92.10) per adult, RM35–RM210 (US$9.20–US$55.25) per child. Peak season (Christmas, New Year's, and Chinese New Year) RM420 (US$110.55) per adult, RM42–RM252 (US$11.05–US$66.30) per child. AE, DC, MC, V.

The world-renowned Club Med occupies a lovely stretch of beachfront property along the coastline here. On 200 private acres, you can expect this resort chain to take complete care of all your holiday needs. This compound of Malay-style wooden houses contains very contemporary but natural furnishings, and nice little balconies with each. Everything is absolutely spotless. *A note:* If you're new to Club Med, they'll require a membership fee of RM80 for adults only, added on to your booking (Club Med really is a club, you see). They'll also be happy to arrange all your transportation from KL for an additional cost.

For fun, try their outdoor swimming pool, sailing activities, windsurfing, kayaking, tennis (six lighted courts), squash, badminton, cricket, archery, volleyball, wall-scaling, and a circus school with flying trapeze! They also coordinate jungle walks and batik lessons. Almost all above activities are included in your daily rate. At extra cost, there's also a nearby golf course. A daily international buffet features Malay, Indian, Korean, Japanese, and Chinese cuisine, while the Pantai features grilled seafood and meats and Vesuvio opens in the evenings for Italian fare. After that, head for the nightclub and bar.

Holiday Villa Cherating. Lot 1303, Mukin Sungai Karang, 26080 Kuantan, Pahang Darul Makmur. ☎ **09/581-9500.** Fax 09/581-9178. 150 units. A/C MINIBAR TV TEL. RM110–RM190 (US$28.95–US$50) double; RM230–RM295 (US$60.55–US$77.65) suite. AE, DC, JCB, MC, V.

What a resort! This 4-hectare (10-acre) coastline property has three different wings to choose from: The Capital Wing houses modern amenities similar to any international-class hotel, while the Village Wing and the Palace Wing have chalets, longhouses, and istanas. The 13 Village Wing chalets are each decorated in the style of one of the thirteen Malay states, and its kampung feel makes it perfect for unwinding. The chalets in both wings range from simple two-bedroom accommodations to a Sarawak longhouse with 10 guest rooms and private balconies to a replica of the Istana Lama Sri Menanti in Negeri Sembilan.

Facilities include two outdoor pools, two outdoor spa pools, a children's wading pool, a game room, three outdoor tennis courts, two indoor badminton courts, a fitness center, sauna, massage, a beauty parlor, and a water-sports center (with windsurfing, beach surfing, catamaran, sailing, parasailing, scuba diving, jet scooters, canoeing, and boating). Also available are sightseeing tours, island excursions, fishing, and golfing.

6 Taman Negara National Park

Malaysia's most famous national park, Taman Negara, covers 434,300 hectares (1,085,750 acres) of primary rain forest estimated to be as old as 130 million years, and encompasses within its borders Gunung Tahan, peninsular Malaysia's highest peak at 2,187 meters (2,392 ft.) above sea level.

Prepare to see lush vegetation and rare orchids, some 250 bird species, and maybe, if you're lucky, some barking deer, tapir, elephants, tigers, leopards, and rhinos. As for primates, there are long-tailed macaques, leaf monkeys, gibbons, and more. Malaysia has taken the preservation of this forest seriously since the early part of the century, so Taman Negara showcases efforts to keep this land in as pristine a state as possible while still allowing humans to appreciate the splendor.

There are outdoor activities for any level of adventurer. Short jungle walks to observe nature are lovely, but then so are the hardcore 9-day treks or climbs up Gunung Tahan. There are also overnight trips to night hides where you can observe animals up close. The **jungle canopy walk** is the longest in the world, and at 25 meters (83 ft.) above ground, the view is spectacular. There are also rivers for rafting and swimming, fishing spots, and a couple of caves.

ESSENTIALS

VISITOR INFORMATION   Call the Kuala Tahan Office, Taman Negara Resort, Kuala Tahan, Jerantut, 27000 Pahang (☎ **609/263-500;** fax 609/261-5000).

GETTING THERE   The entrance to the park is at **Kuala Tembeling,** which can be reached in 3 hours by road from Kuala Lumpur. By far the easiest way to visit the national park is through a **travel operator,** who will arrange your transport to the park, accommodations, meals, and activities. Taman Negara Resort (see below) is the largest operator, with a few others providing excellent packages as well.

Outstation taxis from Puduraya Bus Terminal (☎ **03/238-3525**), will cost about RM150 (US$39.45) to the park entrance. From there you must venture upstream 2 hours by boat to the Taman Negara Resort (below). The **KTM,** Malaysia's rail system, also travels to this area. Get off at the Tembeling station to catch the boat into the park, or at Jerantut if you need a place to stay overnight (there isn't really any place to stay at Tembeling). From KL (☎ **03/274-7434**) there's a special evening train running to Jerantut at 8:20pm. From Johor Bahru, stop at Tembeling. Call KTM at (☎ **07/223-3040**) for inquiries about their morning train. Budget your fare at RM38 (US$10) for second-class passage.

ACCOMMODATIONS

Nusa Camp. Bookings through Kuala Lumpur Office: Malaysia Tourist Information Centre (MATIC), 109 Jalan Ampang. ☎ **03/2162-7682.** Fax 03/2162-7682. Accommodations range from Malay houses at RM100 (US$26.30) per night to A-frame chalets at RM55 (US$14.45) or 4-person hostel for RM15 (US$3.95). You can also rent a tent for RM15 (US$3.95). Meals range from RM11–RM20 (US$2.90–US$5.25), and the boat ride goes for RM38 (US$10), return.

Nusa Camp will send you to the park, put you up in their own kampung house, chalet, or hostel accommodations, and guide your activities for you. See range for accommodations and meals above. Once there, they have numerous guided trips out into the wilds: a night safari (2 hours; RM35/US$9.20 per person), night walk (1 hr.; RM20/US$5.25), a trip to see an orang asli village (4 hrs.; RM45/US$11.85), tubing down rapids (2 hrs.; RM30/US$7.90), overnight hikes (RM90/US$23.70), overnight river fishing trips (RM150/US$39.45), a trip to the canopy walkway (4 hrs.; RM80/US$39.45), or an overnight trip to explore caves (RM220/US$57.90).

Taman Negara Resort. Kuala Tahan Office, Taman Negara Resort, Kuala Tahan, Jerantut, 27000 Pahang. ☎ **09/266-3500.** Fax 09/266-1500. (Or contact Kuala Lumpur Sales Office, Lot G.01A, Ground Floor, Kompleks Antarabangsa, Jalan Sultan Ismail, 50250 Kuala Lumpur; ☎ 03/245-5585; fax 03/245-5430.) Accommodations come in many styles: a bungalow suite for families (RM600/US$157.90); chalet (RM216/US$56.85) and chalet suite RM300/US$78.95, both good for couples; standard guest house rooms in a motel-style longhouse (RM165/US$43.40); and dormitory hostels for budget travelers (RM40.25/US$10.60). All prices above are per night. The Explorer Package runs RM482 (US$126.85) per person for 3 days and 2 nights, or RM775 (US$203.95) per person for 4 days and 3 nights.

Taman Negara Resort, well established in the business of hosting visitors to the park, organizes trips for 3 days and 2 nights or for 4 days and 3 nights, as well as an à la carte deal where you pay for lodging (see above) and activities separately. Explorer visitors check into the chalets, which are air-conditioned with attached bathroom, and enjoy a full itinerary of activities included in the package price. A la carte activities include a 3-hour jungle trek (RM20/US$5.25 per person), a 1½-hour night jungle walk (RM13/US$3.40), the half-day Lata Berkoh river trip with swimming (RM45 (US$11.84) per person), a 2-hour cave exploration (RM35/US$9.20), and a trip down the rapids in a rubber raft (RM25/US$6.60). Shuttle transfers from KL (4 hrs.) are an extra RM50 (US$13.15) per person, and the boat trip to the resort is either RM38 (US$10) for the 3-hour traditional wooden boat or RM60 (US$15.80) for the 1-hour speedboat.

7 Kuala Terengganu

The capital of the state of Terengganu, Kuala Terengganu has far more exciting activities to offer a visitor than its southern capital neighbor, Kuantan. And yet, many travelers to Malaysia often skip this part of the country for the more beaten paths. So why should you consider coming here? **Malaysian crafts.** Kuala Terengganu has the best cottage industries for Malaysian crafts—better than anywhere else on the peninsula. Terengganu artisans specialize in everything from boatbuilding to kite making, and it is here that you can see it all happen.

Kuala Terengganu is small and easy to navigate, clustered around a port at the mouth of the Terengganu River. Many livelihoods revolve around the sea, so most of the activity, even today, focuses on the areas closest to the jetties. Life here is slow paced and comfortable, and very Muslim, owing to its proximity to orthodox Muslim Kelantan in the north. It is a sedate town, so don't come here for the nightlife. As opposed to its west coast contemporaries, this city is mostly Malay (about 90%), so it's here that you see Malay culture in a more pure form, with fewer outside influences.

The local business week is from Saturday to Wednesday, so be prepared for that when you plan your time here. Also important to know: Terengganu is a dry state. Alcoholic beverages cannot be purchased in stores, and there is only one bar in town, at the Primula Parkroyal Resort (listed below). Chinese restaurants are also permitted to sell beer to diners.

ESSENTIALS

VISITOR INFORMATION The Tourism Information Centre is on Jalan Sultan Zainal Abidin just next to the post office and across from the central market. The phone number there is (☎ **09/622-1553**).

GETTING THERE **Malaysia Airlines** has two daily flights from KL to Kuala Terengganu's Sultan Mahmud Airport. The reservations number in KL is ☎ **03/746-3000.** For local airport information call ☎ **09/666-4204.** For Malaysian Airlines bookings from Kuala Terengganu call ☎ **09/622-1415.** From the airport, a taxi to town is about RM15 (US$3.95).

The **MPKT Bus Terminal** is located on Jalan Sultan Zainal Abidin next to the water. **Plusliner** (☎ **03/443-4285**) has two daily buses from KL, departing from the Putra Bus Terminal opposite the Putra World Trade Centre. The trip time is 8 hours, with tickets priced at RM21.60 (US$5.70). From Kuantan you can also catch the Plusliner bus heading from KL to Kuala Terengganu via Kuantan. For buses out of Kuala Terengganu call Plusliner at (☎ **09/622-7067**).

Outstation taxis from Kuantan will cost RM90 (US$23.70). Call ☎ **09/513-6950** for booking. From Kota Bharu taxis will be around RM80 (US$21.05) (RM56/US$14.75 without air-conditioning). The phone number for the taxi stand there is ☎ **09/748-1386.** Outstation taxi bookings from Kuala Terengganu can be arranged by calling ☎ **09/622-1581.**

GETTING AROUND While you can stroll around the downtown areas with ease, getting to many of the bigger attractions will require a **taxi.** To call and arrange for a taxi, dial ☎ **09/622-1581,** or arrange through your hotel concierge. It's a good idea

Kuala Terengganu

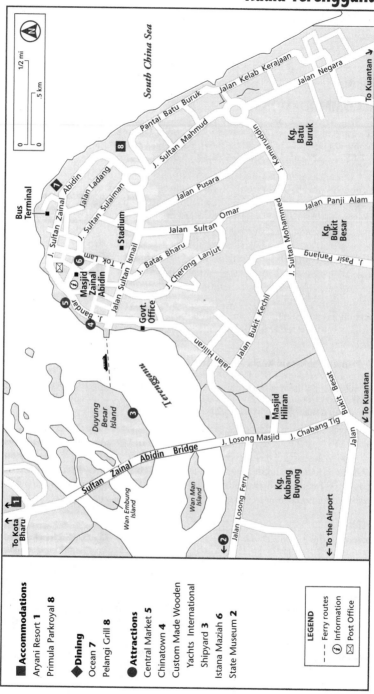

South China Sea

To Kuantan →

Jalan Negara

Jalan Kelab Kerajaan

Pantai Batu Buruk

J. Sultan Mahmud

Kg. Batu Buruk

J. Kamaruddin

Jalan Pusara

Jalan Panji Alam

Abidin

Jalan Ladang

J. Sultan Sulaiman

J. Sultan Zainal

8

7

Bus Terminal

■ Stadium

Jalan Sultan Omar

Kg. Bukit Besar

J. Sultan Mohammed

J. Pasir Panjang

J. Tok Lam

Jalan Sultan Ismail

J. Batas Bharu

6

Masjid Zainal Abidin

ⓘ

⊠

5

J. Cherong Lanjut

J. Cherong Lanjut

4

J. Bandar

Govt. Office ■

Jalan Hiliran

Jalan Bukit Kechil

← To Kuantan

Duyung Besar Island

3

Terengganu

Masjid Hiliran ■

J. Bukit Besat

Sultan Zainal Abidin Bridge

J. Losong Masjid

J. Chabang Tig

Jalan

Wan Embung Island

Wan Man Island

1

← To Kota Bharu

Jalan Losong Ferry

Kg. Kubang Buyong

2

← To the Airport

■ Accommodations
Aryani Resort **1**
Primula Parkroyal **8**

◆ Dining
Ocean **7**
Pelangi Grill **8**

● Attractions
Central Market **5**
Chinatown **4**
Custom Made Wooden Yachts International Shipyard **3**
Istana Maziah **6**
State Museum **2**

LEGEND
- - - Ferry routes
ⓘ Information
⊠ Post Office

to hire these guys for a half or whole day, so you can go around to places and not worry how you'll get back. Rates will be around RM15 (US$3.95) per hour.

FAST FACTS   Most **banks** are on Jalan Sultan Ismail. The main **post office** is on Jalan Sultan Zainal Abidin (☎ **09/622-7555**), next to the Tourist Information Centre.

ACCOMMODATIONS

✪ **The Aryani Resort.** Jalan Rhu Tapai–Merang, 21010 Setiu, Terengganu, Malaysia. ☎ **09/624-1111** or 09/624-4489. Fax 09/624-8007. 20 units. MINIBAR TV TEL. RM560–RM656 (US$147.35–US$172.65) double; RM808 (US$212.65) modern suite; RM1,055 (US$277.65) heritage suite. AE, DC, JCB, MC, V.

Two and a half years ago, Raja Dato' Bahrin Shah Raja Ahmad (a most royal name) opened his dream resort. An internationally celebrated architect, he'd previously designed the State Museum (see below) and wished to translate the beautiful lines of Terengganu style into a special resort. The resulting Aryani is stunning—organic, stimulating, unique, and best of all, peaceful. In a rural 9-acre spot by the sea, the rooms are private bungalows situated like a village. Inside, each is masterfully decorated to suit both traditional style and modern comfort. The Heritage Suite wins the prize: a 100-year-old timber palace, restored and rebuilt on the site, it's appointed with fine antiques. The design of the outdoor pool is practically an optical illusion, and the spa (for massage and beauty treatments) is in its own Malay house. The resort's rural location has both a plus and a minus: On the plus side it's secluded; on the minus side it's 45 minutes from Kuala Terengganu. The resort can arrange boat trips, tours to town, and golfing.

✪ **Primula Parkroyal Kuala Terengganu.** Jalan Persinggahan, P.O. Box 43, 20904, Kuala Terengganu, Terengganu Darul Iman, Malaysia. ☎ **800/835-7742** from the U.S. and Canada, 800/363-300 from Australia (Sydney 02/9935-8313), 0800/801-111 New Zealand, or 09/622-2100 or 09/623-3722. Fax 09/623-3360. 249 units. A/C MINIBAR TV TEL. RM320 (US$84.20) double; RM400 (US$105.25) suite. AE, DC, MC, V.

A top pick for accommodations in Kuala Terengganu is the Parkroyal. The first resort to open in this area, it commands the best section of beach the city has to offer and still is very close to the downtown area. It has full resort facilities, which include three excellent restaurants and the only bar in the city (perhaps even in the state). Make sure you get a room facing the sea—the view is dreamy. Other facilities include an outdoor pool with grassy lawn, water-sports facilities, a lobby shop, and a kid's club.

DINING

Ocean. Lot 2679 Jalan Sultan Janah Apitin (by the waterfront). ☎ **09/623-9154.** Reservations not accepted. RM10–RM25 (US$2.65–6.60); seafood sold according to market prices. MC, V. Daily noon–2:30pm and 5:30pm–midnight. CHINESE/SEAFOOD

One of the most celebrated seafood restaurants in town, Ocean prepares tender prawns, light butterfish, and juicy crab in local and Chinese recipes that are very good. Don't count on much from the al fresco decor. To be honest, the place looks more or less like a warehouse, but the views of the sea help. So does the beer, which Ocean is permitted to serve.

Pelangi Grill. Primula Parkroyal, Jalan Persinggahan. ☎ **09/622-2100.** Reservations not necessary. RM10–RM24 (US$2.65–US$6.30). AE, DC, JCB, MC, V. Daily noon–11pm. LOCAL/CONTINENTAL.

In an open-air lanai facing the sea and the resort's gardens, this delightful multilevel outdoor cafe is good for either family meals or romantic dinners. The main level is set

Terengganu's Wild Side

While the state of Terengganu has its share of natural inland areas, the best nature here is found in the state's **marine parks** (see "Terangganu's Outdoors," below).

A visit to **Redang Island** provides glimpses of an underwater heaven of marine life and coral. And Terengganu's beaches, in addition to being great for sunbathing, have something else to recommend them: **leatherback turtles,** which have been coming ashore to bury their eggs for centuries. Terengganu has a sanctuary to help the babies hatch and get on with their lives free from poachers.

for standard menu items, which include the house specialties, sizzling dishes of prawn or beef, plus pizzas and a great assortment of local and Western entrees. The lower patio is set for steamboat, a fondue-style dinner where you place chunks of fish and meats into boiling broth at your table. A small assortment of international wines is available.

ATTRACTIONS

✪ **Central Market.** Jalan Sultan Zainal Abidin.

Open daily from very early until about 7pm, the central market is a huge maze of shops selling every craft made in the region. There's basket weaving for everything from place mats to beach mats. Batik comes in sarongs (with some very unique patterns), ready-made clothing, and household linens. Songet, beautiful fabric woven with gold and silver threads, is sold by the piece or sarong. Brass-ware pots, candlesticks, and curios are piled high and glistening. Every handicraft item you can think of is here, waiting for you to bargain and bring it home. And when you're done, venture to the back of the market and check out the produce, dried goods, and seafood in the wet market.

Istana Maziah. Jalan Masji. No phone.

Probably one of the least ornate istanas in Malaysia, this lovely yellow and white royal palace, built in 1897, is today mainly only used for state and royal ceremonies. It is not open to the public. Tucked away down the narrow winding street is its neighbor, the Masjid (mosque) Abidin.

Chinatown. Jalan Bandar.

While Terengganu has only a small Chinese population, its Chinatown is still quite interesting. This street of shophouses close to the water is still alive, only today many of the shops are art galleries and boutiques, showcasing only the finest regional arts. Also along Jalan Bandar you can find travel agents for trips to nearby islands.

✪ **State Museum.** Bukit Losong. ☎ **09/622-1444.** Admission RM5 (US$1.30) adults; RM2 (US$0.53) children. Sat–Thurs 9am–5pm. Closed Fri.

The buildings that house the museum's collection were built specifically for this purpose. Designed by a member of the Terengganu royal family, an internationally renowned architect who also built the nearby Aryani resort, it reflects the stunning Terengganu architectural style. Atop stilts (16 of them, the traditional number) with high sloping roofs, the three main buildings are connected by elevated walkways. Inside are fine collections that illustrate the history and cultural traditions of the state.

✪ **Custom Made Wooden Yachts International Shipyard.** 3592 Duyong Besar.
☎ **09/623-2072.**

Abdullah bin Muda's family has been building ships by hand for generations. Now Mr. Abduallah is an old-timer, but he gets around, balancing on the planks that surround the dry-docked hulls of his latest masterpieces. He makes fishing boats in western and Asian styles, as well as luxury yachts—all handmade, all from wood. While Mr. Abdullah doesn't speak any English, he'll let you explore the boats on your own, and even tell you how much money he's getting for them. You'll weep when you hear how inexpensive his fine work is.

TERENGGANU'S HANDICRAFTS

Chendering, an industrial town about 40 minutes' drive south of Kuala Terengganu, is where you'll find major handicraft production—factories and showrooms of batiks and other lovely items. All these places are located along one stretch of highway, but all are too far apart to walk. Plan to hire a taxi by the hour to shuttle you between them; they're about a 5-minute hop between each if you're driving. Also, while you're in the area, stop by the **Masjid Tengku Tengah Zahara,** which is only 5 kilometers outside of the town. The mosque is more commonly referred to as the "Floating Mosque," as it is built in a lake and appears to be floating on the top.

✪ **Terengganu Craft Cultural Centre.** Lot 2195 Kawasan Perindustrian Chendering.
☎ **09/617-1033.** Sat–Wed 8am–5pm; Thurs 8am–12:45pm. Closed Fri.

Operated by the Malaysian Handicraft Development Corporation, The Craft Cultural Center, also called Budaya Craft, not only sells handicrafts, but also has blocks of warehouses where artisans create the work. See batik painting, brass casting, basket weaving, and wood carving as well as other local crafts in progress.

Suteramas. Zkawasan Perindustrian Chendering. ☎ **09/617-1355.** Free admission. Sat–Wed 9am–5pm. Closed Thurs–Fri.

Suteramas specializes in batik painting on fine quality silks. At this, their factory show-room, you can buy their latest creations or just watch them being made. Not only do they dye the cloth, they make it from their own worm stock.

Noor Arfa. Lot 1048 K Kawasan Perindustrian Chendering. ☎ **09/617-5700.** Sat–Thurs 8am–5pm. Closed Fri. AE, MC, V.

Noor Arfa is Malaysia's largest producer of hand-painted batik. This former cottage-industry business now employs 200 workers to create ready-to-wear fashions that are esteemed as designer labels throughout the country. There's also a shop in town at Aked Mara, A3 Jalan Sultan Zainal Abidin (☎ **09/623-5173**).

TERANGGANU'S OUTDOORS

If you are in Terengganu between May and August, you've arrived just in time to see the **baby leatherback turtles.** For hundreds of years, possibly more, giant leatherback turtles have come to the shore here by the thousands. The females crawl to the beaches where they dig holes in which to lay their eggs. Sixty days later, the small turtles hatch and scurry for the water. In recent decades the turtles have had trouble carrying out their ritual, with development and poaching putting severe hardships on the pop-ulation. Of the babies that are hatched, many never make it to the deep sea. At the Department of Fisheries of the State of Terengganu (Taman Perikanan Chendering; ☎ **09/917-3353**) there is a sanctuary that collects the eggs from the beaches, incu-bates them in hatcheries, then sets the babies free. They welcome visitors to their exhibits about turtles and the sanctuary's activities, and to midnight watches to see mothers lay eggs and babies hatch. These activities are free of charge.

The first marine park in Malaysia, the **Terengganu Marine Park,** is situated around the nine islands of the Redang archipelago, 45 kilometers (28 miles) northeast of Kuala Terengganu and 27 kilometers (17 miles) out to sea. Sporting the best coral reefs and dive conditions off peninsular Malaysia, the park attracts divers with its many excellent sites. The largest of the islands is Pulau Redang (Redang Island), where most people stay in resorts on overnight diving excursions. Begin with an hour's drive to the northern jetty town of Merang (not to be confused with Marang, which is in the south), followed by an overwater trip to any one of the islands for scuba, snorkeling, and swimming.

Coral Redang Island Resort is one of the best in Redang, with 40 detached and semidetached bungalows and standard rooms on idyllic gardens next to the beach. They specialize in Eco Diving, with everything from beginner PADI courses to boat dives and night dives, with equipment rental as well. The resort also has snorkeling gear. Contact Coral Redang at 137A, 1st Floor, Jalan Sultan Zainal Abidin, Kuala Terrenganu (☎ **09/623-6200;** fax 09/623-6300).

8 Kota Bharu

In the northeast corner of peninsular Malaysia, bordering Thailand, is the state of **Kelantan.** Few tourists head this far north up the east coast, but it's a fascinating journey for those interested in seeing Malaysia as it might have been without so many foreign influences. The state is populated mostly by Malays and Bumiputeras, with only tiny factions of Chinese and Indian residents and almost no traces of British colonialism. Not surprisingly, Kelantan is the heart of traditional Islam in modern Malaysia. While the government in KL constructs social policies based upon a more open and tolerant Islam, religious and government leaders in Kelantan can be counted on for putting forth a strong Muslim ideal where they feel they may have influence. Indeed, the state has one of only two ministers who are not members of Dr. Mahathir's leading UMNO party.

Kelantan owes its character to the mountain range that runs north to south through the interior, slicing the peninsula in half. Isolated from other Malay areas, Kelantan for most of its history was aligned with Siam, which didn't care one way or another how Kelantan ran its territory. Cut off from the trade traffic on the other side of the mountains, Kelantan, and to some extent its southern neighbor Terengganu, had sufficient peace of mind to form its own Islamic bureaucracy, judicial system, and societal institutions, emphasizing Muslim standards of scholarship and learning. Trade in gold, mined from the interior, provided for business with Chinese and Thais, but Europeans, their mouths watering for the mineral wealth, were not welcome.

Well, Kelantan couldn't keep away the British in 1900. Not only were the Brits interested in all that gold, but also in keeping the region free from French and German interests. Arguments were had and agreements made between London and Siam, and eventually Kelantan came under British rule. Several peasant uprisings disturbed the peace, and the Muslim elite in the cities took to developing their own modern knowledge in hopes of overcoming their Christian infiltrators. Some time after World War II, Malaysia went the way of most other British colonies, and gained independence. However, its strong Muslim roots remain to this day.

Kota Bharu, the state capital, is the heart of the region. The area is rich in Malay cultural heritage, as evidenced in the continuing interest in arts like *silat* (Malay martial arts), *wayang kulit* (puppetry), *gasing* (top spinning), and *wau* (kite flying). For the record, you won't find too much traditional music or dance, as women are forbidden from entertaining in public. Also beware that the state has strict laws controlling the sale of alcoholic beverages, which cannot be purchased in stores, hotels, or most restaurants. You will not find a single bar. Chinese restaurants, however, are permitted to sell beer to their patrons, but will probably not allow you to take any away.

ESSENTIALS
VISITOR INFORMATION
You'll find the Kelantan Tourist Information Centre at Jalan Sultan Ibrahim (☎ 09/748-5534).

GETTING THERE
BY AIR   From KL, Malaysia Airlines (☎ 03/746-3000) flies twice daily. You'll land at Kota Bharu's Sultan Ismail Petra Airport (☎ 09/773-7000), about 20 minutes outside the city. A taxi to town shouldn't be any more than RM25 (US$6.60). The Malaysia Airlines office in town is at Ground Floor, Kompleks Yakin, Jalan Gajah Mati (☎ 09/744-7000).

BY TRAIN   The KTM runs a line through the center of the peninsula all the way to the Thai border. The Wakaf Bharu station is closest to the city, and taxis are available, or you can take local bus no. 19 or 27. For train information in KL call ☎ 03/274-7424.

BY BUS   Kota Bharu's bus terminal is at Jalan Padang Garong off Jalan Doktor. Buses bring you here from all corners of the peninsula. From KL call **Transnasional** at Puduraya Bus Terminal (☎ 03/230-3300). They've got two dailies at a cost of RM22 (US$5.80). From Kuala Terengganu's bus terminal, Transnasional (☎ 09/623-8384) has six buses daily for RM7.50 (US$2). To find out about buses out of Kota Bharu call ☎ 09/747-4330. The taxi stand is just across the street, and you may be hounded by all sorts of gypsy cabs, people with cars who are not proper taxi drivers but who will take you places to make some extra cash. They're basically honest.

BY TAXI   The local taxi stand across from the bus terminal also acts as the outstation taxi stand. To reserve a car the number is ☎ 09/748-1386. Taxis from Kuala Terengganu run about RM80 (US$21.05).

GETTING AROUND
One thing I like about Kota Bharu is how most of the major museums are located in one central area, so walking to them is very easy. For the beach and cottage industry areas you'll need to hire a **taxi**. The main taxi stand is at Jalan Padang Garong; call ☎ 09/748-1386 for booking. Daily and half-day rates can be negotiated for about RM15 (US$3.95) per hour. Trips around town will be between RM5 and RM10 (US$1.30 and US$2.65).

FAST FACTS
Banks are at Jalan Pitum Pong and Jalan Kebun Sultan. The main **post office** is at Jalan Sultan Ismail (☎ 09/748-4033). Look for **Internet service** at Perdana Cyber Café Just inside Perdana Superbowl next to (naturally) the Hotel Perdana.

ACCOMMODATIONS
✪ **Diamond Puteri Hotel.** Jalan Post Office Lama, 1500 Kota Bharu, Kelantan. ☎ **09/ 743-9988.** Kuala Lumpur sales office 03/413-0448. Fax 09/743-8388. 311 units. A/C MINIBAR TV TEL. RM220–RM255 (US$57.90–US$67.10) double; RM320 (US$84.20) suite. AE, DC, MC, V.

Kota Bharu

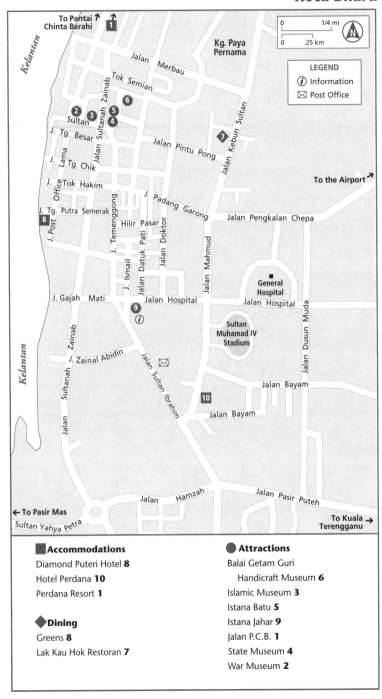

Kelantan

To Pantai ↑ ↑
Chinta Berahi

1

Kg. Paya
Pernama

0 — 1/4 mi
0 — .25 km

LEGEND
ⓘ Information
✉ Post Office

Jalan Merbau

Tok Semian

Jalan Sultanah Zainab

2 Sultan **3** **5** **6**
4

J. Tg. Besar

Jalan Sultan

Jalan Pintu Pong

Jalan Kebun Sultan

7

J. Lama

J. Tg. Chik

J. eTok Hakim

To the Airport ↗

J. Office

J. Tg. Putra Semerak

8 J. Post

J. Padang Garong

Jalan Pengkalan Chepa

Hilir Pasar

J. Temenggong

J. Ismail

Jalan Datuk Pati

Jalan Doktor

Jalan Mahmud

J. Gajah Mati

Jalan Hospital

General
Hospital

Jalan Hospital

Jalan Dusun Muda

9
ⓘ

Sultan
Muhamad IV
Stadium

J. Zainab

J. Zainal Abidin

Jalan Sultan Ibrahim

✉

Jalan Bayam

10

Jalan Bayam

Jalan

Sultanah

Jalan

Kelantan

← To Pasir Mas

Sultan Yahya Petra

Jalan Hamzah

Jalan Pasir Puteh

To Kuala →
Terengganu

■ **Accommodations**

Diamond Puteri Hotel **8**

Hotel Perdana **10**

Perdana Resort **1**

◆ **Dining**

Greens **8**

Lak Kau Hok Restoran **7**

● **Attractions**

Balai Getam Guri
  Handicraft Museum **6**

Islamic Museum **3**

Istana Batu **5**

Istana Jahar **9**

Jalan P.C.B. **1**

State Museum **4**

War Museum **2**

Does Diamond Puteri lead Kota Bharu into the 21st century, or at least bring it up to the 20th? Either way, it's the city's first shiny new five-star hotel, opened just in time for the economic crisis and still struggling to come into its own, but still full of all the modern conveniences. Guest rooms are welcoming and bright. The location by the Kelantan River isn't the fabulous view you'd hope for, which makes the outdoor pool area not as inviting. They also have a fitness center with a sauna.

Hotel Perdana. Jalan Mahmood, P.O. Box 222, 15720 Kota Bharu, Kelantan. ☎ **09/748-5000.** Fax 09/744-7621. 178 units. A/C MINIBAR TV TEL. RM125–RM140 (US$32.90–US$36.85) double; RM600 (US$157.90) suite.

The premier business-class hotel in Kota Bharu for years, Perdana was unrivaled until the Diamond Puteri opened in 1998. Perdana won't seem as fancy anymore, but it's still a good choice for affordable and comfortable accommodations in the city. The small guest rooms need a little refurbishing, but are spick-and-span. Besides, the rates are good for the quality of the facility. Unusual for a hotel, Perdana boasts a bowling alley (!) and more conventional hotel facilities such as an outdoor swimming pool, a fitness center (which is not exactly state-of-the-art), sauna, and steam bath. Sports activities like tennis and squash also make the hotel attractive.

Perdana Resort. Jalan Kuala Pa'Amat, Pantai Cahaya Bulan, P.O. Box 121, 15710 Kota Bharu, Kelantan, Malaysia. ☎ **09/774-4000.** Fax 09/774-4980. 117 units. A/C MINIBAR TV TEL. RM170–RM210 (US$44.75–US$55.25) chalet. AE, DC, MC, V.

For a little beach fun in Kota Bharu, head for Perdana Resort, just about the only beach resort in the area, and perhaps the only beach where you can wear a Western-style bathing suit and not feel out of place. The individual chalets make for great privacy, each with its own porch outside and bathroom inside. They're also spacious, so if you want to put in an extra bed or two for an additional RM30, you'll still have ample room to get around. Perdana will arrange whatever beach activity you desire, from paddleboats to canoeing, beach volleyball, and fishing trips. They also have outdoor tennis, bicycle rentals, horseback riding, kite flying, and a host of other amusements to keep you busy. When you can't take anymore, collapse in the giant free-form pool.

DINING

Greens. Diamond Puteri Hotel, Jalan Post Office Lama. ☎ **09/743-9988.** Reservations not necessary. RM10–RM38 (US$2.65–US$10). AE, DC, MC, V. Daily 7am–midnight. WESTERN/LOCAL.

Done up in a simple cafe style, Greens has yet to grow into its surroundings in the new Diamond Puteri Hotel. Serving as the coffee shop for the hotel, it is open from early in the morning till late at night and features a wide range of dishes. Choose from familiar western favorites or try their specialty local Kelantanese selections (which are the best dishes), such as ayam perchik (chicken in a coconut and fish stock gravy), a favorite in these parts.

Lak Kau Hok Restoran. 2959 Jalan Kebun Sultan. ☎ **09/748-3762.** Reservations not necessary. RM8–RM25 (US$2.10–US$6.60). Daily 11am–2:30pm and 6–10pm. No credit cards. CHINESE/SEAFOOD

Kota Bharu isn't all that boring a town at night. Head down to Chinatown's Jalan Kebun Sultan where the streets get lively. Walk past glowing restaurants, hawker stalls, and friends out for a chat and a stroll, and when you reach the little house that is Lak Kau Hok, head inside. The smells of garlic and chiles will seduce you from the moment you enter, and after specialties like steamed garlic prawns and steamed fish Teochew style (with vegetables and mushrooms sautéed in a rich gravy), you'll be very happy you came. Did I mention they serve beer?

ATTRACTIONS

✪ **Padang Merdeka museums.** At the end of Jalan Hilir Kota. ☎ **09/744-4666.** Sat–Thurs 8:30am–4:45pm. Closed Fri.

Centered around the Padang Merdeka are five of the most significant sights in Kota Bharu, run by the Kelantan State Museum Corporation. At the **Istana Jahar** (adults RM3/US$0.79, children RM1.50/US$0.39), Kelantan traditional costumes, antiques, and musical instruments are displayed in context of their usage in royal ceremonies. **Istana Batu** (adults RM2/US$0.53, children RM1/US$0.26) takes you through a photographic journey of Kelantan's royal family, and offers a peek at their lifestyle through the past 200 years. The **Balai Getam Guri** handicraft museum (adults RM1/US$0.26, children RM.50/US$0.13) showcases the finest in Kelantanese textiles, basketry, embroidery, batik printing, and silversmithing. You'll also be able to buy crafts in the shops within the compound. The **Islamic Museum (Muzium Islam)** (adults RM1/US$0.26, children RM.50/US$0.13) teaches everything you might want to know about Islam in this state, with a focus on Islamic arts and Kelantan's role in spreading Islam in the region. Finally there is the **War Museum (Bank Kerapu)** (adults RM2/US$0.53, children RM1/US$0.26), which tells the story of Kelantan during World War II in a 1912 bank building that survived the invasion.

✪ **State Museum (Muzium Negeri).** Jalan Hospital. ☎ **09/744-4666.** Adults RM2 (US$0.53), children RM1 (US$0.26). Open daily 8:30am–4:45pm. Closed Fri.

It's been a long time since this old building served as the colonial land office, but in 1990 major renovations gave it a new life. It now houses the Kelantan Art Gallery, including ceramics, traditional musical instruments, and cultural pastimes exhibits.

SHOPPING

For great local handicrafts shopping, visitors to Kelantan need go no further than **Jalan P.C.B.**, the road that leads to P.C.B. beach from Kota Bharu's Chinatown area. Hire a taxi and stop at every roadside factory, showroom, shop, and crafts house (the place crawls with them!) and you'll satisfy every shopping itch that needs scratching. Some wonderful places to try are **Wisma Songket Kampung Penambang,** Jalan P.C.B. (☎ **09/744-7757**), for songket cloth and clothing, and to see the ladies weaving the fine cloth. The local kite man, **Haji Wan Hussen bin Haji Ibrahim,** makes and sells kites out of his home at 328-A Kampong Redong Tikat, Jalan P.C.B. (☎ **09/744-0462**), and will invite you in for a look. He'll pack them sturdily so you can airmail them home. Also, **Pantas Songet & Batik Manufacturer,** Kampung Penambang, Jalan P.C.B. (☎ **09/744-1616**), has a nice selection of batik clothing and sarongs, plus some pieces of songket cloth.

In town, if you'd like to buy some silver, good (and inexpensive) filigree jewelry collections and silver housewares are to be had at **Mohamed Salleh & Sons,** 1260B Jalan Sultanah Zainab (☎ **09/748-3401**), and **K. B. Permai,** 5406-C Jalan Sultanah Zainab (☎ **09/748-5661**).

In the small but lively Chinatown area look for **A. Zahari Antik,** 3953-B Jalan Kebin Sultan (☎ **09/744-3548**), where you can shop for old treasures like *keris* (Malay daggers with wavy blades, of which this place has a great selection) as well as pottery, carvings, and brass.

Finally, for a little local shopping experience, check out the giant **Pasar Besar wet market** on Jalan Parit Dalam. Behind the produce and fish stands are shops for cheap bargains.

12 East Malaysia: Borneo

Borneo for the past 2 centuries has been the epitome of adventure travel. While bustling ports like Penang, Malacca, and Singapore attracted early travelers with dollars in their eyes, Borneo attracted those with adventure in their hearts. Today, the island still draws visitors who seek new and unusual experiences, and few leave disappointed. Rivers meander through dense tropical rain forests, beaches stretch for miles, and caves snake out longer than any in the world. All sorts of creatures you'd never imagine live in the rain forest: deer the size of house cats, owls only 6 inches tall, the odd probiscus monkey, and the orangutan, whose only other natural home is Sumatra. It's also home to the largest flower in the world, the Rafflesia, spanning up to a meter (about 3 ft.) wide. Small wonder this place has special interest for scientists and researchers the world around.

The people of Borneo can be credited for most of the alluring tales of early travels. The exotically adorned tribes of warring headhunters and pirates of yesteryear, some of whom still live lifestyles little changed (though both headhunting and piracy are now illegal), today share their mysterious cultures and colorful traditions openly with outsiders.

Add to all of this the fabulous tale of the White Raja of Sarawak, Sir James Brooke, whose family ruled the state for just over 100 years, and you have a land filled with allure, mystery, and romance unlike any other.

Malaysia, Brunei Darussalam, and Indonesia have divided the island of Borneo. Indonesia claims Kalimantan to the south and east, and the Malaysian states of **Sarawak** and **Sabah** lie to the north and northwest. The small sultanate of Brunei is nestled between the two Malaysian states on the western coastline.

1 Sarawak

Tropical rain forest accounts for more than 70% of Sarawak's total land mass, providing homes for not only exotic species of plants and animals, but for the different ethnic groups who are indigenous to the area. With more than 10 national parks and four wildlife preserves, Malaysia shows its commitment to conserving the delicate balance of life here, while allowing small gateways for travelers to appreciate Sarawak's natural wonders. A network of rivers connects the inland

East Malaysia's National Parks

areas to the rest of the world, and a boat trip to visit tribal communities and trek into caves and jungles can prove to be the most memorable attraction going.

The indigenous peoples of Sarawak make up more than half the state's population. Early explorers and settlers referred to these people with the catch-all term *Dyaks,* which didn't account for the variations between the more than 25 different ethnicities. Of these groups, the Iban are the largest, with more than 30% of the population of the state. A nomadic people by tradition, the Ibans were once located all over the region, existing on agriculture, hunting, and fishing. They were also notorious warriors who would behead enemies—a practice now outlawed but that has retained its cultural significance. The Ibans fought not only with other tribes, but within their own separate tribal units as well.

The next largest group, the Bidayuh, live peacefully in the hills. Their longhouse communities are the most accessible to travelers from Kuching. The Melanu are a coastal people who excel in fishing and boatbuilding. Finally, the Orang Ulu is an association of smaller tribes mostly in the northern parts of the state. Tribes like the Kayah, Kenyah, Kelabit, and Penan, while culturally separate entities, formed an umbrella organization to loosely govern all groups and provide representation. These groups are perhaps the least accessible to outsiders.

The indigenous people who still stay in the forest live in longhouse communities, many of which are open for visitors. Most travelers access these places with the help of local tour operators, who have trips that last from an overnight excursion to a week-long adventure. While some tours take you to well-trampled villages for the standard "gawk at the funny costumes" trips, many operators can take you to more remote places to meet people in an environment of cultural learning with a sensitivity that is appreciated by all involved. A few adventuresome souls travel solo into these areas, but I recommend that you stick with an operator. I don't care much for visitors who pop in unexpectedly, and I can't imagine why people in one of these villages wouldn't feel the same way.

Every visitor to Sarawak starts out from **Kuching,** the capital city. With a population of some 400,000 people, it's small but oddly cosmopolitan. In addition to local tribes that gave up forest living, the city has large populations of Malays, Chinese, Indians, and Europeans, most of whom migrated in the last 2 centuries. The city sits at the mouth of the Kuching River, which will be your main artery for trips inland. Before you head off for the river, though, check out the many delights of this mysterious colonial kingdom.

Sarawak was introduced to the Western world by **James Brooke,** an English adventurer who in 1839 came to Southeast Asia to follow in the footsteps of his idol, Sir Stamford Raffles. Like Raffles's Singapore, there was a region waiting for Brooke to settle and start a bustling community. His wanderings brought him to Borneo, where he was introduced to the sultan of Brunei. The sultan was deeply troubled by warring tribes to the south of his kingdom, who were in constant revolt, sometimes to the point of pirating ships to Brunei's port. Brooke provided the solution, initiating a campaign to befriend some of the warring tribes, uniting them to conquer the others. Soon the tribes were calmed. The sultan, delighted by Brooke, ceded Kuching to him for a small annual fee. In 1841, James Brooke became raja and set about claiming the land that is now Sarawak.

Raja Sir James Brooke became a colonial legend. Known as "The White Raja of Sarawak," he and his family ruled the territory and its people with a firm but compassionate hand. Tribal leaders were appointed to leadership and administrative positions within his government and militia, and as a result, the Brookes were highly respected by the populations they led. However, Brooke was a bit of a renegade, turning his nose up at London's attempts to include Sarawak under the crown. He took no money from the British and closed the doors to British commercial interests in Sarawak. Instead, he dealt in local trade and trade with Singapore. Still, Kuching was understood to be a British holding, though the city never flourished as did other British ports in Southeast Asia.

After his death in 1868, Raja James Brooke was succeeded by his nephew, Charles Brooke. In 1917, Charles's son, Vyner Brooke, became the last ruling Raja, a position he held until World War II, when the territory was conquered by invading Japanese. After the war Raja Vyner Brooke returned briefly, but soon after, the territory was declared a crown colony. Eventually Malaya was granted independence by Britain, prompting Prime Minister Tunku Abdul Rahman to form Malaysia in 1963, uniting peninsular Malaya with Singapore, Sarawak, and Sabah. Singapore departed from the union 2 years later, but Sarawak and Sabah happily remained.

KUCHING

The perfect introduction to Sarawak begins in its capital. Kuching's museums, cultural exhibits, and historical attractions will help you form an overview of the history, people, and natural wonders of the state. In Kuching your introduction to Sarawak will be comfortable and fun; culture by day and good food and fun by night. Kuching, meaning "cat" in Malay, also has a wonderful sense of humor, featuring monuments and exhibits to its feline mascot on almost every corner.

Kuching

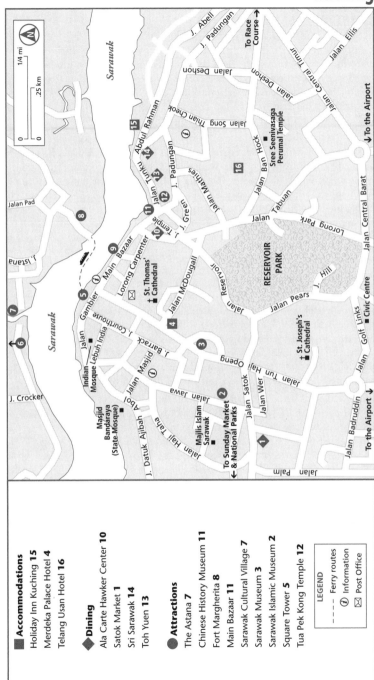

Accommodations
Holiday Inn Kuching **15**
Merdeka Palace Hotel **4**
Telang Usan Hotel **16**

◆ **Dining**
Ala Carte Hawker Center **10**
Satok Market **1**
Sri Sarawak **14**
Toh Yuen **13**

● **Attractions**
The Astana **7**
Chinese History Museum **11**
Fort Margherita **8**
Main Bazaar **11**
Sarawak Cultural Village **7**
Sarawak Museum **3**
Sarawak Islamic Museum **2**
Square Tower **5**
Tua Pek Kong Temple **12**

LEGEND
- - - Ferry routes
ⓘ Information
⊠ Post Office

ESSENTIALS

VISITOR INFORMATION   The Sarawak Tourism Board's **Visitor Information Centre** has literature and staff that can answer any question about activities in the state and city. This is actually the best place to start planning any trips to Sarawak's wonderful national parks, as the main office for the parks board operates from here. Really, they're just incredibly informed and are so welcoming, so feel free to take advantage. You'll find them at the Padang Merdeka next to the Sarawak Museum (☎ 082/423-600).

GETTING THERE   Almost all travelers to Sarawak enter via Kuching International Airport, just outside the city. Malaysia Airlines (☎ 03/746-3000 in KL) flies here about 10 times daily from KL. In addition, there are nonstop flights from the Malaysian cities of Johor Bahru and Kota Kinabalu. Malaysia Airlines also connects Kuching with direct flights from Singapore, Bandar Seri Bagawan in Brunei, Hong Kong, and Manila. The number for Malaysia Airlines in Kuching is ☎ 082/246-622. For airport information call ☎ 082/454-255.

   Taxis from the airport use coupons that you purchase outside the arrival hall. Priced according to zones, most trips to the central parts of town will be RM16 (US$4.20).

GETTING AROUND   Centered around a padang, or large ceremonial field, Kuching resembles many other Malaysian cities. Buildings of beautiful Colonial style rise on the edges of the field; many of these today house Sarawak's museums. The main sights, as well as the Chinatown area and the riverfront, are easily accessible on foot. Taxis are also available, and do not use meters; most rides around town are quoted at RM6 (US$1.60). Taxis can be waved down from the side of the road, or if you're in the Chinatown area, the main taxi stand is near Gambier Road near the end of the India Street Pedestrian Mall. For a taxi call ☎ 082/348-898.

FAST FACTS   The American Express office is located at Cph Travel Agencies, 70 Padungan Rd. (☎ 082/242-289). Major banks have branches on Tunku Abdul Rahman Road near Holiday Inn Kuching, or in the downtown area around Khoo Hun Yeang Road. The central post office is on Jalan Tun Abang Haji Openg (☎ 082/245-952). For a good Internet cafe try Cyber City, No. 46 Ground Floor Block D (☎ 082/428-318), just behind Riverside Complex Shopping Mall, charging RM6 per hour (US$1.60).

ACCOMMODATIONS

Holiday Inn Kuching. P.O. Box 2362, Jalan Tunku Abdul Rahman, 93100 Kuching, Sarawak, Malaysia. ☎ **082/423-111.** Fax 082/426-169. 305 units. A/C MINIBAR TV TEL. RM288–RM345 (US$15.98–US$90.80) double; RM575 (US$151.30) and up suite. AE, DC, JCB, MC V.

Holiday Inn offers Western-style accommodations at a moderate price, and you'll appreciate its location in an excellent part of town. It sits along the bank of the Kuching River, so to get to the main riverside area you need only stroll 10 minutes past some of the city's unique historical and cultural sights, shopping, and good places to dine. Catering to a diverse group of leisure travelers and businesspeople, the hotel has spacious, modern, and comfortable rooms; and while there are few bells and whistles, you won't want for convenience. The outdoor swimming pool and excellent fitness center facility will help you unwind, and the small shopping arcade has one of the best collections of books on Sarawak that can be found in the city.

✪ **Merdeka Palace Hotel.** Jalan Tun Abang Haji Openg, 93000 Kuching, Sarawak, Malaysia. ☎ **082/258-000.** Fax 082/425-400. 214 units. A/C MINIBAR TV TEL.

RM210– RM385 (US$55.25–US$101.30) double; RM646–RM790 (US$170–US$207.90) suite. AE, DC, JCB, MC, V.

Towering over the Padang Merdeka in the center of town is the Merdeka Palace, practically a landmark in its own right (as soon as you see the easily distinguishable tower, you'll always know where you are). This is one of the most fashionable addresses in the city, for guests as well as banquets and functions. From the large marble lobby to the mezzanine shopping arcade stuffed with designer tenants, its reputation for elegance is justified. Large rooms come dressed in European-inspired furnishings and fabrics. Try to get a view of the padang, as the less expensive rooms face the parking lot. The rooftop outdoor swimming pool is small, but the fully equipped fitness center has sauna and steam rooms, plus massage.

✪ **Telang Usan Hotel.** Ban Hock Rd., P.O. Box 1579, 93732 Kuching, Sarawak, Malaysia. ☎ **082/415-588.** Fax 082/245-316. 66 units. A/C TV TEL. RM140–RM200 (US$36.85– US$52.65) double. AE, DC, JCB, MC, V.

While in Kuching I like to stay at the Telang Usan Hotel. It's not as flashy as the higher priced places, but it's a fantastic bargain for a good room. Most guests here are leisure travelers, and in fact, many are repeat visitors. The small public areas sport murals in local Iban style, revealing the origin of the hotel's owner and operator. While rooms are small and decor is not completely up-to-date, they're spotless. Some rooms have only standing showers, so be sure to specify when making your reservation if a long bath is important to you. The coffee shop serves local and Western food from 7am to midnight, and the higher category rooms have minibars.

DINING

In addition to the two conventional restaurants listed below, Kuching's **hawker center** food stalls offer a culinary adventure at affordable prices. A good centrally located center is at **Ala Carte** on Lebuh Temple. It's indoors and air-conditioned. Also try the food stalls at **Satok Market** out at Jalan Satok for excellent Malay, Chinese, and Sarawakian cuisine.

✪ **Sri Sarawak.** Crowne Plaza Riverside Kuching, Jalan Tunku Abdul Rahman. ☎ **082/247-777.** Reservations not necessary. Daily noon–2:30pm and 6–10:30pm. Entrees RM8– RM22 (US$2.10–US$5.80). AE, DC, JCB, MC, V. MALAY.

Sri Sarawak is the only place to find Malay food in a fine-dining establishment. The restaurant occupies the 18th floor of the Crowne Plaza hotel, with views all around to the city below. The friendly and helpful staff is more than happy to help you navigate the menu, which includes Sarawak specialties such as umai, raw fish that's "cooked" in lime juice with onion, ginger, and chile. I'm addicted and want everyone to try it!

Toh Yuen. Kuching Hilton, Jalan Tunku Abdul Rahman. ☎ **082/248-200.** Reservations recommended on weekends. Daily 11:30am–2:30pm and 6:30–10:30pm. RM14–RM48 (US$3.70–US$12.65). AE, DC, JCB, MC, V. CHINESE.

One of the premier Chinese restaurants in Kuching, Toh Yueh serves excellently prepared dishes that are as pleasing to the eye as they are to the palate. Chef's specialties like butter prawns melt in your mouth, as do any of the many bean curd selections and crunchy vegetable dishes. Beware, portions are huge! Call ahead for special promotions for weekend lunch and dinner, which can be surprisingly low priced.

ATTRACTIONS

✪ **Sarawak Museum.** Jalan Tun Haji Openg. ☎ **082/244-232.** Free admission. Sat–Thurs 9am–5pm; Fri 9am–12:45pm and 3–5pm.

Two branches, one old and one new, display exhibits of the natural history, indigenous peoples, and culture of Sarawak, plus the state's colonial and modern history. The two branches are connected by an overhead walkway above Jalan Tun Haji Openg. The wildlife exhibit is a bit musty, but the arts and artifacts in the other sections are well tended. A tiny aquarium sits neglected behind the old branch, but the gardens here are lovely.

Sarawak Islamic Museum. Jalan P. Ramlee. ☎ **082/244-232.** Free admission. Sat–Thurs 9am–5pm; Fri 9am–12:45pm and 3–5pm.

A splendid array of Muslim artifacts at this quiet and serene museum depicts the history of Islam and its spread to Southeast Asia. Local customs and history are also highlighted. While women are not required to cover their heads, respectable attire that covers the legs and arms is requested.

Square Tower. Jalan Gambier near the riverfront. ☎ **082/426-093.**

The tower, built in 1879, served as a prison camp, but today the waterfront real estate is better served by a tourist information center. The Square tower is also a prime starting place for a stroll along the riverside, and is where you'll also find out about cultural performances and exhibitions held at the waterfront, or call the number above for performance schedules.

✪ **The Astana and Fort Margherita.** Across the Sarawak River from town. Museum: no phone. Fort: ☎ **082/244-232.** Free admission. Tues–Sun 9am–5pm.

At the waterfront by the Square Tower you'll find water taxis to take you across the river to see these two reminders of the White Rajas of Sarawak. The Astana, built in 1870 by Raja Charles Brooke, the second raja of Sarawak, is now the official residence of the governor. It is not open to the public, but visitors may still walk in the gardens. The best view of the Astana, however is from the water.

Raja Charles Brooke's wife, Ranee Margaret, gave her name to Fort Margherita, which was erected in 1870 to protect the city of Kuching. Inside the great castlelike building is a police museum, the most interesting sights of which are the depictions of criminal punishment.

Note: The museum/fort closed in April 2000 for renovation; it's scheduled to reopen in April 2001, but call before you go, just to be sure.

Chinese History Museum. Corner of Main Bazaar and Jalan Tunku Abdul Rahman. No phone. Free admission. Daily 9am–5pm.

Built in 1912, this old Chinese Chamber of Commerce Building is the perfect venue for a museum that traces the history of Chinese communities in Sarawak. Though small, it's centrally located and a convenient stop while you're in the area.

Tua Pek Kong Temple. Junction of Jalan Tunku Abdul Rahman and Jalan Padungan. No phone.

At a main crossroads near the river stands the oldest Chinese temple in Sarawak. While officially it is dated at 1876, most locals acknowledge the true date of its beginnings as 1843. It's still lively in form and spirit, with colorful dragons tumbling along the walls and incense filling the air.

Main Bazaar. Along the river.

Main Bazaar, the major thoroughfare along the river, is home to Kuching's antiques and handicraft shops. If you're walking along the river, a little time in these shops is like a walk through a traditional handicrafts art gallery. You'll also find souvenir shops and some nice T-shirt silk screeners.

✪ **Sarawak Cultural Village.** Kampung Budaya Sarawak, Pantai Damai, Santubong. ☎ **082/846-411.** Adults RM45 (US$11.85), children RM22.50 (US$5.90). Daily 9am–5pm.

What appears to be a contrived theme park turns out to be a really fun place to learn about Sarawak's indigenous people. Built around a lagoon, the park re-creates the various styles of longhouse dwellings of each of the major tribes. Inside each house are representative members of each tribe displaying cultural artifacts and performing music, teaching dart blowing, and showing off carving talents. Give yourself plenty of time to stick around and talk with the people, who are recruited from villages inland and love to tell stories about their homes and traditions. Performers dance and display costumes at 11:30am and 4:30 daily. A shuttle bus leaves at regular intervals from the Holiday Inn Kuching on Jalan Abell.

TOURING LOCAL CULTURE

When you come to Sarawak, everyone will tell you that you must take a trip to witness **life in a longhouse.** It is perhaps one of the most unique experiences you'll have, and is a lot easier to arrange than it sounds. Many good tour operators in Kuching take visitors out to longhouse communities, where guests are invited to stay for one or more nights. You'll eat local food, experience daily culture, and view traditional pastimes and ceremonies. On longer tours you may stop at more than one village to get a cross-cultural comparison of two or more different tribes. Good tour operators to speak to about arranging a trip are **Borneo Adventure,** 55 Main Bazaar (☎ **082/ 245-175;** fax 082/422-626), and **Telang Usan Travel & Tours,** Ban Hock Rd. (☎ **082/236-945;** fax 082/236-589). These agencies can also arrange trips into Sarawak's national parks.

TOURING SARAWAK'S NATIONAL PARKS

Before planning any trip into the national parks, travelers must contact the **National Parks Booking Office** at the Visitors Information Centre next to the Sarawak Museum (☎ **082/248-088;** fax 082/256-301). You will need to acquire permission to enter any park, and be advised on park safety and regulations. I recommend you visit the office itself. Situated inside the Tourism Board office, the staff here knows about every trip activity and can advise on accommodations options and all forms of transportation to and from the parks, and can even book your trip for you. They'll also screen tourism videos of the parks for you in their conference room, to help you decide which parks are best for your interests.

Bako National Park, established in 1957, is Sarawak's oldest national park. An area of 2,728 hectares (6,820 acres) combines mangrove forest, lowland jungle, and high plains covered in scrub. Throughout the park you'll see the pitcher plant and other strange carnivorous plants, plus long-tailed macaques, monitor lizards, bearded pigs, and the unique probiscus monkey. Because the park is only 37 kilometers (22 miles) from Kuching, trips here are extremely convenient.

A new project, the **Matang Wildlife Centre,** about an hour outside of Kuching, gives endangered wildlife a home, provides researchers with insights into wildlife conservation, and educates visitors about the animals and their habitat. For day trips, no parks department permission is required.

Gunung Gading National Park, about a 2-hour drive west of Kuching, sprawls 4,106 hectares (10,265 acres) over rugged mountains to beautiful beach spots along the coast. Day-trippers and overnighters come to get a glimpse of the Rafflesia, the largest flower in the world. The flowers are short-lived and temperamental, but the national parks office will let you know if there are any in bloom.

Gunung Mulu National Park provides an amazing adventure with its astounding underground network of caves. The park claims the world's largest cave passage (Deer Cave), the world's largest natural chamber (Sarawak Chamber), and Southeast Asia's longest cave (Clearwater Cave). No fewer than 18 caves offer explorers trips of varying degrees of difficulty, from simple treks with minimal gear to technically difficult caves that require specialized equipment and skills. Aboveground is 544 square kilometers (326 sq. miles) of primary rain forest, peat swamps, and mountainous forests teeming with mammals, birds, and unusual insects. Located in the north of Sarawak, Mulu is very close to the Brunei border.

Niah National Park, while interesting to nature buffs, is more fascinating for those interested in archaeology. From 1954 to 1967 explorers excavated a prehistoric site inside Niah's extensive cave network. The site dates as far back as 40,000 years, and is believed to have been continuously occupied until some 2,000 years ago. The **Niah Great Cave,** which contains the site, revealed sharp stone implements, pottery vessels, and animal and botanical remains. Near the mouth of the cave is a burial ground dating from Paleolithic times. The **Painted Cave,** also within Niah's cave network, is a magnificent gallery of mystical cave paintings and coffins that were buried here between A.D. 1 and A.D. 780. While a visit to the park requires parks department permission, further information on the excavation sites can be obtained from the Sarawak Museum (☎ **082/244-232;** fax 082/246-680).

2 Sabah

Of all the outdoor destinations in Southeast Asia, Sabah by far proves the most exciting. Covering 73,711 square kilometers (48,480 sq. miles) in the northern part of Borneo, the world's third largest island, Sabah stretches from the South China Sea in the west to the Sulu Sea in the east, both seas containing an abundance of uninhabited islands and pristine coral reefs and marine life. In between, more than half of the state is covered in primary rain forest that's protected in national parks and forest and wildlife reserves. In these forests, some rare species of **mammals** like the Sumatran rhino and Asian elephant (herds of them) are hard to spot, but other animals, such as the orangutan, probiscus monkey, gibbon, lemur, civet, Malaysian sun bear, and a host of others can be seen on jungle treks if you search them out. Of the hundreds of **bird species** here, the hornbills and herons steal the show.

Sabah's tallest peak also happens to be the highest mountain between the Himalayas and Irian Jaya. At 4,095 meters (13,432 ft.), it's the tallest in Southeast Asia, and a thrill to trek or climb. Sabah's rivers are also open for **river rafters,** providing whitewater thrills for every level of excitement, from soft adventure to extreme sports.

Not only does this state hold mysterious wildlife and geography, but people as well. Many visitors are attracted to Sabah by the region's 32 different **ethnic groups,** whose cultures and traditions are so different from the Western norm. Divided into four major linguistic families—Kadazandusun, Murutic, Tidong, and Paitanic—certain of these groups were the headhunters that filled past travelers' tales with much intrigue.

The largest group, the Kadazandusun, live on the west coast and in the interior. They are one of the first groups you'll come into contact with, especially if you're in town during their Pesta Kaamatan, or harvest festival, held during May, where the high priest or priestess presides over a ceremony designed to appease the rice spirit. Although it's a Kadazandusun tradition, it is celebrated by all cultures in the state. While this group is the main agricultural producer of the state, these days most members hold everyday jobs and live in cities. The exception to this trend is the Runggus, the last group of Kadazandusun to live in a traditional longhouse community, where they're famous for exquisite basket weaving, fabric weaving, and beadwork.

The Bajau migrated from the Philippines. On the eastern coast of Sabah, these people live their lives as sea gypsies, coming to shore only for burials. On the west coast, they live on land as farmers and cattle raisers. Known as the cowboys of the east, their men are very skilled equestrians, and are usually pictured on horseback. During festivals, their brilliant costumes and decorated ponies almost always take center stage.

The third most prominent tribal group, the Murut, shares the southwest corner of Sabah with the Bajau. Skilled hunters, they use spears, blowpipes, poisoned darts, and trained dogs to hunt their prey. In past days, these skills were used for headhunting, which thankfully is not practiced today (although many skulls can still be seen during visits to their longhouse settlements). One nonlethal Murat tradition involves a trampoline competition. The *lansaran* (the trampoline itself), situated in the community longhouse, is made of split bamboo. During Murut ceremonies, contestants drink rice wine and jump on the trampoline to see who can reach the farthest. A prize is hung above for the winner to grab.

KOTA KINABALU

The best place to begin exploring Sabah's marine wonders, wildlife and forests, adventure opportunities, and indigenous peoples is from its capital, Kota Kinabalu. A speck of a city on the west coast, it's where you'll find the headquarters for all of Sabah's adventure tour operators and package excursion planners. I recommend you spend at least a day here to explore all your options, then set out to the wilds for the adventure of a lifetime.

ESSENTIALS

VISITOR INFORMATION   The best information here can be gotten at the **Sabah Tourism Promotion Corporation office** at 51 Jalan Gaya (☎ **088/212-121**). While MTB has a small office on Jalan Gaya a block down from the Sabah Tourism office, almost all of their information promotes travel in other parts of the country. Still, if you're interested, stop by Ground Floor Bangunan EON, CMG Life, No 1 Jalan Sagunting (☎ **088/242-064**).

GETTING THERE   Because of Sabah's remote location, just about everybody will arrive by air via the **Kota Kinabalu International Airport** in the capital city (☎ **088/238-555**), about a 20-minute drive south of the central part of the city. Malaysia Airlines makes the flight from KL at least five times daily. For reservations information in KL, call the airlines at ☎ **03/746-3000,** or in Kota Kinabalu visit their office at 10th floor, Block C, Kompleks Karamunsing (☎ **088/213-555**).

The most efficient way to get into town from the airport is via **taxi.** The cars line up outside the arrival hall and are supposed to use a coupon system—look for the coupon sales and taxi-booking counter close by. You'll pay about RM12 (US$3.10) for a trip to town. On my last trip, I noticed the drivers trying to wave me over to negotiate a ride without the ticket counter middleman. I didn't go chat them up, but I'm pretty sure they would have quoted me a higher rate if I had.

GETTING AROUND   In the downtown area, you can get around quite easily on foot between hotels, restaurants, tour operators, markets, and the tourism office. For longer trips, a taxi will be necessary. They're easy enough to find cruising the town, or you can go to one of the regular stands around town—the most centrally located one at Jalan Datuk Saleh Sulong between Jalan Haji Saman and Jalan Pantai. I suggest you talk to your hotel concierge before you head out to ask how much you should expect to pay for your particular destination.

FAST FACTS   You'll find your **banks** conveniently located in the downtown area around Jalan Limabelas and along Jalan Gaya and Jalan Pantai. The **post office** (☎ **088/210-855**) is on Jalan Tun Razak. Look for **Internet** at K.K. Internet on Jalan Haji Saman across from Wisma Merdeka (☎ **088/235-219**).

ACCOMMODATIONS

Hyatt Regency Kota Kinabalu. Jalan Datuk Salleh Sulong, 88994 Kota Kinabalu, Sabah. ☎ **800/233-1234** in the U.S. and Canada, 131234 in Australia, 800/441-234 in New Zealand, or 088/221-234. Fax 088/225-972. 288 units. A/C MINIBAR TV TEL. RM402.50–RM448 (US$104.65–$116.50) double; RM863–RM3,450 (US$224.40–US$897) suite. AE, DC, JCB, MC, V.

The only international business-class hotel in town, in some ways the Hyatt seems a little out of place in cozy Kota Kinabalu. Still, it's located close to the waterfront, near all major shopping and travel operators, and has a fantastic assortment of restaurants to chose from. Even if you're staying elsewhere in town, you may appreciate one of their dining options. As modern as you would expect the Hyatt chain to be, rooms here are large, and are presented in up-to-date furnishing styles that are not so Western that they take all the charm away from the room. In-house videos, 24-hour room service, a large outdoor pool, and local tour and car-rental booking in the lobby make the place convenient for leisure travelers. Dining options include Japanese cuisine, Chinese seafood, local hawker fare beside the pool, plus a lounge and coffee shop. One of the high points, however, is Shenanigan's, the best bar in Kota Kinabalu, with live entertainment. It gets packed, mostly with locals and expatriates out for a sip.

⭐ **The Jesselton Hotel.** 69 Jalan Gaya, 88000 Kota Kinabalu, Sabah. ☎ **088/223-333.** Fax 088/240-401. E-mail: jesshtl@po.jaring.my. 32 units. A/C MINIBAR TV TEL. RM322–RM391 (US$86.30–$101.65) double; RM862.50 (US$224.25) suite. AE, DC, MC, V.

Listen to me rave about The Jesselton. It's such a nice surprise to find this quaint boutique hotel in the center of Kota Kinabalu, just about the last real reminder in this city of a colonial presence. Even more lovely is the level of personalized service you receive, and the comfort of the rooms, which, though completely modern, retain their charm with lovely Audubon-style inks and attractive wallpapers and fabrics—sort of a cross between a cozy guest house and a top-class hotel. Due to lack of space in the building, there's no pool, fitness center, or business center, but the staff at the front desk can help you with tour information and transportation. The coffee house serves local and Western food, which is quite good. The Gardenia Restaurant looks more upmarket than it really is.

⭐ **Shangri-La's Tanjung Aru Resort.** Locked Bag 174, 88744 Kota Kinabalu, Sabah. ☎ **088/225-800.** Fax 088/217-155. www.shangri-la.com. 499 units. A/C MINIBAR TV TEL. RM505–RM570 (US$131.30–$148.20) double; RM740 (US$192.40) suite.

A short ride southwest of Kota Kinabalu and you're at Tanjung Aru, an amazingly gorgeous beach resort area—Sabah's Riviera. Shangri-La has two properties here, both of them wonderful; however, I had to pick this one for the highly acclaimed dining you can sample at their Pulau Bayu restaurant. Located on a small island in a most impressive tropical ocean-side setting, it serves the finest local Sabahian cuisine and freshest seafood you can get in the region. I highly recommend you eat here as often as possible. As for the resort, while it's large, as a leisure traveler you'll want to stick to the Tanjung Wing (the Kinabalu Wing, while newer, is more like a hotel block). Every room has a stunning view, with a balcony for full appreciation. Luxuriously decorated, they're at the same time contemporary, convenient, and tropical. Of the many diversions, you've got a bike and jogging track, two outdoor free-form pools, four tennis

Kota Kinabalu

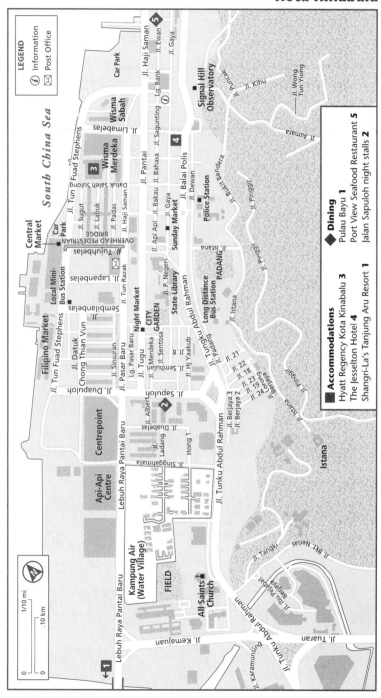

LEGEND
- ℹ️ Information
- ✉️ Post Office

South China Sea

Central Market

Car Park

Wisma Sabah

Wisma Merdeka

Signal Hill Observatory

Local Mini-Bus Station

Filipino Market

Centrepoint

Api-Api Centre

Night Market

CITY GARDEN

State Library

Sunday Market

Police Station

Long Distance Bus Station

PADANG

Kampung Air (Water Village)

FIELD

All Saints Church

Istana

◆ Dining
Pulau Bayu **1**
Port View Seafood Restaurant **5**
Jalan Sapuloh night stalls **2**

■ Accommodations
Hyatt Regency Kota Kinabalu **3**
The Jesselton Hotel **4**
Shangri-La's Tanjung Aru Resort **1**

1/10 mi
.10 km

courts, a children's club and playground, a state-of-the-art fitness center, and all the water sports you can dream of. Their tour desk can arrange everything from scuba to trekking and rafting, and their free shuttle gives you convenient access to town. Now, for the restaurants: In addition to Pulau Bayu there's also Shang Palace Cantonese restaurant, Peppino Italian restaurant, a garden terrace coffee shop, and a poolside cafe.

DINING

If you didn't hear me just above raving about **Pulau Bayu** at Shangri-La's Tanjung Aru Resort (☎ **088/225-800**), then let me recapitulate: All varieties of the freshest fish, lobsters, prawns, squid, crabs, scallops, and clams can be ordered in a great many styles, especially prepared from local recipes or barbecue. My mouth waters just thinking about the hinava (raw fish marinated in lime juice, ginger, shallots, herbs, and chile).

If you're in town, you can also get fresh seafood (selected from tanks on the back wall) at **Port View Seafood Restaurant,** Jalan Haji Saman across from the old Custom's Wharf (☎ **088/221-753**). Prepared primarily in Chinese and Malay styles, dishes are moderately priced and always succulent.

For a more local experience, **food stalls** provide the most authentic local cuisine at the best prices. Check out the night stalls on Jalan Sapuloh. Walk through and peek at all the offerings before ordering, and check for the most popular stalls and dishes. (When approaching a new hawker center, I always stroll around checking out what everybody else is eating. Locals always seem to know what's best.)

ATTRACTIONS

Where to begin? Basically, here in Sabah there's enough to keep you busy for about 6 months solid. Every time I leave, I have a list of about 50 million things I'm dying to do when I return.

We'll start with **scuba diving.** Off the eastern coast of Sabah lies the tiny island of **Sipadan.** If you're a real scuba fanatic, then you already know about it. It is, after all, one of the top-five dive sites in the entire world. This giant coral "garden" just can't be beat by any other site in Southeast Asia. Many outfits in Kota Kinabalu organize short-term and long-term stays out at the dive site, but **Borneo Action,** G19 Ground Floor, Wisma Sabah (☎ and fax **088/246-701;** e-mail: shop@borneoaction.com), in my opinion, is the most exciting and professionally run. They'll take you out for trips either on a live-aboard boat or with night stays at one of the resorts on Sipadan island, and will arrange all transportation and dives. Their special 7-day/6-night live-aboard trip includes not only Sipadan sites but trips all around the region to places other divers don't go. One note about reservations: You're better off booking a Sipadan trip through this local agency rather than through an agent at home. Recent regulations allow only 150 guests on the island each night, and overseas agents constantly overbook. The local firms make sure there's space available before booking.

For shorter trips, **Layang Layang,** while not as incredible as Sipadan, also has some great diving. Borneo Action can take you on this trip as well. Contact them at the address above.

For **snorkeling** and **beach activities,** pick up a boat at the Sabah Parks Jetty just behind the Hyatt to take you out to nearby **Tunku Abdul Rahman Park.** Only 8 kilometers (12.8 miles) from Kota Kinabalu, you can head out for RM10 (US$2.60) round-trip, and spend the day on one of the park's five islands, snorkeling and swimming (you can rent snorkel gear once you're there). Accommodations are available on Pulau Manukan and Pulau Mumutik, and can be booked in advance through any of the tour operators in Sabah.

Customized Adventure

Borneo Action, with both scuba dive and land-adventure divisions, can arrange any activity at any level of extremism you'd like in Sabah, customized to the activities you wish to take advantage of. For further details, see their Web site at **www. borneoaction.com,** e-mail them at enquiries@borneoaction.com, or see the phone number in the "Attractions" section.

Meanwhile, back on dry land, Sabah's spectacular geography draws trekkers, hikers, climbers, rafters, and all sorts of others seeking **adventure travel.** There are a great number of firms that coordinate these trips, but the very creative folks at **Borneo Action Adventure Center,** Lot 3-0-9, Api Api Centre, Lorog Api Api (☎ **088/ 267-190;** fax 088/267-194; e-mail: info@borneoaction.com), put together the most challenging and fascinating trips, designed for all levels of outdoor achievers, with the area's most acclaimed local guides. You can head out to the Crocker Range, Sabah's mountainous range southeast of Kota Kinabalu for either 2 days and 1 night or 5 days and 4 nights of trekking in primary rain forest to kampung villages inhabited by indigenous tribes, either camping in the jungle or staying in the villages. Their 6-day/5-night Jungle Experience includes not only trekking and camping, but educational sessions on the jungle's medicinal plants, fruits, and vegetables, plus wildlife observation and visits to local tribal villages. If that's not enough for you, try their Eco-Challenge: 9 days and 8 nights where you'll learn jungle navigation and survival skills, including the construction of bamboo rafts (that you'll be using to get yourself home!). It's a tough and exciting challenge.

Borneo Action Adventure Center also puts together great **mountain-biking** trips. The Kinabalu and Borneo 6-day/5-night trip takes you to the deepest interior village in Sabah and to many sights along the way. If you're up to it, their Hardcore Mountain Bike Adventure will really kick your butt with 14 days of biking all over the territory, interspersed with a climb up Mount Kinabalu and white-water rafting on the Padas River.

If you prefer a **softer adventure,** talk to the people at **Discovery Tours,** Lot G 22, 433-435 Wisma Sabah (☎ **088/221-244;** fax 088/221-600), with another office at Shangri-La's Tanjung Aru Resort (☎ 088/216-26). They take groups on either 2-day/1-night or 3-day/2-night trips to hike **Mt. Kinabalu** (RM380/US$98.80 and RM540/US$140.40 per person, respectively). They also plan regular trips out to Sandakan, on the eastern coast of Sabah, for 2-day/1-night trips to see the **Sepilok Orang Utan Rehabilitation Center,** the largest orangutan sanctuary in the world, and take a boat trip to see probiscus monkeys and swallows nest caves (RM556/ US$144.55 per person). Or, for about the same price, you can see the orangutan center with a stop at the **Marine Turtle Conservation Park and Hatchery.**

River rafting is also a popular sport here, especially along the Kiulu River, which is an exciting trip for all levels of experience and fitness. A day trip is arrangeable through Discovery Tours and costs only RM150 (US$39) per person. Keep in mind, the best time for rafting in Sabah is between March and September.

Finally, the indigenous peoples of Sabah are happy to welcome visitors to their villages to witness their daily lives and traditions. Discovery Tours offers coach trips to see the Runggus, Bajau, and other tribes in the Kota Kinabalu area. Half-day and day trips cost between RM60 and RM250 (US$15.60 and $65) per person.

Appendix: Singapore & Malaysia in Depth

1 Singaporean History

Dateline

- **1614** Capt. John Smith maps the New England coast, names the Charles River after King Charles I of England, and calls the area "a paradise."
- **3rd Century A.D.** Singapore mentioned by Chinese sailors.
- **5th Century** Tamil (Indian) and Persian traders arrive.
- **1295** Marco Polo visits Sumatra; has a swell time.
- **1349** Siam (Thailand) attacks Temasek (Singapore).
- **1390** Iskander Shah establishes sultanate on Singapura and ascends the "lion throne," but is eventually ousted.
- **1613** Portuguese report having torched a Malay outpost on Singapura.
- **1700s** Temenggongs rule Singapura.
- **1819** Sir Stamford Raffles lands on Singapura, likes what he sees.
- **1820s** First billiards club, first newspaper, first judicial system, first census (counting 4,727 souls).
- **1824** East India Trading Company buys the island.
- **1826** Raffles dies in London.
- **1827** Straits Settlements is formed, which includes

continues

By the 1800s, European powers had already explored much of the world, staking their authority over major trade routes. Southeast Asia's initial attraction was its position in between two seasonal monsoons—one half of the year saw winds that carried sailing vessels from China to Southeast Asia, while the other half of the year favored ships coming from India and Arabia. The English, Dutch, Potuguese, French, and Spanish, reconizing Southeast Asia's advantage, scrambled to set up trading posts to receive valuable tea, opium, silk, spices, and other goods from China.

It was this race for riches that paved the way for the creation of a port in Singapore; however, by the time the outpost was established, Europe's attitudes began to change. By the early 1800s, society was ushering in a new age of romanticism. Europeans no longer saw the world solely for its resources and wealth, but for its promise of adventure, ancient and mysterious cultures, and peoples whose ways were, to the Europeans, curious and uncanny. There was a new breed of officer in the powerful trading companies, the British East India Company included. These new men were dreamers, lured to the Orient's exotic lands not for riches but to satisfy a hunger to experience he unknown. It was one such ambitious dreamer, **Sir Stamford Raffles,** who would found Singapore and set in motion the colony that would exemplify Oriental romance.

The British East India Company, in its rivalry with the Dutch East Indies Company, sought to control the Strait of Malacca, the narrow passage between Indonesian Sumatra and the Malay peninsula. They already had a port at Penang, an island in the north of the Strait, but it was proving an economic failure. The company charged Raffles with the task of locating a new post. Raffles, who knew the area well, had his heart set on a small island at the tip of the Malay peninsula.

At the time of its "discovery," Singapore was occupied by only 1,000 people, mainly Malay residents, orang laut (sea nomads), a handful of Chinese farmers, plus assorted pirates in hiding. The island had little known historical significance. An early settlement on the island, called **Temasek,** had been visited regularly by Chinese merchants, and later the settlement came under the rule of the far-reaching Srivijaya Empire (9th to 13th centuries A.D.), which was based in Palembang in Sumatra. It was the Srivijayas who named the island Singapura, or Lion City, after its leader claimed to have seen a strange lion on its shores. However, the Srivijayas were eventually overtaken by a neighboring power, the Java-based Majapahits. Sometime around 1390, a young Palembang ruler, **Iskander Shah** (aka Parameswara), rebelled against the Majapahits and fled to Singapura, where he set up an independent rule. The Majapahits were quick to chase him out, and Iskander fled up the Malay peninsula to Malacca, where he founded what would be one of the most successful trading ports in the region at the time.

When Raffles arrived in 1819, Singapura had been asleep for nearly 400 years under the rule of the sultan of Johor, of the southernmost province in Malaya, with local administration handled by a Temenggong, or senior minister. It was Temmenggong Abdu'r Rahman who, on February 6, 1819, signed a treaty with Raffles to set up a trading post on the island in return for an annual payment to the Sultanate. After this, Raffles didn't stay around for too long, handing over the Residency of the port to his friend and colleague, **Colonel William Farquhar.**

When Raffles returned 3 years later, Singapore was fast becoming a success story. The ideally situated port was inspired by Raffles's own dream of free trade and Farquhar's skill at orderly administration. The population had grown to

Malaysia and Singapore; first steamship seen in Singapore.
- **1830** The British rule Singapore from India.
- **1833** East India Trading Company loses its foothold in Southeast Asia; population now 20,978.
- **1834** First New Year Regatta.
- **1837** First Chamber of Commerce formed.
- **1839** Launching of first Singapore vessel
- **1840** First bank opened, Union Bank of Calcutta; population 33,969.
- **1845** First Masonic Lodge; arrival of first P&O mail boat.
- **1850** Population 52,891.
- **1854** First Singapore postage stamp printed.
- **1860** Telegraph opened between Singapore and Batavia; population 81,734.
- **1864** First use of gas street lighting.
- **1867** Singapore is declared a British colony.
- **1869** Suez Canal opens; Singapore leaps to prominence.
- **1871** Singapore's population reaches 94,816; visit of the King of Siam; telegraph opened between Singapore and Hong Kong.
- **1877** Experimental rubber seeds smuggled from Brazil; planted at the Botanic Gardens.
- **1877** Chinese Protectorate is formed to curb violence among rival Chinese gangs.
- **1879** First telephone; Gen. Ulysses Grant visits Singapore; first official postcards issued.
- **1881** Population now 137,722.
- **1886** Steam trams begin operation.
- **1887** Statue of Raffles unveiled.

continues

- **1888** Rubber trees introduced into Malaysia as a commercial crop.
- **1891** Singapore Golf Club formed; population 181,602; first concert by Philharmonic Society.
- **1896** First automobile.
- **1901** Population 226,842.
- **1903** Singapore-Kranji Railway opens.
- **1904** Motor vehicle registration and drivers' licensing introduced.
- **1905** First frozen foods arrive in Singapore; electric trams introduced.
- **1907** Singapore Automobile Club founded.
- **1911** Population now 303,321.
- **1914** Outbreak of the Great War in Europe.
- **1915** Singapore Sling invented at the Long Bar in the Raffles Hotel (becomes a smashing success).
- **1916** Slavery abolished.
- **1919** First airplane arrives in Singapore.
- **1921** Britain severs its defense alliance with Japan; population 418,358.
- **1922** Prince of Wales visits.
- **1926** First trolley bus service.
- **1928** Singapore Flying Club formed.
- **1929** Direct Singapore-London telegraph link.
- **1931** Population 570,128.
- **1932** Last tiger on island killed.
- **1936** Anti-Japanese riots by Chinese in Singapore; start of wireless broadcasting.
- **1937** Sultan Mosque installs loudspeakers for muezzin's call to prayer; Kallang Aerodrome opens; opium sales proceeds still providing 25% of Straits Settlements' budget.
- **1938** First set of synchronized traffic lights installed.
- **1939** World War II begins in Europe.

continues

more than 11,000—Malays, Chinese, Bugis (from Celebes in Indonesia), Indians, Arabs, Armenians, Europeans, and Eurasians. The haphazard sprawl convinced Raffles to draft the **Town Plan of 1922,** assigning specific neighborhoods to the many ethnic groups that had settled. These ethnic enclaves remain much the same today—Singapore's Chinatown, the administrative center or Historic District, Little India, Kampong Glam, and other neighborhoods are still the ethnic centers they originally were (of course, with many modern alterations).

This would be the last trip Raffles would make to the island that credits him with its founding. His visit in 1822 was merely a stop on his way back to London to retire. Raffles had had big plans for his career with the East India Company, but never saw any of his ambitions come to fruition. While Singaporeans celebrate him with statues and street names, the truth is he eventually succumbed to syphilis in London, dying a failed and penniless man. He remains, however, a hero to modern day Singaporeans.

In 1824, the Dutch finally signed a treaty with Britain acknowledging Singapore as a permanent British possession, and Sultan Hussein of Johor ceded the island to the East India Trading Company in perpetuity. Three years later, Singapore was incorporated, along with Malacca and Penang, to form the **Straits Settlements.** Penang was acknowledged as the settlements' seat of government, with direction from the Presidency of Bengal in India.

Singapore's first 40 years were filled with all the magic of an Oriental trading port. Squat bumboats cluttered the Singapore river, carting goods from anchored vessels to the dozens of go-downs (warehouses) that lined the banks. Chinese coolie laborers came to Singapore in droves to escape economic hardship at home. Most were from one of four major dialect groups: Hokkien, Teochew, Cantonese, and Hakka, all from southern China. Living in crowded bunks in the buildings that sprang up behind the go-downs, these immigrants formed secret societies, social and political organizations made up of residents who shared similar ancestry or Chinese hometowns. These clan groups helped new arrivals get settled and find work, and carried money and messages back to workers' families in China. But it was the secret societies' other contribution—to gambling, street crime, and violence—that helped fuel Singapore's image as a lawless boomtown, filled with all the excitement and danger of a frontier town in the Wild West.

Indians were quick to become Singapore's second largest community. Most were traders or laborers, but many others were troops carried with the Brits. Most came from southern India, from the mostly Tamil-speaking population, including the Chettiars, moneylenders who financed the building of many places of worship in the early neighborhoods. After 1825, the British turned possession of Bencoolen on Sumatra to the Dutch, transferring the thousands of Indian prisoners incarcerated there to Singapore, where they were put to work constructing the buildings and clearing the land that the fledgling settlement needed. After they'd worked off their sentences, many stayed in Singapore instead of returning home to work their trade as free men.

During this period The Istana Kampong Glam was built in Raffles's designated Malay enclave, along with the Sultan Mosque. The surrounding streets supported a large but modest Malay settlement of businesses and residences.

Despite early successes, Singapore was almost entirely dependent on entrepôt trade, which was literally dependent on the whim of the winds. Dutch trading power still threatened its economic health, and the opening of Chinese trading ports to Western trade placed Singapore in a precarious position. The soil on the island barely supported a small sago palm industry, and with the lack of natural resources Singapore had to constantly look to trade for survival. True economic stability wouldn't arrive until the 1860s.

Major changes around the globe had an enormous effect on Singapore in the second half of the 19th century. In 1869, the Suez Canal opened, linking the Mediterranean and the Red Sea and putting Singapore in a prime position on the Europe–East Asia route. In addition, steamship travel made the trip to Singapore less dependent on trade winds. The shorter travel time not only saw entrepôt trade leap to new heights but also allowed leisure travelers to consider Singapore a viable stop on their itinerary.

The blossoming Industrial Revolution thirsted for raw materials, namely tin and rubber. Malaya was already being mined for tin,

- **1942** Japanese invade Singapore from the north.
- **1945** Japanese surrender; British rule restored.
- **1946** Singapore becomes a Crown Colony.
- **1948** Communist Party of Malaya attempts to take control of the peninsula; emergency powers instituted to discourage such activities.
- **1955** Constitution allows a freely elected parliament; People's Action Party (PAP) is formed; concessions won toward greater political autonomy.
- **1958** Singapore granted internal self-government.
- **1959** People's Action Party (PAP) wins general election; Lee Kuan Yew becomes first prime minister.
- **1961** First oil refinery.
- **1963** Singapore is admitted to the Federation of Malaysia; Internal Security Act passed.
- **1965** Singapore expelled from Federation and becomes an independent state; Singapore admitted into the United Nations.
- **1967** Singapore issues its own currency.
- **1981** PAP monopoly ends; Changi International Airport opens, named the best service in Southeast Asia; East Coast Expressway completed; Pan-Island Expressway opens.
- **1987** Singapore's policy of limiting families to two children reversed due to declining birth rate; hefty incentives given for third children.
- **1988** The Mass Rapid Transit System (MRT), an intraisland subway network built to the tune of S$5 billion, opens.
- **1990** Singapore celebrates 25 years of independence; Prime Minister Yew steps down and

continues

Goh Chok Tong takes over the reins; Ministry for Information and the Arts formed; Placido Domingo first opera star to play Singapore.

- **1992** Chewing gum banned due to vandals plugging up elevator buttons and subway doors.
- **1993** First Christie's auction; Michael Jackson World Tour sellout; *Cats* opens to rave notices and becomes the first of several Broadway road shows in Southeast Asia.
- **1994** Rogue securities trader Nick Leeson turns fugitive and is eventually captured after the US$1.4 billion collapse of Britain's Barings Bank.
- **1996** Passage of Maintenance of Parents Bill, which mandates that children provide for the care of their older parents.
- **1997** Asian Economic Crisis hits. Compared with the economic troubles in neighboring Southeast Asian nations, Singapore weathers the storm effectively.
- **1999** S. R. Nathan declared president without election. No other candidates were certified eligible.

much of which changed hands in Singapore. Rubber didn't enter the scene until 1877, when "Mad" Henry Ridley, director of the Botanical Gardens, smuggled the first rubber seedlings from Brazil to Singapore. After developing a new way to tap latex, he finally convinced planters in Malaya to begin plantations. To this day rubber remains a major industry for Malaysia.

WORLD WAR II

Although the British maintained a military base of operations on the island, Singapore was virtually untouched by the First World War. Just before the Great Depression, however, Britain bowed to U.S. pressure and broke off relations with Japan due to that country's increasing military power. Singapore's defense became a primary concern, and the British, thinking any invasion would come by sea, installed heavy artillery along the southern coastline, leaving the north of the island virtually unprotected.

The British military leaders were deeply divided over the strategy they assumed the Japanese would employ. They were convinced on the one hand that Japan's main intent was to attack Russia, and on the other that Japan's battles with the Chinese had left them battle weary, leaving the British time to prepare. Besides, they thought, nobody in their right mind would mount an invasion during the monsoon season.

In 1941, on the night of December 7, the Japanese attacked Pearl Harbor, invaded the Philippines and Hong Kong, landed in southern Thailand, and dropped the first bombs on Singapore. Still the British clung to their position of maintaining calm among the citizens. No one had any idea of the seriousness of the situation. News censors repeatedly kept insisting there was no alarm and even with the daily air raids, life went on.

Japanese Lieutenant General Yamashita, fresh from battles in Mongolia, saw a definite advantage in Singapore's unprotected northern flank, and stealthily moved three divisions—almost 20,000 troops—down the Malay Peninsula on bicycles. From Johor Bahru, across the Johor Strait, he had a direct view of Singapore and on the evening of February 8th the army quietly invaded the island. For days, the British tried to hold off their attackers, but bit by bit they lost ground. Within days, the Japanese were firmly entrenched.

The occupation brought terrible conditions to multiethnic Singapore, as the Japanese ruled harshly and punished any word of dissent with prison or worse. Mass executions were common- place, prisoners of war were tortured and killed, and it was said that the beaches at Changi ran red with blood. The prisoners that survived were sent to Thailand to work on the railway. Conditions were worst for the island's Chinese, many of whom were arrested indiscriminately just because of their ethnicity, rowed out to sea, and dumped overboard. Little information from the outside world reached Singapore's citizens during this time except when the Japanese were victorious.

In a sense, this behavior lost the Japanese one of the best audiences they could have had for their purported ideals of Asian equality and empowerment. During the occupation, they held exciting rallies, regaling the populace with these ideals, but all to naught, as the Japanese strutted boastfully and arrogantly about the city while the populace cowered in terror. In a country of divided ethnic groups, where the majority Chinese and the underdog Malays had lived for years under British colonial rule, these ideals might've fallen on sympathetic ears; but as it happened, the atrocities the Japanese committed against the Singaporeans only gained them the population's enmity.

Mercifully, the Japanese surrender came before Singapore became a battleground once again. On September 5, 1945, British warships arrived, and a week later, the Japanese officially surrendered to Lord Louis Mountbatten, supreme Allied commander in Southeast Asia.

THE POSTWAR YEARS

Now back under British rule, Singapore spent the next 10 years revitalizing itself, but efforts to become a fully self-governing country were tantamount. Resentment against the British was still very strong for the way they'd abandoned the island to the Japanese in 1941.

The British Military Administration (BMA), setup to efficiently organize and systematically administrate Singapore's postoccupation reconstruction, was neither efficient nor systematic. Disagreements between the British officials in Singapore and those in the Home Office beleaguered efforts to turn Singapore around. On the streets, conditions were terrible. The city was filthy and overrun with squatters living in ramshackle dwellings, food was scarce and high-priced when it was available, hospital facilities were nonexistent, and disease was all around. The BMA eventually got itself under control and proceeded to clean up the port and harbor and return them to civilian control, restore public utilities, and overhaul the distrusted police force. Although food was still scarce, rice was available at a reasonable price.

At the time of the liberation, the Malayan People's Anti-Japanese Army numbered about 4,500, most of them Communists. Sentiment at one time ran high for these heroes among the Singaporeans, but as the reality of the occupation receded, the organization sensed a decline in its popularity and relinquished its hard-line military aims in favor of a political agenda to realize its goal: independence from British rule. One of its prime organizations, the General Labor Union (GLU), had more than 60 trade unions under its banner and was able to organize strikes and mass demonstrations that brought Singapore to a standstill. Although concessions were made on both sides, the GLU eventually decided that overt actions weren't going to win any congeniality contests, and so became more involved with quietly reinforcing the trade union movement.

THE RISE OF LEE KUAN YEW & SINGAPOREAN INDEPENDENCE

In 1949, three years after the British military regime turned Singapore over to a civil administration as a crown colony once again, six Singaporean students in London formed a discussion group aimed at bringing together Malaysian overseas students. A third-generation Straits Chinese, Lee Kuan Yew, was a formidable member of the group. Returning to Singapore, his education completed, Lee made a name for himself as an effective courtroom lawyer during the trials of Chinese students arrested during the anti–national service riots of May 1954. Around this time, he had decided that, although he

Here all is life and activity; and it would be difficult to name a place on the face of the globe with brighter prospects or more present satisfaction."
—Sir Stamford Raffles, 1819

detested their politics, an alliance with the illegal Malayan Communist Party would best serve his aims, and so a new combined party, the **People's Action Party (PAP),** was inaugurated. In the 1955 elections, the long-shot Labour Front, led by David Marshall, won the majority of seats in the Legislative Assembly, shocking the right-wing parties. Lee Kuan Yew also won a seat in this Assembly.

Marshall's demands that his government become more involved in deciding the best course for Singapore provoked the governor and the Colonial Office. To settle the dispute amicably, the office proposed a seven-member Internal Security Council (ISC) comprised of equal seats for Britain and Singapore with the seventh member chosen from the Malay Federation. Although the Assembly accepted the proposal by a large majority, the plan was not to Marshall's liking, as the Federation was definitely pro-Britain, and he resigned.

By 1957, the Federation of Malaysia had won its independence, and around the same time Britain agreed to allow the establishment of a fully elected, 51-seat Legislative Assembly in Singapore. In the first elections for this body, in 1959, the PAP swept 43 of the seats and Lee Kuan Yew became the country's first prime minister.

Lee's agenda was met with distrust by the Federation of Malaysia. His aim was to have Singapore admitted to the Federation, but the Malaysian government was fearful of a dominant Chinese influence and fought to keep Singapore out. In 1963, however, they broke down and admitted Singapore as a member. It was a short-lived marriage. When the PAP looked to becoming a national entity rather than a local Singaporean party, an alarmed Federation demanded Singapore be expelled, and so, on August 9, 1965, Singapore found itself a newly independent country. Lee's tearful television broadcast announcing Singapore's expulsion from the Federation and simultaneous gain of independence is one of the most famous in Singapore's history. In 1971, the last British military forces left the island.

SINGAPORE TODAY

Who would have believed that Singapore would raise to such international fame and become the vaunted "Asian Tiger" it has in recent decades? This small country's political stability and effective government have inspired many other nations to study its methods, and former prime minister Lee Kuan Yew is counted among the most renowned political figures in the world. When asked to explain how Singapore's astounding economic, political, and social success was made possible, Lee always takes the credit—and deservedly so—but in the face of international criticism for dictatorial policies, absolutist law enforcement, and human rights violations, he also stands first in line to receive the blame.

THE GOVERNMENT   In 1954, the procommunist People's Action Party (PAP) was formed during a time when the British colonial government was encouraging local political participation. A year later, the young Peranakan-born and Cambridge-educated lawyer Lee Kuan Yew was elected as the party's secretary-general. In 1955, Mr. Lee was quoted as saying, "Any man in

Singapore who wants to carry the Chinese-speaking people with him cannot afford to be anti-Communist." Master political strategist that he was (and is), Lee used Communism to rally the support of the Chinese population, the largest body of voters in Singapore, though in fact the PAP leaders were moderates. In the election zeal, nobody really noticed. In 1959, the PAP took 43 of the 51 seats in the Legislative Assembly, and Mr. Lee was elected Singapore's first prime minister. Since then, and without debate, it has been his unfailing vision of a First World Singapore that's inspired the policies and plans that created the political and economic miracle we see today. During his tenure he mobilized government, industry, and citizens toward fulfilling his vision, establishing a government almost devoid of corruption, a strong economy built from practically no resources save labor, and a nation of racial and religious harmony from a multiethnic melting pot.

Both critics and admirers refer to Lee Kuan Yew as a strict yet generous "father" to the "children" of Singapore, raising them to a high position on the world stage yet dictating policies that have cost citizens many of their personal freedoms. You'll find that the average Singaporean expresses some duality about this: He or she will be outwardly critical of the government's invasion of privacy and disregard for personal freedoms, and of policies that have driven up the cost of housing and health care, but will also recognize all that Lee has done to raise Singaporeans' standard of living, expand their opportunities for the future, and ensure tranquillity at home—achievements for which many are willing to sacrifice a certain amount of freedom to enjoy. By and large, they wish to see the current government continue its work.

Lee stepped down from the prime minister's chair in 1990, assuming the position of senior minister. Although the new prime minister, Mr. Goh Chok Tong, has created some policies of his own to promote more openness in the political system, it is understood that Lee still drives the car. To his credit, Goh has been a popular leader. In addition to initiating more citizen participation in the politics of the country, he is supporting local visual and performing arts and encouraging an effort to draw internationally acclaimed theater companies to Singapore, all in an attempt to solve Singapore's current brain drain by encouraging more creative and educated Singaporeans to stay in-country rather than emigrate. Unfortunately, he also has to face suspicion that he's nothing more than a seat warmer for Lee's son, Lee Hsien Loong, who is currently deputy prime minister.

Whoever the individual officeholders, one constant of Singaporean politics is that the key players are almost exclusively PAP members. Opposition parties have little chance to grab the prize, as the PAP holds all the cards. Elections are said to be influenced by economic threats and repressive laws. In recent years, the PAP has not been winning the overwhelming majority of government seats it has in the past, but still has enough power to keep its hold.

THE CENSORSHIP QUESTION One infamous feature of Singapore's government is its control over media, both domestic and international. All national news publications have ties to the government, whose philosophy holds that the role of the media is to promote the government's goals. Articles are censored for any content that might threaten national security, incite riot, or promote disobedience or racism. Offenders face stiff fines. After a few days of the *Straits Times,* you'll be sick of cheery reporting that skirts around issues and articles that are grossly transparent in their opinions. The censorship doesn't stop at that old "national security" excuse, either. International publications such as *Time, The Asian Wall Street Journal, Asiaweek,* and

The Economist have all suffered drastically reduced circulation in Singapore after they published articles the government found insulting. Magazines that are banned completely include *Playboy* and *Cosmopolitan,* for their pornographic content and promotion of harmful Western values.

It doesn't stop at the print media, either. Television is also censored, satellite dishes are banned, and there's only one cable provider, which the government keeps a close eye on for anything resembling pornography.

The Internet provided Singapore with a tough dilemma. By design, the Net promotes freedom of communication, which is taken advantage of by, among others, every political dissident and pornographer who can get his little hands on a PC. This thought so terrified the Singapore government that it debated long and hard about allowing access to its citizens. However, the possibilities for communications and commerce and their implications for the future of Singapore's economy won, and the government paved the way for all Singaporeans to have access by the year 2000—though it goes without saying, of course, that access will be heavily censored. Private- and public-sector organizations must register with the government, which clears all content, and Internet providers must block questionable sites and monitor hits to Web sites, reporting to the government who's accessing what.

THE ECONOMY   Singapore's economy is a bizarre marriage between free trade and government control. Lee Kuan Yew's vision and resulting policies have created annual national growth rates of 8.9% going on 3 decades now. The biggest moneymakers are the electronics industry, financial and business services, transportation and communications, petroleum refining and shipping, construction, and tourism. Seventy-six percent of Singapore's exports, exclusive of oil exports, go to the United States, Malaysia, the European Union, Hong Kong, and Japan.

Singaporeans enjoy a high standard of living, with average annual incomes reaching US$23,000. The most commonly heard complaint? The rising cost of real estate.

TOURISM   The Singapore Tourism Board has far-reaching influence that has helped to turn Singapore into a veritable machine for raising foreign cash. More than 7 million tourists visit Singapore annually, spending a total of S$11.6 billion (US$6.96 billion) during their stays.

Not content to rest on its laurels, Singapore has big plans to dramatically increase these numbers in the new century through implementation of its new **Tourism 21 Plan,** which will restore landmarks and create Thematic Zones, areas within the ethnic neighborhoods where the URA (Urban Redevelopment Authority) plans to restore old buildings and block off vehicular traffic to create pedestrian avenues. If their plans succeed, neighborhoods like Chinatown may become more like ChinaWorld, as local shops and colorful street life are replaced by tidy restored buildings, glitzy souvenir shops, and ironic little exhibits describing the vibrant community that once thrived in the neighborhood but was run out by high rents.

The first Thematic Zone is currently being constructed in the streets of Chinatown. Additional Tourism 21 actions will include the construction of a new exhibition center at the World Trade Centre, which was begun in mid-1998, and The Esplanade–Theatres on the Bay, a giant concert hall poised at the edge of the marina and modeled after the Sydney Opera House— a project to which very few Singaporeans feel any personal connection.

2 Malaysian History

If Malaysia can trace its success to one element, it would be geographic location. Placed strategically at a major crossroads between the Eastern and Western worlds and enforced by the northeast and southwest monsoons, Malaysia (formerly known as Malaya) was the ideal center for East-West trade activities. The character of the indigenous Malays is credited to their relationship with the sea, while centuries of outside influences shaped their culture.

The earliest inhabitants of the peninsula were the orang asli, who are believed to have migrated from China and Tibet as early as 5,000 years ago. The first Malays were established by 1000 B.C., migrating not only to Malaya, but throughout the entire Indonesian archipelago as well, including Sumatra and Borneo. They brought with them knowledge of agriculture and metalwork, as well as beliefs in a spirit world (attitudes that are still practiced by many groups today).

Malaysia's earliest trading contacts were established by the 1st century B.C., with China and India. India proved most influential, impacting local culture with Buddhist and Hindu beliefs that are evidenced today in the Malay language, in literature, and in many customs.

Recorded history didn't come around until the **Malay Annals** of the 17th century, which tell the story of Parameswara, also known as Iskander Shah, ruler of Temasek (Singapore), who was forced to flee to Malacca around A.D. 1400. He set up a trading port and, taking advantage of the favorable geographic location, led it to world-renowned financial success. Malacca grew in population and prosperity, attracting Chinese, Indian, and Arab traders.

With Arabs and Muslim Indians came **Islam,** and Iskander Shah's son, who took leadership of Malacca after his father's death, is credited as the first Malay to convert to the new religion. The rule of Malacca was transformed into a sultanate, and the word of Islam won converts not only in Malaya but throughout Borneo and the Indonesian archipelago. Today the people of this region are very proud to be Muslim by conversion, as opposed to conquest.

Malacca's success was not without admirers, and in 1511 the **Portuguese** decided they wanted a piece of the action. They conquered the city in 30 days, chased the sultanate south to Johor, built a fortress that forestalled any trouble from the populace, and set up Christian missionaries. The Portuguese stuck around until 1641, when the Dutch came to town, looking to expand their trading power in the region. For the record, after Malacca's fall to the Portuguese, its success plummeted, and has never been regained.

The **British** came sniffing around in the late 1700s, when Francis Light of the British East India Company landed on the island of Penang and cut a deal with the Sultan of Kedah to cede it to the British. By 1805, Penang had become the seat of British authority in Southeast Asia, but the establishment served less as a trading cash cow and more as political leverage in the race to beat out the Dutch for control of the Southeast Asian trade routes. In 1824, the British and Dutch finally signed a treaty dividing Southeast Asia. The British would have Malaya and the Dutch Indonesia. Dutch-ruled Malacca was traded for British-ruled Bencoolen in Sumatra. In 1826, the British East India Company formed the Straits Settlements, uniting Penang, Malacca, and Singapore under Penang's control. In 1867, power over the Straits Settlements shifted from the British East India Company to British colonial rule in London.

The Anglo-Dutch treaty never provided for the island of **Borneo.** The Dutch sort of took over Kalimantan, but the areas to the northwest were generally held under the rule of the Sultan of Brunei. Sabah was ceded for an annual sum to the British North Borneo Company, ruled by London until the Japanese invaded during World War II. In 1839, Englishman **James Brooke** arrived in Sarawak. The Sultan of Brunei had been having a hard time with warring factions in this territory, and was happy to hand over control of it to Brooke. In 1841, after winning allies and subjugating enemies, Brook became the Raja of Sarawak, building his capital in Kuching.

Meanwhile, back on the peninsula, **Kuala Lumpur** sprang to life in 1857 as a settlement at the crook of the Klang and Gombak rivers, about 35 kilometers (21 miles) inland from the west coast. Tin miners from India, China, and other parts of Malaya came inland to prospect and set up a trading post, which flourished. Forty years later, in 1896, it became the capital of the British Malayan territory.

In 1941, the Japanese conquered Malaysia en route to Singapore. Life for Malays during the 4-year occupation was a constant and almost unbearable struggle to survive hunger, disease, and separation from the world. After the war, when the British sought to reclaim their colonial sovereignty over Malaya, they found the people thoroughly fed up with foreign rule. The struggle for independence served to unite Malay and non-Malay residents throughout the country. By the time the British agreed to Malayan independence, the states were already united. On August 31, 1957, Malaya was cut loose, and Kuala Lumpur became its official capital. For a brief moment in the early 1960s, the peninsula was united with Singapore and the Borneo states of Sabah and Sarawak. Singapore left the federation in 1965, and today Malaysia continues on its own path.

MALAYSIA TODAY

The Malaysia of today is a peaceful nation of many races and ethnicities. The last national census, collected in 1991, placed the population at roughly 17.5 million. Today it's closer to 20 million. Of this number, **bumiputeras** are the most numerous ethnic group (broadly speaking), and are defined as those with cultural affinities indigenous to the region and to one another. Technically, this group includes people of the aboriginal groups native to the peninsula—the orang asli ("original people"), Malays, and other Malay-related groups, more specifically the ethnic groups found in Sabah and Sarawak such as the Iban, Bidayuh, Melanu, and Kadazan, to name a few. A smaller segment of the population is nonbumiputera groups such as the Chinese, Indians, Arabs, and Eurasians, most of whom are descended from settlers to the region in the past 150 years. It is important to know the difference between the bumiputera and nonbumiputera groups to understand Malaysian politics, which favors the first group in every policy. It is equally important to understand that despite ethnic divisions, each group is considered no less Malaysian.

The state religion is Islam, with almost all ethnic Malays following Allah and the word of the Prophet Mohammed in the Koran. The Muslim way of life is reflected in almost every element of Malaysian life. The life of almost every town is centered on its mosque, restaurants serve halal food (prepared according to strict Muslim dietary laws), and every hotel room has an arrow on the ceiling to indicate the direction of Mecca. This strict adherence to Islam will most likely effect your vacation plans in some way. Later in this chapter I'll explain some important rules about etiquette that will simplify your visit.

As for the non-Muslim, life goes on under the government's very serious policy to protect freedom of religion. In multicultural towns such as Georgetown (Penang) or Malacca, you're likely to find churches, mosques, and Buddhist and Hindu temples within a stone's throw of each other. Many of the orang asli tribes and indigenous groups of Sabah and Sarawak practice religions based upon the presence of a spirit world on earth. On the topic of religion, it is vital to note that despite its "freedom of religion" policy, Malaysia is very **anti-Zionist.** Almost daily the local papers report anti-Semitic news, and Israel is the only country in the world to which Malaysian citizens may not travel. If you carry an Israeli passport, you will need to consult your home embassy before considering travel to Malaysia. Jewish people from other countries who still wish to visit are advised to downplay their religion and culture.

Until the **Asian Economic Crisis** that began in July 1997, Malaysia was one of the rising stars of the East Asian Miracle, with an economy built upon the manufacturing sector in electronics and rubber products, as well as on agriculture and mining. Exports in raw rubber and timber also add to the coffers. Though the crisis hit the country hard, the most recent economic reports show that Malaysia's recovery could very well be the strongest in the region.

The government is headed by a prime minister, a post that for the past 17 years has been held by YAB Dato' Seri Dr. Mahathir Bin Mohamad. Dr. Mahathir has been both criticized and praised for his unique efforts to solve his country's economic troubles. When the ringgit, Malaysia's currency, plummeted in mid-1997, Mahathir chose to ignore IMF advice for economic and debt restructuring, which in later months revealed itself to have been very bad advice.

In September 1998, Dr. Mahathir's administration came under international scrutiny when he ousted his deputy prime minister, YAB Dato' Seri Anwar Bin Ibrahim, for alleged sexual misconduct and corruption. While there were brief moments of civil unrest in the nation's capital, the situation never placed travelers in danger. In early 1999, Anwar stood trial for corruption charges, was found guilty of all counts and was sentenced to 6 years imprisonment. His sodomy trial continues at the time of writing, and it appears the present administration is keeping a tight fist on the proceedings. Meanwhile, following the reelection of Dr. Mahathir in late 1999, Malaysians seem little interested in politics anymore. Despite the efforts of Dr. Wan Aziza Wan Ismail, Anwar's wife and leading advocate, plus the emergence of other political parties, most Malaysians have become little convinced that any major changes will come as long as Mahathir is in power. Still, although Malaysians are discouraged from talking politics with outsiders, questions about government transparency and free press are nowadays discussed with a little more freedom.

3 Recommended Books

Singapore publishes quite a few good reads about itself—its history, culture, and people, which can be found in English bookstores are all over the city. The biggest is **MPH,** on the corner of Stamford Road and Armenian Street in the Historic District (☎ 65/336-3633). **Times The Bookshop** has many outlets. The biggest one is in Centrepoint shopping center, at #04-08/16 (☎ 65/734-9022).

While books on **Malaysia** or by Malaysians are hard to find in the West, bookstores in-country as well as in Singapore hold quite a few interesting titles on Malaysian culture, history, and arts written in English. In almost all bookstores you can find gorgeous hardcover picture books featuring Malaysia's beautiful landscape, handicrafts, costumes, and traditions.

For more informational reading, the following books provide a good start.

ARCHITECTURE

Gretchen Liu's *In Granite and Chunam* (Landmark Books) discusses Singaporean architecture, its history, and the origins of its unique character; and Robert Powell's *Living Legacy* (Singapore Heritage Society) is a neat little peek inside restored residential shophouses and bungalows.

THE ARTS

SINGAPORE *The Arts in Singapore: Directory and Guide* (edited by Dora Tay and published by Accent Communications and the National Arts Council) has a great overview of the major influences of Singapore's arts scene, and lists local theater groups, art galleries, dance troupes, and much more. *Singapore: Global City for the Arts* (Singapore Tourism Board and the Ministry of Information and the Arts) provides an overview of Singapore's creative side.

CUISINE

Wendy Hutton's *Singapore Food* (Times Books International) is an anecdotal description of the history and traditions behind the ingredients and preparation involved in Singaporean cuisine, with recipes. *Singapore's Best Restaurants 1998* (Illustrated Magazine Publishing) is a list of the top 100 restaurants as judged by *The Singapore Tattler,* a local high-profile society gossip magazine. Djoko Wibisono and David Wong's *The Food of Singapore* (Periplus Editions) is about the origins and influences of the various cuisines that make up Singapore's favorite dishes, with recipes.

CULTURE

SINGAPORE David Brazil's *Street Smart Singapore* (Times Books International) is a book of vignettes telling the tales that surround the places and people of Singapore, and Pugalenthi Sr's *Myths and Legends of Singapore* (VJ Times) tells the Chinese, Indian, and Malay legends of Singapore. *Portraits of Places: History, Community and Identity in Singapore* (edited by Brenda S. A. Yeoh and Lily Kong, Times Editions) is a fascinating collection of scholarly writings examining the driving social and psychological forces behind the identity of Singaporeans.

For a look at **Chinese festivals,** check out Tan Huay Peng's *Fun with Chinese Festivals* (Federal Publications), which explains the origins of the customs associated with them. Goh Pei Ki's *Origins of Chinese Festivals* (Asiapac) is a cartoon history of China's major festivals and the traditions that make them unique.

If you want to learn about **feng shui,** there are scads of books you can peruse. Kristen M. Newleaf's *Feng Shui: Arrange Your Home to Change Your Life* (Lagatree) is a short read of basic feng shui principles you can apply in your own home, while Sarah Rossbach's *Feng Shui: The Chinese Art of Placement* (Rider) is a deep study and detailed explanation of the principles of feng shui. Derek Walters's *The Feng Shui Handbook: A Practical Guide to Chinese Geomancy* (Thorsen's) is yet another explanation.

MALAYSIA *The Crafts of Malaysia* (Shamira Bhanu, editor, Archipelago Press) is a bulky picture book, but it's packed with color plates and terrific descriptions and histories of this country's little known but beautiful, handicrafts. For music heads, *The Malay Traditional Music* by Mohd. Ghouse Nasuruddin (Dewan Bahasa dan Putstaka) is a little hard to find, but well worth the search for its history, descriptions, and sheet music.

Regarding books on modern culture, Malaysia is not exactly famous for the open expression of opinions; however, a couple of books written by Malaysians shed some light on a few of the more interesting cultural quirks and social dilemmas facing the nation today. Lee Su Kim's *Malaysian Flavors: Insights into Things Malaysian* (Pelanduk Publications) and *Generation: A Collection of Contemporary Malaysian Ideas* by Amir Muhammad, Kam Raslan, and Sheryll Stothard (Hikayat Press), are at times humorous as well.

ETIQUETTE

If you're interested in brushing up on your manners before visiting Singapore and Malaysia, there are a number of books that will help. Elizabeth Devine and Nancy L. Braganti's *The Travelers' Guide to Asian Customs and Manners* (St. Martin's Press) tells you everything you need to know about the region's customs. Raelene Tan's *Chinese Etiquette: A Matter of Course* (Landmark Books) gives concise tips on Chinese etiquette practices, and *Indian & Malay Etiquette: A Matter of Course,* by the same author and publisher, spells out the basic rules of Indian and Malay etiquette.

If you're traveling to Malaysia for an extended period of time, or are planning to work there, I highly recommend *Malaysian Customs & Etiquette: A Practical Handbook,* by Datin Noor Aini Syed Amir (Times Books), for its great advice on how to negotiate any situation.

GOVERNMENT PUBLICATIONS

Singapore Facts and Pictures (Ministry of Information and the Arts) is updated annually and packed with recent statistics and facts about the nation, including trade figures, population estimates, and even unusual and little-known facts. *Singapore 1998* (Ministry of Information and the Arts) is updated annually. It reads like a textbook and will tell you anything you want to know about Singapore's government, economy, and society.

HISTORY

SINGAPORE   *A History of Singapore,* edited by Ernest C. T. Chew and Edwin Lee (Oxford University Press), is a collection of scholarly accounts of the history of Singapore, with chapters on national identity, Singapore's relationship with its ASEAN (Association of Southeast Asian Nations) neighbors, and more. C. M. Turnbull's *A History of Singapore, 1819–1988* (Oxford University Press) tells the story of Singapore from precolonial days to the political and social developments in the 1980s.

MALAYSIA   Regarding the general history of Malaysia, I suggest both Ruud Spruit's *The Land of the Sultans: An Illustrated History of Malaysia* (Pepin Press), for its readability and color plates, and *A History of Malaysia,* by Barbara Watson Andaya and Leonard Y. Andaya (Macmillan), for its thorough attention to detail. Other books I've found interesting and informative include *A Moment of Anguish: Singapore and Malaysia and the Politics of Disengagement* by Albert Lau (Times Academic Press), covering the brief but rocky period of unification between the two neighboring countries; *Old Kuala Lumpur* by J. M. Gulick (Oxford University Press), with its fascinating description of this city's rise from a small mining outpost; and Spenser St. John's *The Life of Sir*

James Brooke, Rajah of Sarawak (Oxford), a historical account by one who was close to the Rajah.

TRAVEL

For a look at what travel to Singapore was like in the old days, check out *Travelers' Singapore, An Anthology* (edited by John Bastin, Oxford University Press), which presents excerpts from old travelogues, with views of Singapore between 1819 and 1942 through the eyes of tourists. Similarly, *Travelers' Tales of Old Singapore* (edited by Michael Wise, In Print) shares the experiences of early travelers.

POLITICS

SINGAPORE While there are many books published about the life and politics of Senior Minister Lee Kwan Yew, he didn't publish his own memoirs until 1998. For the first few months the book was so popular you couldn't find a copy in any bookstore in Singapore, but these days it's easy to find world-wide. Look for *Singapore Story: The Memoirs of Lee Kwan Yew,* by, of course, Lee Kwan Yew (Times International).

MALAYSIA A great number of books have been written by Malaysian leader Dr. Mahathir Mohamad about his political philosophies, and all are easy to find in English anywhere in the country and overseas. Titles like *The Challenge of Turmoil* (Times Books International) and *In Liberal Doses* (Times Books International) cover a wide range of political issues; however, at press time readers are curiously awaiting his latest, *A New Deal For Asia* (Times Books International), to be released sometime in 2000. On the other hand, another interesting read, Anwar Ibrahim's *The Asian Renaissance* (Times Books International), was written prescandal. His views on democracy and Islam are quite interesting and boldly progressive in the face of the country's current policies.

JUST FOR FUN

Jim Aitchinson and Theseus Chan's *The Official Guide to the Sarong Party Girl* (Angsana Books) is a bawdy humor book that pokes fun at Singaporean women who chase Western men. Of a more general nature, Catherine Lim's *O Singapore! Stories in Celebration* (Times Books International) tells witty stories, each designed to make fun of stereotypical Singaporean behavior.

Don't leave without grabbing at least one of the hilarious Mr. Kiasu books—*Everything I Also Want, Everything Also Must Grab, Everything Also Number One,* and *Everything Also Want Extra* (Comix Factory Pte. Ltd.)—a series of comic books starring local comic hero Mr. Kiasu, whose escapades poke fun at many young Singaporeans' overcompetitiveness and terror of missing out on anything new and happening.

Index

See also separate Singapore Accommodations and Restaurant indexes, and the Malaysia indexes, below.

Singapore

SINGAPORE ACCOMMODATIONS

MALAYSIA ACCOMMODATIONS

FROMMER'S® COMPLETE TRAVEL GUIDES

Alaska
Amsterdam
Arizona
Atlanta
Australia
Austria
Bahamas
Barcelona, Madrid &
 Seville
Beijing
Belgium, Holland &
 Luxembourg
Bermuda
Boston
British Columbia & the
 Canadian Rockies
Budapest & the Best of
 Hungary
California
Canada
Cancún, Cozumel &
 the Yucatán
Cape Cod, Nantucket &
 Martha's Vineyard
Caribbean
Caribbean Cruises & Ports
 of Call
Caribbean Ports of Call
Carolinas & Georgia
Chicago
China
Colorado
Costa Rica
Denmark
Denver, Boulder & Colorado
 Springs
England
Europe

European Cruises & Ports
 of Call
Florida
France
Germany
Greece
Greek Islands
Hawaii
Hong Kong
Honolulu, Waikiki &
 Oahu
Ireland
Israel
Italy
Jamaica
Japan
Las Vegas
London
Los Angeles
Maryland & Delaware
Maui
Mexico
Miami & the Keys
Montana & Wyoming
Montréal & Québec City
Munich & the Bavarian
 Alps
Nashville & Memphis
Nepal
New England
New Mexico
New Orleans
New York City
New Zealand
Nova Scotia, New Brunswick
 & Prince Edward Island
Oregon
Paris

Philadelphia & the
 Amish Country
Portugal
Prague & the Best of the
 Czech Republic
Provence & the Riviera
Puerto Rico
Rome
San Antonio & Austin
San Diego
San Francisco
Santa Fe, Taos & Albuquerque
Scandinavia
Scotland
Seattle & Portland
Singapore & Malaysia
South Africa
Southeast Asia
South Pacific
Spain
Sweden
Switzerland
Thailand
Tokyo
Toronto
Tuscany & Umbria
USA
Utah
Vancouver & Victoria
Vermont, New Hampshire
 & Maine
Vienna & the Danube Valley
Virgin Islands
Virginia
Walt Disney World &
 Orlando
Washington, D.C.
Washington State

FROMMER'S® DOLLAR-A-DAY GUIDES

Australia from $50 a Day
California from $60 a Day
Caribbean from $70 a Day
England from $70 a Day
Europe from $60 a Day

Florida from $60 a Day
Hawaii from $70 a Day
Ireland from $60 a Day
Italy from $70 a Day
London from $85 a Day

New York from $80 a Day
Paris from $85 a Day
San Francisco from $60 a Day
Washington, D.C.,
 from $60 a Day

FROMMER'S® PORTABLE GUIDES

Acapulco, Ixtapa &
 Zihuatanejo
Alaska Cruises & Ports of Call
Bahamas
Baja & Los Cabos
Berlin
California Wine Country
Charleston & Savannah
Chicago

Dublin
Hawaii: The Big Island
Las Vegas
London
Maine Coast
Maui
New Orleans
New York City
Paris

Puerto Vallarta, Manzanillo
 & Guadalajara
San Diego
San Francisco
Sydney
Tampa & St. Petersburg
Venice
Washington, D.C.

FROMMER'S® NATIONAL PARK GUIDES

Family Vacations in the
  National Parks
Grand Canyon

National Parks of the
  American West
Rocky Mountain

Yellowstone & Grand Teton
Yosemite & Sequoia/
  Kings Canyon
Zion & Bryce Canyon

FROMMER'S® MEMORABLE WALKS

Chicago
London

New York
Paris

San Francisco
Washington D.C.

FROMMER'S® GREAT OUTDOOR GUIDES

New England
Northern California

Southern California & Baja
Southern New England

Washington & Oregon

FROMMER'S® BORN TO SHOP GUIDES

Born to Shop: China
Born to Shop: France

Born to Shop: Italy
Born to Shop: London

Born to Shop: New York
Born to Shop: Paris

FROMMER'S® IRREVERENT GUIDES

Amsterdam
Boston
Chicago
Las Vegas

London
Los Angeles
Manhattan
New Orleans

Paris
San Francisco
Seattle & Portland
Vancouver

Walt Disney World
Washington, D.C.

FROMMER'S® BEST-LOVED DRIVING TOURS

America
Britain
California

Florida
France
Germany

Ireland
Italy
New England

Scotland
Spain
Western Europe

THE UNOFFICIAL GUIDES®

Bed & Breakfasts in
  California
Bed & Breakfasts in
  New England
Bed & Breakfasts in
  the Northwest
Beyond Disney
Branson, Missouri
California with Kids
Chicago

Cruises
Disneyland
Florida with Kids
Golf Vacations in the
  Eastern U.S.
The Great Smoky &
  Blue Ridge
  Mountains
Inside Disney

Hawaii
Las Vegas
London
Miami & the Keys
Mini Las Vegas
Mini-Mickey
New Orleans
New York City
Paris

Safaris
San Francisco
Skiing in the West
Walt Disney World
Walt Disney World
  for Grown-ups
Walt Disney World
  for Kids
Washington, D.C.

SPECIAL-INTEREST TITLES

Frommer's Britain's Best Bed & Breakfasts and
  Country Inns
Frommer's Britain's Best Bike Rides
The Civil War Trust's Official Guide
  to the Civil War Discovery Trail
Frommer's Caribbean Hideaways
Frommer's Food Lover's Companion to France
Frommer's Food Lover's Companion to Italy
Frommer's Gay & Lesbian Europe
Frommer's Exploring America by RV
Hanging Out in Europe
Israel Past & Present

Mad Monks' Guide to California
Mad Monks' Guide to New York City
Frommer's The Moon
Frommer's New York City with Kids
The New York Times' Unforgettable
  Weekends
Places Rated Almanac
Retirement Places Rated
Frommer's Road Atlas Britain
Frommer's Road Atlas Europe
Frommer's Washington, D.C., with Kids
Frommer's What the Airlines Never Tell You